D1556338

PUBLICATIONS OF THE NEW CHAUCER SOCIETY

THE NEW CHAUCER SOCIETY

Studies in the Age of Chaucer, the yearbook of The New Chaucer Society, is published annually. Each issue contains substantial articles on all aspects of Chaucer and his age, book reviews, and an annotated Chaucer bibliography. Manuscripts should follow the *Chicago Manual of Style*, 14th edition. Unsolicited reviews are not accepted. Authors receive free twenty offprints of articles and ten of reviews. All correspondence regarding manuscript submissions should be directed to the Editor, David Matthews, School of Arts, Histories and Cultures, University of Manchester, Oxford Road Manchester, M13 9PL, United Kingdom. Subscriptions to The New Chaucer Society and information about the Society's activities should be directed to David Lawton, Department of English, Washington University, CB 1122, One Brookings Drive, St. Louis, MO 63130. Back issues of the journal may be ordered from The University of Notre Dame Press, Chicago Distribution Center, 11030 South Langley Avenue, Chicago, IL 60628; phone: 800-621-2736; fax: 800-621-8476, from outside the United States: phone: 773-702-7000; fax: 773-702-7212.

Studies in the Age of Chaucer

Studies in the
Age of Chaucer

Volume 32
2010

EDITOR

DAVID MATTHEWS

PUBLISHED ANNUALLY BY THE NEW CHAUCER SOCIETY

WASHINGTON UNIVERSITY IN ST. LOUIS

The frontispiece design, showing the Pilgrims at the Tabard Inn, is adapted from the woodcut in Caxton's second edition of *The Canterbury Tales*.

ISBN 0-933784-34-1
ISSN 0190-2407

CONTENTS

CONTENTS

REVIEWS

CONTENTS

ix

CONTENTS

Studies in the Age of Chaucer

The Phantasmal Past:

Time, History, and the Recombinative Imagination

Nicholas Watson
Harvard University

The violence of the body reaches the written page only through absence, through the intermediary of documents that the historian has been able to see on the sands from which a presence has since been washed away, and through a murmur that lets us hear—but from afar—the unknown immensity that seduces and menaces our knowledge.

—Michel de Certeau, *The Writing of History*

It seems to me then as if all the moments of our life occupy the same space, as if future events already existed and were only waiting for us to find our way to them at last, just as when we have accepted an invitation we duly arrive in a certain house at a given time. And might it not be, continued Austerlitz, that we also have appointments to keep in the past, in what has gone before and is for the most part extinguished, and must go there in search of places and people who have some connection with us on the far side of time, so to speak?

—W. G. Sebald, *Austerlitz*

Pastness

THIS ESSAY IS A SEQUEL to an earlier one, published in 1999, which set out, by way of a meditation on Caroline Walker Bynum's great *Holy Feast and Holy Fast*, to imagine an alternative to the post-Enlightenment traditions of rationalist hermeneutics that dominate historical scholarship. "Desire for the Past," as the earlier essay is called, suggests that, in order to come to a more compelling understanding of what is at stake in study of the past, historians need to work with, as well as on, the models of thought and feeling they study, adapting these models for historiographic use in order to make visible the rich exchanges between present and past that are an often-repressed feature of our work.[1]

More specifically, the earlier essay shows how premodern conceptions of *affect* might usefully inform the practice of historians. Medieval theories of affect belong within a hermeneutic tradition, displaced to the esoteric margins by the Enlightenment, which thinks of understanding less in rational than in empathetic terms: as the product of a quest for union with the subject of enquiry. Empathetic understanding is underwritten by a double movement of identification and repudiation between the unitary statement *I am you* and its silent shadow, *I am not you*. Considered as an empathetic endeavor, study of the past thus becomes something like the mystic's quest for union with God, and the essay ends by suggesting that close attention to the affective protocols that organize such a quest for thinkers like Julian of Norwich might allow us to understand better, and make more articulate use of, our own passionate investments in the past.[2]

"Desire for the Past" was intended as a thought experiment that would stand on its own as a consciously fervid contribution to the theorization of history. But questions have kept pushing their way out from the corners of the experiment, which cannot quite manage to ignore a looming issue larger than that of the individual scholar's personal investments in the past: that of contemporary culture's relationship to history itself. Where is the past? What has *happened* to the past? Despite the advances of historical scholarship, despite even the eruption of what the *New York Times* persists in calling the "medieval" specter of fundamentalism and other forms of eschatological terror into our new, so-soon-tarnished millennium, the past feels threatened, as though it were disappearing from the cultural imaginary of modernity as rapidly as the polar ice caps are melting from the planet. Not only a matter of professional concern but a challenge to the ethical identity of all historians, as well as a subject of consuming interest in its own right, the apparent vanishment of the past in our present, a phenomenon whose roots must, after all, lie in the past, urgently needs to be understood and confronted.

[1] Caroline Walker Bynum, *Holy Feast and Holy Fast: The Religious Significance of Food to Medieval Women*, The New Historicism: Studies in Cultural Poetics 2 (Berkeley and Los Angeles: University of California Press, 1987); "Desire for the Past," *SAC* 21 (1999): 59–98; reprinted with a new afterword in *Maitresse of My Wit: Medieval Women, Modern Scholars*, ed. Louise D'Arcens and Juanita Feros Ruys, Making the Middle Ages 7 (Turnhout: Brepols, 2004), 149–90.

[2] Karl Morrison, *"I Am You": The Hermeneutics of Empathy in Western Literature, Theology, and Art* (Princeton: Princeton University Press, 1998).

Medievalists might have a role to play here. Our lot is cast with the last centuries of what we may call the deep human past, the epoch whose spectacular ending provides modernity with some of its most enduring myths of origin.[3] The medieval is in a good position to stand both for the senses in which the past can be thought discontinuous with the present and those in which such a thought is a contradiction in terms. Unlike the early modern, an era still understood in teleological relation to the present, the medieval is assumed to have had purposes of its own, an identity not connected in any linear way with the present, notions about its own future quite different from the one we inhabit. Despite, or perhaps because of, the nineteenth-century investment in the medieval as the source of nations, languages, and institutions, the medieval is also regularly vilified as obsolete, fantastic, foundational of modernity only inasmuch as modernity is taken to have established its own heroic identity, its *freedom* from the past, through a violent, life-giving, mythical act of repudiation of the Dark Age from which it emerged.[4]

Considered as an ideology, modernity is a dogma at whose core is a set of beliefs about time (that time is uni-directional, progressive, and so on) in which the postmodern moment has also been quietly invested and which tend strongly to validate the as-yet-nonexistent future at the expense of the past. Hence *The New York Times*'s assumption that any irruption of irrationality into the present is "medieval," for, speaking dogmatically, the medieval *is* the discarded past: the decayed, gothic edifice on whose ruins were built the state, economic progress, secularism, and civil society.[5] All this is, perhaps, obvious. But how did this dogma arise? What are its implications for Western culture's relationship with its history? Medieval studies, with its partner, medievalism, needs to survive modernity's addiction to futurity in part just so that, in alliance with other historical disciplines, it can continue to press such questions.

In light of these concerns, the focus of "Desire for the Past" on schol-

[3] On the sixteenth century as a repository of modernist myths of origin, see James Simpson, *Burning to Read: English Fundamentalism and Its Reformation Opponents* (Cambridge, Mass.: Harvard University Press, 2007).

[4] See Hayden White, *Metahistory: The Historical Imagination in Nineteenth-Century Europe* (Baltimore: Johns Hopkins University Press, 1973).

[5] A point also made by James Simpson, "The Rule of Medieval Imagination," in *Images, Idolatry, and Iconoclasm in Late Medieval England*, ed. Jeremy Dimmick, James Simpson, and Nicolette Zeeman (Oxford: Oxford University Press, 2002), 4–24.

arly affect has come to seem too personal to have much bearing on the larger challenge posed to our relationship with the past by modernity. At the same time, the earlier essay's call to explore the historiographic potential of other intellectual models derived from the premodern past prompts this search for a new approach to the questions it raises.

The present essay thus reflects on the work of history—the work the past does in the present but also the work done by historians in studying and representing the past—through the body of medieval hermeneutic theory that concerns the *imagination*. The Middle Ages are often seen as a repository of the imaginary: an early nineteenth-century topos repackaged not only by modern popular culture and the media but also by historians such as Jacques Le Goff in *The Medieval Imagination*.[6] Yet in contrast to the theory of memory, medieval imaginative theory remains so denigrated that few realize how the idiosyncratic roles played by the imagination in modernity are part of the legacy of the medieval past or appreciate the rational toughness that undergirds this legacy.[7]

The essay sketches a triple response to this situation: first, by gesturing toward the deep links between medieval imaginative theory and the idea of modernity; second, by musing on how this body of theory, with its intense focus on the complexities of any act of mediation, might serve as a guide to our work as historians; third, and at most length, by tracing the consciously innovative narrative forms this theory took in a series of speculative visionary works of the early and late fourteenth century.

[6] Jacques le Goff, *The Medieval Imagination*, trans. Arthur Goldhammer (Chicago: University of Chicago Press, 1988), originally published as *L'Imaginaire médiéval: Essais* (Paris: Gallimard, 1985).

[7] Important recent studies of the medieval imagination include Mary Carruthers, *The Craft of Thought: Meditation, Rhetoric, and the Making of Images, 400–1200*, Cambridge Studies in Medieval Literature 34 (Cambridge: Cambridge University Press, 1998), and, for the later period, Alastair Minnis, "Textual Psychologies: Imagination, Memory, Pleasure," in *The Cambridge History of Literary Criticism, Volume 2: The Middle Ages*, ed. Alastair Minnis and Ian Johnson (Cambridge: Cambridge University Press, 2005), 239–74. For a general survey of the tradition from the Greeks to the Romantics, see J. M. Cocking, *Imagination: A Study in the History of Ideas* (London: Routledge, 1992); still more wide-ranging is Eva T. H. Brann's passionate historical encomium to the faculty, *The World of the Imagination: Sum and Substance* (Lanham, Md.: Rowman and Littlefield, 1991). Generally relevant to this essay are Suzanne Conklin Akbari, *Seeing Through the Veil: Optical Theory and Medieval Allegory* (Toronto: University of Toronto Press, 2004); Sarah Kay, *The Place of Thought: The Complexity of One in Late Medieval French Didactic Poetry* (Philadelphia: University of Pennsylvania Press, 2007). Although its topic is sight, not imagination, I have found also most suggestive Dallas G. Denery II, *Seeing and Being Seen in the Later Medieval World: Optics, Theology, and Religious Life*, Cambridge Studies in Medieval Life and Thought, Fourth Series 63 (Cambridge: Cambridge University Press, 2005).

These English, Italian, and Latin investigations of the uses of the imagination in constructing fictions, uncovering truths, and even constituting realities are at the heart of this investigation.

The more local aim of the essay is to argue that medieval imaginative theory, like medieval empathetic theory, offers a viable way of thinking to those of us whose business is with the past. The larger aim is to suggest a new approach to what may be the single most important assertion premodern historians should be making at present: that the past matters, not only because it underlies the present, nor only because its unsuspected sophistication challenges its dismissal by the present, but because it remains inseparably entangled with the present and will continue to be so however much this fact is forgotten or its relevance denied. The past may, perhaps, be in danger of vanishing from our cultural conversation, but it will not and cannot cease to exist in reconfigured forms. Only the mode of that continued existence is in question.

Like empathetic understanding, imaginative understanding first conceives of the object of inquiry in corporeal terms, and the starting point of these reflections is thus the image of the past as a body evoked by the epigraphs to this essay from Michel de Certeau and W. G. Sebald.[8] But there the resemblances between empathetic and imaginative hermeneutics end. An empathetic approach to the past understands it as an absent object of faith, possible to know only through something akin to the "blinde sterring of love" by which, in *The Cloud of Unknowing*, the soul reaches toward its unknown God.[9] An imaginative approach to the past depends not on its absence but, in some sense, on its presence, allowing us to think about that presence in ways that illuminate both the past's challenge to the dogma of modernity and its vulnerability to that dogma. In so doing, it also gives us the tools we need to consider, from a new angle, the implications and urgencies of our discipline.

---

[8] Michel de Certeau, *The Writing of History*, trans. Tom Conley (New York: Columbia University Press, 1988), 11; originally published as *L'Écriture de l'histoire* (Paris: Gallimard, 1975); W. G. Sebald, *Austerlitz*, trans. Anthea Bell (New York: Random House, 2001), 359–60; originally published in German as W. G. Sebald, *Austerlitz* (Munich: Hanser, 2001).

[9] *The Cloud of Unknowing*, ed. Phyllis Hodgson, EETS o.s. 218 (London: Oxford University Press, 1934). Middle English quotations in this essay normalize thorn and yogh, u/v, i/j, i/y and c/t variation, capitalization, and punctuation, generally along lines proposed by H. A. Kelly, "Uniformity and Sense in Editing and Citing Medieval Texts," *Medieval Academy Newsletter* 152 (Spring 2004). Latin quotations receive analogous normalizations.

Phantasm

One consequence of thus thinking about the past as a body is that it prods the question of the ontological status of this past into unignorable visibility. The status of past bodies themselves is not at issue. They are dead: part of the humus from which new bodies arise. But for scholars digging ever deeper into this past and thinking of it as a time in which beings not quite other than ourselves confidently inhabited their own bodily presents, only a few hundred years behind and a few dozen inches below where many of us now step, past time itself is not easily thought of as dead at all. Progressively opening itself to our gaze, refusing all attempts to fix it into permanent shape, through archives that, incomplete though they are, create the illusion of inexhaustibility as we find new questions to ask, new issues to explore, the past still seems latent: on the way into, not away from, the fullness of being that is the now, almost as though it were the future. Not real: the past is phantasm compared to present actuality; is dependent on that actuality, on present energies and interests, to lend it what, at any moment, it has of life. But still *existent*, and in that sense having an actuality of its own, different from that of the archive, which exists in the present, not the past to which the archive acts as a thin bridge: both less and more, the nearly living spirit to the archive's nearly dead letter.

Where does this spirit subsist? Among other places, in the branch of the cultural imaginary called scholarship. Underpinned by the memory of the archive, tested and retested by research and debate, the mode of existence the past has is, in an exact sense, phantasmic. The past exists in the collective imagination.

Ever since Coleridge, writing Chapter 13 of his *Biographia Literaria* around 1815, called the "primary IMAGINATION" "the living Power and prime Agent of all human Perception," and "a representation in the finite mind of the eternal act of creation in the infinite I AM," the imagination has been linked to Romantic and, later, Modernist poetics, their elevation of the artist to a status next divinity, and their self-conception as evangelists of this new religion in the face of the dead weight of a past that failed to recognize its truth.[10] While it would be wrong to blame most of this on Coleridge himself, a powerfully historical

[10] Samuel Taylor Coleridge, *Biographia Literaria*, ed. James Engell and W. Jackson Bate, Collected Works of Samuel Taylor Coleridge 7, Bollingen Series 75 (Princeton: Princeton University Press, 1983), 304.

reader and anti-elitist thinker, his eschatological proclamation of the creative power of the primary and secondary imagination and relegation of the image-forming and -collating powers long associated with the imagination to the lesser, recombinative faculty of the "fancy," completed a rupture in the West's understanding both of the imagination itself and of the intellectual work associated with it.[11]

It is no accident, either that a long tradition of imaginative historiography flared up brilliantly, then died, a generation after Coleridge, with Thomas Carlyle's *The French Revolution, Heroes and Hero-Worship*, and *Frederick the Great*, or that all these works evince an idea of the past as effectively awaiting its own obsolescence, capable of providing no more than an enfeebled backdrop to the acts of the great men whose vast imaginative energies are credited with bringing the present into being.[12] Creativity and the past, the powers associated with imagination and those associated with memory and reason, were becoming antonyms, and the new empiricist historiography that in many ways still dominates our work confirmed these fissures even as it traced the past's rise to the imperial present, relegating study of the past for the past's sake to antiquarians. The point of this empiricist past resides mainly in the present, which in this new temporal order is separated from the past, both in its presence and in the way it ultimately imagines itself, like Carlyle's heroes, not back toward the past but forward into a future toward which it triumphantly redirects its energies: the future of modernity.

To think of the premodern past as still subsisting in the cultural imaginary, as a phantasmal but active relict of an organism that once enjoyed an existence fully independent of our present and its purposes, promises to unsettle these acts of self-differentiation from the past and perhaps to begin to reframe our relationship with it. An understanding of the past as phantasmal asks us to think horizontally, across the divide between present and past, not teleologically, up through the past into the present. In so doing, it revives the very feature of the past most successfully suppressed and assimilated by modernity: the novelty of the past, both as it was in itself and as we encounter it now, as though for the first time, in a present that is, as Nietzsche long ago argued, the

[11] See James Engell, *The Creative Imagination: Enlightenment to Romanticism* (Cambridge, Mass.: Harvard University Press, 1981).

[12] *The French Revolution* was published in 1837, *Heroes and Hero-Worship* in 1841, *The History of Friedrich II of Prussia* (also *Frederick the Great*) in 1858.

product as much of the past's apparent destruction and forgetting as it is of the process of development framed by teleological historiography.[13]

The pages that follow reflect on the potentiality contained in the idea of the past as a phantasm, and on the mode of historiography it enables, by developing some thoughts about the pre-Coleridgean imagination, the powers attributed to it, and its own association with novelty: that is, both with the announcement or bringing into being of the new, and with the concept of newness itself, one of the crucial underlays of the idea of the modern. The remainder of this section describes, in brutally general form, the place of the imagination in late medieval psychological theory. Subsequent sections then turn to what it calls the "works of the imagination": the literary genres of dream poetry and vision in which encounters with various modes of being are staged through the imaginative faculty and the danger and promise of such meetings are explored. Finally, a brief conclusion returns to novelty, modernity, and the location of the past, arguing that premodern imaginative theory offers a way of thinking about the past and its relations with the present that is still useful.[14]

Reginald Pecock, invoking a late medieval distinction between two levels of imagination, argued that "the office of the fantasye" or higher imagination "is forto forge and compoune [manufacture or combine], or to sette togedir in seeming, thingis whiche ben not togedir and which maken not oon thing in kinde." For *The Cloud of Unknowing*, "imagination is a might thorow the whiche we portray alle images of absent and present thinges."[15] Some of the ways these definitions apply to history will not be immediately apparent, while their invocation of the fraudu-

---

[13] Friedrich Wilhelm Nietzsche, *The Use and Abuse of History*, trans. Adrian Collins, Little Library of the Liberal Arts 11 (New York: Liberal Arts Press, 1949); originally published as *Vom Nutzen und Nachteil der Historie für das Leben* in 1874.

[14] It bears noting that, despite the attempts to police the specifically *visionary* imagination from the fourteenth century on (see below), early modern theories of imagination are closely related to their medieval predecessors, down to Hobbes in the mid-seventeenth century, and to a considerable extent thereafter, as Engell, *Creative Imagination*, shows. For striking examples, drawn from a still largely untapped field, see Koen Vermeir, "The 'Physical Prophet' and the Powers of the Imagination, Part I: A Case-Study on Prophecy, Vapours, and the Imagination (1685–1710)," *Studies in the History and Philosophy of the Biological and Biomedical Sciences* 35 (2004): 561–91, and "The 'Physical Prophet' and the Powers of the Imagination, Part II: A Case-Study on Dowsing and the Naturalisation of the Moral (1685–1710)," in *Studies in the History and Philosophy of Science* 36 (2005): 1–24.

[15] Reginald Pecock, *The Donet*, ed. Elsie Vaughan Hitchcock, EETS o.s. 156 (London: Oxford University Press, 1921); *Cloud of Unknowing*, 117.

lent in the words "forge," "seeming," and "portray" may, at first, even seem actively unhelpful. Yet the association of the imagination in these definitions with the collocation of evidence and re-creation of things absent gives *prima facie* encouragement to an attempt to consider the faculty in relation to history. What follows, then, is an exploration of the role of the imagination in medieval visionary and poetic making whose deepest concern is with its historiographic potential: with how such makings might be induced to offer us a vision of the work of history as an urgent, ongoing, incompletable act of mediation between present and past.

Mediation is of course the main function of the imagination in medieval psychological theory, as the five outer senses transmit impressions of the external world through the *sensus communis* to the *cellula imaginativa* in the front of the brain, which generates meaning-bearing images capable of being sorted and stored by the other inner senses, judgment and memory, in the *cellula estimativa* and *cellula memorativa*. Despite differences in terminology and changes over time, here physicians trained on Galen, scholastic thinkers like Pecock, and hermits brought up to *lectio divina* like the *Cloud*-author all agreed. Writing just after 1300, for example, John of Morigny invoked this basic model in a prayer for knowledge of rhetoric in his *Liber florum doctrine celestis*:

Aperi, Domine, cor meum, mentem meam, et cerebrum perfectum tribus cellulis, ut in prima et in anteriori parte omnia visa et audita velocissime queam imaginari, in secunda omnia imaginata racionari possim, et que racionata sunt ultima perpetue conservet memoria.

Open, Lord, my heart, my mind, and the cerebrum perfected in its three cells, so that in the first and anterior part [of the first *cellula*] I may be able very swiftly to form images of everything seen and heard, in the second I may be able to interpret everything thus imagined and in the last memory may perpetually conserve the things thus interpreted.[16]

[16] *John of Morigny's Flowers of Heavenly Teaching*, ed. with translation and commentary, Claire Fanger and Nicholas Watson (in preparation), II.ii.23.5. For information about this work, see the essays by Claire Fanger, Richard Kieckhefer, and Nicholas Watson in *Conjuring Spirits: Texts and Traditions of Medieval Ritual Magic*, ed. Claire Fanger, Magic in History (University Park: Pennsylvania State University Press, 1998), although all these essays have been partly superseded by subsequent research and by further manuscript discoveries. For a preliminary edition and translation of the first part of the text, see Claire Fanger and Nicholas Watson, "John of Morigny, Prologue to *Liber Visionum* [c. 1304–1318]," *Esoterica* 3 (2001): 108–217, http://www.esoteric.msu.edu.

There were many disagreements in working out the details of this model: over the extent to which the imagination was truly a faculty, a *vis imaginativa*, rather than a mere transmitter of images, as it was for Plato; over the imagination's ability to create by recombination images never presented to it by the senses, especially in dreams; over its role, particularly in Avicennan models, as an instrument of divine revelation, as a mediator between heaven and earth, as well as the material and the mental; and over how the inner senses interact with the soul, comprised of the faculties of reason and will and considered to be nonlocalized because noncorporeal. But even though some of the positions taken on these issues give the imagination true cognitive functions, they all share an awareness of the ambiguous standing of images and the faculty that generates and recombines them: an awareness that, it is proper to say, constitutes an organizing principle for medieval imaginative theories. As we shall see, indeed, it is the field of possibilities opened up by the ambiguous status of the medieval imagination, its powers, effects, and truth claims, that constitutes its usefulness to historiography.[17]

The difficulty of thinking about the imagination, even in the seemingly strictly physiological terms that Chaucer's Knight invokes in describing Arcite's "love-manie," "Engendred of humour malencolic, / Biforen, in his celle fantastic," is that it exists so close to the boundary between corporeal and spiritual, crossing and recrossing that boundary, both in a real sense, as it mediates the external world to the soul, and in a theoretical one, classified as it effectively is on both sides of the divide.[18] Like the other inner senses, imagination is part of the soul, but a part humans share with animals: dying and, in the case of humans, being raised with the body, as Aquinas argues in the *Summa*.[19] As such,

---

[17] For a lucid introduction to late medieval psychology in the Aquinan tradition, see Simon Kemp, *Cognitive Psychology in the Middle Ages* (Westport, Conn.: Greenwood, 1996). More fine-tuned analyses are also available, and, in their interest in the changes in cognitive theory that took place in the late thirteenth and fourteenth centuries, are of considerable potential relevance to this essay, although their findings are not invoked here: see esp. Katherine Tachau, *Vision and Certitude in the Age of Ockham* (Leiden: E. J. Brill, 1988); Robert Pasnau, *Theories of Cognition in the Later Middle Ages* (Cambridge: Cambridge University Press, 1996). The major issues at stake across the millennium separating Augustine from the end of the medieval period are treated in Anthony Kenny, *Medieval Philosophy*, volume 2 of his *A New History of Western Philosophy* (Oxford: Clarendon Press, 2005), chap. 7, pp. 241–51. See also his *Aquinas on Mind*, New Topics in Medieval Philosophy (London: Routledge, 1993).

[18] *Canterbury Tales* I.1375–76. Quotations, with spelling adjusted (see note 9 above), from Larry D. Benson, gen. ed., *The Riverside Chaucer* (Boston: Houghton Mifflin, 1987).

[19] Thomas Aquinas, *Summa theologica*, trans. Fathers of the English Dominican Province (New York: Benziger, 1948), I.77.

it participates both in the limitations inherent in materiality and the more severe ones produced by the Fall, which disordered the physical creation and turned the border between matter and spirit into a scene of intense cosmic battle. Essential but unreliable, imagination is thus figure and symptom of the *miseria condicionis humanae*, the wretchedness of being human, at an especially deep level. Indeed, according to Aquinas, it is precisely the role played by the image-making and -storing faculties of imagination and memory that distinguishes imperfect human intellection from the perfect mode possessed by the angels, who require neither faculty. Angelic being is all but constituted by an intellect that, turned to God by an act of will, intuits imageless truths in a perpetual present, direct from the divine mind.[20]

For humans, by contrast, "imageless truth" is a category under extreme strain even within the discourse dedicated to theorizing it, apophatic theology. True, the influential Augustinian concept of "intellectual vision" seems to offer a ground to stand on for those determined to argue for a mode of human perception that carries certitude. But Augustinian Neoplatonism did not translate well for the later Middle Ages, and most assumed with a visionary like Julian of Norwich that *visio intellectualis* ("gastelye sighte") was still visual, dependent on images stored in memory and derived from imagination.[21] "Bifore er man sinned, was imagination so obedient unto the reson . . . that it ministrid never to it any unordeinde [disordered] image of any bodely creature or any fantasy of any goostly creature," states the *Cloud*. Even for the unfallen Adam, however, truths were conveyed to the *intellectus* through images, "created effects," as Aquinas asserts and even Augustine reluctantly concedes.[22]

For medievals, the mind could thus attain knowledge and under-

[20] Ibid., I.54.

[21] Julian of Norwich, *Writings of Julian of Norwich: A Vision Showed to a Devout Woman and A Revelation of Love*, ed. Nicholas Watson and Jacqueline Jenkins, Brepols Medieval Women Series (University Park: Pennsylvania State University Press, 2006), e.g., *Revelation*, chap. 9. "Gostely sight" is clearly imagistic for Julian, differing from "bodily sight" in its transmission directly into her mind, rather than via the mediation of images perceived through the senses. For the history of *visio intellectualis* and its late medieval decline, see Denys Turner, *The Darkness of God: Negativity in Christian Mysticism* (Cambridge: Cambridge University Press, 1995).

[22] *Cloud of Unknowing*, 117; *Summa theologica*, I.94; Augustine, *The Literal Meaning of Genesis*, trans. John Hammond Taylor, Ancient Christian Writers 42, 2 vols. (New York: Newman Press), XII.33. For analysis, see Gerard O'Daly, *Augustine's Philosophy of Mind* (London: Duckworth, 1987), 106–30; Anthony Kenny, *Aquinas on Mind*, Topics in Medieval Philosophy (London: Routledge, 1993), 31–40.

standing only as a result of its repeated penetration by images assembled in a faculty whose liminal position between body and spirit and sheer accessibility to medical and philosophical as well as theological discourses showed it vulnerably porous to diabolic interference, deterioration as a result of disordered postlapsarian desire, and perceptual error.

It is no wonder that, as Mary Carruthers has so richly shown, such concentrated attention was focused in the contemplative tradition on the management of sense impressions and their orderly translation into images stored in the memory. At its most intense, such attention shaped every aspect of monastic life, from the architectural and pictorial space within which it was lived, to the round of chant, song, and movement that was the liturgy, to the private reading, meditation, and prayer that constituted monastic recreation, even, so far as this was possible, to the regulation of sleep.[23] In this regime, the intrusion of inappropriate impressions on the imagination slid easily into sin. Yet since imaginative activity was of the body as well as the soul, failure to ensure enough impressions, good or bad, led to something worse: the partly physiological condition of boredom, *accidia*, a stagnant pool of immobile images, induced by the noon-day demon, that to all but the inertly despairing sufferer was a clear harbinger of damnation.[24]

Nor is it surprising that this environment should generate a proliferation of visionary experiences and *technes*, vigorously promoted or proscribed by different schools of clerical thought as the science of *discretio spirituum* was developed, especially from the early fourteenth century on, in conjunction with the methodologies of the inquisition, that searcher-out of the false *imaginatiouns* of heretics.[25] Nor, despite this, that late medieval efforts to extend contemplative models to the laity should argue that the *imaginatioun* of "the life of Criste" was a potentially salvific substitute for the "vanitees of the worlde" that constantly sought to

---

[23] See Carruthers, *The Craft of Thought*, a sustained exposition of monastic orthopraxis (1) in relation to such practices as meditation.

[24] See Giorgio Agamben, *Stanzas: Word and Phantasm in Western Culture*, trans. Ronald L. Martinez, Theory and History of Literature 69 (Minneapolis: University of Minnesota Press, 1993); originally published as *Stanza: Le Parola e il fantasma nella cultura occidentale* (Turin: Einaudi, 1977).

[25] See Rosalynn Voaden, *God's Words, Women's Voices: The Discernment of Spirits in the Writings of Late-Medieval Women Visionaries*, York Medieval Press (Cambridge: Boydell and Brewer, 1999): Nancy Caciola, *Discerning Spirits: Divine and Demonic Possession in the Middle Ages* (Ithaca: Cornell University Press, 2003); Dyan Elliott, *Proving Woman: Female Spirituality and Inquisitional Culture in the Later Middle Ages* (Princeton: Princeton University Press, 2004).

infiltrate their lived experiences, as Nicholas Love argued in the *Mirror of the Life of Christ*.[26] Love's understanding of the imagination was at once active, aimed at generating devotion, and defensive, aimed at stopping up the senses by offering alternate images to the *vis imaginativa*, thus turning the mind into a mental cell. As *Ancrene Wisse* would put it, Love made it possible for ordinary lay readers to "wite wel thin heorte, for saule lif is in hire, yef ha is wel i-loket" (guard your heart well, since the soul's life resides in her, if she is well locked), skillfully updating an ancient tradition of self- and soul-care.[27]

Tidinge

Those who policed the medieval imagination thus did so by working with it, providing it with sensory data that had been culturally approved as worthy of a permanent place in the memory in advance of any judgment made by an individual soul's rational power. This might seem an inherently conservative, innovation-refusing pedagogical process. But the medieval imagination was not just a translator of sense impressions into images. In dreams, visions, fantasies, and states of creativity associated with poetic or artistic making, it was a locus of mental activity in its own right. In the intricate mental space of the "higher" imagination of the *fantasie* in particular, images rise up thickly from the storehouse of the memory or are admitted anew by way of the senses. There, they mysteriously combine and recombine to form previously unknown objects—marvels, inventions, novelties, monsters, engines, and all manner of other constructs, "thingis whiche . . . maken not oon thing in kinde," as Pecock put it—with or without the effectual aid of the reason. Any writers who sought to make these unpredictable processes into the ground of art or speculation were opening the door to a mode of thought necessarily quizzical, wayward, and *innovative*: as distant from the security of Love's *imaginatioun* as from Coleridge's harmless *fancy*. The threat represented by the recombinative imagination was quite as evident to these writers as its energetic potentialities. Indeed, in some

[26] Nicholas Love, *The Mirror of the Blessed Life of Jesus Christ: A Full Critical Edition*, ed. Michael G. Sargent, Exeter Medieval Texts and Studies (Exeter: Exeter University Press, 2005), Prologue.

[27] *Ancrene Wisse*, ed. Bella Millett, EETS o.s. 325–26 (Oxford: Oxford University Press, 2005–6), II.3–4.

13

of the most exuberant imaginative works this threat becomes a major theme.

Such is the case, for example, with Chaucer's presentation of the labyrinthine, creaky, rapidly whirling House of Rumour in his eccentric and eloquently incomplete dream poem, *The House of Fame*.[28] The House of Rumour is located immediately adjacent to the orbiting mountain of ice atop which stands the House of Fame itself, wherein the historical understanding of noteworthy deeds and the nature of their place in the collective memory, if any, is determined by the unpredictable, possibly arbitrary, decisions of Fame, *fama*, herself. Nothing even this dignified takes place in the House of Rumour: its roof pitted with holes, its walls basket-woven of twigs, and the whole supple edifice as full of doors "as of leves ben in trees / In somer, whan they grene been," all of which stand open day and night for news of all kinds, *tidinges* of deeds notable and unnotable, real and imaginary, to enter and leave at will (1946–47).

An image aimed at the heart of the eremitic model of the guarded soul that *Ancrene Wisse* derived, ultimately, from Cassian's *Collationes*, the House of Rumour is an imaginative faculty operating in the absence of any guiding influence from reason: ramshackle, viridescent, unjudgmental, and earthbound. Whirling like a watermill (to use Cassian's useful analogue), the House is powered by a constant stream of sensory impressions that it instantly manufactures into phantasms, which represent at once the fleeting impressions of consciousness and the collective tittle-tattle of uncensored social observation we call gossip, and which crowd together, exchange their single tidbit of news, then thrust their way back into the world again.[29] So prolifically does this engine of images gather them in, then pump them out, that its random productivity outdoes even the generative powers of Nature and the destructive powers of her rival, Death:

---

[28] The reading offered here is especially indebted to Steven F. Kruger, "Imagination and the Complex Movement of Chaucer's *House of Fame*," *ChauR* 28 (1993): 117–34, and Ruth Evans, "Chaucer in Cyberspace: Medieval Technologies of Memory and *The House of Fame*," *SAC* 23 (2001): 43–69.

[29] See John Cassian, *Conferences*, trans. Colm Lubheid, Classics of Western Spirituality (Mahwah, N.J.: Paulist Press, 1985), Conference 1.18: "This activity of the heart is compared, not inappropriately, to that of a mill which is activated by the circular motion of water" ("exercitium cordis non incongrue molarum similitudini comparatur quas meatus aquarum praeceps impetu rotante provolvit"; J.-P. Migne, ed. *Patrologia Latina*, vol. 49 [Paris: Migne, 1874], col. 507b).

> But which a congregatioun
> Of folk, as I saugh rome aboute,
> Some within and some withoute,
> Nas never seen, ne shal ben eft;
> That certis, in the world nis left
> So many formed be Nature,
> Ne ded so many creature . . .
> And every wight that I saugh there
> Rounede everich in others ere
> A newe tidinge prively.
>
> (2034–45)

Hammer away at her forge as she may, sweep away with his sickle as he does, the numbers of creatures Nature and Death shape and destroy represent only a fraction of the numbers of *homunculi* born of each word, each eyeblink, in the *cellula imaginativa*.

According to standard medieval ethical and religious discourses, there could be many ways of categorizing the causes and products of this kind of imaginative activity: as good or evil, real or illusory, spiritual or corporeal. Yet *The House of Fame* makes it clear that moral, epistemological, and ontological ambiguities are intrinsic to the "newe tidinges" that are the principal work of the imagination in this unstructured dreaming mode. As the House of Rumour shakes its endless crop of "tidinges" out into the world, throwing them off in ever-increasing numbers, some of its images bear truths, some falsehoods, while others, changed by their jostling conversations and squeezed by the pressures that build up inexorably within this profligate mental machine, bear both:

> . . . Thus north and southe
> Went every word fro mouth to mouthe,
> And that encresing ever mo,
> As fir is wont to quicke and go
> From a sparke spronge amis,
> Til al a citee brent up is . . .
> And somtime saugh I tho, at ones,
> A lesing and a sad soth-sawe,
> That gonne of aventure drawe
> Out at a windowe for to pace
> And, when they metten in that place,
> They were a-checked bothe two,

> And neither of hem moste out go;
> For other so they gonne crowde,
> Tile eche of hem gan cryen loude,
> "Lat me go first!"—"Nay, but let me!
> And here I wol ensuren thee
> With the nones that thou wolt do so,
> That I shal never fro thee go,
> But be thin owne sworen brother!
> We will medle us ech with other . . ."
> Thus saugh I fals and sooth compouned
> Togeder fle for oo tidinge.
>
> (2077–109)

Given this ability of the *fantasie* to combine images, or inability to keep them separate, it seems that the power of the imagination to multiply phantasms is exponential.

In describing a mode of mental activity no more subservient to the *estimativa* (figured perhaps in the instant judgments made in the House of Fame) than it is to the *memorativa* (figured perhaps by the Temple of Glass earlier in the poem, with its images from the *Aeneid*), Chaucer pushes his account of the generative imagination to a characteristic extreme.[30] Just as the images spun by the *imaginativa* exist in an uncertain condition between matter and spirit, body and soul, so the *tidinges* that are their content exist in an uncertain condition between "fals and soth": their status phantasmic, their mode of being merely their facticity as cultural phenomena.

Yet in the endless circulation of "tidinges" between earth and the heavenly House of Rumour, "tidinges" do more than reflect, in more or less distorted form, the truth of what is done and said. Chaucer's simile of the "sparke sponge amis" argues that they are dangerously capable of helping to *create* what is done and said, destroying mighty civilizations through mere reportage, then carrying the news of that conflagration, outrageously varied, back to the shoddy heaven of Rumour to start the process anew.

For all that fact and "tidinge" instantly become indistinguishable, it

---

[30] "Seemingly" decorous because the *Aeneid* also lurks behind the Houses both of Fame and Rumour, and because Chaucer famously imports (and develops) an Ovidian Dido into the Virgilian scene. See Christopher Baswell, *Virgil in Medieval England: Figuring the Aeneid from the Twelfth Century to Chaucer*, Cambridge Studies in Medieval Literature 24 (Cambridge: Cambridge University Press, 1995), chap. 6.

is thus "tidinges," more than the slow work of institution-building or acts of individual heroism, that, in this imaginary cosmos, are seen to bring about change through time. Coming between events and their afterlife, "tidinges" generate differences between one moment and the next by recasting the "soth" of an event within an endless array of alternative versions whose very variance makes its own impact on what happens next. This is an unpredictable process in which, despite the persistence of a kind of cause and effect, any ability to *track* causality is soon lost. Thus does the "fals" become "soth" as well as the other way about; and thus is the future built of the same, fungible but undying phantasmic material that enables the past to survive, constantly transformed, into the future. It is just this effortless capacity of the recombinative imagination to throw off novelties, disrupt orderly continuities, slide the present into seemingly tangential futures, that the monastic cultivation of the imagination was designed to quell, and that strikes readers of *The House of Fame* now as irresistibly prophetic of modernity: the time of the reign of the future and of the omnipresence not of the natural but of the image.

Read alongside a good deal of contemplative writing in the monastic tradition, Chaucer's account of the disruptive power of unregulated imaginative activity is radical, at least to the extent that we understand it as celebration, not satire, energizing Chaucer's future projects even as it brings *The House of Fame* itself to a grinding halt. Nonetheless, the poem's frankness about the ambiguity of imaginative activity is not unusual. On the contrary, we shall see that similar ambiguities are cultivated by those in whom, or by whom, works of the imagination like *The House of Fame* are performed.

The two, overlapping genres of writing tied most closely to the generative imagination and in which the promise or threat of novelty is most real are the dream poem and the religious vision: those twin genres of geographical, intellectual, and epistemological exploration Barbara Newman has shown to be central to the production of the speculative theological constructs she terms "imaginative theology."[31] The rest of this essay meditates on episodes from three further texts in both genres. These texts appear to make very different demands on epistemological

[31] Barbara Newman, *God and the Goddesses: Vision, Poetry, and Belief in the Middle Ages* (Philadelphia: University of Pennsylvania Press, 2003), esp. 24–34.

certitude. But in practice they share Chaucer's sense of the intrinsic ambiguity of the image or "tidinge," moving in related ways between one conception of themselves as truth-bearing, perhaps inspired, and another as fictional, while insisting as clearly as Chaucer on the *power*, the potential efficacy, contained in the image. Part of the point here is to enrich our conception of the medieval imagination by emphasizing the extent to which it was assumed to possess creative as well as mediative capacities, albeit capacities different from those the Romantics were to claim for it, residing as they do for medieval thinkers *within* the mediating function Coleridge was to call "fancy," not in opposition to that function. Understood as the power that brings *tidinges*, false and true, into the world, whether by generating the unnatural images that combine in the *cellula imaginativa* in dreams or by acting as the vehicle for the entry of prophetic truths into the world from the spiritual realm, the medieval imagination indeed forms an essential part of the history of novelty, which is also part of the history of the modern.

Part of the point, however, bears directly on the essay's earlier reflections on imagination and historiography. Here medieval thinking about the imagination as creating by recombination is considerably more helpful than Coleridge's fantasy that the work of the imagination can somehow echo the divine act of *ex nihilo* creation. For medieval imaginative theory admits not only the crucial role imagination plays in all thought, whether based on observation of what exists without the self or reflection on what lies within, but also the consequence of that role: that thought, observation, and reflection are all products of "fals and soth compounded," so that our perception of all reality, past, present, and future, can never be anything other than a negotiation between the false and the true. In the encounters with other worlds staged in dreams and visions, the possibilities for truth and error, certainty and speculation, represented by Chaucer's "fals" and "soth" are indeed combined and recombined, as each is successively shown to be a medium for the other: equally necessary to thought and to the apprehension of whatever mode of reality is in question, but never susceptible of orderly hierarchization, fully definable relation, or final synthesis.

Novità

The first episode is a passage from a poetic text that stops just short of announcing itself as a dream poem, Dante's *Inferno*, from the symbolic center of its thirty-four cantos: the passage at the end of Canto XVI where Dante and Virgil begin their descent from the Seventh Circle (the last of the circles of force) to the Eighth Circle (the first of the circles of fraud), by summoning the monster Geryon from the obscure depths of the great cliff that separates these subdivisions of hell and down which he will later carry them, swimming through the gloomy air in great, wheeling circles.[32] Geryon, described at the beginning of Canto XVII as the "sozza imagine di froda" (foul image of fraud), is a nightmare product of the recombinative imagination, with a saintly human face ("faccia d'uom giusto"), the paws of a beaver, a serpent's body painted all over with knots and whorls ("nodi e rotelle") like a Persian carpet or a weaving from Arachne's looms, and the stinging tail of a scorpion (XVII.7–18). Summoned by a previously unimagined method, the "novo cenno" (new sign) of a rope loosed from Dante's waist (XVI.106–14), and introduced as a *novità* in his own right, Geryon becomes the centerpiece of a carefully constructed textual *aporia* through which Dante articulates his understanding of the epistemological status of this first stage of his poetic project, while also reflecting on the impossibility of knowing truth straightforwardly through the imagination:[33]

> "E' pur convien che novità risponda,"
> dicea fra me medesmo, "al novo cenno
> che 'l maestro con l'occhio sì seconda."
> Ahi quanto cauti li uomini esser dienno
> presso a color che non veggion pur l'ovra,
> ma per entro i pensier miran col senno!
> El disse a me: "Tosto verrà di sovra
> ciò ch'io attendo e che il tuo pensier sogna:
> tosto convien ch'al tuo viso si scovra."
> Sempre a quel ver c'ha faccia di menzogna
> de' l'uom chiuder le labbra fin ch'el puote,
> però che sanza colpa fa vergogna;
> ma qui tacer nol posso; e per le note

[32] Quotations and translations are from Dante Alighieri, *The Divine Comedy*, ed. and trans. Charles S. Singleton, 6 vols., Bollingen Series 80 (Princeton: Princeton University Press, 1970–75), vol. 1.

[33] On Geryon, see Roberto Mercuri, *Semantica di Gerione: Il motivo del viaggio nella Divina Commedia di Dante* (Rome: Bulzoni, 1984). On the summoning of Geryon by means of a cord, see Christopher Bennett Becker, "Dante's Motley Cord: Art and Apocalypse in *Inferno* XVI," *MLN* 106 (1991): 179–183, with bibliography, although the interpretation given here differs considerably from Becker's.

> di questa comedìa, lettor, ti giuro,
> s'elle non sien di lunga grazia vòte,
> ch'i' vidi per quell'aere grosso e scuro
> venir notando una figura in suso,
> maravigliosa ad ogne cor sicuro,
> sì come torna colui che va giuso
> talora a solver l'àncora ch'aggrappa
> o scoglio o altro che nel mare è chiuso,
> che 'n sù si stende, e da piè si rattrappa.
>
> (XVI.115–36)

"Surely," I said to myself, "something strange will answer the strange signal which the master follows so carefully with his eye."

Ah, how careful one should be with those who not only see the deed, but have the wit to read one's thoughts! "Soon will come up what I look for and what your mind dreams of," he [Virgil] said to me; "soon must it be discovered to your sight."

To that truth which has the face of a lie a man should always close his lips so far as he can, for through no fault of his it brings reproach; but here I cannot be silent; and, reader, I swear to you by the notes of this Comedy—so may they not fail of lasting favor—that I saw, through that thick and murky air, come swimming upwards a figure amazing to every steadfast heart, even as he returns who sometimes goes down to loose the anchor that is caught on a reef or something else hidden in the sea, who stretches upwards his arms and draws in his feet.

The "ver c'ha faccia di menzogna," the truth with the face of a lie, here is Geryon, a lie with the face of a truth, whose "maravigliosa" arrival from below, a "figura" swimming through the air, is so unlikely that Dante stakes the success of his poem on its veracity, in the process naming the poem a "comedìa" for the first time. As he does so, the poem becomes entangled in the winding beauty and stinging tip of Geryon's fraudulence, introduced as he is at the exact halfway point of the *Inferno* like a sinister or comic revelation of the poem's fictionality. At the same instant, fraudulence threatens to undo even itself through its representation by an "imagine" that reveals, through the partial legibility of its monstrosity, the truth about Geryon's falsity: a truth the poem can only make manifest if it continues to assert its own veracity, naming Geryon not as a shadow self but as an eternal, mendacious opposite. This is the childish terrain of the Cretan paradox: Is the true image of fraud true, or does its truth make it fraudulent?

Epistemology and ontology labor under conditions of compromise in hell, a place whose human inhabitants, like Geryon himself, are condemned to the eternal absurdity of their chosen inauthenticity. Since in Christian theology sin is no more than an absence, a *privatio boni* (privation of good), sinners unite themselves substantially with a principle of nonbeing when they disorder their souls into the shape of one of the forms of evil. Even though their sufferings still take a grossly measurable corporeal form, words like "veracity" and "reality" thus cannot strictly apply to them or their habitation, deformed as even their spirits have become into an obscene simulacrum of bodilyness.

But hell here is also a name for a complex sequence of images, some of which are caught, in this passage, in the moment of their generation in Dante's imagination, as one of those images, Virgil, describes himself as waiting for Dante to imagine another, Geryon, in the faculty Virgil calls the "pensier": "Tosto verrà . . . ciò . . . che il tuo *pensier sogna*" (Soon will come up . . . what I look for and what your mind dreams of). Virgil sees not only Dante's deeds but the flow of images that are his thoughts ("non veggion pur l'ovra, / ma per entro i pensier miran col senno"), and it is as he gazes on these that they formulate the "figura" who becomes, at first only through simile, the image of Geryon.

What, then, is Geryon? On the one hand, he is a product of the recombinative imagination, knit together from the pool of images available to Dante's mind by the rope he throws down to summon him and by his "pensier," described here as *dreaming*. The final simile suggests that Geryon first appears less like something arriving from below than like something *returning* to Dante and Virgil after slipping an anchor that has become snagged. Such a view of his role is consistent with an understanding of the *Inferno* as a fiction in which Geryon essentially represents an involuted rhetorical solution to a literary problem: the problem of how to represent fraud in a poem that, in its fictitious depiction of a real otherworldly place, itself inhabits a space dangerously close to the uncertain barrier separating invention from fraudulence.

On the other hand, however, the passage also supports the reading that Dante's imagination prophetically *apprehends* Geryon, as it does the rest of hell, including Virgil himself. When Virgil announces Geryon's imminent arrival ("tosto convien ch'al tuo viso *si scovra*" ["soon must it uncover itself to your sight"]), he does so in language that assumes

Geryon's objective being, using a phrase ("si scovra") that derives from the terminology of revelation and lends support to the improbable oath Dante then takes that all he describes is true.

Not that this oath is without cost. The price of the strange dalliance with lying ("menzogna") played out through the passage is the shame ("vergogna") that someone without fault can feel, Dante notes, at how closely truth resembles falsity: a striking linkage between the visionary imagination and the experience of *embarrassment*, an emotion that is equally associated with being wrongly suspected (by a lie) and being caught out (by the truth). "Vergogna" both inhibits and, when it has to, obliges speech, here in the form of an oath grounded in the mere "note" from which the narrative situation is constructed; an oath, then, and a shame, as involuted as the lying truth of Geryon himself. Even in his attempt to overcome "vergogna," it seems that Dante cultivates epistemological uncertainty, allowing the work of the imagination to unanchor itself from the constraints of rationality, since only so can his poem truthfully convey the ontological conditions under which beings of pure fraudulence might persist.[34]

In the process, he not only summons one of his poem's most compelling series of imaginative novelties: a mythological helicopter as redolent of the technological marvels that are a principal product of the recombinative imagination in modernity as any of Leonardo da Vinci's prophetic doodles. He radicalizes the distinctive late medieval visionary understanding of the fictive, deploying Chaucer's moral language of "soth" and "fals" in a moral environment so harsh that these opposing categories must be understood as mutually constitutive, not merely indistinguishable, and in which forward progress is possible only through the solidification of an impossible object, a fraud, the *novità* Geryon. A notion of the fictive akin to that found in that essential, fraudulent modern genre, the "novel," hovers nearby.

At the end of *The House of Fame*, Chaucer offers a vision of history in which reconstructing the truth and trajectory through time of any event in the past would involve the collation of endlessly dispersed voices

---

[34] On the close relationship between imagination and shame in medieval psychological theory, see Ernest N. Kaulbach, *Imaginative Prophecy in the B-Text of "Piers Plowman"* (Cambridge: D. S. Brewer, 1993), 65–66; Nicolette Zeeman, *"Piers Plowman" and the Medieval Discourse of Desire*, Cambridge Studies in Medieval Literature 59 (Cambridge: Cambridge University Press, 2006), 146–47.

whose rumorous falsifications appear so powerful as to overwhelm normal models of historical causality, if indeed they do not constitute a bizarre version of that causality. Not that historical collation could ever keep up with such a proliferation of images or offer any workable reconstruction either of the event or its afterlife, given the fundamental irresponsibility of cultural processes as described in this poem, the absolute powerlessness of *memoria* or other sources of "auctoritee." All the historian might ever achieve in this world would be the production of yet another set of recombined images: an outcome Chaucer chooses not to represent, preferring the suicide of the interrupting blank page, the end of imagination, to any attempt to sift the cultural bric-a-brac his dream quest has uncovered for usable nuggets of truth.

At the center of *Inferno*, Dante is no more sanguine than Chaucer about the possibility of separating truth and error, at least in the corrosive conditions of hell. But where Chaucer abandons his quest to earn the right to plant a kiss on "the next laure I see" in gratitude to Apollo (*House of Fame,* 1107), Dante plows on, red-faced, using the fictive and mendacious materials that lie to hand to forge the machine that will carry him down the abyss to confront yet darker images of the fraudulent. Sustained by the presence of Virgil, on the one hand, and the promise of Beatrice, on the other, Dante has resources unavailable to Chaucer. Here the images he summons to constitute hell solidify as he passes through into the shapes of "giustizia" (III.4), frozen into meaning by narrative need, bold acts of historical interpretation, and theological hypothesis.

Historians, like artists, are familiar with those stalled moments when the great gulfs of evidentiary lacunae, of "aere grosso e scuro," threaten to block our progress, and with the dubious methodological technologies it is necessary to assemble from whatever lies to hand in order to continue. Indeed, as de Certeau implies in the first epigraph at the beginning of this essay, the fragments washed up on the "written page" of the archive—a page his beachcombing image suggests may be as terrifyingly blank as the nonconclusion of *The House of Fame*—there is never any other way to translate the "murmur" we may still just hear of "the unknown immensity" that is the violent, bodily past than to summon Geryon, the *figura* of fraud, to our aid. To produce new working models of the past capable of resonating with that immensity, and so bring it into such presence as it may have, we must speak for, as well as of, it, and in the process involve ourselves in the ethical uncertainties attendant upon invention; on our projection of our own dreams onto the past; on our embarrassed knowledge that the vehicle we create to continue our journey is not really a truth about the past but a *novità*, an assemblage of images of the past into a form that never was.

Experimentum

The last two sections of this essay turn away from the rhetorical tradition as exemplified by Chaucer and Dante, in which engagement with fraud is, in a sense, a matter of course, and in which it is claims to *truth* that constitute the serious problem, to read passages of two visionary writers who might be thought particularly sensitive to threats to facticity, John of Morigny and Julian of Norwich. Establishing a clear relationship between facticity and fraud is crucial to John's so-called *experimentum visionis habende* (experiment for having a vision), which serves a series of functions in his *Liber florum doctrine celestis* (book of the flowers of heavenly teaching), a complex tripartite work of visions, prayers, and *experimenta*, written in two versions at Orléans and Morigny in the early fourteenth century, at the same time as Dante was writing the *Commedia*.[35]

If for Chaucer in *The House of Fame* the *vis imaginativa* has a correspondence with the human world as consensually constructed through the endless repetition of *tidinges*, and if for Dante it has a useful correspondence with the phantasmagorical ontology of hell, for John of Morigny, as for many religious visionaries, the imagination is the unreliable but vitally important borderland between the beings that people earth and heaven. This borderland was coming to be fiercely patrolled in the early 1300s, as the science of *discretio spirituum* was systematized around a belief that any error in communication between divine and human was likely to be diabolically inspired and would bring ruin in its wake: a belief that may have been a factor in the condemnation of the *Liber florum*, which was burned in Paris in 1323.[36] For John, however, the risk

[35] John's use of the term *experimentum* derives from his principal source, the *Ars notoria*. Both the phrase *experimentum visionis habende* and the experiment itself have analogues in medieval ritual magic texts, but no immediate source has been identified. The versions of *Liber florum* contain an array of dates difficult to arrange in a clear way, but it seems to have been begun around 1301 and was completed in October 1315.

[36] Enthralling testimony to the emergence of a hermeneutics of suspicion as John was writing is provided by the *De spiritu guidonis*, whose second, expanded version by Jean Gobi dates from the mid-1320s. See Jean Gobi, *Dialogue avec un fantôme,* trans. Marie-Anne Polo de Beaulieu (Paris: Belles Lettres, 1994).

of error was acceptable, partly because the project around which he evolved the *experimentum visionis habende*, his method of communication with heavenly beings through the imagination, was so urgent to him, partly because he did not share the dualistic understanding of error gaining ground in the literature of *discretio spirituum*.

The *experimentum* is a system for generating meaningful dreams, typically involving apparitions of the Virgin and exchanges with her initiated by the operator, which can be predicted to occur in response to a set of divinely inspired rituals involving recitation of certain prayers, inspection of certain images, and a prayerful focus of the mind at the point of sleep on questions to which one desires answers. These answers are then revealed in the same part of the mind the rituals are designed to prepare, the *cellula imaginativa*.[37] Although it is the reason that frames the questions and interprets their answers, the *experimentum* is itself a product of the *imaginativa*, both in its focus on dreams and inasmuch as its prayers and figures were created under the guidance of the same visionary process they generate; the most important *experimenta* concern gaining permission to write or use the prayers that will then, inter alia, enable further *experimenta*. This process renders the entire pyramidal construct experimental in a proto-scientific sense, since any error made in analyzing a given *experimentum* can be corrected through further *experimenta*, even if the error is diabolical in origin.[38]

The dreams are as varied as their status as products of the recombinative imagination would suggest. But many of them fit a common pattern in which an image of the Virgin appears to the dreamer, not in the flesh but rather as an artwork, most often a statue that may then change or half-change into flesh, moving, gesturing, speaking, within the dream itself in response to the operator's desires and needs:

Et aliquando apparet virgo Maria ante portam ecclesie . . . aliquando in obviam dum itur ad ecclesiam; aliquando in ecclesia in loco suo ubi imago sua ponitur. . . . Et aliquando apparet in forma regine nobilissime; aliquando in

---

[37] Crucial is the recitation of a set of prayers (the Seven Prayers) that John composed while attaining his own vision of Mary with a specific visionary prayer, "O revelatrix," and preexisting liturgical prayers such as "O intemerata"; see NC III.i.10–15. (References to *Liber florum* distinguish between John's two versions, the Old Compilation [OC] and the New Compilation [NC], only in parts of the texts where these differ, i.e., where the New Compilation discarded portions of its predecessor or added its own material.)

[38] The first part of the work, *The Book of Visions* (Prologue) is an account of the composition of the Seven Prayers central to the production of visions.

forma religiose mulieris pulcherrime; aliquando in forma nativitatis Ihesu; aliquando in imaginis sue forma nova et depicta . . . aliquando in forma antiqua
et deleta ab omni pictura. . . . Aliquando pulchra, aliquando turpis. . . . Aliquando loquitur et aliquando non vult loqui. . . . Et aliquando videtur et aliquando non, set vox eius auditur. Aliquando in alto loquitur, aliquando in imo,
ita quod vox eius est quasi sibilus aure tenuis, et vix auditur.

(OC I.iv.10)

Sometimes the virgin Mary will appear before the church door . . . sometimes
in the path on the way to church, sometimes in the church, in the place where
her image is located. . . . And sometimes she appears in the form of the noblest
queen; sometimes in the form of a most beautiful nun; sometimes in the form
of the nativity of Jesus; sometimes in the form of her newly painted image . . .
sometimes in an ancient form with all the painting rubbed away. . . . Sometimes beautiful, sometimes ugly. . . . Sometimes she speaks, and sometimes she
does not wish to speak. . . . And sometimes she is seen, and sometimes not,
but her voice is heard. Sometimes she speaks in a high voice, sometimes in a
low one in such a way that her voice is thin as a whisper in the ear, and is
scarcely heard.

What the Virgin says, or how she says it, or the gesture that she makes
with hand, foot, shoulders, or eyebrow, then provides raw material for
interpretations that assume a great deal, from the fact that the dream
must be understood supernaturally to the pertinence of a dream to the
questions that frame it. These questions the dream may not explicitly
answer or even ask, since the operator's own behavior within the dream
is, for reasons to do with the nature of dreaming itself, as unpredictable
as is that of the Virgin:

Opifex vero, quando apparet ei, tunc aliquando genibus flexis rogat eam ut
loquatur secum, loquendo aliquando in alto, aliquando in imo; aliquando
flendo, aliquando ridendo; aliquando per plura verba, aliquando per pauca,
aliquando per nulla.

(OC I.iv.10)

But the operator, when she appears to him, then sometimes on bent knees asks
her to speak with him, speaking sometimes in a deep voice, sometimes in a high
voice; sometimes weeping, sometimes smiling; sometimes with many words,
sometimes with few, sometimes with none.

26

In interpreting this difficult imaginative material, the operator must thus use the rational language of exegesis and disputation to mold it into the desired form. This is a highly interventionist process in which, if the Virgin promises something tomorrow ("crastina die"), she can be understood to refer to next year, while her refusal to allow something "adhuc benedicemus tibi" (until we shall bless you) gives implicit permission to act now (NC III.iii.2, NC III.i.4). When the Virgin responds smilingly "non" to a question and holds her foot out to be kissed, the operator may proceed as though her smile implies a *qualified* no, or, in other words, a provisional yes (OC III.3). Conversely, when she gives permission "quasi invitus et graviter et quod se tederet loquendo" (as though unwillingly and heavily and as if she tired herself by speaking), the operator accepts the permission but understands her reluctance as a counsel of delay (I.ii.5).

The *Liber florum* uses similarly drastic techniques in arguing its own validity in the face of its critics, interpreting Gratian's claim that dreams produce only illusions *a contrario sensu* as implying the opposite of what it says:

Quod [ista sciencia] sit stabilis, sancta, et vera . . . potest probari auctoritate illa canonum . . . unde dicitur, *ex turpi enim cogitacione vigilantis oritur illusio luxurie in mente dormientis*. . . . Ex quibus verbis datur intelligi a contrario sensu subtiliter intuenti: quia *ex munda et pulchra cogitacione vigilantis oritur veritas castitatis summa in mente dormientis*. . . .[39] Set ista sciencia ex ineffabili et pulchra cogitacione vigilantis in contemplacione imaginis Virginis gloriose et rerum super celestium. . . . Ergo sequitur ex hoc quod oriatur visio veritatis in mente dormientis, et ita patet in animo a sompno excitato visionem veritatis vidisse non illusionem fantasticam.

(NC III.i.5)

For that [this science] is stable, holy, and true . . . can be proved by the authority of the canon where it is said, *the illusion of lust arises in the mind of the dreamer from his sinful thoughts when awake*. It is possible to those of subtle understanding to understand these words in the opposite sense: that *out of the pure and beautiful cogitation of the waker is born the truth of highest chastity in the mind of the sleeper*. But this science consists in an ineffable and beautiful cogitation on the part of the waker, in contemplation of the image of the glorious Virgin and of supercelestial things. . . . Thus it follows from this that a vision of truth is born in the

[39] From Gratian's *Decretum*, Pars I, Dist. VI, Cap. 1(*PL* 187: 41).

27

mind of the sleeper, and so it is clear that a vision of truth, not a fantastic illusion, is seen in the mind by the awakened sleeper.

The strong claims made for the prophetic content of dreams here suggest how important it is to the *Liber florum,* whose success depends on the ultimate viability of the imagination as an instrument of the *visio veritatis,* to distance the *experimentum visionis habende* from the epistemological ambiguities Dante finds himself obliged to embrace, lest the shape-shifting Virgin be revealed as only another manifestation of Geryon.

Despite its quest for certitude, however, the *Liber florum* makes it clear that the mode of the *experimentum* has a vexed and provisional relation to truth, for two reasons. First, the Virgin's appearance in dreams must be carefully vetted for diabolical deception. When she appears not in a church but in a place "unclean, filthy, dark and of ill repute, as in a tavern, or ditch, or dark cavern, or in a brothel" ("immundus, sordidus, obscurus et diffamatus, ut in taberna, vel fossa, vel caverna obscura, vel in lupanari"), or incites lust in the operator, clearly all she says and does will be evil (OC I.iv.10). But even true visions may contain a whiff of the diabolic, an intermingling of truth and error. Sometimes the Virgin's true appearance is followed by a deceptive one; sometimes Virgin and demon actually appear together, the latter "speaking first with her permission, always falsely persuading against salvation" ("preveniens verba illius, ea permittente, semper contra salutem fallaciter persuadens"), in a test of the operator's faith, hope, and charity (NC I.iv.3). Interpretations of dreams thus always stand to be corrected by new evidence, improvements in the operator's understanding of a dream and the balance of good and evil within it, or changes in external circumstance.

Second, the dreams themselves are in any case explicitly constructs, generated by a collaborative process of creation, in which the operator's imagination, under the Virgin's guidance, invents a shape for her in the form of a work of devotional art, which then enables her to communicate, imperfectly but urgently, with his mind. Indeed, it is said to be only in such constructed forms that such heavenly beings as the Virgin, the saints, even Christ himself are able to manifest themselves to humans on earth:

Christus, Maria, sancti, et angeli, secundum formam in qua hominibus apparent, in ipsis est ficta transmutatio, quia alio modo nobis apparere non possunt;

sed secundum naturam divinam et essenciam in qua sunt et in perfeccione eterna manent. Tunc apud ipsos *nulla est transmutatio nec vicissitudinis obumbratio* (Jas. 1:17). Et hec que prediximus . . . cum ista vel aliquod predictorum videris, scias et cognoscas me verum dixisse et in nullo mentitum fuisse.

(OC I.iv.10)

With regard to the form in which Christ, Mary, the saints, and angels appear to human beings, they undergo a fictitious transmutation, since they cannot appear to us in any other way; but with regard to the divine nature and essence in which they exist, they still remain in eternal perfection. So where they are in themselves *there is no transmutation nor shadow of vicissitude* (Jas. 1:17). And about these things which we have just said . . . when you see these things or anything of the aforesaid, you may know and understand that I have spoken truth and lied in no respect.

Despite the echoes of the Pygmalion story (or the resurrection of Hermione in *The Winter's Tale*), there is a clear hierarchy of creation here, with the operator responsible only for a deaf and dumb idol that the Virgin turns into a speaking image by animating it with miraculous life. Yet the passage also offers a suggestive understanding of the obscurity of the Virgin's appearances as produced by difficulties on *both* sides of the divide between earth and heaven, human and divine: as a kind of static, caused by the vast spiritual distances being bridged and the fallibility and openness to diabolic interference of the place where the bridge is built, the operator's dreaming imagination.

The truth about the *experimentum* of the shape-shifting Virgin is that it is no lie ("me . . . in nullo mentitum fuisse") but a meaning-bearing fictional ("ficta transmutatio"), inherently vulnerable to error, through which the Virgin's voice may indeed be heard no louder than a whisper ("quasi sibilus aure tenuis"). Hence the open-endedness not only of the *experimentum* John passes on to his successors, who are free, with the Virgin's guidance, to take his heavenly research in new directions, but also of the *Liber florum* itself, despite its real artistry. For all its claims to an unusually collaborative form of divine inspiration, the *Liber florum* provides little new knowledge but rather a method of study, endlessly susceptible of improvement, in which the imagination is at once the principal medium through which knowledge may pass and a barrier whose partial impermeability both constitutes and symbolizes the gulf between earthly contingency and the eternal truths in which "nulla est transmutatio nec vicissitudinis obumbratio."

29

* * *

Operators of the *Liber florum*, then, are very much like historical scholars, understanding the *figurae* they fashion for the Virgin and the meanings they find in her manifestations merely as models, hypotheses, always liable to be supplemented and corrected by new data once they are available. These *figurae* offer a necessary environment in which the search for that stable yet flexible thing, truth, can continue, but it is also only a temporary one. Times change; new evidence emerges; new needs demand new questions; the Virgin's baffling responses to these questions in turn require that they be reunderstood—much as historical hypotheses, often also based on present concerns, may initially be rebuffed by the evidence of the archive, but then be given back to the historian in a form made over, as the study of the past again transforms the present.

Meanwhile, the medium itself, the mode of investigation, is suspect in ways that can be isolated neither from the manner in which the past survives nor from the biases of the historical operator. Yet according to the *Liber florum*, the Virgin must address the needs and desires of operators in the present, albeit in her own, obstinately slant way. This is not in the end because—her being elsewhere, where "nulla est transmutatio"—she can reach into the present only as a phantasm made of present needs and desires. To reason thus, as John says, "secundum auctoritates physicas naturales" (according to the authorities of the natural sciences), is possible only by sacrificing the operator's sense of the independent coherence and truth of the phenomena (OC I.iv.10). In the same way, to think of the construction of the past as no more than a projection of modernity's needs and desires, doing away with any trace of the metaphysical, carries the cost of eliminating any sense of the past's once-separate identity—any sense that in its many and various modes of manifestation it still exerts pressure on the present.

Not that we can rely on the past we can apprehend through *experimentum* to be benign, tell us helpful truths, or tell us truths at all. The Virgin's manifestations may be demonic, not divine, and will as often as not be both. In the second epigraph at the beginning of this essay, from Sebald's last great fictional study of the catastrophic interpenetration of Europe's past and present, *Austerlitz*, the eponymous hero insists that the past, an object of almost extinguished but just recoverable memory, might still serve as a "meeting place" between modernity and its history, the place where we "keep," "so to speak," our "appointments . . . in the past." But even though Austerlitz lives in mortal need of what the past can and does tell him, the novel also represents the encounter with the past as the product of chance or grace as much as of effort or receptivity. What is more, the truth that perhaps redeems Austerlitz also destroys him; for Sebald, modernity needs its rapprochement with the past mainly because only so can it understand the violent sources of its own immeasurable destructiveness. In the search for historical truth through the mode of urgent and demanding summoning that is *experimentum*, only the persistence of question and answer, not the result, is certain.

Shewing

If Chaucer understands the imagination as a vital but explosively unpredictable engine of a vision of history whose lurching progress takes place under the sway of "tidinges," not orderly event, Dante and John of Morigny use the faculty to move beyond the here and now into far-distant places whose status is in important ways non-natural, having either almost infinitely less, or almost infinitely more, of being. Their projects serve different ends and their emphases fall in different places. Where Dante's use of the terminology of truth and fiction constructs an anxious literary aporia to demonstrate the impossible epistemological strain under which his poem labors, John, resisting total collapse into uncertainty, insists on the partial possibility of reaching truth through fiction by repetition and elaboration of visionary *experimenta*. Yet the two writers share an understanding of the capacity of the imagination to communicate with realms outside the range of the physical senses, agreeing on its prophetic ability to transmit information about forms inaccessible to these senses, even as they concede that this can only be done through fraud or *figura*, as the imagination invents, by recombination, images of things not found in nature as its means of representing these inaccessible forms.

As we have seen, there are complex analogies between these deployments of the idea of imagination and our own activities as historians summoning past forms into the present as we inventively recombine the information surviving in our collective *memoria*, the archive. This is a process in which prophecy and invention, here taking the forms of scholarly intuition and synthesis, both play their necessary roles, lending temporary life to the past in order to perform the unpredictable, essentially experimental, act of summoning that allows us to talk about and with this past as though it were still capable of presence on our own temporal plane. As we have seen, too, medieval imaginative writers are fully aware of the dangers of these procedures, even as they insist that the dangers are both necessary and surmountable: necessary because, in the nature of things, truth must be mediated through the image; surmountable because images, these writers optimistically insist, can in practice conjure the presence of things absent, the phantasm, at least temporarily, can bear the weight of the real.

The passage whose discussion concludes this essay, from the second of the sixteen revelations that make up Julian of Norwich's *Revelation of Love,* offers both a more direct medieval counterpart to the aspirations, ambiguities, and possibilities involved in the modern historian's attempt to summon the distant past and a particularly incisive analysis of the role of the phantasm in this attempt. The past in question here is the past of Christ's passion, which represents itself to Julian during the course of the long vision her text describes and analyzes, playing itself out on the surface of a cross that is being held before her face, throughout the revelation, as she lies sick in bed, attended by her friends and family (her "evencristen"), and waiting, as she thinks, to die:

And after this, I saw with bodely sight in the face of the crucifixe that hung before me, in the which I beheld continually a parte of his passion: dispite, spitting, solewing [soiling], and buffeting, and many languring paines, mo than I can tell, and often changing of colour. And one time I saw how halfe the face, beginning at the ere, overyede [spread over] with drye bloud till it beclosed into the mid face. And after that the other halfe beclosed on the same wise, and therewhiles it vanished in this party, even as it cam . . .

This secounde shewing was so lowe and so little and so simple that my spirites were in great traveyle in the beholding: morning, dredful, and longing. For I was sometime in a feer whether it was a shewing or none. And then diverse times our lord gave me more sight, wherby that I understode truly that it was a shewing. It was a figur and a liknes of oure foule, black, dede hame [skin] which our faire, bright, blessed lord bare for our sinne. It made me to thinke of the holy vernacle of Rome, which he portrude with his owne blessed face when he was in his hard passion, wilfully going to his death, and often changing of coloure.

(10.1–7, 25–32)

Julian's imaginative experience of the divine differs in obvious ways from John's, although it, too, is summoned by petition (a petition made long before the revelation, to experience actual presence at the past of the passion), and susceptible to the vagaries of imaginative activity: in this case, the problem of evanescence, the imagination's periodic inability to summon the images it desires or, once summoned, to hold them steady (2.5–16). Julian's first revelation of the blood of Christ dripping from the cross "hot and freshely, plentuously and lively," does not suffer from this problem, but her revelation as a whole is much prone to it, even more so than is true for John. This is both because there are many modes of revelation in operation at once, and because her represented response to her experience, even while in progress, is so quizzical, as her reason pointedly interrogates the procession of images from her *vis imaginativa* and the abstractions of "gostely sight" crowd out the presence of "bodily sight" (4.2, 9.24–25).

Apart from the opening sequence of the outpouring blood, Julian's "bodily sight" is indeed always most at home in scenes of absence and withdrawal. This is true again in the "harre" account of the "drye dying" that befalls "alle the lively spirites of Cristes flesh" in the eighth revelation, the intense culmination of *A Revelation*'s presentation of the passion. Here the slow death of Christ's "swete body" and the slow withering of her apprehension of it—as it grows "browne and blacke, alle changed and turned oute of the faire, fresh, and lively coloure of himself"—take place in tandem, as if her failure to keep Christ imaginatively alive were in some manner causing him to die, and the entire creation with him (16.7–9, 17). On this occasion, Julian's rationalism allows her to track the minute changes that accompany the withdrawal of color and life from revelation and dying body at once, as Christ's "lippes" appear to her "as it were drye and blodeles with pale dying; and sithen more deade pale, languring. And than turned more deade into blew; and sithen more browne blew, as the flesh turned more depe dede" (16.2–5). Yet reason intervenes to shut off sight of the death itself completely—"And I loked after the departing with alle my mightes and wende to have seen the body all dead" (21.5–6)—as though to allow the imagination to generate a phantasm of a scene from which all life is withdrawn would be a contradiction in terms. Rather as with John's *experimenta*, it seems axiomatic to this visionary mode that Julian's revelation will at once "enform" her "of alle that me neded" and refuse to correspond to her ideas about its shape and meaning, as image is supplanted by abstraction, easy answer by fierce question (27.9).

Indeed, Julian has internalized the hermeneutics of visionary suspicion advocated by the discourse of *discretio spirituum* so much more thoroughly than John, seven decades earlier, that her first instinct, on awakening to find herself still sick near the end of her revelation, is to deny her experience in its entirety, reluctant to feel the "vergogna" that, as Dante notes, falls to those who must assert improbable truths:

Then cam a religious person to me and asked me how I fared, and I saide I had raved to day. And he loght loude and enterly. And I saide: "The crosse that stode before my face, methought it bled fast." And with this worde, the person that I spake to waxed all sad and merveyled, and anone I was sore ashamed and astoned for my rechelesnesse.

(66.12–16)

Only her participation within a community of belief represented by the "religious person" saves the revelation from destruction, generating a confirmatory sixteenth revelation. Here Christ is no longer the fragmentary vision from the past he sometimes is earlier but is fully absorbed into Julian's own being, sitting "in the soule even righte in peas and rest," so that "the soule is alle occupied with the blessed godhed," seemingly accessing it directly, through intellectual vision, no longer by means of phantasms (68.1–10). This final vision is end-stopped by diabolic apparitions meant to induce despair, as the devil appears as "a yonge man," his face a parody of that of the dying Christ in the eighth revelation, "red, like the tilestone whan it is new brent, with blacke spotes therein like freknes, fouler than the tilestone": an image of what refusal of the truth of the revelation, the decision to treat it as subjective or fraudulent, would make it into (67.2–4). Fantastic as it is, skeptical as she is, the revelation requires Julian's belief to make it true, and also needs to be true if this demonic vision of meaninglessness is to be kept at bay.

A revelation showed to a devout rationalist, Julian's vision thus fails to summon the richly realized past she was hoping for in her petition, demanding a sometimes corrosively high level of self-awareness about the implications of summoning itself: about what it means to attempt to cross between present and past time. The imaginary archive that nonetheless accumulates through the thirty hours of her experience—for Julian is, in the end, convinced to treat her revelation as an archive of authenticated data, an indispensable collection of evidence for the study of sacred history—becomes the basis of the lifelong research project that is the *Revelation of Love* itself.

Returning now to the passage of the second revelation quoted earlier, we can observe the use to which Julian puts one small and initially most unpromising fragment of her archive: a fragment that her early version, *A Vision Showed to a Devout Woman*, dispenses with in a sentence (*Vision* 8.1–8). In the much-expanded later version given here, the evanescence of the imagination, its failure to live up to its image-making role in depicting the past, is understood as a truth about the past, as a phantasm of dried blood appears and disappears on either side of the physical crucifix at which Julian is gazing, as though the image were almost failing to cross the gulf of time.

This is an effect similar to one we noticed in the *Liber florum*. But where John's response to such difficulties might have been to undertake further *experimenta*, Julian's interpretive response is to make absence an aspect of revelation itself. Both the glimpsed image of the dried blood and the anxiously uncertain process of glimpsing are hence folded into a single image: the "figur and . . . likness of oure foule, black, dede hame which our faire, bright, blessed lord bare for oure sinne." The "dede hame," dead skin or membrane, is Christ's incarnate but dying flesh, in which his "bright, blessed" divinity is hidden, here almost to the vanishing point, just as divinity lies hidden in the wastes of history, figured here by the "foule, black, dede" quality of Christ's blood, and the blurring that impedes Julian's vision of it. The passage compares this effect to that of the Vernicle, a relic that, faded as it is, also testifies as eloquently to the passage of time as it does to the miracle of its portrayal of Christ's frail, human image. It is as if Christ's "willful" journey toward "his death" on Golgotha to suffer for all human history's sins had been stretched out to encompass the entirety of time thereafter; as if time itself, or the damage to presence wrought by time, were a "figur and . . . likness" of sin.

Here the imaginary archive is so "lowe . . . little and . . . simple" that it would fail to be an archive, were it not asked the one set of questions it can at this point answer, questions about time, memory, and loss. Asked those questions, however, the passage can contribute to Julian's overall project, which is to understand how this image of history can coexist with the vision of presence and plentitude presented early in her revelation. There, Christ's blood, not "foule" and "black" but "fair" and "rede," flows through the world "like to the droppes of water that falle of the evesing of an house after a grete shower of raine, that falle so thicke that no man may nomber them with no bodely wit" (7.17–19):

an image of the fecundity not only of his embodied life, but of sacred history and the endless procession of images by which it first represents itself to Julian.

This is not the place to describe Julian's full theories of history and the epistemology of vision, although both are of potential relevance. I conclude instead with a few thoughts about the past as phantasm, just figured for us again in the drops of blood from the past of the Passion that Julian initially sees as present, as "quick and lively." Like Julian's experience of her revelation, our lives as scholars of archives or textual *corpora* tend to involve severe alternations of presence and absence: places at which our evidence and our work is "foul, black, and dede," and others at which it seems to stream as thick as the blood of Christ before Julian's visionary gaze. This is of the nature of our work with material that, whatever it is we research, has always, one way or another, suffered devastating loss, while also leaving us, once we can learn to see them, with glimpses of thoughts, experiences, and lives lived in the bodies that are no longer here.

Our work on these bodies does not bring them back. But it does temporarily summon their phantasms, making novelty, *tidinges* of the past. Moreover, it does so in the face of a process, which this essay has dystopically called modernity, through which the past may have tended, over the last two centuries, to become inert: more and more like those accumulations of lifeless images that, in monastic imaginative regimes, were once taken to herald the onset of *accidia*. Conceivably the vanishment of the deep past from the consciousness of the collective cultural imaginary would not be a mortal loss to the present, at least on the scale of some losses. Mortal loss can no longer befall the past, both because it already has and because its phantasmic presence, if no longer sustained by historical research, must continue in other forms; premodern imaginative theory assures us that the processes underlying cultural change are recombinative. Nonetheless, it falls to historical scholars to make the case for the necessity of the past: for the value, if not predictable utility, of keeping even deep history in cultural circulation.

Always aware of *accidia* and its consequences, medieval visionaries and dream poets agree that circulation, the process of question, answer, and exchange that John calls *experimentum*, is vital to the mode of imaginative thought that is their concern, since phantasms are unpredictable and mobile and the thinking that can be done with them must be open and provisional. Even Julian's intensively researched revelation ends by stating that its work is only "begonne . . . not yet performed" (86.1–2). Historical research undertaken under the sign of the phantasm might think of itself very differently in this respect than if it understood itself, as historical writing generally has, only in relation to the fixed systems of worth and the certainties of fact associated with the *memoria*. Yet visionaries and dream poets alike assert the necessity of treating the phantasm as a vehicle of the real: for *belief* in the imaginative constructs that allow visionary journeys to continue serve to link the other world with this one, reach out mysteriously to or from the past to renew the life of the present. Their faith, seriousness, urgency, and inventiveness challenge our own.[40]

[40] Versions of this essay were read at venues at the following universities, April 2006 through 2009: Calgary, California–Berkeley, California–Davis, Chicago, Connecticut, Harvard, Manchester, New York, Ottawa, Toronto, and Virginia. My thanks to all who organized and attended these events, providing a body of commentary that has significantly influenced this revision. Special thanks are due Suzanne Akbari, Amy Appleford, Andrew Cole, Claire Fanger, Barbara Newman, and James Simpson; also to Mary Carruthers and a second, anonymous reviewer for *SAC* for trenchant thoughts and suggestions.

Religious Practice in Chaucer's
Prioress's Tale:

Rabbit and/or Duck?

Helen Barr
Lady Margaret Hall, University of Oxford

N OTHING IN CHAUCER'S *Prioress's Tale* explicitly refers to four-teenth-century religious controversy. The tale is set in Asia, and in the past. This geographical and temporal dislocation, however, disguises only very thinly the extent to which the narrative is steeped in devotional issues greatly disputed by Chaucer's contemporaries. The tale manages to pre-sent both an orthodox, and a heterodox, account of religious practice. In so doing, it toys with the perceptions of the reader, rather like Jastrow's famous Duck-Rabbit illustration.[1] The observer of the duck-rabbit image produces either a duck or a rabbit, or alternates between the two; but nothing changes materially in the lines of the image itself. So too, in reading the lines of the verbal text of *The Prioress's Tale*, the duck of ortho-doxy or the rabbit of heterodoxy are both present, depending on the inter-pretative presuppositions of the reader.[2] But while neither we, nor Chaucer's contemporary audience, can experience alternate readings at the

[1] See J. Jastrow, "The Mind's Eye," *Popular Science Monthly* 54 (1899): 299–312.
[2] "The subject of a gestalt demonstration knows that his perception has shifted because he can make it shift back and forth repeatedly while he holds the same book or piece of paper in his hands. Aware that nothing in his environment has changed, he directs his attention increasingly not to the figure (duck or rabbit) but to the lines of the paper he is looking at. Ultimately he may even learn to see those lines without seeing either of the figures, and he may then say (what he could not legitimately have said earlier) that it is these lines that he really sees but that he sees them alternately *as* a duck and *as* a rabbit. . . . As in all similar psychological experiments, the effective-ness of the demonstration depends upon its being analyzable in this way. Unless there were an external standard with respect to which a switch of vision could be demon-strated, no conclusion about alternate perceptual possibilities could be drawn." Thomas Kuhn, *The Structure of Scientific Revolutions* (Chicago: University of Chicago Press, 1970), 114.

same time, we can switch from one reading to another with increasing rapidity. As E. H. Gombrich argues, "We will also remember the rabbit when we see the duck."[3] Polarity of interpretation shades into uncertainty of meaning; to the process of response, not to its summation.

It is exactly this phenomenon that Norman Rabkin explores in his essay on *Henry V* in *Shakespeare and the Problem of Meaning*. Audiences arriving for the first performance of *Henry V* in 1599 would have been unsure what to expect of the figure of Henry had they seen both *1 Henry IV* and *2 Henry IV*. From their knowledge of the first part, they would recall a broadly comic Hal, "potentially larger than his father, possessing the force that politics requires without the sacrifice of imagination and range that Bolingbroke has to pay." But if they had watched the second part, they would have seen "the study of an opportunist who has traded his humanity for his success, covering over the ruthlessness of the politician with the mere appearance of fellowship."[4] Perhaps, if we were members of that 1599 audience, Rabkin argues, we hope that the new play will resolve our doubts, give us a single gestalt to replace the antithetical images before our mind's eye. "But instead, we are made to see a rabbit or duck . . . leaving the theatre at the end of the first performance, some members of the audience knew that they had seen a rabbit, others a duck. Still others, and I would suggest that they were Shakespeare's best audience, knew uneasily that they did not know what to think."[5]

Chaucer's *Prioress's Tale* poses a very similar problem of meaning dependent on the response of an audience to a work derived from material they already knew. But in this case, the audience's prior knowledge lay not in conflicting experiences of prequels to a new play, but in cultural knowledge of the values of liturgical practices and the keywords that describe them. What follows is not an intervention into *The Prioress's Tale* that simply poses a choice between an "orthodox" and a "Lollard" way of reading the poem. While I shall contend that the materials of the tale do present the potential for this interpretive polarity, my argument is more fundamentally concerned with the process of response: how the gestalt of previously acquired knowledge informs the reading of new phenomena; how in the case of *The Prioress's Tale*, the reconstruc-

---

[3] E. H. Gombrich, *Art and Illusion: A Study of the Psychology of Pictorial Representation* (New York: Pantheon Books, 1960), 5–6.

[4] Norman Rabkin, "Either/Or: Responding to *Henry V*" in *Shakespeare and the Problem of Meaning* (Chicago: University of Chicago Press, 1981), 33–62 (43).

[5] Ibid., 43–44.

tion of available cultural knowledge of social practice, most fundamentally its language, can help us to read the past in ways that the past might have recognized. I want to argue not so much for a particular reading of the tale as to show how the mode of narration and clusters of diction in *The Prioress's Tale* act as prompts for readers to interpret the poem depending on their prior cultural knowledge and values.

I make use here of a context of reception that is informed by the model of cultural linguistics based on Gricean pragmatics and relevance theory—namely, "inferencing." Inferencing, through a refinement of the concept of decoding, affords great scope for the existence of competing interpretations of a text. Reception depends on the cultural knowledge and competence of the reader. The words of a text are only part of what the recipient has to work with in producing a response to it. One does decode it, but through drawing on other information, both that which is included in the communicative context and that which is available as cultural knowledge about the world.[6] While, of course, all acts of interpretation require inferencing, what is especially pertinent in this approach to meaning for *The Prioress's Tale* is that inferencing involves the recognition of meanings that may not be available to all readers, or whose value is differently regarded. Recipients respond to prompts in a text, which leads them to inference certain values or even "messages," most importantly where these values or issues are not explicit. In her

---

[6] Deborah Cameron invokes the concept of inferencing in her discussion of language, sexism, and advertising standards in *On Language and Sexual Politics* (London: Routledge, 2006), 36. My treatment here is indebted to that discussion. H. P. Grice's linguistic research argued for a mode of communication in which the recovery of meaning depended both on speakers sharing the same code and the expectations surrounding the speech event. Grice described those expectations in terms of a cooperative principle existing between speakers where communication was governed by maxims of Quality (truthfulness), Relation (relevance), and Manner (clarity).

Relevance theorists have refined Grice's pragmatics through further attention to cognitive processing. An utterance is an "input"—like a sound, a sight, or a memory. An input becomes relevant to an individual when it connects to background information that he or she has available to yield conclusions that are significant to that individual. A conclusion is deductible from input and context together, but from neither input nor context alone. There is no shortage of potential inputs that might have relevance, but an individual cannot attend to them all. The recovery of the most relevant input from competing stimuli is based on a mix of linguistic and nonlinguistic clues, including perception, categorization, memory, encyclopedic knowledge, and cognitive mechanisms. See H. P. Grice, "Logic and Conversation," in *Syntax and Semantics 3: Speech Acts* (New York: Academic Press, 1975), 41–58; see also Dan Sperber and Deirdre Wilson, *Relevance* (Oxford: Blackwell, 1986), and Deirdre Wilson and Dan Sperber, "Relevance Theory," in *Handbook of Pragmatics*, ed. G. Ward and L. Horn (Oxford: Blackwell, 2004), 607–32.

study of the inferencing of cultural values in language, sexism, and advertising, Deborah Cameron analyzes captions and images from a series of lingerie advertisements, in which the copy is dependent on sexual innuendo. Responses to these advertisements depended on recipients' recognition of coded references to sexual practices and being able to forge connections (inexplicit in the advertisements) between text and image. A wide range of responses was generated: at one extreme, complaints were made to the advertising standards agency, while at the other end of the scale, some respondents found the advertisements not only funny but sexually empowering to women.[7] At each end of the spectrum, readers' responses to exactly the same advertisements were contradictory. Readers made sense of the texts by drawing on their cultural knowledge of prompts or signals.[8]

In *The Prioress's Tale,* these prompts are its generic affiliations, the collocational patterns of its diction and their experiential and relational values.[9] There are no cookery japes about transubstantiation, or whiffs of "Lollere[s] in the wynd."[10] A Wycliffite reading of the tale becomes available only if a reader has the cultural knowledge of religious dissidence to inference a critique from the connotations of words and phrases, which, together with the stylistic formality of the tale, accrete

[7] In an extension of this inferencing, Cameron demonstrates how responses were influenced, consciously or not, by the degrees of heteronormativity to which the advertisements could be seen to conform. *On Language and Sexual Politics,* 37, 41.

[8] This cultural knowledge functions as the "environment" or "external standard" that Kuhn argues is lacking when the subject of a gestalt demonstration views the duck-rabbit image. See note 2 above. How would the image be perceived if the subject had never seen one or other animal?

[9] Experiential values are the kinds of experiences to which the language of the text refers and relational values are the interpersonal relationships set up between text and recipient. See Norman Fairclough, *Language and Power* (London: Longman, 1989), 110–11.

[10] See *The Pardoner's Tale,* VI.538–39; *Epilogue to the Man of Law's Tale,* II.1172. Quotations are from Larry D. Benson, gen. ed., *The Riverside Chaucer* (Oxford: Oxford University Press, 1988). The Prioress's oath may be considered an exception, see note 73 below. For discussion of Wycliffism in Chaucer's oeuvre, see Anne Hudson, *The Premature Reformation* (Oxford: Clarendon Press, 1988), 390–92; Paul Strohm, "Chaucer's Lollard Joke: History and the Textual Unconscious," *SAC* 17 (1995): 23–42; Fiona Somerset, "'As just as is a squyre': The Politics of 'Lewed Translation' in Chaucer's *Summoner's Tale,*" *SAC* 21 (1999): 187–208, and "Here, There, and Everywhere? Wycliffite Conceptions of the Eucharist and Chaucer's 'Other' Lollard Joke" in *Lollards and Their Influence in Late Medieval England,* ed. Fiona Somerset, Jill C. Havens, and Derrick G. Pitard (Woodbridge, Suffolk: Boydell, 2003), 127–40; Alcuin Blamires, "The Wife of Bath and Lollardy," *MÆ* 58 (1989): 224–42; Alan J. Fletcher, "Chaucer the Heretic," *SAC* 25 (2003): 53–122; Andrew Cole, *Literature and Heresy in the Age of Chaucer* (Cambridge: Cambridge University Press, 2008), 75–100.

to suggest the spiritually empty "ornament" that is the object of so much Lollard complaint. For another reader, a practitioner perhaps of orthodox liturgical practice, the repetitive stylistic virtuosity and projection of affective piety connote the dignity of felt church ritual. One reader's duck is another reader's rabbit. But even to polarize thus is an oversimplification. For a reader possessed of both gestalts, the image shifts from one to the other, so much so that the defining lines disappear altogether, leaving perhaps just an area shaded gray.[11]

One further caveat before turning to *The Prioress's Tale* in detail. While I shall trace the process of interpretative polarity, this is not done in disregard of scholarship that has gone so far in demonstrating that religious culture in late medieval England cannot be understood simply in terms of a binary of orthodoxy or Lollardy.[12] Furthermore, as Kathryn Kerby-Fulton has demonstrated, Wycliffite heresy is not a lonely narrative of radical religious thought. The religious climate in late medieval England was unsettled and diverse. While Wycliffism might have dominated the attention of modern scholars because of its high profile in official records, late medieval authors, Chaucer among them, were aware of other strands of suspect religious thought, both Latin and continental.[13] *The Prioress's Tale* is situated within a complex web of religious writings in which Wycliffism is but one thread. And even then, the social value of writing informed by Wycliffite debate is not straightforward. While I shall argue that the writing of *The Prioress's Tale* presents the potential for interpretative polarity, this is not to set up a model of judgment in which Wycliffism is somehow a "backdrop" to the tale, possessing negative value, while orthodoxy tests positive. Rather, the existence of Wycliffite debate renders the linguistic and extralinguistic signs of the tale open to potentially oppositional inferencing. It is a work that can be seen to have been produced within the imaginative registers of late medieval writing that Wycliffism and other heterodox strands of religious thought made

[11] A reference, of course, to Anne Hudson's celebrated term, the "grey area" between orthodoxy and heterodoxy, *Premature Reformation*, 21–24.

[12] In addition to Hudson, see the essays by Jill Havens, Annie Sutherland, Fiona Somerset, and James Simpson in *Text and Controversy from Wyclif to Bale: Essays in Honour of Anne Hudson*, ed. Helen Barr and Ann M. Hutchinson (Turnhout: Brepols, 2005); Cole, *Literature and Heresy*, 47–53. This issue was also debated in many of the papers at the "After Arundel" conference, University of Oxford, 2009. Kantik Ghosh and Vincent Gillespie are editing the proceedings for Brepols, forthcoming 2010/11.

[13] Kathryn Kerby-Fulton, *Books Under Suspicion: Censorship and Tolerance of Revelatory Writing in Late Medieval England* (Notre Dame, Ind.: University of Notre Dame Press, 2006).

possible,[14] even though the tale itself does not appear to encroach on the major subjects of religious controversy: clerical endowment, the place of the sacraments, or biblical translation, for example. I want to argue that one of the possibilities for late fourteenth-century readers of *The Prioress's Tale* was the potential for inferencing polarity of religious attitudes from a single work within a much broader context of other available responses. That is, I am not trying to unweave the threads of religious expression in all their striated colors, but to argue that within late fourteenth-century orthodoxy, there existed the interpretative potential for the expression, and recognition, of apparently conflictual views.[15] While my intervention into *The Prioress's Tale* does not engage some of these wider polemical issues, nor does it negotiate the much broader context, I hope to show that discussion of the ways in which Chaucer's contemporaries might have inferenced the presentation of liturgy and song in this text might do work applicable elsewhere.

First, generic affiliations: the tale that Chaucer assigns to the Prioress is a miracle of the Virgin story afforced by elements of martyr-tales and saint's lives.[16] An explicit parallel is drawn between the killing of the little "clergeoun" and the martyrdom of Saint Hugh the Younger of Lincoln.[17] The tale is Marian not only in its plot but in its verbal texture; the Virgin is referenced insistently. In the *Prologue,* the Prioress frames her telling of the tale with a praise of the Virgin Mary (460–87), and throughout the tale the name of Mary, or the Mother of God, occurs with a repetitiveness that exceeds the strict demands of the plot. In a tale of 238 lines there are ten instances of the phrase "the mother of God." The boy learns his song in reverence of the mother of God (537–38); the song itself is in praise of the Virgin (552–57), and the boy's whole devotion is set on reverencing Mary (550). Whenever he sees an image of the Virgin, he kneels down and says the Ave Maria (505–8),

---

[14] See Cole, *Literature and Heresy,* especially 186–87.

[15] Rather as in the responses to the advertisements Cameron analyzed: within a range of opinions, some of them culturally inexplicit, contradictory polarity was registered at each end of the scale.

[16] Roger Ellis notes that "the miracle is the momentary expression of what the saint's life represents in fully extended form." *Patterns of Religious Narrative in the "Canterbury Tales"* (London: Croom Helm, 1986), 70. On the tale's affiliations, see also Roger Dahood, "English Historical Narratives of Jewish Child-Murder, Chaucer's *Prioress's Tale,* and the Date of Chaucer's Unknown Source," *SAC* 31 (2009): 125–40.

[17] *The Prioress's Tale,* VII.684–86.

and he cannot stop singing his song because the sweetness of the Virgin Mary has so pierced his heart (555–56). When the boy's mother learns of his fate, she calls ever on Christ's mother (597–98), and the provost, hurrying to the terrible scene of the murdered boy, praises the Virgin Mary as he goes (619). The boy's narration of his torture at the hands of the Jews is laced with Marian praise (654–69), and after the boy's death the abbot and the whole convent salute "Cristes mooder deere" (678). The final line of the tale, spoken by the Prioress, is "[f]or reverence of his mooder Marie" (690).

Clearly, there is what linguists would call Marian "overwording" in this tale.[18] That is, a dense cluster of vocabulary returns again and again to a single issue above the strict demands of the events of the story. This Marian overwording is reinforced through allusions that create parallels between the boy and Jesus, and his mother and Mary. After telling us that the "clergeoun" is taught to reverence Mary by his mother, the Prioress interrupts the narrative to draw attention to Saint Nicholas's reverencing of Christ (514–15). The reference in line 542 to the beating of the boy "thries in an houre" reminds of the scourging of Christ before his Crucifixion. The labeling of the Jews, as they form their conspiracy to attack the boy, as "cursed folk of Herodes al newe" (574), refers to the massacre of the innocents from Matthew 2:18. The diction of line 672—"[a]nd he yaf up the goost ful softely"—recalls Christ's death on the cross.[19] Jesus' revelation to the mother of her murdered son's location—"of his grace / [he] Yaf in hir thoght inwith a litel space" (603–4)—is based on an incarnational topos.[20] The mother's distress for

---

[18] Overwording is "an unusually high degree of wording, often involving many words which are near synonyms. Overwording shows preoccupation with some aspect of reality—which may indicate that it is a focus of ideological struggle." Fairclough, *Language and Power*, 115.

[19] Three of the gospels record Christ's death using this diction: Mark 15:37, "And Jesus having cried out with a loud voice, gave up the ghost"; Luke 23:46, "And Jesus crying out with a loud voice, said: Father, into thy hands I commend my spirit. And saying this, he gave up the ghost"; and John 19:30, "Jesus therefore, when he had taken the vinegar, said: It is consummated. And bowing his head, he gave up the ghost," *The Douay-Rheims Bible*, http://www.drbo.org/index.htm accessed 25 August 2008.

[20] See the Marian religious lyric that includes the lines "For in this rose conteynyd was / Heven and erthe in lytyl space" in *A Selection of Religious Lyrics*, ed. Douglas Gray (Oxford: Clarendon Press, 1975), 12, lines 4–5. This topos is discussed in Jacqueline Tasioulas, "'Heaven and Earth in Little Space': The Foetal Existence of Christ in Medieval Literature and Thought," *MÆ* 76 (2007): 24–48.

her boy parallels that of Mary for her son; her swoon by his bier recalls Mary's grief at the foot of the cross (625).[21]

This Marian devotion is bolstered with liturgical reference. The chronological background of the story consists of the three seasons of the Christian year devoted to the nativity: Advent, Christmas, and Epiphany. The boy's song, the *Alma Redemptoris* (518), is an antiphon to Mary in the breviary sung in the liturgy from Advent to Candlemas. Lines 580–85 are based on Revelation 14:1, which was read at the Feast of the Holy Innocents (28 December), and line 627, referring to the boy's mother as "This newe Rachel," is based on Matthew 2:18 and was part of the Gospel reading for the same Mass. The ceremonial sprinkling of the clergeoun's body with "hooly water" (639) recalls the blessing with holy water in the burial ritual that followed the requiem before the corpse was taken from the church. Maltman has argued that the "greyn" placed on the child's tongue at the end of the story derives from a commemoration of Saint Thomas sung during the second Vespers of the Feast of the Holy Innocents, where it is a symbol both of martyrdom and the soul winnowed from the body.[22] The framework of the tale is drawn from Marian liturgy. As has been well documented, lines 453–59 of the Prioress's *Prologue* are a paraphrase of Psalm 8:1–2. These were the opening lines of matins in the Little Office of the Virgin, though it has also been argued that Chaucer may have had the Mass of the Holy Innocents also in mind.[23]

Saturated with Marian devotion and liturgical reference, then, the tale appears overwhelmingly orthodox. Worship of Mary is reinforced through a narrative poetics that foregrounds affective devotional piety.[24] The persistent patterning of the tale creates a texture akin to the repeti-

---

[21] Ellis analyzes the biblical analogues and archetypal references in *Patterns of Religious Narrative*, 76–77. Carolyn P. Collette argues that the parallels between the mother-child and Virgin-Christ relationship "call to mind the most human aspect of the most ineffable mystical relation the world has known, the love of a virgin-mother for a God-child." "Sense and Sensibility in the *Prioress's Tale*," *ChauR* 15 (1981): 138–50 (144).

[22] Sr. N. Maltman, "'The Divine Granary,' or the End of the Prioress's 'Greyn,'" *ChauR* 17 (1976): 163–70 (164).

[23] These liturgical references are noted in *The Riverside Chaucer*, 913–16, and are discussed by Beverly Boyd, *Chaucer and the Liturgy* (Philadelphia: Dorrance and Company, 1967), 65–75.

[24] The affective piety of the tale is discussed by John C. Hirsh, "Reopening *The Prioress's Tale*," *ChauR* 10 (1975): 30–41 (37–39); and see R. O. Payne's observation that "in the *Prioress's Tale*, the story is in effect frozen into a kind of basic situation and the major effort is in the rhetorical elaboration of its emotional implications." *The Key of Remembrance* (New Haven: Yale University Press, 1963), 166.

tion of liturgical practice.[25] One of the repeated words is "reverence" (473, 515, 537, 564, 690); the word's connotations of orchestrated veneration are entirely appropriate to the narrative style that is assigned to the teller. The resounding of words and phrases also constructs a religiosity akin to that found in devotional lyrics. Seen at its most virtuosic in the poems of Richard Rolle, language in this kind of religious writing attains to a song-lyric state, in which repetition creates affective intensity:

> Jhesu, my dere and my drewry, delyte ert þou to syng.
> Jhesu, my myrth and melody, when will þow com, my keyng?
> Jhesu, my hele and my hony, my whart and my comfortyng,
> Jhesu, I covayte for to dy when it es þi payng.[26]

Such iterative devotion targets the heart, not the head. The somatic is the semantic; lyrics such as Rolle's are, in the words of Susan Sontag, "an experience, not a statement or an answer to a question."[27] So, too, the textuality of *The Prioress's Tale* offers not explanation, but orthodox affective excitation.

Or does it? What happens when we look at exactly the same phe-

---

[25] As Richard Osberg observes, "Almost everyone who comments on the tale notes its salient stylistic features: the frequency with which certain words are repeated, its rhyme royal stanza and the character of its syntax," Richard H. Osberg, "A Voice for the Prioress: The Context of English Devotional Prose," *SAC* 18 (1996): 25–54. For analysis of this stylistic artifice, see Payne, *Key of Remembrance*, 169. On liturgical practice in the poem, see Dorothy Guerin, "Chaucer's Pathos: Three Variations," *ChauR* 20 (1985): 90–112; Alfred David, "An ABC to the Style of the Prioress," in M. Carruthers and E. Kirk, eds., *Acts of Interpretation: The Text in Its Contexts, 700–1600: Essays on Medieval and Renaissance Literature in Honor of E. Talbot Donaldson* (Norman, Okla: Pilgrim Books, 1982), 147–57, and Derek Pearsall, *The Canterbury Tales* (London: G. Allen and Unwin, 1985), 247.

[26] Richard Rolle, *Ego Dormio*, lines 341–45, in *English Writings of Richard Rolle: Hermit of Hampole*, ed. Hope Emily Allen (Gloucester: Alan Sutton, 1988). On Rolle's affectivity, see Vincent Gillespie, "Mystic's Foot: Rolle and Affectivity," in *The Medieval Mystical Tradition in England: Papers Read at Dartington Hall, July 1982*, ed. Marion Glasscoe (Exeter: Exeter University Press, 1982), 199–230.

[27] "A work of art encountered as a work of art is an experience, not a statement or an answer to a question. Art is not only about something; it is something. A work of art is a thing in the world, not just a text or commentary on the world. . . . [T]he distinctive feature of [works of art] is that they give rise not to conceptual knowledge (which is the distinctive feature of discursive or scientific knowledge—e.g. philosophy, sociology, psychology, history) but to something like an excitation, a phenomenon of commitment, judgment in a state of thraldom or captivation. Which is to say that the knowledge we gain through art is an experience of the form or style of knowing something rather than a knowledge of something (like a fact or a moral judgment) in itself." Susan Sontag, "On Style," *Against Interpretation* (London: Vintage, 1994), 21–22.

nomenon but with different prior cultural knowledge? A straightforward orthodox reading of the textuality of *The Prioress's Tale* is problematized by the fact that its repetitive signification clusters around the very religious practices that are the subject of Lollard polemic: hostility toward the veneration of images, devotion to saints,[28] belief in reports of miracles.[29] Given that reading the gospel and preaching it are considered the foundation of true Christian belief, Lollards express extreme skepticism about the value of anything that might distort the scriptures or distract from true understanding of the Bible.[30] The generic affiliations of *The Prioress's Tale*, with the narrative denouement achieved through Marian miracle, suggest a prime example of a "fable ungrounded upon truth." Anything that distracts from the supremacy of scripture is a superfluity, founded by man's law, not God's, and a pernicious invention that encumbers the ordained apostolic work of the church and the true understanding of its members. Important among such excrescences is liturgical spectacle, and especially song, both inventions of the devil:

Also bi song þe fend lettiþ men to studie & preche þe gospel; for siþ mannys wittis ben of certeyn mesure & myȝt, þe more þat þei ben occupied aboute siche mannus song þe lesse moten þei be sette aboute goddis lawe.

[28] See, for example, among Wycliffite writings, the opinion that "merueile it is þat synful foolis doren graunte ony þing of meritis of syntis; for al þat euere seynt dide may not brynge o soule to heuene wiþouten grace & myȝt of cristis passioun." Among the false fables that curates tell are how "þis seynt or þis lyuede in gay costy cloþis & worldly aray ȝit is a grete seynt." Compare the opinion, "þes prestis schulden witness opynly þat alle þe seyntis in heuene may not brynge a man to heuene wiþouten his owen goode lif, kepynge þe hestis of God, & endynge in charite." F. D. Matthew, *The English Works of Wyclif Hitherto Unprinted*, EETS o.s. 74 (London: Trübner & Co. for the EETS, 1880), 83, lines 11–14; 153, lines 16–18; 177, lines 18–20.

[29] The Wycliffite text "The Office of Curates" inveighs against fables and "seyntis dedis, or lesyngus putt on seyntis." Matthew, ed. *English Works of Wyclif*, 153, lines 5–6; see also the description of miracles of the saints as "foule leesyngis for to dissyue þe comune puple for coueytise of worldly muk." Anne Hudson, *Selections from English Wycliffite Writings* (Cambridge: Cambridge University Press, 1978), 87, lines 171–72. In *The Premature Reformation*, Anne Hudson relates two anecdotes that are symptomatic of Lollard attitudes toward saints and miracles: one, the comment of a Thomas Garenter in 1428, who held that only the Bible was true, for "the legendes and lyves of saintes, I helde been nought and the miracles wryten of hem I helde untrewe," and Knighton's account of the Leicester Lollard William Smith and his friends, who used an image of Saint Katherine to cook their supper, and commented on her second martyrdom (303).

[30] "[P]oul in his pistel [says] þat ȝif ony man, ȝee apostil or angel of heuene prech oþer þing þan is tauȝte of crist & his spostelis he is cursid. And Seint Jon seiþe, in þe ende of þe apocalips, þat ȝif ony man adde þus to goddis wordis, god schal brynge vpon hym alle þe vengauences wryten in þe apocalips." Matthew, ed. *English Works of Wyclif*, 37–38, lines 29, 1.

Also þe ordynalle of salisbury lettiþ moche prechynge of þe gospel; for folis chargen þat more þan þe maundementis of god to studie & teche cristes gospel.

A lord, ȝif alle þe studie & traueile þat men han now abowte salisbury vvs wiþ multitude of newe costy portos, antifeners, graielis, & alle oþere bokis weren turned in-to makynge of biblis & in studiynge & techynge þer-of, how moche schulde goddis lawe be forþered & knowen & kepte.[31]

The *Prioress's Prologue and Tale* is swollen with reference to targets of Wycliffite polemic.[32] What can be read one way as intense devotional piety can be read another as a sustained litany of religious malpractices. The distended orthodoxy of this tale inscribes its own critique. And here, the repetition of diction that describes the boy's song and the process through which he comes to learn it are crucial. I have placed the key vocabulary in bold:

> This **litel** child, his **litel book lernynge**,
> As he sat in the scole at his prymer,
> He *Alma redemptoris* herde synge,
> As children lerned hire antiphoner;
> And as he dorste, he drough hym ner and ner,
> And herkened ay the **wordes and the noote**,
> Til he the firste vers koude *al by rote*.
>
> **Noghte wiste he what this Latyn was to seye,**
> For he so **yong** and **tendre** was of age.
> But on a day his felawe gan he preye
> **T'expounden** hym this song in his langage. . . .
> (516–26)
>
> His felawe, which that elder was then he,
> Answerde hym thus: "This song, I have herd seye,

---

[31] Matthew, ed. *English Works of Wyclif*, 191, lines 4–7; 192, lines 33–35; 194, lines 4–9). These are not isolated criticisms; see also ibid., 77, lines 24–31; 112, lines 15–19; 169, lines 14–29; 170, lines 8–16; 177, lines 7–11.

[32] It should be noted, however, that for all the invective against liturgy, Lollard sermon collections often have liturgically organized lectionaries or calendars included; a point noted by Bruce Holsinger, "Liturgy," in *Middle English: Oxford Twenty-First Century Approaches to Literature*, ed. Paul Strohm (Oxford: Oxford University Press, 2007), 295–314 (308). See also the study of the Lollard Mass celebrated by the Lollard "priest" William Ramsbury, which used the established Sarum rite (if abbreviated), but appears to have left no room for a sermon. Anne Hudson, "A Lollard Mass," in *Lollards and Their Books* (London: Hambledon Press, 1985), 111–24.

Was maked of our blisful Lady free,
Hire to salue, and eek hire for to preye
To been oure help and socour whan we deye
I kan namoore expounde in this mateere.
I lerne song: I kan but smal grammeere."

"And is this song maked in reverence
Of Cristes mooder?" seyde this innocent
"Now, certes, I wol do my diligence
To **konne it** al er Cristemasse be went.
Though that I for my prymer shal be shent
And shal be beten thries in an houre,
I wol it **konne Oure Lady for to honoure!**'

His felawe taughte hym homward prively,
Fro day to day, til he koude it *by rote*,
And thanne he **song** it wel and boldely,
Fro **word to word, acordynge with the note**,
Twies a day it passed **thurgh his throte**,
To scoleward and homward whan he wente;
On Cristes mooder set was his entente.

(530–50)

These passages contain collocational patternings that stress littleness, tenderness, childlike innocence, and ignorance of book learning. The "konnyng"—understanding—of the boy falls outside the exposition provided through words. Grammar is explicitly contrasted to song.[33] The overwording of the lexis of youth and smallness contrasts with the adult sense of Latin and learning. Sense and song exist in antinomy. How do we read this discourse patterning? On the one hand, it might be read to foreground the boy's sweet innocence and to place stress on miraculous learning. Katherine Zieman has argued that the Prioress champions Latin song as a pure speech act—"as objectified language selflessly rendered to God to which understanding is subordinated."[34]

---

[33] Bruce Holsinger notes that the boy's musical learning is "anything but a product of classroom discipline." *Music, Body, and Desire in Medieval Culture: Hildegard of Bingen to Chaucer* (Stanford: University of Stanford Press, 2001), 271.

[34] Katherine Zieman, *Singing the New Song* (Philadelphia: University of Pennsylvania Press, 2008), 186. Zieman further characterizes the boy's singing as "an act of prelingual innocence" (187); the clergeon's singing is motivated "by his unique piety rather than his privileged access to Latin texts" (190), and hence, "the ideal Christian utterance

This is not an isolated example of a reading that prioritizes the purity of the boy's singing.[35] But might the collocational patterning be read differently? Might it simultaneously produce what linguists call negative semantic prosody; that is, lexical patternings whose connotations would be recognized as pejorative even if none of the individual words immediately arouses attention as a socially marked term?[36] How do we distinguish between true, innocent faith and blind, ignorant devotion, especially in light of Wycliffite criticisms of the way in which song (including the hours of the Virgin), invented by sinful men, impedes proper understanding of the meaning of the words?

Þan were matynys & masse & euen song, placebo & dirige & comendacion & matynes of oure lady ordeyned of synful men, to be songen wiþ heiȝe criynge to lette men fro þe sentence & vnderstondynge of þat þat was þus songen & to maken men wery & vndisposid to studie goddis lawe for akyng of hedis . . . þes foolis schulden drede þe scharpe wordis of austyn, þat seiþ: as ofte as þe song likiþ me more þan doþ þe sentence þat is songen, so oft I confesse þat I synge greuously.

lecherous lorellis schullen knacke þe most deuout seruyce þat noman schal here þe sentence.[37]

This criticism of song is not without precedent, however. As Bruce Holsinger notes, Christian writers on liturgy consistently emphasized the subordination of musical sonority to the salvational language it supports, using the same sentence from Augustine to back their argument.[38] The history of the relationship between music and verbal

---

is thus defined by the Prioress as unsullied not only by grammatical reading but by human intention altogether" (193). A rather different approach is taken by Nicolette Zeeman, who shows how the boy is one of a number of Chaucerian male singers whose narcissism in singing ultimately causes them to be victims of violence. "The Gender of Song in Chaucer," *SAC* 29 (2007): 141–82.

[35] For instance, the readings of Collette, "Sense and Sensibility," and Sherman Hawkins, "Chaucer's Prioress and the Sacrifice of Praise," *JEGP* 63 (1964): 599–624.

[36] My reading of the cultural work of collocational patterns derives from the methodology of Deborah Cameron's essay, "Narrow Church," *Critical Quarterly* 45 (2003): 109–12, in which she shows, through analysis of the collocability of "openly," "blatantly," and "actively" in disparaging contexts that include "false," "stupid," "rude," "defiant," "contemptuous," and "incredulous," that collocations of "openly" and "gay" demonstrate the extent to which "negative constructions of homosexuality are naturalised in our everyday discourse"; redolent of a subtle, more genteel kind of prejudice than overtly homophobic comment (111–12).

[37] Matthew, ed., *English Works of Wyclif*, 191, lines 20–33; 192, lines 23–25.

[38] Holsinger, *Music, Body, and Desire*, 266.

language in the liturgy is one of extended commentary. As Anne Yard-ley observes, while there would have been some monks and nuns who sang the office and read and chanted psalms without real understanding of the meaning of the Latin, the majority did seem to have reading and understanding of liturgical texts; "reading and singing are always mentioned in tandem, the assumption being that you cannot sing the services unless you can read the words."[39] Wycliffite writers opposed to song draw on this debate, but take its implications further in order to vilify the rituals of the material church, its priests, and especially its "unfounded" orders.

In *The Prioress's Tale*, the inferencing of the relationship between words and song is further complicated by the use of the phrase "by rote." It occurs twice in this tale to describe the boy's learning of the song (522, 545; italicised above). The sense of the phrase "by rote" in Middle English usage is not straightforward. As Mary Carruthers has argued, " 'By rote' appears in English in the fourteenth century meaning both 'reciting (prayers, speeches and the like) from memory' (an essentially neutral usage) and, in a pejorative way, 'reciting unintelligently or by formula.' " Carruthers remarks further that "for Chaucer, the word on its face is neutral, meaning 'from memory exactly', a synonym of verbatim memory. The first clearly pejorative uses of the word (which are from the fifteenth and sixteenth centuries) modify 'rote' with 'mere' or 'pure.' "[40] While the first statement, attributing contesting usages for "bi rote," is accurate; the second, with reference both to Chaucer's usage and the dating of the term, is open to question.

Using electronically searchable texts and the *Middle English Diction-ary*, I have traced the collocability of "rote," and found that, in contrast to twentieth- and twenty-first-century usage, there is no overwhelm-ingly pejorative discourse associated with the word in Middle English. However, it *does* occur in what can be seen as pejorative contexts both within Chaucer's works and in texts closely contemporary with them. "By rote" can refer to the word-for-word memorizing that is an essential part of the process of learning grammar,[41] and it can also signal a me-

[39] Anne Bagnall Yardley, *Performing Piety: Musical Culture in Medieval English Nunneries* (New York: Palgrave Macmillan, 2006), 76–77.

[40] Mary Carruthers, *The Book of Memory: A Study of Memory in Medieval Culture*, 2nd ed. (Cambridge: Cambridge University Press, 2008), 330.

[41] "Word-for-word rote memorizing of a number of outstanding literary and Scriptural texts was also always considered to be the essential base of education." "[W]ord-for-word rote memorizing is associated particularly with grammar, the fundamental work in language upon which both dialectic and rhetoric built." Ibid., 111, 113.

chanical empty exercise. The phrase occurs four times in Chaucer's work, two of them in *The Prioress's Tale*, as signaled above. One of the other examples comes in *The General Prologue* and describes the Man of Law's prodigious memory:

> Nowher so bisy a man as he ther nas.
> And yet he semed bisier than he was.
> In termes hadde he caas and doomes alle
> That from the tyme of kyng William were falle.
> Thereto he koude endite and make a thyng
> Ther koude no wight pynche at his writyng;
> And every statut koude he pleyn *by rote*.
>
> (I.321–27)

At face value, this is a description of formidable learning in the execution of legal practice. But the statements are riddled with hyperbole and simulation. The "sergeant of the lawe" *seems* busier than he was. He has learned the terms of *all* the cases of judgments from the time of William the Conqueror and he has learned *every* statute "by rote." It is the voice of the Man of Law we implicitly hear making this exaggerated claim; the pilgrim narrator is simply reporting. Could it have been possible to have learned all of this, even for such an apparently busy man? Even if we allow for the much more highly developed memory skills of the Middle Ages, the overstatement, together with the comment that the Man of Law is not all that he seems, destabilizes a straightforward acceptance of his claims. The implied voice of the speaker is important here and its subjectivity; we hear an exaggerated boast, a *performance* of legal knowledge. How much integrity is there in a claim to know *every* statute "by rote"?[42]

Similar conditions attend the fourth usage of the phrase, in the *Prologue to The Pardoner's Tale*:

---

[42] As Lee Patterson has argued, "Chaucer persistently filters into the narratorial description of each pilgrim an individualizing voice." Here as elsewhere, *The General Prologue* "is . . . saturated with the pilgrims' professional jargon," such as "the Sergeant of Law's 'patente', 'pleyn commissioun', 'termes' and 'caas' and 'doomes alle.'" *Chaucer and the Subject of History* (London: Routledge, 1991), 27, 29. Jill Mann argues that the stress in the portrait falls on the face that the Serjeant presents to the world, "and the narrator makes sure we know it is a face." *Chaucer and Medieval Estates Satire* (Cambridge: Cambridge University Press, 1973), 91.

> "Lordynges," quod he, "in chirches whan I preche,
> I peyne me to han an hauteyn speche
> And rynge it out as round as gooth a belle,
> For I kan al *by rote* that I telle.
> My theme is alwey oon, and evere was—
> *Radix malorum est Cupiditas."*
>
> (VI.329–34)

The Pardoner's boast that he preaches what he has learned all "by rote" has been likened to the educational practice of committing material to memory with reference to the "Rota Virgilis," or wheel diagram, which was a pedagogic tool used to facilitate learning.[43] But as with the Man of Law, the phrase "by rote" is placed in the mouth of an unreliable speaker, a notoriously duplicitous figure.[44] His use of language in his prologue and in his tale blends fraudulence with morality so that it becomes impossible to distinguish the one from the other. In the lines quoted above, the focus falls on performance.[45] The Pardoner takes pains to offer dignified speech, making his language as sonorous as a bell. Hyperbole is present once again: "I kan *al by rote* that I telle. / My theme is *alwey* oon, and *evere* was." The Pardoner makes an impressive claim about performance, but here, as with the Man of Law, rote learning appears in a context where the sincerity of the speaker is in doubt. There is nothing openly pejorative in the use of "by rote." That is exactly the point: the contexts in both these portraits suggest that the phrase could be claimed both positively and negatively.

This semantic tug of war is seen elsewhere. Unquestionably, "by rote" does occur in contexts in which the learning described is entirely praiseworthy—as, for example, when referring to a herald's knowledge, or a physician's memory of herbs.[46] But there are also instances where dis-

---

[43] Carruthers, *Book of Memory*, 330.

[44] David Lawton comments that "Chaucer intends us to recognise in his Pardoner a type of Faux-Semblant, or rather the quintessence of false seeming." *Chaucer's Narrators* (Cambridge: Brewer, 1985), 31.

[45] H. Marshall Leicester accounts for the subjectivity of the Pardoner as a performance of "deliberate self-presentation." *The Disenchanted Self: Representing the Subject in the "Canterbury Tales"* (Berkeley and Los Angeles: University of California Press, 1990), 61.

[46] *MED* "rote" (n.(2)), (b) *a1325(?c1300) Caiphas (Sln 2478)* 148: Ich may noȝt synge hym al bi rote Vorto tele eche note. *a1400 Cursor (Trin-C R.3.8)* 7408: Dauid coude of dyuerse note, he couþe mychel of harpe birote. *a1450 Parton.(1) (UC C.188)* 5925: Alle maner of Spyces I know by rote, How in phisike they haue her worching. *(a1460) Vegetius(2) (Pmb-C 243)* 555: An heraude expert by roote, The Centrions other the Centenaryis In ordre forth hem calle. *a1500(?a1400) KEdw.& S.(Cmb Ff.5.48)* 249: I shalle tech þe a gamme; I can hit wel be rote.

tinction is made between outward mechanical recitation and sincere feeling:

> I saugh a kevell, corpulent of stature
> Lyk a materas redlyd was his coote
> And theron was sowyd this scripture:
> "A good be stille is weel wourth a groote."
> It costith nat mekyl to be hoote,
> And paye ryght nought whan the feyre is doon.
> Suych labourerys synge may *be roote*
> Alle goo we stille, the Cok hath lowe shoon.[47]

This stanza is from a world-upside-down poem. Laborers sing a song of social quietism; they sing sentiments that keep them firmly in their social place, "be roote." To perform such proverbial conservatism against their social interests suggests a divorce between production of song in this topsy-turvy world and the way things operate in reality. Even more clearly, in Lydgate's *Reson and Sensuallyte*, the figure of Deduit, or pleasure, is said to have masterly command of singing skill; he is an "expert" (2402). There is unmistakeable antithesis between learning, craft—or skill—and the production of song "be rote."

> . . . he *kan* hem euerychon . . .
> Touche be *crafte*, and nat *be rote.*
> Harpe and lute, fythel and Rote,
> And synge songes of pleasaunce,
> Maisterly revel and Daunce,
> Pipe and floyte lustely,
> And also eke ful konyngly
> In al the crafte and melody
> Of musyke and of Armonye.[48]

In each of these Lydgate poems, rote learning collocates pejoratively. But Lydgate of course is writing later than Chaucer. What evidence, if any, is there to suggest that "by rote" could have been used with shades

---

[47] John Lydgate, *The Cok Hath Lowe Shoon*, lines 65–72, in H. N. MacCracken, ed., *The Minor Poems of John Lydgate, Part II: The Secular Poems*, EETS o.s. 192 (London: Oxford University Press, 1934).

[48] Ernst Sieper, ed. *Lydgate's Reson and Sensuallyte*, 2 vols. EETS e.s. 84, 89 (London: Kegan Paul, Trench, Trübner for the EETS, 1901–3), vol. 1, lines 2392–400.

of pejoration before 1400? Intriguingly, the phrase occurs in two poems certainly written before the fifteenth century, and in both the context is religious.

In *The Cuckoo and the Nightingale*, possibly written by John Clanvowe, the nightingale is characterized as a flighty, preening bird with shallow sense. This is how the narrator describes the way in which the nightingale's flock of birds sing the hours of divine office:

> Thei koud þat service al *bi rote*;
> Ther was many a loueli note:
> Some song loude, as þei hadde pleyned,
> And some in oþer maner voys *i-fayned*.
> And some al oute, with al the ful throte.
>
> They *preyned* hem, & made hem riȝt gay,
> And davnseden and lepten on þe spray . . .[49]

The service produced "bi rote" is accompanied by lovely notes, dancing and leaping. "Bi rote" here collocates with feigning and preening and the emphasis falls on self-satisfied outward performance. Where is the devotional integrity in such singing? The picture is not one of firm faith but of feathered frolicking. It has been argued that this poem is informed by Wycliffite diction and debate, and that the treatment of the liturgy in this stanza is of a temper with Wycliffite criticism.[50]

Pierce the Ploughman's Crede—an overt denunciation of the spiritually empty practices of the friars—is indisputably Lollard. So excrescent are the four orders in this poem's view that at one point Peres argues they were "put in by the devell" (506), and so stupid are they, they cannot read their rule, or responses in a church service, except "be rote."

> Loke a ribaut of hem þat can nouȝt wel reden
> His rewle ne his respondes but *be pure rote*.[51]

---

[49] *The Cuckoo and the Nightingale*, lines 71–77, in John W. Conlee, ed., *Middle English Debate Poetry: A Critical Anthology* (East Lansing, Mich.: Colleagues Press, 1991).

[50] See Helen Barr, *Socioliterary Practice in Late Medieval England* (Oxford: Oxford University Press, 2001), 175–87.

[51] *Pierce the Ploughman's Crede*, lines 377–78, in *The Piers Plowman Tradition: A Critical Edition of Pierce the Ploughman's Crede, Richard the Redeles, Mum and the Sothsegger, and The Crowned King*, ed. Helen Barr (London: Everyman, 1993).

While one of the targets of rote learning is the familiar jibe against the otiose "rule"[52] of the fraternal orders, a foundation that places them outside the structures of the institutional church, it is also significant that this is bracketed with the responses of divine office. The collocation of "rewle" and "respondes" and "rote" is not simply a matter of alliterative convenience; rather, the phonemic patterning groups together useless superfluities that run counter to apostolic purity and spiritual integrity. *Pierce the Ploughman's Crede* is the sole unambiguously Wycliffite text in which I have been able to locate the phrase "by rote." But its sentiments, and those of *The Cuckoo and the Nightingale*, are of a piece with Wycliffite tracts that stress the baselessness of singing in church. In "Of Prelates," an early fifteenth-century tract, liturgical song is contrasted to meekness of heart. Concern with costly church ornamentation, of which singing is part, results in churches having walls covered in gold and poor men left with naked sides:

Of Prelates
for þei don not here sacrifices bi mekenesse of herte & mornynge & compunccion for here synnes & þe peplis, but wiþ knackynge of newe song, as orgen or deschant & motetis of holouris, & wiþ worldly pride of costy vestymentis & oþere ornementis bou3t wiþ pore mennus goodis, & suffren hem perische for meschef & laten pore men haue nakid sidis & dede wallis haue grete plente of wast gold.[53]

An antinomy is set up between song, on the one hand, and contrition and charity, on the other. Other Lollard texts set up a clear contrast between song and devotion in heart:

The Order of the Priesthood
it semeþ þat god seiþ bi þes newe singeris as he dide in þe gospel to pharisees, "þis peple honoureþ me wiþ lippis but here herte is fer fro me, þei worshipen me wiþouten cause, techynge lore & comaundementis of men."[54]

Of Feyned Contemplative Life
god in all þe lawe of grace chargiþ not siche song but deuocion in herte, trewe techyng & holy spekynge in tonge.

[52] Wycliffite texts figure the obedience of friars to their Rule as one of the reasons for their superfluity, and contrast this obedience to the rule of Christ or to the gospel, or to secular lords, e.g. Matthew, ed., *English Works of Wyclif*, 51, lines 15–35.
[53] Matthew, ed., *English Works of Wyclif*, 91, lines 27–33.
[54] Ibid., 169, lines 25–29; internal quotation from Matthew 15:8.

crist . . . tauȝt not ne chargid vs wiþ sich bodely song ne ony of his apostlis, but wiþ deuocion in herte, holy lif & trwe prechynge.[55]

The use of the word "herte" is crucial, and here I want to turn to think about collocation from a different perspective: not syntagmatic but paradigmatic. Often, in the glossing of Middle English, "by rote" is rendered as "by heart" and vice versa.[56] *The Riverside Chaucer* glosses "by rote," as spoken by the Pardoner and the Man of Law, with "by heart."[57] But to do this obscures an important, and available, semantic distinction. In devotional contexts, these two phrases are not synonymous, especially in the description of the devotional work of singing divine office. The Wycliffite stress on devotion in heart, rather than outward bodily song, is also found in orthodox texts. *The Myroure of Oure Lady* is an early fifteenth-century text that instructs the nuns at the newly established Brigittine house of Syon in proper observance of religious practice. While this text was written later than Chaucer's *Prioress's Tale*, the diction it uses to discuss the correct practice of religious singing is still, I think, relevant to consideration of how the boy's singing in that tale might be read.

The new monasteries of Sheen and Syon were established by Henry in 1415, though preparations for the Brigittine order at Syon can be seen to have started as early as 1407.[58] It is well known that Henry V was an enthusiastic reformer of the church in an attempt to combat the threats of Lollardy, and his founding of the new Brigittine houses was part of an endeavor to restore prayer and order to the church from within. Another of his key endeavors was to promote liturgical practice, especially the Sarum Rite, in order to provide unity and focus within the church. Catto notes that the Sarum Use was "a subject of conscious pride . . . in the early years of the fifteenth century, and . . . attests the vitality and importance of public communal worship in the church's response to Lollardy."[59] There is extended discussion of singing in *The Myroure*, discussion that can be seen to defend the orthodoxy of the practice against its critics. Its diction is revealing:

[55] Matthew, ed., *English Works of Wyclif*, 191, lines 11–12; 191–92, lines 34, 2.

[56] *MED* "rote" (n.(2)) (b) bi ~, by heart; according to form; expertly.

[57] *Riverside Chaucer*, 28 (gloss to line 327), 194 (line 332). Riverside does not gloss "by rote" in *The Prioress's Tale*.

[58] See David Knowles, *The Religious Orders in England,* 3 vols. (Cambridge: Cambridge University Press, 1949–59), 2 (1957):157–82.

[59] Jeremy Catto, "Religious Change Under Henry V," *Henry V: The Practice of Kingship,* ed. G. L. Harriss (Oxford: Oxford University Press, 1985), 97–116 (107, 108–9).

. . . ye ar bounde to synge euery day these holy houres of oure lady solempnly. And this solempnyte asketh both inwarde besynes to haue deuocyon *in harte,* and also in syngyng and redyng with tongue, and in other outwarde obseru- aunce.

[God] taketh more hede of the *harte* then of the voyce. But when bothe accorde in hym then is yt beste. And yf ether shulde fayle, yt is better to lacke the voyce then the harte from hym.

It profyteth but lytel, to syng only with the voyce, or to say only with the mouthe, withoute *entendaunce of the hart.*[60]

While the writer is at pains to stress the importance of singing the liturgy, especially the hours of the Virgin, he can be seen also to fend off exactly the opposition to such practice recorded in Lollard polemic. *The Myroure* endorses outward observance and bodily song only if they are accompanied by true understanding and devotion in heart. The writer establishes a potential opposition between the heart and the voice, and also between voice and understanding, not, as the Lollards did, to vilify the practice of singing divine office, but to ensure its spiri- tual integrity. *The Myroure* can be seen to wrest discursive territory from the Lollards and to wield it with all the power of orthodoxy to uphold the value of liturgical practice.[61]

From examination, then, of the discursive contexts of "in herte" and "by rote" in devotional settings, I would argue that there is the potential for a semantic distinction, one that would have been available in the fourteenth and early fifteenth centuries. In the context of devotional practice, "in herte" unequivocally suggests sincere understanding and spiritual integrity, whereas "by rote" is more ambivalent. While I have not found an example of the exact phrases "by rote" and "in herte" used oppositionally within the same text, the larger textual environment indicates that "by rote" has the potential to suggest ignorant perform- ance, music without spiritual matter. Depending on the collocational

---

[60] *The Myroure of Our Ladye*, ed. J. H. Blunt, EETS e.s. 19 (London: Trübner & Co. for the EETS, 1873), 22, lines 5–9; 35, lines 3–5; 40, lines 6–9.

[61] Such statements do not appear solely in defensive contexts; however, see note 38 above. The same sentiment appears in all three versions of the Rule of Saint Benedict collected in editions of the *Three Middle-English Versions of the Rule of St Benet*, ed. E. A. Kock, EETS o.s. 120 (London: K. Paul, Trench, Trübner & Co, for the EETS, 1902): "And lokis, when ye sing þat yure herte acorde wid yur voice; for þan sing ye riht" (19, lines 18–20); cf. 80, lines 1167–69, and 126, lines 31–33.

company it keeps, the word "song" and its cognates can signify both sincere church practice and empty outward performance.

To return to *The Prioress's Tale* in light of this evidence, I would suggest that the collocational patternings of ignorance, youth, and lack of understanding, together with the use of the phrase "by rote," create the potential to read the Marian devotion of the tale two ways. An orthodox reading would respond to the patterning as an expression of miraculous, innocent sweetness.[62] A reader attuned to those collocations in more dissident texts would see the description of the boy's singing as a projection of sentimentalized, vapid ritual. There is only one place in the tale where the boy's song is associated with the heart:

> As I have seyd, thurghout the Juerie
> This litel child, as he cam to and fro,
> Ful murily wolde he synge and crie
> *O Alma redemptoris* everemo.
> The swetnesse his herte perced so
> Of Cristes mooder that, to hire to preye,
> He kan nat stynte of syngyng by the weye.
>
> (551–57)

An affective reading of this stanza would be attracted to the image of the pierced heart, suggestive as it is of the piercing of Christ's side on the cross. In its expression of compassion and feeling ("swetnesse"), we have, in miniature, a vignette of innocent devotion that touches the heart. Reason is bypassed because this is the simple, pure response of faith.[63] Read in light of a discursive context, however, which establishes hostile opposition between the heart and understanding, the stanza becomes more subversive. The word "litel" connotes sentimentality, not sentiment; the boy sings the song he has learned by rote, not with devotion in heart, or with compunction, but "murily." The singing is arguably extreme and, indeed, unstoppable. The antiphon in praise of Mary can be seen, in the words of Bruce Holsinger, as "an excessive rhetorical performance—a 'musical delivery' from the body and voice of an un-

---

[62] Alfred David characterizes the tale as one of "sentimentalised religion that worships beauty as a version of truth characteristic of the new and fashionable religiosity of Chaucer's day that combines gentility with emotion, decorousness with enthusiasm." "An ABC to the Style," 156.

[63] Compare the account in Collette, "Sense and Sensibility," 142.

trained but thoroughly indoctrinated Christian *actor*."[64] The boy is a performer.

But the value of devotional *performance* is also tricky to calibrate. While modern English connotations of the verb "perform" include simulation or lack of integrity,[65] these are much harder to detect conclusively in Middle English. The primary senses of the verb appear to be to complete a work or a task, to act, perform a duty or an office, or to conduct an operation. Where there is a sense of fraudulence, the verb collocates with "falsnesse."[66] Likewise, the performance of liturgical texts in the Middle Ages was not intrinsically associated with insincerity. The outward production of prayer and devotion, especially the Psalms, was seen as an act of inward devotion.[67] It has been argued that the true significance of the liturgy is "realised only in its recitation and enactment."[68] Even within this cultural matrix of religious performance, how-

[64] Holsinger, *Music, Body, and Desire*, 291. Holsinger does not here associate the boy's singing with Wycliffite opposition, but he does note the potential for Lollard critique in "Liturgy," 308.

[65] *OED* "perform" (v) dates the first recorded use in the sense "to present (a play, ballet, opera, etc.) on stage or to an audience; to play or sing (a piece of music) for an audience" to 1567. Additionally, it dates the first recorded use of "perform" in the sense of "to act or play (a part or role in a play, ballet, etc.); to represent (a character) on stage or to an audience" to 1598.

[66] *MED* "performen"(v.) 1.(a) To complete (work, a task, a course, etc.); 2(a) To act; accomplish (a deed, task, service, etc.), carry out from beginning to end, achieve, perform (a duty, an office, a crime, penance, etc.); make (a pilgrimage); ~ up, ~ out; (b) to carry out (a promise, agreement, command, threat, law, etc.), fulfill, comply with; satisfy (desire, lust); put into effect or into practice (a plan, purpose); follow (advice); of a dream: come true; ~ wille, carry out the request or desire (of sb.), act under the sway (of sb. or sth.); (c) to execute (the provisions of a will or testament); pay (costs, debts), provide for paying for (sth.); also *fig.* [quot.: (?a1430)]; ~ wille; (d) to conduct (an examination, operation); make use of (powers); (e) ~ to falsnesse, to speak deceitfully; ppl. performed, of a text: discoursed or lectured upon.

[67] See Susan Boynton, "Prayer as Liturgical Performance in Eleventh- and Twelfth-Century Monastic Psalters," *Speculum* 82 (2007): 896–931, and Clifford C. Flanigan, Kathleen Ashley, and Pamela Sheingorn,, "Liturgy as Social Performance: Expanding the Definitions," in *The Liturgy of the Medieval Church,* ed. Thomas J. Heffernan and Ann E. Matter (Kalamazoo: Medieval Institute Publications, 2001), 695–714; and more recently Jessica Brantley's wide-ranging discussion of the nature of devotional performance and the connections between private reading and public communal action, *Reading in the Wilderness: Private Devotion and Public Performance in Late Medieval England* (Chicago: University of Chicago Press, 2007). She discusses the social and lexical meaning of performance (14–21) and gives an extended discussion of reading as performance (167–268).

[68] Bridget Nichols, *Liturgical Hermeneutics: Interpreting Liturgical Rites in Performance* (Frankfurt, 1996), 15; and Annie Sutherland, "Performing the Penitential Psalms in the Middle Ages," in *Aspects of the Performative in Medieval Culture,* ed. Manuele Gragno-

ever, the intensity of the focus on the boy's production of song in *The Prioress's Tale* is open to question, not least because of the tale's framing. The opening lines of the prologue to the tale, spoken of course by the Prioress, are (as has already been noted) a paraphrase of the lines of Psalm 8, which began Matins in the Little Office of the Virgin. Here, as in the tale itself, the repetitive diction causes problems with interpretation:

> O Lord, oure Lord, thy name how merveillous
> Is in this large world ysprad—**quod she**—
> For noght oonly thy laude precious
> **Parfourned** is by men of dignitee,
> But by the **mouth of children** thy bountee
> **Parfourned** is, for on the **brest soukynge**
> Somtyme shewen they thyn heriynge.
>
> Wherfore in laude, **as I best kan or may,**
> Of thee and of the whyte lylye flour
> Which that the bar, and is a mayde alway,
> **To telle a storie I wol do my labour;**
> **Nat that I may** encressen hir honour,
> For she hirself is honour and the roote
> Of bountee, next hir Sone, and soules boote.
>
> O mooder Mayde! O mayde Mooder free!
> O bussh unbrent, brennynge in Moyses sighte,
> That ravyshedest doun fro the Deitee
> Thurgh thyn humblesse, the Goost that in th'alighte,
> Of whos vertu, whan he thyn herte lighte,
> Conceyved was the Fadres sapience,
> **Help me to telle it in thy reverence!**
>
> Lady, thy bountee, thy magnificence,
> Thy vertu and thy grete humylitee,
> **Ther may no tonge expresse in no science,**
> For somtyme, Lady, er men praye to thee,
> Thou goost biforn of thy benyngnytee,

---

lati and Almut Suerbaum (New York: De Gruyter, 2010); I am indebted to Dr. Sutherland's paper for the shape of argument in this section of my essay.

And getest us the lyght, of thy preyere,
To gyden us unto thy Sone so deere.

My konnyng is so wayk, O blisful Queene,
For to declare thy grete worthynesse
That I ne may the weighte nat susteene;
But as a child of twelf month oold, or lesse,
That kan unnethes any word expresse,
Right so fare I, and therfore I yow preye,
Gydeth my **song that I shal of yow seye.**

(453–87)

The Prioress's very first words contain significant overwording: in this instance, of expressions that foreground the act of telling.[69] One-third of the thirty-five lines is concerned with the production of speech. Many of the expressions are modal, for example, "as best I kan"; "that I ne may." While the overt content of the prologue is a praise poem to Mary, the diction assigned to the teller positions this praise as a recitation: not just praise, but the reproduction of praise. Twice, in the opening stanza, the word "parfourned" is used. Lines 466–72 are a recital of conventional tropes addressed to the Virgin. The praise is inseparable from speaking about how it is produced, as is indicated by "quod she" (454), and two appeals for assistance ("Help me to telle it," "Gydeth my song"). Furthermore, the Prioress's shaky confidence in her recitation is aligned with the innocence and weak "konnyng"—or understanding—of children. In lines 457–59, the precious lauding is performed not just by men of dignity but by the mouths of children sucking on the breast. In the final stanza, the Prioress specifically aligns her own production of "song" (487) with that of a child. She declares that she may not sustain the weight of telling the great worthiness of the Virgin. She proceeds as a child of twelve months or less, a child that can scarcely express a single word. No tongue, she says, can express the bounty, magnificence, virtue, and great humility of the Virgin with any "science"—that is, with any knowledge or true understanding (476).[70]

[69] Holsinger, *Music, Body, and Desire* emphasizes the Prioress's concern with performance (264); see also Brantley, *Reading in the Wilderness* (16–17).

[70] Zieman's interpretation of this line is that in "claiming the insufficiency of 'science', [the Prioress] implies that infantile devotion, undefiled by human knowledge (Lat. *scientia*), comes closest to praising the ineffable Virgin. It is more valuable than performances by men of dignity." *Singing the New Song,* 188.

This lexical patterning creates a tale teller who is a proleptic projection of the boy within.[71] Like the boy, the Prioress produces song to reverence the Virgin. Like the boy, she performs conventional praise of the Virgin. But also like the boy, her focus on performing Marian devotion is reliant on diction that stresses tender innocence at the expense of adult understanding. Once again, as with the diction in the tale itself, it is perfectly possible to read the prologue as an emphatic assertion of orthodox Marian piety, but the insistent focus on performance, on the act of telling, and on childlike language also has the potential to be read oppositionally. The prologue fronts a sentimentalized, sensational story that celebrates, at its heart, a little child who performs Marian reverence with no understanding of the words that he produces.[72] It is very significant that the last line of the prologue describes the forthcoming tale as "song" (487). The semantic and devotional unruliness of the tale is prefigured by the lexical pointing of this prologue.

More accurately, the problems of interpretation start much earlier—in the portrait of the Prioress in *The General Prologue*, details of which bear significantly on issues of devotional piety:

> Ther was also a Nonne, a PRIORESSE,
> That of **hir smylyng was ful symple and coy;**
> **Hire gretteste ooth was but by Seinte Loy;**
> And she was cleped madame **Eglentyne.**
> **Ful weel she soong the service dyvyne,**
> **Entuned in hir nose ful semely . . .**
>
> (118–23)

It is now a critical commonplace to see the characterization of a simpering, sentimental, aristocratic woman in this portrait of a nun.[73] Especially important for my purposes, however, is diction that describes her devotional practices. She sings the divine office[74] "ful weel" and "ful

---

[71] See Louise Fradenburg, "Criticism, Anti-Semitism, and *The Prioress's Tale*," *Exemplaria* 1 (1989): 69–115.

[72] Florence Ridley argues that "only from the Prioress . . . could we expect a humorless display of naïveté, ignorance, blind, vehement devotion; and suppressed maternal longing, and that is precisely what we get." *The Prioress and Her Critics* (Berkeley and Los Angeles: University of California Press, 1965), 29.

[73] The worldliness of the portrait and Chaucer's indebtedness to courtly sources is documented in full by Mann, *Chaucer and Medieval Estates Satire*, 128–37.

[74] Which, as Boyd argues, is part of the liturgy of the canonical hours. *Chaucer and the Liturgy*, 61. Boyd comments that the liturgical orientation of the Prioress's prologue and tale "show[s] the emotionalism of her personality" (62).

semely" (112–13); the double intensifiers suggest exaggeration. In line 113, the verb "entuned" foregrounds sound and the adverb "semely"—attractively—points to outward show and performance. There is none of the understanding of heart urged by the writer of *The Myroure of Oure Lady* and other defenders of liturgical practice. Spiritual matter or inward devotion is replaced by liturgical nasal. While the Prioress's swearing by Saint Loy might have pricked up the ears of a Wycliffite, so too might her bodily singing.[75] And the anatomical detail matters; the nose, unlike the heart, is not capable of sapiential devotion.[76]

Cumulatively, then, if we approach *The Prioress's Tale* in light of its repetitive diction, its prologue, and the description of its teller in *The General Prologue*, it would be entirely possible to read it as a Lollard critique of institutional church practices rather than an orthodox account of affective practice and miracle. When we think of how cultural meaning is inferenced, however, the situation is rather more complicated. While the sexual possibilities afforded by the sporting of Gossard lingerie and Lollard lamentation over religious luxury might seem unlikely bedfellows in one essay, the methodology of inferencing allows us to calibrate not just available cultural responses to text and/or image, but also the ways in which those responses are valued. To view *The Prioress's Tale* as Lollard critique, or as an orthodox Marian miracle story, is to see only the duck—or should that be the rabbit? More to the point is that Chaucer's contemporary audience, if knowledgable both about orthodox devotion and dissident critique, would be in a position to inference both meanings, if not exactly at the same time, then certainly sequentially. Perhaps, like the audience at that 1599 performance of *Henry V*, and perhaps like me, they realized that they are unsure what to think.

Which is the rabbit here, and which the duck?[77]

---

[75] For Wycliffite opposition to swearing oaths, see Hudson, *The Premature Reformation*, 371–74, and cf. the Epilogue to *The Man of Law's Tale*, "What eyleth the man, so synfully to swere?" (II.1171).

[76] And here we might recall that the little boy, like the birds in Clanvowe's *Cuckoo and the Nightingale*, sings through his *throat*.

[77] Cf. Portia's question in the courtroom, "Which is the merchant here? And which the Jew?" *Merchant of Venice*, IV.i.171.

The Wife of Bath's Marginal Authority

Theresa Tinkle
University of Michigan

T O READ *The Wife of Bath's Prologue* in glossed manuscripts is to become keenly aware of how much scripture Chaucer translates and comments on through this unlikely woman preacher. Throughout the fifteenth century, scribes regularly call attention to Alison's many biblical sources, usually by copying into the margin some part of the original Latin, creating a *mise-en-page* that highlights her (Chaucer's) acts of vernacular translation. The simplest glossing programs scatter several Latin notes through the work, while the most extensive crowd glosses into barely adequate margins.[1] Each glossed manuscript selectively emphasizes the scriptural borrowings (as well as other features), and a number reveal how closely the English follows the biblical Latin. When Alison argues that "god bad vs *wexe and multiple*," for instance, the scribe of Oxford, New College 314 (Ne), links her words to Latin scripture: "*Crescite et multiplicamini*" (Increase and multiply, Gen. 1:28).[2] Scribes

---

[1] Considered together, existing studies reveal the diversity in glossing programs: Susan Schibanoff, "The New Reader and Female Textuality in Two Early Commentaries on Chaucer," *SAC* 10 (1988): 71–108; Christopher Baswell, "Talking Back to the Text: Marginal Voices in Medieval Secular Literature," in *The Uses of Manuscripts in Literary Studies: Essays in Memory of Judson Boyce Allen*, ed. Charlotte Cook Morse, Penelope Reed Doob, and Marjorie Curry Woods (Kalamazoo: Medieval Institute Publications, 1992), 121–60; Beverly Kennedy, "Contradictory Responses to the Wife of Bath as Evidenced by Fifteenth-Century Manuscript Variants," in *The Canterbury Tales Project Occasional Papers,* ed. N. Blake and P. Robinson, 2 vols. (London: Office for Humanities Communication Publications, 1997), 2:23–39; Beverly Kennedy, "The Rewriting of the *Wife of Bath's Prologue* in Cambridge Dd.4.24," in *Rewriting Chaucer: Culture, Authority, and the Idea of the Authentic Text, 1400–1602*, ed. Thomas A. Prendergast and Barbara Kline (Columbus: Ohio State University Press, 1999), 203–33.

[2] *The Wife of Bath's Prologue*, lines 26–29; my emphasis. All citations are from Peter Robinson, ed., *The Wife of Bath's Prologue on CD-Rom* (Cambridge: Cambridge University Press, 1996); the base text, Hengwrt (Aberystwyth, National Library of Wales, Peniarth 392 D), is cited, unless otherwise noted, by the use of the manuscript sigils in the next note. I take the liberty of simplifying and modernizing orthography (silently expanding abbreviations, regularizing thorns and yoghs, deleting virgules), and of supplying modern punctuation to improve readability, particularly of the Latin glosses.

continue to draw attention to scriptural translations in the *Prologue* long after Thomas Arundel's 1407/9 *Constitutiones* declare the possession of vernacular scripture potentially heretical. Despite the prohibitions, Alison's vernacular project was apparently not censored, and biblical glosses survive in nineteen of the fifty-eight extant manuscripts and incunabula.[3] Some scribes also identify Alison's biblical sources (not always correctly), further highlighting her translations of the Word.[4]

At the time of Chaucer's composition, and throughout the work's early reception, this treatment of scripture is unusual. Vernacular literature typically develops narratives drawn from scripture, usually with considerable elaboration of noncanonical detail, as famously occurs in the Corpus Christi plays.[5] Such "popular Bibles" are not considered threatening to orthodoxy. In fact, verse translations and adaptations of the Word are exempt from ecclesiastical strictures on vernacular theology, even at the height of Lollard persecutions.[6] By contrast, *The Wife of*

[3] In addition to Ne, already mentioned, these are: Alnwick Castle, Northumberland MS 455 (Nl); Cambridge, Trinity College R.3.15 (595) (Tc²); Chicago, University of Chicago Library 564 (Mc); Lichfield Cathedral 29 (Lc); Lincoln Cathedral 110 (Ln); London, British Library, Additional 5140 (Ad¹), Additional 35286 (Ad³), Egerton 2864 (En³), Harley 1758 (Ha²), Lansdowne 851 (La), and Sloane 1685 (Sl¹); Oxford, Bodleian Library, Laud 600 (Ld¹), Rawlinson poet. 141 (Ra¹) and Arch. Selden B.14 (SC 3360) (Se); Oxford, Corpus Christi College 198 (Cp); San Marino, Calif., Henry E. Huntington Library, Ellesmere 26 C 9 (El); Paris, Bibliothèque Nationale, Fonds anglais 39 (Ps); and Sussex, Petworth House MS 7 (Pw). Other manuscripts occasionally mentioned in this essay are: Cambridge, Fitzwilliam Museum, McClean 181 (Fi); Cambridge, University Library, Mm.ii.5 (Mm); and Oxford, Bodleian Library Bodley 414 (SC 27880) (Bo¹). A number of scholars mention the presence of Chaucer's *Canterbury Tales* in a suspected heretic's library but consider his work "unexceptionable," as John A. F. Thomson does, *The Later Lollards, 1414–1520* (London: Oxford University Press, 1965), 243. I find the work more provocative than it is sometimes considered: although the fictional Wife would have aural access to scripture, the glossed texts flag Chaucer's citations of scripture as translations. For the vernacular scripture controversy, see Anne Hudson, "Lollardy: The English Heresy?" *Studies in Church History* 18 (1982): 261–83; and Nicholas Watson, "Censorship and Cultural Change in Late-Medieval England: Vernacular Theology, the Oxford Translation Debate, and Arundel's Constitutions of 1409," *Speculum* 70 (1995): 822–64, which should be read with his later remarks, "Cultural Changes," *ELN* 44 (2006): 127–37.

[4] E.g., "Poule durst nat commaunden at the leste / A thyng of which his mayster yaf noon heste / The dart is set vpon virgynyte" (73–75, En³) is glossed, "Non enim audeo aliquid loquo eorum que per me non efficit Christi, *Apostolus ad Romanos*. Si [sic] currite vt comprehendatus, *Apostolus ad Corinthios*" (74, En³; my emphasis).

[5] For typical biblical literature, see Margaret Deanesley, *The Lollard Bible and Other Medieval Biblical Versions* (1920; rpt. Eugene: Wipf and Stock, 2002), 146–87; Brian Murdoch, *The Medieval Popular Bible: Expansions of Genesis in the Middle Ages* (Cambridge: D. S. Brewer, 2003).

[6] See Deanesley, *Lollard Bible*, 146–55.

Bath's Prologue recites few biblical stories, and even those are condensed versions, notably lacking in colorful narrative detail: "Crist ne wente neuere but ones / To weddyng in the Cane of Galilee" (10–11). Nor does Alison draw on a psalter or Book of Hours, detail the Ten Commandments, recite the Creed, or list the seven deadly sins, all of which would be entirely acceptable for the laity of her class.[7] Instead, she focuses on vernacular translation and literal interpretation of canonical scripture, detached from conventional Latin glosses.

Although vernacular translation is controversial at the time, most ecclesiastics would theoretically consider Alison's literal hermeneutics suitable to her class and gender, and appropriate for a lay audience.[8] Literal interpretation finds contemporary support among lowly preachers, influential exegetes, and controversial theologians alike, all of whom favor what they call literal interpretation, though what they mean by "literal" varies from exegete to exegete, and sometimes even within the work of one exegete.[9] Although the "letter of the text" is a fluid concept, Alcuin Blamires and Lawrence Besserman astutely propose that the nuances of Alison's literal hermeneutic align her with Lollardy, an

---

[7] That is, "acceptable" to some conservatives. Chaucer elsewhere exposes weaknesses in this standard for lay piety: see Alan J. Fletcher, *Preaching, Politics, and Poetry in Late–Medieval England* (Dublin: Four Courts Press, 1998), 239–46.

[8] See, e.g., Henri de Lubac, *Medieval Exegesis: Volume 1, The Four Senses of Scripture,* trans. Mark Sebanc (Grand Rapids, Mich.: Eerdmans; Edinburgh: T. and T. Clark, 1998), 1:12; Deanesley, *The Lollard Bible,* 31, 36–37, 45–46.

[9] For preaching, see Beryl Smalley, *The Study of the Bible in the Middle Ages,* 3rd ed. (Oxford: Basil Blackwell, 1983), 281–308, with the qualifications set forth in the Preface to that edition, xiii–xvi; A. J. Minnis, *Medieval Theory of Authorship: Scholastic Literary Attitudes in the Later Middle Ages,* 2nd ed. (Philadelphia: University of Pennsylvania Press, 1988), 73–117; L.-J. Bataillon, O.P., "Early Scholastic and Mendicant Preaching as Exegesis of Scripture," in *Ad Litteram: Authoritative Texts and Their Medieval Readers,* ed. Mark D. Jordan and Kent Emery Jr. (Notre Dame, Ind.: University of Notre Dame Press, 1992), 165–98. For exegetes, see Douglas Wurtele, "Chaucer's *Canterbury Tales* and Nicholas of Lyra's *Postillae litteralis et moralis super totam Bibliam,*" in *Chaucer and Scriptural Tradition,* ed. David Lyle Jeffrey (Ottawa: University of Ottawa Press, 1984), 89–107; Philip D. W. Krey and Lesley Smith, eds., *Nicholas of Lyra: The Senses of Scripture* (Leiden: E. J. Brill, 2000); Deeana Copeland Klepper, *The Insight of Unbelievers: Nicholas of Lyra and Christian Reading of Jewish Text in the Later Middle Ages* (Philadelphia: University of Pennsylvania Press, 2007), 32–43. For the controversial theology of Wyclif, see G. R. Evans, "Wyclif on Literal and Metaphorical," in *From Ockham to Wyclif,* ed. Anne Hudson and Michael Wilks (Oxford: Basil Blackwell, for The Ecclesiastical History Society, 1987), 259–66; Kantik Ghosh, *The Wycliffite Heresy: Authority and the Interpretation of Texts* (Cambridge: Cambridge University Press, 2002), 11–14, 22–66, 101–2, 135. For the various and complex senses of the literal in, e.g., Nicholas of Lyra's works, see Krey and Smith, eds., *Nicholas of Lyra*; Klepper, *The Insight of Unbelievers,* 32–43.

alignment strengthened by her acts of vernacular scriptural translation.[10] She is also orthodox, as evidenced by her role in the Canterbury pilgrimage. In other words, Chaucer's Alison ambiguously references both Lollardy and orthodoxy, enacting a hybrid religion increasingly common in late medieval England.[11] Chaucer clearly designs his feminine persona to engage unsettled contemporary debates about vernacular scripture and lay hermeneutics. The persona allows Chaucer to enter the debates behind a mask, safely distanced from "Alison's" vernacular theology and hermeneutic positions.

The feminine persona is hardly a neutral choice in this cultural context. Speaking through the Wife of Bath, Chaucer reaccentuates scripture in the most controversial possible voice, that of a laywoman from the artisan class.[12] Alison's class and gender mark her as one of the unlearned people ("Lollards") whose exegesis, officials fear, could dangerously unsettle society. With her feisty rejection of apostolic, patristic, and spousal authority, Alison appears unlikely to calm those fears. Chaucer's Wife of Bath is indeed a provocative exegete in an age filled with controversies over lay access to vernacular scripture, yet a significant number of scribes throughout the fifteenth century appear undaunted by her exegetical daring. Instead of deleting or minimizing potentially

[10] Respectively, "The Wife of Bath and Lollardy," *MÆ* 58 (1989): 224–42; *Chaucer's Biblical Poetics* (Norman: University of Oklahoma Press, 1998), 138–59. See also Besserman, "'Glosynge Is a Glorious Thyng': Chaucer's Biblical Exegesis," in *Chaucer and Scriptural Tradition,* ed. Jeffrey, 65–73. For Lollardy, see Deanesley, *Lollard Bible,* 268–97, 319–73; Rita Copeland, *Pedagogy, Intellectuals, and Dissent in the Later Middle Ages: Lollardy and Ideas of Learning* (Cambridge: Cambridge University Press, 2001), 99–140.

[11] My conclusion agrees with Blamires, "The Wife of Bath and Lollardy," 224–42. Peggy Knapp details the mix of orthodoxy and Wycliffism in Chaucer's time in *Chaucer and the Social Contest* (New York: Routledge, 1990), 63–76. For the "grey area" between Lollardy and orthodoxy, see the essays in Helen Barr and Ann M. Hutchison, eds., *Text and Controversy from Wyclif to Bale: Essays in Honour of Anne Hudson* (Turnhout: Brepols, 2005). Gail McMurray Gibson establishes the continuing vigor of this mix: *The Theater of Devotion: East Anglian Drama and Society in the Late Middle Ages* (Chicago: University of Chicago Press, 1989), esp. 19–43. Among the many excellent studies of Chaucer and Lollardy, I would single out: Paul Strohm, "Chaucer's Lollard Joke: History and the Textual Unconscious," *SAC* 17 (1995): 23–42; Alan J. Fletcher, "Chaucer the Heretic," *SAC* 25 (2003): 53–121; Alan J. Fletcher, "The Criteria for Scribal Attribution: Dublin, Trinity College, MS 244, Some Early Copies of the Works of Geoffrey Chaucer, and the Canon of Adam Pynkhurst Manuscripts," *RES,* n.s. 58, no. 237 (2007): 597–632. The emerging consensus, with which I agree, is that Chaucer was familiar with and engaged by Wycliffite ideas, and could be perceived as sympathetic to Lollards, but was finally too ambivalent to be closely identified with Lollardy.

[12] I adopt M. M. Bakhtin's theory of "reaccentuation": *The Dialogic Imagination: Four Essays,* ed. Michael Holquist, trans. Caryl Emerson and Michael Holquist (Austin: University of Texas Press, 1981), 419–22.

heretical material, many scribes highlight the passages most vulnerable to heresy charges: her English scriptural references.

If the Wife of Bath figures, in Chaucer's age, the perceived threat of lay access to scripture, the circulation of the glossed *Prologue* throughout the fifteenth century demonstrates readers' interest in its biblical teachings, and their apparent immunity from heresy prosecution. These characteristics neatly define the fifteenth-century gentry, who are an important market for *Canterbury Tales* manuscripts, and who, by virtue of their social status, can explore vernacular theology with relative safety.[13] In fact, members of the gentry possessed and presumably read vernacular scripture—including the Wycliffite Bible—throughout this period.[14] This fact implies their serious commitment to religious education of the sort Wyclif advocated, though it would be a mistake to label them Lollards on that account. Many members of the gentry practice orthodox customs (such as devotion to saints), while investing in vernacular scripture and "dabbling in theology"—much as Alison herself does.[15] Gentry religion blurs distinctions between the "orthodox" and "heterodox": the gentry can be both. That they are rarely accused of heresy testifies to their protected social status, not to their pious conventionality. It is not a stretch to hypothesize that these adventurous lay readers would be intrigued by the *Wife of Bath's Prologue*. Alison's focus on the bare biblical text, her expertise in vernacular translation, and her moderate teachings in the interesting realm of marital relations mirror gentry readers' own interests. Indeed, the poem seems made to order for just such an audience.[16]

[13] See, e.g., John M. Bowers on two manuscripts of the *Canterbury Tales* produced for high-ranking Lancastrian courtiers, "Two Professional Readers of Chaucer and Langland: Scribe D and the HM 114 Scribe," *SAC* 26 (2004): 113–46.

[14] From the official point of view, the problem was not vernacular scripture per se, but rather open challenges to orthodoxy and structures of power; such challenges were associated with the lower class, not the gentry: see Watson, "Censorship and Cultural Change," 831, 847, 857; Margaret Aston and Colin Richmond, eds., "Introduction," *Lollardy and the Gentry in the Later Middle Ages* (Stroud: Sutton; New York: St. Martin's Press, 1997), 19–21; Shannon McSheffrey, "Heresy, Orthodoxy, and English Vernacular Religion, 1480–1525," *Past and Present* 186 (2005): 47–80.

[15] See Aston and Richmond, eds., "Introduction," *Lollardy and the Gentry*, 1–27 (18); and, in the same volume, J. A. F. Thomson, "Knightly Piety and the Margins of Lollardy," 95–111.

[16] A great deal has been written about the Wife's exegesis, and many scholars have followed D. W. Robertson's negative assessment of Alison as a "carnal" exegete: *A Preface to Chaucer: Studies in Medieval Perspectives* (Princeton: Princeton University Press, 1962), 317–31. This line of thought requires us to accept a normative clerical and monastic context for the work. My argument aligns rather with those who allow for the Wife's exegetical competence (according to the standards of the time), and who empha-

STUDIES IN THE AGE OF CHAUCER

By recognizing the possibility of readers sympathetic to some aspects of Lollardy, we gain a fresh purchase on the biblical glosses that frame the *Wife of Bath's Prologue* in many manuscripts. It is historically possible, perhaps even likely, that the glosses express a Lollard-inspired respect for vernacular scripture and literal lay exegesis. Comparable glossing programs appear in other works designed for the laity, and imply a horizon of expectations shaped by positive attitudes toward some aspects of Lollardy, particularly vernacular biblical translation. Nicholas Love's *Mirror of the Blessed Life of Jesus Christ,* for instance, explicitly argues against Lollardy; but manuscripts display Latin source notes beside his vernacular biblical citations, exhibiting his own acts of translation and thus turning him into something of a Lollard.[17] A number of Chaucer manuscripts exhibit Latin source notes in ways likely to suggest a Lollard scriptural agenda to readers, and to inflect the Wife's reception in ways Chaucer could not have anticipated.[18]

The many biblical glosses on the Wife's *Prologue* clearly speak to readers' interest in religious education, and appear to address members of the gentry influenced by some aspects of Lollardy. Almost all the biblical glosses call attention to the Wife's sources, allowing a close comparison of her vernacular translations with the original biblical language, and mapping her exegetical arguments. I will argue that most of the biblical glosses endorse the Wife's authority as an exegete, and that a scribal consensus emerges in the fifteenth century: in thirteen manuscripts (a substantial percentage of the nineteen glossed works), scribes use the margins of the text to invent the Wife of Bath as a reliable biblical

---

size the text's challenge to sacralized clerical knowledge: e.g., David Aers, *Chaucer, Langland, and the Creative Imagination* (London: Routledge and Kegan Paul, 1980), 83–88; Peggy A. Knapp, "'Wandrynge by the Weye': On Alisoun and Augustine," in *Medieval Texts and Contemporary Readers,* ed. Laurie A. Finke and Martin B. Shichtman (Ithaca: Cornell University Press, 1987), 142–57; Carolyn Dinshaw, *Chaucer's Sexual Poetics* (Madison: University of Wisconsin Press, 1989), 113–31; Ralph Hanna III, "*Compilatio* and the Wife of Bath: Latin Backgrounds, Ricardian Texts" (1989), rpt. in *Pursuing History: Middle English Manuscripts and Their Texts* (Stanford: Stanford University Press, 1996), 247–57; Susan Crane, "The Writing Lesson of 1381," in *Chaucer's England: Literature in Historical Context,* ed. Barbara Hanawalt (Minneapolis: University of Minnesota Press, 1992): 201–21; Alastair Minnis, *Fallible Authors: Chaucer's Pardoner and the Wife of Bath* (Philadelphia: University of Pennsylvania Press, 2008), 253–64.

[17] Ghosh, *The Wycliffite Heresy,* 168–70.

[18] Helen Cooper perceptively analyzes other issues that contribute to the Wife's reception: "The Shape-Shiftings of the Wife of Bath, 1395–1670," in *Chaucer Traditions: Studies in Honour of Derek Brewer,* ed. Ruth Morse and Barry Windeatt (Cambridge: Cambridge University Press, 1990), 168–84.

expert.[19] Alison is not, however, the only biblical authority speaking through these material works. What the scribes gloss—and, as significantly, what they pass over in silence—expresses their own partial versions of Alison's biblical argument. The glosses illuminate sometimes surprising ways of reading the poem in relation to scripture and can contribute substantially to our understanding of historical attitudes toward vernacular lay exegesis.

Reception study must steer a course somewhere between the Scylla of the individual, possibly eccentric work, and the Charybdis of unmanageable detail. Each glossed manuscript holds a particular reading of the work, but a single manuscript leads to only limited and tentative conclusions about reception. To comprehend the early reception of Chaucer's most unlikely exegete, we need to compare various manuscripts, seeking to discern how scribes usually highlight Alison's teaching, what they typically gloss, and which glosses they tend to repeat. Only then can we infer anything about historical attitudes toward Alison's exegesis. The New College manuscript (dated to the third quarter of the fifteenth century) is an obvious place with which to begin this project: as it has just five short glosses, all biblical, it offers a coherent site for close textual analysis.[20] The biblical glosses are, moreover, entirely typical of the time and agree in principle with those of a dozen other manuscripts. New College can therefore lead to credible conclusions about how one scribe frames the text for anticipated readers and to supportable conclusions about historical reception. Not all manuscripts develop the same program, of course, and it is instructive also to mark the limits of scribal consensus. Egerton 2864 (from the end of the century) may serve this purpose. It is an atypical manuscript: packed with forty-six glosses, almost all of them biblical, and many quite long, it resembles just one other manuscript (British Library Additional 5140, copied from the same exemplar). Egerton 2864 can protect us from overgeneralization and hint at a possible range of attitudes toward Chaucer's work. The more famous Ellesmere and related manuscripts

[19] B. Kennedy discovers "contradictory responses" to the Wife in fifteenth-century manuscripts, with a split between a misogynous reception and a relatively "sympathetic" response: "Contradictory Responses to the Wife of Bath," 23–39. As I understand her argument, the "contradictory responses" center on issues other than exegesis.

[20] Stephen Partridge describes New College as professionally and carefully copied. Since the work is not a private copy for personal consumption, it allows for plausible inferences about historical reception beyond a single individual: "A Newly Identified Manuscript by the Scribe of the New College *Canterbury Tales*," *EMS* 6 (1997): 229–36.

must, regrettably, be marginal to this study. Chaucer probably wrote the Ellesmere notes, so the manuscript reveals authorial intention, mixed with scribal intention in the process of copying, which unnecessarily complicates a study of historical reception.[21] The Ellesmere and closely related works therefore enter this study only to confirm an existing pattern of reception.

Reading Like a Scribe

The New College manuscript establishes the Wife's marginal biblical authority in ways characteristic of almost all other substantively glossed manuscripts. All but one of the New College glosses concern the Wife's teaching about marriage, potentially the most provocative aspect of the work, and, it turns out, the aspect that receives the most marginal comments in other manuscripts as well. By comparing the New College glosses with those of other manuscripts, we may comprehend both its unique glossing program and areas of agreement across manuscript groups.[22]

[21] Chaucer's authorship of Latin glosses has been the subject of some controversy. Accepting Chaucer's authorship of some glosses are Aage Brusendorff, *The Chaucer Tradition* (London: Oxford University Press, 1925), 82, 127–28; J. S. P. Tatlock, "*The Canterbury Tales* in 1400," *PMLA* 50 (1935): 103–4; Daniel S. Silvia Jr., "Glosses to *The Canterbury Tales* from St. Jerome's *Epistola adversus Jovinianum*," *SP* 62 (1965): 28–39. Charles A. Owen Jr. contends that the glosses are part of the editorial finish added to the work after Chaucer's death, "The Alternative Reading of *The Canterbury Tales:* Chaucer's Text and the Early Manuscripts," *PMLA* 97 (1982): 237–50. To date, the most exhaustive and definitive study inclines toward Chaucerian authorship of some glosses: Stephen Partridge, "Glosses in the Manuscripts of Chaucer's 'Canterbury Tales': An Edition and Commentary" (Ph.D. dissertation, Harvard University, 1992), chap. 2. Recent research argues that Chaucer supervised early manuscripts; this evidence would support the possibility that he wrote some glosses. See N. F. Blake, "Geoffrey Chaucer and the Manuscripts of the *Canterbury Tales*," *JEBS* 1 (1997): 96–122; Peter Robinson, "A Stemmatic Analysis of the Fifteenth-Century Witnesses to the *Wife of Bath's Prologue*," *The Canterbury Tales Project: Occasional Papers* 2 (1997), 126–27; Linne R. Mooney, "Chaucer's Scribe," *Speculum* 81 (2006): 97–138; Estelle Stubbs, "'Here's One I Prepared Earlier': The Work of Scribe D on Oxford, Corpus Christi College, MS 198," *RES* n.s. 58, no. 234 (2007): 133–53.

[22] The subject of manuscript groups is complicated. Manly and Rickert's groupings and lines of descent have been partially disproven, partially confirmed by computer analysis: see Peter M. W. Robinson, "An Approach to the Manuscripts of the 'Wife of Bath's Prologue,'" in *Computer-Based Chaucer Studies,* ed. Ian Lancashire (Toronto: Centre for Computing in the Humanities, University of Toronto, 1993), 17–47; Robert O'Hara and Peter Robinson, "Computer-Assisted Methods of Stemmatic Analysis," in *The Canterbury Tales Project: Occasional Papers* 1 (1993): 53–74; and Robinson, "A Stemmatic Analysis," 69–132. When I refer to manuscript groups in this essay, I mean manuscripts connected by Robinson's stemmatic analysis. The glosses present particularly challenging stemmatic issues. For informative arguments on this point, see Stephen Partridge,

Early in her marriage sermon, the Wife alludes to the traditional procreative rationale for marriage:

> Men mowe deme & glose vp & doun
> Wel I wot expresse withoutyn lie
> That god bad vs wexe and multiple
> That gentil text can I vnderstonde.
>
> (Ne, 26–29)

The lines are glossed: "Crescite et multiplicamini et cetera" (28, Ne) [Increase and multiply, Gen. 1:28]. The Wife distinguishes between what "men deme" and what "god bad," between men's glosses and the "gentil text," locating authority in the text rather than in scholastic commentaries like the *Glossa Ordinaria*.[23] From her perspective, men's busy glossing up and down produces more smoke than light (a number of Chaucer's contemporaries would agree). Brushing these glosses aside, she emphasizes literal interpretation. This is not perforce a failing on her part. The brief Latin gloss provides a conventional source citation for her text, confirming her point and, not incidentally, her ability to translate Latin ("crescite et multiplicamini") into English ("wexe and multiple"). This source citation appears in eight other manuscripts, spread across several manuscript groups.[24] The scribes' response to this passage suggests a consensus validating the Wife's understanding of scripture. At the same time, the scribes' selection of this particular gloss demonstrates willingness to authorize the Wife's teaching on the subject of procreative intercourse. What is not glossed is also important to the Wife's reception: no manuscript supplies even a brief tag from the many men who "glose vp & doun." That is, the scribes do not cite scholastic or other exegetes who might oppose Alison's take on scripture. The margins represent her as a competent exegete and concur with her in preferring the divine commandment to men's glosses.

"The *Canterbury Tales* Glosses and the Manuscript Groups," in *The Canterbury Tales Project: Occasional Papers* 1 (1993): 85–94; and Partridge, "Wynkyn de Worde's Manuscript Source for the *Canterbury Tales*: Evidence from the Glosses," *ChauR* 41 (2007): 325–59.

[23] Other scholars fully demonstrate this point in Chaucer's canon: see Besserman, *Chaucer's Biblical Poetics*, 138–59; John A. Alford, "Scriptural Testament in *The Canterbury Tales*: The Letter Takes Its Revenge," in *Chaucer and Scriptural Tradition*, ed. Jeffrey, 197–203; Robert W. Hanning, " 'I Shal Finde It in a Maner Glose': Versions of Textual Harassment in Medieval Literature," in *Medieval Texts and Contemporary Readers*, ed. Finke and Shichtman, 27–50.

[24] Ad¹, Ad³, El, En³, Mc, Ps, Ra¹, Tc².

The New College manuscript also authorizes the Wife's teaching about marriage:

> For wel y woot that myn husbonde
> Sholde leve fader and moder & take to me.

> Propter hoc relinquet homo patrem et matrem ei et cetera.
> [For this cause shall a man leave his father and mother, Eph. 5:31]
>
> (Ne, 30–31)

The Latin source displays her adherence to biblical language ("leve fader and moder"; "relinquet patrem et matrem"), and again confirms her teaching. The choice of gloss is intriguing. Ephesians quotes Genesis, and the difference between the verses is just one word ("propter," *for this cause*, replaces "quamobrem," *wherefore*). By citing Genesis, which context suggests is the Wife's obvious source, the scribe would simply support her point. Most scribes do just that.[25] The New College scribe, however, selects the more complicated Ephesians citation, which imposes a specific Christian meaning on the union of man and woman: a man leaves his parents in order ("propter") to love his wife as Christ loves the church. In this reading, the "cause" of marriage is self-sacrificial love. By choosing Ephesians for the gloss, the scribe subtly recalls this implication. On a literal level, moreover, the gloss emphatically supports the Wife's procreative rationale for marriage: "for this cause"—procreation—a man shall leave his father and mother. The gloss turns the elevated metaphor of Christ marrying the church into a defense of sexual generation.

Where the Wife makes a potentially arcane reference to a minor biblical figure, Lamech—"What Reckith me though men say welaway / Of shrewd lameth and of his bigamey" (Ne, 53–54)—New College provides a marginal explanation: "Lameth primo induxit bigamiam" (Ne, 54) [Lameth married bigamously first]. The reader is expected to be less a biblical expert than the Wife, in need of a Latin gloss to comprehend

---

[25] If the first word of either verse is omitted, the source becomes ambiguous. Cp, Ha², Ld¹, N¹, Pw, Ps, and Sl¹ clearly quote from Genesis at one point; Lc probably quotes Genesis; En³ quotes from Genesis but misidentifies the quote ("Apostolus ad Philipenses," 28, En³); Ad¹ quotes both books and also misidentifies the Ephesians passage.

her learned aside. Similar informative glosses appear in six other manuscripts, some of which link Lamech not only to bigamy but also to homicide.[26] The introduction of homicide implies diverse possible interpretations for "welaway": do men decry him for bigamy, homicide, or both? Are the two sins related? In these cases, far from stabilizing her meaning, glosses open the text to multiple interpretations.

Lamech gains a diverse reception across the manuscript groups, and the New College scribe does not in this instance represent a clear consensus. Most scribes (fourteen, to be precise) are more interested in the proverbial verse immediately before the Wife mentions Lamech: "Bet is to be wedded than to brynne" (52). Scribes typically highlight the proverb by translating it back into Latin: "Melius est nubere quam vri" (El, 54).[27] The marginal Latin once again supports the Wife's biblical teaching. This particular gloss also testifies to scribes' interest in proverbial expressions: in fact, proverbs get more attention than scripture in most manuscripts, whether that interest is signaled by a Latin translation or a "Nota." (Chaunticleer was not alone in valuing Latin proverbs.) Hence the Wife's misogynistic confession, "Deceite wepyng spynnyng god hath yeue / To wommen kyndely whil they may lyue" (401–2), is popular with scribes, many of whom mark it with a "Nota" or Latin translation.[28]

Serenely distinct from the masses, the New College scribe ignores this and all other proverbs. Even if he were marking proverbs, he would miss "Bet is to be wedded than to *brynne*," for the New College text reads "Bettir it is to be weddid than to *wynne*" (Ne, 52; emphasis added)—a misprision that may make sense but lacks either apostolic authority or proverbial cogency. The misprision would not actually prevent a Latin

---

[26] Ad[1], Ad[3], El, En[3], Ra[1], Tc[2].

[27] Ad[3], Cp, El, En[3], Ha[2], La, Lc, Ld[1], Nl, Ps, Pw, Ra[1], Sl[1], Tc[2]. Several manuscripts also explicitly note the verse's biblical authority ("Apostolus ad Corintheos," Ad[3], 59, compare En[3]; "Secundum Paulum," Tc[2], 60), making the Wife's reference to "thapostle seith" (base text, 49) more specific.

[28] "Fallere nere flere cepit deus in muliere," Ad[1], 401. A Latin version appears in Cn, Cp, En[3], Ha[2], La, Lc, Ld[1], Ma, Nl, Pw, Ra[3], Sl[1], Tc[2]. "Nota" appears in Fi and Mm, each manuscript's only gloss on the *Prologue*. Another proverb of broad interest in the manuscripts reminds men of their disciplinary role in marriage (632–38). Although the Wife dismisses the "old sawe," many scribes mark it with a "Nota," "Nota bene," or "Nota prouerbium": Ad[3], Bo[1], Cp, Dd, El, Gg, Ha[2], Hg, La, Ln, Ma, Nl, Ph[3], Pw. Two manuscripts (Ad[3], El) also identify a biblical source (Ecclesiasticus 25:34), making the Wife dissent from scripture itself.

gloss, if one were in the exemplar; other manuscripts with similar variations include a mismatched Latin gloss.[29] We may safely conclude that
the New College scribe is simply not interested in proverbs.

As New College continues, Alison again cites the Apostle Paul, who
counsels virginity but permits marriage:

> The Apostil whenne he spak of Maidenhede
> He saide that ther of precept had he noon
> Men may counsel awomman to be oon
> But counsel is no maner comaundement.
>
> (Ne, 64–67)

Paul testifies from the margin: "De virginibus preceptum domini non
habeo" (Ne, 63) [Concerning virgins, I have no commandment of the
Lord, I Cor. 7:25]. As we by now expect in this manuscript, her "precept" and "comaundement" accurately translate "preceptum," and the
gloss substantially affirms her interpretation. The source citation is entirely proper and seemingly sober-minded, though we might pause over
the fact that the scribe chooses to authorize yet another of the Wife's
scriptural precedents for a nonvirginal lifestyle. The selection of glosses
argues that the scribe uses source notes to enhance the Wife's biblical
argument about marital sexuality. Eight other manuscripts exhibit similar citations, so the affirmation of marital sexuality appears a commonplace, at least among scribes.[30] The scribes' focus on conjugal sexuality
accords well with the interests of the married gentry, who constitute
an important market for the manuscripts, and who would doubtless
appreciate this validation of their life choices.

The next New College gloss, the only nonbiblical marginal note, attributes to Alison an exemplum:

> Ful wel y knowe a lord in his houshold
> Hath meny a vessel of siluer & of gold.
> Exemplum
>
> (Ne, 99–100)

---

[29] Nl reads "Bettir it is to be weddit then to blyn," and Tc[2] agrees (Tc[2], 52). Both
nonetheless include a version of the Latin proverb: "Secundum Paulum Melius est nubere quam vri" (Tc[2], 60; compare Nl, 52).

[30] Ad[1], Ad[3], El, En[3], Mc, Ps, Ra[1], Tc[2].

As the passage continues, the Wife distinguishes between the perfection of virginity and the (lesser) good of marriage, a consistent theme in her biblical teaching. "Exemplum" marks this passage as having moral, didactic value. The implication is unique to this manuscript. Only two manuscripts identify her biblical source for the exemplum,[31] while most scribes pass over this point entirely and concentrate instead on her reference to Jesus' advice about financial management, clearly a point of great interest to these scribes' expected readers:

> But Crist that of parfeccioun is welle
> Bad nat euery wight he sholde go selle
> Al that he hadde and yeue it to the poore
> And in swich wise folwe hym and his fore
> But swynke with his hondis and labore
> He spak to hem that wol lyue parfitly
> And lordynges by youre leue that am nat I.
>
> (107–12)

The direct citation of Christ garners considerable scribal attention, and some version of the source appears in thirteen manuscripts: "Dixit dominus vende omnia que habes et da pauperibus" (Mc, 108; The Lord said, sell all you have and give to the poor, Matt. 19:21).[32] Interestingly, the gloss quotes scripture in a way that turns the passage into an apparently universal command to "sell all." A correct understanding of Christ's teaching (*if you would be perfect,* sell all) becomes entirely dependent on the Wife's exegesis, and the reader is here expected to privilege her account rather than the source note. By putting the reader in this subordinate position, the gloss heightens Alison's authority. The New College manuscript is therefore relatively conservative in its marginal construction of her exegetical expertise; other manuscripts not only document her biblical citations more fully but also script readers' deference to her in more complex ways.

The next New College gloss calls attention to the Wife's announcement that men are sexually subject to their wives:

[31] Ad[1], En[3].

[32] Versions of this gloss appear in Ad[1], Cp, En[3], Ha[2], Lc, Ld[1], Ln, Nl, Ps, Pw, Ra[1], Sl[1]. Se marks the passage with "Nota bene."

> The power wol I haue during al my lif
> Both of his propir body and nat he
> Right thus the Apostil tolde it me
>
> (Ne, 158–60)

With another nod to Latin authority: "Vir non habet potestatem sui corporis set mulier" (Ne, 158) [The man does not have power over his own body, but the wife [does], I Cor. 7:4]. As usual, the Wife competently translates scripture ("power" for "potestatem," "body" for "corporis"), and the gloss confirms her teaching. The New College scribe thus consistently presents the Wife as a reliable biblical authority. At the same time, his careful attention to her biblical support for sexual intercourse suggests a sense of humor akin to Chaucer's and perhaps even a covert pleasure in the lessons that can be derived from scripture.

In contrast to the New College scribe, modern scholars interpret this citation as evidence of the Wife's so-called exegetical failing. They point out that whereas she insists on her own power, scripture makes the obligation mutual. Modern readers regularly conclude that her "partial" citation establishes her self-interested reading practices.[33] Manuscript evidence demonstrates that this conclusion is based entirely on modern standards of citation and hermeneutic expectations. The New College scribe in fact represents a medieval consensus. This passage gathers considerable attention in manuscripts, and the most often repeated gloss agrees with New College in affirming that a married man does not have power over his own body, but the wife does.[34] If medieval scribes conformed to modern expectations, at least one would correct the Wife's gendered reading of scripture; none does. Indeed, no medieval reader could possibly perceive her citation as "partial": scripture is not yet divided into verses (that will happen in the sixteenth century), and she simply begins, as medieval exegetes do, with the part of the text that pertains to her argument. Far from countering her gendered exegesis, a number of scribes enhance her position by adding one or more glosses depicting husbands as their wives' sexual debtors, without noting that

[33] E.g., Robertson, *Preface to Chaucer,* 329; Graham D. Caie, "The Significance of the Early Chaucer Manuscript Glosses (With Special Reference to the *Wife of Bath's Prologue,*" *ChauR* 10 (1976): 354–55; Dinshaw, *Chaucer's Sexual Poetics,* 124; Robert Longsworth, "The Wife of Bath and the Samaritan Woman," *ChauR* 34 (2000): 372–87 (382).

[34] A similar gloss appears in Ad¹, Ad³, El, En³, Ha², La, Lc, Ld¹, Ln, Nl, Ps, Pw, Ra¹, Se, Sl¹, Tc².

wives are also their husbands' debtors.[35] In short, most scribes unambiguously support Alison's point about a husband's sexual subjection to his wife. Lopsided scriptural arguments are apparently the norm, not the exception.

Alison continues to interpret apostolic teachings about marriage, with her New College scribe accompanying her:

> Right thus the Apostil tolde it me
> And bad our husbondis for to love vs weel
>
> Viri diligite vxores vestras et cetera
> [Men, love your wives, Eph. 5: 25 or Col. 3:10]
> (Ne, 160–61)

Although in the Wife's mouth "love" carries an unavoidable sexual innuendo, the margin affirms that scripture commands just that ("diligite"). Here as elsewhere in New College, both text and gloss argue that the Bible legitimates sexual love in marriage, a message well suited to the manuscript's probably devout but not ascetic gentry readers. By calling attention to just these biblical injunctions, the New College scribe implies his appreciation of the argument.[36] The Wife's emphasis on men's roles and responsibilities in marriage, highlighted by these glosses, reverses clerics' characteristic attention to women's duties. Scriptural hermeneutics is obviously gendered, but that does not invalidate Alison's focus. The New College manuscript, along with many others, uses Latin glosses to display her scriptural foundations, in the process cloaking her in the aura of authority.

The New College margins trace the main points in the Wife's teaching about marriage. Some of these points are gendered: men should leave father and mother, give power over their bodies to their wives, and love their wives. Other points apply equally to men and women: God commands procreation; bigamy is reprehensible; Paul permits marriage. The gendered aspect of her exegesis would be remarkable for her earliest audiences, yet I find no resistance to it in these manuscripts, no pattern of marginal contestation with the text (with the exception of Egerton 2864 and British Library Additional 5140, discussed below).

---

[35] Ad¹, Ad³, El, En³, Ln, Mc, Ps, Ra¹, Tc².

[36] Several other manuscripts similarly exhort men to love their wives: see Ad¹, Ad³, El, En³. This gloss does not appear in Ra¹ or Tc², which otherwise follow El closely; the omission is suggestive.

While the glosses do not argue with the Wife's exegesis, neither do they closely mirror the poetic text. Rather, the glosses evidence partial and simplified readings of the poem. New College and most other glossed manuscripts highlight just a few of the many threads in Alison's argument against marriage. Hence, according to the glosses, marriage makes a man sexually indebted and subject to his wife—not because she is a shrew but because scripture commands his subjection. The manuscripts are not concerned with the wife's subjection to her husband; perhaps they take that for granted.

In these manuscripts, Alison clearly interprets the "wo that is in mariage" as the product of man's sexual debt to his wife, his so-called tribulation in the flesh. The glosses lend intellectual authority to Alison's antimatrimonial argument. Glosses also reveal her witty and highly original deviation from similar arguments. Antimatrimonial literature typically points out the domestic distractions of crying babies, difficult servants, and a complaining wife; a wife's unending material desires, satisfied only with great labor; and the continual threat of cuckoldry, poisoning, and lesser betrayals. These domestic trials are memorably detailed in Jerome's polemic against Jovinian, and would have been prominent in Jankyn's book of wicked wives.[37] In a striking reversal of Jerome and subsequent antimatrimonial literature, Alison makes sexual intercourse the sole—and surely comical—trial of married life. The glosses that call attention to this deviation from patristic authority can hardly be coincidental. The scribes presumably recognized and appreciated Chaucer's ludic revision of the discourse.

In the New College manuscript, the poetic text and marginal glosses reinforce each other, creating the *Prologue* as a sermon aimed at men. Many manuscripts obviously agree. Indeed, on the topic of marital sexuality, many other scribes similarly treat the Wife as a persuasive exegete in command of authoritative scriptural lessons. Yet we must be clear about the character of her exegesis: she is not a scholastic, nor, judging from their glosses, are her scribes. The manuscript margins nowhere disclose the kind of commentary developed in a contemporary monas-

---

[37] For the relevant part of Jerome's diatribe, see *Against Jovinianus,* in *The Principal Works of St. Jerome,* trans. W. H. Fremantle, A Select Library of Nicene and Post-Nicene Fathers of the Christian Church, 2nd series, 14 vols. (rpt. Grand Rapids, Mich.: Eerdmans, 1989), 6: book 1, chap. 47, pp. 383–84. For the tradition of misogamy and the contexts of Jankyn's book, see Robert A. Pratt, "Jankyn's 'Book of Wikked Wives': Medieval Anti-Matrimonial Propaganda in the Universities," *Annuale Mediaevale* 3 (1962): 5–27.

tery or university context. Alison's authority, like that of her scribes, is limited. Near the beginning of the Prologue, for instance, she recalls Jesus' words to the Samaritan woman at the well, but forestalls interpretation: "What he mente therby I can not sayn" (Ne, 20). Although this line appears in almost all manuscripts, it gathers no gloss: apparently Alison's scribes cannot or will not say "what he mente" either. In fact, she and her scribes typically respect a clear division of labor. The Wife elucidates the meaning of scripture; the scribes copy her sources.

The scribes' respect for the Wife's biblical learning could be a reaction to intratextual hints from Chaucer. Within the *Prologue,* the Pardoner dramatically declares himself convinced by Alison's teaching, modeling a semiserious response to the argument:

> Vp stert the pardoner & that anon
> Now dame quod he be god & be saint Iohn
> Ye be an nobil prechour in this caas
> I was aboute to wedde awif alas
> What sholde I bye it my self so dere
> Yit hadde y lever wedde no wif tw yere.
>
> (Ne, 163–68)

The Pardoner heeds the "nobil prechour" and decides against marriage: the sexual threat puts him off. His conversion to misogamy establishes the Wife's effectiveness as a biblical teacher. This is a remarkable moment in the history of antimatrimonial literature. Arguments against marriage are almost always, as Jill Mann notes, a "purely male affair . . . addressed to a man by another man." The arguments are also consistently "ineffectual," "redundant," and "ignored." Thus in *The Merchant's Tale*, Justinus tries halfheartedly to dissuade January from marriage, but the marriage proceeds apace.[38] Similarly, Alison's fifth husband, Jankyn, reads to her from a book intended to dissuade Oxford clerks from marriage. Since the clerk is reading to his wife, his book is obviously and ludicrously redundant. When Alison takes the reins, however, arguments against marriage prove remarkably persuasive. Indeed, one historical reader concurs with the Pardoner's distaste for the marriage debt: "Nota seruitutem in matrimonio" (Ra³, 155).

Chaucer develops another antimatrimonial argument in "Lenvoy de

[38] *Geoffrey Chaucer* (Atlantic Highlands, N.J.: Humanities Press International, 1991), 55–70, quotes respectively 51, 56, 58, 58.

Chaucer a Bukton," which, like most such works, anticipates having as little impact on the reader as Justinus has on January. "Lenvoy a Bukton" continues the Wife's development as an exegete and possibly further inspires some of the scribes' biblical glosses. "Lenvoy a Bukton" quotes Alison twice: first in Chaucer's promise to speak of the "sorwe and wo that is in mariage," and later in his recollection of a proverb she recites ("Bet ys to wedde than brenne").[39] These quotations, together with a reference to the *Prologue,* construct the Wife as an established authority worthy of citation. Like the *Prologue,* "Lenvoy a Bukton" follows scripture in representing marriage as masculine subjection to women. In marriage, a man:

> shal have sorwe on thy flessh, thy lyf,
> And ben thy wives thral, as seyn these wise;
> And yf that hooly writ may nat suffyse,
> Experience shal the teche.
>
> (19–22)

Jill Mann calls attention to the comedy of this poem, implicit in its assumption that the advice will not be heeded: "experience shal the teche."[40] The poem nonetheless concludes by directing Bukton to read the Wife of Bath in order to escape imminent sexual thralldom. The Wife appears a trustworthy exegete, using "hooly writ" to teach the "wo that is in mariage" for men; and her *Prologue* remains Chaucer's best hope (tongue in cheek) for male freedom from the "sorwe" of sex. By discrediting the Wife's exegesis, modern critics have missed the point. The force as well as the comedy of Alison's antimatrimonial argument lies precisely in its valid scriptural authority. The joke is not on the Wife but on men like Jankyn and Bukton who refuse to be dissuaded by scriptural warnings, and who, as a consequence, "shal have sorwe on [their] flessh."

Both the Wife's *Prologue* and "Lenvoy a Bukton" grant a laywoman the capacity to cite scripture persuasively, at least in an argument about marital sexuality. Chaucer's own reception of Alison's exegesis establishes a coherent foundation for the New College and other scribes' biblical glosses. Through the glosses, then, we may perceive Chaucer slyly

---

[39] Larry D. Benson, gen. ed., *The Riverside Chaucer* (Boston: Houghton Mifflin, 1987), 6, 18.

[40] Mann, *Geoffrey Chaucer,* 57–58.

winking at readers capable of appreciating the humor in the scriptural lesson. The New College scribe gets the joke and in turn uses biblical glosses to point out the comic implication of Alison's sermon: marriage means sex, so men had better run the other way! Only an earnestly ascetic (or impotent) reader would be turned from marriage by this argument, while most members of the gentry would likely discover in the glossed sermon an acceptable biblical rationale for their nightly labors in bed.

A Historical Consensus

The vast majority of biblical glosses, like those of New College, never question or undermine the Wife's exegetical authority. On the contrary, most manuscripts that supply source notes support her biblical references at every turn, and most call attention to her accuracy of citation. This is obviously true of twelve manuscripts ranging from the first to the last quarter of the fifteenth century, all of which reinforce the impression created by the New College glosses.[41] In fact, these manuscripts allow us to extend our conclusions about biblical citations to other kinds of glosses. Each of these manuscripts includes several glosses on the Wife's biblical teachings, confirming that Jesus went to a wedding in Galilee,[42] that the Bible commands men and women to increase and multiply,[43] that a man should leave his father and mother when he marries,[44] that it is better to marry than burn,[45] that Paul had no precept about marriage,[46] that a man has no power over his own flesh,[47] that the married man owes his wife a debt,[48] and that Jesus spoke about selling all you have and giving to the poor.[49] Although the twelve manuscripts differ in their selection of biblical glosses, each affirms the Wife's treatment of scripture in much the way New College does. This set of manuscripts points toward a clear historical consensus: these fifteenth-century scribes present the Wife of Bath as an authoritative exegete.

[41] Cp, Ha², La, Lc, Ld¹, Ln, Mc, Nl, Ps, Pw, Se, Sl¹.
[42] Mc, Ps.
[43] Cp, Ha², Ld¹, Mc, Nl, Ps, Pw.
[44] Cp, Ha², Lc, Ld¹, Nl, Ps, Pw, Sl¹.
[45] Cp, Ha², La, Lc, Ld¹, Nl, Ps, Pw, Sl¹.
[46] Mc, Ps.
[47] Ha², La, Lc, Ld¹, Ln, Nl, Ps, Pw, Se, Sl¹.
[48] Ln, Mc, Ps.
[49] Cp, Ha², Lc, Ld¹, Ln, Mc, Nl, Ps, Pw, Sl¹.

Unlike New College, some of these manuscripts also briefly gloss others of the Wife's learned remarks. When the Wife claims that even Argus, with his hundred eyes, could not keep track of her, scribes sometimes mark the passage, albeit with some uncertainty about just how many eyes Argus is supposed to have.[50] A mention of Pasiphae, queen of Crete, prompts marginal notations specifying that Crete is an island.[51] And, like most manuscripts other than New College, all of these works make note of proverbs, probably regarding them as serious wisdom literature.[52] One manuscript pays attention as well to the Wife's scientific learning, noting her reference to "Protholome" (Se, 182), and commenting on an astrological passage: "Nota the diuersite bitwex Mercurie and Venus" (Se, 675). Taken together, these manuscripts establish a clear pattern of reception. In these dozen manuscripts, as in New College, the Wife is represented as a learned authority over several discourses. The margins of these pages evidence no hint of anxiety about how she uses sources, biblical or other. To the contrary, the margins construct her authority across traditionally masculine fields of learning, including but not restricted to the biblical.

In short, a significant number of medieval scribes represent Alison of Bath as a dependable (and sometimes amusing) biblical authority: thirteen of the nineteen scribes who include biblical glosses foster a positive reception of the Wife's exegesis, and the number would go up if we included Ellesmere and related works.[53] Hence manuscript study requires us to recognize that this particular laywoman was represented as authoritative over scripture and other learned discourses throughout the fifteenth century. This does not mean that these scribes would regard actual lay women as persuasive exegetes. The scribes who write and select glosses are aware of Chaucer's authorial status and deferential

[50] "Argus habuit mille oculos," 358, Cp (also Nl); compare "Argus habuit . C. oculos," 358, Ha². La reveals a correcting hand at work. Se just marks "Argus" (358).

[51] "Creta insula," 707, Ha²; also Lc.

[52] "Fallere flere nere dedit deus in muliere," 402, Cp; also Ha², La, Lc, Ld¹, Nl, Pw, Sl¹. "Solo melius est habitare," 748, Cp; also Ha², Lc, Ld¹, Mc, Nl, Pw, Se, Sl¹. Similarly, "Whoso that buyldeth his hous al of salwes" (633) is noted in Cp, Ha², La, Ln, Nl, Pw. And finally, "Tria sunt que expellunt hominem a domo sua . fumus stillicidium et mala mulier," 278, Mc; also Ps. The idea that proverbs were considered "a source of wisdom" is advanced by Julia Boffey, "Proverbial Chaucer and the Chaucer Canon," in *Reading from the Margins: Textual Studies, Chaucer, and Medieval Literature,* ed. Seth Lerer (San Marino, Calif.: Huntington Library, 1996), 37–47 (46).

[53] As I think Chaucer probably wrote the El glosses on the *Prologue,* I exclude El and closely related manuscripts from this section of my argument, though these manuscripts confirm the historical pattern.

toward the arcane learning so prominently displayed in this text. Whether they are authorizing the Wife or Chaucer is an open question (they may, like modern readers, occasionally confuse the two). They nonetheless inscribe material pages that support the Wife's claims to authority over scripture. In the realm of fiction at least, a woman preaches to men, and does so with acknowledged authority and persuasive force. Fifteenth-century Chaucer manuscripts serve as midwives to the idea of an authoritative woman exegete—so long, at least, as she recommends marital sex.

Peter Shillingsburg cogently remarks that "a literary work is only partially represented in each of its physical manifestations."[54] The New College manuscript witnesses to one scribe's partial reading of the text, and discloses his appreciation for the Wife's lessons about men's sexual bondage. Other manuscripts (also partially) concentrate on other discourses, from the biblical to the patristic, proverbial, astrological, and mythological. Collectively, the margins of these glossed manuscripts call attention to the work's astonishing erudition, emphasize the Wife's wide-ranging intellectual authority, and evidence a consistently positive reception of her gendered exegesis. By studying these many partial representations, we may appreciate anew Chaucer's unusual reaccentuation of scripture, and more fully apprehend the work's historical potential for meaning. The Wife's exegetical authority is literally marginal: that is, constructed in and through the Latin margins of material works.

Manuscript margins witness to scribes' interest in Alison's exegesis and to the authority they grant her vernacular translations. By choosing to highlight these particular features of the text, scribes lead us to infer the presence of buyers who seek precisely these treatments of vernacular scripture. In other words, most manuscripts of the *Prologue* address readers who accept, as Alison herself does, a mix of Lollardy and orthodoxy, and who more than likely mirror her in their questioning of conventional clerical authority and in their desire for lucid biblical hermeneutics. The glosses at once reveal and direct the interests of their intended readers.

Egerton 2864 Reconsidered

At the end of the fifteenth century, one small manuscript group takes a radical departure from the dominant pattern of reception exemplified by

---

[54] *From Gutenberg to Google: Electronic Representations of Literary Texts* (Cambridge: Cambridge University Press, 2006), 49.

New College. Or, to be more precise, Egerton 2864 and British Library Additional 5140 supply the expected biblical glosses—but only for the first half of the work.[55] The glossing program for the two manuscripts is almost identical, evidencing just a few meaningful variations. Since Egerton 2864 offers a better text, I cite it in this section; the conclusions apply as well to Additional 5140, which contains the same glosses at these points.[56] Egerton 2864 glosses Jesus' presence at the wedding in Galilee, his reproof to the Samaritan woman, his suggestion about selling all and giving to the poor, the divine command to increase and multiply, a woman's freedom to remarry after her husband's death, a husband's sexual debt, a woman's power over her husband's body, and so on. Many of these glosses are notably fuller than in their appearances elsewhere—Jesus' direction for those who would live perfectly is documented in three gospels rather than just one—but otherwise conform to the horizon of expectations evidenced by the New College and other manuscripts.

The Egerton 2864 glosses can help us better apprehend how biblical citations can support the Wife's sermon. One gloss, for instance, gives two sources for a mere three lines of poetry:

Poule durst nat commaunden at the leste
A thyng of which his mayster yaf noon heste
The dart is set vpon virgynyte.

> Non enim audeo aliquid loquo eorum que per me non efficit Christi,
> Apostolus ad Romanos. Si [sic] currite vt comprehendatus, Apostolus ad
> Corinthios.
> [For I dare not to speak of any of those things which Christ does not
> work through me, Rom. 15:18; Know you not that they that run,
> 1 Cor. 9:24]

(En³, 73–75)

As with many source notes, the citations are elliptical, giving the reader enough information to find the passage but not enough for the note to make sense on its own. The more elliptical the source note, the more

---

[55] I am indebted to Schibanoff's analysis of the Egerton manuscript ("The New Reader and Female Textuality," 71–108) but differ from her in my conclusions.

[56] Interestingly, a similar glossing program was added by hand to an early print edition, for which see Daniel W. Mosser, "The Manuscript Glosses of the *Canterbury Tales* and the University of London's Copy of Pynson's [1492] Edition: Witness to a Lost Exemplar," *ChauR* 41 (2007): 360–92.

dependent the reader becomes on the Wife's commentary. Each citation specifies where in canonical scripture the full account may be found, making it obvious that Alison translates the Vulgate and not some secondhand vernacular source. In fact, she translates the Vulgate as it appears in Jerome's *Against Jovinian;* it is the scribe who constructs her as a straightforward biblical translator. The scribe also credits her exegesis: the source note from Romans confirms her assertion that "Poule durst not commaunden," and emphasizes her close adherence to scripture. As the note continues, it alludes as well to her biblical authority for the idea of virginity as a race won by few. The margin endorses Alison's representation of virginity as a heroic endeavor, a standard never meant for all believers.

The next glosses similarly buttress her claims that Paul wishes all to be as he is himself, though he gives them leave to marry:

> He wolde that euery wight were such as he.

> Volo autem omnes homines esse sicut me ipsum, Apostolus
> ad Corinthios.
> [For I would that all men were even as myself, 1 Cor. 7:7]
> (En³, 81)

> And for to been a wyf he yaf me leve
> Of Indulgence so it is no repreve.

> Hoc autem dico secundum Indulgenciam non secundum Imperium,
> Apostolus ad Corinthios.
> [But I speak this by indulgence, not by commandment, 1 Cor. 7:6]
> (En³, 83–84)

The margins scrupulously distinguish between apostolic commands and invitations to extraordinary virtue. The manuscript next offers marginal reflections on the proverbial caution against touching women, further detailing the work's engagement with scripture:

> Al were it good no womman for to touche
> He mente as in his bed or in his chouche
> For pereyl is bothe fyr and touh tassemble.
> (En³, 87–89)

This passage gains two glosses, the first emphatically brief:

> Bonum est mulierem non tangere.
> [It is good not to touch a woman, 1 Cor. 7:1]
>
> (En³, 87)

And the second extensive:

Numquid potest homo abscondere ignem in sinu suo vt vestimenta illius non ardeant? aut ambulare super prunas et non comburentur plante eius? Sic qui ingredatur ad mulierem proxi sui non erit mundus cum tetigerit eam et cetera, pabole Salamonis; et alibi, bonum est homini mulierem non tangere, Apostolus ad Corinthios.

[Can a man hide fire in his bosom, and his garments not burn? Or can he walk upon hot coals, and his feet not be burned? So he who goes in to his neighbour's wife, shall not be clean when he shall touch her, Prov. 6: 27–29; It is good for a man not to touch a woman, 1 Cor. 7:1]

(En³, 89)

In the Wife's account, to touch a woman is inevitably to light a fire. The context makes it clear that she refers to a married couple. The gloss is more prurient, for it imagines a man attempting to hide his "fire," overconfident about his resistance to the flames, eventually touching his neighbor's wife and becoming sexually impure. The Wife's comment on married life turns into a marginal reflection on man's temptations to adultery. The scribe repeats Alison's point—"it is good not to touch a woman"—twice, as if to ward off the imagined temptation.

Some readers may discover in these glosses invitations to separate from the Wife and side with the more heroic apostle, and in this event the glosses would serve as prompts for ascetic self-denial. There is, however, no moment at which Alison's authority over the biblical text is in doubt, anymore than it is in the briefer New College program. The more extensive glosses are probably best interpreted as the scribe's performance of his own expertise, his ability to identify all possible biblical allusions. These glosses look to me more like a learned game of identifying biblical sources or allusions than an attempt to argue with the exegesis: there is nothing glossed that is not in the poem, and none of the glosses contradicts Alison. If the New College scribe most concisely captures her focus and demonstrates her authority, thus far this manuscript similarly presents her as a respected expert on scripture.

For the first half of the work, the Egerton scribe stands out only in his extraordinary diligence, searching out sources wherever they may hide. In this manuscript group alone, for instance, do we get the biblical citation for the Wife's allusion to a great lord's household:

> For wel ye knowe a lord in his houshoolde
> Ne hath nat every vessel al of golde
> Som been of tree and doon her lord servise.

> In magna autem domo non solum sunt vasa
> aurea et argentea sed et liquea et fictilia et
> cetera, apostolus ad Titum.
> [In a great house there are not only vessels of gold and
> silver, but also of wood and earth, 2 Tim. 2:20[57]]
>
> (En[3], 99–101)

The vessels of wood, with which the Wife identifies, seem equal in merit to those of gold and silver. The gloss authorizes not only her biblical knowledge but also her exegesis, her idea that virgins and wives differ only as gold and wooden vessels do, their service similarly welcome to the lord.

Such diligence with biblical sources leads at several points to distinctly laughable affirmations of the Wife's teaching, though even these glosses may be meant as seriously as the rest appear to be. The Wife promises to persevere in the married state to which she has been called, unashamed of being the barley bread with which Jesus "refreisshed many a man" (En[3], 146). A gloss treats her commitment to sex as a holy vocation: "Vnusquisque in qua vacacione vocatus est in ea permaneat, apostolus ad Corinthios" [En[3], 146; Let every man abide in the same calling in which he was called, 1 Cor. 7:20]. At least one advocate of chastity, Jerome, would surely disapprove of this notion of spiritual vocation, and even proponents of diverse vocations in the Church might protest that this goes too far. Similarly, when the Wife expresses willingness to accept her husband's "payment," the scribe reminds readers of

---

[57] For the sake of readability, I omit from my translations all scribal additions to biblical verses: references to books ("apostolus ad Titum"), the typical conclusion to a quotation ("et cetera"), and transitions within the gloss ("et postea," "et alibi," etc.).

her Christian obligation to do just that: "Vxori vir debitum reddat similiter autem et vxor viro, Apostolus ad Corinthios" [En³, 153; Let the husband render the debt to his wife, and the wife in like manner to the husband, 1 Cor. 7:3]. According to this scribe, scripture unambiguously enjoins the exchange of the conjugal debt. This manuscript also includes a gloss reminding husbands that they do not have power over their bodies, but their wives do (En³, 162). Fully visible in the margins, the reciprocal marriage debt equalizes the sexual duties of each spouse. The Wife evidently practices what she preaches, making her a lay (but not necessarily ironic) version of the poor Parson: "But Cristes loore and his apostles twelve / He taughte; but first he folwed it hymselve."[58]

Eager to discover sources, the Egerton scribe can create mere farce, as in a gloss on the Wife's claim that all is for sale:

> Wynne who so may for al is for to selle
> With empti hond men may noon hawkes lure
> For wynnyng wolde I al his lust endure.
>
> Donum hominis dilatat viam eius, parabole Salamonis.
> [A man's gift enlarges his way, Prov. 18:16]
> (En³, 414–16)

In the Bible, the proverb recommends gifts in order to get the prince's attention. The scribe turns "Solomon's" advice to a new purpose: getting sex from wives—or perhaps, literally, seducing hawks. The gloss hovers ambiguously between literal and figurative meanings. However we interpret it, the Latin margin locates power in the man who enlarges his own way and exercises power over hawks and/or women. The note in effect reduces Solomon to advocating marital prostitution. Significantly, this gloss does not document a source but introduces scripture as a commentary on the poetic text.

More typically, however, to this point the biblical glosses simply track down the Wife's sources with unusual thoroughness. After spending about 400 lines in this fashion, Egerton 2864 takes a startling and un-

---

[58] *General Prologue*, I.527–28. I find Chaucer's treatment of the Parson ambivalent. Although the Parson has been much idealized, Aers persuasively reads the Parson portrait as satiric, *Chaucer, Langland, and the Creative Imagination*, 106–14. As H. Ansgar Kelly proposes, the Parson is both sympathetic and "unduly sanctimonious and narrowminded": "Sacraments, Sacramentals, and Lay Piety in Chaucer's England," *ChauR* 28 (1993): 5–22 (12).

precedented turn: for the rest of the *Prologue*, biblical glosses create explicitly misogynous commentaries on the poem. The change in glossing strategy is not absolute—several biblical sources in the remaining lines are glossed as usual—but that convention is now a trifling part of the scribal agenda. For the last half of the work, the scribe deploys scripture as a polemical weapon, and fills the margins with extended biblical commentaries on Alison's accounts of married life. The most obvious explanation for such a change would be that a new scribe took over half way through the work; since one hand writes both text and gloss, this explanation does not serve. Perhaps further research will explain the sudden appearance of a new glossing strategy. In the meantime, we can try to understand exactly how the glosses change, and how those changes contrast with the work's usual historical reception.

In the latter half of the Egerton 2864 commentary, Chaucer's feminine persona becomes the focus of considerable animosity. The turn comes soon after the hawking gloss, when the Wife's boast about matching her husbands in verbal combat gives rise to an extended commentary on feminine loquaciousness:

> I wolde nat spare hem at her owne boord
> For bi my trouthe I quytt hem woord for woord.

Qui profert contumeliam insipiens est, et parabole Salamonis; et postea, Melius est sedere in angulo domatis quam cum muliere litigiosa et in domo comuni. Et postea, melius est habitare in terra deserta quam cum muliere rixosa et Iracunda; et alibi, Ascensus arenosus in pedibus veteram sic mulier lignata homini quieto, Ecclesiastica; et alibi, liagnam [sic] autem mulierum nullus homini domari potest, Iacobi Apostoli.

[He who utters reproach is foolish, Prov. 10:18; It is better to sit in the corner of the housetop, than with a brawling woman, and in a common house, Prov. 21:9; It is better to dwell in a wilderness, than with a quarrelsome and passionate woman, Prov. 21:19; As the climbing of a sandy way is to the feet of the aged, so is a wife full of tongue to a quiet man, Eccl. 25:27; But a woman's [nonsense word] no man can tame, James 3:8]

(En³, 421–22)

The scribe turns abruptly into a patronizing commentator and corrects the Wife with biblical aphorisms. Ironically, due to a copying error, women's untamable feature—her tongue (*linguam*) in scripture—becomes aporetic nonsense (*liagnam*).

The scribe's patronizing strategy continues in commentaries on her drinking. When she refers to her youthful taste for sweet wine, the scribe cries "woe":

Ve qui potentes estis ad bibendum vinum et cetera, Ysaye; et ibidem autea, Ve qui consurgitis mane ad ebrietatem sectandam et potandum vsque ad vesperam vt vino estuetis et cetera.

[Woe to you that are mighty to drink wine, Isaiah 5:22; Woe to you that rise up early in the morning to follow drunkenness, and to drink till the evening, to be inflamed with wine, Isaiah 5:11]

(En³, 460)

Several potentially objectionable behaviors are mentioned in the general vicinity of this gloss, including her fourth husband's adultery. The adultery passes unnoticed, for the target is not sin but the Wife herself, who has become a prompt for marginal editorializing. Later, "A likerous mouth must have a likerous tayl" (En³, 466) gets similar attention: "Ecclesiasticus, Mulier ebriosa ira magna et contumelia et turpitudo illius non tegetur" (En³, 469) [A drunken woman is a great wrath: and her reproach and shame shall not be hid, Eccl. 26:11]. These glosses are not incited by the Wife's use or misuse of biblical sources, nor do they challenge her exegesis. Rather, they use scripture to condemn her quarrelsome and drunken tongue. After presenting her as a reliable exegete, the scribe turns the Wife into a negative moral exemplum.

As the commentary continues, glosses similarly judge her memory of youthful sexual pleasures (flee youthful desires; En³, 472); her habit of betraying her husbands' confidences (keep your counsel in bed; En³, 533); her distaste for reproof (correction is good for the soul; En³, 639); her ripping pages out of her husband's book (a wicked woman harms a man; En³, 765); and her husband giving "the bridle" into her hands (a woman is contrary to her husband; En³, 787). More conventionally, the margins reinforce the book of wicked wives with source glosses about Eve and Delilah (En³, 693). Finally, notes translate two proverbs into Latin.[59]

[59] It is better to live with a lion or dragon than with a wicked woman; En³, 749; fair and foolish women are like gold rings in swine's noses; En³, 760.

The margins clearly target the Wife at some of these points, as when the scribe comments on the untamable quality of a woman's *liagnam*, the shame of a drunken woman, or married women's contrariness. Yet the commentary is not always directed at the Wife or even at women. One gloss literally addresses men: *"He who* utters reproach is foolish" (*"Qui* profert contumeliam *insipiens* est"). This gloss presents men with a choice between better domestic arrangements (a wilderness) and worse (a space with a woman in it). The gloss concludes with a reminder about man's domestic powerlessness: no man can tame woman. None of these glosses seeks to change woman's behavior; rather, they caution men about the woes of marriage. Together, these glosses shift attention away from the Wife's ludic emphasis on the sexual woes of marriage and return the reader to the commonplaces of antimatrimonial literature: misogynous warnings about domestic turmoil, the distractions of married life, and so on. Interestingly, the glosses recall a memorable passage in Jerome's antimatrimonial treatise *Against Jovinian*.[60] Whereas Chaucer deliberately reaccentuates and revises Jerome's argument, the scribe reinstates the patristic *auctor*'s voice in the margins.[61] The glosses align less with Chaucer's revisionary text than with all the other "ineffectual" and "redundant" antimatrimonial lectures delivered by men to men.[62]

The scribe's address to men is most apparent in a long gloss that admonishes a "son" ("fili mine") to accept correction for the good of his soul. The reader, grammatically gendered male, is required to choose between the Wife's resistance to correction and the proper masculine role of heeding reproof:

> Ne I wolde nat of hym corrected be
> I hate hem that my vices telle me.

Disciplinam autem domini fili mine abicias, parabole Salamonis. Et postea ibidem, Qui arguit in idipsum [sic] sibi maculam generat; et postea ibidem, Qui increpaciones relinquit er[r]at. Et postea Egestas et ignominia ei qui deserit

---

[60] See note 37 above.

[61] For Chaucer's revisions of Jerome, see my "Contested Authority: Jerome and the Wife of Bath on I Timothy 2," *ChauR* 44 (2010): 268–93.

[62] The same can be said of a gloss exhorting men to "keep the doors of your mouth from her that sleeps in your bosom" (En[3], 533; "Ab ea que dormit in sinu tuo custodi claustra oris tui, Michee prophete," Michaea 7:5); and of another gloss enjoining men not to let women "gad about" (En[3], 615; "nec modicum nec mulieri nequam veniam prodeundi," Eccl. 25:34).

disciplinam. Et postea, Qui increpaciones odit morietur. Et postea, Non amat pestilens eum qui se corripit et cetera. Et postea, Qui abicit disciplinam despicit animam suam. Et postea, Qui enim inpaciens est odit disciplinam.

[My son, reject not the correction of the Lord, Prov. 3:11; He who censures himself gets himself a blot, Prov. 9:7 (corrupted); He who forsakes reproofs goes astray, Prov. 10:17; Poverty and shame to him who refuses instruction, Prov. 13:18; He who hates reproof shall die, Prov. 15:10; A corrupt man loves not the man who reproves him, Prov. 15:12; He who rejects instruction despises his own soul, Prov. 15:32; He who is impatient hates correction[63]]

(En[3], 639–40)

The gloss addresses a male reader and exhorts him not to imitate the Wife (apparently a real possibility). He reminds the reader to exercise proper humility when reproved. The scribe's emphasis on masculine humility and obedience most likely addresses a monastic or clerical audience—obliged by their vows to perform precisely those virtues—rather than the lay gentry.

The last half of the commentary in Egerton 2864 makes scripture a supplement to the Wife's sermon. Although this is a misogynous supplement, once again it does not contest her exegetical practice, although it does revise her narrow focus on men's sexual woe in marriage. The final two glosses exemplify the pervasive effect of this scribal supplement. When the Wife reports ripping pages out of Jankyn's book of wicked wives, the scribe takes the opportunity to point out women's depressing domestic effect: "Cor humile et facies tristis et plaga mortis mulier nequam Ecclesiasticus" (En[3], 765; A wicked woman abates the courage, and makes a heavy countenance, and a wounded heart, Eccl. 25:31). From the scribe's perspective, woman is responsible for domestic turmoil and men's unrest. Woman is also inevitably set against her husband, or so the final gloss on the work tells us: "Mulier si primatum habeat contraria est viro suo Ecclesiasticus" (En[3], 787; A woman, if she have superiority, is contrary to her husband, Eccl. 25:3). In this marginal commentary, a woman is a terrible domestic burden and marriage a wretched state—not, as Alison would have it, because men are re-

---

[63] The gloss suggests that this last verse falls later in the same book ("et postea"), but my search of the Vulgate does not find a match: *Liber Proverbium, Patrologia Latina*, vol. 28, ed. J.-P.Migne (Paris, 1844–49).

quired to have sex with their wives, but because women are as proud, noisy, and unruly as a drunken tongue.

This is, then, a very complex representation of the Wife. More fully than any other manuscript, Egerton 2864 grants the Wife authority as a biblical exegete. Throughout the work, the scribe develops a complementary supplement to the Wife's sermon, shoring up the biblical support for her position that marriage promises men nothing but hell (or perhaps purgatory), and mirroring from the margins her address to an imagined male audience. For the first half of the work, the Latin commentary and poetic text substantially cohere. In the latter half of the work, however, the Bible becomes a source not only of admonition to men but also of sharp words about the inadequate second sex. Egerton 2864 at once enhances Alison's authority over scripture, rewrites her argument about men's woe in marriage, and frames her through misogynistic stereotypes. While Chaucer uses Alison to reaccentuate scripture, the scribe employs the margins to reaccentuate both Alison and scripture.

The latter half of this commentary registers a sudden, dramatic shift away from the historical consensus, perhaps hinting at a change in the horizon of expectations at the end of the fifteenth century, or maybe implying a greater anxiety about feminine authority in the anticipated reader. Whereas almost every earlier scribe treats the Wife as a neutral stand-in for Chaucer, glossing her scripture teachings as if they came from an *auctor,* the Egerton scribe phenomenalizes her, focusing on the fictional mask rather than the poet behind it, and evidencing an unusually imaginative and apprehensive awareness of the sexualized feminine speaker. At the same time, biblical citations are transformed from bare source notes into a vivid commentary on the work, which substantially revises the character of Chaucer's antimatrimonial arguments.

Egerton 2864 therefore signals shifts in strategies for reading both fiction and scripture. It evidences new ideas about how scriptural passages can be deployed polemically, and about how scripture can become a source of moral teaching in relation to vernacular poetry. This conclusion needs to be carefully qualified, however, for the strategy is new only in the context of Chaucer manuscripts. The method of using biblical citations as a gloss (often on the Bible) was invented in the universities and was commonly used by preachers from the thirteenth century forward. Likewise, the strategic deployment of biblical references in academic disputations during the same period suggests a university context for this manuscript's glossing program.[64] In other words, these glosses testify to the specific textual expectations of university-trained readers, accustomed to seeing the Bible used as a gloss, often polemical, on other texts. These expectations are obviously not shared by the other scribes studied here, nor, so far as I can discern, in any other manuscript group. The Egerton scribe's marginal revision of Alison's antimatrimonial arguments further testifies to a university context, for the margins of this work develop precisely the arguments traditionally addressed to university students.[65]

Significantly, the Egerton scribe's treatment of scripture depends on the letter of the text, in much the way that the poem itself does. The scribe does not turn the Bible into moral allegories; he implies moral teachings through the literal meaning of the verses. Like the other fifteenth-century scribes, this one typically privileges the plain text of scripture in marginal source notes. For the first half of the notes (the marriage sermon), the scribe simply affirms the Wife of Bath's literal translations and hermeneutic method. This consistent emphasis on the letter of the text argues for a diffuse Lollard influence over all of the glossing programs. Late medieval academic culture both elevates and derides the literal sense of scripture, but Lollards appropriate it as a crucial foundation for lay religion. As Rita Copeland demonstrates: "Lollardy redefines the fundamental conditions of scriptural knowledge by asserting that what non-clerical adult audiences can know [the literal meaning of scripture] is the very horizon of an adequate and politically enabling hermeneutics. It refuses pastoral formulas that equate laity with puerility; and it does so by rejecting the historical baggage of pastoral condescension, the association of pedagogical literalism with presumptions of childish limitation."[66] Since Alison's exegesis is regularly annotated by scribes sympathetic to this aspect of Lollardy, if to no other, manuscripts of the *Wife of Bath's Prologue* show the far reach and appeal of this redefinition. In each of the manuscripts studied here, literal exegesis appears the accepted standard for adult lay religion and a fully adequate basis for scriptural knowledge. Although Egerton 2864

---

[64] For the development of these academic models, see Gillian Rosemary Evans, "Gloss or Analysis? A Crisis of Exegetical Method in the Thirteenth Century," in *La Bibbia del XIII Secolo: Storia del Testo, Storia dell'Esegesi,* ed. Giuseppe Cremascoli and Francesco Santi (Florence: Sismel edizioni del Galluzzo, 2004), 93–111.

[65] See Pratt, "Jankyn's 'Book of Wikked Wyves,'" 5–27.

[66] Copeland, *Pedagogy, Intellectuals, and Dissent,* 140.

adds another, specifically university standard for biblical discourse, it does not at any point challenge the sufficiency of the letter.

Marginal Authority

All the manuscripts studied here reveal a close relationship between glossing programs and anticipated readers. New College and the group of twelve manuscripts address readers, most likely among the gentry, who are expected to be deferential toward Alison's (Chaucer's) learning, and to take it at face value. Egerton 2864 speaks to readers with less deference toward the scholarship and with a more complex aesthetic response to the literary persona. The latter half of the Egerton glosses conform to particular standards for how scripture may and should be used in polemical debates among the *literati*, inviting a kind of textual pleasure that is hard to replicate at our own cultural distance from the work. The twin of Egerton 2864—Additional 5140—has been connected with Henry Dene, Archbishop of Canterbury (1501–3).[67] That connection merits further study, for it could significantly advance our understanding of the fit between the unusual gloss apparatus and anticipated clerical readers.

Egerton 2864 and its twin signal a shift in the horizon of expectations, perhaps marking the point at which Chaucer's work enters serious consideration in a new market, or perhaps evidencing the eccentric interests of a few readers. The two manuscripts certainly signal changes in reception. The Egerton style of glossing does not, however, replace that of New College, any more than university-trained readers suddenly replace Lollard-sympathizing gentry. Both glossing strategies coexist in the late fifteenth century, and they testify to the range of contemporary readers' interests and horizons of expectations. In the late fifteenth century, moreover, both strategies are actually on the wane; the manuscripts studied here bear witness to the end of a cultural era. Caxton dismisses glosses from the roughly contemporary first print editions of *The Canterbury Tales* (1476–77, 1483), anticipating readers remote from the controversies that Chaucer engaged so provocatively in the late fourteenth century, and addressing readers wholly uninterested in university polemics. Subsequent editors follow Caxton's lead. We should note the historical irony: sixteenth-century Protestants, eager for vernacular

---

[67] See the description of Ad¹ in Robinson, ed., *The Wife of Bath's Prologue on CD-Rom*.

scripture, did not have ready access to the biblical text available to gentry of an earlier age. From Caxton onward, readers are scripted as humanists whose literary tastes cannot bear the imposition of scholastic glosses—an editorial agenda that obviously depends on serious misunderstandings about medieval glossing programs.

So far as I can discern, none of the manuscripts challenges Alison's specific readings of biblical texts, supplements her hermeneutic with traditional allegoresis, or imports moralizing comments from scholastic glosses. This does not mean that medieval readers never supplemented her literal interpretations with spiritual, typological, anagogical, or tropological analyses; but no manuscript evidence of such a practice survives. Instead, manuscripts that include biblical glosses typically do nothing more than identify selected sources, often focusing on those passages that instruct men about the "woes" of marriage: the obligation to procreate, pay the marriage debt, and be submissive to a wife's sexual desires. On these points, the Wife appears an entirely capable exegete—even as she drolly redefines the "woe" and "tribulation" of marriage as sexual intercourse. Chaucer's tongue-in-cheek antimatrimonial argument depends on his persona's persuasive treatment of scripture, and scribes' glosses wholly support the improbable authority he fashions for her.

For that matter, the marginal notes lend credibility to the work's playful engagement with scriptural teachings about marriage. Chaucer gives us an ambivalent, comic portrait of a matrimonial specialist, and the New College and other scribes often echo him from the margins, selecting biblical sources so as to emphasize the Wife's risible exegetical competence. At other times, scribes seriously gloss her biblical sources, proverbs, and astrological or mythological references, in effect reinventing her as a more or less straightforward authority figure. Manuscripts can thus heighten or mute the notorious Chaucerian irony (and sometimes do both in the same work). For all the variety of these glosses, however, none of them supports the often-repeated modern idea that Alison is an inadequate or heterodox exegete.

The Wife of Bath's Prologue nonetheless does dramatize the potential threat of a laywoman exegete, and Chaucer uses the *Prologue* to explore contemporary ecclesiastical apprehensions that laywomen, if given access to scripture, would become irreverent and unruly. Alison affirms these fears, proving concerned officials right. At the same time, Chaucer defuses the danger, for he makes this laywoman entirely orthodox in her exegesis. She agrees, for instance, with Jerome's main argument in *Against Jovinian:* virginity is better than marriage.[68] She avoids a (Lollard) condemnation of clerical celibacy or rejection of virginity.[69] Her exegesis is not eccentric (by the standards of the time), nor do her human foibles jeopardize the received truths of religion. She resists masculine authority but not direct scriptural teachings (with one notable exception[70]). To the extent that she represents feminine exegetical authority, she makes that prospect unfrightening, if not entertaining. Chaucer turns the threat of feminine exegesis into broad comedy, and many of his scribes seem to appreciate his humor and lend their quills to the cause. Ultimately, however, the *Prologue* confirms the strength of orthodoxy, and expresses the conviction that if women took over exegesis, nothing much would change. Chaucer crafts a remarkably double-edged representation of a feminine exegete: at once authoritative and marginal, credible and risible. That representation is further complicated by each scribe who comments on it from the margins.

Scribal glosses sometimes point out Alison's rebellion or highlight her fulfillment of misogynous proverbs. For the most part, though, scribes grant her an authoritative grounding in canonical scripture and call attention to her lessons on marital sexuality. Scribes translate Chaucer's persona into various representations of "auctoritee," creating new implications for the work through their choice of glosses. Although each material work is unique, some general patterns clearly emerge from most of the glossed manuscripts: the Wife of Bath appears bold in her translation of extensive scriptural passages, reliable in her biblical references, sure-footed in her understanding of fine distinctions (as between counsel and commandment), and persuasive in her account of men's marital obligations. Scribal biblical glosses give us access to the Wife of Bath's marginal and marginalized potential for meaning. In the material works, Alison represents not just a supposedly feminine "experience" but also the masculine authority of Chaucer and his scribes. She embodies both the threat and the pleasures of a gendered (s)exegesis.

---

[68] Warren S. Smith makes this case, "The Wife of Bath Debates Jerome," *ChauR* 32 (1997): 129–45.

[69] See Blamires, "The Wife of Bath and Lollardy," 233–34.

[70] See my "Contested Authority."

Where Chaucer Got His Pulpit:

Audience and Intervisuality in the *Troilus and Criseyde* Frontispiece

Joyce Coleman
University of Oklahoma

Among the many puzzles that scholars have debated in the famous *Troilus and Criseyde* frontispiece (Cambridge, Corpus Christi College 61, fol. 1v; Fig. 1), the most puzzling may be the placement of Geoffrey Chaucer in a draped pulpit, from which he is apparently reciting his text to a courtly audience.[1] Similar pulpits could be (and have been) found in many other illuminations, but one significant difference stands out. All those other pulpits hold religious men—bishops, priests, friars. This one holds a layman. The other pulpits appear in manuscripts containing Christian scripture, theology, sermons, devotional texts; this one adorns a story of love, sex, and betrayal set in pagan Troy. The purpose of this essay is to suggest a previously unexplored iconographic source for the pulpit imagery of the *Troilus* frontispiece. This new explanation "saves the appearances," I think, more successfully than any yet offered. It also suggests further connections that lead to some new ideas about the role of both author and audience in the frontispiece, and perhaps in *Troilus* itself.

I will begin with a quick overview of current critical thought on the

[1] Research for and writing of this article was supported by a Fletcher Jones Foundation Fellowship at the Huntington Library, San Marino, California. I am very grateful to the Library, as well as to Michelle Brown, Nancy Regalado, and Jocelyn Wogan-Browne for their recommendations. The work has been enriched by interdisciplinary conversations with Alan Fletcher, John Fyler, Anne D. Hedeman, Sylvia Huot, Meradith McMunn, Elizabeth Morrison, Stephen Partridge, Dan Ransom, Nancy Regalado, Mary Robertson, and Kathryn Smith. I would also like to thank the anonymous reviewers of this article for their helpful comments. I learned much from these wise and generous colleagues, but made all and any errors on my own.

Fig. 1. Geoffrey Chaucer, *Troilus and Criseyde*. Cambridge, Corpus Christi College 61, fol. 1v, early 15th century. By permission of the Master and Fellows of Corpus Christi College, Cambridge.

frontispiece.[2] The creator of the miniature—dubbed by Kathleen Scott the "Corpus Master"[3]—is generally supposed to have been either a foreign artist working in England or an English artist who had been exposed to much continental work.[4] The frontispiece and manuscript are universally dated, on both artistic and paleographic grounds, to the first quarter of the fifteenth century.[5] The manuscript is obviously a luxury item, employing fine parchment, wide margins, and an unusually elaborate script,[6] and introduced by an outstanding frontispiece. While space was left for some ninety illuminations in the body of the text, however, none was produced.[7] The general assumption is that the manuscript was

[2] A complete digitization of the manuscripts owned by Corpus Christi College, including Corpus 61, is available at "Parker Library on the Web," a joint project of Corpus Christi's Parker Library and Stanford University Libraries. The URL is parkerweb.stanford.edu/parker (access to high-resolution images requires a subscription). The ability to view the Corpus 61 frontispiece at a very high level of magnification has been of great help to me in researching and writing this essay.

[3] Kathleen L. Scott, *Later Gothic Manuscripts, 1390–1490*, 2 vols. (London: Harvey Miller Publishers, 1996), 2:182.

[4] Elizabeth Salter, "The '*Troilus* Frontispiece,'" in M. B. Parkes and Elizabeth Salter, intro., "*Troilus and Criseyde": A Facsimile of Corpus Christi College Cambridge MS 61* (Cambridge: Brewer, 1978), 15–23 (17–21); Elizabeth Salter and Derek Pearsall, "Pictorial Illustration of Late Medieval Poetic Texts: The Role of the Frontispiece or Prefatory Picture," in *Medieval Iconography and Narrative: A Symposium*, ed. Flemming G. Andersen et al. (Odense: Odense University Press, 1980), 100–123 (120); K. Scott, *Later Gothic Manuscripts*, 2:182; Kathleen L. Scott, "Limner Power: A Book Artist in England, c. 1420," in *Prestige, Authority, and Power in Late Medieval Manuscripts and Texts*, ed. Felicity Riddy (York: York Medieval Press, 2000), 55–75 (55). Gerhard Schmidt has recently argued that an Italian artist created the Corpus frontispiece, citing some Italian precedents for the image. Schmidt's analogues, however, are not as convincing as the French and Flemish ones offered in Salter's 1978 article, which Schmidt does not cite ("Chaucer in Italy: Some Remarks on the 'Chaucer Frontispiece' in Ms. 61, Corpus Christi College, Cambridge," trans. Holger Klein, in *New Offerings, Ancient Treasures: Studies in Medieval Art for George Henderson*, ed. Paul Binski and William Noel [Stroud: Sutton, 2001], 478–91).

[5] Montague Rhodes James, *A Descriptive Catalogue of the Manuscripts in the Library of Corpus Christi College, Cambridge*, 2 vols. (Cambridge: Cambridge University Press, 1909–11), 1:126; Robert Kilburn Root, "Introduction," in *The Book of Troilus and Criseyde by Geoffrey Chaucer*, ed. Root (Princeton: Princeton University Press, 1926), xi–lxxxix (liii); M. B. Parkes, "Palaeographical Description and Commentary," in Parkes and Salter, intro., "*Troilus and Criseyde": A Facsimile*, 1–13 (2); Salter, "The '*Troilus* Frontispiece,'" 15 n. 2; K. Scott, *Later Gothic Manuscripts*, 2:182; K. Scott, "Limner Power," 56.

[6] Malcolm Parkes identifies the script as *littera quadrata*, which he describes as "primarily a 'display' script reserved for liturgical books, de-luxe manuscripts, and for 'display' purposes" (Parkes, "Palaeographical Description," 5).

[7] John H. Fisher and Philippa Hardman have tried, with differing results, to identify the possible subjects of these missing pictures. Fisher, "The Intended Illustrations in MS Corpus Christi 61 of Chaucer's *Troilus and Criseyde*," in *Medieval Studies in Honor of Lillian Herlands Hornstein*, ed. J. B. Bessinger Jr. and R. R. Raymo (New York: New

initiated on orders from a commissioner and suspended when that person's misfortune or death cut off funds to complete the project. Who that patron was is unknown; no coats of arms or other recognizable features have been identified. Kathleen Scott has proposed that Corpus 61's patron and thus also the gold-clad figure standing before Chaucer in the frontispiece (on the viewer's left) was Charles d'Orléans. Subsequently, Kate Harris suggested Henry, third Baron Scrope, as manuscript patron and chief frontispiece audience-member.[8] Most recently, Anita Helmbold has placed the patronage issue in a neohistoricist context, arguing that Henry V commissioned Corpus 61 and its introductory image "as a tool in the Lancastrian propaganda campaign for the promotion of English as the national language of England."[9]

For the purposes of my essay, the identity of the patron of Corpus 61 is not important, other than to acknowledge that he or she was probably someone of considerable wealth and standing, associated with or at least cognizant of the interests of the Lancastrian court.[10] What does require notice here, however, is the late datings for the manuscript implied by these proposed patrons; production on Corpus 61 was halted, it is suggested, by Scrope's execution in 1415, by Henry V's death in 1422, or by Charles d'Orléans's financial problems in the early 1420s.[11] Yet as English tomb effigies and pictorial evidence reveal, the high collars and small female headdresses in the Corpus frontispiece clearly date to c. 1400–1415; after c. 1415, women's hairstyles, particularly, become very different. The fashion historian Margaret Scott dates the *Troilus* frontispiece itself to c. 1400.[12]

The image of Geoffrey Chaucer, nearly dead center in the picture, is

---

York University Press, 1976), 111–21; Hardman, "Interpreting the Incomplete Scheme of Illustration in Cambridge, Corpus Christi College MS 61," *EMS* 6 (1997): 52–69.

[8] K. Scott, *Later Gothic Manuscripts*, 2:183; K. Scott, "Limner Power," 56, 73–75; Kate Harris, "The Patronage and Dating of Longleat House MS 24, a Prestige Copy of the *Pupilla Oculi* Illuminated by the Master of the *Troilus* Frontispiece," in Riddy, ed., *Prestige, Authority, and Power*, 35–54 (42).

[9] Anita Helmbold, "Chaucer Appropriated: The *Troilus* Frontispiece as Lancastrian Propaganda," *SAC* 30 (2008): 205–34 (208).

[10] I plan to discuss patronage, dating, and related issues further in an article in process.

[11] The Orléans dating is from K. Scott, "Limner Power," 74.

[12] See Margaret Scott, *A Visual History of Costume: The Fourteenth and Fifteenth Centuries* (London: Batsford, 1986), 53 (plate 44), 56–57 (plates 49–51), 63–66 (plates 58–62); her comments on the *Troilus and Criseyde* frontispiece are in the unpaginated color plate 45.

recognizable as a younger version of his two other famous portraits (astride a horse as a Canterbury pilgrim in the Ellesmere Chaucer, and pointing to the text in the margin of his disciple Thomas Hoccleve's *Regement of Princes*).[13] The man in cloth of gold before Chaucer's pulpit is usually thought to represent Richard II; certainly any fifteenth-century viewer would have made that assumption.[14] If there was an attempt at a likeness, we cannot tell, since some long-ago viewer smudged the face. Most of the women in the picture wear tight little hairdos topped by gold *bourrelets* (padded rolls).[15] Two ladies near Richard add diadems to their headdresses, suggesting they represent the king's mother, Joan of Kent, and his queen, Anne of Bohemia. Early, overreaching attempts to assign a historical identity to every person in the frontispiece have left scholars cautious about trying to name other audience members.[16].

What the lower register of the frontispiece seems to provide, overall, is a vision of mutually reinforcing literary and social value, an evocation of Chaucer in his prime set within a *locus amoenus* and invoking, even literally in the king's costume, a sort of golden age. A similar feeling of richness and order attends on the upper scene, though its cast has been harder to pinpoint. The prevailing idea is that it represents an episode from the poem itself: Troilus escorting Criseyde from Troy and Diomede kneeling to greet her.[17] While that explanation has flaws, it is beyond the scope of this essay to explore the issue further. The question of whether Chaucer ever did actually recite or read to courtly audiences and the issue of Corpus 61's possible role in Lancastrian politics are similarly outside my present remit. The focus here will be on the artistic and literary affiliations of the lower register's iconography, starting with the puzzle of the poet's pulpit and continuing on to relate the proposed solution of that puzzle to the broader meanings of the scene.

[13] Ellesmere Chaucer: San Marino, Calif., Huntington Library, EL 26 C 9, fol. 167v; Hoccleve, *Regement*: London, British Library, Harley 4866, fol. 88.

[14] Donald C. Baker notes that "however unspecific the royal and noble personages depicted [in the Corpus frontispiece] might be, one cannot imagine a fifteenth-century reader interpreting them other than as members of a royal outing, and of the court with which Chaucer was known to have been associated" (Donald C. Baker, review of Parkes and Salter, intro., *"Troilus and Criseyde": A Facsimile, SAC* 1 [1979]: 187–93 [191]).

[15] M. Scott, *Visual History*, 141.

[16] Margaret Galway, "The *Troilus* Frontispiece," *MLR* 44 (1949): 161–77; George Williams, "The *Troilus and Criseyde* Frontispiece Again," *MLR* 57 (1962): 173–78.

[17] E.g., Salter, "The '*Troilus* Frontispiece,'" 22; Salter and Pearsall, "Pictorial Illustration," 123; K. Scott, *Later Gothic Manuscripts*, 2:183–84.

The Poet in the Pulpit

Current understanding of the pulpit imagery in the lower register of Corpus 61's frontispiece trace back to a series of influential works written in the late 1970s and early 1980s by Alfred David, Derek Pearsall, and Elizabeth Salter. Pearsall explored the parallels from the iconography of religious authorship, citing particularly a manuscript of Petrus de Aureolis's *Compendium super Bibliam* (London, British Library, Royal 8 G.iii; c. 1421). Not only is this Anglo-Latin text prefaced with a picture of its author in a pulpit (fol. 2; see Fig. 2), but the scene above Petrus parallels what Pearsall considered the plot-visualization of the frontispiece's upper register by illustrating the theme of the work itself (in Petrus's case, men seeking to ascend the mountain of God).[18]

Of course, Petrus de Aureolis was a bishop and his text is a commentary on the Bible. David and Salter moved closer to the Corpus frontispiece with Guillaume de Deguileville's *Pèlerinage de la vie humaine*.[19] The first recension of this text, composed in 1330, begins with a summons to "rich, poor, wise, or foolish / Be you kings or be you queens."[20] The incipit illuminations in a number of Deguileville manuscripts accordingly visualize Guillaume in a pulpit addressing the mixed audience just summoned (Fig. 3). Reinforcing the likelihood that the Deguileville iconography influenced that of the Corpus frontispiece, for both David and Salter, was the presence in the background of images such as Figure 3's of what David called "a château" and Salter described as "intricate castle architecture."[21] Like the upper register of the frontispiece, therefore, the Deguileville images backed the pastoral scene of the performance itself with a structure suggestive of courtly elegance—and power.

Although the Deguileville miniatures do move the pulpit into a context of narrative, as opposed to exegesis or homily, the parallel falters somewhat when one considers that Deguileville was a monk and his

---

[18] Derek Pearsall, "The *Troilus* Frontispiece and Chaucer's Audience," *YES* 7 (1977): 68–74 (72); K. Scott, *Later Gothic Manuscripts*, 2:185–86. Scott attributes the border of Royal 8, fol. 2, to the same artist who did the outer border of the Corpus frontispiece, whom she considers to be the Corpus Master himself (2:184).

[19] Alfred David, *The Strumpet Muse: Art and Morals in Chaucer's Poetry* (Bloomington: Indiana University Press, 1976), 10; Salter, "The '*Troilus* Frontispiece,'" 17, 19.

[20] "Riches poures sages ou fol / Soient roys ou soient roynes" (lines 4–5; BnF fr. 823, fol. 1). (All Deguileville translations are mine.)

[21] David, *Strumpet Muse*, 10; Salter, "The '*Troilus* Frontispiece,'" 19.

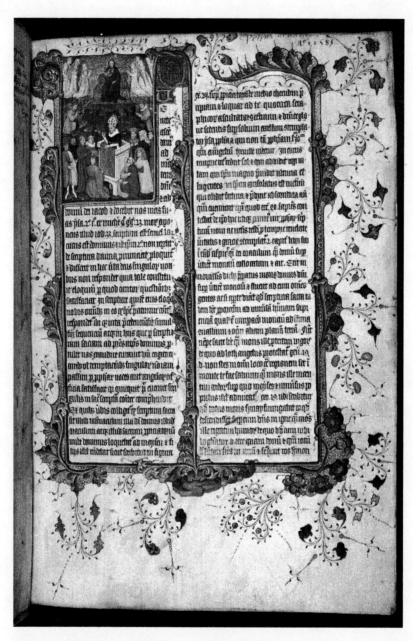

Fig. 2. Petrus de Aureolis, *Compendium super Bibliam*. London, British Library, Royal 8 G.iii, fol. 2, c. 1421. © The British Library Board.

Fig. 3. Guillaume de Deguileville, *Pèlerinage de la vie humaine*. London, British Library, Add. 38120, fol. 1, c. 1400. © The British Library Board.

narrative a minimally fictionalized religious allegory. Moreover, a closer look at the structure in Figure 3 casts doubt on the supposedly courtly context created by the "castle." A gateless wall surrounds a building with a transept jutting out midway, flying buttresses, round clerestory windows, and a large cross at the far end. These details strongly suggest that the walled structure is not a castle but a cathedral, and not just any cathedral but one to which (as the lack of gate suggests) access is far from easy. This imagery finds its explanation in Deguileville's text, where the author relates how in his dream vision he saw reflected in a mirror the ultimate goal of the pilgrimage of human life: the Celestial Jerusalem.[22] Later in the dream, Grace presents the Pilgrim with the staff of Hope, on which is set a mirror that perpetually reflects the city of Jerusalem. The unblemished mirror, a figure of Jesus, is a guide to salvation for the Pilgrim, while the Pilgrim's quest, in turn, is meant to serve as a mirror for his audience.[23] Some Deguileville incipit illustrations set up a mirroring of these mirror images, by placing a scene of the author asleep dreaming of Jerusalem before the scene of author and audience with a structure representing Jerusalem in the distance (Fig. 4). The artist of Figure 4 emphasizes the continuity of the two Jerusalems by placing them at the same height in the picture and using the same rose-pink for the walls. The *Pèlerinage* and the *Troilus* scenes are thus broadly parallel but have a fundamentally different orientation: the landscape of the Deguileville pictures is configured not as courtly pleasance but as *via peregrinorum*.

A few other explanations have been offered for the puzzle. James McGregor argued that the pulpit contributed to a portrayal of Chaucer as counselor to the king and court. *Troilus and Criseyde* is thus interpreted as a *de casibus* plot, charting the misguided behavior and consequent fall of a prince.[24] Laura Kendrick, citing a common medieval assumption about the performance of classical plays, proposed that the frontispiece's lower register depicted a dramatic performance. Chaucer is supposedly acting as *lector* while the two figures standing before his pulpit silently

---

[22] "En vn myrour ce me sembloit / Qui sans mesure grant estoit / Celle cite apperceue" (lines 39–41; BnF fr. 823, fol. 1v; "It seemed to me I saw this city [Jerusalem] in a mirror that was immeasurably large").

[23] Eugene Clasby, "Introduction," in Guillaume de Deguileville, *The Pilgrimage of Human Life (Le Pèlerinage de la vie humaine)*, trans. Clasby (New York: Garland, 1992), xiii–xxxiii (xx).

[24] James H. McGregor, "The Iconography of Chaucer in Hoccleve's *De Regimine Principum* and in the *Troilus* Frontispiece," *ChauR* 11 (1977): 338–50.

Fig. 4. Guillaume de Deguileville, *Pelèrinage de la vie humaine*. Paris, Bibliothèque Ste-Geneviève 1130, fol. 2, last third of 14th century. © Bibliothèque Ste-Geneviève, Paris.

enact the characters of Troilus and Criseyde.[25] Seth Lerer saw the upper register as a royal entry (perhaps specifically reminiscent of Richard II's entry to London in 1392) progressing down to the lower register, where Chaucer presides, Lydgate-like, as laureate and pageant master.[26] None of these experimental readings has dislodged the interpretation developed by Pearsall and Salter, in their intersecting articles of 1977–80, from its dominance in modern scholarly understanding of the Corpus frontispiece.

Corpus and the *Rose*

Yet it remains difficult to see the pulpit as the proper environment for a lay author and for a text whose content hardly meets the standards of Christian morality. A story set in pagan times and focused on illicit

[25] Laura Kendrick, "The *Troilus* Frontispiece and the Dramatization of Chaucer's *Troilus*," *ChauR* 22 (1987): 81–93.

[26] Seth Lerer, *Chaucer and His Readers: Imagining the Author in Late Medieval England* (Princeton: Princeton University Press, 1993), 53–56.

love is an unlikely vehicle for spiritual uplift.[27] No intertextuality or intervisuality links the Aureolis or Deguileville and Chaucer images beyond, perhaps, practical suggestions about how to arrange an author and an audience in a space. Yet there is another, iconic text whose imagery and content not only align much more satisfactorily with *Troilus and Criseyde* but in fact underlie much of Chaucer's (and Deguileville's) creative enterprise: the *Roman de la Rose* of Guillaume de Lorris and Jean de Meun.[28] The *Rose* had established the game or religion of love as a deeply rooted metaphor and major pastime in late medieval culture. It inaugurated or influenced many expressive genres, from a wide variety of literary forms and competitions through actual or pretended courts of love, tournaments, music, dances, and minor games of every sort.[29] The fact that, as some scholars point out,[30] the game of love may have been as much a vehicle for inter-male competition as for heterosexual flirtation adds to rather than depletes the complexity of the game. It could serve its practitioners in many ways, from simple entertainment to actual attempts at seduction or marriage through self-aggrandizing display or competition through various forms of social critique. The love culture may not have been "real" in any hard sense—as a principle affecting political or economic action. But it was a literary, cultural, and social reality. It channeled perception, influenced behavior, and took up real time in people's lives. In fact, one could interpret *Troilus and Criseyde* as, precisely, Chaucer's attempt to set the two realities at odds. Laura L. Howes argues that in that work, "Chaucer juxtaposes the highly devel-

[27] Alan J. Fletcher observes that in reading sermon texts from this period, he has not personally encountered the *Troilus* material used for preaching purposes, though he also notes that some preachers drew on the resources of this sort of pagan culture and that their efforts in this regard were not universally approved of. One Wycliffite critic, for example, chided those who in their preaching spoke about the "batel of Troye" (personal communication, February 21, 2009). I am very grateful to Professor Fletcher for his generous response to my emailed inquiry.

[28] For the *Roman de la Rose*'s influence on Deguileville, see, e.g., Sylvia Huot, *The "Romance of the Rose" and Its Medieval Readers: Interpretation, Reception, Manuscript Transmission* (Cambridge: Cambridge University Press, 1993), 207–30; on Chaucer and the *Rose*, see, e.g., Dean Spruill Fansler, *Chaucer and the "Roman de la Rose"* (New York: Columbia University Press, 1914); Winthrop Wetherbee, *Chaucer and the Poets: An Essay on "Troilus and Criseyde"* (Ithaca: Cornell University Press, 1984), 53–86.

[29] John Stevens, *Music and Poetry in the Early Tudor Court* (Lincoln: University of Nebraska Press, 1961), 154–202; Richard Firth Green, *Poets and Princepleasers: Literature and the English Court in the Late Middle Ages* (Toronto: University of Toronto Press, 1980), 101–34.

[30] E.g., Richard Firth Green, "Women in Chaucer's Audience," *ChauR* 18 (1983): 146–54 (150).

oped conventions of courtly love with a world of social and political circumstances that exist separately from this system. . . . Chaucer portrays both a well-defined system and a world that does not mesh with that system."[31]

Of the 326 surviving manuscripts or fragments of the *Roman de la Rose*, and the 248 that have or were intended to have illuminations, some 68 include one particular scene that, I suggest, is the source of Chaucer's pulpit:[32] Genius's sermon. The failure of l'Amant and the barons of Love to storm the Rose's castle has alarmed Nature, who summons her priest, Genius. After confessing to him, she dictates a sermon and a pardon that she orders him to deliver to the god of Love and his army. Love welcomes Genius, providing him with chasuble, ring, crosier, and miter. Venus places a burning torch in his hand: "Without taking any more time, Genius then mounted a large platform, the better to read the text. . . . The barons sat on the ground and didn't want to seek any other seats. Genius unfolded the charter, made a sign with his hand all around him, and called for silence. Those whom his words pleased looked at and nudged one another. Then they quieted down immediately and listened."[33]

Genius's sermon runs over a thousand lines, but its essence is this: Nature, God's vicar on earth, seeks to ensure the renewal of the world by encouraging reproduction. Anyone whose practices do not promote reproduction shall be excommunicated, while anyone who serves Nature will be pardoned and "go off to paradise decked with flowers."[34] Genius describes this paradise later as "the park of the lovely field where the son of the virgin ewe in all his white fleece leads his flock with him,

---

[31] Laura L. Howes, *Chaucer's Gardens and the Language of Convention* (Gainesville: University Press of Florida, 1997), 81.

[32] Meradith McMunn, personal communication, September 8 and 16, 2009. I am very grateful to Professor McMunn for generously sharing images of Genius's sermon and information about them. The following observations are based on thirty-two versions of Genius's sermon (from twenty-seven manuscripts) that I have seen to date.

[33] The translation is from Guillaume de Lorris and Jean de Meun, *The Romance of the Rose*, trans. Charles Dahlberg (Princeton: Princeton University Press, 1971), 321–22. The original text reads: "Genyus, san plus terme metre, / s'est lors por lire mieuz la letre . . . / seur un grant eschaufaut montez, / et li baron sidrent par terre, / n'i vostrent autres sieges querre. / Et cil sa chartre leur desploie / et sa main antour soi tournoie / et fet signe et dit qu'il se tesent; / et cil, qui ses paroles plesent, / s'antreguignent et s'antreboutent. / Atant s'apesent, si escoutent" (Guillaume de Lorris and Jean de Meun, *Le roman de la Rose*, ed. Félix Lecoy, 3 vols. [Paris: Champion, 1968], lines 19461–62, 19464–72).

[34] Trans. Dahlberg, 322; "floriz en paradis s'en aille" (ed. Lecoy, line 19508).

leaping over the grass,"[35] and more Christianized imagery follows. "In many ways," notes Sylvia Huot, "Genius does seem to offer Love's followers a more noble goal, a higher quest. The problem, of course, is Genius' insistence on heterosexual coupling as the means of reaching this goal."[36] His sermon concluded, Genius vanishes. Venus shoots her burning arrow into the Rose castle, which takes fire; its defenders run away, and l'Amant takes possession of his rose.

At first glance some of the depictions of Genius's sermon could pass for ordinary preaching scenes. But of course, Genius's sermon is not an ordinary, or indeed a real, sermon—any more than Chaucer's is. Where the distinction becomes visible is in the audience, in which many Genius-sermon miniatures, such as that in New York, Pierpont Morgan Library M.324 (fol. 129; c. 1350; Fig. 5), place a winged and crowned male figure, often seconded by a woman who may herself wear a crown. The fact that the foremost members of such congregations are the god of Love and Venus alerts viewers that this particular sermon is urging its auditors not to spiritual repentance but to physical copulation.

Some illustrations of Genius's sermon, like M.324, show a plainly (though clerically) dressed preacher standing in a draped pulpit with no book or script—the visual configuration most clearly reminiscent of Chaucer and his pulpit. More often, illustrators follow the text by depicting Genius as a mitered bishop holding an open or closed scroll (Nature's dictated sermon) or a charter with a seal (her pardon). Genius may or may not also have a crozier and/or Venus's torch. He stands variously in or on a ground-level pulpit, a raised pulpit, or an open platform.[37] (In BL Harley 4425, a late manuscript, he sits on a platform supported by four wine barrels [fol. 167v].) After the turn of the fifteenth century, the audience becomes more courtly. The god of Love is almost always present, frequently accompanied by Venus and sometimes

---

[35] Ibid., 328; "[le] parc du champ joli / ou les berbiz conduit o li, / saillant devant par les herbiz, / li filz de la Vierge, berbiz / o toute sa blanche toison" (ed. Lecoy, lines 19905–9).

[36] Huot, The "Romance of the Rose," 225. The alignment of Chaucer with Genius sets up potential resonances that may or may not have been part of the Corpus designers' intent. For Genius as a type of the poet, see ibid., 267–72; for discomfort with Genius's advocacy of fornication, which fed into the early fifteenth-century querelle de la Rose, see Sylvia Huot, "Bodily Peril: Sexuality and the Subversion of Order in Jean de Meun's Roman de la Rose," MLR 95 (2000): 41–61 (and further references in 41 n. 1).

[37] Jean de Meun calls the structure on/in which Genius stands an eschaufaut (Roman de la Rose, ed. Lecoy, line 19464). Lecoy glosses the word as estrade, which can mean "platform," "rostrum," or "pulpit."

Fig. 5. Genius's sermon; Guillaume de Lorris and Jean de Meun, *Roman de la Rose*. New York, Pierpont Morgan Library, M.324, fol. 129, c. 1350. The Pierpont Morgan Library, New York.

by other women as well (appropriately, since Love's barons, being personifications such as Franchise and Bien Celer, are of mixed sex). Also around 1400, the abstract background (as in Fig. 5) gives way to landscape, if usually a rather simple one. As samples of the range of iconography, and of that iconography's congruence with the Corpus frontispiece, I reproduce three further Genius-sermon pictures that are more or less contemporary with Corpus 61. Oxford, Bodleian Library, Douce 371, fol. 127v (c. 1400; Fig. 6), presents a fashionable audience whose courtly attire is not dissimilar to that in the Corpus frontispiece. BnF fr. 12595, fol. 140 (1400–1416; Fig. 7), places Love and Venus prominently in the back of the auditory in a "couple" pose; note that someone has partly rubbed out Love's face. Finally, Philadelphia Museum of Art, Collins 1945–65–3, fol. 135 (early fifteenth century; Fig. 8), illustrates the development of landscape as a major feature of the image.

Obviously, none of these miniatures approaches the scale or the sophistication of the Corpus frontispiece's lower register. But the basic action is strikingly similar: a priest-who's-not, in a pulpit, in a pleasant outdoor setting, delivering a faux-sermon on a decidedly noncanonical subject to the acolytes of Love, led by their king and his consort. It is

Fig. 6. Genius's sermon; Guillaume de Lorris and Jean de Meun, *Roman de la Rose*. Oxford, Bodleian Library, University of Oxford, Douce 371, fol. 127v, c. 1400.

also true that the intent of Genius's sermon does not completely match the announced intent of Chaucer's *Troilus*. Genius is summoning the army of Love to help storm the Rose's castle in order to promote the reproduction crucial to Nature. Chaucer states in his prologue that his goal is to edify the servants of Love with an exemplary tale of Love's sorrows. But it is enough to validate the parallel, I think, that both messages are embedded in the culture of love: they are issued in service of Love, are addressed to Love's servants, and concern Love.

The hypothesis that the iconography of Genius's sermon lies behind the placement of Chaucer in Corpus 61 resolves the "poet in the pulpit" dilemma. The pulpit is not simply a convenient place to put a speaker but a deliberate intervisual reference that powerfully connects the text and its frontispiece to the foundational text of medieval love culture, the *Roman de la Rose*. The crossover seems to reflect recognition of Chaucer's profound debt to and ongoing relationship with the *Rose*.[38] As Larry D. Benson notes, "Geoffrey Chaucer was more deeply influenced by the

[38] See Fansler, *Chaucer and the "Roman de la Rose"* (conclusions summarized on 229–34).

Fig. 7. Genius's sermon; Guillaume de Lorris and Jean de Meun, *Roman de la Rose*. Bibliothèque nationale de France, fr. 12595, fol. 140, 1400–1416.

Roman de la rose than by any other French or English work."[39] Chaucer's literary career seems to have begun with at least a partial translation of the text, *The Romaunt of the Rose*.[40] In Chaucer's earliest known composition, *The Book of the Duchess*, the poet's dream vision begins with him waking in a chamber whose windows are glazed with "al the story of

[39] Larry D. Benson, Introduction to *The Romaunt of the Rose*, in Benson, gen. ed., *The Riverside Chaucer* (Oxford: Oxford University Press, 1987), 685–86 (686).

[40] Chaucer acknowledges this translation in the prologue to *The Legend of Good Women* (*LGW*, F: 328–31, 441, 470; LGW, G: 254–57, 431, 460; all references to and quotations from Chaucer's texts are from Benson, gen. ed., *Riverside Chaucer*). The only surviving manuscript, Glasgow, Hunter 409 (olim V.3.7; dated first quarter of the fifteenth century), contains three fragments, some or none of which may be Chaucer's (see Derek Pearsall, *The Life of Geoffrey Chaucer: A Critical Biography* [Oxford: Blackwell, 1992], 82; Charles Dahlberg, "Introduction," in *The Romaunt of the Rose*, ed. Dahlberg, Variorum Chaucer Series 7 [Norman: University of Oklahoma Press, 1999], 3–70; www.memss .arts.gla.ac.uk/html/pilot.htm). There is a striking, though speculative, connection between Hunter 409 and Corpus 61. Folio 101v of Corpus 61 has a much-discussed inscription: "neuer foryeteth: Anne neuyll." Of three possible women with this name, one often suggested as author of the inscription is Anne Neville (?1411–80), duchess of Buckingham. Folio 139 of Hunter 409 bears an inscription that A. I. Doyle has read as: "my lorde monjoy my lady your wyffe." Doyle tentatively suggests that the Lady Montjoy so commemorated is the same Anne Neville, who after the duke of Buckingham's death, married Walter Blount, first Baron Montjoy (Doyle, "Appendix B: A Note

Fig. 8. Genius's sermon; Guillaume de Lorris and Jean de Meun, *Roman de la Rose*. Philadelphia Museum of Art, Collins 1945-65-3, fol. 135, early 15th century. Workshop of Maître François. The Philip S. Collins Collection, gift of Mrs. Philip S. Collins in memory of her husband, 1945.

Troye" (*BD*, line 326), while the walls are "peynted, bothe text and glose, / Of al the Romaunce of the Rose" (333–34). The young author thus frames his first attempt at sustained poetic narrative between the origin myth of European culture and the originary text of one of that culture's central paradigms.

---

on St. John's College, Cambridge, MS. H. 5," in *The Epistle of Othea, Translated from the French Text of Christine de Pisan by Stephen Scrope*, ed. Curt F. Bühler, EETS o.s. 264 [London: Oxford University Press, 1970], 125–27). As daughter of Joan Beaufort and thus granddaughter of John of Gaunt, this Anne Neville was, as it were, in direct cultural descent from the literary milieux of the late fourteenth and early fifteenth centuries. It is thus quite interesting to think that she may have owned or at least "visited" two very important Chaucer manuscripts.

Chaucer's other two earliest surviving works are also dream visions, and even the more realistic *Troilus and Criseyde* salts its love narrative with references to the familiar *Rose* personification, Dangier (*TC,* 2:384, 399, 1243, 1376; 3:1321). At one point, Chaucer implicitly aligns himself with Genius's pulpit, via the ironic comment that his alter ego, Pandarus, was an unsuccessful lover, "koude he nevere so wel of lovyng preche" (2:59). The prologue to *Troilus* (1:1–56) is particularly imbued with the love culture of the *Rose* tradition. It deploys a complex set of postures and motifs focused around the image of a stern god of Love, of the lovers who serve him, and of the simultaneously humble and powerful author through whom these roles are filtered. Never addressed directly, Love is mentioned by name eight times in the prologue's eight stanzas (lines 15, 16, 27, 31, 34, 42, 46, 48) and twice pronominally (lines 18, 28). The unspecified "god" to whom lovers are urged to pray in lines 32, 40, and 44 may or may not also be the god of Love; if not, the Christian god is being enlisted in Love's service, since he is asked to help lovers please their ladies.

A *Rose*-influenced *Troilus* frontispiece would speak not only retrospectively, to the author's literary formation, but also prospectively, to a fifteenth-century English audience for whom the *Roman* remained a fundamental cultural text. As Kathryn Lynch notes, "A French heritage, . . . during the late Middle Ages, was the common cultural property of all educated, well-placed Englishmen."[41] Julia Boffey's investigation of manuscript ownership has demonstrated that fifteenth-century readers of Chaucer would have recognized his "indebtedness to French sources including the *Roman* and poems by Froissart and Machaut" and would "have had access to these texts outside Chaucer's reformulations of them."[42] In pivoting their iconography off of the *Rose*, the Corpus team could thus be confident that their target audience would recognize and appreciate the intervisuality.[43] Only the *Rose* conclusively resolves the

[41] Kathryn L. Lynch, "Dating Chaucer," *ChauR* 42 (2007): 1–22 (13).

[42] Julia Boffey, "English Dream Poems of the Fifteenth Century and Their French Connections," in *Literary Aspects of Courtly Culture: Selected Papers from the Seventh Triennial Congress of the International Courtly Literature Society*, ed. Donald Maddox and Sara Sturm-Maddox (Cambridge: Brewer, 1994), 113–21 (113).

[43] The Corpus frontispiece may have been the artist's conception start to finish, or he may have been acting partially or completely in collaboration with or under the direction of the patron, of an intermediary representing the patron, and/or of a workshop supervisor. As a result, like other scholars, I speak here of "designers" or of a "design team," except in cases where the focus is on the artistic realization of an idea rather than on the idea itself.

key paradox of the poet in the pulpit. Love and sex, anathema as topics in Petrus de Aureolis's or Guillaume de Deguileville's pulpit, are right at home in Genius's.

Concatenated Identities

If Chaucer inhabits the place of Genius in the Corpus frontispiece, it follows that his audience is in some sense doubling for the lords and barons of Love. If so, we do not have far to look to find the god of Love and Venus. The gold-clad Richard II seems to echo, in prominence and masterfulness, the god of Love from the *Rose* illuminations. Splitting Venus's attributes—difficult to combine in mortal women—of beautiful young woman and mother of an adult son may be the two diademed females near Richard. The conservatively dressed woman standing behind the king suggests his mother, Joan of Kent, whom Froissart had described as "in her time the most beautiful lady in all the realm of England, and the most amorous."[44] The young woman sitting "downstage" from Richard wears a more elaborate and revealing dress, and likely represents Richard's queen, Anne of Bohemia. The rest of the audience includes three young wooing couples, a female attendant on Anne, and eight other men engaged to varying degrees in the address from the pulpit. It is like a mix of Love's barons with the lovers envisioned in the text's prologue.

These carefully deployed iconographic elements suggest that in the *Troilus and Criseyde* frontispiece, three imaginations of speaker-and-audience have coalesced seamlessly. Probably the first layer was the desire to memorialize Geoffrey Chaucer, who in the early fifteenth century was assuming the elevated status of "[f]airest in our tonge, as the laurer grene" (Lydgate, c. 1401) and "[t]hys landes verray tresour and rychesse" (Hoccleve, c. 1411–12) that he was to occupy until our own day.[45] If one accepts the earlier dating of the frontispiece indicated by the hair and clothing styles, Corpus 61 falls into the same period during

[44] Joan "fu en son temps la plus belle dame de tout le roiaulme d'Engleterre, et la plus amoureuse." Jean Froissart, *Oeuvres: Chroniques*, ed. Kervyn de Lettenhove, 16 vols. (Brussels: Devaux, 1867–72), 2(1867): 243.

[45] Quotes from, respectively, John Lydgate, "The Flour of Curtesye," in Walter W. Skeat, ed., *The Complete Works of Geoffrey Chaucer*, vol. 7: *Chaucerian and Other Pieces* (Oxford: Clarendon Press, 1897), no. 9, line 238; Thomas Hoccleve, *Works*, vol. 3: *The Regement of Princes . . . and Fourteen of Hoccleve's Minor Poems*, ed. Frederick J. Furnivall, EETS e.s. 72 (London: Kegan Paul, Trench, Trübner, 1897), line 2081.

which the other two manuscripts with likenesses of Chaucer were created: the Ellesmere (c. 1400–1410) and Harley 4866 (c. 1410–20).[46] Unlike those images, however, which show Chaucer on his own, Corpus 61 augments his status by depicting him addressing king and court. The second layer of the frontispiece elides that royal assembly with the court of Love invoked so persistently in *Troilus*'s prologue. The third and final layer, by placing Chaucer in Genius's pulpit, invests Richard's court—and Richard's poet, at least in this picture—with the glamour of the ur-text of courtly love, the *Roman de la Rose*. The three layers feed into and out of each other, exhibiting that productive play with identities, postures, and attributes that games, including the game of love, exist to facilitate.

The importance of audience to the frontispiece team's conception of Chaucer appears most immediately in the brilliant individuation of the people around him. In his prologue, Chaucer himself addresses an undifferentiated group of happy lovers, and most preaching, teaching, or prelection illuminations depict the audience as a more or less anonymous conglomeration of auditors distinguished at most by sex and status (see, for example, Figs. 2–8). But the Corpus team chose, and the Corpus Master was able, to portray a fascinating assortment of distinct individuals. One finds oneself—especially now that the image can be viewed on a computer at high magnification—scanning across the scene, scrutinizing faces, headdresses or hats, clothing, hand positions, pondering the elusive characters and relationships of these vividly realized humans. This audience gives the social life of the text and the image great visual reality and great interest—one by-product of which has been the now-discredited but understandable impulse to *name* everyone, to attach a historical identity to each person. One source of that fascination, I think, is that the artist has managed to capture the double reality configured in *Troilus*'s prologue. From the opening of the third stanza, when the god of Love is first invoked, the game of Love begins in "earnest" as everyone starts, as it were, putting on their Love identities. Chaucer defines his as "I, that God of Loves servantz serve" (*TC* 1:15), thus assigning to himself an accessory situation analogous to that of Genius. Stanza 4 uses direct address to invest the audience with its role, labeling them "ye loveres, that bathen in gladnesse" (line 22). The rest of the

---

[46] The Ellesmere has been variously dated to c. 1400–1410 (Pearsall, *Life*, 285) and 1400–1405 (K. Scott, *Later Gothic Manuscripts*, 2:140); and Harley 4866 to the early 1410s (Pearsall, *Life*, 285) and c. 1415–20 (K. Scott, *Later Gothic Manuscripts*, 2:160).

prologue calls on these lovers to employ their memories and prayers in service to Love. In the Corpus frontispiece, we seem to see "real" people folding their complex human realities into the game of being Love's servants. Some are immersed in it completely, some are just having fun, some are savoring and deploying the status it gives them, and some are maintaining a skeptical distance.

The most important member of the audience, of course, is the king. It is complimentary to the poet (and to the patron of Corpus 61) to imagine that *Troilus and Criseyde* was presented to King Richard himself. Accordingly, the man in gold stands before Chaucer, their gazes locked, the poet's speaking gesture aimed directly at his chief auditor. At the same time, historical events had made the idea of celebrating Richard II a little awkward; the frontispiece was painted during the reign either of the man who dethroned Richard or of that man's son. Seeing the poet in Genius's pulpit, though, we are invited to imagine this Richard rather less as king of England than as king of Love—to place him in the *Rose* context of chief auditor in Genius's audience, and into the *Troilus and Criseyde* prologue context of offstage deity. That this king figure sports a gold hat rather than a gold crown splits the difference, as it were: it directs us away from accessories suggestive of political power but retains the implication of splendor. At the same time, historicity or pseudohistoricity is not completely undermined, as it would be if the figure bore Love's wings. The designers evidently sought, and achieved, a careful balance between realism and romance that combined the best of both identities for their purposes. In this context, it is fascinating to note that the smudging of this figure's face—always attributed to anti-Ricardian sentiments—also seems to have been a treatment meted out sometimes to the god of Love, as in Figure 7. Was it as Love rather than as Richard that the man in gold was defaced—or as both? The Corpus team have managed to cover themselves very cleverly; their image glorifies the deposed Richard, but in a manner that underlines his unfitness for royal power. He made a great play-king of Love, the frontispiece implies, and as such properly honored the great Chaucer with his attention; but he was so busy playing and posing that he was a disastrous king of England, thus meriting his displacement.

Similar considerations seem to influence Chaucer's location in the frontispiece, which flouts a basic rule of visual rhetoric: that the most important person in a picture stands the highest. Since Chaucer is by far the highest person in the lower register, we are evidently being told that this plainly dressed commoner was more important than the king and all his gorgeously attired nobles. The implications are, again, flattering to Chaucer but seem rather harsh toward Richard—and might even offend other, successor kings and nobles. But again, the possibility of offense is offset by resort to the *Rose*. As spokesmen for divine authority, preachers properly stand above their audience, whether the king of England or the god of Love.[47] Thus, in his Genius identity as Nature's priest, Chaucer can fairly stand higher than Richard as Love, since Love is subject to God's vicar, Nature. A glance at the illustrations of Genius's sermon (see Figs. 5–8) shows that Genius consistently stands higher than Love (though in Figure 7 he wins only by the tip of his miter). *Rose* iconography thus helps rationalize the diminishment of royal power. Simultaneously, it contributes to the enhancement of the poet, visualizing the double role Chaucer assigns himself in his prologue: as definer and as servant of the audience he invokes.[48]

Two other iconographic details may reflect a "negotiation process" between the Genius–Love model and the Chaucer–Richard scene. Although one tends to think of the Corpus frontispiece's lower register as set in a garden, it is more aptly described, in Salter's words, as "a wooded parkland."[49] There are no flowers, no fountain, no structures, and no other inhabitants, human or animal. Chaucer in a pulpit in a garden might have too obviously suggested the *Rose*'s Garden of Delight; a more pastoral landscape with, for instance, fleecy lambs might recall Genius's Heavenly Park. Since both landscapes might carry distracting connotations, the iconography resolves itself into a neutral setting amid rather serious-looking trees. The other, more important detail is Chaucer's textlessness. Why memorialize the father of English literature while not showing us the books he wrote? (Compare this memorial conception with John Gower's decision to pillow the head of his tomb effigy on his three major works.) The answer might involve a conception of literature as an aural process, but it may also represent a similar trian-

---

[47] Cf. Helmbold, "Chaucer Appropriated," 206–7, 222–24, where she attributes the poet's placement above Richard to Chaucer's propaganda value for Henry V (whom she argues is the manuscript's patron).

[48] Another, probably coincidental, parallel lies in the fact that Geoffrey Chaucer's son, Thomas, also held a prominent speaker's post as five times speaker of the House of Commons, beginning in 1407 (Carole Rawcliffe, "Chaucer, Thomas (c. 1367–1434)," *Oxford Dictionary of National Biography* [Oxford: Oxford University Press 2004]; online edition, www.oxforddnb.com/view/article/5192, accessed August 13, 2008).

[49] Salter, "The '*Troilus* Frontispiece,'" 15.

gulation among the options available in depictions of Genius's sermon. Chaucer with a book might look too little like Genius. But Chaucer with a scroll might look too much like Genius—given that the content of Genius's scroll was a summons to fornication. Apart from any English qualms about advocating outright immorality, the fact that Genius urged fornication in the interests of reproduction would clash with the figure of Love/Richard, given that Richard had had no children—and that no loyal Lancastrian could possibly wish he had.

Finally, the depiction of Richard II in his play identity as the god of Love may have one further resonance. In modern terminology, it could be that an "Easter egg" lurks among the data.[50] In the very next text that Chaucer created after *Troilus and Criseyde*, the F-prologue to the *Legend of Good Women* (between 1386 and 1388),[51] the poet reverts to dream vision. In his dream, the god of Love appears with his consort, here the Greek heroine Alceste. Love is angry with Chaucer because

> Thou hast translated the Romaunce of the Rose,
> That is an heresye ayeins my lawe,
> And makest wise folk fro me withdrawe;
> And of Creseyde thou hast seyd as the lyste,
> That maketh men to wommen lasse triste.
>
> (*LGW*, F: 329–33)

Alceste gently pleads on Chaucer's behalf and as penance assigns him to translate the legends that become the body of the text. Scholars are almost unanimous in accepting Love and Alceste as allegorized versions of Richard II and Anne of Bohemia.[52] Chaucer signals such an identifi-

---

[50] The *OED* defines an "Easter egg" in this sense as "an unexpected or undocumented feature in a piece of software, intended as a joke or bonus; (now also) a feature of this kind in a sound or video recording, esp. on DVD."

[51] Date per M. C. E. Shaner and A. S. G. Edwards, notes to *The Legend of Good Women*, in *Riverside Chaucer*, 1059–75 (1060).

[52] Scholars who accept the Richard/Love and Alceste/Anne equation in the *Legend of Good Women* prologue—with various shadings—include Andrew Taylor, "Anne of Bohemia and the Making of Chaucer," *SAC* 19 (1997): 95–119; Ann W. Astell, *Political Allegory in Late Medieval England* (Ithaca: Cornell University Press, 1999), 94; Helen Barr, *Socioliterary Practice in Late Medieval England* (Oxford: Oxford University Press, 2001), 89–105; Helen Phillips, "Register, Politics, and the *Legend of Good Women*," *ChauR* 37 (2002): 101–28 (104); Jenni Nuttall, *The Creation of Lancastrian Kingship: Literature, Language, and Politics in Late Medieval England* (Cambridge: Cambridge University Press, 2007), 162 n. 20; see also Shaner and Edwards, notes to *LGW*, 1060–61; and Joyce Coleman, "'A bok for king Richardes sake': Royal Patronage, the *Confessio*, and the *Legend of Good Women*," in *On John Gower: Essays at the Millennium*, ed. R. F.

cation by having Alceste remind Love that he is "a god and eke a kyng" (line 431). She also names two royal castles when instructing the poet to deliver the finished *Legend* to "the quene, / On my byhalf, at Eltham or at Sheene" (496–97). The unusual choice of Alceste as Love's consort is another clue; the archetype of devoted wives, and thus duly complimentary to the royal consort, Alceste also has the advantage of a name beginning, like Anne's, with the letter A.

Chaucer was not the only poet in this period to cast the royal couple as the king and queen of Love. Gower's *Confessio Amantis* (begun c. 1386), which opens with an account of Richard commissioning the work,[53] presents a more traditional pair. In a structure redolent of *Rose* influence, the distraught Amans prays to Cupid and Venus, who appear before him. Cupid angrily strikes Amans with his dart, while Venus sympathetically sends her priest, Genius, to hear Amans's confession (I.124–202).[54] At the end of the book, Queen Anne is invoked with an indirectness similar to Chaucer's, as young lovers appear adorned after "the newe guise of Beawme," or Bohemia (VIII.2470).[55] Finally, also around 1386, John Clanvowe began his *Book of Cupid* with an invocation to the titular deity,[56] continuing into a love debate between an idealistic Nightingale and a skeptical Cuckoo. The two birds ultimately decide to meet next near another royal castle: "Vnder the maple that is feire and grene, / Before the chambre wyndow of the Quene / At Wodestok . . ." (283–85).

In an earlier article I have argued that more than chance lies behind three poets' simultaneous decision, around 1386, to begin Middle English love poems presenting a god/king and queen of love, along with hints aligning these figures with King Richard and Queen Anne.[57]

Yeager (Kalamazoo: Medieval Institute Publications, 2007), 104–23 and references therein.

[53] *Confessio Amantis*, Prol.: 35*–53*. All quotations from the *Confessio Amantis* from G. C. Macaulay, ed., *Complete Works of John Gower*, vols. 2–3: *Confessio Amantis* (Oxford: Clarendon Press, 1901).

[54] The illustrations of Amans confessing to Genius in the *Confessio Amantis* very likely derive from those of Nature confessing to Genius in *Roman de la Rose* manuscripts; the images resemble each other in all but the gender of the confessant.

[55] On Gower's royal allegory, see Hans-Jürgen Diller, " 'For Engelondes sake': Richard II and Henry of Lancaster as Intended Readers of Gower's *Confessio Amantis*," in *Functions of Literature: Essays Presented to Erwin Wolff on His Sixtieth Birthday*, ed. Ulrich Broich, Theo Stemmler, and Gerd Stratmann (Tübingen: Niemeyer, 1984), 39–53 (49–50); Green, *Poets and Princepleasers*, 91–92.

[56] Sir John Clanvowe, *The Boke of Cupide*, in *The Works of Sir John Clanvowe*, ed. V. J. Scattergood (Cambridge: Brewer, 1965), 33–53; lines 1–20.

[57] Coleman, " 'A bok for king Richardes sake.' "

Whether or not Richard II commissioned all these poems, this striking congruence suggests that the king was encouraging a fashion in the mid-1380s—when he and Anne were just reaching the age of twenty—of equating the young couple with these *Rose* divinities. The heavy emphasis placed on the god of Love in the *Troilus and Criseyde* prologue and text might also align with this fashion. It is true, as scholars have noted, that the portrayals of Love/Cupid seem to contain critiques of Richard II.[58] But it would be surprising if three English authors independently conceived the idea of allegorizing the teenaged Richard II as the god of Love purely in order to comment on his faults as a ruler. More likely, the impulse behind these courtly texts was primarily to flatter the young king, while also using the allegory, as one might use proverb or parable, to smuggle in some discreet moral and political advice. Allegory allowed the authors to express but simultaneously disavow critique: it is Cupid who is arbitrary and unreliable, not Richard—but Richard could learn from Cupid's excesses to become more thoughtful and consistent. Such play with identities and attributes is entirely consonant with the game of love as inaugurated by the *Rose*.

Fast-forward some fifteen to forty years (from c. 1385 to c. 1400–1425), and we have the Corpus frontispiece, in which the pulpit and the prologue both key us to see in Richard and Anne the king and queen of Love. The "Easter egg" would be the informed viewer's recognition that this equation is not a new idea but a deliberate invocation of a lost Ricardian moment. Informed viewers would not have been hard to come by; even at the latest proposed date for the frontispiece, 1425, Richard II himself, had he lived, would have been under sixty; at the more likely date of c. 1400–1415, he would have been in his thirties or forties. An upper-class commissioner of Richard's age or even older could have drawn on memories of the court c. 1385—the king in his late teens, remodeling his palaces to add dancing rooms and extravagantly rewarding his inner circle of young courtiers;[59] the Wonderful Parliament still a year or so in the future. Although Richard Firth Green has pointed

[58] E.g., Lee Patterson, "Court Politics and the Invention of Literature: The Case of Sir John Clanvowe," in *Culture and History, 1350–1600: Essays on English Communities, Identities, and Writing*, ed. David Aers (New York: Harvester Wheatsheaf, 1992), 7–41 (11); see also Lynn Staley, "Gower, Richard II, Henry of Derby, and the Business of Making Culture," *Speculum* 75 (2000): 68–96 (69–77).

[59] Michael J. Bennett, "The Court of Richard II and the Promotion of Literature," in *Chaucer's England: Literature in Historical Context*, ed. Barbara A. Hanawalt (Minneapolis: University of Minnesota Press, 1992), 3–20 (9).

out that we have little evidence about court life in the period,[60] the evidence we do have—the mini-explosion of Cupid allegories, the chronicler Thomas Walsingham's comparison of Richard's court to "knights of Venus"[61]—supports the idea that in the earlier 1380s Richard was promoting a *Rose*-tinged culture of Love. What we may see in the frontispiece, then, is a reminiscence and a carefully framed celebration of that time, caught in all its complex weave of glory and futility. The fact that Chaucer is shown as a youngish man, rather than the old man seen in the Ellesmere and Harley portraits, reinforces the theory that the Corpus designers were deliberately historicizing the frontispiece. The goal was to show us Richard's reign and "Richard's poet" in their heyday. But though the king stands tall and golden, the poet rises above him, and the book in whose introductory image the king presides is itself a monument not to the failed Plantagenet but to the triumphant "first findere of our fayre langage"[62] who happened to live during his reign.

This conclusion seems to return my argument to its beginning, the initial claim that the lower register of the frontispiece presents a golden-age view of Chaucer and his king. What I can hope to have accomplished in the intervening pages is to deepen our understanding of that vision. I have proposed that the lower register of the Corpus frontispiece presents an intricate concatenation of identities, roles, games, and realities, built around and off of a pulpit that clues the informed viewer to remember Genius's sermon and the *Roman de la Rose* in general, as source of the late medieval culture of love.

---

[60] Green, *Poets and Princepleasers*, 5–7.

[61] Richard's favorites "milites plures erant Veneris quam Bellonae" (were more knights of Venus than of Bellona) (Thomas Walsingham, *Historia anglicana*, 2 vols., ed. Henry Thomas Riley [London: Longman, Green, Longman, Roberts, and Green, 1862, 1864], 2:156).

[62] Hoccleve, *Regement*, line 4978.

"It may nat be":

Chaucer, Derrida, and the Impossibility of the Gift

Kyle Mahowald
New College, Oxford

C HAUCER'S MOST LIKELY SOURCE for his *Summoner's Tale*, Jacques de Baisieux's fabliau *Le dis de le vescie a prestre*, tells of a dying priest who promises to bequeath to two corrupt friars a "jewel" so precious that, while he were alive, he would "not let another have it for two hundred marks."[1] The friars are crushed when the priest reveals that the precious jewel "locked in [his] possession" is his bladder.[2] The tale concludes shortly after the friars learn of their misfortune. As T. W. Craik notes, however, *The Summoner's Tale* diverges from its source and portrays not only the revelation of the friar's unwelcome gift—in this case a fart—but also the aftermath of the gift's reception, which includes the friar's reporting the gift of the fart to the town's lord, whose squire then proposes a solution to the task of dividing the fart into twelve parts.[3] This coda represents a marked departure from the rest of the tale, the plot of which mainly concerns the friar's attempt to obtain money from Thomas. It seems, in many ways, a non sequitur. Why

---

[1] Jacques de Baisieux, "The Tale of the Priest's Bladder," in *The Literary Context of Chaucer's Fabliaux: Texts and Translations*, ed. Larry Dean Benson and Theodore Murdock Andersson (Indianapolis: Bobbs-Merrill, 1971), 354–59.

[2] The introduction to the Variorum Edition of *The Summoner's Tale* includes an extensive discussion as to whether Chaucer worked directly from *Le dis de la vescie a prestre*, or whether both were responding to an earlier common source (John F. Plummer III, "Introduction," *The Variorum Edition: The Summoner's Tale* [Norman: University of Oklahoma Press, 1995], 3–51 [8–10]). Either way, critics seem to agree that the final scene is Chaucer's own addition.

[3] T. W. Craik, *The Comic Tales of Chaucer* (London: Methuen, 1964), 118.

Chaucer concludes his tale with such a bizarre scene has been the subject of much critical attention.[4]

The purpose of the coda, I argue, comes into focus through the word *inpossible*, which the lord of the town uses to describe the division of the fart: "Who evere herde of swich a thyng er now? / To every man ylike? Tel me how. / It is an inpossible; it may nat be."[5] While few critics have drawn attention to the word, according to the *Middle English Dictionary*, Chaucer was the first English writer to use the word *inpossible*—also in the form *impossible*—as a noun. The occurrence is not isolated: similar expressions appear in both *The Franklin's Tale* ("[T]his were an inpossible" [V.1009]) and *The Wife of Bath's Prologue* ("For trusteth wel, it is an impossible / That any clerk wol speke good of wyves" [III.688–89]). The *Middle English Dictionary* lists this particular usage under the noun's primary meaning: "something which cannot be or be done; impossible thing, impossible action, etc." Although the *MED* suggests that Chaucer's usage of the word predates the next usage in this context by thirty years,[6] the *Oxford English Dictionary* lists a similar occurrence in Usk's *The Testament of Love* (c. 1387–88). The next listed occurrence of the word as a noun, however, is not until c. 1440.[7] Thus, while Chaucer may not have been the first to use *impossible* as a noun, he was certainly among the first.[8] This usage of *impossible* might have been novel, but the thirteenth-century Latin noun *impossibile*—more commonly seen in the

[4] Plummer, ed., *Variorum Edition*, summarizes the ongoing critical discussion about the ending (14). Among major readings, Derek S. Brewer argues that the last scene is intended to parody an arithmetic handbook ("Chaucer and Arithmetic," in *Medieval Studies Conference Aachen 1983: Language and Literature*, ed. Wolf-Dietrich Bald and Horst Weinstock [Frankfurt am Main: Peter Lang, 1984], 111–20). R. F. Green argues that the division of the fart has a parallel in a collection of riddles from northern France ("A Possible Source for Chaucer's Summoner's Tale" *ELN* 24.4 [1987], 24–27). Alan Levitan claims that the fart is "a brilliant and satirical reversal of the Holy Ghost at Pentecost" ("The Parody of Pentecost in Chaucer's Summoner's Tale," *UTQ* 40 [1971], 236–46). Karl P. Wentersdorf suggests that the division of the fart into twelve parts on the carousel represents the "twelve winds of heaven" ("The Motif of Exorcism in the Summoner's Tale," *Studies in Short Fiction* 17 [1980], 249–54). Despite the copious criticism on the subject, no clear consensus exists as to the source or function of the coda.

[5] *The Summoner's Tale*, III.2229–31. Chaucer quotations are from Larry D. Benson, gen. ed., *The Riverside Chaucer* (Boston: Houghton Mifflin, 1987).

[6] *Middle English Dictionary*, s.v. "Impossible."

[7] *Oxford English Dictionary*, s.v. "Impossible."

[8] Roy J. Pearcy suggests the possibility that the Usk usage was in fact based on Chaucer's. "Chaucer's 'An Impossible' ('Summoner's Tale' III, 2231)," *N&Q* 14 (1967): 322–25 (322n). The precise ordering is less important than the fact that the usage was, in Chaucer's time, still innovative.

plural, *impossibilia*—was well established. It is perhaps from this Latin word that Chaucer's *impossible* derives. That is, Chaucer employs *impossible* not in the modern sense, but to refer to a now-obscure scholastic exercise that Roy J. Pearcy defines as "a proposition, advanced by a self-acknowledged sophist, which violates the dictates of common sense or is clearly incapable of demonstration, but which is nevertheless vigorously defended or 'proved' by a series of such paralogical arguments as the sophist's ingenuity can devise." For example, a sophist might begin with the proposition, as the thirteenth-century philosopher Siger von Brabant does in a classic example of an *impossible,* that "the Trojan war is still in progress," and then use logic to prove his clearly impossible claim.[9] The goal of these exercises was to train students to identify errors in logic that could lead to erroneous conclusions.

Pearcy's reading of the word "inpossible" is appropriate in this context. Thomas's order to divide his fart among twelve friars, with each getting as "muche as oother" (III.2134), resembles a sophist's presentation of an *impossible*—as does the friar's own presentation of the problem to the lord. As Pearcy notes, the problem of the fart has "the requisite effect of violently challenging common-sense presuppositions about the nature of the physical world" but, like an *impossible*, is ultimately "proved" through the ingenuity of the squire who proposes that the fart be divided up using a cartwheel.[10] The squire suggests that Thomas be placed on the hub of the wheel with a friar at each of the twelve spokes. That way the sound and smell of Thomas's fart will travel through the hollow spokes of the wheel to reach each friar. Although Pearcy convincingly argues that this method of dividing a fart functions as an example of an *impossible*, he does not fully explain why Chaucer concludes his tale with this odd parody of a scholastic exercise. A closer examination of *The Summoner's Tale*, however, reveals that the structure of the *impossible* applies not only to the lord's discussion of the fart. The friar's impossible attempt to acquire a gift of money from Thomas represents a second *impossible*. Through a series of parallels, Chaucer links Thomas's fart to the money that the friar tries to attain. As such, the impossibility of the fart serves as an analogue for the impossibility of the friar's obtaining money as a gift in exchange for heavenly rewards. Through this juxtaposition of flatulence and money, *The Summoner's Tale* raises a broader ques-

[9] Pearcy, "Chaucer's 'An Impossible,'" 322–23, 323.
[10] Ibid., 324.

tion as to the possibility of the gift in general. That is, the skeptical attitude toward the friar's attempt to extract a gift from Thomas invites the reader to consider whether all gifts are undermined by similar principles of economic exchange.

Insofar as Chaucer complicates and questions the notion of the pure gift, *The Summoner's Tale* independently discovers the idea set forth by Derrida in *Given Time: I. Counterfeit Money* that the gift is "the very figure of the impossible."[11] Derrida suggests that, for a gift to take place, a donor must intentionally give something to a donee and receive nothing in return. If the donee knows that it is a gift, he will necessarily feel indebted to the donor. As soon as the donor knows he has given a gift, he will "make a return payment" to himself with the "gratifying image of goodness or generosity."[12] Consequently, for a gift to be a pure gift, neither the donor nor the donee can know that it is a gift. But, by its very nature, a gift requires that someone intentionally give something to someone else, that both parties know that a gift event is transpiring. Thus, says Derrida, the gift "could not take place except on the condition of not taking place." It is *"the* impossible."[13] I will argue that, in the context of this argument, Chaucer's concluding *The Summoner's Tale* with an *impossible* is not only relevant but crucial. It serves as a model for "the impossible" that lies at the tale's heart: the impossibility of the gift. Indeed, Derrida's thought on the gift gives us a new way to conceive the ending of *The Summoner's Tale*. But every gift demands a return, and, just as Derrida gives us a new lens through which to examine Chaucer's work, *The Summoner's Tale* reciprocates by discovering a type of gift unthought in Derrida's *Given Time*.

Before exploring such connections, however, we must first return to the vexing question of how to divide a fart into twelve parts. Pearcy observes that the entire problem of dividing the fart—from its proposal to its eventual solution—assumes the form of a logical *impossible*. According to the traditional structure of *impossibilia*, a "master propos[es] and defend[s] his sophistical argument before a critical audience of students." That is, a sophist makes a proposition that "violently challenges common-sense presuppositions about the nature of the physical world" and then proves it.[14] The role of the audience is to express "wonderment

[11] Jacques Derrida, *Given Time: I. Counterfeit Money,* trans. Peggy Kamuf (Chicago: University of Chicago Press, 1992), 7.
[12] Ibid., 21–23.
[13] Ibid., 35.
[14] Pearcy, "Chaucer's 'An Impossible,'" 323, 324.

at the ingenuity which devised so outlandish an assertion, and incredulity that its validity should be susceptible of proof."[15] Pearcy claims that, in *The Summoner's Tale*, the role of sophist is shared by Thomas, who initially poses the seemingly impossible problem of dividing a fart among twelve friars, and the squire, who solves Thomas's problem through his suggestion that a cartwheel be used to divide the fart. The lord assumes the role of audience by expressing astonishment at the proposition. Pearcy posits a number of linguistic clues that Chaucer leaves to connect the tale to sophistical *impossibilia*. For instance, the friar rejects the title of "master" but reminds Thomas that he is a university graduate. He also points to the use of Latinate technical terms like "reverberacioun" and "perturbynge" as further support for a mockingly academic tone. In the end, though, Thomas's fart cannot be divided using a cartwheel or any other means because it is already dissipated with no conceivable means of ever being reassembled. This basic flaw in the squire's logic dovetails neatly with the structure of the *impossible*, which has as its goal the demonstration of logical fallacy in order to train the audience in "recognizing and refuting false arguments."[16] Regardless of what the sophist argues, he cannot change the truth that, while the division of the fart has a solution in the context of the *impossible*, it remains impossible in reality.

While Pearcy claims only that Chaucer depicts the division of the fart as the subject of the *impossible*, implicit in Chaucer's *impossible* is a second "illogical proposition"—that a fart can be given as a gift. Regardless of whether or not it has been divided, the idea of giving a fart to someone else is absurd. The fart-gift would be impossible even if the fart were "whole"—if a fart can be said to be capable of existing in such a state. A fart is a noise, an odor, a gas, what Chaucer's lord calls "but of eir reverberacioun" (III.2234). As a result, when the squire proposes the cartwheel solution, he solves not only the *impossible* of how to divide a fart but implicitly solves the more fundamentally impossible problem of how a fart can be given as a gift at all. This illogical idea of the fart-gift, one that the sophistical characters Thomas and the squire both embrace, comes to serve as a metaphor for the gift in general.

While it requires little imagination to see the illogic in a fart's being given as a gift, it is not immediately obvious how a fart symbolizes the

[15] Ibid., 324.
[16] Ibid., 323.

impossibility of the gift as a phenomenon of human culture. In his classic anthropological work *The Gift*, Marcel Mauss explains that the giving of a gift represents more than just the exchange of an item. Mauss observes that the law of the Maori culture accounts for a gift's being endowed with a *hau* or a spirit that it retains even when a given item changes hands. He goes on to argue that his observations of these primitive cultures reflect a broader truth: even in societies like ours and Chaucer's, which do not recognize an actual spirit in a gifted item, a gift still represents "a part of one's nature and substance"—and receiving a gift is equivalent to receiving "a part of one's spiritual essence."[17] Besides the humorous surface parallel that a fart, like Mauss's gift, is both quite literally a "part of one's nature and substance" as well as an "essence," Chaucer's rendering of the fart in *The Summoner's Tale* resembles Mauss's argument that the gift is something that exceeds mere physical representation.

In that sense, Thomas's inelegant fart serves as a surprisingly elegant model for the impossibility that Derrida sees as characterizing the gift, since Derrida not only follows Mauss in perceiving the gift as something intangible but also argues that the gift itself is, paradoxically, ungivable. Thomas's fart is an apt metaphor for such an event. As the lord says when he hears the problem of the fart, "The rumblynge of a fart and every soun / Nis but of eir reverberacioun, / And evere it wasteth litel and litel awey" (III.2233–35). Like a gift, a fart lacks a physical form and it, too, exists for "a paradoxical instant" before "wasting away." Thus, similar reasoning in each case underlies the fact that both the fart and the gift are ungivable. Derrida writes, "It is perhaps in this sense that the gift is the impossible. Not impossible but *the* impossible [non pas impossible mais *l*'impossible]. The very figure of the impossible."[18] Derrida's use of "impossible" as a noun, a usage he emphasizes by italicizing the article in "*l*'impossible," recalls Chaucer's own innovative use of "impossible" as a noun.

An understanding of the way in which the *impossible* of the fart reflects back on the impossibility of the gift illuminates the odd ending of *The Summoner's Tale*. The *impossible* at the tale's end serves as a model for the friar's similar, albeit more subtle, *impossible* when he attempts to attain

---

[17] Marcel Mauss, *The Gift*, trans. Ian Cunnison (Glencoe, Ill.: The Free Press, 1954), 10.

[18] Ibid., 7. French from Jacques Derrida, *Donner le temps: 1. La fausse monnaie* (Paris: Éditions Galilée, 1991), 19.

a gift of money from Thomas. In this case, the *impossible* concerns not the division of a fart among twelve friars but the acquisition of a gift of money, a gift that would ordinarily be recognized as possible. Mirroring his presenting the fart problem to the lord and the lord's wife, the friar presents his proposition for money to the parallel audience of Thomas and Thomas's wife. Furthermore, just as the lord says that "it may nat be" (III.2231) upon hearing that the fart must be divided, Thomas is also skeptical when he hears the friar's request for money:

> As help me Crist, as I in fewe yeres,
> Have spent upon diverse manere freres
> Ful many a pound; yet fare I never the bet.
> Certeyn, my good have I almoost biset
> Farwel, my gold, for it is al ago!"
>
> (III.1949–53)

Significantly, Thomas states not only that he does not want to give the friar money but also implies that his gold is "al ago" or completely gone. As a result, when the friar later demands, "Yif me thanne of thy gold, to make oure cloystre" (III.2099), he quite literally demands the impossible since Thomas has no gold. The friar's demand for a gift represents the seemingly illogical proposition necessary as the starting point of an *impossible*.

Despite the hopelessness of obtaining money from Thomas, the friar engages in the logical progression that the form of the *impossible* demands, the same logical progression the squire practices when he describes how to distribute the fart by cartwheel. The friar outlines what Pearcy calls "a series of . . . paralogical arguments" to prove why Thomas should donate. He explains that the friars' supposed asceticism makes them the most godly, that other clerics are not worthy, and that giving the friars money will lead to spiritual salvation. The friar's argument culminates in the outrageous claim that the world itself could end if he does not: "And if yow lakke oure predicacioun, / Thanne goth the world al to destruccioun" (III.2109–10). The fart and the money share parallel structures in their respective *impossibilia* insofar as both represent the impossible end that the sophist figure seeks to prove. Consequently, shortly before beginning his "proof" of the *impossible*, the friar remarks, "Thou shalt me fynde as just as is a squyre" (III.2090). The "squyre" in question is ostensibly a measuring square: a symbol of justice and balance. But at the time Chaucer wrote the tale, the *y* in "squyre," meaning "square," and the *i* in "squier," meaning "squire," would likely have already phonetically merged to [i].[19] As such, the text may play on the similarity between "squyre" and "squier" in order to link the friar, the man who "proves" the *impossible* about the gift of money, to the squire, the man who "proves" the *impossible* about the fart.[20]

A more blatant linguistic hint connects the tale's two *impossibilia* when the friar says, "What is a ferthyng worth parted in twelve?" (III.1967). Drawing upon an ancient correspondence between feces and money, the reference to a "ferthyng parted in twelve" seems a foreshadowing of the "farting," also to be "parted in twelve."[21] The tale confirms this connection when Thomas invites the friar to reach behind him "in hope for to fynde there a yifte" (III.2146). Identifying the fart as a "yifte" aligns it with the gift of money that the friar seeks. And just as the fart is impossible, Chaucer subtly alludes to the impossibility of money as gift when the friar says to Thomas, "A, yif that covent half a

---

[19] *The Cambridge History of the English Language,* vol. 2, ed. Norman Blake (Cambridge: Cambridge University Press, 1992), 57. Furthermore, *The Merchant's Tale* refers to a squire by the alternate spelling "squyer" instead of the more usual "squier" (III.1772).

[20] Bernard F. Huppé is perhaps the first to suggest that the line contains "unconscious word-play involving the squire's suggestion for a just distribution of Thomas' gift," in *A Reading of the Canterbury Tales* (Albany: State University of New York Press, 1967), 208.

[21] Numerous critics have pointed to the farting/farthing pun, most notably J. Edwin Whitesell in "Chaucer's Lisping Friar," *MLN* 71 (1956): 160–61; Paull F. Baum in "Chaucer's Puns: A Supplementary List," *PMLA* 73 (1958): 167–70; Earle Birney in "Structural Irony Within the Summoner's Tale," *Anglia* 78 (1960): 204–218; and according to Plummer, ed., *Variorum Edition,* "all commentators since" (note to line 1967, p. 160). Valerie Allen points to the pun and explains away an apparent phonetic difference. She also points to the pun of *ars-metrike* on "arithmetic" and "arse-metrics" (*On Farting* [New York: Palgrave Macmillan, 2007], 139–40). The fart and gold may also be linked on a psychological level. According to Sigmund Freud, "Wherever archaic modes of thought predominate or have persisted—in ancient civilizations, in myth, fairy-tale and superstition, in unconscious thoughts and dreams, and in the neuroses—money comes into the closest relation with excrement." Money, according to Freud, comes to serve as a substitute for the "original erotic interest in defecation" that is "destined to be extinguished in later years." He cites a folk figure known as the "excretor of ducats" and a Babylonian myth in which gold is the "excrement of Hell" ("Character and Anal Erotism," *Collected Papers,* trans. Joan Riviere [New York: Basic Books, 1959], 49–50). For an extensive list of works that make the connection between feces and money, see Marc Shell, *Money, Language, and Thought: Literary and Philosophical Economies from the Medieval to the Modern Era* (Baltimore: Johns Hopkins University Press, 1993), 196–97. Because psychoanalysis bases this argument in part on a notion of sublimated anal eroticism, the same reasoning that links excrement and money may also link the fart and money.

quarter otes! / A, yif that covent foure and twenty grotes! / A, yif that frere a peny, and lat hym go! / Nay, nay, Thomas, it may no thyng be so!" (III.1963–66). Although the friar mocks Thomas for giving small donations to many different friars, he also impugns the possibility of the gift insofar as the pronoun "it" in "it may no thyng be so" may subtly refer not to the division of the gift among various clerics, but to the act of giving money in general. By claiming that even these smallest of gifts "may no thyng be so," Chaucer suggests that, like the division of the fart, Thomas's gift of money is impossible. Indeed, the lord's description of the dividing of the fart, "it may nat be," echoes the friar's description of the gift, "it may no thyng be so."

The parallels that Chaucer constructs between the gift of the fart and the gift of money reveal why he goes to such lengths to align the final scene of *The Summoner's Tale* with sophistry. For Chaucer, the "impossible proposition" taken as the starting point of each of the tale's two *impossibilia* is a gift—first a gift of money and then a gift of flatulence. *Impossibilia*, however, represent a "perversion of the proper ends of logic."[22] They are intended to train students in "recognizing and refuting false arguments." So it is no surprise that Chaucer uses the *impossible* of the fart to expose the perversion in the friar's logic. By connecting the friar's attempt for money with a sophist's argument for the division and distribution of a fart, Chaucer mocks the friar's attempt to use the logic of economic exchange to obtain a gift. The appeal to the flawed logic of sophistry serves not only to mock the friar but reflects a broader erasure of the gift.

One might object that the problematic of the gift in *Given Time*, which is that it demands reciprocity, differs from the problematic of the fart, which is that it cannot be given at all. But the impossibility of full presence underlies both impossibilities. According to *Given Time*, the gift can take place only if the donor and donee simultaneously know that a gift event has occurred, but also simultaneously not know it. That is, a gift can take place only through a "forgetting so radical that it exceeds even the psychoanalytic categoriality of forgetting"—a forgetting so extreme that it is fundamentally impossible.[23] For that reason, Derrida writes, "The 'present' of the gift [le 'présent' du don] . . . is no longer thinkable as a now, that is, as a present bound up in the temporal

[22] Pearcy, "Chaucer's 'An Impossible,'" 323.
[23] Derrida, *Given Time*, 16.

synthesis. . . . That a gift is called a present [un présent] . . . will not be for us just a verbal cue."[24] The text suggest that the polysemy of "le présent," that it means both "gift" and "now," reveals that the gift can exist only in a "paradoxical instant [that] tears time apart"—a paradoxical and thus impossible instant.[25] A *present* necessitates the full *presence* that Derrida's philosophy famously denies.

As such, the impossibility of the gift is related to Derrida's idea of logocentrism: the privileging of the spoken word or *logos* over the written. As explored in "Plato's Pharmacy," logocentrism demands the (impossible) *presence* of the "speaking subject": "*Logos* is a son, then, a son that would be destroyed in his very *presence* without the present *attendance of his father*."[26] Instead, literature and language must be given.[27] To that end, *Given Time* includes the example of Baudelaire's "Counterfeit Money," to which Baudelaire appends a dedication to his "dear friend" Arsène Houssaye. That is, he *gives* his story to someone. But by making it available to the public, Baudelaire "gives" it "above and beyond any determined addressee, donee, or legatee." Derrida writes, "The accredited signatory delivered it up to a dissemination without return" because the "structure of trace and legacy of this text" inevitably "surpasses the phantasm of return and marks the death of the signatory."[28] The text enters into a system. Similarly, the gift is destroyed by the presence of its "father," the giver, and can exist only within a system of exchange that is, not coincidentally, analogous to the weave of signification that exists among texts or even within a monetary system. He writes, "That is why there is a problematic of the gift only on the basis of a consistent problem of the trace and the text."[29] The necessarily absent author/giver places his work/gift into the scene of writing/system of exchange. Upon entering, it becomes not a gift.

The gift of a fart remains necessarily absent from this system. As such, it resembles Derrida's idea of *logos*. Valerie Allen's *On Farting* posits

---

[24] Ibid., 9–10. French from Derrida, *Donner le temps*, 21–22.

[25] Derrida, *Given Time*, 9.

[26] Jacques Derrida, "Plato's Pharmacy," in *Dissemination*, trans. Barbara Johnson (New York: Continuum, 2004), 67–186 (82).

[27] Derrida is not the first to conceive of literature as a gift. Marc Shell notes that Faust identifies poetry with "cornucopian dispensation." He continues, "This association is as old as Aristotle and Alcidamous, and was common among many eighteenth-century thinkers, such as Alexander Gottlieb Baumgarten." *Money, Language, and Thought*, 94. See also Lewis Hyde, *The Gift* (London: Vintage Books, 1983).

[28] Derrida, *Counterfeit Money*, 99–100.

[29] Ibid., 100.

this very connection between the fart and *logos*: "Farts supplement shit as does living speech to the archive of writing."[30] Allen's Derridean language—"supplement" and "the archive of writing"—points to a deeper correspondence. Unlike a gift, which can leave its author and enter into a system, a fart exists only in the act of its production and thus as a supplement in the full Derridean sense of the word. Like the spoken word, the fart has no tangible form but is mere sound and "reverberacioun." The fart is a gift that cannot be given or received outside the presence of its "giver." Thomas calls it "swich thyng . . . that may *I* yeve, and *noon other*" (III.2124–25; emphasis added). Even the squire, who otherwise has no problem with the idea that a fart can be given as a gift, recognizes that Thomas must be "sette . . . on the wheel right of this cart" (III.2269) for the fart to be given. Like *logos*, the fart needs its "father," its farter, to exist. This explains Allen's connection between spoken word and fart, writing and shit. With its own system of signification, money—including the gold that the friar so persistently demands—falls on the shit/writing side of that divide because it exists within a system independent of its source. Perhaps this link illuminates the long-standing connection between feces and money proposed by Freud and others.[31] But as *logos*, the fart is denied a place in such a system.

Indeed, Thomas's fart represents a gift more radically impossible than that discussed by Derrida and consequently illuminates a subtlety in his argument. While *Given Time* states that the gift is impossible because it is necessarily enmeshed in a circle of exchange, it does not address what it would be like to think a gift that must remain outside that system. Unable to enter the circle of exchange—represented quite literally by the circular cartwheel—the fart is a gift that cannot be separated from its giver. But the inherently impossible nature of the fart-gift reveals that the gift cannot exist outside the circle either. This raises the question of whether these two competing models of the gift's impossibility are in some fundamental way the same.

Indeed, a comparison of the way Chaucer treats the gift in *The Summoner's Tale* with his treatment of it in other tales suggests a deep equivalency between the two competing models for the gift's impossibility. *The Franklin's Tale* links the gift and the impossible in a way more

---

[30] Allen, *On Farting*, 3.
[31] See Shell, *Money, Language, and Thought*, and note 16 above.

strictly similar to Derrida's model of reciprocity as explored in Britton Harwood's reading of *The Franklin's Tale* and *The Squire's Tale* in his "Chaucer and the Gift (If There Is Any)." Harwood claims that both "make a problem of the gift"—that, in both tales, Chaucer anticipates Derrida and tries to "erase unproductive expenditure—what Georges Bataille called *dépense*—by safely framing and containing it by economy and exchange."[32] Both Harwood and Derrida seek to show how every gift is subsumed in a cycle of reciprocity.

Besides just questioning the status of the gift, *The Franklin's Tale* also has an *impossible*. This is no coincidence. *The Franklin's Tale*, in fact, features an even clearer example of an *impossible* than the Summoner's. Aurelius presents the task of removing rocks from the coast—a feat that Dorigen explicitly deems "agayns the proces of nature" (V.1345)—to a man that Chaucer refers to as a "philosophre." While "philosophre" in this case ostensibly means "magician" or "alchemist," the *MED* notes that it could also refer to a sophist, the exact type of person who might have practiced *impossibilia*.[33] The philosopher's actions align him more with a sophist or scholar than a magician insofar as he uses not magic but scientific knowledge to make the rocks disappear: "Whan he hadde founde his firste mansioun, / He knew the remenaunt by proporcioun, / And knew the arisyng of his moone weel, / And in whos face, and terme, and everydeel" (V.1285–88). The philosopher uses his astrological charts to find the position of the moon and then calculates the "remenaunt by proporcioun" to see where it will be in the future. Presumably he uses this knowledge to calculate when the tides will completely cover the rocks. By using logic to solve the seemingly impossible problem with which Aurelius presents him, the philosopher neatly follows the structure of *impossibilia*—just as the squire does when he solves the problem of dividing the fart. Not surprisingly, Aurelius's response to Dorigen's demand that he either move the rocks or cease loving her draws upon the same peculiar nominal usage of "impossible" that we see in *The Summoner's Tale*: "'Madame,' quod he, 'this were an inpossible" (V.1009). Implicit in both instances is the idea of scholarly *impossibilia*.

The similarities, however, do not end with semantics. As in *The Summoner's Tale*, the *impossible* in *The Franklin's Tale*, in this case not the division of a fart but the removal of rocks, is aligned with a scenario in

---

[32] Britton J. Harwood, "Chaucer and the Gift (If There Is Any)," *SP* 103:1 (2006): 26–46 (26–27).

[33] *MED*, s.v. "Philosophre."

which the gift is depicted as the impossible. Harwood argues that "the solicitation of a return comes right to the surface" in *The Franklin's Tale*.[34] Arveragus gives up his wife. As a return, Aurelius gives her back. And, as a return for Aurelius's return, the philosopher refuses to accept payment for his services. Thus, each would-be gift is negated and contained within a circle of exchange. But the Franklin describes all three of these actions as gifts, referring to their "gentilesse," crediting the spirit of giving, asking "Which was the mooste fre?" (V.1622). Read through the lens of the *impossibilia*, however, no one was "fre." The apparent exchange of generosity breaks down. Just as the friar's gift of money "may no thyng be so," impossibility pervades each display of generosity in *The Franklin's Tale*. Alan T. Gaylord argues that the tale is a "satiric masterpiece," that Chaucer fills it with intentional contradictions to show "how ludicrously and inadequately the Franklin grasps the essence of gentle behavior."[35] Although the tale is indeed filled with intentional contradictions, they result not—as Gaylord suggests—from the Franklin's inadequacy but from the text's exposure of the contradictions inherent in the gift.

Gaylord identifies one such contradiction when he observes that Dorigen's promise to sleep with Aurelius if he can move the rocks is not really a promise at all.[36] Indeed, Dorigen uses *adynaton*—a rhetorical device in which a speaker describes an impossible event as a means of hyperbole—when she says that she will love Aurelius only if he can clear the coast of rocks.[37] After stating as much, she says, "For wel I woot that it shal never bityde. / Lat swiche folies out of youre herte slyde" (V.1001–2). By making such a promise and then insisting on its impossibility, telling Aurelius to give up his "folies," Dorigen does not make an earnest promise at all, but uses the impossible condition as a rhetorical device to express the impossibility of her ever loving Aurelius. Perhaps her claim that it "shal never bityde" even subtly hints that, according to her understanding, there "shall never *be tide*" at which the rocks are covered.

Chaucer establishes a precedent for using the movement of rocks as just such a hyperbolic device through a similar statement in *Troilus and*

---

[34] Harwood, "Chaucer and the Gift," 33.
[35] Alan T. Gaylord, "The Promises in the *Franklin's Tale*," *ELH* 31.4 (1964): 331–65 (332).
[36] Ibid., 347.
[37] Christopher Brookhouse, "Chaucer's Impossibilia," *MÆ* 34 (1965): 40–42 (40).

Criseyde: "That first shal Phebus fallen fro his speere, / And everich egle ben the dowves feere, / *And everich roche out of his place sterte*, / Er Troilus oute of Criseydes herte."[38] In this instance, the rocks' disappearing from their usual places is an example of something as impossible as the sun's dropping from the sky or an eagle's befriending a dove. All are items that Chaucer lists to show the strength of Criseyde's love for Troilus. Just as the reader would be foolish to interpret the statement about Troilus and Criseyde literally—that is, by assuming that if the sun were to fall from the sky Criseyde would stop loving Troilus—Aurelius acts absurdly in taking Dorigen's promise at its word. In doing so, Aurelius violates a basic tenet of speech-act theory: Searle's treatise that a binding promise necessitates that the speaker intend her speech act to obligate her to do something and that the speaker intend that the listener understands said obligation. Searle explains, "If a speaker can demonstrate that he did not have this intention in a given utterance, he can prove that the utterance was not a promise."[39] Dorigen, who repeatedly states that Aurelius will never achieve the conditions she sets, clearly lacks this intention, and, as a result, her promise is not a promise.[40] Because the promise is founded on an unsound speech act, Aurelius's claim to Dorigen is faulty, and his supposed generosity in giving her up is not generosity at all because she is not his to give.

Even if the flawed promise is accepted as legitimate, Aurelius lacks a rightful claim to Dorigen because he fails to meet her stated conditions that he remove all the stones from the shore and instead only makes it *"seme* . . . that alle the rokkes were aweye" for a "wyke or tweye" (V.1295–96; emphasis added). Presumably, though, they remain just below the surface and thus do not allow ships the safe passage that Dorigen desires. Also, Aurelius does not personally remove the rocks

---

[38] *Troilus and Criseyde* III.1495–98; emphasis added.

[39] John R. Searle, *Speech Acts: An Essay in the Philosophy of Language* (Cambridge: Cambridge University Press, 1969), 60.

[40] R. F. Green argues that Dorigen's rash promise may have been valid according to medieval law since medieval "common law stands foursquare behind the principle that *pacta sunt servanda* [agreements must be kept]." He writes that what Gaylord calls "fanatical literalism" in *The Franklin's Tale* is "precisely the kind of thinking on which a medieval serjeant would have most prided himself." Nonetheless, Green admits that this type of thinking was opposed to that of both the "canonist" and "civilian"—who would have required intent from both sides for a promise to be binding. *A Crisis of Truth: Literature and Law in Ricardian England* (Philadelphia: University of Pennsylvania Press, 1999), 324. Whether Chaucer favored the common-law interpretation of such a promise or was—more likely—satirizing it, he certainly would have been cognizant of its special status as a promise without intent to bind.

"stoon by stoon" as Dorigen requests but instead pays a philosopher to make them disappear from sight. Gaylord observes that, in all of these aspects, Chaucer departs markedly from the source for the tale, the fifth story of the tenth day in Boccaccio's *The Decameron*. In it, the lady demands that a garden "full of green grass, flowers, and leafy trees" appear in the month of January[41]—a task that the suitor in the tale miraculously achieves. Whereas Boccaccio's version of the impossible feat requires a miracle, Chaucer's task is solved through the prosaic process of calculating tides. Chaucer's substitution of a task with such an easy— although technically inadequate—solution seems a decision to show how the suitor and his philosopher fail to meet the lady's conditions, to show how they fail to accomplish her impossible task but merely give the appearance of doing so.[42] Consequently, when Aurelius shows apparent generosity by relinquishing his right to Dorigen, he gives up something that was never his to give. And, for the same reason, the philosopher's excusing Aurelius's debt fails as a gift because the philosopher does not do what was requested of him either—that is, to remove the physical rocks. In this sense, despite the appearance of generosity in both instances, the gifts cannot take place. Chaucer foreshadows these strangely impossible gifts when Aurelius tells the philosopher, "This wyde world, which that men seye is round, / I wolde it yeve, if I were lord of it" (V.1228–29). His suggestion that he would give something that does not belong to him anticipates his "generously" relinquishing Dorigen despite her never actually having made a truly binding promise—and his not even fulfilling it. Thus, like the fart that Thomas gives the friar, and even like the money that the friar tries to wrest away from Thomas, the gifts given by Aurelius and the philosopher do not—and cannot—exist.

More extensive analysis of *The Franklin's Tale* reveals that Chaucer sees economic exchange pervading even the most seemingly legitimate generosity. Although Arveragus hands his wife over to Aurelius in order to maintain the value of her word, the Franklin narrates the event as if it were a gift, describing Arveragus as "fre" (V.1622) and of "grete gentillesse" (V.1527). But Arveragus's generosity is so extreme as to seem false. Gaylord observes that the first promise Dorigen makes in the tale is not to love Aurelius if he moves the rocks, but to be true to

[41] Giovanni Boccaccio, *The Decameron*, trans. Mark Musa and Peter Bondanella (New York: New America Library, 2002), 731.
[42] Gaylord, "Promises," 360.

her husband: "Sire, I wol be youre humble trewe wyf—/ Have heer my trouthe—til that myn herte breste" (V.758–59). Her speech almost exactly parallels her words to Aurelius when she promises to love him if he meets her impossible request: "Have heer my trouthe" (V.998). But when Arveragus instructs his wife to be true to her word—"Ye shul youre trouthe holden, by my fay!" (V.1474)—he refers only to the "trouthe" of her promise to Aurelius and forgets the promise that she has made to him. Her dilemma becomes a struggle between chastity and truthfulness instead of a struggle between one "trouthe" and another, between her "trouthe" to Aurelius and her "trouthe" to her husband. Gaylord notes, "This omission, when noticed, gives [Arveragus's] speech to her a strange quality of unreality."[43] By applying the lessons of the sophistical *impossible* in *The Summoner's Tale*—that is, by seeking a logical fallacy in the nature of the gift, this seeming contradiction, this "strange quality of unreality," becomes not only understandable but central to the tale's theme. Although Gaylord argues that Chaucer builds the contradiction into the tale to show the Franklin's ignorance of "gentilesse," it also leads to the representation of a gift that Arveragus has no reason to give, a gift that Chaucer portrays as necessarily strange.

Furthermore, the word "trouthe" itself may imply an unexpected absence of generosity insofar as it retains shades of its proto-Germanic etymological meaning: a mutual understanding arising from a promise between two parties. This meaning exists in all early Germanic cognates of the word,[44] and R. F. Green notes that, even as the semantics of the word shifted over time, some "fundamental concept of reciprocity" persisted even when it was used to denote primarily what the *MED* defines as "nobility of character" and "adherence to the chivalric ideal"—both of which resemble the idea of "gentilesse." Chaucer traded in both senses of the word.[45] In fact, in certain instances in *The Franklin's Tale*, such as "Have heer my trouthe" and "Ye shul youre trouthe holden," the contractual meaning may crowd out the more chivalric

[43] Ibid., 343.
[44] D. H. Green's investigation of the origin of the word "truth" reveals that this meaning, which he calls a "mutual agreement or treaty on the basis of a promise between two parties," is present in Old High German, Gothic, Old Saxon, Old Norse, Old English, and even such non-Germanic languages as Latin and Old French. *The Carolingian Lord: Semantic Studies on Four Old High German Words: Balder, Frô, Truhtin, Hêrro* (Cambridge: Cambridge University Press, 1965).
[45] Green, *A Crisis of Truth*, 11–16.

meaning. When Dorigen and Arveragus refer to Dorigen's "trouthe," their overtones of generosity are tempered by the language of a potentially binding legal contract. Whereas the former suggests the idea of the gift, the latter reduces it to terms of exchange, contractual obligation, and reciprocation—the very concepts that Derrida sees as destructive of the gift.

Thus, the three gifts in *The Franklin's Tale* involve a man who gives up his wife for an absurd and paradoxical reason, a squire who gives up a woman who does not belong to him, and a philosopher who gives up a thousand pounds that he could never rightfully claim anyway. Because of these contradictions that undermine all the tale's gifts, the Franklin's final question as to "which was the mooste fre" (V.1622) rings hollow. As Harwood suggests, there is no real generosity in *The Franklin's Tale* because every gift exchange is trapped in a circle of economy and reciprocity. That even a tale purportedly *about* "gentilesse" and "being fre" negates the gift resolves the debate as to whether Chaucer's text applies the impossibility of the gift only to farts and corrupt friars.

The two impossibilities in *The Franklin's Tale* and *The Summoner's Tale* are essentially the same. In *The Franklin's Tale*, as in Derrida's model, every gift is negated by reciprocal demand. In *The Summoner's Tale*, the fart cannot be given because it requires the presence of its giver. But, in Derrida's argument, that impossibility of the giver's absenting himself is universal and is the very reason that the specter of reciprocity can never be eluded. The apparently competing impossibilities of the traditional gift and the fart-gift are merely two sides of the same coin—perhaps quite literally if one accepts the farthing/farting pun and the connection between feces and money so central to *The Summoner's Tale*.

Ultimately, it is this unified impossibility of the gift that unifies *The Summoner's Tale*, that makes its strange ending with its farts, cartwheels, and *impossibilia* a fitting conclusion. Throughout the first part of the tale, the words "yif" and "yifte" are a constant focus: "A, yif that covent half a quarter otes! / A, yif that covent foure and twenty grotes!" (1963–64), "Yif me thanne of thy gold" (III.2099), "And doun his hand he launceth to the clifte / In hope for to fynde there a yifte" (III.2145–46). But, of course, the only thing the friar receives is a fart—that which literally cannot be given because it is intangible and nontransferable. Only through the coda, which so closely follows the form of the sophistical *impossible*, does the full import of Thomas's fart become clear. By paralleling the squire's explanation of how to divide a fart with the friar's attempt to get money from Thomas, the coda serves as a model for the illogicality of the friar's actions. As such, the coda does exactly what an *impossible* is supposed to do: it demonstrates a seemingly sound, but inherently flawed, premise and trains the audience—in this case, the reader—to apply the same process of "recognizing and refuting false arguments" to other scenarios, such as the impossibility of the friar's obtaining a gift of money. Without the "practice" that the squire's clearly defined *impossible* provides at the end of *The Summoner's Tale*, and without the parallels that Chaucer uses to tie the gift to the *impossible*, the reader would not have sufficient evidence to understand the impossibility of the gift in the main text of *The Summoner's Tale*—or anywhere else in the *Canterbury Tales* for that matter.

Still, throughout this analysis, the question of why we should consider any of these transactions gift events at all arises. Why should the corrupt friar's attempt to *exchange* heavenly rewards for monetary ones be considered a gift? And if each display of generosity in *The Franklin's Tale* is reciprocation for a previous response, why should we call them gifts? Why not just call everything exchange and render it in terms of debt and repayment? Why not just call the fart a fart instead of a gift? Derrida asks the same question about Mauss's text by questioning why Mauss insists on referring to certain transactions as gifts instead of merely as exchanges: "Mauss tries to restitute, so to speak, the value of the gift . . . where others wanted to describe the same operation of exchange with purely economic, commercial, or fiduciary operation, without needing in the least to have recourse to the category of the gift."[46]

Derrida briefly raises—but quickly rejects—this possibility that the concept of "gift" should be dismissed and replaced with the logic of exchange. He asks: "And since we are saying with such insistence that [the pure gift] is impossible, why not denounce it as an illusion, even as sophism or paralogism, as well as a pseudo-problem that reason would require us, in good logic, to evacuate? Does it not suffice in fact to describe scientifically the objective exchange of values with usurious supplement, in short, the logic of credit, of interest rates, and of repayment due dates?"[47] Eventually, Derrida decides that the gift should not be denounced as an illusion because it is merely the impossible and not

[46] Derrida, *Counterfeit Money*, 42.
[47] Ibid., 42.

the unthinkable. Derrida insists that the gift must be thought. It must be named. Derrida vigorously defends the value of "thinking" the gift and explains that, while the gift is impossible, it is certainly not "unnameable or unthinkable."[48] He even goes so far as to suggest that the gift is among the only things that can be properly named or thought:

Perhaps there is nomination, language, thought, desire, or intention only there where there is the movement still for thinking, desiring, naming that which gives itself neither to be known, experienced, nor lived—in the sense in which presence, existence, determination regulate the economy of knowing, experiencing, and living. . . . One can desire, name, think in the proper sense of these words . . . *only* to the *immeasuring* extent . . . that one desires, names, thinks *still* or *already*, that one still lets announce itself what nevertheless cannot *present itself* as such to experience, to knowing: in short, here *a gift that cannot make itself (a) present* [un don qui ne peut pas se faire présent]. This gap between, on the one hand, thought, language, and desire and, on the other hand, knowledge, philosophy, science, and the order of presence is also a gap between gift and economy.[49]

That is, Derrida maintains that only that which is not measurable can be rightfully named or thought. Economy, with its system of debts and values, can be definitively measured. Therefore, it cannot be properly "thought" or "named" since it is already "known." "In this gap between the impossible and the thinkable a dimension opens up where *there is* gift."[50]

The fart of *The Summoner's Tale* resides in the gap between the impossible and the thinkable. The idea of the fart's being divided by cartwheel can be named, thought, and desired (assuming of course that someone had a reason to desire one-twelfth of a fart). But, like Derrida's gift, it remains impossible. Just as Chaucer invites the reader to "think" the division of the fart, Derrida insists that the reader must "think" the gift even while recognizing that it can never be attained, even while recognizing that the gift will never be "(a) present." But *The Summoner's Tale* thinks the gift in a way that even Derrida's wide-ranging philosophy does not. For Derrida, the gift must be thought in a system of

[48] Ibid., 10.
[49] Ibid., 29.
[50] Ibid., 10. Derrida later notes that the German *es gibt*, literally "it gives," is an idiomatic expression equivalent to English *there is* or French *il y a* (20).

exchange divorced from the giver. *The Summoner's Tale,* however, invites the reader to think the gift in an even more impossible form: as a *logos*-like fart that cannot exist away from its giver but is still somehow a gift.

Perhaps *The Summoner's Tale* can think the gift in this way because the *Canterbury Tales* exists as part of a tradition that Derrida would deem logocentric. The *Canterbury Tales* is a text, and many critics have pointed to references that call attention to the tales' status as material objects, such as when Chaucer invites any displeased readers to "turne over the leef and chese another tale" (I.3177).[51] At the same time, the tales are presented as oral works told by pilgrims on a journey. When the host agrees to ride with them on the condition that each pilgrim tell four tales, he says that whoever wins the contest "[s]hal have a soper at oure aller cost" (I.799). The tales themselves become items of exchange. Harwood, building on a commonplace in Chaucer criticism, notes, "The pilgrims enter into exchange by hearing a tale and thus incurring a determinate obligation."[52] Every tale is told as reciprocation for a previous tale and in turn demands its own reciprocation. Harry Bailey reveals the extent to which economic exchange pervades the structure of tale-telling when he tells the Monk, "Now telleth ye, sir Monk, if that ye konne, / Somwhat to quite with the Knyghtes tale" (I.3118–19). The word "quite" in this case means "to match." But it derives from the earlier meaning "to repay a debt,"[53] a usage that Chaucer himself employs in *The Monk's Tale*: "And she that bar the ceptre ful of floures / Shal bere a distaf hire cost for to quyte" (VII.2373–74). When this earlier meaning is considered, Harry Bailey's suggestion that the monk "quite with the Knyghtes tale" indicates that the tales are quite literally recast as part of an economy, as payment for debt.

R. Allen Shoaf claims that this repayment of debt, this "quiting," is central to the structure of the *Canterbury Tales*, noting that the Miller echoes Harry Bailey's use of *quite*: "'I kan a noble tale for the nones, / With which I wol now quite the Knyghtes tale'" (I.3126–27). Shoaf argues that the Miller then "quites" the Knight by recasting *The Knight's Tale* in his own parodic way: "It cannot be denied that he pays

---

[51] For one such reading, see V. A. Kolve, *Chaucer and the Imagery of Narrative: The First Five Canterbury Tales* (London: Edward Arnold, 1984), 17.

[52] Harwood, "Chaucer and the Gift," 27.

[53] *MED*, s.v. "Quiten."

the Knight back, 'quites' him, by almost retelling *The Knight's Tale*."[54] Insofar as the Miller repays the Knight by retelling a version of the same tale, the exchange exemplifies what Derrida sees as the impossibility of the gift in its most obvious form: "If the other *gives* me *back* or *owes* me or has to give me back what I give him or her, there will not have been a gift. . . . This is all too obvious if the other, the donee, gives me back *immediately* the same thing."[55] The donee's giving back "immediately the same thing" is exactly what happens when the Miller "quites" the Knight by immediately retelling his tale. This event is an "all too obvious" example of how each pilgrim must "quite" the debt in which the previous tale has placed him, how the concept of exchange is woven into the very fabric of the *Canterbury Tales*.

The notion of these oral tales as elements in a system of exchange arises within a world that Derrida would consider logocentric. As with the fart, there is no physical "text" and thus no hope that the gift of the tale will survive the death of its "donor agency." The pilgrims' oral tales cannot exist without the presence of their tellers, their "fathers." But the tales still enter into a giftlike system of exchange. This doubleness informs Chaucer's representation of the fart-gift in the *Canterbury Tales* and allows him to think the gift in a way more extreme than Derrida. In a sense, the fart is its own oral tale, and thus the idea of fart as gift represents the tension that arises from allowing oral tales to enter into a system of exchange. The very idea is in a sense impossible, but the fact that it is thought in *The Summoner's Tale* requires it to exist.

That is, even as *The Summoner's Tale* resists the idea of the gift, it cannot escape it. The text's very attempt to place the gift under erasure necessitates its existence. The occupatio, a ubiquitous rhetorical device for Chaucer, nicely models this paradox. When an author describes something by saying that he cannot describe it, he recognizes the inadequacy of his description. But at the same time, he describes it. Chaucer uses occupatio in *The Squire's Tale* to depict the opulence of Genghis's feast:

---

[54] R. A. Shoaf, *Dante, Chaucer, and the Currency of the Word: Money, Images, and Reference in Late Medieval Poetry* (Norman, Okla.: Pilgrim Books, 1983), 168. Shoaf is referring to what he calls a "long recognized" critical opinion that the Miller "tells, in effect, a parody of [*The Knight's Tale*]—complete with an old man who is a father figure, two suitors, a pretty young woman for them to compete over, etc." *Chaucer's Body: The Anxiety of Circulation in the "Canterbury Tales"* (Gainesville: University Press of Florida, 2001), 96.

[55] Derrida, *Counterfeit Money*, 12.

"I wol nat tellen of hir strange sewes, / Ne of hir swannes, ne of hire heronsewes . . . Ther nys no man that may reporten al. / I wol nat taryen yow, for it is pryme / And for it is no fruyt but los of tyme" (V.67–74). The paradoxical construction, "I wol nat tellen of hir strange sewes," resembles Derrida's "paradoxical instant" since, as soon as the narrator claims that he "wol nat tellen" of the "sewes," he has told of them. Considered in the context of Harwood's argument, the similarity between the squire's occupatio and the gift is not a mere structural coincidence. Harwood argues that Genghis's opulent feast in *The Squire's Tale* represents the excess of the gift. As such, the occupatio applies not only to the banquet, but to the gift in general. Just as the claim that the banquet is indescribable provides a description of the banquet, albeit one unattainable for the narrator, Chaucer's erasure of the gift names the gift. The text's framing of every gift transaction in terms of economic exchange invites the reader to imagine a "gentilesse" that breaks that circle, invites the reader to *think* the gift just as it invites the reader to think the division of the fart.

Given this model of tales as gift, the consideration of the text itself as a gift is inevitable. Could the *Canterbury Tales* themselves be placed into a circle of economic exchange? Probably: after all, Chaucer has received lasting fame in exchange for his work. But perhaps the best answer is simply to heed Derrida and think the gift: a work that has *given* itself to generations of readers, an opus that has opened itself up to centuries of critical *reception*, a *present* from the past that will persist into the future.

Religion, Alchemy, and Nostalgic Idealism in Fragment VIII of the *Canterbury Tales*

Jennifer L. Sisk
The University of Vermont

I
T HAS BEEN SAID of Fragment VIII of the *Canterbury Tales*—the Second Nun's legend of Saint Cecilia and the Canon's Yeoman's exposé of alchemical failure and fraud—that "no other part of the *Tales* contains in two ostensibly unrelated stories such a tight unity of theme and imagery."[1] Long familiar to Chaucerians, this unity paradoxically has been anatomized in terms of a set of oppositions. These oppositions correlate with the overarching contrast established by the two tales between the heavenly clarity of spiritually advantageous activity, illustrated in the Nun's account of Cecilia, and the confusion and deception surrounding alchemy, revealed in the Yeoman's confession and tale.[2] The Yeoman's "elvysshe craft" (751) stands against Cecilia's "feithful bisynesse" (24), raising the specter of sin in the face of the Nun's expression of Christian piety.[3]

I would like to thank Lee Patterson, Traugott Lawler, Isaac Cates, and the anonymous readers for *SAC* for their helpful feedback and encouragement during the various stages of this essay's development.

[1] Glending Olson, "Chaucer, Dante, and the Structure of Fragment VIII (G) of the *Canterbury Tales*," *ChauR* 16 (1982): 222–36 (222–23).

[2] Few analyses of the tales in Fragment VIII leave these contrasts unremarked. Notable among the studies that consider them in detail are Joseph Grennen, "Saint Cecilia's 'Chemical Wedding': The Unity of the *Canterbury Tales*, Fragment VIII," *JEGP* 65 (1966): 466–81; Bruce A. Rosenberg, "The Contrary Tales of the Second Nun and the Canon's Yeoman," *ChauR* 2 (1967–68): 278–91; Olson, "Structure of Fragment VIII"; John Scattergood, "Chaucer in the Suburbs," in *Medieval Literature and Antiquities: Studies in Honour of Basil Cottle*, ed. Myra Stokes and T. L. Burton (Cambridge: D. S. Brewer, 1987), 145–62; Lee Patterson, "Perpetual Motion: Alchemy and the Technology of the Self," *SAC* 15 (1993): 25–57; and John M. Fyler, *Language and the Declining World in Chaucer, Dante, and Jean de Meun* (Cambridge: Cambridge University Press, 2007), 155–88.

[3] All quotations of Fragment VIII of the *Canterbury Tales*, cited parenthetically by line number, are from Larry D. Benson, gen. ed., *The Riverside Chaucer*, 3rd ed. (Boston: Houghton Mifflin, 1987).

Despite the soundness of these observations, the long-standing critical preoccupation with the ways these performances contrast runs the
risk of obfuscating important similarities between them.[4] Although the
Nun and Yeoman have radically different speaking styles and interests,
they share certain habits of thinking about the past, and both—though
in significantly different ways—are idealists.[5] The Nun's legend expresses an ideal in its representation of the purity of the primitive church
and the simple clarity of its Christianity. This portrait resonates with
the idealism underlying certain strains of religious reformist thinking
that looked to early Christianity to criticize the contemporary church
and urge its improvement through a reclamation of an idealized past.
The Nun's tale thus bespeaks a kind of nostalgia.[6] The Yeoman, as we
will see, similarly betrays nostalgia, although in his case it is for alchemy
perfected as he believes it once to have been by the philosophers of a
bygone era. Whereas the Nun merely expresses her nostalgia, the Yeoman draws attention to the impossibility of realizing the object of his
desire and the potential perils of acting upon nostalgic idealism. In this
way his performance casts a shadow on the Nun's otherwise bright tale
and the modes of reformist thinking to which it is obliquely related.

Saint Cecilia and the *ecclesia primitiva*

The Second Nun's Tale stands in sharp contrast to previous Canterbury
tales told by members of the religious establishment because it explores
contemporary religious thinking without actually depicting an aspect of
life in the contemporary church. The Nun instead offers an idealized
portrait of the early church in a hagiographic legend set in the distant
past. She offers no commentary on the reformist discourse to which her

[4] David Raybin also draws attention to this problem, but subsequent criticism has
largely neglected to follow his lead. See " 'And Pave It Al of Silver and of Gold': The
Humane Artistry of the Canon's Yeoman's Tale," in *Rebels and Rivals: The Contestive
Spirit in the "Canterbury Tales,"* ed. Susanna Greer Fein, David Raybin, and Peter C.
Braeger (Kalamazoo, Mich.: Medieval Institute Publications, 1991), 189–212 (190).

[5] My argument takes its inspiration from Donald R. Howard, who years ago stated
very succinctly that "The Second Nun's Tale depicts an ideal; the Canon's Yeoman's
Tale that follows depicts a *failed* ideal" (*Chaucer: His Life, His Works, His World* [New
York: E. P. Dutton, 1987], 493), and from more recent work by James Dean: *The
World Grown Old in Later Medieval Literature* (Cambridge, Mass.: Medieval Academy of
America, 1997), 271–313 (esp. 273).

[6] James Dean observes that while the word *nostalgia* was unavailable to writers in the
later Middle Ages, the attitude toward history revealed in many of their works indicates
that the emotion was familiar to them. See *World Grown Old*, 17.

tale seems to allude but merely engages its ideal by presenting a version of it in her legend of Saint Cecilia.

Cecilia's world, as the Nun depicts it, is one in which truth is both accessible and communicable. Despite the Nun's temporal and cultural separation from this world, her tale-telling is clearly an attempt to participate in it. Her performance is marked as a pious utterance from the outset, opening with a moral exhortation to her listeners to eschew "Ydelnesse" (2) in favor of a life of "leveful bisynesse" (5). She practices what she preaches, personally avoiding sloth by recounting Saint Cecilia's life of pious works. Her prologue makes no reference to Harry Bailly's tale-telling contest, and her performance seems to have nothing to do with any game or competition.[7] Our sense of her presence as tale-teller—weak from the outset, since there is no headlink introducing her and she does not open with any remark that can be construed as self-revealing—weakens further over the course of her prologue until she explicitly removes herself from authorship by insisting that she is not a subtle innovator but merely a reteller of a venerable story:

> Foryeve me that I do no diligence
> This ilke storie subtilly to endite,
> For bothe have I the wordes and sentence
> Of hym that at the seintes reverence
> The storie wroot, and folwen hire legende. . . .
>
> (79–83)

The Nun trusts the "wordes" and the "sentence" of the legend to communicate the transcendent truth of Saint Cecilia's story.[8] This trust in linguistic efficacy enables her, at the conclusion of her prologue, to allow her presence as the narrating "I" to recede almost entirely, leaving her tale to speak for itself. The legend's truth is preexisting and transcendent; she is simply the vehicle by which it is transmitted.

Much of what the Nun understands to be the legend's truth inheres in the figure of Cecilia, whose life and martyrdom the story celebrates.

---

[7] The Nun's performance never actually signals itself as a Canterbury tale, and more than once it calls attention to its existence as a written text rather than a spoken performance (see lines 32–35 and 78–80).

[8] For a more detailed account of the linguistic immediacy underwriting *The Second Nun's Tale*, particularly as it contrasts with the use of language in the Canon's Yeoman's performance, see Patterson, "Perpetual Motion," 32–34. On the role of language in the two tales, see also Fyler, *Language and the Declining World*, 155–88.

She is an emblem of purity uncomplicated by the emotions and desires that motivate most people. When her marriage is arranged according to the custom of her society, she demonstrates her renunciation of worldly pleasure by wearing a hair shirt beneath her gown. Continually in prayer, she fasts every second and third day for the love of Christ and avoids consummating her marriage by orchestrating her new husband's conversion to Christianity. She then persists in a life of faith and good works until her martyrdom, which occurs in a context that literalizes her chastity as immunity to worldly heat. Consigned to a bath of flames, she sits "al coold," feeling "no wo" (521).

Cecilia's life of "leveful bisynesse" consists of relentless work to spread her faith. In the world of the legend—far removed from the debates about Lollard women preachers that exercised the church in Chaucer's day—Cecilia's "prechyng" is openly celebrated (375).[9] The tale implies that in these early days of Christianity it is completely acceptable for women to engage in this manner of doctrinal pedagogy, and that it is in fact the best kind of "bisynesse" because it increases the community of Christians by effecting the conversion of pagans. It is thus through her preaching, rather than wedlock, that chaste Cecilia is fruitful.[10] Her "wise loore" (414) is so persuasive, in fact, that the people she converts go on to become preachers in their own right, bringing still others to the faith in a blessed contagion of conversion. Her husband, Valerian, and brother-in-law, Tiburce, after being brought to their own conversions by Cecilia, convert their pagan tormentors, one of whom then converts his fellows with a report of the brothers' visible ascent to heaven after their martyrdom. The Nun stresses that Cecilia herself—even in the bath of flames to which she is finally consigned, and even after three strokes to her neck have left her "half deed" (533)—still

[9] Explicit references to Cecilia's preaching also occur at lines 342 and 539. Lynn Staley Johnson rightly notes that the tale neither criticizes Cecilia's "ecclesiastical voice" nor makes an explicit argument in favor of contemporary women preachers ("Chaucer's Tale of the Second Nun and the Strategies of Dissent," *SP* 89 [1992]: 314–33 [330]). On the contested issue of female preaching, see Alcuin Blamires, "Women and Preaching in Medieval Orthodoxy, Heresy, and Saints' Lives," *Viator* 26 (1995): 135–52 (see 151 for a discussion of this debate as it pertains specifically to *The Second Nun's Tale*). On the relevance of this debate to Chaucer's tale, see also Sherry L. Reames, "Artistry, Decorum, and Purpose in Three Middle English Retellings of the Cecilia Legend," in *The Endless Knot: Essays on Old and Middle English in Honor of Marie Borroff*, ed. M. Teresa Tavormina and R. F. Yeager (Cambridge: D. S. Brewer, 1995), 177–99 (180–81).

[10] V. A. Kolve emphasizes Cecilia's spiritual fecundity in "Chaucer's *Second Nun's Tale* and the Iconography of Saint Cecilia," in *New Perspectives in Chaucer Criticism*, ed. Donald M. Rose (Norman, Okla.: Pilgrim Books, 1981), 137–74 (151).

never ceases "the feith to teche" (538). The work of preaching, teaching, and conversion is Cecilia's raison d'être, and she persists in it until the moment of her death.

The method and extent of Cecilia's preaching are revealed in greatest detail in the lessons she gives to Tiburce. She teaches him, in turn, about the Trinity, the life of the soul in heaven after death, Christ's life and passion, and Christian redemption. But the lessons themselves are delivered in rudimentary form. When Tiburce asks Cecilia how she, who preaches the existence of a single God, can bear witness to "Fader," "Sone," and "Goost," she answers,

> Right as a man hath sapiences three—
> Memorie, engyn, and intellect also—
> So in o beynge of divinitee,
> Thre persones may ther right wel bee.
>
> (338–41)

Cecilia here draws upon an Augustinian analogy,[11] but she sets forth the comparison without explication, barely scratching the surface of Trinitarian theology. Such a lesson, however, is perfectly adequate. The simplest of doctrinal teaching suffices to sustain the early Christians' clear, uncomplicated faith.[12]

Conversion in the tale is correspondingly unfraught. Valerian's experience is emblematic of the speedy ease with which pagans renounce their former religious commitments to embrace new teachings that convey the clear and simple truth of Christianity. His conversion occurs when an old man (generally taken to be Saint Paul) miraculously appears and reads to him an English version of Ephesians 4:5–6. Isolated as it is from

---

[11] See Fyler, *Language and the Declining World*, 160.

[12] Sherry Reames demonstrates that Chaucer's legend places less emphasis than its sources on the ability and need for a convert to have sophisticated theological understanding, and that he consistently reduced those passages in the sources that provide such explanations. See "The Cecilia Legend as Chaucer Inherited It and Retold It: The Disappearance of an Augustinian Ideal," *Speculum* 55 (1980): 38–57. C. David Benson argues that what Chaucer offers is not so much a reduction of theological ideas as a "dramatized version suitable for poetry" that suggests rather than suppresses the full extent of the theological ideas being conveyed (*Chaucer's Drama of Style: Poetic Variety and Contrast in the "Canterbury Tales"* [Chapel Hill: University of North Carolina Press, 1986], 141). My reading of the tale is more in keeping with Reames's than with Benson's, although the point I wish to make is that the simplicity of doctrine in the tale supports the tale's overall celebration of an early church unencumbered by the burdens of complicated theology, ecclesiology, and ecclesiastical politics.

its larger biblical context, the text conveys a brief and straightforward message:

> O Lord, o feith, o God, withouten mo,
> O Cristendom, and Fader of alle also,
> Aboven alle and over alle everywhere.
>
> (207–9)

This passage does little more than proclaim universal monotheism and a unified Christian community, but for Valerian it is enough. The scriptural part communicates the truth of the whole, and he immediately professes absolute belief: "sother thyng than this, I dar wel say, / Under the hevene no wight thynke may" (214–15). With his voicing of this simple credo, the old man vanishes, and Valerian is baptized on the spot. It is an uncomplicated lesson, an easy miracle, and a quick and conclusive conversion.[13] Tiburce adopts Christianity with similar ease: after only slightly more extensive teaching from Cecilia, he instantly responds, "Whoso that troweth nat this, a beest he is" (288). In this world, conversion is absolute. No one is a Christian in name only, and there is no apostasy.

The black-and-white world of the tale—with its depiction of conversion as an easy and absolute transformation and its ready miracles—lends the legend the overtones of a folktale in which magical wonders are common. People of faith see angels, emissaries from the "bettre lif in oother place" that Cecilia promises Tiburce (323). And the faithful are privy to visions that others cannot see, as evidenced by Tiburce's inability to see Cecilia's and Valerian's floral crowns until after his conversion, even though before it he is able to smell their heavenly bouquet through Valerian's prayer. Miracles occur frequently, and many are indistinguishable from wishes granted. As a reward for his conversion, Cecilia's angel tells Valerian, "Sey what thee list, and thou shalt han thy boone" (234). Tiburce, too, after his conversion is the frequent recipient of miracles: "every maner boone / That he God axed, it was sped ful soone" (356–57). Lest we worry that this mystical-magical realm of wish-fulfillment is too good to be true, Tiburce anticipates our concern,

---

[13] Relating this passage to the tradition going back to Augustine's *Confessions* of conversions catalyzed by reading, Patterson points out that, in contrast to the scene in *The Second Nun's Tale*, "what these scenes usually stress is the complexity of the process and its attendant perils" ("Perpetual Motion," 32).

responding to Valerian's explanation of a miracle by asking, "Seistow this to me / In soothnesse, or in dreem I herkne this?" (260–61). "In dremes . . . han we be / Unto this tyme," Valerian replies, "But now at erst in trouthe oure dwellyng is" (262–64).

As Valerian's words attest, in this early Christian world it is entirely possible to "Bileve aright and knowen verray trouthe" (259). James Dean argues that Cecilia incarnates—and I would add that *The Second Nun's Tale* as a whole expresses—"the simplicity and economy of absolute truth"; here, as he puts it, "we recognize distinctions between truth and falsehood, and truth swiftly triumphs over error."[14] Valerian's immediate assent to the message in the old man's book, with its repetition of the word "one"—"o feith," "o God," "O Cristendom"—is the paradigmatic example. Truth exists, and it is the *one* truth, the only truth that matters. As the tale draws to its conclusion, this unity is repeatedly emphasized.[15] It is reflected in the unified cries of the new Christian converts, who proclaim their faith "with o voys" (420), and in Cecilia's final dialogue with Almachius, which likewise draws attention to the unity that characterizes her faith. When he asks her to tell him of her "religioun" and "bileeve" (427), she protests,

> Ye han bigonne youre questioun folily,
> . . . that wolden two answeres conclude
> In o demande; ye axed lewedly.
> (428–30)

Cecilia speaks in the tradition of bold virgin martyrs facing their tyrant-persecutors, but here she is not merely splitting hairs to make Almachius appear a fool. She in fact voices a version of the ideal that underwrites the Second Nun's performance as a whole. Her religion and her belief are one, just as the tale's depiction of Christianity is unfractured by the presence of sects or competing versions of the faith.

This articulation of idealized Christian unity reminds us that the Nun's portrait of the early church is far removed from the church as it existed in late medieval England. In the world of the tale, the faithful are a persecuted minority, the underdogs in a struggle with authority.

---

[14] James Dean, "Dismantling the Canterbury Book," *PMLA* 100 (1985): 746–62 (748).

[15] Fyler also discusses the tale's emphasis on unity. See *Language and the Declining World*, 164–66.

The Christian leader in the poem, "hooly olde Urban" (185), to whom Cecilia sends her converts to receive baptism, cannot even lead a normal public life but must remain in hiding in the catacombs. Nevertheless, he is part of a network of strong and cheerful Christians who communicate with one another as they work to spread the faith. The church of the tale may not be politically powerful, but it is spiritually strong, composed of faithful believers who are connected through personal relationships forged by teaching and conversion.[16] It is based on human bonds and an experience of shared religion, not on any conceptualization of the church as an institution.

For this reason, it comes as a surprise at the end of the tale when Cecilia's final act on earth is to ask Urban to make her house "perpetuelly a cherche" (546). Cecilia seems to imagine her "feithful bisynesse" continuing even after her death, as the work of preaching, teaching, and conversion continues in the very home she once occupied. To the Nun, this bequest provides evidence of the continuation of Cecilia's truth-spreading mission. She concludes her tale by witnessing to the permanence of the saint's benefaction:

> Hir hous the chirche of Seint Cecilie highte;
> Seint Urban halwed it, as he wel myghte;
> In which, into this day, in noble wyse,
> Men doon to Crist and to his seint servyse.
>
> (550–53)

The Nun asserts an unbroken religious tradition extending from the time of Saint Cecilia up to the present day. But the tale's ending bespeaks the absence of the continuity it imagines. Although the Roman persecution of Christians presumably does not cease with Cecilia's death, the donation of her house as a church symbolizes the emergence of the underground Christian community into the light of day, an emergence into public acceptance and finally the social and political dominance, with its attendant wealth and complexity, that made the church the most powerful institution in the medieval West.[17] The Nun's depiction of Cecilia's purity and the ease and efficacy of her evangelical mission

---

[16] See Johnson, "Strategies of Dissent," 326.

[17] Johnson suggests that, by concluding his version of the legend on this note, Chaucer may mean to signal the tale's relevance to contemporary debates about the church's temporalities. Ibid., 329–30.

paints an idealized portrait of the "radical simplicity" of early Christianity, but in Chaucer's day it was a simplicity that no longer existed.[18]

Idealization of the early church was a vital part of religious reformist discourse in medieval Europe, where, by the high Middle Ages, the church had achieved a level of cultural dominance and material prosperity that led many thinkers to question its purity and integrity. In their criticism of the contemporary institution, these thinkers—and likewise their intellectual descendants in the late Middle Ages—looked back in time to the simplicity of the early church and saw in the *ecclesia primitiva* a Christian ideal that had deteriorated over the course of history.[19] Beginning with Gregory VII's reform efforts, the ideal of the primitive church was conceived as a goal that could be recaptured. This belief spawned various efforts at institutional purification that attempted to return religious practice to such earlier standards as the full common life of the early Christians in Jerusalem, a model most relevant to cloistered religious. In the twelfth century, however, the *ecclesia primitiva* took on a different interpretation that found its authority in the passage in Luke's Gospel describing Christ's sending of the seventy to wander as poor preachers.[20] This interpretation spread widely, influencing such heretical and heterodox groups as the Cathars, Waldensians, and Humiliati, and finding its orthodox realization in the rise of the mendicant orders.[21] In Chaucer's lifetime, it was represented in the thinking of John Wyclif, whose later writings advocate a return to the ideals of the early church and the development of a new religious order, the Ordo Christi, which would consist of poor, simple men in the apostolic tradition, who would devote their lives to pastoral care and Christian teaching.[22]

Reformist thinkers had recourse to the *ecclesia primitiva* as an ideal

---

[18] I borrow the phrase from Johnson (ibid., 327).

[19] For a historical account of the use of the term *ecclesia primitiva* and a discussion of the development of the ideal of the primitive church, including its role in the reform efforts of the high Middle Ages, see Glenn Olsen, "The Idea of the *Ecclesia Primitiva* in the Writings of the Twelfth-Century Canonists," *Traditio* 25 (1969): 61–86.

[20] My discussion of this development follows Malcolm Lambert, *Medieval Heresy: Popular Movements from the Gregorian Reform to the Reformation*, 2nd ed. (Oxford: Blackwell, 1992), 42. The sending of the seventy is described in Luke 10:1–20.

[21] See Lambert, *Medieval Heresy*, on the importance of the *vita apostolica* and the ideal of the primitive church for the Cathars and Waldensians (56–57, 63) and for the Franciscans (91–92, 189–90).

[22] On Wyclif's adoption of the *ecclesia primitiva* as an ideal, see Michael Wilks, "John Wyclif, Reformer, c. 1327–1384," in *Wyclif: Political Ideas and Practice* (Oxford: Oxbow, 2000), 1–15 (11–14).

precisely because it provided them with a useful point of contrast that could be brought to bear on theological and ecclesiological debates as well as on less learned discussions of latter-day problems in the church. It functioned for them as a model to use in comparison with—and in criticism of—contemporary Christianity. These reformers all sought to perfect the Christian religion, its institution and faithful members, through a conscious return to the purity and clarity of the church's originary moment. Attempts to model contemporary existence on the *vita apostolica*, diverse though they were, all were grounded in a desire for simplicity that was a recurrent theme of medieval Christianity— although, as Malcolm Lambert notes, it was sometimes "an illusory simplicity" of a "romanticized early Church."[23]

By placing the legend of Saint Cecilia in the context of the *Canterbury Tales*, Chaucer sets the tale's idealized portrait of the early church into sharp relief against the complexity of the church that forms the religious world of Chaucer's pilgrims. On account of this contrast, and although her tale overtly displays no reformist impulse, the Nun's performance resonates with contemporary reformist thinking. The contemporary church within which Chaucer's tale-tellers make their pilgrimage— unlike Cecilia's church—features schism, a complicated ecclesiastical hierarchy, competing versions of the faith expressed through internal debate, and various failings that some of the pilgrims have already exposed. This contrast would not have escaped Chaucer's original audience, for whom the tale's religious idealism bears witness to a kind of nostalgia for a world in which absolute truth is accessible and the question of how to be a good Christian has a simple and clear answer: in life, the faithful business of evangelism; in death, the crown of martyrdom.[24] It is into this context of nostalgia that the Canon's Yeoman intrudes to offer his own description of longing for a lost ideal.

The Canon's Yeoman and the "slidynge science"

The Canon's Yeoman exhibits nostalgic idealism similar to the Second Nun's, although his pertains to the esoteric medieval science of alchemy, which he believes to have been perfected by ancient philosophers. Alchemy's marginalized status might make the Yeoman's longing appear to

[23] Lambert, *Medieval Heresy*, 86.

[24] David Aers rightly argues that the Second Nun's portrait of the early church is "crucial to the poem's contemporary force." *Faith, Ethics and Church: Writing in England, 1360–1409* (Cambridge: D. S. Brewer, 2000), 40.

be far removed from the Nun's and the concerns of medieval reformist thinkers. Nevertheless, a significant connection becomes evident on consideration of the philosophical side of the medieval science—particularly, its understood spiritual aspects. The craft of alchemy was not only an enterprise aiming to transform base metals into gold but also a philosophy that shared a practical goal with religious reform: the transformation and spiritual improvement of the present world.

Alchemy had been introduced into the Latin west through Arabic learning brought to Spain by the Muslim conquerors. Friars became acquainted with this body of knowledge and played an important role in its dissemination by translating, compiling, and composing alchemical treatises both theoretical and practical in character.[25] From its very beginnings, alchemical discourse had possessed a "quasi-religious tone" that took on a decidedly Christian flavor in the hands of these clerical translators.[26] Drawing on their knowledge of scripture, they used elaborate biblical allegories to describe the mysterious workings of the alchemical *opus*, often comparing the mystical aspects of alchemy to the central mysteries of Christianity.[27] In the words of Petrus Bonus of Ferrara, describing the philosopher's stone, "Alchemy is supernatural and Divine, and in this Stone consists the whole difficulty of the Art. We have need of faith in this matter, just as much as we have need of it in regard to God's miraculous dealings in Scripture."[28]

The treatises repeatedly relate alchemy to the Christian work of re-

[25] In addition to being translators and theoreticians, some of these churchmen were also practitioners, if we accept as evidence the promulgation of acts forbidding clerics and friars from engaging in alchemical endeavors. Legislation against alchemy was periodically passed by the General Councils of the mendicant orders, and it is also the focus of a papal bull issued by Pope John XXII. See Edward H. Duncan, "The Literature of Alchemy and Chaucer's Canon's Yeoman's Tale: Framework, Theme, and Characters," *Speculum* 43 (1968): 633–56 (635–36).

[26] Joseph E. Grennen, "Chaucer and the Commonplaces of Alchemy," *Classica et Mediaevalia* 26 (1965): 306–33 (307).

[27] See Joseph E. Grennen, "The Canon's Yeoman's Alchemical 'Mass,'" *SP* 62 (1965): 546–60 (552–53). A sequence of Christian allegories can be seen in the alchemical treatise *Aurora consurgens*. Its author refers to alchemy as a gift from God, describes the philosopher's stone in words taken from the Song of Songs and Psalms, draws a parallel between the alchemical trinity of body, spirit, and soul and the Christian Trinity, and identifies the alchemical microcosm with Christ. C. G. Jung provides excerpts from this text and an accompanying analysis in *Psychology and Alchemy*, trans. R. F. C. Hull, 2nd ed. (Princeton: Princeton University Press, 1993), 376–96. The first part of the text has been edited and translated as *Aurora Consurgens: A Document Attributed to Thomas Aquinas on the Problem of Opposites in Alchemy*, ed. Marie-Louise von Franz, trans. R. F. C. Hull and A. S. B. Glover (New York: Pantheon, 1966).

[28] Petrus Bonus, *The New Pearl of Great Price*, trans. Arthur Edward Waite (London: J. Elliott and Co., 1894), 124.

demption, and one extensive branch of alchemical allegories even goes so far as to relate the philosopher's stone to the Christian savior.[29] In its most extreme manifestation, the parallel between the alchemical *lapis* and Christ leads to a comparison of alchemical transmutation and transubstantiation. A change in essential substance occurs, and the philosopher's stone, like Christ, effects a species of redemption.[30] The ninth chapter of an alchemical *Codicillus* offers a concise expression of this relation: "And as Jesus Christ, of the House of David, took on human nature for the deliverance and redemption of mankind, who were in the bonds of sin on account of Adam's disobedience, so likewise in our art that which has been wrongfully defiled by one thing is absolved by its opposite; cleansed and delivered from that stain."[31] Medieval alchemists and writers of alchemical treatises understood their discipline as an endeavor devoted to the improvement of created matter, a purification from defilement not unlike Christ's redemption of fallen humanity. Moreover, they believed that the purification accomplished by means of the philosopher's stone would affect not only base metals but also the alchemist's own soul.[32]

[29] The allegorical comparison of the philosopher's stone to Christ appears, for example, in an early fourteenth-century alchemical treatise, *De secretis naturae*, attributed to Arnold of Villanova (a supposed alchemical authority whom Chaucer names in *The Canon's Yeoman's Tale*). The same parallel is drawn in the *Exempla de arte philosophorum*, also a fourteenth-century composition. See H. L. Ogrinc, "Western Society and Alchemy from 1200 to 1500," *JMH* 6 (1980): 103–32 (107).

[30] Jung writes, "One might be tempted to explain the symbolism of alchemical transformation as a parody of the Mass were it not pagan in origin and much older than the latter" (*Psychology and Alchemy*, 313). He goes on to discuss the parallel drawn in alchemical treatises between the philosopher's stone and Christ (345–431). Jung's work is inspired by the discovery of an early sixteenth-century text by Nicholas Melchior of Hermannstadt, which expounds the alchemical process explicitly in the form of the Christian mass, with Introit, Kyrie, Collect, Gradual, etc. He provides excerpts from this text with an accompanying discussion (396–406). While this text clearly postdates Chaucer, the basic ideas underlying Melchior's presentation of the alchemical *opus*, as well as allegories describing alchemy specifically in terms of Christ's death and resurrection, were common in alchemical tracts contemporary with Chaucer. On this point, see also Grennen, "Alchemical 'Mass,'" 552–53.

[31] "Et ut Jesus Christus de stirpe Davidica pro liberatione et dissolutione generis humani, peccato captivati, ex transgressione Adae, naturam assumpsit humanam, sic etiam in arte nostra quod per unum nequiter maculatur, per aliud suum contrarium a turpitudine illa absolvitur, lavatur et resolvitur." Jean Jacques Manget, ed., *Bibliotheca chemica curiosa*, vol. 1 (Geneva, 1702; repr., Bologna: A. Forni, 1976), 884; cited in Jung, *Psychology and Alchemy*, trans. Hull, 358. The text has been attributed to Raymond Llull but may have been written by a Spanish or Provençal devotee of the science.

[32] Sheila Delany offers a description of this aspect of medieval alchemical thinking: "The transmutation of metal into gold became an effort by one part of nature to help another to become its best self. It was seen as a charitable and redemptive act whose

Belief in alchemy was ubiquitous in medieval Europe. Even such learned authorities as Albertus Magnus and Thomas Aquinas accepted it as a theoretical possibility, and others believed that the alchemical *opus* had actually been achieved.[33] The thirteenth-century *Summa perfectionis* models the response of such believers to an implied audience of skeptics: "If they say that philosophers and leading men of this world have desired this science and have not found it, we answer that they lie. For we read that certain leaders (though few) and especially the ancient, and wise men of our time have by their own industry found out . . . this science, but would not either by word or by writings discover it to such men because they are unworthy of it."[34]

By Chaucer's time, skepticism about the possibility of achieving alchemical success had increased, but the theoretical feasibility of transmutation continued to be generally recognized.[35] The legislation against alchemical practice that was promulgated by religious authorities never attacked the basic premises of the philosophy. Even the papal bull issued by Pope John XXII did not define alchemical belief as heresy but instead took issue with men merely posing as alchemists while practicing fraud and counterfeiting money.[36] Some late medieval poets echoed this denunciation, similarly focusing on alchemical deceit.[37] But this sort of objection does not bespeak disbelief. Alchemy remained a tantalizing

---

successful performance also required the transmutation of human nature into its refined and perfected Possible: a moral as well as a scientific discipline, whose interior laboratory was the practitioner's soul." "Run Silent, Run Deep: Heresy and Alchemy as Medieval Versions of Utopia," in *Medieval Literary Politics: Shapes of Ideology* (Manchester: Manchester University Press, 1990), 1–18 (12).

[33] For a discussion of the belief in alchemy among medieval scholars and poets, see Ogrinc, "Western Society and Alchemy," 104–14.

[34] Cited by Duncan, "Literature of Alchemy," 642. The *Summa perfectionis* is attributed in the manuscripts to Jabir or Gerberus (Geber).

[35] See Duncan, "Literature of Alchemy," 643. England was a locus of alchemical enthusiasm, so famous for the quality of its alchemists that continental scholars began traveling there in order to translate English treatises. As Christine Chism notes, "So widespread was the mania that soon after Chaucer's death, King Henry IV passed his edict of 1404 banning alchemical gold-making, for fear of the effect it would have on the national economy should even a fraction of its practitioners succeed." "I Demed Hym Som Chanoun For to Be," in *Chaucer's Pilgrims: An Historical Guide to the Pilgrims in the "Canterbury Tales,"* ed. Laura C. Lambdin and Robert T. Lambdin (Westport, Conn.: Greenwood, 1996), 340–56 (350).

[36] See Ogrinc, "Western Society and Alchemy," 114.

[37] Dante, in cantos XXIX and XXX of the *Inferno*, treats alchemy as a variety of deceit by placing alchemists in the circle of hell where falsifiers are punished. Langland, in Passus 10 of the B-text of *Piers Plowman*, likewise describes alchemical experiments as false endeavors designed to deceive people.

possibility. The simple fact that spurred interest and sustained belief was that no one was able to offer definitive proof that it was a pseudoscience, that the transmutation of base metals was in fact an impossible dream.

In the absence of solid evidence disproving alchemy, medieval alchemists had to find a way to rationalize their repeated failures. Rather than taking their lack of success to mean that transmutation could never happen, they drew upon their awareness of the long history of their craft to assert the idea that their current difficulties signaled a deterioration in alchemical philosophy over the ages. In this interpretation, medieval alchemists were not unlike contemporary churchmen, as the reformers saw them, in that the passage of time had brought them further away from the original truth of their discipline. For alchemists, this felt distance from the truth was compounded by the cryptic obscurity of the very language used in the treatises to explain alchemical philosophy and practice.[38] Efforts by these writers to describe the complex mystery of the *opus*, and to do so in figurative language that would protect it from the profanation of the unworthy, resulted in a richly impenetrable discourse so replete with specialized terminology that clear description of alchemy and naming of the philosopher's stone was impossible.[39] As a result, latter-day alchemists faced a task of recovery that, if not likewise impossible, was very difficult indeed. Chaucer's contemporary John Gower, for instance, writes of modern alchemists that they futilely seek the philosopher's stone with no returns on their labor:

> Thei speken faste of thilke Ston,
> Bot hou to make it, nou wot non
> After the sothe experience.[40]

---

[38] As John M. Fyler points out, "The alchemist's nostalgia, from his world of confusion, proliferative materials, and opaque jargon, is in some part a longing for the world of transparent language before Babel." "Domesticating the Exotic in the Squire's Tale," *ELH* 55 (1988): 1–26 (12).

[39] The *Morienus*, a twelfth-century alchemical treatise, asserts that "it is only the multitude of terms which causes the masters in this operation to err"; likewise, Petrus Bonus of Ferrara acknowledges in the *Pretiosa margarita novella* that the philosopher's stone "has as many names as there are things, or names of things" (cited by Patterson, "Perpetual Motion," 40, 41–42).

[40] John Gower, *Confessio Amantis*, ed. Russell A. Peck (New York: Holt, Rinehart and Winston, 1966; repr., Toronto: University of Toronto Press, 1980), book 4, lines 2581–83.

The idea of loss is prevalent in alchemical literature, conveying a sense of longing for the ancient philosophers' knowledge of how to achieve alchemical perfection.

Loss and longing permeate the Canon's Yeoman's performance. Nostalgia for a bygone golden age, in which practicing alchemists—the "Philosophres"—concluded their *opus* successfully, underwrites his confession and receives full expression near the end of his tale:[41]

> Philosophres speken so mystily
> In this craft that men kan nat come therby,
> For any wit that men han now-a-dayes.
> They mowe wel chiteren as doon jayes,
> And in hir termes sette hir lust and peyne,
> But to hir purpos shul they nevere atteyne.
>
> (1394–99)

His depiction of the present state of alchemical affairs—the way things are "now-a-dayes"—conveys the idea of a world lacking what it once possessed in a better past that was richer in learning.[42] The Yeoman's concluding citations of alchemical philosophers likewise emphasize that the old knowledge is now shrouded in mystery and therefore, for all practical purposes, inaccessible. Arnold of the Newe Toun, the Yeoman says, admonishes would-be alchemists not to pursue the craft if they cannot understand "th'entencioun and speche / Of philosophres" (1443–44). The Yeoman cites a dialogue between Plato and his disciple Senior Zadith to dramatize the extreme difficulty of deciphering the philosophers' language. "Telle me the name of the privee stoon," Senior

---

[41] Although *The Riverside Chaucer* follows the rubrication of the Ellesmere manuscript by printing the text as *The Canon's Yeoman's Prologue* (lines 554–719) followed by a two-part *Canon's Yeoman's Tale* (consisting of *Prima Pars*, lines 720–971, and *Pars Secunda*, lines 972–1481), this editorial choice poses significant interpretive problems, since the obvious dividing point marking the end of the Yeoman's "prologue" occurs at the break between *Prima Pars* and *Pars Secunda*. It is more useful for my purposes to follow E. Talbot Donaldson, who prints the three parts of the text as Introduction, Prologue, and Tale in *Chaucer's Poetry: An Anthology for the Modern Reader* (New York: Ronald Press, 1958). On the soundness of Donaldson's choice, see Patterson, "Perpetual Motion," 25 n. 1. What I call the Yeoman's "confession" consists of his Introduction and Prologue, since he speaks about himself in both.

[42] On the connotations of the expression *nowadays* in Middle English literature including Chaucer, see J. D. W. Crowther, "'Now-Adaies': A Rhetorical *Topos*," *Revue de l'Université d'Ottawa* 48 (1978): 270–82.

requests of his master (1452). But each answer that Plato supplies requires a further definition, until Senior accuses him of proceeding *"igno-tum per ignocius,"* explaining what is unknown by means of something even more unknown (1457). Rather than allow this frustrating explanatory process to continue indefinitely, Plato finally reveals to his disciple the underlying cause of their linguistic impasse:

> The philosophres sworn were everychoon
> That they sholden discovere it unto noon,
> Ne in no book it write in no manere.
> For unto Crist it is so lief and deere
> That he wol nat that it discovered bee,
> But where it liketh to his deitee
> Men for t'enspire, and eek for to deffende
> Whom that hym liketh; lo, this is the ende.
> (1464–71)

Alchemy, in other words, is part of "Goddes pryvetee"—it is one of the mysteries of the faith that modern practitioners must trust in but cannot understand without divine revelation.

The Yeoman's performance on the road to Canterbury suggests a deep frustration with his difficulty gaining access to "the secree of the secretes" that is the philosopher's stone (1447). It is clear that he and the Canon have spent the past seven years operating under the assumption that alchemical transmutation is feasible in theory and might even be realizable in the laboratory. The Yeoman's lengthy description of their ingredients, equipment, and alchemical procedures provides a glimpse of men engaged in all-consuming work. "Ascaunce that craft is so light to leere?" the Yeoman asks the other pilgrims (838), emphasizing the difficulty of alchemy but simultaneously implying that it is a legitimate craft that *could* be learned. This sense of possibility underwrites the numerous admissions of longing and "good hope" (870) that punctuate his confession, and it explains why he has become addicted to the alchemical pursuit. He understands, with utter psychological clarity, why he has persisted:

> The philosophres stoon,
> Elixer clept, we sechen faste echoon;
> For hadde we hym, thanne were we siker ynow.
> (862–64)

For the Yeoman, alchemy offers something true and real: a fundamental security that he currently lacks. Possession of the philosopher's stone would for him be similar to the direct experience of truth that Cecilia and her converts enjoy, but such secure truth remains beyond his ken. And so he says, as if with a sigh, "Now wolde God my wit myghte suffise / To tellen al that longeth to that art!" (715–16). His wish to tell the whole art bespeaks his much deeper desire to know the whole art.

While the Yeoman's hopes and desires reveal his belief in the theoretical feasibility of alchemy, the portrait of practical alchemy in his confession is one of profound failure, for not only does he possess incomplete knowledge of the craft, but so does his master, the Canon. A laboratory accident he describes reveals not only the "wo," "rancour," and "ire" (919) that ensue after an alchemical mistake but also the confusion, as each apprentice and his master offers a different explanation of what went wrong, and it is clear that no one really knows. The Yeoman quotes the Canon's indecisive conclusion: "Ther was defaute in somwhat, wel I woot" (954). The Yeoman's speech is peppered with expressions of alchemical failure and despair, which counterbalance the hope he also admits. Again and again he reiterates their disappointment: "For alle oure sleightes we kan nat conclude" (773); "Noght helpeth us; oure labour is in veyn" (777); "lost is al oure labour and travaille" (781); "We faille of that which that we wolden have" (958). Hope in the possibility of success and desire for the goal sustain these alchemists, but they are trapped in a relentless cycle of trial and error.[43]

The necessity of repeatedly trying again—of making new and varied attempts to get it right this time—seems to underlie the Yeoman's obsessive attention to the various materials of his craft. His confession is in effect a series of autobiographical vignettes interspersed within an inordinately long list of the things that alchemists need for their work. But this fixation on the material aspects of alchemy points up a significant absence in the Yeoman's account. His description of his alchemical efforts with the Canon lacks the characteristic religious overtones of contemporary alchemical treatises, suggesting that their work possesses a spiritual barrenness parallel to its material fruitlessness. He does not use the typical religious allegories to describe their purposes, nor does he draw any analogy between their efforts and Christian redemption. As

---

[43] Traugott Lawler describes the "interplay of hope with loss and failure" in the Yeoman's speech, noting that the subject "provides a kind of refrain for him." *The One and the Many in the "Canterbury Tales"* (Hamden, Conn.: Archon, 1980), 134–35.

far as we can tell from his confession, their work carries no moral or spiritual force. They apparently fail to achieve the purifying and redemptive effects of alchemy not only for the materials upon which they work but also for their own souls. This absence is made the more conspicuous by the Yeoman's reference at the end of his performance to Christ as the keeper of alchemy's secret. Only in this concluding gesture—which he makes by way of renouncing his craft once and for all— does he acknowledge any relation, literal or allegorical, between alchemy and Christianity.

The Yeoman's tale is even further from depicting alchemy's spiritual mission: in contrast to his confession, his tale is not an account of genuine alchemical effort but rather a story of alchemy as a cover for fraud. The tale describes a canon who dupes a priest by merely pretending to perform the alchemical *opus*, convincing the priest to buy his fraudulent secret for forty pounds. Unlike the confession, the tale carries considerable religious significance, but it does not pertain to the spiritual value or peril that may inhere in alchemy itself. Instead, it has to do with the diabolical nature of deceit, for which the canon is the tale's emblem.[44] The Yeoman calls him "this feendly wrecche" (1158) and describes his itinerancy—"he is heere and there; / He is so variaunt, he abit nowhere" (1174–75)—in a way that suggests an affiliation with the devil. There is no evidence that this canon actually understands the secrets of alchemy or even desires them as the Yeoman and his Canon clearly do.[45] The tale's would-be alchemist is actually the priest, who is fooled not only by the canon but also by his own wishful thinking. The tale thus

[44] See Patterson, "Perpetual Motion," 38. A more extreme view is set forth by Bruce Rosenberg, whose argument that the canon of the tale is a figure for Antichrist revised the former speculation that Chaucer himself was favorably inclined toward alchemy. See "Swindling Alchemist, Antichrist," *Centennial Review* 6 (1962): 566–80, esp. 578. See also Grennen, who reads the tale as a parody of the Christian mass and therefore evidence of "Chaucer's vision of alchemy as a diabolical betrayal through what is at best an amusing mimicry, at worst a profane parody of the Work of Creation and Redemption" ("Alchemical Mass," 553).

[45] Lawler draws a careful distinction between the activities and motivation of the canon in the Yeoman's tale and the canon who is the Yeoman's former master. The canon in the tale is "a typical confidence man, an out-and-out cheat," and the tale gives "no indication that he actually practices alchemy"; instead, as Lawler points out, "he practices only on his victims; his only aim is to enrich himself by cheating others." By contrast, the Yeoman's former master wants to enrich himself as much as does the canon in the tale, but "he focuses his hope not on a confidence game but on experiment," attracting others to his work, who "become his associates rather than his victims" (*The One and the Many*, 130).

illustrates how someone susceptible to idealistic hopes may be duped by pragmatic charlatans, and by extension how such idealism can blind its victims to the realities in the world around them.

With the tale's portrait of alchemical deception, the Yeoman draws our attention retrospectively to a passage in his introduction that suggests his own rather different complicity in deceit. Describing the frustrations that he and the Canon have experienced, he admits,

> To muchel folk we doon illusioun,
> And borwe gold, be it a pound or two,
> Or ten, or twelve, or manye sommes mo,
> And make hem wenen, at the leeste weye,
> That of a pound we koude make tweye.
>
> (673–77)

The Yeoman and the Canon have never achieved the kind of success that would pay for their continued efforts, so they have needed to persuade others to invest in their experiments. The Yeoman even admits to being "endetted so therby" (734) that he will "it quite nevere" (736). His talk of borrowing and debt suggests honest transactions entered into with good intentions, but the specter of deceit is raised by his reference to the "illusioun" they perform to make people suppose they can succeed despite their formidable record of failure.[46]

The Yeoman does suggest that alchemical failure and deceit are inextricably linked. Explaining to his audience the financial perils of his craft, the Yeoman warns,

> What maner man that casteth hym therto,
> If he continue, I holde his thrift ydo.
> For so helpe me God, therby shal he nat wynne,
> But empte his purs and make his wittes thynne.

[46] Duncan fails to recognize the ambiguity in the passage, arguing that the Yeoman and his Canon are simply con-men, who "have overtaken the Canterbury pilgrims with the rather obvious intent of wangling money from them, the yeoman acting as a come-on man by hinting at his master's marvelous powers" ("Literature of Alchemy," 638). The textual evidence does not support this claim, however. A more nuanced reading is provided by Lawler, who points out that if the Yeoman and Canon are playing their own confidence game, "it is so infinitely more elaborate, long-term, committed, and communal an enterprise, so much closer to the wellsprings of hope and trust, so much more 'ernest' than 'game,' as to constitute in any case an utter contrast to the second canon's simple bilking of the priest, the brief work of a few hours" (*The One and the Many*, 131).

And whan he thurgh his madnesse and folye
Hath lost his owene good thurgh jupartye,
Thanne he exciteth oother folk thereto,
To lesen hir good as he hymself hath do.

(738–45)

The phenomenon that the Yeoman describes here is a different kind of betrayal of innocence from that featured in his tale—not outright fraud but the involvement of others in alchemy's expenses and attendant losses. The hypothetical alchemist depicted by the Yeoman cannot cease his pursuit upon losing his own wealth but, even when bankrupt, continues his quest for the elusive philosopher's stone by drawing upon the wealth of others and ultimately losing it forever—and all on account of his belief that what the philosophers of old claim to have possessed might actually be attainable now. Thus, what starts out as a good-faith effort to investigate a mysterious science grows into the alchemist's all-consuming effort to reclaim a lost ideal—an effort that causes him to squander his present goods and even lose touch with basic moral instincts to the extent that he feels no compunction about ruining his friends. This almost inescapable descent into abuse may be what prompts the Yeoman to call his craft a "slidynge science" (732). As he describes it, even the best-intentioned alchemists are at risk. Indeed, the point of the Yeoman's strange performance seems to be that "now-a-dayes" it is very hard to tell when alchemy is, and when it is not—to borrow the Second Nun's language—"leveful business."

The Yeoman's recognition of his susceptibility to the perils of alchemy provides the subtext of his entire performance, which concludes with his renunciation of his craft. But what he renounces is only the pursuit and not his belief in alchemy per se. In the words of Robert Longsworth, "At the conclusion of his tale, for all his disillusionment, the Canon's Yeoman remains a true believer."[47] After reciting the dialogue between Plato and Senior Zadith that ends with the identification of Christ as the keeper of the philosopher's stone, the Yeoman concludes,

sith that God of hevene
Ne wil nat that the philosophres nevene
How that a man shal come unto this stoon,

[47] Robert M. Longsworth, "Privileged Knowledge: St. Cecilia and the Alchemist in the *Canterbury Tales*," *ChauR* 27 (1992): 87–96 (89). See also Fyler, *Language and the Declining World*, 172.

> I rede, as for the beste, lete it goon.
> For whoso maketh God his adversarie,
> As for to werken any thyng in contrarie
> Of his wil, certes, never shal he thryve,
> Thogh that he multiplie terme of his lyve.
>
> (1472–79)

His ability to say good riddance to the Canon—"the foule feend hym quelle!" he exclaims upon his master's departure (705)—suggests that as far as his own alchemical pursuit is concerned, he hopes to take his own advice to let it go and not offend God. But his persisting belief in alchemical feasibility and his need to articulate a divine prohibition in order to realize his renouncement of the practice reveal his inability to overcome his longing for what he believes the ancient philosophers possessed. His desire remains, and with it his nostalgic attitude toward the past. Nevertheless, he declares that he will no longer act upon the nostalgic idealism that previously has driven him. His abandonment of alchemical practice is thus a pragmatic rejection of a quest for an inaccessible ideal, which—in its effect on his daily life—causes him to deny the moral and practical exigencies of his current situation. The renunciation draws attention to the potential perils of willful ignorance and self-deception that may be attendant upon pursuits grounded in nostalgic idealism. Such nostalgic idealism is at the root of the Yeoman's problems, and, as we have seen, it is a way of thinking about the past that the Second Nun shares, although the focus of her interest is different and she exhibits none of the Yeoman's evident anguish.

Veneration and Imitation of the Past

An analogy can therefore be drawn between the Nun's and Yeoman's performances and between medieval alchemy, esoteric and marginalized though it was, and a central strain of religious reformist thinking. Alchemy was an enterprise focused on reclaiming the crippling loss of the knowledge and practices of its originary moment. Alchemists understood their ultimate goal, the philosopher's stone, as the attainment of the highest philosophical and spiritual truth: it was the elixir, the quintessence, the knowledge of the philosophers, the wisdom of God. And the effort to achieve this goal entailed the redemption, purification, and perfection of both nature and the self. Many religious reformers, in comparison, desired a return to the spirituality of the church's originary moment, represented by the *ecclesia primitiva* and manifested in the *vita apostolica*, ideals that defined Christian identity for these thinkers. Their goal, like the alchemists', was spiritual improvement that would bring them closer to God, and their efforts likewise sought purification and refinement, a stripping away of the base accretions that wealth and worldly power had brought to the church. Just as the alchemical *opus* was believed to improve both the natural world and the alchemist's soul, so too religious reform, as the reformers conceived it, was work that would improve both the church and the practicing Christians within it.

The nostalgic idealism expressed by the Second Nun and described and criticized, with respect to alchemy, by the Canon's Yeoman grows out of a fundamental way of thinking about history and human potential that was dominant in Chaucer's time. A model of decline, though not universally embraced, formed the basis of most medieval theories of historical change.[48] According to this model, the past was a golden age of simplicity and moral rectitude, when truth was accessible and people were stronger. This way of thinking was foundational to Christian orthodoxy, which viewed the time from creation to the present as an ongoing process of estrangement from God, precipitated by the Fall and bound to continue in the current age until Christ's second coming. The standard outline of history accepted by most medieval intellectuals divided the time since creation into six ages, the last of which had been inaugurated by Christ's life and passion. Although the Christian dispensation had introduced to humanity the possibility of salvation, the world in the Christian era had degenerated from the time of the early church, as could be witnessed in the decline in Christian virtues among the faithful and the institutional problems that plagued the contemporary church. Attendant upon this conceptualization of history, in which the current era was understood to lack the fundamental goodness of the past, was a profound sense of loss and longing for what once was.

---

[48] For an introduction to this topic of intellectual history, see Dean, *World Grown Old*, 1–111. Dean notes that models of progress were never dominant in the intellectual climate of the Middle Ages, though they surfaced from time to time in such schemata as the tripartite division of history before the law, under the law, and under grace; in Anselm of Havelberg's idea of the progress of the church; and in Joachim of Fiore's belief that the world was entering upon a third age of spiritual men (109–10). However, such views of history stood in sharp contrast to the usual medieval view, which was based instead on a model of decline. Dean provides a basic outline of history according to this model (3–4).

This model of historical decline provided the context for a great number of intellectual enterprises in the Middle Ages, including both religious reform and alchemy. For reformist thinkers, it authorized a look back to the *ecclesia primitiva* for models with which to illuminate by contrast the problems of the contemporary church. In Chaucer's time, the connection between the idea of historical decline and reformist impulses was articulated with particular force in the thinking of Wyclif, who castigated the contemporary ecclesiastical hierarchy for corrupting the traditions of the early church, all the while recognizing this degeneration as a feature of the world's senescence.[49] For Wyclif, as for so many reformist thinkers, the early church was a better church—simpler, purer, and closer to God—to whose values and practices he longed for the church of his own day to return. For medieval alchemists, the attitude toward the past was similar. The model of historical decline authorized their belief in the feasibility of their craft, whose secrets, they believed, were once known by philosophers but had become indecipherable through the figurative language used to convey alchemy's spiritual significance and through the linguistic accretions of increasingly feeble attempts to explain its practice. For alchemists, as for reformist thinkers, the world had degenerated and something precious had been lost.

The case of medieval alchemy is instructive because it illuminates with particular clarity a fundamental problem dooming enterprises motivated by nostalgic idealism and contextualized within a model of historical decline. The problem with alchemy is abundantly clear, as medieval theoreticians and practitioners conceived it, and as the Canon's Yeoman's renunciation vividly illustrates. The world was degenerating, but alchemy, performed successfully with complete knowledge of the craft, could reverse this decline by helping the elements in nature and human souls achieve their physical and spiritual perfection. However, in order to use alchemy successfully, one had to possess the very knowledge that had been lost due to the historical decline that alchemy sought to reverse. Medieval alchemy thus was fueled by two incompatible attitudes toward human potential: one pessimistic, located within the context of a world that had degenerated and lost the advantages of an earlier era, and one optimistic, grounded in the utopian premise that

---

[49] Ibid., 76. On Wyclif's ideas about the degeneration of the world, see also chapter 4 of Penn R. Szittya, *The Antifraternal Tradition in Medieval Literature* (Princeton: Princeton University Press, 1986), esp. 161–67.

perfection was possible in the here and now through human intervention in the established order of things.[50]

This fundamental contradiction within alchemy points to a similar problem in the strain of reformist thinking I have been considering. For reformist thinkers, too, the world was degenerating, and even in the Christian dispensation things had been better at the beginning. Hence derived the numerous attempts to recuperate the *vita apostolica*, the practices, habits, and values of the early Christians. But the very context of historical decline—the inescapable consequence of the Fall—doomed this attempted recuperation because it required reversing the thrust of salvation history. And, for Chaucer's audience, not only the logic of decline but also the state of affairs in the medieval world revealed the impossibility of such a reversal. By Chaucer's day, history had transformed not only the world but also the church within it far beyond any easy identification with the *ecclesia primitiva*. The conditions that had pertained then—when Christians were a minority in Europe and actively persecuted by powerful political institutions—no longer existed. The late medieval church was itself a dominant political institution possessing both property and power, splintered since 1378 and plagued by debates on issues ranging from sacramentalism to the relation between papal and royal authority. As Lynn Staley Johnson aptly notes, it had become "no longer either simple or one."[51] In light of what history had done to the church, the reformist yearning for the *ecclesia primitiva* appears as futile as a quest for the philosopher's stone.

The juxtaposition of the Second Nun's and Canon's Yeoman's performances thus calls our attention to the unbridgeable distance between the idealized pasts represented or alluded to in these tales and the contemporary world of Chaucer's pilgrims. *The Second Nun's Tale*, with its depiction of the age of the martyrs when Christianity was young, provides a moment of respite from the contemporary scene. But the modernity of the Yeoman's performance—its belatedness, its sense of urgency,

---

[50] As Chism puts it, alchemy is a discipline that "acknowledges corruption, but stresses its power to transform, enliven, and recuperate" ("I Demed Hym Som Chanoun," 353). Patterson discusses how Chaucer manifests this alchemical paradox in the character of the Canon's Yeoman, who "prefigures a disenchanted rationalism eager to dominate the natural world" and simultaneously "bespeaks a yearning, heightened by the possibility of loss, for the value-laden, animated universe of traditional religion" ("Perpetual Motion," 55). For a description of alchemy's utopianism, see Delany, "Run Silent, Run Deep," 11.

[51] Johnson, "Strategies of Dissent," 329.

and its consciousness of historical contingency—marks an abrupt return to the present, to the difficulties of the here and now.[52] As Dean points out, the Yeoman's performance "posits a more complex view of reality" than the Second Nun's Tale,[53] and in so doing it draws attention to the problems implicit in the Nun's apparent longing for an idealized past. Such a portrait of the early church is different indeed from the reality of Chaucer's pilgrims, whose piety will not be rewarded with the crown of martyrdom lovingly held out to Cecilia's converts, and whose church faces internal problems far more complex than abuse from outsiders. The Nun's assertion of continuity between the church of Saint Cecilia and the contemporary church therefore not only draws attention to the contrast between them—thereby, for reformist thinkers, opening up a means of critique—but also lays open the impossibility of the fantasy it expresses. In the context of the *Canterbury Tales*, the legend suggests a willed denial of the difficulties of modern life. Its representation of the early church may be the expression of a venerable ideal, but—as the modernity of the Yeoman's performance will not allow us to forget—it is an ideal whose time has passed.

The Yeoman's performance thus carries critical implications for the Second Nun's tale. While he admits that he is unable to let go of his longing for what he believes men possessed in the past, he recognizes that what he desires is inaccessible and therefore renounces his destructive efforts to achieve it. His renunciation—based as it is on his recognition of the perils of a nostalgia that focuses so obsessively on the past that it ignores the problems and responsibilities of the present—obliquely hints at the similar perils that might endanger an attempt to recuperate the past idealized in the Nun's tale. The Nun's and Yeoman's performances are grounded in similar nostalgia for a time when truth was more accessible, knowledge greater, and spirituality purer. But while Chaucer allows the Nun simply to voice nostalgia, he uses the Yeoman's performance to critique it. Had Chaucer's legend of Saint Cecilia not been included in the *Canterbury Tales* and joined with the Canon's Yeoman's performance, the hagiography would not resonate with these concerns.[54]

[52] On the Canon's Yeoman as the "irresolute spokesman" of Chaucerian modernity, see Patterson, "Perpetual Motion," 57.

[53] Dean, "Dismantling the Canterbury Book," 749.

[54] It is thus unproductive to view the Second Nun's performance as "unmediated by larger context," as V. A. Kolve has claimed. While I disagree with this statement, Kolve is otherwise right to point out that "second only to *The Parson's Tale*, . . . *The Second*

I do not mean to imply by the analogy I have drawn between medieval alchemy and reformist thinking that Chaucer's use of the legend of Saint Cecilia in the context of the *Canterbury Tales* suggests that religious reform per se is misguided. It is clear that Chaucer, like so many thinkers of his age, saw reasons to reflect critically on the contemporary church and recognized that one way to do so was through a comparison with the *ecclesia primitiva*.[55] But the eighth fragment of the *Canterbury Tales* suggests that, while such a comparison can illuminate contemporary problems, an attempt to recuperate the early model is an unlikely solution, particularly when it cannot apply to contemporary circumstances. As the Yeoman's performance implies, such an attempt may do more harm than good if it becomes an obsession that blinds the devotee to present realities. In the context of the *Canterbury Tales*, then, the portrait of the early church in the legend of Saint Cecilia emerges as one to be revered but not imitated: *non imitanda set veneranda*.[56] The Yeoman's performance functions as a cautionary reminder of the possible danger in confusing veneration of the past with potentially harmful attempts at its imitation.

But if recuperative efforts motivated by nostalgic idealism are risky, then what possibilities for positive action remain in the face of contemporary problems? An understanding of history as a process of decline offers no theoretical space for a concept of progress. Invention that goes against the grain of nostalgia, however enticing, is itself colored by pessimism: the model of a declining world, while dictating the impossibility of cultural recuperation, simultaneously testifies against the hope of novel action, since innovation can only arise in the already fallen present moment. But for Chaucer, the poetic enterprise seems to have offered a third alternative. It is true that, while he allows his art to register contemporary woes, including the problems facing the church, in the

---

Nun's Tale is the most absolute of the Canterbury narratives—uncompromised by irony . . . and uncolored by the idiosyncrasies of a personal narrative voice" ("Iconography of Saint Cecilia," 156–57).

[55] See Aers, *Faith, Ethics and Church*, 50.

[56] This formula was used by medieval canon lawyers to discuss, among other things, certain kinds of hagiographic precedents that were considered to be potentially disruptive. See Bruce C. Brasington, "*Non Imitanda set Veneranda*: The Dilemma of Sacred Precedent in Twelfth-Century Canon Law," *Viator* 23 (1992): 135–52 (esp. 142–48). Although the formula was usually used in relation to saints who exhibited problematic behavior, it is similarly appropriate here. For a reading of Cecilia not as a role model but rather as "a measure of the limits of possibility," see David Raybin, "Chaucer's Creation and Recreation of the *Lyf of Seynt Cecile*," *ChauR* 32 (1997): 196–212 (209).

end he stops short of espousing a clear agenda for real-world change. Nevertheless, a kind of change—an effort somewhere in between invention and recuperation that we might call renovation—is unmistakable in his poetry. In the realm of the literary, Chaucer is nothing if not renovative, characteristically deploying with a difference inherited narratives and genres. This approach seems to run athwart the ideology of a world in decline in that it allows the materials of the past to be accessed and recast in new ways as present innovations. Chaucer's engagement with literary possibility thus holds significant cultural implications, suggesting as it does novel uses of the past that do not stem from nostalgic idealism.

But if, for much of his career, the realm of the literary for Chaucer represented a safe arena in which he could experiment with renovation as an approach to the burdens of history, it did not finally remain for him a consequence-free space for experimentation. We see this most clearly in the *Canterbury Tales* when he departs from his renovative approach and risks breaking wholly new ground. His Canon's Yeoman, despite being associated with nostalgic idealism, is paradoxically also a figure for invention. He is an interloper, a late arrival to the preexisting fiction of the *Tales*, and his performance is an act of novelty for which there is no discernible generic precedent. This is one sense in which he represents Chaucerian modernity. But it is significant that Chaucer does not allow this emblem of invention to escape from the fetters of his own nostalgia or to succeed in making the past fruitfully new. And the position of his performance in the *Tales*—right before the Manciple's tale against tale-telling and the Parson's refusal of the art of fiction in favor of a spiritually edifying treatise—likewise suggests that this move toward more radical innovation is precisely what triggers the dimming of the Chaucerian dream. Chaucer's daring novelty may be the aspect of his poetry that modern readers most appreciate, but it is not the note on which the *Canterbury Tales* ends. The text's conservative closure does not permit a celebration of innovation—or even renovation—as an antidote to nostalgic idealism with valuable real-world applications. Instead, Chaucer turns his attention to penance, which for him was perhaps the only true recuperative transformation available in the real world—not, however, to society and its institutions, but only to the individual, isolated soul.

Naming the Pilgrim:

Authorship and Allegory in Guillaume de Deguileville's *Pèlerinage de la vie humaine*

Stephanie A. Viereck Gibbs Kamath
University of Massachusetts, Boston

G UILLAUME DE DEGUILEVILLE'S FOURTEENTH-CENTURY PILGRIMAGE allegories—the *Pèlerinage de la vie humaine* [Pilgrimage of Human Life], *Pèlerinage de l'âme* [Pilgrimage of the Soul], and *Pèlerinage de Jhesucrist* [Pilgrimage of Jesus Christ]—were among the most widely traveled literary texts of the Middle Ages. Before the mid-sixteenth century, portions of the trilogy had inspired translations in English, Dutch, German, Latin, and Castilian, in addition to adaptations into drama and prose forms in French.[1] Philippe de Mézières proclaimed Deguileville's

All modern English translations are my own, unless otherwise noted. I am grateful to members of the British Academy's Poetic Knowledge in Late Medieval France project for feedback on earlier versions of this work, to the anonymous reviewers for *SAC* for their useful comments, and to my university and the Neil Ker Memorial Fund for supporting manuscript research. This article refers to the author of the trilogy as "Guillaume de Deguileville," the spelling used predominantly in the manuscripts and editions consulted, but the modernized spelling, "Guillaume de Digulleville," is also current.

[1] A number of the adaptations and translations from Deguileville's trilogy are available in critical editions or in facsimile. Editions of the English prose *Vie* and John Lydgate's English verse translation of the *Vie* recension appeared in the Early English Text Society series as *The pilgrimage of the lyfe of the manhode*, ed. and intro. Avril Henry, 2 vols., EETS 288, 292 (London: Oxford University Press, 1985–88), and *The Pilgrimage of the Life of Man*, ed. F. J. Furnivall and Katharine B. Locock, 3 vols., EETS 77, 83, 92 (London: Kegan Paul, Trench, Trübner and Co., 1899, 1901, 1904), respectively. An edition of the English prose translation of the *Pèlerinage de l'âme* was begun as *"The Pilgrimage of the Soul": A Critical Edition of the Middle English Dream Vision*, ed. Rosemarie Potz McGerr, 2 vols. [projected, only one completed] (New York: Garland, 1990). An edition of one Middle Dutch prose translation of the *Vie*, with accompanying study of three other Middle Dutch translations, appeared as *Die pilgrimage vander menscheliker creaturen*, ed. Ingrid Biesheuval (Hilversum: Verloren, 2005). There are editions of two different German verse translations of the *Vie*—*Die Pilgerfahrt des träumenden Mönchs*, ed. Adriaan Meijboom (Bonn: Schroeder, 1926), and *Pilgerfahrt des träumenden Mönchs Aus der Berleburger Handschrift*, ed. Aloys Bömer (Berlin: Weidmann, 1915)—as well as a color microfilm of a German prose translation of the *Vie*, *Die Pilgerfahrt des träumenden*

allegory necessary to those seeking the holy sites of the East, and although the crusade urged by Mézières never materialized, Deguileville's allegory did touch the far West, when Christopher Columbus drew names for new-world islands from the Castilian translation.[2] But the foreign land offering the warmest literary reception to Deguileville's pilgrim was certainly England. Deguileville's allegory shares structural and thematic elements with *Piers Plowman* and had an indisputable influence on Geoffrey Chaucer, whose only known complete translation from a single French source, the *ABC*, renders an acrostic lyric from the *Pèlerinage de la vie humaine*.[3] In fifteenth-century England, prose translations

---

Mönchs: Farbmikrofiche-Edition der Handschrift Hamburg, Staats- und Universitätsbibliothek, Cod. germ. 18, intro. Ulrike Bodemann (Munich: H. Lengenfelder, 1998). A Latin translation of the entire trilogy survives in Paris, Bibliothèque de l'Arsenal, MS 507, dated 1504; for a brief discussion of this manuscript's context, see Florence Bourgne, "Medieval Mirrors and Later Vanitas Paintings," in *The Middle Ages After the Middle Ages in the English-Speaking World*, ed. Marie-Françoise Alamichel and Derek Brewer (Cambridge: D. S. Brewer, 1997), 79–90. The Roxburghe Club printed in facsimile Anthoine Vérard's pre-1499 print edition of the French prose *Vie* as *"Le Pelerinaige de vie humaine": Reproduced in Facsimile from the Printed Book in the Library of the Earl of Ellesmere*, intro. Alfred Pollard (Manchester: Roxburghe Club, 1912); Anne-Marie Legaré offers color facsimiles from a manuscript of the French prose *Vie* in *Le Pèlerinage de Vie Humaine en prose de la Reine Charlotte de Savoie*, ed. Anne-Marie Legaré (Rotthalmünster: Antiquariat Heribert Tenschert, 2004). The dramatic adaptations of Deguileville's allegories are described in Fabienne Pomel, "La théâtralité des *Pèlerinages* de Guillaume de Digulleville," in *Maistre Pierre Pathelin: Lectures et contextes*, coll. Denis Hüe and Darwin Smith (Rennes: Presses Universitaires de Rennes, 2000), 159–70. The modern English translation of Deguileville's *Vie* collates lists of manuscripts and incunables from various editions at its opening; see *The Pilgrimage of Human Life*, trans. and intro. Eugene Clasby (New York: Garland, 1992). Although a useful starting point for study, many of the references collated here were unfortunately already outdated at the time of printing (the library of Lord Aldenham, for example, was dispersed through sale in 1937). A new list, restricted to manuscripts of the French trilogy, appears in *Guillaume de Digulleville: Les Pèlerinages Allégoriques, Actes du Colloque de Cerisy-La-Salle, 5–8 Octobre 2006*, ed. Frédéric Duval and Fabienne Pomel (Rennes: Presses Universitaires de Rennes, 2008), 425–53. I am grateful to the volume editors and the list preparers (Géraldine Vesseyre, with Émilie Fréger and Julia Drobinsky) for making this resource available to me in advance of publication.

[2] For Philippe de Mézières's references to Deguileville as an exemplar, see Philippe de Mézières, *Le Songe du Vieil Pelerin*, ed. G. W. Coopland, 2 vols. (Cambridge: Cambridge University Press, 1969), 1:278, 304, 307, 377, 404, 405, 452, 455, 546, 572, 588, and 2:203, and Philippe de Mézières, *Le Livre de la vertu du sacrament de mariage*, ed. Joan B. Williamson (Washington, D.C.: Catholic University of America Press, 1993), 258–59, 332, 382. On the relation to the new world, see Valerie I. J. Flint, "Columbus, 'El Romero' and the so-called Columbus Map," *Terrae Incognitae* 24 (1992): 19–30. An unpublished edition of Vincente de Mazuelo's Castilian translation of the *Vie* is available in Maryjane Dunn-Wood, *"El pelegrinage de la vida humana*: A Study and Edition" (Ph.D. diss., University of Pennsylvania, 1985).

[3] If later manuscript attributions are correct in identifying Blanche of Lancaster as the recipient, the *ABC* is also one of the earliest datable Middle English works addressed

---

of the entire *Vie* and the later *Âme* circulated along with verse translations from Deguileville's allegory by John Lydgate and Thomas Hoccleve, two self-proclaimed disciples of Chaucer. Widely recognized for
its role in popularizing the literary pilgrimage genre, Deguileville's allegory also witnesses another feature important to English readers: like
the "Will" who narrates the vision of *Piers Plowman*, or the "Geoffrey"
who recounts travel in *The House of Fame*, the narrator of Deguileville's
allegory bears a name that readers interpreted as an authorial signature.

Deguileville's narrator reflects the author's source of inspiration as
well as his name: Deguileville's *Vie* identifies itself through citation as
one of the earliest substantial responses to the *Roman de la rose*, the first
major vernacular allegory to make extensive use of first-person narration. The *Rose* presents a dramatic development in creating a first-person
narrator who acts diegetically not only as the poem's protagonist but
also as an author, or rather as two authors, specific in identity and name,
since the *Rose* acknowledges within its allegorical narrative that Jean de
Meun continued and ended the poem more than forty years after the
death of Guillaume de Lorris, who began the poem in about 1230.
Forms of signature practice that require reader interpretation are not
new to the late Middle Ages, but the manner of signature popularized
by the *Rose* marks a significant change. Although twelfth-century romance writers, including Chrétien de Troyes, Béroul, Thomas d'Angle-
terre, and Marie de France, name themselves within their works, such
naming typically appears as exterior to the story in some fashion, in a
third-person prologue or colophon, or as an aside within the text. These
writers' names are not presented as part of the protagonist's identity
and their texts do not present the entire narrative primarily as a subject
for readers' interpretation, frequently affiliating their matter with history instead.[4] Naming in the *Rose* links authorial identity to the first-

---

to a member of the upper aristocracy. On Chaucer's *ABC* translation and its dissemination, see Helen Phillips, "Chaucer and Deguileville: the 'ABC' in Context," *MÆ* 62.1
(1993): 1–19, and John Thompson, "Chaucer's *An ABC* in and out of Context," *PoeticaT* 37 (1993): 38–48. For study of Deguileville's relation to *Piers Plowman*, see Guy
Bourquin, *"Piers Plowman": Études sur la genèse littéraire des trois versions"* (thesis, University of Paris, 1970), 2 vols. (Paris: Champion, 1978), and Emily Steiner, *Documentary
Culture and the Making of Medieval English Literature* (Cambridge: Cambridge University
Press, 2003).

[4] For study of Chrétien de Troyes's naming and narration, representing this alternative tradition of authorial self-reference, see David F. Hult, "Author/Narrator/Speaker:
The Voice of Authority in Chrétien's *Charrete*," in *Discourses of Authority in Medieval
and Renaissance Literature*, ed. Kevin Brownlee and Walter Stephens (Hanover, N.H.:
University Press of New England, 1989), 76–96.

person narrator-protagonist through readers' interpretation, and the significance of this development to later representations of authorship has been widely recognized.[5]

By contrast, Deguileville's *Vie* has won little recognition for its influence on models of vernacular authorship, despite its explicit citation of the *Rose* and the breadth of its medieval reading community.[6] The lack of modern editions may have contributed to the low profile of these allegories in literary studies today, but the common description of Deguileville's work as "moralizing" may also play a role in obscuring the complexity of Deguileville's response to the *Rose* and his allegory's subsequent influence.[7] Both the 1331 *Pèlerinage de la vie humaine* and its 1355 recension have been characterized as monastic correctives to the *Rose*'s questionable morality. Scholarship on the *Rose* imagery reworked in Deguileville's allegory has concentrated on the moral implications of alterations, at times noting the differences between the version of 1331 (hereafter *Vie1*) and its subsequent and less widely dispersed recension

---

[5] Michel Zink, citing H. R. Jauss, argues that in the *"Roman de la Rose*, allegory for the first time expresses not the movements of the soul in general, but rather the narrator's own subjectivity." See Michel Zink, "The Allegorical Poem as Interior Memoir," trans. Kevin Brownlee and Margaret Miner, *Yale French Studies* 70 (1986): 100–126 (118). Zink speaks of Guillaume de Lorris's *Rose*; this article will also discuss Jean de Meun's continuation of the *Rose*. Cynthia Brown's account of authorial development in sixteenth-century France similarly emphasizes the seminal role of the conjoined *Rose*, claiming "the narrator's voice gained prestige . . . through its association with the first-person voice of the protagonist." See Cynthia J. Brown, *Poets, Patrons, and Printers: Crisis of Authority in Late Medieval France* (Ithaca: Cornell University Press, 1995), 202.

[6] Recent works that alter this situation, appearing too recently for substantial consideration here, are: Philippe Maupeu, *Pèlerins de vie humaine: Autobiographie et allégorie narrative, de Guillaume de Deguileville à Octovien de Saint-Gelais* (Paris: Champion, 2009), and Ursula Peters, "Geistliche Kontrafaktur des *Roman de la Rose*: Die Eingangsbilder des französischen und deutschen *Pèlerinage de la vie humaine*," in *Das Ich im Bild: Die Figur des Autors in volkssprachigen Bilderhandschriften des 13. bis 16. Jahrhunderts* (Cologne: Böhlau, 2008), 140–62.

[7] In contrast to adaptations of Deguileville's allegories, the allegories themselves are less accessible to modern scholars. The Roxburghe Club's nineteenth-century editions of Deguileville's trilogy are rare books themselves and do not include the recension of the *Vie*. Moreover, the projected fourth volume of notes was never completed due to the deteriorating mental stability of the editor, J. J. Stürzinger. No modern edition of the 1355 recension of the *Vie* exists, although two printed editions appeared in the sixteenth century. David F. Hult suggests this lack of textual access reflects modern distaste when he characterizes the allegory as unpalatable today due to its "moral" focus: "The medieval corpus that we have assembled is largely beholden to modern tastes in fiction. . . . Were we to give popular works their due in our survey courses, we would have to include such moralizing fictions as the *Pèlerinage de la vie humaine*"; see Hult, *Self-Fulfilling Prophecies: Readership and Authority in the First "Roman de la Rose"* (Cambridge: Cambridge University Press, 1986), 305.

(hereafter *Vie2*).[8] Studies of Deguileville's influence on English writers have also been couched in terms of shared moral or religious interests, often to the exclusion of attention to poetic practice.[9] Yet Deguileville's interest in the *Rose* extended beyond moral reformation and Deguileville's signature practice within this "edifying" allegory reveals its importance to the development of authorial representation. The allegories inspired by the *Rose* form the very first coherent, interreferential tradition of narratives routinely employing the device of a first-person narra-

[8] Most studies focus on the more critically available first version. See, for example, Steven Wright, "Deguileville's *Pèlerinage de Vie Humaine* as 'Contrepartie Édifiante' of the *Roman de la Rose*," *PQ* 68.4 (1989): 399–424, or Rosemond Tuve, *Allegorical Imagery: Some Mediaeval Books and Their Posterity* (Princeton: Princeton University Press, 1966), 145–218. Exceptions that give detailed attention to both versions have been limited: Pierre-Yves Badel suggests that Deguileville's original, despite its description of the *Rose* as "biau" [fair] was "implicitement . . . déjà un *Anti-Roman de la Rose*" [implicitly . . . already an *Anti-Romance of the Rose*]. John Fleming relies upon the autobiographical hypothesis of "slowly maturing personal pique" to explain the difference in *Rose* characterization. Sylvia Huot's groundbreaking study of the *Rose* presents a more extended codicological consideration of Jean de Meun's and Deguileville's texts, speculating that Deguileville's "greater uneasiness in 1355 might even be explained by his having encountered the *Rose* in an unexpurgated, non-*B* manuscript." See Pierre-Yves Badel, *Le "Roman de la rose" au XIVe siècle: Étude de la réception de l'oeuvre* (Geneva: Librairie Droz, 1980), 375; John Fleming, "The Moral Reputation of the *Roman de la Rose* Before 1400," *Romance Philology* 18.4 (1965): 430–35 (433); and Sylvia Huot, *The "Romance of the Rose" and Its Medieval Readers* (Cambridge: Cambridge University Press, 1993), 228.

[9] William Calin proposes Deguileville's importance to Chaucer as the influence of "sacred allegory . . . the idea of a great pilgrimage poem in the vernacular, with the crucial motifs of quest, transformation, true and false seekers, edifying and satirical discourse, the growth of the individual, and the judgment of Christian society as a whole" and presents Thomas Hoccleve's Deguileville translation as evidence of his "gift for sacred poetry." See William Calin, *The French Tradition and the Literature of Medieval England* (Toronto: University of Toronto Press, 1994), 302, 403. Roger Ellis comments on the way both Deguileville and Hoccleve depend for their effect upon the Christian perspective of scriptural history in his Hoccleve anthology, *"My compleinte" and Other Poems* (Exeter: University of Exeter Press, 2001), 35–36. The importance of Deguileville to John Lydgate's poetry has been less studied, perhaps in part because of the lack of an edition of the French recension from which Lydgate translated. Susan Hagen's study of the *Pèlerinage* draws its quotations from John Lydgate's translation rather than Deguileville's poem on the grounds that the translation is more "readily available to readers"; see Hagen, *Allegorical Remembrance: A Study of "The Pilgrimage of the Life of Man" as a Medieval Treatise on Seeing and Remembering* (Athens: University of Georgia Press, 1990), ix. Piero Boitani similarly conjoins Deguileville's poetry with its translation in his article, "'His desir wol fle withouten wynges': Mary and Love in Fourteenth-Century Poetry," in *Chaucer's Frame Tales: The Physical and the Metaphysical*, ed. Joerg O. Fichte (Cambridge: D. S. Brewer, 1987), 83–128. Religious stance remains the focus in Michael Camille's study, which claims Lydgate's translation "sought to emphasize orthodox attitudes" through imagery; see "The Iconoclast's Desire: Deguileville's Idolatry in France and England," in *Images, Idolatry, and Iconoclasm in Late Medieval England: Textuality and the Visual Image*, ed. Jeremy Dimmick, James Simpson, and Nicolette Zeeman (Oxford: Oxford University Press, 2002), 151–71 (167).

tor-protagonist ever to arise in French or English literary history, so the relationship between the new role of the narrator and authorial self-naming merits careful consideration. After a brief discussion of the naming strategy within the *Rose*, I will demonstrate how Deguileville's engagement with the *Rose* shapes his own use of naming and develops from *Vie1* to *Vie2*. Given the importance of readers' interpretation to the discovery of the author's identity within these allegories, I support the conclusions reached through literary analysis with brief references to codicological evidence of reception. A closer examination of Deguileville's narrator and his naming ultimately offers us a new understanding of how—and why—this form of signature within allegory traversed not only linguistic boundaries but also sacred and secular agendas in the late Middle Ages.

Allegorical and Authorial Logics in the *Roman de la rose*

The opening of the thirteenth century, the context in which the *Roman de la rose* emerges, is typically depicted as a time of expanding interest in human authorship and of a simultaneous decline in the extensive allegorical exposition of scripture, exegesis that directed attention away from human writers' intentions toward God as author of all.[10] Allegorical exegesis like that applied to scripture, however, becomes the means of directing attention to the human author within the narrative of the *Rose*. In a passage written by Guillaume de Lorris, the narrator promises readers a *glose* that will reveal the hidden meaning of his work, repeating this promise immediately before he recounts the commandments of the *dieu d'Amours*. The promise almost replicates the typology of scriptural exegesis, arguing that the *glose* will demonstrate the fulfillment of all that happens in the dream. Jean de Meun's continuation of *Rose* takes the narrator's exegetical role further and greatly develops the role of the *dieu d'Amours*. A speech delivered by the *dieu d'Amours*, significantly

[10] This view is most directly expressed in A. J. Minnis's classic account of historical developments in medieval authorship theory. Minnis claims that in the twelfth century "the primacy of allegorical interpretation had hindered the emergence of viable literary theory [concerning authorship]," by attributing authorship to God, a connection unfathomable by human understanding. Exegetes, in Minnis's terms, "cleverly allegorised away" the role and problems of human authorship and a new interest in human authorship arose only in the wake of the "decline in extensive allegorical exposition of Scripture." See A. J. Minnis, *The Medieval Theory of Authorship: Scholastic Literary Attitudes in the Later Middle Ages* (London: Scolar Press, 1984), 5, 48, 143.

positioned at the midpoint of the expanded *Rose*, refers to the text itself, declaring the *Rose* to be worthy of the new title, "Le *Miroër aus Amoreus*" (10621) ["The Mirror for Lovers" (188)].[11] This same speech, renaming the work, is also the only passage that records the names of the *Rose*'s authors, indicating authorial control through the words attributed to the allegorical Amours, who claimed emotive control over the narrator from the start of the *Rose*.[12]

Amours names the *Rose*'s authors yet usurps their authority. He laments that Guillaume de Lorris, who began the work, is on the point of dying, and that Amours's other literary servants, including Ovid, have died. Amours then predicts that Jean de Meun, who is not born, will finish the work by writing the words Amours plans to sing over Jean's cradle. Speaking of the writing of the *Rose* in the future, and the action of the quest in the present, Amours depicts the roles of both Guillaume de Lorris and Jean de Meun not as compositors but as scribes and exegetes. He declares that once the quest of the dream has finished:

> Puis vodra si la chose espondre
> que riens ne s'i porra repondre.
> Se cist conseill metre i peüssent,
> tantost conseillié m'en eüssent;
> mes par cestui ne peut or estre,
> ne par celui qui est a nestre,
> car il n'est mie ci presanz.
>
> (10573–79)

[Then he (Jean de Meun) will want to explicate the affair in such a way that nothing can remain hidden. If they (Jean or Guillaume) could have given their counsel in this matter, they would have given it to me immediately; but that cannot now take place through Guillaume nor through Jean, who is yet to be born, for he is not here present. (188)]

---

[11] All quotations from the *Rose* refer by line number to *Le Roman de la rose*, ed. Félix Lecoy, 3 vols. (Paris: Champion, 1965–70, repr. 1982–85). Modern English translations refer by page number to *The Romance of the Rose*, trans. Charles Dahlberg, 3rd ed. (Princeton: Princeton University Press, 1995).

[12] Daniel Heller-Roazen similarly calls attention to this passage as central in staging "a double movement in which identification and the loss of identity, the ascription of names and their withholding, cannot be told apart, a movement in which the constitution of the poetic subject provokes his simultaneous deconstitution as such" in *Fortune's Face: The "Roman de la Rose" and the Poetics of Contingency* (Baltimore: Johns Hopkins University Press, 2003), 53.

Jean de Meun thus uses Amours to signal the text's authorship within its allegory, simultaneously presenting the authors' names and denying their presence and control within the narrative frame. Rather than being overtly explained by an authorial "master," the meaning of the text is registered obliquely through the dramatic interaction and dialogue of personifications.[13]

The apparent absence of the author position within the allegory at this point is a literary device that draws attention to voice, like the first-person dream-vision frame itself. The explicit declaration within the narrative that Guillaume de Lorris and Jean de Meun are absent, not *ci presenz*, points to their authorial presence and extradiegetic control of the narrative. Here the practice of signature is exploiting the semantic duality of allegory, a mode of writing that promises a meaning that exceeds and can even contradict the words of the text. Staging the meaning of the text as beyond the interpretative control of the author invites the interpretative control of the reader, but the subject of interpretation here is the author's identity. Rather than allegory directing attention away from the conditions of human authorship, nonliteral interpretation of this passage is the only method of discovering the author(s) of the text.

Medieval readers noted attentively the authorial claims established by the first-person voice and the prophecy of the *dieu d'Amours*; as the pioneering codicological work of scholars including Lori Walters and Sylvia Huot demonstrates, visual markers such as rubric divisions distinguish perspectives within the first-person voice in medieval manuscripts, and various kinds of authorial portraits are inserted, both in the passage of Amours's central speech and at the earlier point of transition that it indicates.[14] Particularly striking evidence of attention to Amours's speech is found in the case of Gui de Mori, celebrated by Sylvia Huot as the "only known *Rose* poet who preserved the distinction between Guillaume and Jean while still creating his own explicit presence in the

---

[13] On the political and ideological implications of this unstable signature passage, see Noah Guynn, *Allegory and Sexual Ethics in the High Middle Ages* (New York: Palgrave Macmillan, 2007), 137–67.

[14] On rubrics, see Sylvia Huot, "'Ci parle l'aucteur': The Rubrication of Voice and Authorship in the *Roman de la Rose* Manuscripts," *SubStance* 56 (1988): 42–48, and on portraits, see Lori Walters, "Illuminating the *Rose*: Gui de Mori and the Illustrations of MS 101 of the Municipal Library, Tournai," in *Rethinking the "Romance of the Rose": Text, Image, Reception*, ed. Kevin Brownlee and Sylvia Huot (Philadelphia: University of Pennsylvania Press, 1992), 167–200.

text."[15] Gui recognizes that the speech Jean attributes to Amours indicates authorial presence through describing Jean's (and Guillaume's) absence. Gui, revising the poem, mimics Jean's strategy to create his own textual signature by adding another prophecy to this passage. Gui first claims his name is present at the opening of the dream, through linguistic play on the gate or "gui-chet" that leads to the garden of Love.[16] Yet Gui also depicts himself as absent and unborn, for Amours declares:

> desci en sui devins.
> Guis de Moiri avra a non,
> Mais il n'ert pas de tel regnon
> Com cis Jehans ne chil Guillaumes . . .[17]

[I know of him through divination. He will have the name Gui de Mori, but he will not be of such renown as this Jean nor that Guillaume . . .]

Like Jean's use of proper names or Guillaume's first-person voice, Gui's manner of adding his name here conveys knowledge of his poetic role only through readers' figurative interpretation: his identity as a reviser becomes recognizable only through disruption of the literal sense and linear temporal progression in Amours's speech. The staking of authorial claims within the allegory of the *Rose*, rather than in a literal manner, was not only noted but imitated by its medieval readers.[18]

---

[15] Huot, *The "Romance of the Rose" and Its Medieval Readers*, 332.

[16] See Hult, *Self-Fulfilling Prophecies*, 48–49.

[17] *Le Roman de la rose*, ed. Ernest Langlois, 5 vols. (Paris: Champion/Firmin-Didot, 1919–24), 2:256. Further citations of Gui de Mori's additions to the *Rose* by volume and page number are to this edition.

[18] Indeed, Hult's *Self-Fulfilling Prophecies* ascribes medieval interest in the *Rose* to the very aspect of the text enlarged upon by Gui de Mori. Observing this new authorial inscription within the first-person voice of the allegory, Hult remarks: "Considering that Jean de Meun performs precisely the same reversal on Guillaume de Lorris, who in turn predicated his account on the intimate and interchangeable relationship established between lover and writer at the outset, we might here be approaching an understanding of the fascination exercised by the *Rose* fiction on its succession of readers" (50). Of course, the *Rose* itself may have developed its technique through borrowing from Raoul Houdenc's *Songe d'enfer*, which opens with a meditation on the truth of dreams, features a first-person narrator-protagonist who travels to hell as a "pilgrim" and serves as a clerk by reading aloud for the king of Hell, who names him as Raoul only in the context of revealing that he comes from everywhere on earth. See *The "Songe d'Enfer" of Raoul de Houdenc: An Edition Based on All the Extant Manuscripts*, ed. Madelyn Timmel Mihm (Tübingen: Max Niemeyer, 1984), lines 1–7, 411–16, 613–29.

Rewriting Raison: Self-Naming in *Vie1*

Guillaume de Deguileville's *Vie1* and *Vie2* constitute the first extended creative response to this allegorical technique of naming, reproducing the textual as well as the codicological effects of the *Rose*. Deguileville's representation of his own authorial role and his discussion of authorial-naming in *Rose* once again insert attention to authorship in the context of allegoresis, negotiating the complex interaction between divine inspiration and human intention, the present and absent function of the author, and the relative authority granted to personifications and narrating personae in order to create allegory.

One character takes a central role in guiding the narrator through Deguileville's first exploration of authorship within allegory: Raison, the personification of reason. In the *Roman de la rose*, the character Raison claims to be the daughter of God, acts as an unsuccessful rival to Amours, and memorably explores the logical relation of divine creation and human language in a discussion sparked, in most manuscripts, by Raison's explicit and colloquial naming of male genitals as "coilles" (5537) ["testicles" (113)], much to the narrator's surprise. In Deguileville's *Vie1*, Raison does not rival the *dieu d'Amours* but rather Grace de Dieu [Grace of God], the character Deguileville names as God's daughter, to whom Raison is ultimately subordinate.[19] Deguileville's Grace de Dieu names Raison, grants her the commission she needs to carry out her task, and at times exceeds Raison's comprehension and power to interpret for the narrator. Although Deguileville's Raison thus no longer claims all the authority of Christian divinity, she retains from the *Rose* both her interest in the logic of naming and her ability to surprise the narrator. In *Vie1*, Raison's explorations of naming relate specifically to the formation of allegorical and authorial identity, and this former rival of Amours assumes a role in authorial presentation like that held by Amours in the *Rose*.

Raison's reasoning through the difference between the human and the divine in Deguileville's text provides the most explicit clue to the author's name, and the manner in which Raison suggests the author's name is reminiscent of the *Rose* moment of naming. Both transpire in

[19] The debate over the Eucharist between Aristotle, ally of Raison and Nature, and Sapience, ally of Grace de Dieu, establishes the greater authority of Grace de Dieu. Grace de Dieu's authority is also reflected in the extension of her role in Deguileville's recension.

an allegorical context that requires rhetorical estrangement; to discover the author's name and to understand the narrator's role, readers must consider the meaning of the claims within the narrative and their converse, extradiegetic meaning. Moreover, codicological evidence demonstrates medieval readers' particular interest, and even participation, in the strategy of authorial naming voiced by Deguileville's Raison, reinforcing the significance of the attention to authorial naming witnessed in *Rose* manuscripts.

The opening of Deguileville's *Vie1* explicitly cites "li beau roumans de la Rose" (11) ["the beautiful *Romance of the Rose*" (3)].[20] The narrator claims that he read the *Rose* immediately before falling into the sleep that produced the *Vie*'s allegorical dream, thus weaving the intertextual relation into the frame of the allegory.[21] Codicological study demonstrates that the relation of the texts was also emphasized in many manuscripts by a colophon reminding readers that Deguileville's allegory was inspired by the *Rose*.[22] Aside from such rubrics, however, after the initial mention of the *Rose*, Raison is the only character to invoke the *Rose* explicitly within Deguileville's *Vie1*. She cites the *Rose* as a demonstration of her opposition to Carnal Love: "Amor charnel tout hors m'enchace. . . . Ce verrez vous tout sans glose / Ou roumans qui'est de la Rose" (879–82) ["Carnal Love drives me out completely. . . . You can see this plainly in the *Romance of the Rose*" (14)].[23] Raison's citation of

---

[20] Quotations for the 1331 *Pèlerinage* are cited by line number from *Le Pèlerinage de la vie humaine de Guillaume de Deguileville*, ed. J. J. Stürzinger (London: Roxburghe Club, 1893). Modern English translations for the 1331 *Pèlerinage* are cited by page number from Guillaume de Deguileville, *Pilgrimage*, trans. Clasby.

[21] The narrator declares "bien croi que ce fu la chose / Qui plus m'esmut a ce songier / Que ci apres vous vueil nuncier" (13–14) ["I am sure that this was what moved me most to have the dream I will tell you about in a moment" (3)].

[22] "Chi fine le romans du moisne / Du pelerinage de vie humaine . . . Prins sur le roman de la rose / Ou lart damours est toute enclose" [Here finishes the monk's romance of the pilgrimage of human life . . . drawn from the romance of the rose in which the art of love is entirely enclosed] (423). Stürzinger lists other colophons on this page as well. Arras, Bib. Mun. MS 845, which incorporates selected excerpts from the *Rose*, among other texts including *Vie1*, offers a more specific interpretation of the relation between the two texts: a rubric describes Deguileville's text as "fais par poeterie, comme li Livres de le Roze, qui est en grant partie de philozofie, mes cilz pelerinages est de theologie" [composed in poetry, like the book of the *Rose*, which concerns philosophy for the most part, but this *Pilgrimage* concerns theology] (fol. 103r). For analysis and description of the scribe's work, see Huot, *The "Romance of the Rose" and Its Medieval Readers*, 231–38.

[23] Contemporary scholars have read Raison's citation of the *Rose* here in differing ways; as noted earlier, John Fleming sees it as rather neutral, whereas Pierre-Yves Badel sees it as implicitly condemnatory. Whether or not the allusion constitutes a critique of the *Rose*'s contents, this naming of the *Rose* demonstrates Deguileville's interest in the

the *Rose* as a source that demonstrates her nature encourages readers to examine the action of her personification in Deguileville's work in the specific context of the *Rose*. Moreover, it is Raison, the character who names the *Rose*, who encodes Deguileville's name within the allegory in a debate with the narrator concerning the relation of body and soul.

The context of Raison's speech on this matter within *Vie1* establishes both the complexity of the identification and its resemblance to the logic of the *Rose*'s naming. The narrator wonders why he finds the armor of virtues that Grace de Dieu entrusted to him too heavy to bear, given that his maidservant, Memoire, can carry it with ease. Immediately thereafter, Rude Entendement [Poor Understanding] obstructs the way until Raison counters his obstruction. The narrator then asks Raison to help him understand his weakness in comparison to Memoire. In good philosophic tradition, Raison answers the question with another set of questions: Did he pay attention to the earlier teaching of Grace de Dieu, who gave him both the armor and Memoire? Does he know whether he is single or dual in nature? As the confused narrator begs explication from her, Raison unfolds an account of internal division, claiming that he cherishes an enemy who destroys his strength. The narrator twice asks Raison to tell him the name of this enemy, so the narrator can find and kill him (5802, 5843). Raison then names the enemy as the narrator's own body, declaring "autrement nommer ne le sai" (5874) ["I do not know what other name to call him" (80)]. The narrator cries out: "Ai je songie ou songiez vous?" (5876) ["Have I been dreaming? Or are you dreaming?" (80)], but Raison insists that this is not "c'on doie appeler songe" (5886) ["anything that could be called a dream" (80)] and through further questioning displays the narrator's self-division through conflicting desires for his spiritual goal and for his physical comfort. When the narrator asks who he is, if he is not his physical body, Raison's response is an emphatic negation of human lineage: "Dieu est ton pere et tu son fil, / Ne cuides pas que soies fil / (A) Thomas de Deguileville" (5963–65) ["God is your father and you are his son. You must not think that you are the son of Thomas de Deguileville" (81)]. These lines naming Thomas de Deguileville, the father of Guillaume de Deguileville, are the most explicit clue to authorial identity found in *Vie1*.

Readings of the allegorical relation of body and soul in this passage

---

earlier work's poetic techniques, borrowing a salient rhyming pair ("rose / glose") from the *Rose*.

must therefore recognize that the moment at which the narrator learns who he is not—his body—is simultaneously the moment at which the author reveals to his readers who he is—the son of Thomas de Deguileville. The "literal" identification of the narrator in this passage is the fragmented "Everyman," the universal soul of psychomachiac drama; the "figurative" meaning affirmed by the specificity of the overt denial is in fact the author's personal name. The logic bears a striking resemblance to the moment in the *Rose* when the allegory of the quest becomes a figure of the text's composition, and the personification Amours denies both authors' presence in order to inscribe record of it. In the *Rose*, the first-person narrator (and initial author) is named as Guillaume de Lorris only after death disrupts the united identity of Guillaume and the narrator; Amours declares that the bodies of his servants, including Guillaume, will be "morz porriz" (10495) ["dead and decayed" (187)] before Jean's portion of the narrative begins. In Deguileville's *Vie1*, the naming scene suggests that the narrator within this dream must "kill" his body in order to be himself, revealing identity through rupture. Like its counterpart in the *Rose*, this naming scene also clashes with the dream-frame device as, once again, a personification argues for a reality that exceeds the framing fiction. Amours within the *Rose* insists that both narrators dreaming him are absent, their bodies rotting or unformed; Raison insists that the narrator of Deguileville's dream is neither dreaming the debate with her nor defined by his bodily identity, the enemy who has his name. Moreover, this dialogue explicitly sets up the debate between the narrator's body and soul at the allegorical crossroads that falls at the midpoint of Deguileville's text, the point that Amours's author-naming speech occupies in the *Rose*.

Looking at the context of the passage enclosing the authors' names in Jean's *Rose* reveals how Deguileville's own self-naming takes form through rewriting it. Immediately prior to Amours's speech, the narrator of the *Rose* complains of a doubled self, lamenting his confusion about how to act: "Ainsinc m'entencion double oi, / n'onc mes nul jor ne la doubloi" (10271–72) ["In this way I had a double intention, but it was never I, on any occasion, who made it double" (183)]. When Amours thereafter accuses him of treachery for listening to Raison, the narrator declares that he will henceforth never follow Raison but will live and die according to the law of Amours (10337–38). Intending to die in the service of love, he imagines those who behold his corpse saying:

or est il voirs, sanz point de fable,
bien iert ceste mort convenable
a la vie que tu menoies
quant l'ame avec ce cors tenoies.

(10351–54)

[now it is true, without any fable whatever, that this death is indeed suitable
to the life that you led when you kept your soul together with this body. (184)]

These lines, which announce an involuntary division within the first-
person narrator and imagine his corpse after he rejects Raison, are traditionally read as ironic foreshadowing of the following speech in which
Amours announces that Guillaume will die after writing the first debate
with Raison. Deguileville's allegory takes up this program of elaborating
upon fissures in the universal or moral self—the opposition between
Love and Reason, the discord between body and soul—to signal allegorically a specific poetic identity for the increasingly fragmented first-person voice. Jean's narrator imagines himself as a deserted corpse before
Amours names the authors and denies their bodily presence; Deguileville's allegory echoes the strategy of naming and denying and enacts the
Rose narrator's vision as well, since Raison concludes her negation of
human lineage by temporarily extracting the soul of Deguileville's narrator from his body, enabling him to see it as a corpse.

Deguileville's allegory, like the *Rose*, thus depends on the fragmentation of the speaking subject in creating moments of authorial identification.[24] Deguileville's first-person voice combines the perspective of
dreamer, narrator, and protagonist; of soul and body; of the universal
pilgrim in whose identity the reader can participate and also of Thomas
de Deguileville's son, the individual poet. Codicological attention to the
authorial naming passage of Deguileville's work does not witness quite
the same level of activity as the *Rose*'s moment of authorial naming,
perhaps in part due to the smaller number of extant manuscripts.[25]

[24] Sarah Kay draws attention to the way in which the debate concerning the nature
of body and soul relates to other elements within the poem—most notably, the Eucha-
ristic debate between Sapience and Aristotle—representing an idea of the medieval subject as inherently fragmented. See *The Place of Thought: The Complexity of One in French
Didactic Poetry* (Philadelphia: University of Pennsylvania Press, 2007). I am grateful to
Sarah Kay for sharing with me portions of her book in advance of publication.

[25] Certain manuscripts of *Vie1*, including Paris, Bibl. de l'Arsenal 5071, do place a
marginal "nota" beside this passage.

Nonetheless, the debate between Raison and the narrator was recognized as a naming scene, as is demonstrated by an emendation found in at least two fifteenth-century manuscripts of a French prose translation of the text. Here a name has been added to the line denying the narrator's human identity: "Tu es filz et enfant de dieu ne cuides pas que tu soyes filz a thomas de deguilleuille *ne a pierre gaultier*" [You are son and child of God; do not think that you are son to Thomas de Deguileville *or Pierre Gaultier*] (italics added). This may be the name of the person who adapted the poem into prose but refused to name him- or herself in the prologue; the insertion is not witnessed in all prose manuscripts, so its relation to the adaptor is not certain.[26] The presence of the insertion where it does occur, however, shows that this passage acted as an authorial signature for at least one medieval receiver of the text, who sought to participate in the text through the adoption of this technique. Like Gui de Mori's insertion of his name when the *Rose*'s authors are identified as absent, the addition of Gaultier's name beside Deguileville's denied paternal name supports the idea that the interpretation-inviting placement of proper names in the mouths of personifications was a significant method of marking authorial identity within allegorical narrative. But does the evidence of one medieval French reader who denies his father and forswears his name prove this allegory as sweet as any *Rose*?

Interestingly, both the *Rose* and the *Vie* also found similar responses in instances of foreign-language translation, although these translations frequently replace the proper names found in passages of these works with different names, instead of adding to the names that appear. One

---

[26] Rosemond Tuve noted the appearance of this emendation in the 1504 Lyons Nourry edition and argued for its adoption as the name of the prose translator. See Tuve, *Allegorical Imagery*, 216. Having examined the manuscripts as well as the editions, I am more cautious about such attribution, as the name appears in only two of the eight extant manuscripts with known whereabouts: Geneva, Bibl. Pub. et Univ., MS fr. 182, fol. 75v and Paris, BnF, MS F. Fr. 1646, fol. 72r. I have also seen the additional name in two early print editions of the prose adaptation, produced by Matthias Huss in Lyons, 1485, and by Anthoine Vérard in Paris, pre-1499. For a more extensive comparison between this prose translation and the authorial recension, see my "Deversifying Knowledge: The Poetic Alphabet of the Prose *Pèlerinage de la vie humaine*," in *Poetry, Knowledge, and Community in Late Medieval France*, ed. Rebecca Dixon and Finn E. Sinclair, with the participation of Adrian Armstrong, Sylvia Huot, and Sarah Kay (Woodbridge: Boydell & Brewer, 2008), 111–24. Philippe Maupeu suggests that the translator may be the daughter rather than son of Gaultier, proposing attribution to the Jehanne Maillart named in the colophon of a *Vie1* manuscript based on his research in genealogical tables. Maupeu, *Pèlerins de vie humaine*, 303–5.

Middle Dutch translation of the *Rose*, for example, replaces the naming of Guillaume de Lorris with a passage in which Amours gives the narrator the name of the translator and prophecies the creation of a Dutch (rather than French) text: "Siet hier van Brusele Henrecke . . . / noch wille dienen alse mijn vrient, / Ende maken te Dietsch, daer in sal staen / Mine gebode" ["See here Henrecke from Brussels . . . [who] still wants to serve as my friend, and write in Dutch, in which my commands will be written"].[27] The medieval Italian adaptation of the *Rose* similarly erases the proper names; the god of Love asks his court "pur convien ch'i' soccorra Durante" [to offer help to Durante] rather than Guillaume de Lorris.[28] Deguileville's self-naming in the *Vie* meets an equivalent fate in one of its German translations, which renders Raison's line about the narrator's not being the son of Thomas de Deguileville with the line "dencke neit dat du son sijs / Peters van Meroede" [do not think that you are the child of Peter van Meroede], leading Rosemond Tuve to concur with editor Adriaan Meijboom's suggestion that this German version was created by the son of Peters van Meroede of Cologne.[29] Like

---

[27] Quotation from this Middle Dutch *Rose* translation refers to *Die "Rose" van Heinric van Aken, met de fragmenten der tweede Vertaling*, ed. Eelco Verwijs ('s Gravenhage /Den Haag: Martinus Nijhoff, 1868), lines 9901, 9918–20. English translation is drawn from Karin Lesnik-Oberstein, "Adapting the *Roman de la Rose*: Was the Middle Dutch Adaptor Careless or Ambitious?" *Tr&Lit* 1 (1992): 134–40 (135). Lesnik-Oberstein's perceptive study argues for the Dutch translator's complex appropriation of authorial identity within the poem and demonstrates the way in which the translator reworks not only the presence of proper names and linguistic reference but also the allegorical allusion to pagan deities in order to render the passage appropriate to his identity and intention; she also repeats earlier scholars' theory that the name "Mechiel" that occurs within this passage in one manuscript of this translation refers to "a scribe (or assistant?) anxious to have his work recognized," claiming that "this further suggests the importance medieval writers attached to having their efforts acknowledged" (140). The inserted ascription to Heinric is discussed in relation to the fragments of a different, Flemish, Dutch medieval translation in Dieuwke van der Poel, "The *Romance of the Rose* and I: Narrative Perspective in the *Roman de la Rose* and Its Two Middle Dutch Adaptations," in *Courtly Literature: Culture and Context*, ed. Keith Busby and Erik Kooper (Philadelphia: John Benjamins, 1990), 573–83.

[28] Quotation from the Italian *Rose* translation refers to *"Il Fiore" e "Il Detto d'amore,"* ed. Claudio Marchiori (Genoa: Tilgher, 1983), Sonnet 82, line 9.

[29] Quotation from this German translation of the *Vie* refers to *Die Pilgerfahrt des träumenden Mönchs*, ed. Adriaan Meijboom (Bonn: Schroeder, 1926), lines 5988–89. In addition to her observation about the German translator "Petrus," Rosemond Tuve convincingly interprets the addition of the name "Richard" within this same passage in a seventeenth-century prose version of the *Vie* as an identification of its scribe as William Baspoole (mentioned as a scribe of the work in another manuscript's colophon), specifically the William Baspoole recorded as the son of a Richard Baspoole by documents from that period and locality. See Tuve, *Allegorical Imagery*, 215–16. One manuscript

the scribal addition of names to these poems, these translations' insertion of new names suggests that the technique of signaling authorship through the voice of the personifications describing an allegory's narrator was both recognized and widely adopted in the Middle Ages.

Other readers and scribes responded visibly to the internal divisions of the *Vie*'s narrator, just as they had to the first extended use of first-person voice in the *Rose*. Many manuscripts of the poem repeatedly divide the first-person discourse of the narrator between the rubrics of "l'acteur" [the author] and "le pelerin" [the pilgrim], reminiscent of the famously innovative rubric divisions of "l'acteur" [the author] and "l'amant" [the lover] found in *Rose* manuscripts.[30] Further division of the first-person voice between the speech of "le corps" [the body] and "l'esperit" [the spirit] of the narrator occurs at the dramatic moment of self-debate at the midpoint of *Vie1* when the narrator must decide whether to follow the path of Oiseuse [Idleness] or that of Labour. Raison's earlier speech also alludes to the different directions pursued by the body and the soul and Deguileville's division at the crossroads may reflect his reading of the *Rose*; in the *Rose*, the narrator is led into the garden of Amours by Oiseuse, heedless of Raison's urging.[31] But Deguileville takes the fragmentation of the self and the psychomachiac logic of personification further through extended meditation on the relationship between the narrator and the personification Raison.

---

containing a fifteenth-century Middle Dutch translation witnesses another kind of attempt to transform this name: "God es dijn vader, du best zijn soene. En wanet niet dattu bist Thomas's Backers sone" [God is your father, you are his son. Do not think you are son of Thomas Baker] (Berlin, SPK, MS germ. fol. 624, fol. 28r). For discussion of this manuscript in terms of two other Middle Dutch translations, see Ingrid Biesheuval's introduction to *Die pilgrimage vander menscheliker creaturen*, 130. I have also seen the insertion of the name "Claes" in a Middle Dutch translation of the *Vie* printed in 1498 by Hendrik Eckert van Homberch (Oxford, Bodleian Library, Douce 46, fol. 66v), not discussed by Biesheuval. Interest in participation through this technique by persons involved in adapting and disseminating Deguileville's text thus extends across Europe and reaches from the Middle Ages into the era of the English reformation.

[30] On *Rose* rubrics, see Huot, "'Ci parle l'aucteur.'" The treatment of naming and identity in the French prose redaction of the text is particularly worthy of closer consideration at this point. In five manuscripts of the 1465 prose version of the *Vie*, the moment of denying Thomas de Deguileville is the moment when the rubric for the first-person voice switches from being consistently "l'aucteur" [the author] to being marked by the rubric "le pelerin" [the pilgrim] as well.

[31] For further consideration of the motif of two paths, see Fabienne Pomel, "Le *Roman de la rose* comme voie de paradis. Transposition, parodie et moralisation de Guillaume de Lorris à Jean Molinet," in *De la Rose: Texte, Image, Fortune*, ed. Catherine Bel and Herman Braet (Louvain: Peeters, 2006), 355–76.

Raison's Clerk: Personification and Persona in *Vie1*

In *Vie1*, as we have seen, Raison is the only character to cite the *Rose* by name and the only character to introduce Deguileville's name within the text, in a manner similar to author identification in the *Rose*. Moreover, just as the *Rose*'s Amours had claimed both Guillaume de Lorris and Jean de Meun as scribes of his words when naming them, Raison calls forth the narrator as her "clers" (5205) ["clerk" (71)] in the passage immediately preceding the debate that contains the author's name. Deguileville's *Vie1* thus adopts from the *Rose* the strategy of having a personification define the narrator's identity and claim to control textual meaning. Acting as a clerk to a personification, Deguileville's narrator encounters the antiphrastic logic found in the corresponding portion of the *Rose*'s allegory, allowing the words of the text to hold a figurative meaning that is in contradiction to their literal meaning. Deguileville also develops the *Rose* strategy of depicting portions of verse as separate documents within the allegory, using such "embedded" texts to direct attention beyond the immediate narrative.

In *Vie1* the passage that identifies the narrator as Raison's clerk and the subsequent debate between the narrator and Raison are both introduced by the narrator's contemplation of his weakness in relation to Memoire.[32] As we have seen, the question is answered within the debate by Raison's (un)naming of the narrator, fragmented by both his human and his textual condition. Questioning the relationship between the narrator and Memoire illustrates the difference between the divine and the human, willing intellect and weak flesh, as well as the difference between the voice of "l'acteur," who remembers and recounts his dream, and the un-dreaming, incomplete voice of "le pelerin," who is separate in identity from Memoire and reads and writes only under the direction

[32] Questioning the nature of the personification Memoire leads to the simultaneous introduction of the author's name and denial of his human identity in Deguileville's poem. Deguileville's allegorical investigation of memory's role thus resembles Augustine's influential presentation of himself as a paradox in the face of the divine: "Et ecce memoriae meae vis non comprehenditur a me, cum ipsum me non dicam praeter illam" ["Yet the power of memory in me I do not understand, though without memory I could not even name myself"]. See Augustine, *"Confessions": Text and Commentary*, ed. James J. O'Donnell, 3 vols. (Oxford: Clarendon Press, 1992), vol. 1, X.16.25, and Augustine, *Confessions*, trans. F. J. Sheed, 2nd ed. (Indianapolis: Hackett, 2006), 202. For a brief recent consideration of the importance of Augustinian semiotics to Jean de Meun's *Rose*, see Noah D. Guynn, "Authorship and Sexual/Allegorical Violence in Jean de Meun's *Roman de la Rose*," *Speculum* 74.3 (2004): 628–59, esp. 639–40.

of Raison. The divided voice and clerkly service of the narrator-protagonist become a subject for interpretation; the revelation of the author's identity and intention does not preclude the readers' role as interpreters but rather depends on it.

The narrator's subjection to the process of allegoresis lies at the heart of his encounter with Rude Entendement, from whom he escapes by acting as Raison's clerk. Situated between the first question concerning Memoire and Raison's response, the narrator's encounter with Rude Entendement draws attention to the significance of names and how they are understood within allegory. Rude Entendement, like Memoire, appears as a function of the self dramatized externally, declaring: "la destourbance / Vient de ta outrecuidance" (5119–20) ["the trouble comes from your insolence" (70)]. Rude Entendement criticizes the narrator's foolish boldness in adopting the staff and satchel of a pilgrim since, according to Rude Entendement, the New Testament prohibition of literal staffs and satchels also prohibits figurative items like the narrator's staff of Hope and the satchel of Faith.[33] Rude Entendement assumes that every name names a thing to which it uniquely corresponds—a staff is a staff is a staff—and insists on a literal, corporal reading of the narrator's quest. This personification is thus doubly obstructive, refusing to let the narrator progress on his journey within the narrative frame and also denying the figurative aspect of language upon which the allegory's meaning depends. In order for both allegory and allegoresis to progress, both this character and the aspect of the subject he represents must be controlled and corrected.

To allow the narrator to pass Rude Entendement, Deguileville's Raison must demonstrate not only that the quest should not be read literally but also that a word can be used antiphrastically, to name its opposite.[34] These demonstrations grant the personification Raison her

[33] The scriptures to which Rude Entendement appears to refer are Matthew 10.9–10 and Luke 10.4. Julia Bolton Holloway remarks on the importance of these same scriptures in "The Pilgrim in the Poem: Dante, Langland, and Chaucer," in *Allegoresis: The Craft of Allegory in Medieval Literature*, ed. J. Stephen Russell (New York: Garland, 1988), 109–32.

[34] Deguileville's Raison, intertextually linked to the *Rose* and advocating antiphrastic reading, anticipates the figure of Raison in Christine de Pizan's *Cité des dames*, who also draws attention to the antiphrastic reading of allegory, specifically in terms of the *Rose*. Christine de Pizan's Raison counsels her to read the *Rose* and other misogynistic poets' fables "par la rigle de grammaire qui se nomme antifrasis . . . quel que fust leur entente" [according to the grammatical principle named antiphrasis . . . whatever their [the poets'] intent was]; see Maureen C. Curnow, "The *Livre de la Cité des dames* of Christine

identity and authority. When Rude Entendement refuses to recognize who Raison is, interpreting her according to an alternative meaning of "raison" in use at the time, Raison denies the singular identity of her name and her person: "Je tenoie une opinion / Que n'est pas un moi et mon nom" (5365–66) ["I was of the opinion that my name and I were not the same thing" (73)]. Raison argues that she is not the unjust lack of measure called "raison" by fraudulent millers but is rather its opposite. Indeed, the unjust measure is so named because of this opposition, as Raison declares:

> Entre no*n* et existence
> Vueil (je) bien faire difference . . .
> Ainciez est signe que bonne est,
> Quant le vice s'en pare et vest.
> (5307–8)

[I would like very much to distinguish between name and existence (. . .) it is a sign that it {virtue} is good when vice dresses and clothes itself in it. (72)][35]

Describing how her name can also refer to her opposite, Raison explicitly encourages textual allegoresis, which operates antiphrastically. These lines have been discussed in terms of Raison's "scandalous" insistence on a separation between name and thing when proclaiming the innocence of names signifying sexual members in the *Rose*.[36] But these lines are not simply important markers of the intertextual resonance between Deguileville's and Jean de Meun's Raison; they also prepare the reader for the immediately subsequent debate between Raison and the narrator, in which antiphrastic reading of the denied father's name is the only reading with the power to reveal the author's identity and intent.[37]

---

de Pizan: A Critical Edition" (Ph.D. diss., Vanderbilt University, 1975), sec. 4a. For a brief consideration of Christine's position on "antiphrasis" and a proposed antiphrastic reading of the *Rose*, see Douglas Kelly, *Internal Difference and Meanings in the "Roman de la Rose"* (Madison: University of Wisconsin Press, 1995), 40–44, 157–58.

[35] As Huot suggests, perhaps this is also a commentary on the "dishonest" use of pilgrim satchel as scrotum in the *Rose*; see Huot, *The "Romance of the Rose" and Its Medieval Readers*, 215.

[36] See Huot, *The "Romance of the Rose" and Its Medieval Readers*, 218–20, or Steiner, *Documentary Culture*, 35–47.

[37] These lines also examine personification as a device, creating characters through the correct interpretation of their names. Steiner offers closer analysis of the use of documents as a strategy of identity and its relation to personification, arguing that "the scene of Reason's commission questions the method by which documents authenticate persons and, by extension, the various ways in which personification may be received, recognized and named" and ultimately concluding that "Reason's commission effec-

Raison's argumentation here is thus integral to figuring Deguileville's identity; her discussion of her name represents a development of allegorical logic found within the *Rose*, as does her employment of the narrator as a clerk in her triumph over Rude Entendement.[38] Amours, when describing the *Rose*'s authors as his literary servants or scribes, renames the text itself as a "Mirror of Lovers." Assigning this new title, Amours claims control not only of "l'amant," the first-person narrator of the *Rose,* but also the text's extradiegetic authors and its audience, whose experiences as lovers are reflected and predicted in his text. Deguileville's text exhibits a similarly complex representation of composition through the drama of personification in the *Vie*, but the effect is created not by renaming the text but by figuring the text within the allegory, in the form of the charter that Raison asks the narrator, as her clerk, to read. The *Vie* depicts the charter as a document authored by Grace de Dieu, who grants Raison authority over Rude Entendement. Yet this charter figuratively signifies Deguileville's entire *Vie*, which presents itself from the start as a project made possible by the grace of God.

Moreover, this passage in which Raison identifies the narrator as her clerk also plays upon the temporal relation of the allegorical narrative and its recording as text, as Amours's speech naming the poets as his clerks in the *Rose* had done. Raison's charter concludes with a date: "Donne en nostre an que chascun / Dit M. CCC. et xxxj" (5255–56) ["Given in our year that everyone calls 1331" (71)]. Frequent marginal rubrication draws attention to the charter's date as revealing the text's date of composition, showing that medieval readers interpreted Grace de Dieu's charter as figurative of Deguileville's entire text. One scribe, for example, writes, "Note icy lan qui ce liure du pelerin fut fait" [Note here the year that this book of the pilgrim was made].[39] Medieval read-

---

tively reconciles allegoresis and hermeneutics: it proves that the pilgrim in a personification allegory-*cum*-psychomachia may literally carry stick and satchel because Luke is meant to be read allegorically." *Documentary Culture*, 35, 45.

[38] Huot compares Deguileville's churlish Rude Entendement to the *Rose*'s churl, Dangier [Mistrust], perceptively noting that Dangier accuses the narrator in the *Rose* of "rude antandement" [misunderstanding] in interpreting the courtesy of Bel Acueil [Fair Welcome] as carnal invitation; see Huot, *The "Romance of the Rose" and Its Medieval Readers*, 220. The subject of misunderstanding in Deguileville's allegory is no longer the delicate phrasing of the *Rose*'s amatory quest but the corporal/spiritual meaning of the pilgrimage quest. In Deguileville's allegory, the narrator's misunderstanding itself takes corporal form, is the personification of, Rude Entendement. This churl's obstruction is removed not by literal treasure, like the gold that silences the *Rose*'s Dangier, but by the charter treasured in Raison's coffer.

[39] See Paris, BnF, MS F. Fr. 1646, fol. 62v.

ers were as attentive to this figuration of composition as they were to the textual relevance of Amours's prophecy about his literary servants in the *Rose*. Discovering the date of the poem in the date of the charter means identifying the author with the first-person narrator at the moment when he becomes Raison's clerk. Interpretation connecting intradiegetic and extradiegetic time frames renders this passage oddly prophetic; the *Je* of the poem, acting as Raison's clerk within a dream, reads a charter issued by Grace de Dieu, which teaches how to understand the poem that he is to write when he awakens and also shares its future date. Most significant, the charter encodes the correct reading of Deguileville's allegory by granting authority to the allegorical reading practices of Raison rather than the literalist assertions of Rude Entendement, an endorsement of antiphrastic reading that also ensures the recognition of Deguileville's self-naming. Authorial presence is thus the product of readers' interpretation in Deguileville's 1331 *Pèlerinage*; the figurative action of the narrator, who reads the "document" of a personification as her clerk, signals the date of composition for the *Pèlerinage* and the means of discovering the name of its composer.

After the narrator's reading in *Vie1*, Rude Entendement foolishly concedes to Raison that he is described in her charter, becoming angry when she adopts the rhetorical ploy of pretending not to recognize him.[40] She then declares that the distinction she claimed between herself and her name must not operate in his case, quipping that he must indeed be one and the same as his name. Since the allegorical character Rude Entendement admits to being one and the same as the Rude Entendement named and described in Raison's charter, he must submit himself to the authority of the charter, to Raison, and to Grace de Dieu. Ultimately, Rude Entendement loses his authority through his literal reading, insisting that each name refers exactly and only to one thing, since he concedes the power of literal definition to the figurative charter held by Raison; it contains his name and thus refers to him. Raison gains control over Rude Entendement through the text spoken by the narrator, which establishes the correct reading of Deguileville's work, employing the multiple meanings of allegory, both antiphrastic and di-

---

[40] More unredeemable and uncontrollable in *Vie2*, Rude Entendement denies that he is the figure described in the charter as well as his name. He claims "ceulx qui mappellent ainsi / sont plus rudes que ie ne suy" [those who call me thus are more ignorant than I am] (48r). In this version, the churl is vanquished only by being ignored after Raison gives her court summons to him.

rect, championed by Raison. When Raison invokes the narrator as her clerk to rescue him from Rude Entendement's literal reading, she teaches the multiple readings of his own first-person voice. Grace's charter is the key to finding the correct level of interpretation not only for doctrinal scripture but for the narrator himself, his satchel and staff, as well as his participation in the natures of the personified Reason and Poor Understanding. Only after the text within the text has given the correct level of reading, affirming reason and rebuking poor understanding, can the narrative progress.

Raison in *Vie1* acts as the central figure in representing authorial identity within the allegory, employing similar logic to that found in the *Rose*. Raison's explicit citation of the *Rose* suggests the textual connection, and her identification of the narrator demonstrates a sophisticated response to the figuration of authorship in the *Rose*. Her authority to name, however, as seen in her encounter with Rude Entendement, is ultimately authorized by the charter that resembles Deguileville's entire allegory (bearing its date of composition and voiced by its narrator), and this charter is in turn authorized by the personification Grace de Dieu. By ascribing the figurative charter to Grace, Deguileville secures a spiritual "author" and authority for his allegory even as his narrator signals human authorial identity, reworking the *Rose*'s innovative creation of a first-person voice that is both specific and universal within its allegory.

Venus's Clerk: Personification and Persona in *Vie2*

The link between authorial naming and *Rose* allusions in Deguileville's *Vie1* remains present in the later recension (*Vie2*), although aspects of Raison's function are reassigned to other characters. The *Rose* is not cited by name in *Vie2*'s opening lines, so Raison's citation becomes the first direct reference to the *Rose* in *Vie2*.[41] Yet Raison is no longer the only allegorical character to call upon the *Rose* as a source demonstrating her nature. *Vie2* expands the discourse of Venus, who now not only cites the *Rose* but takes a role in the text's exploration of authorial naming, since her citation introduces a debate over the name of the *Rose*'s author. In

[41] The intertexual resemblance to the opening of the *Rose* is arguably stronger in *Vie2*, as the relation of the waking and dreaming self is explored more deeply. For another interpretation of the changes between the openings, see Fabienne Pomel, "Enjeux d'un travail de réécriture: Les incipits du *Pèlerinage de vie humaine* de Guillaume de Digulleville et leurs remaniements ultérieurs," *MA* 109.3–4 (2003): 457–72.

Vie2, Venus appears to usurp Raison's role in interpreting the *Rose* and the allegorical author. Deguileville's narrator is not invoked as Raison's clerk in *Vie2*, but Venus assigns the *Rose* author the posture of her clerk. Venus, not Raison, claims to demonstrate the relationship of personifications and persons to textual creation. The debate with Venus now exposes the authorial control hidden in the *Rose*'s device of a narrator who claims to be controlled by a personification, even as Deguileville adopts the same device to serve his own ends.

In Deguileville's allegory, Venus appears in a series of personified sins, representing "Luxure" [Lust]. She gives this as an alternate name for herself and is sometimes rubricated by this name. Several *Vie2* manuscripts also employ the term "Luxure" in place of "Amors Carnal" [Carnal Love] within Raison's citation of the *Rose*, so the name links the two *Rose* citations and sharpens the contrast between Venus and Raison. Moreover, in *Vie2*, Venus (or Luxure) also opposes Raison in textual interpretation as she seeks to supplant any reading of the *Rose* that does not depend on her nature and "authorial" intent. Citing the *Roman de la rose* as her own work, Venus admires the way it reflects her hatred of Chastite by its slanderous depiction of Chastite in the character Faux Semblant [False Seeming].[42] The narrator directly questions her startling assumption of the text's authorship:

> Pour quoy (dis ie) reputes tien
> Le rommant quas dit, que scay bien
> Qui le fist, et comment ot nom.[43]

[Why, I said, do you call the romance you mention yours, for I know well who made it and what his name is?]

Venus's prompt reassertion of her right to the *Rose* redefines the understanding of textual ownership. The romance is rightly hers, she claims,

---

[42] Deguileville is perhaps thinking here of both Faux Semblant [False Seeming] and Abstinence Contrainte [Constrained Abstinence], who travel as a pair in the *Rose*.

[43] In *Le Romant des trois Pelerinaiges*, fols. 55v–56r, printed circa 1510–11 or 1514–18 in Paris by Barthole Rembolt and Jean Petit. I use this—one of the earliest printed editions—as there is no modern edition of the *Pèlerinage de la vie humaine*'s 1355 recension. For a discussion of the relative dating of this edition and the 1511 *Pelerinage de l'homme* printed in Paris by Anthoine Vérard, see Edmond Faral, "Guillaume de Digulleville, Jean Galloppes et Pierre Virgin," in *Études Romanes Dédiées à Mario Roques* (Paris: Droz, 1946), 89–102 (96–97 n. 2). I have compared the edition for sense agreement with multiple manuscripts of the recension (Paris, BnF, F. Fr. MSS 829, 825, 1138, 3646).

because from beginning to end it speaks of her; Lust is its substance. In speaking of her "scribe" for the *Rose*, however, Venus immediately cites an exception to her control. She admits that her scribe, against her will, digressed from her description and stole from others' works, rather than writing of his own invention. She then reports that a Norman accused her scribe of this theft. Venus claims her scribe hated Normans for this reason and argues that this hatred motivated his lying description of the character Male Bouche [Bad Mouth] as a Norman.[44] Both the statement inviting the narrator's question and its answer thus suggest that ulterior, deceitful purposes govern the depictions of *Rose* personifications: whether praising her enemy Chastite's slanderous portrayal under a false name or alleging that Male Bouche's Norman origin is a grudge-driven lie, Venus opens doubt as to the credibility of her own characterization, particularly her claim of a voice independent from that of her "scribe," the allegory's author.[45]

This assertion of authorial control on the part of Venus imitates the assertion of control by Amours at the midpoint of the *Rose*; indeed, the passage containing Venus's assertion falls at the new midpoint in Deguileville's much extended *Vie2*. Once again, authorial presence is discovered by reading for contradictions: Venus presents herself as a personification with intertextual and even extratextual reality, claiming authorship of the *Rose*, yet she also complains of her lack of full control over mortal writers. Both her assertion and her complaint reveal the biases of authorial intention that can direct an allegory's use of sources and manner of identifying allegorical personifications. The narrator responds to this puzzle of who is speaking by once more asserting his ability to name the author of the *Rose*. But when the narrator at last names the author of the *Rose*, he does not untangle the relation of Venus and her scribe/author or reveal the nonallegorical names of Jean de Meun or Guillaume de Lorris. Instead he declares that the human

[44] For brief references to anti-Norman satire in the *Rose*, written by both Guillaume de Lorris and Jean de Meun, see Matthew Bennett, "Stereotype Normans in Old French Vernacular Literature," *Anglo-Norman Studies* 9 (1987): 25–42. Norman satire is well attested from the earliest surviving manuscripts; whatever the motivation for either author's depiction of Normans, criticism of plagiarism within the *Rose* is thus unlikely. Venus's claim in the *Vie2* challenges the order of temporality as flagrantly as Amours's celebrated speech in the *Rose*.

[45] Venus, in fact, openly informs the narrator that she will lie to him; her aim is to deceive: "ie te mentiray / Et en mentant te deceuray" [I will lie to you and in lying I will deceive you] (56r).

"scribe" and the personification claiming authorship must share the identity of Male Bouche, the most ill-speaking allegorical character. Discounting the alleged Norman origin of Male Bouche, Deguileville gives Male Bouche a new origin of his own choosing by having the narrator declare that both Venus's scribe and she herself are recognizable as no one other than Male Bouche, precisely because of their manner of creating this character:

> . . . veritablement dy
> Male bouche est ton escripuain
> En male bouche son prochain
> Appellant . . .
> Et tu male bouche as aussi
> Quant contre chastete mesdy
> Tu as, et ton clerc fait mentir.
> (56r)

[truly I say Bad Mouth is your scribe when he calls his neighbor Bad Mouth. . . . And you have a bad mouth also since you spoke ill of Chastity and made your clerk lie.][46]

Edmond Faral's 1962 study and most subsequent considerations of this passage note Deguileville's probable Northern origin as a reason why he might have taken offense at the depiction of Normans as drunken soldiers and companions of Male Bouche in both Guillaume de Lorris's and Jean de Meun's sections of the *Rose*.[47] My interest in the passage renaming the *Rose* authors as their personification Male Bouche lies not in Deguileville's extratextual biography, however, but in how this passage shapes Deguileville's presentation of authorship within allegory. It shows a close reading of the *Rose*'s allegory and authorial play and asks some of the same questions that Christine de Pizan would later explore

[46] Certain manuscripts (including Paris, BnF, F.Fr. 829 and 12466) have the reading "Male bouche ot ton escripuain" or "Male bouche a ton escripuain" [Your scribe has an evil mouth]; the association of the poet and this personified quality, however, remains strong. The most complete medieval manuscript of the English verse translation, British Library, Cotton Vitellius C.xiii, renders the lines as "trewly thy skriyveyn / Hihte malë bouche"; see *The Pilgrimage of the Life of Man*, ed. Furnivall and Locock, lines 1327–28.

[47] See Faral, "Guillaume de Digulleville," 2, 37 n. 2. Badel, for example, refers to Guillaume's patriotism and says "la réaction du Normand peut faire sourire" [the reaction of a Norman is perhaps risible]; see Badel, *Le "Roman de la rose" au XIVe siècle*, 374.

concerning the authorial stance within allegory.[48] Venus's debate with the narrator in *Vie2* concerning the writing of the *Rose* calls to mind Amours's inversion of personification and author roles in the *Rose* and Raison's similar inversion in *Vie1*. In this conversation with Venus, the worlds of author and allegory intersect: the creation of the Male Bouche character in the *Rose* becomes an act of Male Bouche that leads to the *Rose* author's renaming as Male Bouche. This passage borrows the impossible allegorical logic of the *Rose* to reinvent the *Rose* author as a personification invented by the *Rose* author.

Deguileville thus playfully challenges the *Rose*'s slippery use of the supposedly neutral role of the exegete or compiler in medieval allegory. In Deguileville's allegory, personifications again claim to control the authorial persona, and the midpoint is again a place of renaming, renaming not the *Rose* this time, but its authors. The function of renaming remains an allegorical invitation to envision the first-person narrator as at once specific and universal, fragmented in identity by the multiple levels of allegorical reading. As noted, when the *Rose* is renamed as a "Mirror for Lovers" by Amours, the new name invites readers to see themselves as the lovers mirrored in the text at the same moment that Amours identifies another, individual name for the internal character of the lover (Guillaume de Lorris), simultaneously assigned the role of textual creator. In the midpoint renaming passage from *Vie2*, Male Bouche is simultaneously identified as an abstract quality any reader may embody, as a character in the *Rose* revealing authorial intention, and also as the *Rose* author who is both the narrator posing as scribe and the abstract personification claiming authorial control. Male Bouche, a means of satire upon Normans in the *Rose*, becomes a means of mocking the satire's author as lustful and deceitful in Deguileville's *Vie2*, recasting the *Rose* allegory through antiphrasis to mean its opposite. Responding to the *Rose* through the very strategies the *Rose* inspired, Deguileville's allegory reveals intertextual affiliation and offers intertextual critique in a figurative, rather than explicit, manner.

---

[48] Christine's first critique of the *Rose*, in her *Epistre au dieu d'amours* (c. 1399), is launched not in her own voice as a woman author but in the voice of the *dieu d'Amours*, challenging Jean de Meun's pretense that the personification of Love controlled and appreciated the work of the *Rose*'s authors. See Lori Walters, "The Woman Writer and Literary History: Christine de Pizan's Redefinition of the Poetic *Translatio* in the *Epistre au Dieu d'amours*," *French Literature Series* 16 (1989): 1–16.

Given by Grace: Self-Naming in *Vie2*

Deguileville's recension of the *Vie* not only renames the *Rose* author as it reopens the question of personification and narrator relations, however; it also expands Deguileville's self-naming strategies. Just as Venus expands the once-singular role of Raison by naming the *Rose*, Grace de Dieu supplants Raison by naming Deguileville no fewer than three times in *Vie2*. As Deguileville enlarges the role of Grace de Dieu, he elaborates upon the allegorical play of author presentation begun by borrowing personifications from the *Rose* to increase recognition of his own name. *Vie2* not only introduces Deguileville's name more fully than *Vie1*, but the process of naming also begins sooner. Early in *Vie1*, the narrator follows Grace de Dieu to her house suspended over water; entrance into the house of Grace requires passing through water, a figuration of baptism. The narrator asks if he can avoid the water, but Grace declares he is filthy from his nine-month home (the womb). In *Vie2*, immediately after this exchange, the narrator desires to know more about the necessity of washing. Grace, referring to Adam and Eve as his father and mother, explains "la damnation / Que tout lhumain lignaige auoit" (fol. 5r) [the damnation that the entire human lineage shares]. But describing how Christ allows her to cleanse those who keep their marriage vows, Grace declares "ton pere et ta mere lauez / Y furent" (fol. 5v) [your father and your mother were washed here]. The parentage Grace invokes thus slips from the biblical universals of Eden to a respectable medieval couple. When the narrator submits to Grace and finds he is unable to do anything other than cry loudly, he introduces his namesake godparent as his surrogate voice:

> ung aduocat me suruint
> Qui pour moy la parole print
> Disant que pour moy parleroit . . .
> Icellui guillaume auoit nom
> Mais pas ne sauoie son surnom.
>
> (5v)

[a godparent (*lit.* advocate) served me, who took the oath for me, saying that he spoke for me . . . this one had the name Guillaume, but I do not know his surname.]

Like Jean de Meun, whom Amours claims will be unable to write the *Rose* unless Amours gives words to Jean while he is a child in a cradle, Guillaume de Deguileville, posturing as the speechless narrator of his own baptism, calls in another voice to speak for him and to name him when a child. The narrator's posture of speechlessness at this moment of his naming resembles Jean de Meun's depiction of his own birth through the voice of one of his characters, the one who gives his name.

Deguileville's narrator is given a name, and an unforgettable tie of kinship, at the very moment of seeking escape from sinful human lineage through baptism:

> Adonc cest aduocat me prit
> Et ie luy dis auil mapellast
> Tout ainsi com luy, et nommast . . .
> Et laduocat sen fut ale
> Qui me fist si grant courtoisse
> Quobiler iamais ne doy mie.
>
> (5v)

[then this godparent took me and I asked him to call me after him and he named me . . . and the godparent departed, who did me a service so courteous that I should never forget it.]

The narrator's renunciation of human lineage thus introduces the author's first name as a unique individual, albeit voiced and bestowed by another human relation. Deguileville's depiction of the narrator as an infant remains open to readers' allegorical participation even as it reveals the author's name. The conjoined universal and individual nature of the narrator is clearly visible in the index added to the early sixteenth-century *Vie2* edition from which I quote. This passage, marked by the exact same folio number and alphabetical tabula, is listed in section B, as "Baptesme est le premier sacreme(n)t de chascun pelerin.fo.v.B" [Baptism is the first sacrament of each pilgrim, fol. 5b] and in section G, as "Guillaume parrain du pelerin se presente a laider a lauer par le sacrement de baptesme foeillet.v.B" [Guillaume godparent of the pilgrim presents himself to help to bathe him in the sacrament of baptism, fol. 5b]. Readers are thus invited to identify the narrator both as a universal representative of "each pilgrim" and as the godson of "Guillaume," the author Guillaume de Deguileville.

The surname Deguileville, the final clue to authorial identity, is with-held, however, until the debate about the narrator's division between body and soul, also significantly revised. The debate now takes place immediately after Memoire's introduction and before the encounter with Rude Entendement. The same exchanges transpire between the narrator and Grace de Dieu, rather than Raison.[49] Although the name of the author's father is presented in much the same way as in *Vie1*, the assigning of these lines to Grace instead of Raison subtly shifts the text's presentation of how identity is formed. In *Vie2*, Grace introduces both the first name and the surname of Guillaume de Deguileville in *Rose* style: like Amours at Jean de Meun's cradle, Grace de Dieu now in-structs the voiceless but narrating "Guillaume" from his allegorical birth.[50] This alteration, in which Grace de Dieu replaces Raison as an authority on the author's name, appears to work in concert with *Vie2*'s use of Venus to replace Raison's function as a personification who reads and challenges the *Rose*.

Despite Venus's complaints depicting the *Rose*'s literary borrowing as theft, however, Deguileville's recension includes more lines borrowed from other authors' compositions than his allegory had originally con-tained, including Latin lines from Ovid, the author whose writings are the most widely influential sources of the *Rose*.[51] Indeed, the introduc-tion of Ovid as a character provides the context for the final instance of naming in *Vie2*, the instance perhaps most overtly concerned with intertextual authorial relations. The narrator encounters Ovid after he is attacked by personifications representing envy, conspiracy, detraction,

---

[49] These changes follow from suggestions seen in *Vie1*. The debate with Raison origi-nally concluded with the narrator claiming that he now understands what Grace de Dieu taught him earlier, clarified by Raison's teaching, and Raison insists that she can do nothing without Grace, from whom all her teaching comes. Substituting Grace for Raison as the guiding interlocutor in the debate eliminates the need for such clarification of allegorical relation, as does the change of context that places the debate directly after Memoire's introduction, rather than referring back to these scenes after the encounter with Rude Entendement.

[50] At the close of the fourteenth century, perhaps reflecting the influence of Deguile-ville's use of this image, Jean Molinet's commentary on the *Rose* interprets the *Rose* narrator's early crossing of a river as an allegory representing the narrator's birth and interprets the fountain of Narcissus in the *Rose* as "le saint fons de baptesme" [the sacred font of baptism] (8r). Citations from Molinet's commentary in his *Le "Roman de la rose moralisé"* refer to the early print edition produced by Guillaume Balsarin in Paris, circa 1503, according to folio number. Jean Devaux is currently preparing a modern edition, forthcoming from Champion.

[51] On the extent of Ovidian borrowing in the *Rose*, see Thérèse Bouché, "Ovide et Jean de Meun," *MA* 83 (1977): 71–87.

and treachery. As he suffers, Ovid delivers a curse upon the narrator's attackers: Latin verse from Ovid's *Ibis*, the curse composed in exile, appears as an insertion. The narrator responds warmly to Ovid's affection but refuses to curse, hoping instead for the return of a king who will redress his wrongs. When the ancient poet departs, the pensive narrator voices a lament.[52] Declaring that no one knows his sorrow save himself, he requests the reader: "ne tienne nul a despit / Sen icelluy dueil iay assises / Les lettres de mon nom" (84r) [do not despise it, if I have placed in this lament the letters of my name]. The lyric conveys the author's name in a stanzaic acrostic of twenty-four stanzas with a rhyme scheme of couplets systematically linking alternating Latin and French lines. In this manner, the lyric is not only metrically but linguistically distinguished from the rest of Deguileville's text, suggesting the influence of Latin verse, like the lines just attributed to Ovid. The lyric's contents, however, summarize the allegorical action: the acrostic describes the narrator's entry into monastic life with the aid of Grace de Dieu, the attacks he then suffered, and his plea for succor.

In *Vie1*, the narrator's reading of Grace de Dieu's charter enables him both to interpret and be interpreted correctly. In *Vie2*, the narrator's reading of his own acrostic lyric, authorized by knowledge that he claims only he can have, still invokes the allegorical authority of Grace de Dieu, who also appears in the earlier passages signaling the author's first and last names. The lyric's second stanza introduces Grace de Dieu as the character who calls the narrator by name from within writing, drawing attention to the author's name and to the process of interpretation:

> Vidi scriptum in margine
> Ou cestuy escript s'enracine

---

[52] The departure of Ovid at this point echoes the departure of Raison in the *Rose* after her rejection by the narrator, so this passage could be considered to display Deguileville's critical response to the "unreasonable" inspiration of the *Rose* by pagan poetry. There is a warmth of affection expressed for Ovid here, however, and the sixteenth-century printed editions of *Vie2* contain a prologue that compares the style of Ovid and Deguileville explicitly, as two worthy poets: "Touteffois ainsi quen latin / Ouide son langaige fainct / Semblablement de pres attainct / Poesie nostre deguileuille" [Just as Ovid made Latin his language, similarly to attain esteem our Deguileville used poetic discourse]. As a preface to *Le Romant des trois Pelerinaiges*, these lines appear on fol. 1r–1v; with some variation, the lines also appear before the 1511 *Vie2* printed by Anthoine Vérard, on fol. 1r. Early readers, it seems, would not necessarily have viewed Ovid as an entirely rejected influence in Deguileville's allegory.

> Mirandam pulchritudine
> Grace dieu du ciel royne digne
> Me vocantem ex nomine
> Vien auant, et si tachemine
> Mecum, quia regimine
> Tu as mestier, et de doctrine.
>
> (84r–85r)

[I saw written in the margin where this writing roots itself a wonderful beauty. Grace de Dieu, worthy queen of heaven, called me by name: "Come forth and I will lead you to me since you need direction and teaching."]

What the reader calls forth from the writing along the marginal edges of these folios, in a typically laid-out manuscript with marked initial letters for each stanza, is the Latin form of the poet's name, GVILLERMVS DE DEGVILVILLA. (The V beginning the stanza quoted above, for example, marks the second letter of the author's name.) Deguileville presents the narrator as a master of Ovid's language and literature, but ultimately chooses Grace de Dieu once again as the naming authority; Deguileville's readers reenact Grace de Dieu's role by calling forth his name from the textual margin. The process of exegesis, far from being inimical to interest in human authorship, provides Deguileville with the means of signaling his identity within his allegory, greatly developing the *Roman de la rose*'s playful presentation of its author as an exegete and as a narrator created through interactions with personifications.[53]

In Deguileville's allegory, passages depicted as separate compositions—Grace's charter, the narrator's lament—figure the text in which they are contained and teach readers how to read texts figuratively.[54]

[53] In light of the text's play upon marginal exegesis, it is interesting that the imagery of Deguileville's trilogy was adopted as a marginal gloss upon liturgical texts at least in one medieval book of hours. Michael Camille notes how the recognizable illumination cycle developed for Deguileville's trilogy is painted into the margins of Cambridge, Fitzwilliam Museum, MS 62. See Michael Camille, "The Illustrated Manuscripts of Guillaume de Deguileville's 'Pèlerinages,' 1330–1426" (Ph.D. diss., University of Cambridge, 1985), 2:227–34. More study of the integral role that Deguileville's images play in this manuscript's schema of textual interpretation and reader representation can be found in Hagen, *Allegorical Remembrance*, 126–28, and Richard Emmerson, "A 'Large Order of the Whole': Intertextuality and Interpictoriality in the Hours of Isabella Stuart," *SIcon* 28 (2007): 51–110. I am grateful to Richard Emmerson for sharing with me a draft in advance of his article's publication.

[54] In *Vie2*, the narrator's relation to texts within the allegory shifts from the role of reader toward that of author: Raison, not the narrator, reads the charter in the revised scene with Rude Entendement and, as we have seen, the narrator is introduced as the author of *Vie2*'s acrostic complaint.

This innovation may also have a root in Deguileville's *Rose* reading, if Grace de Dieu's authorship of Raison's dated charter and naming authority within the narrator's acrostic lament took shape as a response to the activity of the *Rose*'s priest Genius, who writes and reads aloud Nature's charter, which similarly acts as a textual microcosm. Genius acts as a writer who seeks control of the entire *Rose* allegory, explicitly contrasting the garden described in his charter with the *Rose*'s initial depiction of Amours's garden. His speech thus seeks to replace Guillaume de Lorris's opening, and his intradiegetic character seeks to replace the extradiegetic author, as Kevin Brownlee has noted.[55] Deguileville's development of Grace de Dieu's role in literary activity may reflect his appreciation of how Genius's "charter" raises the question of authorial identity in the *Rose*, as well as Deguileville's desire to differentiate his own work. Deguileville's techniques of signaling authorial control within allegory are drawn from the intensely Ovidian *Rose*, as the love of the character Ovid for the narrator suggests, but Deguileville's self-naming in the recension establishes that the *Rose*'s source, Ovid, is neither fully departed nor the father of Deguileville's narrator, a child of God named by Grace.

Deguileville thus contests the *Rose* on its own terms, masterfully creating a specific authorial identity within an allegory that nonetheless functions as an allegory. Imitating the complexities of authorial signature in the erotic allegory of the *Rose*, Deguileville first signs his own name as the clerk of reason rather than a foolish lover in *Vie1* and then revises his work to incorporate his full name in *Vie2*, in more extensive figurative passages that challenge Jean's scribal posture and dependence on Ovid. The pan-European distribution of Deguileville's allegory extends the influence of the complex first-person voice of the *Rose* well beyond the French *dits amoureux* tradition, and also merits comparison with the many later responses to the *Rose*, such as Chaucer's *Legend of Good Women*, Christine de Pizan's *Epistre au dieu d'Amours*, Thomas Hoc-

---

[55] Brownlee describes the reversal of personification and author persona positions, stating that "Genius the character (in Jean de Meun's text) becomes a poet figure. But, at the same time, Genius's rewriting of Guillaume de Lorris works to transform the latter (a 'real' poet, with a privileged extratextual existence in terms of the entire *Rose* enterprise) into a 'character,' also 'contained' by Jean de Meun's poetic *summa*." See Kevin Brownlee, "Jean de Meun and the Limits of Romance: Genius as Rewriter of Guillaume de Lorris," in *Romance: Generic Transformations from Chrétien de Troyes to Cervantes*, ed. Kevin Brownlee and Maria Scordilis Brownlee (Hanover, N.H.: University Press of New England, 1985), 114–34 (129).

cleve's *Epistola Cupidinis*, and Alain Chartier's *Excusacion aux dames*. Recognition of Deguileville's sophisticated authorial signature practice should revise the idea that "Deguileville's capacity to absorb the literary techniques of the *Roman de la Rose* was much more limited than Chaucer's."[56] Deguileville's 1331 *Pèlerinage de la vie humaine* and its 1355 recension reveal to us that the rhetorical play of claiming authorship within an allegory, moral or otherwise, was one of the *Rose*'s most important legacies for the vernacular writers of late medieval France and England.

Conclusion: The Tradition of Authorship in Allegory

A. C. Spearing's *Textual Subjectivity* recently argued that "we are living through a reversal of the process experienced in the later Middle Ages. For us, the notion that every text must have its speaker, every narrative its narrator, may be beginning to dissolve; for late medieval writers . . . it was a new discovery."[57] Spearing seeks to recapture a reading of early texts without the anchor of an individual authorial voice, but it is fair to say that our current understanding of the movement that yoked narration and the representation of authorship is at best incomplete. Deguileville's *Rose*-inspired allegory has been noted for its popularizing—and bowdlerizing—of the *Rose* narrator's climactic role as a pilgrim. But if we are to recognize how Deguileville's allegory also disseminated the *Rose*'s practice of naming the author by means of this figure, we must begin to take allegorical narrative seriously as the means, rather than the enemy, of developing interest in authorship.

On closer examination, what George Kane once described as a curious and ambiguous "practice of signature" ultimately yields a vision of how late medieval writers conceived of vernacular authorship.[58] Defin-

---

[56] This claim perhaps reflects the predominant focus on the 1331 allegory in Wright, "Deguileville's *Pèlerinage de Vie Humaine*," 399.

[57] *Textual Subjectivity: The Encoding of Subjectivity in Medieval Narratives and Lyric* (Oxford: Oxford University Press, 2005), 30.

[58] In making the case for the narrator's name of "Will" as a signature in *Piers Plowman*, Kane cited the wider tradition without delving into its analysis: "Thirteenth- and fourteenth-century French and English authors, writing various kinds of narrative poems in which a first-person narrator recounts a succession of fantastic incidents represented as experienced either awake or in a dream, would conventionally identify the narrators with themselves. . . . They created the ambiguous situation where encouragement to identify poet and narrator is given by their possession of the same name and checked by the character of what is narrated; that they did this suggests that the ambiguity had a purpose. To speculate about this purpose is not part of the present discussion." See George Kane, *"Piers Plowman": The Evidence for Authorship* (London: Athlone

ing the position of the vernacular writer within the medieval literary tradition did not always transpire through expanding "realistic" reference to historical life outside the narrative; instead, vernacular writers claimed recognition through weaving their identities into the matter for interpretation. An image of authorial identity takes shape within the mind of the reader exploring the conflicting elements of narration, and later writers reveal themselves as readers through their ability to signal their own identities through this same structural vehicle. Allegory provided a uniquely communal model of authorship: writers reenter the same visionary landscapes and character voices and reform them as their own, implanting their proper names or features in a way that begs individual attribution and yet leaves their voices open to symbolic and universal interpretations. As in the cases of the *Rose* and Deguileville's trilogy, the allegories employing this practice reflect a wide array of ethical, social, and political agendas. Yet the identity of the first-person narrator-protagonist within these late medieval allegories consistently functions as a means of authorial attribution, recoverable through interpretation but ensconced within a communal, interreferential tradition. This signature practice renders not only the vernacular author but also vernacular literary history a subject worthy of readers' attention.

Press, 1965), 53, 57. Subsequent studies of signature in *Piers Plowman* have built upon Kane's suggestions, primarily in terms of its English sociohistorical context, notably Anne Middleton, "William Langland's 'Kynde Name': Authorial Signature and Social Identity in Late Fourteenth-Century England," in *Literary Practice and Social Change in Britain, 1380–1530*, ed. Lee Patterson (Berkeley and Los Angeles: University of California Press, 1990), 15–82, and James Simpson, "The Power of Impropriety: Authorial Naming in *Piers Plowman*," in *William Langland's "Piers Plowman": A Book of Essays*, ed. Kathleen M. Hewett-Smith (New York: Routledge, 2001), 145–65.

The Ends of Excitement in *Sir Gawain and the Green Knight:*

Teleology, Ethics, and the Death Drive

Mark Miller
University of Chicago

Holding Still

I N THE FOURTH FITT of the fourteenth-century alliterative romance *Sir Gawain and the Green Knight*, when our hero has finally arrived at the Green Chapel to receive the promised blow from his giant adversary, the poet describes his stillness as he awaits the ax's descent upon his neck:

> Gawayn grayþely hit bydez and glent with no membre
> Bot stode stylle as þe ston oþer a stubbe auþer
> Þat raþeled is in roché grounde with rotez a hundreth.[1]
>
> (2292–94)

As the moment immediately preceding this one emphasizes, such stillness is by no means an easy thing for Gawain to manage. In that previ-

An early version of sections I–III was presented to the Medieval Studies Colloquium at the University of California at Santa Barbara, and an even earlier version of some of the material in sections III and IV was presented at the University of Pennsylvania and Harvard University. I would like to thank the members of all three audiences for their insightful engagement and suggestions for revision.

[1] All citations of *Sir Gawain and the Green Knight* and *Pearl* are from *The Poems of the Pearl Manuscript*, ed. Malcolm Andrew and Ronald Waldron, 4th ed. (Exeter: University of Exeter Press, 2002), and will be given by reference to line numbers in the body of the text.

ous moment, as the Green Knight prepares to strike his blow, Gawain does something that later gets called "flinching":

> Bot Gawayn on þat giserne glyfte hym bysyde,
> As hit com glydande adoun on glode hym to schende,
> And schranke a lytel with þe schulderes for þe scharp yrne.
>
> (2265–67)

In the reading that both Gawain and the Green Knight will soon give of these moments, they stand in sharp contrast. In the earlier moment— that is, the one I cited second—Gawain succumbs to fear, and in so doing betrays nearly everything that constitutes his chivalric identity: "þou art not Gawayn" (2270), chides the Green Knight in a refrain we hear throughout the poem, and one that Gawain accepts. By this, both figures understand that what makes Gawain who he is are his courage and self-control in the face of danger and death, his commitment to his *trawthe*, and his commitment to Arthur to stand for him, and in so doing to stand for the virtue of Camelot. In the later moment, however, by holding still Gawain returns to himself, manifesting his inner integrity by holding himself to his word and by making good both on his sacrificial commitment to his lord and on the representational burden that has been placed on him—in short, by doing his duty.

Such an account is right enough as far as it goes, and it is the one most critics have followed in understanding the import of this scene for the poem and for the chivalric ethos it embodies. But the lines I have cited suggest that there is a lot more going on here than a straightforward contrast between betrayal and integrity. The notion of integrity at issue here is closely tied to a conception of autonomy as a special form of aliveness.[2] What makes Gawain an icon of knightly *trawthe* is that he refuses to be compelled by the most compelling forces at work in him— here, his natural desire for self-preservation; earlier in the poem, his equally natural desire for sexual pleasure. According to Paul, Augustine,

---

[2] My argument concerning a special form of chivalric aliveness in the poem is indebted to Aranye Fradenburg's account of the prestige of chivalric sacrifice, in *Sacrifice Your Love: Psychoanalysis, Historicism, Chaucer* (Minneapolis: University of Minnesota Press, 2002). See especially her chapters "Sacrificial Desire in Chaucer's *Knight's Tale*," 155–75, and "'Oure Owen Wo to Drynke': Dying Inside in *Troilus and Criseyde*," 199–238). Fradenburg extends and rearticulates that account in helpful ways in "Pro Patria Mori," in Kathy Lavezzo, ed., *Imagining a Medieval English Nation* (Minneapolis: University of Minnesota Press, 2004), 3–38.

and others working in the Christian moral tradition, to be compelled in such a way is to become passive, to become a victim of one's *pathe* or passions, of desire in the mode of what comes upon or befalls us; and to do that is to become subject to a living death.[3] If Gawain flinches—if he allows his desire for the sheer continuance of life to control him—then he has lost the very thing that animates him, that makes his life rise above a condition of mere temporal extension. He is no longer "Gawain." Holding still is thus a way of resisting the pull of death-in-life; or, to put it another way, of resisting the fragmenting force of passion in the name of a unifying ideal, a self-conception that gives him form and purpose. The lines describing Gawain's stillness, however, tell a more complicated story. As he waits for the blade "grayþely," in the way that is due from him and appropriate to him, he stands "stylle as þe ston": his integrity is that of the hard, inanimate object. Or he is like a "stubbe," a dead thing that can only be identified by referring back to the life it once had—and if that lost life offers an image of being, as Gawain is now, unmoved, that is because its condition was already one of fixity, of being "raþeled . . . in roché grounde, with rotez a hundreth," clinging to an existence entwined with the stoniness from which it

---

[3] Paul's main discussion of living death is in Romans; see especially his discussion of the relation between sin and law in chapters 7–8. Augustine's main discussion of living death comes in *City of God*, books 12–14, where it emerges from his argument for the insubstantiality of evil and his account of the Fall. Peter Brown helpfully traces the tradition of Christian thinking along these lines from Paul to Augustine: see Brown, *The Body and Society: Men, Women, and Sexual Renunciation in Early Christianity* (New York: Columbia University Press, 1988). It is crucial to remember that desire as such is not the culprit here; nor is passion, except in a technical sense narrower than that of common usage. Every act is in some sense a function of desire, and on the theological accounts under discussion here, desire is perhaps the central term for describing the human relation to its normative principle in the divine. The problem, rather, is one of being moved in a way you do not want to be moved. This is one way of describing what it means to be moved against your will, in those cases of being so moved in which you are moved by something in you rather than by an external force. To be moved, and even flooded or driven, by a desire that you *would* endorse is not on such an account "pathological." For a further explication of such an account and its relevance to a four-teenth-century chivalric ethos, see my discussion of Chaucer's *Knight's Tale* in *Philosophi-cal Chaucer: Love, Sex, and Agency in the Canterbury Tales* (Cambridge: Cambridge University Press, 2004), 82–110. For the connection between such thinking about agency and passivity to accounts of the political grounds of aristocratic power, see John of Salisbury, *Policraticus*, vol. 5, ed. and trans. C. J. Nederman (Cambridge: Cambridge University Press, 1990); and Aquinas, *De regimine principum*, in *St. Thomas Aquinas on Ethics and Politics*, ed. and trans. Paul E. Sigmund (New York: W. W. Norton, 1988), 14–29. For the intimate bonds among chivalric integrity, the broader Christian ethics of integrity, and the death drive, see Fradenburg, *Sacrifice Your Love* and "Pro Patria Mori."

emerges. If holding still is Gawain's way of laying claim to a special form of aliveness, then, the absence of *pathe* it entails would also seem to link him with the impenetrability of the unliving, and with life's tendency toward, and even need for, immobility, for rooting itself in inanimacy.

A similar complication emerges from Gawain's earlier, unwanted movement. To call that movement a flinch motivated by fear is to read it in the terms the Green Knight and Gawain have for it after the fact. What the lines say, first, is just that Gawain takes a look at the blade as it descends to destroy him. He wants to see it coming; he wants, as it were, to be present at the scene of his own death, to bear witness to it; he does not want his death to be something that just happens to him, as it happens to a tree that it gets broken, leaving only a stump. In this sense, Gawain succumbs less to fear than to anticipation, to the desire to register the coming of this unimaginable, long-awaited event, to let it have an impact on him. His movement is thus closely tied to, rather than opposed to, his desire for a special form of aliveness, for being the one whose life is more than a condition of mere temporal extension. Next, the poem says that Gawain "schranke a lytel with þe schuldres for þe scharp yrne." This is not quite the same as saying "his shoulders shrank." *That* would be closer to a flinch, closer to a case of pure *pathe*—as we might say, something his body does whether he wants it to or not. What the poem describes is rather something *Gawain* does, a movement he makes, *with* his shoulders. And why "for þe scharp yrne"? The line is sometimes glossed "for fear of the sharp iron," but that adds something the poem does not say.[4] What it does say is just that Gawain shrinks on account of, or for the sake of, the sharp iron. In the context of his anticipatory glance, this line certainly suggests fear; but it also suggests anticipation, or perhaps something stranger, a movement that, while a drawing away, involves a certain sort of welcoming. There is excitation and even a shudder of pleasure here, as Gawain moves his shoulders to shrink from, but also to relish, the fearful, violent blow approaching him, the last one (or so he thinks) he will ever feel—his final moment of life, a moment to which he wants to be fully alive.

I begin with these moments of stillness and movement because they

[4]See, for instance, Thomas J. Garbaty, *Medieval English Literature* (Lexington, Mass.: D. C. Heath, 1984), 324.

both evoke and complicate some of the most fundamental ways in which we have understood this poem and the late medieval aristocratic culture it engages. As many critics have noted, the poem here represents the space of the aristocratic subject's formation around ideals of integrity, self-command, and chivalric duty, a space in which to come up short with respect to those ideals can so evacuate one's life that an honorable death seems preferable, and so charge one's life with shame that it can only continue under an indelible stigma. The ethical weight of duty and shame here associates Gawain's stillness with the core values of the poem and of chivalry itself, values reflected most clearly in the poem's central figure of ethical value, the "endless knot" of the pentangle depicted on Gawain's shield.[5] To the extent that Gawain manages or desires to manage such a stillness, he is then understood to live up to or to desire to live up to that ethos, and to the extent that he does not, he is understood, at least in the poem's terms, to be guilty of an ethical failure.[6] This is not to say that such an ethos has uniformly seemed unproblematic. To some, it is a reflection of chivalry's ideological stasis and outmodedness, and the pentangle an expression of totalizing fantasy.[7] Further, a number of critics have argued that the poem gives us access to a mobility of desire that cannot be assimilated to pentangular totality. But even when such mobility has been understood as itself internal to chivalric desire rather than something whose possibility chivalry must foreclose, mobility is seen as entering into the poem from

[5] John Burrow offers a nuanced account of "trawthe" as a broad virtue of chivalric integrity represented in the pentangle, and of the issues surrounding Gawain's motives and the evaluation of his ethical failure in these terms. See *A Reading of "Sir Gawain and the Green Knight"* (London: Routledge and Kegan Paul, 1965), esp. 41–51 and 122–49.

[6] This is one of the main reasons why so much energy has been devoted to measuring the seriousness of Gawain's fault, or as the question is often conceived, to determining whether to grant authority to the very different judgments of Gawain's culpability offered by Bertilak, Gawain himself, and Arthur's court. Burrow's account stands out as an early example of refusing to grant one or another of these judgments final authority: see *A Reading of "Sir Gawain and the Green Knight,"* 122–59. A. C. Spearing is also helpful on this point: see *The Gawain-Poet: A Critical Study* (Cambridge: Cambridge University Press, 1970), esp. 219–36.

[7] For the pentangle as an expression of totalizing fantasy associated with ideological stasis, see, for instance, Sheila Fisher, "Taken Men and Token Women in *Sir Gawain and the Green Knight,"* in *Seeking the Woman in Late Medieval and Renaissance Writings: Essays in Feminist Contextual Criticism,* ed. Sheila Fisher and Janet E. Halley (Knoxville: University of Tennessee Press, 1989), 71–105; and Carolyn Dinshaw, "A Kiss Is Just a Kiss: Heterosexuality and Its Consolations in *Sir Gawain and the Green Knight,"* *diacritics* 24 (1994): 205–26.

outside its core pentangular ethos.[8] On this kind of account, the poem's own resistance to fantasies of stasis and totality has its home in a competing ethos that recognizes the value of feminine desire and the pleasures of improvisation, and whose central figure is the girdle given to Gawain by the Lady of Bertilak's castle, a girdle whose knot, far from being static and endless, is open to, and in fact requires, the perpetual movement of retying and thus of resignification.

Each of these ways of reading the poem has done much to help us understand the structure of chivalric ethics and desire, and the ideological work on which chivalry depends. In one way or another, however, each of the accounts I have sketched depends on a fundamental trope of thought, in which the ethical and ideological import of the poem is determined by assigning distinct and opposed values to the text's figurations of stasis and movement. Gawain's reactions to the descent of the Green Knight's blade suggest something that, I shall argue, the rest of the text elaborates: while the poem and chivalry itself in many ways trade on such an opposition, we will not be able to understand how they do so unless we attend to the poem's mergings of stasis and movement, undergoing and activity, suffering and enjoyment, and even death and life. If Gawain's autonomy, the pentangle that represents the terms in which he understands it, and the various formalisms that give shape to the poem's productions of beauty and refinement can be associated with an ideological stasis linked to the rejection of life, the excitations that course through the poem's engagements with these matters, as well as through its more direct engagements with death, are intimately tied to the subject's desire to be fully alive, to have a life that exceeds the deathly repetitions of mere quotidian existence. At the same time, while the poem's reach for aliveness is central to its interests in the pleasures and ethics of improvisation, this reach does not oppose pentangular fantasies of totality; the poem is still fully inhabited by death here.

---

[8] Both Fisher and Dinshaw see the poem as alive to desires that cannot be assimilated to pentangular totality; their arguments involve seeing the poem as strategically seeking to foreclose such desires in the interests of maintaining ideological intelligibility. For accounts of the mobility of desire in the poem as articulating an alternative to pentangular stasis to which the poem seeks to remain alive, see Geraldine Heng, "A Woman Wants: The Lady, *Gawain*, and the Forms of Seduction," *Yale Journal of Criticism* 5 (1992): 101–34, and Christine Chism, *Alliterative Revivals* (Philadelphia: University of Pennsylvania Press, 2002), 66–110. My account owes much to their discussions of the ways pleasure and danger feed each other in the poem. Tison Pugh helpfully emphasizes both the poem's foreclosure of non-normative desire and its queer energies, in *Queering Medieval Genres* (New York: Palgrave Macmillan, 2004), 107–50.

As these formulations suggest, my discussion owes a great deal to Aranye Fradenburg's work on the forms of enjoyment and prestige produced by the imperative to chivalric sacrifice, and the work of Fradenburg, Jacques Lacan, and Slavoj Žižek on the ideological productivity of desire's tight bond with the law.[9] More broadly, this essay is informed by psychoanalytic and queer thinking about the interpenetration of pleasure and pain, the ecstatic undoing of identifications, and the vicissitudes of the drives, in particular the death drive.[10] But while the death

[9] Fradenburg's arguments throughout *Sacrifice Your Love* concerning the death drive and its relation to an attachment to life, and concerning the relations among death, the gift, and sacrifice both within and beyond chivalric contexts, has been important to many paths of thought in this essay. So too has been her recent account of romance's ways of fostering an interest in life: see Fradenburg, "Simply Marvelous," *SAC* 26 (2004): 1–27. My thinking about the relation between death and an attachment to life in medieval culture has also been informed by D. Vance Smith, *Arts of Possession: The Middle English Household Imaginary* (Minneapolis: University of Minnesota Press, 2003), particularly his argument that "the chivalric economy" is one in which "death and enjoyment, surplus and void, possession and relinquishment, are dangerously convertible" (215). My argument here is that the enjoyment of such danger is central to the chivalric ethos, at least as the *Gawain*-poet understands it. More broadly, this essay also responds to Smith's discussion of the way the interminable mystery of earthenness in the Harley poem "erthe toc of erthe" gives voice at once to the death drive and to the perpetual foundering of thought that constitutes a mode of human liveness, in his as-yet-unpublished "Thinking Earth." For Lacan on the tight bond between desire and the law, see among other places *The Seminar of Jacques Lacan, Book VII: The Ethics of Psychoanalysis*, trans. Dennis Porter (New York: W. W. Norton, 1992), esp. 71–84, 167–204. On the ideological productivity of that bond, see Lacan's discussion of sublimation in *The Ethics of Psychoanalysis*, 87–164; see also Žižek, *The Sublime Object of Ideology* (New York: Verso, 1989), esp. Che Vuoi? 87–129, and You Only Die Twice, 13–149.

[10] For the classic Freudian discussion of the death drive and the convertibility of the drives, see Sigmund Freud, *Beyond the Pleasure Principle*, trans. and ed. James Strachey (New York: W. W. Norton, 1961); Freud, *The Ego and the Id*, trans. and ed. James Strachey (New York: W. W. Norton: 1960); Freud, "Instincts and Their Vicissitudes," in *General Psychological Theory: Papers on Metapsychology*, ed. Philip Rieff (New York: Simon and Schuster, 1991), 83–103; and Freud, "The Economic Problem in Masochism," in *General Psychological Theory*, 190–201. For Lacan's discussion of the death drive, see *The Seminar of Jacques Lacan, Book II: The Ego in Freud's Theory and in the Technique of Psychoanalysis*, trans. Sylvana Tomaselli (New York: W. W. Norton, 1991); while that entire year of the Seminar involves a critique of ego psychology from the perspective opened by Freud's attempt to move beyond the pleasure principle, see esp. 36–90, 171, 206–34. Something similar is true of *The Ethics of Psychoanalysis*; while there is a direct discussion of the death drive on 203–17, Lacan's discussions of *Das Ding* and of the problem of sublimation throughout *The Ethics of Psychoanalysis* are discussions of our relation to that which insists beyond the pleasure principle, and therefore of whatever might be meant by a "death drive." Other psychoanalytic discussions of the death drive that have been especially important for this essay include Jean Laplanche, *Life and Death in Psychoanalysis*, trans. Jeffrey Mehlman (Baltimore: Johns Hopkins University Press, 1976), esp. "Why the Death Drive?" 103–24; Leo Bersani, *The Freudian Body: Psychoanalysis and Art* (New York: Columbia University Press, 1986); Tim Dean, *Beyond Sexu-*

drive is the central psychoanalytic concept for this essay, I will not be deploying a specific theory of the death drive that locates it as a technical concept with strong explanatory power. In fact, as Lacan argues in great detail, the very notion of a death drive, both in Freud and in his own work, resists such technicalization.[11] Both Freud and Lacan are drawn to the term because something in the psychic economy or in the play of signification pushes the subject beyond its seemingly natural inclination to seek pleasure and avoid pain. As both Freud and Lacan argue, not only can the insistence of this drive not be accommodated to the pleasure principle; it cannot be accommodated to any of the traditional theories of motive that modify the pleasure principle in terms of prudence, virtue, or duty. Neither Freud nor Lacan developed a satisfying theory of what that something is. Lacan's work on the matter might best be understood as an account of why we could not in principle develop a theory of what insists beyond the pleasure principle.[12] Partly for this reason, I will not proceed by deploying Lacanian technical terms as an explanatory apparatus for the textual phenomena I discuss. Lacan himself warned against such a procedure, calling it psychoanalysis for dentists—that is, for those who want to be trained in the kind of technical knowledge that holds its objects still in order to provide a professionally replicable method for working on them.[13] Such knowledge is just

---

ality (Chicago: University of Chicago Press, 2000); and Lee Edelman, *No Future: Queer Theory and the Death Drive* (Durham: Duke University Press, 2004).

[11] See the discussions, cited above, in Books II and VII of the *Seminar*. In each case, the discussions of the death drive are discussions of the *problem* that motivates Lacan's sense of what remains elusive in (respectively) the analytical attempt to move beyond the pleasure principle and in the Thing; they are not moments in which Lacan proffers a technical concept that explains those matters. This is true of most of Lacan's key terms, as well as of his understanding of Freud. As he puts it in opening what has come to us as the first year of the Seminar (that is, 1953–54, the first year it was transcribed by a stenographer), "This kind of teaching is a refusal of any system. It uncovers a thought in motion—nonetheless vulnerable to systematization, since it necessarily possesses a dogmatic aspect." See *The Seminar of Jacques Lacan, Book I: Freud's Papers on Technique*, trans. John Forrester (New York: W. W. Norton, 1991), 1.

[12] Again, Lacan's discussion of *Das Ding* in relation to the death drive is a good place to turn for such an account.

[13] See Lacan, *The Ego in Freud's Theory*, 6–7. After referring to "the kind of people that we shall define, using a conventional notation, as dentists" because of their "confiden[ce] about the order of the universe" (6), Lacan goes on to offer the formula "I is an other" (7), and then immediately warns: "Don't let this impress you! Don't start spreading it around that *I is an other* . . . it doesn't mean anything. Because, to begin with, you have to know what an other means. The other—don't use this term as mouthwash" (7).

what we want in a dentist—no one wants their dentist pausing in the middle of a root canal to call into question the very nature of a tooth. But both in psychoanalysis and in literary and cultural studies, we *do* want the kind of thinking for which the very nature of the object remains one of the central questions. To pursue such thinking, I will proceed as Lacan himself does, and as he urges his students to: by tracing the contours of the text's significant insistence, and by gradually developing an account out of the paths of the signifier, always with an eye on the unresolved mystery those paths encounter.[14]

Another reason for proceeding in this way is that allowing the critical encounter with the object to disturb our thinking can be as productive theoretically as it can be critically. In fact this was the case for Freud and Lacan, whose conceptual work was always developing in relation to their ongoing engagement with psychoanalytic phenomena, and it has continued to be the case with the best psychoanalytic criticism. The main conceptual agenda here centers on the problem of teleology. Teleology is a complicated issue for psychoanalysis, both because of the challenge psychoanalytic thought poses to traditional understandings of human ends and our relations to them, and because that challenge has always relied on normative imperatives of its own that have remained undertheorized.[15] One purpose of this essay is to suggest some terms for understanding a psychoanalytic reliance on teleology, which are not subject to the *critique* of teleological thinking so powerfully articulated in Freud and Lacan. I venture such a suggestion in an essay with the focus of this one because of the centrality of the problem of teleology both to psychoanalysis and to the intellectual traditions central to this poem, namely, medieval theology and ethics and the classical traditions on which they draw. Another purpose of this essay, then, is to extend the work I began in *Philosophical Chaucer*, in which I argued that medieval thinking about human ends occupies much of the same ground as

[14] Throughout Book II of the *Seminar*, "significant insistence" is Lacan's formula for repetition compulsion, understood as a feature of the functioning of signification rather than as being anchored in individual psychology. Elizabeth Scala helpfully focuses on the compulsive repetitions of *Sir Gawain and the Green Knight* at the level of both theme and form as indices of the poem's textual unconscious, in *Absent Narratives, Manuscript Textuality, and Literary Structure in Late Medieval England* (New York: Palgrave Macmillan, 2002), 37–70.

[15] Lacan himself was well aware of this problem and gives it ample discussion throughout the *Ethics of Psychoanalysis*.

psychoanalysis, and exhibits a sophistication we have sometimes been reluctant to accord it.[16] There are of course important differences between how we, in the wake of Lacan, might formulate the issues I raise in this essay and how the *Gawain*-poet might have, and I will turn to some of them at the end of the essay. But a medieval understanding of teleology can provide avenues for thinking about what we would call the death drive, avenues that, I will argue, this poem quite forcefully opens. In order to follow those avenues, we must attend as closely as possible to the relations this poem charts among carnality and mortality, excitation and deferral, seduction by life and the desire to see it come to an end. One result of such attention will be to trouble a presumptive clarity concerning the contrast between modern or postmodern thought and the kind of thinking being done by our medieval interlocutors.[17]

Dead Meat and Living Flesh

Let me take as a second point of departure some lines describing the third stroke of the Green Knight's ax. Having determined that Gawain will hold still for the blow, the Green Knight finally makes contact with his flesh:

> Þaȝ he homered heterly, hurt hym no more
> Bot snyrt hym on þat on syde, þat seuered þe hyde.

---

[16] Mark Miller, *Philosophical Chaucer*; see especially "Agency and Dialectic in the *Consolation of Philosophy*," 111–51, and "Sadomasochism and Utopia in the *Roman de la Rose*," 152–90.

[17] The idea that we should *not* presume terms for an antecedently clear contrast between medieval and modern culture and thought has been central to medieval studies at least since the early 1990s and the publication of Lee Patterson's "On the Margin: Postmodernism, Ironic History, and Medieval Studies," *Speculum* 65 (1990): 87–108, and David Aers's "A Whisper in the Ear of Early Modernists: Or, Reflections on Literary Critics Writing the 'History of the Subject,'" in Aers, ed., *Culture and History, 1350–1600: Essays on English Communities, Identities, and Writing* (Detroit: Wayne State University Press, 1992), 177–202. Curiously, however, while the force of the point has been relatively well taken as regards narratives of historical change, highly conceptual work, especially when it engages with psychoanalytic theory, is often treated with suspicion in ways that replicate just such a presumption. Fradenburg's work has been exemplary in pushing us to rethink such presumptions on this score. For other recent work that asks us to reconsider the relation between theory and historicism, see Paul Strohm, *Theory and the Premodern Text* (Minneapolis: University of Minnesota Press, 2000); Bruce Holsinger, *The Premodern Condition: Medievalism and the Making of Theory* (Chicago: University of Chicago Press, 2005); Erin Felicia Labbie, *Lacan's Medievalism* (Minneapolis: University of Minnesota Press, 2006); and Elizabeth Scala and Sylvia Federico, eds., *The Post-Historical Middle Ages* (New York: Palgrave Macmillan, 2009).

> Þe scharp schrank to þe flesche þurʒ þe schyre grece,
> Þat þe schene blod ouer his schulderes schot to þe erþe.
>
> (2311–14)

The description is wonderful for its slow-motion aestheticism: we are asked to see the ax descend, sever the skin, and cut through the fat to the flesh beneath it, sending blood shooting over Gawain's shoulders to the earth, as the next line tells us, to gleam on the snow. It is in response to that image that Gawain springs once again into motion: "[a]nd quen þe burne seʒ þe blode blenk on þe snawe, / He sprit forth spenne-fote more þen a spere lenþe" (2315–16). The description also contains one of the most pointed repetitions in this poem of repetitions, as the ax cuts through Gawain's "hyde" and "schyre grece."[18] "Grece" appears in two other places in the poem. The first comes in the description of the ax's flight through the Green Knight's body at the end of Fitt I: "þe scharp of þe schalk schyndered þe bones / And schrank þurʒ þe schyire grece and schade hit in twynne" (424–25), such that "[þ]e blod brayd fro þe body, þat blykked on þe grene" (429). The second comes, this time paired with the poem's other use of the term "hyde," in the description of the butchering of the deer after Bertilak's first hunt, as the hunters

> Gedered þe grattest of gres þat þer were
> And didden hem derely undo . . .
> Two fyngeres þay fonde of þe fowlest of alle.
> Syþen þay slyt þe slot, sesed þe erber,
> Schaued wyth a scharp knyf, and þe schyre knitten.
> Syþen rytte þay þe foure lymmes and rent of þe hyde;
> Þen brek þay þe balé, þe bowelez out token,
> Lystily for laucyng þe lere of þe knot.
>
> (1326–34)

[18] Marie Borroff notes that the phrase "schyre grece" is original to the *Gawain*-poet, that it "links the Green Knight, the hunted deer, and Sir Gawain as fleshly beings" (109), and that "the noun *grece* itself denotes the fatty flesh of human beings only in *Sir Gawain and the Green Knight*" (110). For Borroff, these "descriptive and verbal repetitions" (109) have to do with the poem's exploration of the vulnerability as "an embodied mortal creature" (109) that humans share with other animals, and support a lenient judgment of Gawain's fault at the end of the poem. Borroff's is one of a very few critical studies of the poem that seeks to understand the aesthetic and ethical value of the hunting scenes in their own right rather than assimilating them to the bedroom scenes with which they are paired. See "*Sir Gawain and the Green Knight*: The Passing of Judgment," in *The Passing of Arthur: New Essays in Arthurian Tradition,* ed. Christopher Baswell and William Sharpe (New York: Garland, 1988), 105–28.

The description continues for another twenty-seven lines in poetry that is astonishing for its viscerality and technical precision.[19] In the context of the scenes Gawain's nick on the neck invokes, his wound becomes an instance of a topos—call it the topos of the body's capacity to be slit open. The poem's fascination with such opening has several features. One is a desire for mastery over the life and death of the other, a desire for the satisfaction that comes from seeing the deer, felled in droves, begin their transformation into meat, from feeling the ax cut through that monstrous intruder's threatening body, from seeing that impudent, frightening head of his bounce across the room and, as Arthur's courtiers do, giving it a good kick. Another is a desire to stick one's hand down inside the opened body, to measure its fingers of fat, itself related to a desire to see how the body is put together, what pieces it is made of, how it works and how we can work it. Yet another is a desire to see what the body emits when the fragile container of skin is pierced, and to aestheticize that emission, garishly (as in the Green Knight's spurting blood and the tacky Christmasy contrast it makes of red on green) or beautifully (as in the graceful arc of Gawain's blood as it shoots over his shoulders to land in lovely red on the white snow). And another is a desire for the delivery of that witnessing of one's own mortality expressed in Gawain's movement under the impending ax, of living through the moment when the blow makes mortal contact with one's flesh—though also, as always, a deflection of that witnessing, since if

---

[19] In saying that this poetry is astonishing, I do not mean to suggest that it is unique. As I say above, this passage participates in a *topos*, and one that extends well beyond *Sir Gawain and the Green Knight*. In particular, the butchering of the deer is a romance convention, and the ability to display technical precision in pursuing the activity is a traditional sign of aristocratic know-how and class belonging. For the other most extended example of the butchering of the deer in Middle English poetry, which shares some of the same language as the description in *Sir Gawain*, see *The Parlement of the Thre Ages*, lines 21–96, in Warren Ginsburg, ed., *Wynnere and Wastour and The Parlement of the Thre Ages* (Kalamazoo, Mich.: Medieval Institute Publications, 1992). For an account of the importance of hunting and butchering in the making of chivalric subjects, see Nicholas Orme, *From Childhood to Chivalry: The Education of English Kings and Aristocracy, 1066–1530* (London: Methuen, 1984), 191–97. The conventionality of the *topos*, however, says nothing by itself about what is at issue in it, or whether we might find what is at issue astonishing. Astonishing things are often widely shared, and in their sharedness are often naturalized. My argument above is meant to suggest a way of understanding the appetite for technical precision in the pursuit and poetic description of the hunting and butchering of animals, an understanding that this poem opens for us through the contexts and resonances it builds around those descriptions. This is a poem that denaturalizes conventions in a number of ways, including those of the hunt and those of courteous love-talk.

mortal contact were made, no one would be around to do the witnessing.[20]

While these are, as I have said, distinct forms of a topos, since we are dealing with a topos here the poem does not represent the desires these forms express as fully discrete. The desire to see how the deer is put together is related to the desire to "undo" it (or as the poem puts it later, "vnbynde" it [1352]), and in taking it apart to turn once-living flesh into what can finally be called "venysoun" (1375). But the Green Knight and Gawain too have "grece" and flesh, revealed as the ax cuts into them; they too are made up of meat, even if the poem will not put them through the technologizing of their further capacity to be broken apart that transforms the deer into food. And the subjection of the deer to the techne of butchery is so full of the fleshy enjoyment of cutting open the belly, "lystily" removing the bowels, gripping the windpipe and separating it from the esophagus, and so on—all of which, in addition to its eroticism, refers back to the living functionality of the animal, its capacity for breath, digestion, and movement, a capacity shared by the human body by way of more or less the same interior structures— that it cannot only be doing the work of establishing technical mastery over death and bringing the dead body into culture as food, although that is certainly one of its functions. The butchering of the deer is thus a way of elaborating what the poem shows by association in the human case: a desire to undo or unbind, but also to be undone or unbound; a wish to see and touch the interior stuff that is living flesh, but that can only be made accessible as dead meat.

In referring to desires and wishes that inform this poetry, I want to be clear that I am not suggesting, for instance, that the hunters pursue their elaborate, stylized, and utterly conventional butchering of the deer

[20] In pursuing the relations among the various instances of this topos, I am developing what I see to be at stake both in Borroff's understanding of the poem's repetitions of corporeal violence and in Spearing's discussion of the "closeness of the connection between delight and death" in the hunting scenes, including the delight in the transformation wrought on the animal by death: "previously they were living creatures, full of violent energy; now they are unmoving lumps of meat, completely transformed from subjects to objects" (*The Gawain-Poet: A Critical Study*, 214–15). Like Dinshaw, I understand "the violent dismemberment of the hunt" as one of the poem's ways of staging the phantasmatic "unlacing" of chivalric identity ("A Kiss Is Just a Kiss," 211); like Spearing, I see both the poem and the inner workings of chivalry itself as invested in producing the excitement of such unlacing. My account is in this respect close to Chism's argument that "pleasurable splits in chivalric identity are literalized in the actual penetrations and dismemberments of the hunting scenes" (*Alliterative Revivals*, 100), although I am less confident than Chism is in the redemptive power of such splits.

because it occurs to them that it would be fascinating to look inside the dead bodies and see what makes them tick. As far as they are concerned, this is simply what they do with the spoils of the hunt, and such descriptions appear in romance precisely as markers of aristocratic group belonging, *not* as signs of the distinctive psychologies of individuals. Nor did I mean to suggest earlier that it occurs to Gawain to relish the feel of the ax slicing through his neck. It is not a question of reading the minds of fictional characters, but rather of the forms of desire figured in these characters and the structures of representation surrounding them. What's more, neither Gawain nor the hunters are figures for a so-called perverse organization of desire around avowable masochistic or sadistic pleasures. A central feature of the poem's interest in them is that within their communities they are about as normal, even normative, as can be. But the forms of desire exhibited in any signifying structure are hardly exhausted by the avowable motives, aims, and wants of the subjects inhabiting it. To put the point in more technical terms, the forms of desire are not to be found in anything that takes the form of a mental object present to consciousness—and this is so both on the best modern accounts (such as those found in the work of thinkers as diverse as Lacan and Wittgenstein) and on the best medieval accounts (as found in Augustine, Boethius, Aquinas, and others).[21] The desire I am discussing here is not anchored in anything represented in the text as an individual

---

[21] Lacan's most extended and direct argument in this respect comes in his critique of ego psychology in Book II of the *Seminar*, although it is a constant theme of his writings; a good place to begin is "A Materialist Definition of the Phenomenon of Consciousness," *The Ego in Freud's Theory*, 40–52. Wittgenstein develops his argument in this respect throughout the *Philosophical Investigations*, trans. G. E. M. Anscombe (New York: Macmillan, 1958), most famously in what gets called the "private language argument" in §§243–71. The medieval case is less obvious, since medieval thinkers did not take themselves to be opposing the philosophical traditions (which were only developed later) that treated desires as mental objects present to consciousness. Still, it has been a persistent feature of the modern engagement with medieval and ancient philosophy that it has been characterized both by a tendency to misread those texts as having a consciousness-based view of desire and of the mind more generally, and, for instance, in the work of philosophers as different as Heidegger, Gilbert Ryle, and Elizabeth Anscombe, by an effort to turn to Aristotle in particular as a resource for thinking in other terms. Two discussions that are especially helpful in clarifying how different medieval thinking about desire and action is from modern ways of doing so are Daniel Westburg, *Right Practical Reason: Aristotle, Action, and Prudence in Aquinas* (Oxford: Clarendon Press, 1994), esp. "The Distinctiveness of Thomist Psychology," 95–115, and "Stages in Human Action," 119–35; and Candace Vogler, *Reasonably Vicious* (Cambridge, Mass.: Harvard University Press, 2002), esp. "In Some Sense Good," 26–52, and "Medieval and Modern," 53–73, although in each case the broader arguments of the books are entirely relevant as well.

mind or soul (such as Gawain's), but is rather to be found in the signifying structures of the text, in its repetition of tropes across its represented
figures and narrative moments, and in the underlying logic that informs
those repetitions. What I have to say along the way about individual
represented figures such as Gawain and the hunters will be informed
by an ongoing account of those structures, rather than the other way
around.

What I am after, then, is a form of desire alive in the text's signifying
chains, and animating much that is central to the poem, including the
hunting scenes, the scenes of bedroom flirtation, the ethical and ideological work figured in the pentangle on Gawain's shield, and the formal
structures of the poem itself; and a full account of that desire will itself
depend on substantial discussion of each of these matters. The hunting
scenes bear the most direct relation to what I have been discussing,
especially in the way they problematize any clear lines between domination and being violated. Listen, for instance, to the way alliteration functions during the hunting of the deer:

> Þer myȝt mon se, as þay slypte, slentyng of arwes;
> At vche wende vnder wande wapped a flone,
> Þat bigly bote on þe broun with ful brode hedez.
> What! þay brayen and bleden, bi bonkkez þay deȝen,
> And ay rachches in a res radly hem folȝes,
> Hunterez wyth hyȝe horne hasted hem after
> Wyth such a crakkande kry as klyffes haden brusten.
> What wylde so atwaped wyȝes þat schotten
> Watz al toraced and rent at þe resayt.
>
> (1160–68)

These are, to be sure, lines that revel in sadistic pleasure. As the "s"
sounds of the first line mimic the hissing of arrows on their release, the
"w" sounds of the second the duller, breathier noise of the arrows as
they approach their target, and the explosive "b" sounds of the third
the impact of the arrows on flesh, we are given access not just to the
sound but to the viscerality of the moment. When the arrowheads
"bigly bote on þe broun" of the deer, we can feel the impact. But we
are feeling that impact not just in the excitement of the violence and
power it unleashes, but from the perspective of the quarry.[22] Those "w"

---

[22] See Borroff, "*Sir Gawain and the Green Knight:* The Passing of Judgment," 111.

sounds are the sounds of arrows coming near, and the feel of their impact registers on our flesh. By the time the deer are orgiastically "toraced and rent," the poem's energies are as much on the side of being torn apart as they are on that of the tearing. This is less a shift of perspectives than a fusion of them that reveals the underlying structure of the pleasures of the hunt itself. The excitement of seeing and hearing the arrows bite on the soft brown flesh of the deer, of hearing them cry out and seeing them bleed, depends on an aliveness to their suffering, not just as something the hunters can cause, but as something they can undergo. The fusion of perspectives on which the pleasure of violence depends is captured as well in the hunters' orgasmic horn-blowing, which makes a "crakkande kry, as klyffes haden brusten." What is unleashed here is the excitement of destructivity as such, and it does not much matter any more which side of the destruction we are on. This fusion is reinforced with another associative link between the hunt and the end of the poem: when the horns cry out with the joy of the hunt, they make the sound Gawain hears as the Green Knight, whom he has yet to see, sharpens his ax: "a wonder breme noyse. / Quat! hit clatered in þe clyff as hit cleue schulde" (2200–2201). This is more than the sound of an individually impending mortality; it is as though, in the cliff-bursting sounds of blowing horns and sharpening ax, we could hear the sound of the end of the world.[23]

The wish to hear that sound—to *make* it, but also to be there when it happens, perhaps to survive it, perhaps to be undone by it—is part of what the poem at its beginning calls the warrior's love of "baret" (21), a love those early lines link to suffering and the causing of suffering, to "blysse and blunder" (18), and to pride and treachery not to be distinguished from the founding of empire. At issue here is the very basis of the chivalric order's capacity to rule. As a number of critics have noted, the description of Aeneas's treachery, instrumental both in the fall of Troy and the *translatio imperii* that leads to the making of Britain, is knotty, hard to make out both syntactically and semantically. Here is how the lines, stripped of the punctuation added by modern editors, read:

Siþen þe sege and þe assaut watz sesed at Troye

---

[23] Cf. Burrow's ongoing account of the poem's invocation of apocalyptic imagery throughout *A Reading of Sir Gawain and the Green Knight*. Spearing also reads the cracking of cliffs in apocalyptic tones, as the poem's way of registering what the breaking of the pentangle might sound like: see *The Gawain-Poet: A Critical Study*, 218.

> Þe borȝ brittened and brent to brondez and askez
> þe tulk þat þe trammes of tresoun þer wroȝt
> Watz tried for his tricherie þe trewest on erthe
> Hit watz Ennias þe athel and his highe kynde
> Þat siþen depreced prouinces and patrounes bicome
> Welneȝe of al þe wele in þe west iles
>
> (1–7)

The difficulty stems from the way the phrase "þe trewest on erthe" simultaneously stands in apposition to "tricherie," as though the point is that this is the greatest treachery the earth has ever seen, and initiates the passage's turn to naming "Ennias þe athel," the noble one who, along with "his highe kynde," founded the cornerstones of European polity and civilization, including the British chivalric order, which, for most of the poem, Gawain and his "trawthe" will represent.[24] The poem's blurring of these possibilities suggests that "trawthe" and "tricherie," despite the obvious opposition between them on which chivalry and the poem's plot depend, are quite deeply interlaced. Both chivalric virtue and its failure emerge from the poem's opening as articulations of an underlying love of "baret"—of battle, but more broadly of conflict or sheer strife—a love that is the condition for the "breeding" of the class of men with the violent energy to rule: "Bolde bredden þerinne, baret þat lofden, / In mony turned tyme tene þat wroȝten" (21–22).

The poem gives us a further sense of the character of that energy in

---

[24] Editors of the poem have often tried to clean up its syntax by placing a strong pause after "þe trewest on erthe." Andrew and Waldron render the central lines as follows:

> þe tulk þat þe trammes of treson þer wroȝt
> Watz tried for his tricherie, the trewest on erthe.
> Hit watz Ennias þe athel and his hyghe kynde,
> Þat siþen depreced prouinces . . .
>
> (3–6)

The problem with this rendering is that, while it provides syntactic clarity, it makes the contrast between the description of destruction and treachery in lines 1–4 and the description of *translatio imperii* in line 5 and following so sharp that it only heightens the feeling in hitting line 5 that we must suddenly be reading another poem with another history in mind, or perhaps that the poem is now referring to a different person, leaving the traitor of lines 1–4 unnamed. Andrew and Waldron note that "it has been argued that Antenor is the traitor referred to here," but dismiss that possibility, partly perhaps because of their sense of the lines' ambiguity, but certainly because, as they note, "medieval legend associated Aeneas with the traitor Antenor in plotting with the Greeks" (*The Poems of the Pearl Manuscript*, 207).

the way its opening lines associate the love of "baret" with the production of life as a site of "wonder" (16) and "ferlyes" (23), of the marvels that make life elusive and fascinating.[25] This is an association on which the poem's initial plot structure depends as well, as the Green Knight's intrusion on Camelot's holiday festivities comes in answer to Arthur's wish for an "auenturus thing" (93) without which those festivities would be incomplete. The hunting scenes capture this package of affect in a range of other ways as well, from the excitation of men being torn apart by the wild boar they have purposefully driven into a frenzy, an animal with whose fierce but doomed body the lord will merge in an indistinguishable heap while shattering its heart with a well-placed strike of the sword, to that of seeing the world frantically on the move, in the form of the fox whose darting speed repeatedly escapes the hunters' aim, only to be felled not by the lord's misplaced blow, but by the pack of dogs that descends on it in his wake. In each case, as with deer and cliffs and the strife whereby cities are razed to the ground and new nations are founded, the pleasures involved are those of mastery. But the pleasures of mastery do not, as they are sometimes thought to, serve simply as a buttress against unpleasure, powerlessness, and mortality. They depend on an identification with mortality, not in a melancholic mode, but in a mode in which death's approach marks the point of ultimate visceral contact with the world, of maximum exposure to its impact—even as that impact, to be registered at all, must be phantasmatically displaced onto the suffering body of the other, or the otherness of one's own anticipated end, a "treachery" distinguished by its opposition to the "trawthe" it sets in motion.

Anticlimax and Teleology

One way of putting this structure, in which the height of excitation is marked by an extinction that must be displaced to be registered at all, would be to say that *Sir Gawain and the Green Knight* is a poem of anticlimax.[26] Such a formulation has the advantage of being literally true when it comes to the poem's narrative structure. Gawain lives through all that buildup, all that anticipation, focusing himself on the final moment

[25] On the function of marvel and *ferlye* in romance generally as producing an attachment to life through a mode of wonder related to violence, see Fradenburg, "Simply Marvelous."

[26] Cf. Spearing, *The Gawain-Poet: A Critical Study*, 190 and 229.

when he will make good on his word no matter what the cost; and it turns out that all the Green Knight was going to do was give him a nick on the neck. Then Gawain is told, after all the excitement and danger of the bedroom, after all his delicate and frustrating efforts not to go too far, and not to insinuate that the Lady was going too far, that it was not even her idea to be there, that the whole thing was a put-on. Gawain thought that he was going to die triumphantly, in the service of his lord, in the defense of Camelot's reputation, and in a definitive exhibition of his own ethical integrity; or, if avoiding death, he was going to do so in the mode of courageous survival against all odds. He also thought that back in the castle he had been putting on a virtuoso performance of *cortaysye*, living through the most thrilling erotic encounter of his life while simultaneously getting to rescue not just himself but the Lady, too, from moral disaster. But all these payoffs evaporate at once at the poem's end, leaving Gawain with only the comfort of self-aggrandizement to help him through the non-end-stopped time of his disappointment and shame.[27]

Gawain's position is not the only one from which a promised climax meets with disappointment. The entire plot of the poem, and every subject-position within it, becomes utterly nonsensical right when everything seems to get tied up.[28] Bertilak says that nothing was going on in that bedroom, that he just put his wife up to it to test Gawain. But this so evacuates the erotic tension and pleasure of those scenes—which seemed, after all, to be the locus of the poem's interest in them—that it smells like an alibi.[29] Then there is that other alibi, as Bertilak tells Gawain that he did not really want to chop off his head, it was all Morgan's idea: she wanted to test the Round Table and distress Guenevere so much that she would die, and anyway she is your aunt, so come on back home with me, "[m]ake myry in my hous," (2468). Is Bertilak just a pawn of Morgan's, shoring up his compromised masculine pride by claiming to be behind his wife's bedroom advances?[30] Or is Bertilak

---

[27] Spearing is also helpful on the matter of the interpenetration of Gawain's self-aggrandizement and shame: ibid., 227–30.

[28] Cf. Burrow, *A Reading of Sir Gawain and the Green Knight*, 169: "Bertilak's relation to Morgan, insofar as it can be made out at all, seems quite eccentric and unlikely."

[29] One way to put this point is that Bertilak's account suspiciously evacuates the Lady's pleasure and agency from those scenes. See Fisher, "Taken Men and Token Women," esp. 86–97, and Geraldine Heng, "Feminine Knots and the Other *Sir Gawain and the Green Knight*," *PMLA* 106 (1991): 500–514, esp. 507–8.

[30] Cf. Fisher, "Taken Men and Token Women," 89–92.

blaming it all on Morgan to preserve chivalry's homosocial bond with Gawain? Neither possibility makes any sense. If this is Morgan's plan, it is a pretty bad one, and one no one ends up caring about. By Bertilak's own measure, Gawain passed the test better than anyone else would have, and the idea of Guenevere dying of distress is so ludicrous that the narrative never even bothers to mention whether or not she is upset.[31] On the other hand, if Morgan is not behind it all, how did Bertilak talk out of that severed head of his, and what was the point of this whole charade?[32] At the end of the poem, the narrative gesture is that of opening onto a world of shadowy conspiracy that, as readers, we might have suspected would be part of this story given its setting in Arthurian history, and that would seem to lend Gawain's trials the *gravitas* of that history's larger tragedy. But, as with many conspiracy theories, the explanations it offers are incoherent, and if they *were* true, they would evacuate the things they promise to explain (the secret of the bedroom, the secret of Gawain's doom) of the very features that create an appetite for explanation.

The relation of this odd feature of the poem's narrative structure to the forms of desire I have been discussing becomes clearer when we note that each involves a complicated relation to teleology. This is a feature not only of its narrative structures but of its broader engagements with temporality. I have already suggested that there is a structure of anticlimax in the ways that excitement in the poem depends on life's inhabita-

[31] It is possible to square these considerations with an account in which Morgan remains the real power behind Gawain's trials. As Fisher argues, the rendering of Morgan's power as ludicrous in the narrative serves ideological ends, as a way of reestablishing patriarchal domination in the face of a feminine power that threatens it. I agree with Fisher that Bertilak's account of things takes something like this shape. My argument is that finally there is no "real" answer concerning the agency or agencies behind the events of the narrative, or at least not an answer that locates such agency in any nameable figure in the poem. What we are reading at the poem's end is the constitution of a phantasmatic space through and through, *not* a phantasmatic space designed to cover up a real one. Scala is helpful on this score as well; see *Absent Narratives,* 61–68. Spearing also argues that the conclusion does not explain anything it purports to, and the Green Knight remains an unintelligible figure; see *The Gawain-Poet: A Critical Study,* 236. For a helpfully antiliteralizing argument that emphasizes the phantasmatic logic of the poem's explanations, and that locates the confused status of its narrative payoffs in terms of ethnic and colonial anxieties, see Patricia Clare Ingham, *Sovereign Fantasies: Arthurian Romance and the Making of Britain* (Philadelphia: University of Pennsylvania Press, 2001), 107–36.

[32] Besides Fisher's reading of such questions, see Burrow's argument that Morgan becomes a "dumping-ground for all the suspicions and resentment which we have stored up on Gawain's behalf in the course of his adventure," in *A Reading of Sir Gawain and the Green Knight,* 64.

tion by death, an inhabitation that takes the form of anticipation and displacement of the event that would, obviously enough, put an end to the excitement it enables. Something similar is true of the poem's interest in sex. The erotics of those bedroom scenes does not easily fit a teleological understanding of sexuality as pointed toward, and deriving its meaning from, a genital sexual act.[33] They are not exactly scenes of temptation, or of seduction, as they are usually called. To call what happens there "temptation" is to locate the Lady as an agent of moral threat, and to locate Gawain's aim as one of resistant virtue, successful or not as the case may be. But, as Geraldine Heng and Christine Chism argue, it is not at all clear that the poem is entirely on the side of the prudish moralization of the bedroom, or the demonization of the Lady and her desire, particularly if her desire is not necessarily aimed at genital intercourse. To call what happens "seduction" can level the moral field somewhat: the Lady might be seducing Gawain into an acknowledgment of feminine desire as well as into an illicit affair. But this still figures her as the agent of the erotic encounter and Gawain as the recipient of her action, and like the language of temptation, it remains rather too knowing about what either of them wants.[34] This is not to deny that in a straightforward sense the Lady takes the lead, or that these scenes are full of risk. But right from the start, Gawain's engagement with her is more than merely responsive, and more than merely risk-averse. He is acting not so much to preserve his chastity and her honor as to load their interaction with the maximum possible excitation.

The poem gives a good indication of the way Gawain enters into those scenes in the description of his actions at the beginning of the first one, before the Lady has had a chance to do much more than open the door:

[33] Much of what follows builds on, and is in conversation with, Heng's account of a nonteleological desire alive in the bedroom scenes, in "A Woman Wants: The Lady, *Gawain*, and the Forms of Seduction," and Chism's sense of the poem as invested in the pleasures of risk, uncertainty, and improvisation. The notion that the Lady is seducing Gawain into an acknowledgment of feminine desire is also Heng's. Despite my disagreement with Dinshaw's sense of the poem's ethics and aesthetics as engaged in a "labor of limitation—the reduction of polyvalent signs to the monovalent meaning" ("A Kiss Is Just a Kiss," 205), my argument here is in some ways closer to hers that "normative masculine gender and sexual behavior . . . is problematized" in the poem without being "organized into an alternative sexuality" ("A Kiss Is Just a Kiss," 208).

[34] Note, however, that in Heng's account, the question *what* the woman wants is precisely what needs to be suspended in an account of those scenes, in favor of an acknowledgment *that* she wants.

And as in slomeryng he slode, sleȝly he herde
A littel dyn at his dor and derfly vpon;
And he heuez vp his hed out of þe cloþes,
A corner of þe cortyn he caȝt vp a lyttel,
And waytez warly þiderwarde quat hit be myȝt.
Hit watz þe ladi, loflyest to beholde,
Þat droȝ þe dor after hir ful dernly and stylle
And boȝed towarde þe bed; and þe burne schamed
And layde hym doun lystyly and let as he slepte.

(1182–90)

Even in the midst of being surprised, Gawain is lying in wait: he "[l]ur-kkez" in bed (1180), he hears the noise at his door "sleȝly," and as the Lady approaches his bed he "layde hym doun lystyly." The energy of the scene comes partly from the way Gawain's wondering, wary antici-pation gets converted into a flood of pleasure in no small part powered by uncertainty: "What could it be? . . . *It was the Lady*, loveliest to behold," framed in her radiant beauty both by the doorway and by Gawain's slightly lifted bedcurtain. If Gawain simply wanted to put a stop to things, he could easily have reduced the tension somewhat by yawning loudly, sitting up in bed, looking surprised, and asking the Lady what brings her there. Lying down and pretending to sleep is in some sense a defensive gesture: Gawain does not know what is going on, so he waits to see what happens before deciding what to do. But waiting to see what happens is also a "lysty," desiring act here.

One might think, on reading the further fact that as Gawain lies down in this way he does so in shame, that he is nursing some illicit sexual hope or goal, and that *that* is what he is waiting for and ashamed of. But that would be to miss the way both his desire and his shame are bound up in a gesture of deferral and prolongation. What Gawain does here, and throughout the bedroom scenes of Fitt III, is to avoid anything that would confer a definitive meaning on his or the Lady's actions, in order to remain in the delicious suspension of flirtatious innuendo, a suspension in which every gesture is charged with erotic possibility pre-cisely because no gesture singularly expresses it.[35] The event of genital intercourse would put an end to this excitement as fully as would an

[35] Scala also emphasizes the indeterminacy of these scenes, although she reads Ga-wain as trying to overcome that indeterminacy rather than as purposefully and pleasur-ably heightening it; see *Absent Narratives*, 56–60.

outright refusal of the Lady's advances. But so would imagining that genital intercourse was anyone's ultimate goal in these scenes: if Gawain were to think *that*, not only would he be robbing the scenes of their constitutive uncertainty, but he would be failing in *cortaysye*. And for that matter, this form of excitement would come to an end just by the attribution to the Lady, or for that matter to Gawain, of *any* determinate goal as the object of desire driving their actions.[36] For Gawain to find his pleasure in "luf-talkyng," he must maintain it as a space of erotic intersubjectivity in which the meaning of what they are doing and of who they are in the scene remains up for grabs, in which desire aims not at the resting place of an orgasmic act or erotic possession or for that matter of moral rectitude, but at the multiplying of desire, and its unfolding through uncertainty, risk, and shame.

In making this argument, I do not, however, mean to locate the pleasure of courteous flirting as a generative, life-affirming alternative to a closed-off, pentangular ethos.[37] For one thing, Gawain's lying in wait is still, as I have said, a defensive gesture. Through all his deferrals, he is still preserving a certain chastity, still keeping things from "going too far," and so doing his duty to lord and host. The very same gestures thus give him a way of prolonging his enjoyment of the risk of the encounters and of gaining a measure of control over them.[38] Further, while the excitement of those encounters depends on the possibility of Gawain's violating his duties to lord and host, the convergence of preserving his dutifulness with the hyping-up of his excitation makes his erotic investment in the bedroom a *source* of his commitment to those duties rather than simply a competing commitment. The fact that flirting with the Lady is a tricky business thus does the same kind of ideo-

---

[36] Note in this respect that even while "remaining in the delicious suspension of flirtatious innuendo" is clearly in one sense what Gawain wants to do, it cannot provide a substantive *telos* for his activity, that is a *telos* in the form of a definitive and singular object of desire. If it did, the activity of flirting would be robbed of the excitement and danger that comes from the possibility that either or both of the participants in it might turn out to want something more, or for that matter less, than that. In what follows above, I distinguish between a substantive teleology and a purely formal one that is, I think, central to the energies of these scenes.

[37] As in the reading of Heng, for whom the pentangle stands for the totalizing fixities of patriarchal desire, while the girdle stands for the open-ended, generative possibilities of a nonteleological desire that can acknowledge the feminine. Chism's argument for the poem's investment in an ethics of improvisation and risk follows similar paths.

[38] See Joseph Gallagher's argument that Gawain's double entendre in the bedroom is for the sake of safety as much as for titillation, in " 'Trawthe' and 'Luf-Talkyng' in *Sir Gawain and the Green Knight*," *NM* 78 (1977): 362–76.

logical work as the pentangle: it heightens the pleasure and the prestige of duty, and so functions as an engine of chivalric subjection, the making of a chivalric subject bound to his lord.

Notice also that, on such an account, teleology is not exactly set to the side. For the danger of the bedroom encounters to be real enough to lend them any pleasure, "luf-talkyng" must preserve a formal structural relation to some further sexual act. This is not to reinvoke the clumsy teleology of temptation or the tyranny of a genital goal. For one thing, the "further sexual act" is nonspecific: it need not be intercourse or any other particular act. For another, the relation to that nonspecific act is nonpsychological: it need not correspond to anything anyone in the scenes determinately wants, that is, to a "desire" in the sense of "psychological object." These two provisos are what I mean to invoke in saying that the teleological relation is purely *formal*. What is necessary for such a formal relation is just that this unspecified potential development occupy the position of a "something more" than flirting, a "more" to which flirting may or may not lead as the case may be, or even, as here, a "too far" from which flirting shies away even as it refers to it. This structural relation of reference and withdrawal is what makes the bedroom scenes anticlimactic. They are literally so, in the sense that climax is avoided in the joint service of the elaboration of pleasure and the regulation of conduct. But they are also anticlimactic in the *form* of pleasure they elaborate, in which the telic potentiality to which pleasure's buildup refers also represents the condition of pleasure's extinction, an "end" to the suspensions and deferrals that animate it.

The notion of a purely formal teleology is what I had in mind at the beginning of the essay in saying that a discussion of teleology in this poem might help us better understand the place of teleology in psychoanalysis. There are two issues here. One is the death drive, to which I will soon turn more directly. The other is the place of teleology in psychoanalytic thinking about sexual arousal. Feminist and queer readers of Freud—including Heng, who pursues a helpful discussion of the issue—have for some time urged that psychoanalytic thinking about sexuality involves two forms of suspect teleology.[39] One form of teleology emerges in the invocation of a narrative of "normal" sexual development that depends on naturalizing reproductive heterosexual intercourse as a developmental goal and pathologizing forms of sexuality

---

[39] For Heng's discussion of the issue, see "A Woman Wants."

that deviate from that goal. The other has to do with the directionality of sexual activity itself, and takes heterosexual genital activity aimed at orgasm as the informing goal of the normal process of sexual arousal. Such critiques are misplaced with respect to Lacan, who mounted his own critique of the normalizing ambition of much (especially American) psychoanalysis. But the issue with Freud is more complicated. Critiques of psychoanalytic teleology have often centered on Freud's *Three Essays on the Theory of Sexuality*, and it is true that one does find teleological language there, particularly in the third essay, "The Transformations of Puberty."[40] In the first two essays, however, when Freud contrasts heterogenitality with non-normative forms of sexuality, he is careful to offer formulations such as "what is referred to as normal sexuality" and "the so-called perversions." Further, the force of his argument in the first, "The Sexual Perversions," is that the way such contrasts typically get deployed depends on an empty concept. The sexual instinct is widely imagined to bloom in adolescence, with the effect of establishing a powerful attraction to the opposite sex. But Freud argues that this notion of a "sexual instinct" cannot do the work it is popularly supposed to do, of establishing a natural sexual goal or a developmental path toward a subject's having such a goal.[41] The question remains, then, what to do with the teleological language that nevertheless appears throughout Freud's work.

One answer is to think of it as a residue of the psychiatric traditions from which Freud's work emerged; as radical as Freud was, he remained in some ways attached to the very notions he was problematizing.[42] That much seems true, but saying that much tells us little about *why* his thought was divided in this way, except to say that he remained a man of his time. A distinction of the kind I have made here between a formal and a substantive teleology can help to clarify the issue. Freud himself does not make such a distinction, and that is part of the problem: his discussion of teleology imports contents where they do not be-

---

[40] Freud, *Three Essays on the Theory of Sexuality*, trans. James Strachey (New York: Basic Books, 1975), essay three, "The Transformations of Puberty," 73–96.

[41] See Freud, *Three Essays*, essay one, "The Sexual Aberrations," 1–38.

[42] See Leo Bersani, *The Freudian Body: Psychoanalysis and Art* (New York: Columbia University Press, 1986), esp. 29–47, and Arnold Davidson, "How to Do the History of Psychoanalysis: A Reading of Freud's *Three Essays on the Theory of Sexuality*," *Critical Inquiry* 13 (1987): 252–77. Bersani and Davidson are particularly helpful in bringing out the conflict in Freud between a teleological view of sexuality and a nonteleological view that also emerges from *Three Essays*.

long. The aim here, as Lacan argues is always the case with reading Freud, is to see the direction of his thinking, especially when Freud himself does not. To make sense of the way much preorgasmic sexual pleasure involves an element of unpleasurable tension, a "compulsion to make a change in the psychological situation," Freud invokes the distinction between "forepleasure," understood as the pleasure of preorgasmic activity, and "endpleasure," understood as the pleasure of orgasm. In doing so, he would seem to be harnessing his account of sexual arousal to the goal of genital orgasm.[43] But if we think of the notion of a *telos* in purely formal rather than substantive terms, that is, if we detach it from any specification of acts and from a naturalizing account of desire's relation to specifiable acts, we might reconceive the relation between forepleasure and endpleasure as a purely formal relation. Such a relation would have no absolute poles and no relation to a substantive teleology, either in the form of positing genital pleasure in orgasm as the ultimate end of sexual activity, or in the sense of a developmental theory that takes as a goal the organizing of infantile polymorphousness by the forms of adult genital sexuality. Gawain's flirting offers a model for such a purely formal relation since, as I have argued, the structure of his excitation depends on any given moment's relation to an unspecified "something more" that does not depend on anyone's having a substantive desire aimed at any particular goal. That is no more than an example, and as such it is hardly enough to offer much leverage on psychoanalytic theory; and this is hardly the place to embark on an extended account of the matter. But the provocation to thought that the example offers does suggest a distinction that, I think, can help clarify matters in this notoriously difficult area.

I will return to the notion of a purely formal teleology later, when I return to the death drive. For now, the distinction between a formal and a substantive teleology is crucial for making out the structures of excitation in *Sir Gawain and the Green Knight*. The structures of excitation informing its representations of sexual activity are in this respect homologous to those informing its representations of the excitement of death and the excitement of the plot. Gawain's anticipation of his end under the ax, his wish to experience the moment of his ultimate sacrificial integrity, would only be frustrated by its literalization, since he would

---

[43] For Freud's discussion of "forepleasure" and "endpleasure," see *Three Essays*, "The Transformations of Puberty," 74–78.

not be there to have the experience. More strongly, literalizing that wish as an empirical desire to die evacuates the scene of the excitement produced by the way that wish is informed by Gawain's reach for a special form of aliveness. Yet the forms of desire, subjectivation, and ideological investment here are unintelligible absent the notion that Gawain is engaged in end-directed activity. A similar structure obtains in the plot. This is a narrative that requires some explanatory payoff to make good on its insistently mounting suspense and sense of mystery. But as soon as a literalized explanation gets offered, the suspense and mystery tip over into unintelligibility and farce. In each case, a teleological structure is formally necessary to the production of the affect and energy in question, but the presence of a substantive, content-laden *telos* would deaden that affect and energy.

This reach for a presence that would deaden the very reach that extends to it is what I had in mind in saying, in the discussion of the hunts, that much of the poem is organized around a wish figured there as the wish to see and touch the interior stuff that is living flesh, but that can be made seeable and touchable only as dead meat. I have argued that such a wish is central both to the chivalric ethos the poem elaborates and to the production of the chivalric subject as a bearer of that ethos. Such a wish is alive as well, I think, in the poem's interest in ethics proper. In distinguishing ethos and ethics, I mean to distinguish an account of particular values and social forms from an account of the conceptual structure of value. While the pentangle on Gawain's shield participates in the former, I will now argue that it also participates in the latter, and in ways that do not reduce to its ideological function, although they certainly help to buttress that function.

The Excitement of Virtue

As mentioned earlier, when the pentangle has been understood as something other than an unproblematic chivalric emblem, it has been identified with ideological stasis and obsolescence, with a fixity of identity and desire caught up in misrecognition, and with defensive claims to ethical perfection. In short, the pentangle has been read as a figure of the bad-faith wish to guard against or contain or foreclose uncomfortable social and psychic realities, including the more unruly energies and desires that course through this poem.[44] Such accounts of the figure's function

[44] See Fisher, "Taken Men and Token Women," 74–75; Heng, "Feminine Knots," 504–6, and Dinshaw, "A Kiss Is Just a Kiss," 213–16.

respond to the way the pentangle represents chivalric "trawthe" as an "endeles knot" (630), composed of five subsidiary virtues, each of which "vmbelappez and loukez in oþer" (628), such that "vchone halched in oþer, þat non ende hade, / And fyched vpon fyue poyntez þat fayld neuer" (657–58), as though virtue were some kind of self-guaranteeing formal totality. A full understanding of the place of virtue in the poem must take account of such a fantasy. But in its representation of the unity of the virtues, the pentangle is also registering a claim about the conditions of virtue as such. As Aristotle and Aquinas among others have argued, virtues do not stand or fall one by one, but rather depend on one another.[45] On the one hand, this means that they support each other. To take an example from the central virtues at issue in this poem, a capacity for courtesy is enhanced by a capacity for courage, for there will be situations in which courtesy calls for courage, as when Arthur responds to the Green Knight's initial intrusion into Camelot's festivities—an intrusion that leaves some if not all of the members of the court dead silent with fear—by welcoming him into the company rather than, as a less courageous king might have, treating him as a hostile intruder. On the other hand, this also means that if one virtue fails, others are compromised. Courtesy will not stand up in all situations without courage's support, and that means that courtesy without courage remains imperfect no matter how assiduously cultivated. For this reason, the person who aims at virtue cannot be understood as aiming at distinct territories of goodness or individual ethical attributes one by one. While virtue is in a sense made up of parts—we can define courage and courtesy and distinguish many of their occasions—it is not composed of those parts atomistically, and they cannot be pursued or cultivated atomistically. To aim at virtue is to aim at goodness in its entirety.[46]

To the extent that such an account is compelling, it suggests that the

---

[45] Burrow and Spearing discuss the relevance of the unity of the virtues to the poem; see Burrow, *A Reading of "Sir Gawain and the Green Knight,"* 49–50, and Spearing, *The Gawain-Poet*. As Burrow points out, the idea "is quite common in patristic and medieval writers" (49). For Aquinas's discussion of the idea, see *Summa Theologiae* I–II, q. LXV, in *Treatise on the Virtues*, trans. John A. Oesterle (South Bend, Ind.: Notre Dame University Press, 1966), 139–48. Aquinas cites versions of the idea from Ambrose, Augustine, and Gregory.

[46] This is not to say, as it is sometimes thought, that a commitment to the unity of the virtues entails a denial of the possibility of real conflicts of value. One might rather think that in cases of conflicts of value there is a loss that cannot just be measured in terms of the value that gets sacrificed, but is rather a loss to the entirety of the ethical field.

perfectionism of pentangular virtue is not just a projection of the specific conditions of chivalric ideology, but is also a register of the holistic character of virtue. What is particularly interesting about the poem's ethical holism is that it tends to focus on scenes in which value in some important way gets socially bestowed.[47] An example that will return us to some earlier concerns of this chapter comes at the beginning of the second flirtation scene. The Lady teases Gawain that he seems not to understand the rules of polite society, since he failed to claim a kiss from her when she first entered his bed, even after she had taught him the previous day that that is just what a courteous knight should do. Gawain responds "þat durst I not do, lest I deuayed were. / If I were werned, I were wrang, iwysse, ȝif I profered" (1493–94). In the spirit of an older, moralizing critical tradition, one might imagine criticizing Gawain for not appealing here to some absolute moral standard by which the rightness or wrongness of kissing the Lady might be determined. But doing so would miss both the fun of Gawain's response—he is not only putting the Lady off, he is keeping their flirtation going by turning her tease back on her, asking in a coy, roundabout way if she would *like* to be kissed—and the ethical aptness of his formulation. In flirting of the kind these two are pursuing, the question whether or not to act in a particular way cannot always be answered by an appeal to absolute standards, since the answer can depend entirely on how the act in question would be received. Of course, absolute standards can still be in play. Given the ethical values of the communities to which Gawain and the Lady belong, if he were to try to have intercourse with her, or if he were to dry up and prudishly treat all of her advances as untoward behavior unbecoming of her, he would be acting in ways that are culpable independently of her response. But all the excitement of these scenes, and everything that is ethically interesting about them, occurs in between these extremes.

If Gawain attempts a kiss and is refused—at least if the refusal is not itself in flirtatious mode, but involves a genuine desire not to be kissed—then it *was* wrong for him to do so, *just because* it turned out not to be what the Lady wanted. This would not necessarily be because Gawain meant anything he should not have meant in kissing. It might have been the most innocent of flirtatious acts from his end of things;

[47] See Burrow, "Honour and Shame in *Sir Gawain and the Green Knight*," in his *Essays on Medieval Literature* (Oxford: Clarendon Press, 1984), 117–31.

but if the Lady is offended or disturbed by it, the playful mood has been broken, everyone is embarrassed, and Gawain is the culpable party. This need not occur as a result of Gawain misreading the situation or the Lady's desire. She might have no definitive desire about the matter prior to his attempt. It might just turn out that that's not what she wants, in what could be a surprise even to her. Still, in such a case Gawain has committed an embarrassing act, failing in his regard for the Lady, his duties to his host, and his own erotic comportment—in a word, failing in *cortaysye*, the social finesse for which he is most renowned. This goes along with the poem's elaboration of a purely formal teleological structure for flirting. What makes flirting exciting is that, while it has the *form* of "potentially going somewhere," no one involved in it needs to have any determinate desire at any point as to where that might be. Not knowing what you might turn out to want, and not knowing what the other party might turn out to want, and so being able to be surprised at what either of you turns out to want, is central to the enjoyment of this sort of flirting, as well as to its potential for embarrassment. In ethical terms, what this means is not only that virtues are not individually determinate attributes of the ethical subject, since any given virtue, no matter how assiduously cultivated, is vulnerable to failure with respect to another, but that, at least for the ethical concerns most central to this poem, virtues are not determinately possessable attributes of the individual subject at all, since nothing in the individual finally decides whether or not he is the bearer of the virtues in question. The pressure toward a holistic account of ethical value does not stop, as it were, at the border of Gawain's body, or of his acts at the moment they issue forth from him, but includes the social scenes in which those acts get constituted as the acts they are.

The connection between pentangular holism and the chivalric excitation that I have been tracing throughout this essay should now be clear. On such an account of the constitution of ethical value, the ethical field becomes almost unbearably exciting. Something you might otherwise regard as a minor failure, assignable to some relatively unimportant corner of your ethical conduct, can radiate out into the whole of your ethical substance, making it seem compromised at the core. Everything you do is thus potentially charged with enormous significance, and there is no way of telling where that significance might come from. This is especially so because the significance might come from the way others receive your actions, which in some cases at least is essentially unpredictable, since there may be no antecedently knowable desire behind it. With its pentangular picture of virtue, then, the poem occupies the same space as it does when it registers the deathly thrills of ax's descent and arrows' impact, of opened flesh and cracking cliffs. For seen this way, the pentangle is a register of the desire, not for prophylaxis in the face of the world's dangers or containment of one's own wild excitations, but for maximizing the world's impact, making it impinge on you, and being alive to the thrill of the wildness with which you meet it. Pentangular virtue is yet another form of the chivalric love of "baret." Or, to put the point the other way around, the various forms of "baret" this poem traces are its ways of imagining the field of the ethical.

The Stain of the Animate

In discussing Gawain's pleasure in flirting and the excitations of chivalric ethics, I have mainly been discussing features of the poem that give expression to the chivalric subject's preferred self-understanding, and to the ways that self-understanding is shaped in relation to the signifying forms and normative structures of chivalric culture. In this respect, my argument has been that *Sir Gawain and the Green Knight* locates the features of chivalry that usually get grouped under the rubric of "courtly love"—the "masochistic" character of the chivalric subject, its love of suspension and delectation in suffering—as homologous with the chivalric ethos of violent domination, self-command, and sacrificial commitment; and I have argued that both derive key features of their underlying structure from the ethical holism that informs the poem's formal teleologies. That says a lot about the structures of desire informing the poem, but by itself it does not return us to the topic with which I began, namely, the death drive. The death drive pushes us past the register we have mostly been examining; it concerns the subject's relation to that in it which cannot be accommodated to the ego's organization or to the structures of signification in which it is embedded. For this reason, the death drive is largely unconscious. While I have engaged unconscious, death-driven desire throughout this essay (for instance, in Gawain's enjoyment of the ax's descent, or in the hunter's horns heralding the end of the world), we are not going to find the source of that desire in an ethical problematic that is largely conscious, or at least preconscious. I will conclude by turning to these considerations. In doing so I will offer necessarily quick sketches of how the notion of a formal teleology might help us better understand Lacan, and of the proximity and distance between a Lacanian account of the death drive and an account rooted in the *Gawain*-poet's thoroughly orthodox medieval theology.

Lacan's interest in the Freudian notion of a "death drive"—a concept, as I have said, that he in many ways finds obscure—stems in part from his interest in understanding the scope and trajectory of unconscious desire. On a thin reading of the Freudian unconscious—or indeed, on the understanding of the unconscious that Freud developed early in his own work—psychic conflict is understood as conflict between competing systems or "spaces" in the mind. The subject has a set of mental objects (desires, beliefs, intentions, and so on) that are available to consciousness, and that form the basis of her "ego," the organized structure of mental processes that characterizes her sense of self. Now of course there can be plenty of psychic conflict within a subject's consciousness. But hysterical symptoms, dreams, slips of the tongue, and other psychopathologies large and small point to another, deeper kind of conflict, between conscious motives and another set of unconscious, repressed mental objects (paradigmatically, desires) that nevertheless motivate her. This is a brilliant and powerful insight, but by the time of *The Ego and the Id*, Freud had come to see this contrast between two realms of mental objects, one in the conscious ego and the other in the unconscious repressed, as clumsy. As he argues there, some of what constitutes the ego is unconscious, and not everything that is unconscious is repressed. The result is that the entire picture of the mind as an interior space populated by mental objects that could in principle become objects of consciousness looks a lot less compelling than it used to. One of Lacan's great contributions lies in the way he radicalizes the Freudian trajectory away from thinking of psychic conflict as a conflict between two systems or realms in the mind, on the one hand consciousness, and on the other an unconscious understood in effect as just like consciousness, only repressed, that is an inner realm with a set of contents that take the form of mental objects.

Lacan has a number of ways of pursuing this insight, among them the idea that the unconscious takes its form from signifying structure rather than from anything in the individual subject's mind.[48] What this

---

[48] Lacan develops this idea throughout his work in a number of ways. The critique of ego psychology in Book II of the *Seminar*, to which I have already referred, is one place to turn for such an argument. For some other paradigmatic instances, see *The Seminar of Jacques Lacan, Book XI: The Four Fundamental Concepts of Psychoanalysis*, trans. Alan

means is that the conflict between conscious and unconscious desire cannot be understood in any terms organized by the trope of the individual subject's mind as a discrete inner realm. The subject only comes into being in the first place in relation to the impersonal and limitless workings of signification and normativity; and there is no end to the ways in which signifiers can hook up with one another in signifying chains, and no way to specify and delimit all of the conflicting normative messages so produced. Psychic conflict in the individual thus ultimately stems from the incoherence of what Lacan calls the Symbolic order, together with the fact that everything in the subject is invested by its relation to the Symbolic. But the incoherence of the Symbolic order also means that nothing in the subject's experience can ever fully answer to her desire. The subject is driven beyond any determinate form that desire can take, whether conscious or unconscious, whether taking part in the organization of the ego or in conflict with it. Another way of putting this is to say that there is more to desire than its symbolic and imaginary structuration. That is why Lacan has recourse to the notion of a psychic Real, to refer to that toward which desire drives, but which remains in excess of anything figurable or signifiable. It is crucial to note here that the Real has no positive content: all psychic objects are caught up in misrecognition and in the incoherence of the Symbolic. But that also means that objects as such are finally inadequate to desire, and the subject is driven not simply beyond any objects it happens to have, but beyond anything objectifiable. That is why desire's drive can be called a death drive. The subject is driven beyond every way, conscious or unconscious, that it has of recognizing itself and its objects, beyond anything that can fall within a representational field. It is driven outside life and everything that participates in life. In this sense, desire aims at death.

This is where the notion of a purely formal teleology that I have been developing throughout this essay can help us better understand Lacan. In one sense, Lacan's account of desire is pitched directly *against* teleological thinking. Nothing that can be posited as an "end" is adequate to desire; desire aims at no good. Yet the very idea that desire *drives* is

---

Sheridan (New York: W. W. Norton, 1981), most pointedly, "The Unconscious and Repetition," 17–65; and from *Écrits*, trans. Bruce Fink (New York: W. W. Norton, 2006), "The Instance of the Letter in the Unconscious, or Reason since Freud," 412–43, "The Signification of the Phallus," 575–84, and "The Subversion of the Subject and the Dialectic of Desire in the Freudian Unconscious," 671–702.

in some sense a teleological one, even if it drives with no destination in mind. The trick is to see how this might be so, in a way that does not obscure the account by importing content where it does not belong, and so reinvoking a traditional notion of the goods toward which desire aims. When Lacan, attempting to dislodge that very notion, speaks of desire aiming at death or at evil, despite the gothic and transgressive appeal of such formulations, he *cannot* mean that death or evil offer substantive, content-bearing ends for desire, except in the same way that any *other* goods do. We do indeed aim at both death and evil, but we do so only in the way we aim at other ends, namely, insofar as they are embedded as Imaginary and Symbolic goods, and therefore only insofar as they are partial goods that fail to answer fully to the desire that reaches for them. The death drive is something else. It is still teleological, but only in the sense that desire aims beyond all goods, beyond any end with positive content. That beyond is the Real. For this reason, the death drive in Lacan is not what it was for Freud, who still had a strong tendency to think of it as taking inanimacy or quiescence as its final target. The distinction between substantive and formal teleology can help us here by giving us terms for avoiding not only the Freudian tendency to substantialize the death drive by making it a literal drive toward death, but also any tendency to turn the object of the drive into yet another good (in the technical sense), however discomfiting or "evil."

There are a number of ways in which we have seen *Sir Gawain and the Green Knight* tread upon this ground. The slipperiness of the way "death" functions as a trope in the poem, together with the conflicting identifications that inform the poem's representations of violence and suffering, indicate that what we are dealing with here is an unstable phantasmatic field, *not* some set of reportable attitudes with determinate contours. As I have argued, it is not as though the poem represents Gawain as consciously relishing the descent of the Green Knight's ax even as he fears it, or the hunters as identifying with the stricken deer, whose conquest they so thoroughly enjoy. Rather, these complications emerge from the signifying structures the poem puts in play around those moments, and while they emerge in one sense as part of what the poem represents as character psychology, they do so even more powerfully in the scene of the poem's aesthetic effects, as consequences of its formal structures and of the career of its tropes. Further, the poem's narrative anticlimax leaves it markedly without a perspective from which the events of the plot make sense: neither Gawain, nor Arthur's court, nor Bertilak, nor Morgan, nor the narratorial voice itself provides anything but local, and strongly motivated, gestures at sense-making that both undercut themselves and conflict with one another. But this is a poem that will not set teleology to the side: desire continues to drive, even if nowhere does the poem represent a destination, narrative, erotic, ethical, or otherwise, that is adequate to that drive. Perhaps that is the reason for the otherwise odd eschatological overtones in the poem's representation of the orgiastic horn-blowing in the hunt and the equally thrilling sound of the Green Knight sharpening his ax. Something can be heard here, even if there is no language for it, and whatever it is, it sounds like the end of things, an end both ecstatic and fearful.

Left as such, this is of course no more than suggestive. To fill out a bit this sketch of the intrusion of the Real into the poem, and to indicate how the poem's own engagement with it both brushes up against, and swerves away from, Lacanian insights, let me return to some terms the poem itself offers. One such term, drawn from the scene of Gawain's stillness under the ax with which we began, is that of "rootedness in inanimacy." I have argued that one of the consequences of this poem's ethical holism lies in a species of indeterminacy. In the kind of scenes of interest here, there is often no empirically determinable fact of the matter about the right thing to do, about what you desire in acting, or about the desires others have with respect to your action. You just have to take your best shot and see how it comes out, and in the process see how you and your desire come out. That is what the social virtuosity of *cortaysye* consists in, and it is a principal source of the thrill of aliveness that courses throughout this poem. That being said, it remains the case that in order to have a field of aliveness such as this, an agent must hold much of the deliberative field still. Everything cannot be in the air at once, or there will be no way of acting intelligibly at all. Much of what Gawain desires is perfectly clear; he also has certain obligations to the Lady and his host, and has a particular kind of care throughout the poem for his own ethical condition. The hunters too have some perfectly clear desires, and must meet certain standards of skill and courage and finesse. None of this is ever allowed to enter a space of "delicious indeterminacy," and such foreclosures of indeterminacy are a condition of there being such a space at all. It makes sense, then, that Gawain should be rooted in inanimacy in the moment of his stillness under the ax. This is the moment when he must forbid himself access to the thrills of a flesh quivering in anticipation of the world's impact, the thrills that motivated his earlier glance at the descending blade. Otherwise he will not be able to make good on a commitment that is absolutely central to his sense of who he is and what he must do, a commitment that makes the thrills he longs for possible in the first place.

This sense of "rootedness in inanimacy" might also help explain another foreclosure that is central to this poem's mode of excitation, the foreclosure of Gawain's sodomitical relation with Bertilak. As Carolyn Dinshaw has argued, if Gawain and the Lady go "too far" in the bedroom, and Gawain is true to his word in the exchange-of-winnings game with Bertilak, then he will have to make himself sexually available to Bertilak in the way the Lady has made herself sexually available to him. This is part of what makes those bedroom activities exciting, and it is also part of what defines a "too far" that is absolute there—not because Gawain could not go that far, and even perhaps take pleasure in doing so, but because if he did then he would be in another territory of pleasure altogether, one that must be kept off the map for him to maintain the territory he has established with the Lady, and one that his entire culture works to keep off the map as well. Both Gawain's sacrificial stillness under the ax and the poem's foreclosure of sodomitical relations should be understood as ideological operations, *not* as ethical necessities. But what an ethical analysis reveals is that these ideological operations are *enabled* by an ethical necessity. For there to be an intelligible field of action at all, there must be many possibilities that, as Dinshaw puts it quite precisely, are not so much repressed as foreclosed, never allowed to enter a representational field. The necessity of such foreclosure in turn guarantees that the forms of "rootedness in inanimacy" will predictably occupy sites of ideological work.

The *Gawain*-poet has another way of understanding the necessity and import of such "rootedness in inanimacy," although it will require a significant shift of terms to unpack it. I have argued that a purely formal teleology is central to this poem's explorations of the chivalric love of "baret." But the poet has another teleology in mind as well, one he explicitly links to "baret" in *Sir Gawain and the Green Knight*, and explores at fuller length in his equally brilliant poem *Pearl*. The other appearance of the term "baret" in *Sir Gawain and the Green Knight* occurs as Gawain searches in the wilderness for the Green Chapel; it is Christmas Eve, and he wanders "[c]arande for his costes, lest he ne keuer schulde / To se þe seruyse of þat Syre þat on þat self nyȝt / Of a burde watz borne oure baret to quelle" (750–52). Christ was born "oure baret to quelle," to put an end to everything that makes us a site of strife, that marks our separation from the divine. "Quelle" is a strong term to use here: its principal meanings are to kill, slaughter, or destroy.[49] But it is not too strong a term to use in a poem in which the love of this thing that Christ comes to destroy is constitutive of so much pleasure and excitement, and is central to so much that gives us energy and purpose. To remove the impediments to union with God would be to eradicate one of the principal ways the human is bound to its life. But such an eradication, the poem intimates, is also an end in store for us, a *telos* that determines the core structure and trajectory of the subject's desire, perhaps the only *telos* in the poem that is *not* anticlimactic.

We can better understand the connection between the teleologies that are the principal focus of *Sir Gawain and the Green Knight* and the Christian one that appears only around the poem's edges by borrowing some terms from the *Gawain*-poet's other great poem, *Pearl*.[50] That poem too is built around anticlimax. Throughout, the dreamer-narrator articulates his longing for his lost "pearl." Perhaps the pearl is his daughter, although the poem never definitively says so, and many of its ways of figuring her value are, at the least, uncomfortable from such a literalizing perspective. Given the multiple and fractured forms of figuration through which the dreamer tries to bring her into focus, the "pearl" emerges as simultaneously radiant and obscure, the lost thing which in its lostness functions as an image of the precious, unattainable object constitutive of desire. Late in his vision, the dreamer sees his pearl across an impassable river, among Christ's company "wyth lyf . . . laste and lade" (*Pearl* 1146), overflowing with the life that is proximity to the divine. The sight overwhelms him:

> Delyt me drof in yȝe and ere,
> My manez mynde to maddyng malte;
> Quen I seȝ my frely, I wolde be þere,
> Byȝonde þe water þaȝ ho were walte.
>
> (1153–56)

---

[49] *Middle English Dictionary* online, http://ets.umdl.umich.edu/m/med/.

[50] My discussion here is indebted to the accounts of Pearl's ungraspability in George Edmondson, "*Pearl*: The Shadow of the Object, the Shape of the Law," *SAC* 26 (2004): 29–63, and D. Vance Smith, "The Physics of Elegy," paper presented to the Medieval Studies Colloquium at the University of California, Santa Barbara, February 3, 2006.

Penetrated by an unmanageable excitation that melts his mind into madness, all the narrator can think of is his desire to "go beyond the water," to cross the impassable barrier, "þaȝ I þer swalte" (1160), even if it means his death. But just as he is about to enter the stream, he is thrown out of his vision and awakes, left to offer himself a series of unconvincing assurances that after all he is happy "in þys doel-doun-goun" (1187) that is life, that it is quite easy to be a good Christian and obey God's will, since God apparently was not happy with his importunate desire to join his pearl. The poem thus ends with a fantasy of access to the lost thing that would fulfill desire, an access imagined to bring with it madness or death, and to be impossible or forbidden, and in relation to which *this* life looks like imprisonment, bitter ashes, living death. This is the same structure of anticlimax we found in the central pleasures of *Sir Gawain and the Green Knight*. As in *Gawain*, the buildup of excitation in *Pearl* refers to a *telos* that must remain unliteralized for that excitation to persist in its dominant mode of suspension and deferral. The narrator is rooted in inanimacy, able to act and imagine only from a place of death-in-life, longing to reach a place of life that itself would seem to entail his death.

The *Pearl*-poet understands this to be a condition of what he calls "spottiness." *Pearl* is structured in stanza groups, each of which is built around a central term whose semantic range is made to bear conceptual and figurative weight. The central term or figurative *topos* for the opening stanza group is "spot." "Spot" is, first of all, the blemish or stain whose absence defines the pearl's perfection as the "perle withouten spot" (12, 24, 36, 48, 60). As the stanza group develops, however, it becomes clear that the spot is also the place of loss, the spot on which the pearl "sprang" from the narrator (13), and the place of the production of life in the pearl's absence, the spot on which spices must grow now that the pearl has fallen to rot there (25). A reading of "spot" as place in turn suggests another reading of the repeated phrase "perle withouten spot": "spot" is the place the pearl no longer has, since it is now no place, defined by its lack of location. The term also appears as the "spot þat I in speche expoun" (37), the spot about which I speak, but also the rhetorical *topos* itself, the space of figuration in which the narrator tries to give form to his sense of lack, and so, on yet another reading of the repeated phrase "perle withouten spot," the representation the pearl does not have, since nothing sayable, no figuration, is adequate to it. Finally, in a development of "spot" as place and as rhetorical *topos*, it is also the place the narrator tries to "grasp" as "[b]ifore þat spot my honde I spenned / For care ful colde þat to me caȝt" (49–50), in what is both a failed gesture of capture and an expression of woe. The woefulness of the "spot" thus emerges as its siting of the pearl's ungraspability, both its unholdability and its unthinkability.

A stain that is the condition of life's production, of its having a place and a mode of figuration, of its being manipulable and thinkable, all of which points to a condition of ungraspable perfection determined by its absence of such "spots": this is the *Pearl*-poet's understanding of the basic ontology of the human. The Christian teleology that defines this understanding, like the teleologies of chivalric desire, is in a sense purely formal. In the Christian case, there is of course a determinate end that gives shape to the whole, an end that is an object of desire, namely, union with the divine. But the poem insists that we can only articulate or imagine a relation to that end in figurative terms, phantasmatic "spots" that are imbedded in our spottiness, our place that is also our blemish. Any moment in which we imagine our relation to our end will thus be anticlimactic: it will read as the loss of a precious object, of something or someone dear to us; or, as in the dreamer's sense of God's rejection of him, or the parable of the vineyard that occupies much of the poem's middle, as the suffering of an injustice; or as a vision of the foreclosure of the most ecstatic fulfillment of desire, since that fulfillment takes place, as it seems, across an impassable barrier that we must at all costs pass.

The poet understands the chivalric occasions of *Sir Gawain and the Green Knight* in terms of this ontology and the phenomenology of anticlimax that emerges from it. *Gawain* is a poem concerned with a specific kind of "spot," that of the chivalric love of "baret," the condition Christ came to destroy, a condition in which *trawthe* and treachery, excitation by life and boundedness to death, are inseparably mixed. In conventional theological terms, this is the condition of sin. The poem's purpose is not to level a condemnation of chivalry as sinful; surely David Aers is right to see critical discussions weighing the severity of Gawain's sinfulness, or that of Arthur's court, as overblown and as missing the authority the poem grants to chivalric values.[51] The poet rather seeks to

[51] See David Aers, "Christianity for Courtly Subjects: Reflections on the *Gawain*-Poet," in *A Companion to the Gawain-Poet*, ed. Derek Brewer and Jonathan Gibson (Cambridge: D. S. Brewer, 1997), 91–101, and Aers, *Community, Gender, and Individual Identity: English Writing 1360–1430* (London and New York: Routledge, 1988), 153–78.

understand the shape of chivalry's directedness on an unfigurable *telos*, its ways of imagining and foreclosing ecstatic fulfillment, and of producing impassable barriers and anticlimaxes. Where discussions of Gawain's sinfulness go awry, then, is not in overvaluing the religious and theological discourses of sin, but in restricting the scope of an interest in the topic to questions of moral evaluation. This poet's interest in sin, at least in these two poems, is analytical and phenomenological rather than moralistic. He is interested in exploring, in quite different but complementary ways, the condition of a creature in love with strife and loss, a creature for whom the very condition of being animate is a stain. While such a condition can easily produce moralism, it is in no way the enemy of desire. As both *Gawain* and *Pearl* help us to see, the human's animacy and its stainedness sustain each other, in no small part because while its desire demands figuration, and so helps to substantialize a world in which it can intelligibly act, no figuration is adequate to desire's drive beyond all "spots," beyond any satisfaction it can picture and any subject-position it might inhabit.

It is clear that desire's drive beyond signification as it is represented in *Pearl* is not the same thing as the Lacanian death drive. For Lacan, as I have said, the Real toward which desire drives has no substance whatsoever. The Real is not a name for a distinct metaphysical realm from which we are debarred; it is not a metaphysical concept at all, which is what makes it so hard to articulate. The fact that the Real is, in terms of the reality constituted by the subject's psychic economy, an emptiness or absence, is part of why desire's drive toward the Real is a death drive. For the *Pearl*-poet, however, the something beyond all objects that constitutes the target of desire's drive—that is, the divine—*is* substantial, in fact is the very substance of substance, the only substance not shadowed by its own fall into some species of nonbeing, and as such the principle of life. Further, the divine substance is also the Sovereign Good, the ground of the subject's principles of action, and of the being of all of the subject's objects; whereas Lacan argues that for modern subjects there is no Sovereign Good, or to put the point more strongly, it is a mistake to think there has ever been one. These differences are enormous. To posit a divine substance at the heart of the metaphysical structure of reality, of the structure of the human psyche, and of the nature of the good, is on a Lacanian account to shield oneself from the incoherence of the Symbolic order and the emptiness of the Real. This does not mean, however, that psychic life is somehow more ordered or "safer" for medieval subjects than it is for modern ones. Given the mess humans tend to make of things—an obsessive object of thought in medieval texts—the thought of a Supreme Good persistently calling forth a desire that responds to it in fitful and perverted ways (the term is Augustine's) opens up possibilities for abjection, paranoia, and the enjoyment of punishment that course through medieval culture. These possibilities are present in medieval texts in more than merely symptomatic ways; they are the object of sophisticated thought. There is a strong tendency in modern engagements with medieval culture to imagine that that culture's theological commitments somehow foreclose the possibility of medieval subjects having a complicated relation to, or complex understandings of, desire—a tendency into which medieval studies has fallen all too often. Those commitments should certainly not be ignored. But neither should we presume that we know what they tell us about the life of desire or its conceptualization in medieval culture.

That is partly because, as Lacan argued, we should not presume that we know what modernity's lack of theological commitments tells us about our own desire. If God is dead, then God has always been dead, and there has never been a Sovereign Good. But at the same time, we moderns (or postmoderns) are all still creationists, even if we are atheists. The very possibility of psychic and social functionality depends on our investment in the fantasy of a Sovereign Good, no matter what we think we believe about the farcical emptiness of the Big Other. That is part of what it means to be a constitutively split subject on Lacan's account.[52] To read the difference between medieval and modern is to read the difference between ways of handling a simultaneous lack of and commitment to a Supreme Good that is, in some form, constitutive of the human. As Lacan's own work reflects, one crucial value of an engagement with medieval texts is that they can help us see the shape and consequences of phantasmatic commitments we retain, but to which we remain systematically blind because of our strong investment in under-

---

[52] See *The Ethics of Psychoanalysis*, "On Creation *Ex Nihilo*," 115–27; *Encore: The Seminar of Jacques Lacan, Book XX: On Feminine Sexuality, the Limits of Love and Knowledge*, trans. Bruce Fink (New York: W. W. Norton, 1998), esp. 64–77. Lacan's argument that psychic functionality depends on the conjuring of an Other taken to be the source of coherent signification and normativity goes to the same point; see, for instance, "Signification of the Phallus" and "Subversion of the Subject." Bruce Holsinger helpfully argues that, at least in *The Ethics of Psychoanalysis*, Lacan's historicism cuts directly against the grain of the strongly periodizing historicism often attributed to him; see *The Premodern Condition*, 57–93.

standing ourselves to have left them behind. This is especially so given how self-congratulatory modernity remains, both in its glamorous sense of the supposedly newfound psychic fragmentation modern subjects suffer, and in its tendency to turn our necessarily partial and incomplete ways of theorizing that fragmentation into technologies for keeping it at arm's length. As I have argued here, the problem of teleology occupies one such blind spot, and as such offers fertile ground for further thinking.

Saint George, Islam, and Regional Audiences in *Sir Gawain and the Green Knight*

Su Fang Ng and Kenneth Hodges
University of Oklahoma

BEFORE HIS TALE, which begins with Islamic merchants carrying stories between Syria and Rome, Chaucer's Man of Law offers this apostrophe to merchants: "Ye seken lond and see for yowre wynnynges; / As wise folk ye knowen al th'estaat / Of regnes; ye been fadres of tidynges / And tales . . ."[1] Thus Chaucer notes that trading networks spread stories as well as merchandise, stories Chaucer himself appropriates and retells. If we take Chaucer's remarks seriously, we need to expand the area of literary exchange beyond Western Europe. One work that may have been shaped, unexpectedly, by such exchanges is *Sir Gawain and the Green Knight*. Although European analogues and sources for it exist, there have been hints over the decades of possible non-European contexts for the poem. In 1916, George Lyman Kittredge noted that in a number of the analogues the supernatural challenger is black or Turkish.[2] These analogues thus link the challenger of the beheading plot to racial otherness. In 1974, Alice Lasater, in her work on the influence of Spanish literature (Christian, Islamic, and hybrid) on Middle English literature, noted extensive parallels between a

We would like to thank Michael Bennett for so generously sharing with us his notes on BL Harley MS 3988 and Thomas Burman for sharing his transcription of Theodorus Bibliander's 1550 edition of Robert of Ketton's Latin translation of the Qu'ran. We have benefited from a conversation with Michael Twomey about our paper at Kalamazoo. We would also like to thank Bernadette Andrea and Christina Fitzgerald for reading an early draft of this essay.

[1] *Canterbury Tales,* II.127–30, in Larry Benson, gen. ed. *The Riverside Chaucer* (Boston: Houghton Mifflin, 1987).

[2] The relevant stories are *La Mule Sanz Frain, Humbaut,* and *Sir Gawain and the Turk.* See Kittredge, *A Study of "Sir Gawain and the Green Knight"* (Cambridge, Mass.: Harvard University Press, 1916), 44, 62.

well-known popular Islamic folk figure, al-Khidr[3] (the Green One), and the Green Knight.[4] Evidence for the *Gawain*-poet's interest in the east has been detected in the other poems as well. The heavenly city of *Pearl*, as Mahmoud Manzalaoui has noted, has close parallels to the description in an Islamic text known to Europeans in Latin translation as the *Liber Scalae* or *Book of the Ladder* (a copy of fourteenth-century English provenance was found at Oxford). It recounts Mohammed's ascent into the heavens (*mi'rāj*), and scholars now largely agree that this text was a source for Dante's *Commedia*.[5] Further suggesting interest in the east, *Cleanness* draws on Sir John Mandeville's description of the Dead Sea.[6]

Since the poem is elusive in questions of authorship, date, and circumstances of composition, criticism has necessarily proceeded speculatively. Most critics have understandably focused on Northern European (especially Irish and French) sources and analogues. Given recent scholarly interest in medieval romance's engagement with the east and with Islam, however, the Green Knight's non-European analogues and particularly Lasater's intriguing suggestion of al-Khidr need to be reconsidered. While the poem's many unknowns prevent any absolute identification of the Green Knight as al-Khidr, especially since the Green Knight is most probably a composite character with elements taken from several traditions as well as the poet's imagination, the possibility that the *Gawain*-poet may have, in his typically allusive manner, borrowed from an Islamic figure nonetheless leads to a fruitful reexamination of the poem's commitments and affiliations. The seminal works of Dorothee Metlitzki and María Rosa Menocal have demonstrated that

---

[3] Spellings of the name الخضر range widely: Khidr, Khadir, Chadir, and so on. Hizr and Hizir are Turkish variants. Because Khidr was identified with Elijah (Elias), he was also known as Khidr-Elias or Chidrelles.

[4] Alice Lasater, *Spain to England: A Comparative Study of Arabic, European, and English Literature of the Middle Ages* (Jackson: University of Mississippi Press, 1974), esp. 168–96. Several recent articles acknowledge Lasater's work: Joseph Skaria, "*Sir Gawain and the Green Knight* and the Matter of Araby," *South Asian Review* 19.16 (1995): 49–58; Zacharias Thundy, "Classical Analogues—Eastern and Western—of *Sir Gawain*," in *"Sir Gawain" and the Classical Tradition*, ed. E. L. Risden (Jefferson, N.C.: McFarland, 2006), 135–81. Suggested links between al-Khidr and the devil in Chaucer's *Friar's Tale*, however, seem improbable.

[5] Mahmoud Manzalaoui, "English Analogues to the *Liber Scalae*," *MÆ* 34 (1965): 21–35; for a translation of the *Liber Scalae*, see *The Prophet of Islam in Old French Romance: "The Romance of Mohammad" (1258) and "The Book of Mohammad's Ladder" (1264)*, trans. Reginald Hyatte (Leiden: E. J. Brill, 1997).

[6] Malcolm Andrew and Ronald Waldron, eds., *The Poems of the Pearl Manuscript* (Berkeley and Los Angeles: University of California Press, 1978), 154 n. 1025ff.

Islamic literature must be taken seriously as an influence on and source for medieval Christian literature: intellectual engagement with Islam went far beyond the caricatured Muslims of bad romances.[7] Religious antipathy did not prevent medieval Christians from studying the sacred book of their enemies: Robert of Ketton's twelfth-century translation of the Qu'ran circulated widely and continued to be read into the early modern period. As Thomas Burman shows in his study of Latin translations of the Qu'ran, Robert of Ketton and other translators incorporated Islamic commentary into their translations and their glosses in order to elucidate obscure Qu'ranic passages, and in so doing they strove to understand a difficult, alien text in its own terms: Christian response to the text was not simply polemical—though it certainly was that—it was also deeply philological.[8] Since medieval engagements with Islam are starting to be understood as doing more than simply recycling old stereotypes or caricaturing Muslims, Lasater's suggestion of al-Khidr as an analogue for the Green Knight must be more thoroughly considered.

As medievalists also turn, increasingly, to questions of postcolonialism, a reconsideration of the literary markers of *Sir Gawain and the Green Knight*'s possible engagement with the Islamic world in relation to the likely historical and political contexts of its composition may point us to a new, international reading of the poem. For, while literary study was turning up intriguing evidence of Islamic and international connections, historical scholarship showed that Chester had significant and sustained political and economic ties to the outside world. Though regional, Cheshire was not provincial in the sense of being on the cultural periphery of a national center. Ralph Hanna III suggests that London is best understood not as a central court setting a cultural model for the rest, but as the point of contact where regional court cultures intersected.[9] In later work, Hanna goes further to decentralize London, suggesting that "before Chaucer, London may truly have been 'provincial,' among England's vernacular literary backwaters, just another locality," as distressing as this may be to "master narratives of national culture

---

[7] Dorothee Metlitzki, *The Matter of Araby in Medieval England* (New Haven: Yale University Press, 1977); María Rosa Menocal, *The Arabic Role in Medieval Literary History: A Forgotten Heritage* (Philadelphia: University of Pennsylvania Press, 1987).

[8] Thomas E. Burman, *Reading the Qu'ran in Latin Christendom, 1140–1560* (Philadelphia: University of Pennsylvania Press, 2007).

[9] Ralph Hanna III, "Sir Thomas Berkeley and His Patronage," *Speculum* 64.4 (1989): 878–916 (912–13).

[that] require that London reflect a universal metropolitanism."[10] Cheshire's relation to the larger world thus need not be defined by its relation to London and the royal court. Michael Bennett's invaluable study of fourteenth-century Chester shows that not only a number of the lords and military men had significant international experience, including in Muslim lands or the hybrid kingdoms of Spain, but also that Cheshire was firmly connected to the mercantile web that extended through and beyond Britain.[11] We suggest that a closer look at a number of the lords proposed as possible patrons for the *Gawain*-poet shows extensive international interests and experience. As Bennett argues, "The links between literary activity [in the northwest Midlands] and increasing mobility are all too evident. . . . Few works of the alliterative revival are provincial in their outlook."[12]

As postcolonial readings have begun to suggest, *Sir Gawain and the Green Knight* is a border poem. But the borders are not simply between Wales and England: Cheshire was affected by borders between England and Europe, Christendom and Dar al-Islam. The possible link between al-Khidr and the Green Knight (even if inconclusive, given the elusiveness of the author and his poem) allows the poem to explore these boundaries and show how the chivalry of the young King Arthur and his court is profoundly shaped by an encounter that goes beyond his kingdom and even beyond Christendom. Yet the poet's playfulness and delicate handling of the theme of the simultaneous allure and threat of the foreign mean that geopolitical allusions are provocative rather than programmatic statements for particular ideologies or interests. In proposing this reading, however, we emphasize an understanding of international encounters that depends upon regional politics. Cheshire's international ties must be viewed within the context of multiple powerful aristocratic courts with their own foreign engagements. Thus our reading is not singular but several—we look at the courts of three possible patrons of the *Gawain*-poet—as the several courts provide intriguing contexts that give very different meanings to the poem's international engagements. Nonetheless, one common thread runs through all three courts of the poem's possible patrons: their surprising cosmopolitanism.

[10] Ralph Hanna, *London Literature, 1300–1380* (Cambridge: Cambridge University Press, 2005), 2–3, xvii.
[11] Bennett, *Community, Class, and Careerism: Cheshire and Lancashire Society in the Age of "Sir Gawain and the Green Knight"* (Cambridge: Cambridge University Press, 1983).
[12] Michael Bennett, "The Historical Background," in *A Companion to the Gawain-Poet*, ed. Derek Brewer and Jonathan Gibson (Cambridge: D. S. Brewer, 1997), 79.

The Order of the Garter, Al-Khidr, and Saint George

A fruitful starting point for exploring *Sir Gawain and the Green Knight*'s international engagements is the Order of the Garter. The unique manuscript of the poem ends with a variant of the motto of the Order of the Garter, "Honi soyt qui mal pence," in a medieval hand (perhaps scribal, perhaps added by an early reader).[13] It urges readers not to think badly of Gawain, and it comments on the creation of a knightly honor out of ambiguous origins. Whether this explicit connection is intrinsic to the work or the result of reader response, it provides a powerful context for the poem, and recent criticism is increasingly persuaded that the poem should be considered as a Garter poem.[14] Given the prestige and strong Arthurian associations of the Order of the Garter, and the thematic similarities in the poem, Leo Carruthers is almost certainly correct to conclude that "any English poet writing in the Arthurian mode at this date would necessarily see, and know that an aristocratic audience would see, a parallel between the Round Table and the Order of the Garter."[15] While there is agreement about the importance of the Garter, there is not agreement about specific historical contexts involving the Garter that the poem may refer to, and thus suggested dates vary widely. Michael Bennett's contextualizing of *Sir Gawain and the Green Knight* in the Ricardian period has been widely accepted, but more recently Francis Ingledew dates it to midcentury, arguing that a poem in which a society of the green girdle is founded out of an erotic test is in fact responding to reports of Edward III's rape of the Countess of Salisbury. In Ingledew's reading of the Order's motto, this alleged rape is also imbricated with the Order's founding as Edward tries to deflect such criticism. This dating would put the poem's composition close to the foundation of the Order of the Garter.

[13] Francis Ingledew, *"Sir Gawain and the Green Knight" and the Order of the Garter* (Notre Dame, Ind.: University of Notre Dame Press, 2006), 224 n. 10.

[14] Besides Ingledew, see Leo Carruthers, "The Duke of Clarence and the Earls of March: Garter Knights and *Sir Gawain and the Green Knight*," *MÆ* 70.1 (2001): 66–79; W. G. Cooke and D'Arcy J. D. Boulton, "*Sir Gawain and the Green Knight*: A Poem for Henry of Grosmont?" *MÆ* 68.1 (1999): 42–54; and Hugh E. L. Collins, *The Order of the Garter, 1348–1461: Chivalry and Politics in Late Medieval England* (Oxford: Clarendon Press, 2000), 256–57. Ann R. Meyer notes that Edward and Thomas Despenser were both Knights of the Garter as she makes a case for their possible patronage in "The Despensers and the *Gawain* Poet: A Gloucestershire Link to the Alliterative Master of the Northwest Midlands," *ChauR* 35.4 (2001): 413–29.

[15] Carruthers, "Duke of Clarence," 66.

From the beginning, the Order of the Garter was an international Order, with "Stranger Knights" included since its founding in 1348. The Order of the Garter was modeled on the Castilian Order of the Band, whose device was worn as a baldric (like the green sash in the poem) and whose purpose was to restore knights to high chivalry because of the perception that men had fallen away from its ideals.[16] Its founder, Alfonso, was Edward III's cousin, and it is likely that Edward's ambassadors Henry, earl of Derby, and William de Montague, earl of Salisbury, who went to Castile in 1343 and assisted Alfonso in the siege of Arab-held Algeciras, reported to Edward on the Order of the Band just before Edward decided to refound the Round Table—an idea that probably evolved into the Order of the Garter.[17] Derby has been suggested as a possible patron of the *Gawain*-poet.[18] If this reconstruction of the origins of the Order of the Garter is correct, the Order's origin itself is imbricated with the politics of fighting against Muslim others. These politics would transfer as well to a Garter poem written close to the period of the Order's founding.

However, *Sir Gawain and the Green Knight* need not be so linked to the Order's founding to be associated with crusade against Islam. Attempts to pin down a date more precise than the second half of the fourteenth century remain speculative. While it is an intriguing historicization of *Sir Gawain and the Green Knight*, the connection Ingledew makes between the poem's composition and Edward's sex scandal requires a series of substitutions and even reversals (Gawain is substituted for Arthur so that Gawain can represent Edward, while the Lady's seduction of Gawain is substituted for Edward's rape of the Countess) that tend to detract from the historical parallels Ingledew tries to find. Ingledew himself concedes that the poem could well have been written later, and that other sex scandals may have prompted its "thematization of chastity," including Edward's later affair with Alice Perrers in the 1360s, Edward's son John of Gaunt's sexual promiscuity, or even the immorality of the Ricardian court.[19] Since most critics consider the poem to be late Ricardian, we will propose possible political scenarios in that

---

[16] D'Arcy J. D. Boulton, *The Knights of the Crown: The Monarchical Orders of Knighthood in Later Medieval Europe, 1325–1520* (Woodbridge: Boydell; New York: St. Martin's Press, 1987), 52–53.

[17] Boulton, *Knights of the Crown*, 109; Collins, *Order of the Garter*, 8.

[18] Cooke and Boulton, "Poem for Henry of Grosmont?"

[19] Ingledew, *"Sir Gawain and the Green Knight,"* 94.

period; however, since English engagement with the Mediterranean and Islamic world was long-standing, an earlier date would change some specifics but not our overall argument.

It is the Order of the Garter's primary patron saint, George, that provides the connection to al-Khidr and the Green Knight.[20] Venerated not only throughout Latin Christendom but also in Orthodox Christian and Islamic lands, Saint George cannot be read as wholly English. In the fourteenth century, his adoption as patron saint of England was still fairly new—it was not until 1416 that Archbishop Chichele officially made Saint George's Day a high feast day to recognize him as patron saint of England and not just of the king and his knights.[21] The elevation of Saint George was also part of a complex negotiation of England's (and Christendom's) relations to the east, since his origin was in the Levant, in Cappadocia, while the earliest accounts of him were in Greek, Coptic, and Syriac.[22] He was known in England in Anglo-Saxon times, but it was the crusades that popularized his cult; several chronicles give stories of George's miraculous aid at Antioch and Jerusalem, and by the Third Crusade George had become the patron of English Crusaders.[23] Edward I made extensive use of Saint George in heraldry and pageantry in Britain, helping to make George a patron of the English beyond the

[20] While George was the primary patron of the Order of the Garter, Mary and Edward the Confessor were also patron saints. Gawain's devotion to Mary reinforces the poem's connection to the Garter.

[21] Jonathan Bengtson, "Saint George and the Formation of English Nationalism," *JMEMSt* 27.2 (1997): 317–40 (326).

[22] For Saint George as a contested mediator between East and West during the Renaissance, see Jerry Brotton, "St. George Between East and West," in *Re-Orienting the Renaissance: Cultural Exchanges with the East*, ed. Gerald MacLean (New York: Palgrave, 2005), 50–65. For the history of George, see Ernest A. Wallis Budge, ed. and trans., *The Martyrdom and Miracles of Saint George of Cappadocia: The Coptic Texts* (London: D. Nutt, 1888); and *St. George of Lydda, The Patron Saint of England: A Study of the Cultus of St. George in Ethiopia* (London: Luzac, 1930); John E. Matzke, "Contributions to the History of the Legend of Saint George, with Special Reference to the Sources of the French, German, and Anglo-Saxon Metrical Versions," Part 1 in *PMLA* 17.4 (1902): 464–535, and Part 2 in *PMLA* 18.1 (1903): 99–171; and "The Legend of Saint George: Its Development into a Roman d'Aventure," *PMLA* 19.3 (1904): 449–78.

[23] Maurice Keen, *Chivalry* (New Haven: Yale University Press, 1984), 47; Matzke, "Contributions to the History of the Legend of Saint George," Part II, 150–56. For discussion of how George became England's patron saint, see Samantha Riches, *St George: Hero, Martyr, and Myth* (Stroud: Sutton, 2000), 101–39; David Scott Fox, *Saint George: The Saint with Three Faces* (Shooter's Lodge, Berks.: Kensal Press, 1983), 59–96; Cornelia Steketee Hulst, *St. George of Cappadocia in Legend and History* (London: David Nutt, 1909), 40–58, 71–83; and Bengtson, "Saint George and the Formation of English Nationalism."

crusading context. The decision of his grandson Edward III, however, to give Saint George preeminence over native saints as patron of the Garter, including the royal Saint Edward the Confessor, lent a crusading glamour to the new society. Edward III was not alone, however, in turning to George for a patron of knighthood: the Hungarians had already founded a knightly order of Saint George, and early plans for the French Order of the Star had saints George and Mary as patrons (Mary was a secondary patron of the Garter).[24]

Saint George was, then, always more than English. To understand *Sir Gawain and the Green* Knight as a possible Garter poem, we need to recapture the medieval sense of George as being not quite English but rather a knight of crusade and foreign encounter.

This is especially true given that Saint George transcended Christianity. Muslim and Christian scholars considered Saint George and al-Khidr to be versions of each other. In medieval Anatolia, shrines dedicated to Saint George, to Saint Theodore, and to Elijah were slowly converted into Islamic shrines to al-Khidr after the Byzantine defeat at the hands of the Seljuk Turks at the Battle of Manzikert in 1071. In that process of conversion these shrines became shared sacred spaces and, between the mid-thirteenth and early fifteenth centuries, al-Khidr became identified with the Christian saint and the Old Testament prophet.[25] In Turkey, al-Khidr's feast day is April 23, celebrated in Western Europe as Saint George's day.[26] That al-Khidr was linked to these Christian figures was known in the Middle Ages. In the late fourteenth century, the Byzantine Emperor Cantacuzenus wrote that Saint George was honored among the Muslims as "Χετηρ ήλιάς" [Khidr-Elias], and George of Hungary tells of "Chidrelles" in the early fifteenth century.[27] Haghia Sophia had its own "sweating column" associated with al-Khidr.[28] Since

[24] Boulton, *Knights of the Crown*, 174–77.

[25] Ethel Sara Wolper, "Khidr, Elwan Celebi, and the Conversion of Sacred Sanctuaries in Anatolia," *The Muslim World* 90.3/4 (2000): 309–22; Elizabeth Key Fowden, "Sharing Holy Places," *Common Knowledge* 8.1 (2002): 124–46; and Frederick [and Margaret] Hasluck, *Christianity and Islam Under the Sultans*, 2 vols. (New York: Octagon Books, 1932), 1:326–27, 320–36.

[26] Hasluck, *Christianity and Islam*, 1:320; Patrick Franke, *Begegnung mit Khidr: Quellenstudien zum Imaginären im traditionellen Islam* (Beirut: Orient-Institut der DMG; Stuttgart: Franz Steiner Verlag, 2000), 85.

[27] See Hasluck, *Christianity and Islam*, 1:322; Franke, *Begegnung mit Khidr*, 3, 159; Carl Göllner, ed., *Chronica und Beschreibung der Türckey mit eyner Vorrhed D. Martini Lutheri* (Cologne: Böhlau Verlag, 1983), 57.

[28] Hasluck, *Christianity and Islam*, 1:10–11; Franke, *Begegnung mit Khidr*, 266–69.

Constantinople was a major stop on the pilgrimage to Jerusalem and lay on the Arm of Saint George, as the Hellespont was called, it is not hard to imagine curious English pilgrims bringing stories of George known in Constantinople back to England. Something similar certainly happened in 1555, when the ambassador Ghiselin de Busbecq in Anatolia heard stories of al-Khidr, whom he and his Muslim hosts readily identified as Saint George.[29] Al-Khidr was also popular in Spain, offering a nearer location where English travelers might hear accounts of him.

An immortal, being the only man to have drunk the water of life (which in some versions of the story turns him green), al-Khidr predates Islam, going back as far, perhaps, as Sumeria.[30] Islam adopted him as a friend of God, and he became the guide for Alexander the Great in the eastern (Islamic) Alexander romances. In the Qu'ranic commentaries, he is linked to the unnamed figure in Sura 18 of the Qu'ran, to whom God sends Moses for instruction. Although Moses promises not to question al-Khidr but to learn humbly, he fails to keep his word when in a series of adventures al-Khidr acts inexplicably; in each case, unbeknown to Moses, al-Khidr has a benevolent reason. For instance, after they cross the sea with poor fishermen, al-Khidr destroys their boat: as al-Khidr later explains, a king was going to commandeer the fishermen's boat to invade the country. Moses' rational horror at al-Khidr's actions in each case is shown to be misplaced, and al-Khidr thus demonstrates that God's benevolence exceeds human reason. After his appearance in the Qu'ran, stories of encounters with al-Khidr spread. He appears in the *Arabian Nights*, stories that probably circulated widely in oral form, and may have been sources for Chaucer.[31] As the stories spread, some fea-

[29] Interestingly, Busbecq did not recognize al-Khidr's association with Elijah (Elias) even though he heard the form Chedreles (Khidr-Elias); he declines the name as Chederle, Chederlis, Chederlem. Saint George, not Elijah, is thus the primary point of contact between the eastern and western traditions, and it is images of George that draw Muslims to "Greek" temples to venerate al-Khidr. See Busbecq, *Aug. Gislenii Besbequii quae extant omina; quibus accessit epitome de Moribus Turcarum* (London: R. Danielis, 1660), 52–54.

[30] The ninth-century historian al-Tabari surveys the Islamic al-Khidr tradition in *The History of al-Tabari*, trans. William Brinner, 40 vols. (Albany: State University of New York Press, 1991), 3:1–18. For modern studies, see Franke, *Begegnung mit Khidr*; Hasluck, *Christianity and Islam*, 1:319–336; Israel Friedländer, *Die Chadhirlegende und der Alexanderroman; eine sagengeschichtliche und literhistorische Untersuchung* (Leipzig: B. G. Teubner, 1913); and Irfan Omar, "Khidr in the Islamic Tradition," *The Muslim World* 83.3–4 (1993): 279–294.

[31] Metlitzki, *Matter of Araby*, 159; see the headnote to *The Squire's Tale* in *The Riverside Chaucer*, 890.

tures became common: he is able to disguise himself (despite his name, he frequently does not appear as green), and he is a patron of travelers, attributes that fit the middle sections of *Sir Gawain and the Green Knight*. An inscrutable figure of wisdom, he teaches people to see God's meaning in seemingly cruel or random events; he appears suddenly and vanishes to who-knows-where, much as the Green Knight is last seen going "Whiderwarde-soeuer he wolde" (2478).[32]

Given his widespread popularity, it is unsurprising to find traces of al-Khidr and of Islamic legends of Saint George in Christian medieval literature. The *Gesta Romanorum*, a collection of stories in Latin compiled at the end of the thirteenth or the beginning of the fourteenth century, includes a version of the story about al-Khidr and Moses from the Qu'ran, though the characters are Christianized into an angel and a hermit.[33] By 1498, William Caxton, although not mentioning al-Khidr, felt it necessary to expand the description of Saint George when he published his translation of Jacobus de Voragine's *Golden Legend*: probably drawing on an earlier fifteenth-century manuscript of the *Gilte Legende*, he adds details about Saint George's tomb as a place where Saracens go to be cured of madness, before noting George's status as protector of England and patron of the Order of the Garter.[34] Thus, for Caxton, George was a saint owing associations both to the East and the West, performing miracles for Christians and Muslims. The Islamic version of Saint George had fully entered Western European consciousness by the late seventeenth century at the latest when Barthélemy d'Herbelot compiled his massive *Bibliothèque Orientale* with entries on George, al-Khidr, and Elias or Elijah, noting the conflation of these three figures in the Islamic tradition.[35] Thus, in his familiar guise of

---

[32] These traits are described in Hasluck, *Christianity and Islam*, 1:320, and Franke, *Begegnung mit Khidr*, 23–35. All quotations of *Sir Gawain and the Green Knight* are from Andrew and Waldron, eds., *Poems of the Pearl Manuscript* (Exeter: University of Exeter Press, 1996), and cited parenthetically by line numbers.

[33] Tale LXXX, "Of the Cunning of the Devil, and of the Secret Judgments of God," in *Gesta Romanorum*, trans. Charles Swan (London: George Routledge & Sons, 1905), 194–96.

[34] Manfred Gorläch, *"The South English Legendary," "Gilte Legende," and "Golden Legend"* (Braunschweig: Technische Universität Carolo-Wilhelmina zu Braunschweig Institut für Anglistik und Amerikanistik, 1972), 92–93; *Legenda Aurea* (London: William Caxton, 1483), STC (2nd ed.) 24873, leaves clvii–clix.

[35] D'Herbelot's entry on George reads: "George & en particulier saint-George, Martyr, fort connu dans l'Orient & même par les Mahometans, qui le mettent au nombre des Prophetes & le confondent avec Elie; car ils lui donnent le nom ou surnom de Khedherles & de Khizir Elia, qui est celuy du Prophete Elie." *Bibliothèque Orientale, ou*

militant saint and patron saint of the crusaders, Saint George mediated a military form of East-West contact, while his assimilation into the tradition of al-Khidr involved him in a far more complex set of negotiations between Islamic and western Christian identities.

Saint George's appropriation by Islam might lead the *Gawain*-poet, mindful of the Garter, to the enigmatic figure of al-Khidr. He might explain the Green Knight's greenness, which has not been definitively derived from the British or Celtic traditions. The mature, civilized Bertilak does not make a fully convincing woodwose or wild green man, even if elements of his description may be drawn from them.[36] Woodwoses tend to be young, they do not have their own courts, and when Gawain meets woodwoses on his journey (721), there is no evident connection to the Green Knight.[37] Nicolas Jacobs concludes that while the beheading game most probably comes from the Celtic tradition, the greenness "is a secondary development in the English poem and designed to make a particular thematic point unconnected with any of the [French or Irish] analogues."[38] Al-Khidr—green, immortal, teacher of divine grace through actions that initially seem hostile, master of disguise, unexpected host in the wilderness, and representative of countries ancient and sophisticated in comparison to the relatively young England— seems a better fit than green men. It is thus possible that the Green Knight combines a Celtic tradition with Islamicized legends of Saint George.

Fourteenth-century English interest in Saint George was growing rapidly. After George became patron of the Garter, "England was caught up in a kind of George-mania," in Jonathan Bengtson's words.[39] It is possible that this is when Saint George became a fixture in Christmas mummers' plays, in which a character is often killed and brought back to life, which have been discussed in connection with *Sir Gawain*

Dictionnaire Universel Contenant Tout ce qui fait connoître les Peuples de l'Orient (J. Neaulme and N. van Daalen, 1777–79), vol. 2 (1782): 109, sig. O3.

[36] Derek Brewer, "The Colour Green," in *Companion to the Gawain-Poet*, ed. Brewer and Gibson, 181–89; in the same volume, see Helen Cooper, "The Supernatural," 286–87; Susan Crane, *The Performance of Self: Ritual, Clothing, and Identity During the Hundred Years War* (Philadelphia: University of Pennsylvania Press, 2002), 167–68. For a counterview, see Piotr Sadowski, "The Greenness of the Green Knight: A Study in Medieval Colour Symbolism," *Ethnologia Polona* 15–16 (1991): 61–79.

[37] See Lasater, *Spain to England*, 185–86.

[38] Nicolas Jacobs, "*Fled Bricrenn* and *Sir Gawain and the Green Knight*," in *"Fled Bricrenn": Reassessments*, ed. Pádraig Ó Riain (London: Irish Texts Society, 2000), 43.

[39] Bengtson, "Saint George and the Formation of English Nationalism," 328.

and the Green Knight.[40] In a climate of "George-mania," Englishmen seeking stories of Saint George would likely also discover stories of al-Khidr, green, wise, and inscrutable. They would also find stories of Saint George's severed head, which Richard II sought as a relic. The head was in Livadia in central Greece, which was controlled by the Catalan Grand Company, a group of Aragonese and Catalan mercenaries who had come to Asia Minor to fight the Turks.[41] In 1393, it was reported that the alleged owner of the head was interested in selling it to Richard II. This came to nothing, and ultimately the head passed into the possession of the Venetians. (The Order of the Garter finally acquired a relic of Saint George when Emperor Sigismund donated his heart to the English in 1416).[42] Looking for relics of George in the Levant and the Iberian Peninsula would have meant English and European contact with eastern traditions of Saint George, both Orthodox and Islamic, and with them stories of al-Khidr. While *Sir Gawain and the Green Knight* is much more than a topical poem, it may have coalesced in an environment where tales of Saint George's head, the Order of the Garter, and al-Khidr, Saint George's green avatar, were all circulating. Nonetheless, the appearance of al-Khidr in a western English poem is not simply the product of one-time circumstance but is part of the negotiation of important, long-term relationships between England and the older, eastern Mediterranean powers.

The Geography of *Sir Gawain and the Green Knight*

If *Sir Gawain and the Green Knight*'s original courtly audience recognized the Green Knight as al-Khidr, then the geographic engagements of the poem shift. Medievalists approaching *Sir Gawain and the Green Knight* from postcolonial perspectives have so far focused on internal colonization, particularly relations between England and Wales. While this has been a productive and illuminating approach, there is also a need to put

---

[40] E. K. Chambers suggests a link between the Green Knight and sword dances, rather than the closely related mummers' plays (*The Medieval English Stage* [Mineola, N.Y.: Dover, 1996], 186 n. 1, 211–27). Sir James Frazier, of course, analyzes the "Green George" as a vegetation spirit, providing, perhaps, a vague mythological link to the Green Knight (*The New Golden Bough*, ed. Theodor Gaster [Garden City, N.Y.: Anchor Books, 1961], 47).

[41] Details of the competition for Saint George's head comes from Kenneth Setton, "Saint George's Head," *Speculum* 48.1 (1973): 1–12.

[42] Collins, *Order of the Garter*, 224–25.

the poem in an international context, one in which England is not a self-evident center of culture. *Sir Gawain and the Green Knight* opens with the fall of Troy, not only a temporal disjunction from the rest of the poem but one that hints at an eastern perspective:

> Siþen þe sege and þe assaut watz sesed at Troye,
> . . .
> Hit watz Ennias þe athel and his highe kynde,
> Þat siþen depreced prouinces, and patrounes bicome
> Welneȝe of al þe wele in þe west iles.
>
> (1, 5–7)

The "west iles" founded by Aeneas and his descendants include not just Britain but also Rome, Tuscany, and Lombardy, western not from the perspective of England but of the Near East.

Medieval England imagined itself not as the center of the world but on the edge of it. Medieval maps of the world centered on Jerusalem or Rome, with England on the margins, as Kathy Lavezzo notes: "We can cite literary examples of this trend as well, from the time of Bede, who describes Britain as 'an island sundered so far from the rest of mankind' in his *Ecclesiastical History of the English People* (721), to the time of the Gawain-poet, who locates Britain 'fer ouer þe French flod' in *Sir Gawain and the Green Knight* (ca. 1375–1400). The English were not simply self-conscious of their marginality in the Middle Ages; English writers and cartographers actively participated in the construction of England as a global borderland."[43] When the Green Knight asks scornfully, "What, is þis Arþures house . . . / Þat al þe rous rennes of þurȝ ryalmes so mony?" (309–10), it may not be a matter of a metropolitan fame reaching the hinterlands, but of a distant kingdom's fame reaching more central realms. If the Green Knight's depiction owes something to the multivalent Saint George/al-Khidr, with his roots nearer the center of the medieval map, his curiosity in testing Arthur's court seems less presumptuous, and his violation of the court's protocols may have less to do with wildness than with arrogant cultural superiority.

That the poem opens with Arthur's British court, at the end of a sequence that rehearses the establishment of various successor kingdoms of Troy, suggests the climax of a western *translatio imperii*. On the other

---

[43] Kathy Lavezzo, *Angels at the Edge of the World: Geography, Literature, and English Community, 1000–1534* (Ithaca: Cornell University Press, 2006), 7.

hand, its placement at the end of successive displacements also suggests its youthfulness and untested mettle, as the Green Knight's dismissive characterization of Arthur and his court indicates, especially when compared to more ancient civilizations in the East. As Iain Higgins has shown, the East—the location of Eden, Jerusalem, Troy, and Rome— was seen as the place of origin in medieval culture: "The East as it was known to Latin Christendom between the twelfth and the fifteenth centuries . . . was the fertile ground of an imagined community's noblest hopes, wildest dreams, and worst fears—at once the distant source of its chivalry, learning, and historical covenant with God, the outlandish source of its most sacred, coveted and finally unattainable sites, and the slowly expanding theater of its most reverent, bewildered, disgraceful and disturbing encounters with Otherness."[44] Arthurian literature was one way of mediating between native British pride and the awareness of eastern origins.

Sylvia Federico argues: "Sometimes Arthurianism is viewed as a native tradition, one that supports the notion of a home-grown British hero, whereas Trojanness, by contrast, takes on the flavor of the foreign, exotic, decadent Other. But just as easily, Arthurianism may be glossed as a bit rough—uncivilized and "out-there"—compared to the fashionableness and sophistication of Troy and its European offspring."[45] In any case, Arthur's court is one of many, compared both to rival continental European courts as well as to all these courts' ultimate origins in the East.[46] The result, as Kathy Lavezzo suggests, is that "isolated England requires the validating desire of authorities hailing from world capitals. England cannot authorize itself . . . but requires the legitimizing approval of the center."[47] In some works, legitimacy comes from Rome— either imperial desire for English conquest or papal desire for English conversion—or from further east, with the Trojans or Joseph of Arimathea. In medieval romance, often it is Constantinople, the second Rome. As Geraldine Heng argues, Constantinople is the "magical location that precedes, and haunts, medieval Europe, and Europe's capacity to envi-

[44] Iain MacLeod Higgins, *Writing East: The "Travels" of Sir John Mandeville* (Philadelphia: University of Pennsylvania Press, 1997), 5.

[45] Sylvia Federico, *New Troy: Fantasies of Empire in the Late Middle Ages* (Minneapolis: University of Minnesota Press, 2003), 58–59.

[46] Ibid., xii; cf. Thorlac Turville-Petre, "The Brutus Prologue to *Sir Gawain and the Green Knight*," in *Imagining a Medieval English Nation*, ed. Kathy Lavezzo (Minneapolis: University of Minnesota Press, 2004), 345.

[47] Lavezzo, *Angels at the Edge of the World*, 87.

sion aureal places, majestic grandeur, and a puissant past under threat"
and thus functions "as a point of orientation," serving, for instance, as
the model for Arthur's Caerleon (later Camelot) in Geoffrey of Monmouth's *History*.[48] Reading *Sir Gawain and the Green Knight* with the
possibility of Islamic borrowing in mind allows us to see how the poem
dramatizes Britain's relation to the larger world, especially the old and
great Mediterranean civilizations.

While the poem's opening harks back to the mythic origins of Arthur
and the British, it also has contemporary geopolitical resonances. If *Sir
Gawain and the Green Knight* is in some ways looking east at the Byzantine Empire, as Heng's argument for Constantinople's centrality in
medieval romance might suggest, it was looking at a Byzantine Empire
whose territory was steadily encroached upon by the Ottomans. Constantinople was besieged long before its fall in 1453, with the Seljuk
Turks' victory at the Battle of Manzikert in 1071 being the signal event
that started the decline of the Byzantine Empire. Indeed, the victory
of Timur the Lame over the Ottoman Sultan Bayezid in 1402, which
temporarily halted the Ottoman advance, was welcomed by Europeans
who saw the Mongols as God's scourge on the Turks. In the fourteenth
century, ancient Troy was located in lands that were in the hands of the
Ottomans. Some European authors and artists trying to discover the
origins of these Central Asian peoples associated the Turks with Trojans
both geographically and historically. In the seventh century, Pseudo-
Jerome traced Turks back to a Trojan named Torquatus.[49] The association between Turk and Trojan, though contested in historical writing,
nonetheless became strong enough that from the late fourteenth century

---

[48] Geraldine Heng, *Empire of Magic: Medieval Romance and the Politics of Cultural Fantasy* (New York: Columbia University Press, 2003), 9.

[49] James Harper, "Turks as Trojans; Trojans as Turks," in *Postcolonial Approaches to the
European Middle Ages*, ed. Ananya Jahanara Kabir and Deanne Williams (Cambridge:
Cambridge University Press, 2005), 151–79. Other scholars also note the medieval idea
of Trojan origins of the Turks: A. Eckhardt, "La Légende de l'origine troyenne des
Turcs," *Körösi Csoma Archivum* 2 (1926–32): 422–33; T. Spencer, "Turks and Trojans in
the Renaissance," *MLR* 47 (1952): 330–33; S. Runciman, "Teucri and Turci," in *Medieval and Middle Eastern Studies in Honor of Aziz Suryal Atiya*, ed. S. A. Hanna (Leiden:
E. J. Brill, 1972), 344–48. For a contrary opinion, see Margaret Meserve, *Empires of
Islam in Renaissance Historical Thought* (Cambridge, Mass.: Harvard University Press,
2008), 26–64: Meserve argues that in the Renaissance the idea was not as widespread
as believed and largely confined to poetic texts, while in the Middle Ages the idea was
contested and had lost its credibility by the start of the fifteenth century in serious
historical writing. *Sir Gawain and the Green Knight* is not of course historical writing but
a narrative poem.

into the fifteenth, artists depicted Trojans dressed as Turks. In one early example, an illustrated manuscript from Castile dated 1350, the Trojans are given *morisco* costumes (we shall have more to say about possible connections between *Sir Gawain and the Green Knight* and Castile).[50] Indeed, the Trojan connection was invoked in a spurious letter to the pope purportedly from a Muslim ruler, "Sultan Morbisanus," calling for him to call off the crusade because they are both descended from Trojans; revived many times over a century, the earliest version is dated 1345 and addressed to Pope Clement VI (r. 1342–1352), who in 1344 was directing a crusade against Smyrna, capital of the Turkish emirate of Aydin.[51] While this letter is part of an antipapal agenda, the invocation of the Trojan Turks suggests a capacity to consider Muslim foes within a classical framework that links Europeans with Turks. Even if ultimately meant to satirize the pope by claiming his kinship with Muslim foes, the spurious letter presents a different view of Turkish or Muslim enemies, perhaps making possible a double perspective of them as both foreign and kin. Since a number of sources and analogues of *Sir Gawain and the Green Knight* have a black or Turkish challenger, this mix of foreignness and kinship might have suggested to the *Gawain*-poet the intriguing possibilities of delicate allusions to George's Islamic avatar.

While the beginning of *Sir Gawain and the Green Knight* places Arthur's court in a large, globalized expanse of place and time, quickly reviewing the cycles of history, the Green Knight's arrival makes these concerns more specific. When the Green Knight arrives to test the "surquydrye" (311) of the young court, his role as a mature man in contrast to the "berdlez chylder" (280) of the court could be read as a test of the young British civilization in front of the challenging eyes of the older Mediterranean civilizations, a personalizing of the narrative of historical transition of Trojan honor from East to West. His flamboyant entrance is wild, but it may be the wildness of arrogant cultural superiority, not primitiveness. It is suggestive of Farīd ad-Dīn 'Attār's story of al-Khidr, who humbles human pride by reminding kings of the cyclic nature of history. In the guise of a camel driver, al-Khidr comes to the court of

[50] Harper, "Turks as Trojans," 157–58.

[51] MS Florence, Biblioteca Medicea-Laurenziana, Ashburnham 1182, fols. 51v–53r, letter from "Morbosiano" to Clement VI; a version printed in *Prose antiche di Dante, Petrarcha, Boccaccio et di molti altri nobili et virtuosi ingegni*, ed. A. F. Doni (Florence, 1547), 15–16 (Meserve, *Empires of Islam*, 36, 272 n. 61; part of a later version is also quoted on 35–36).

Ibrāhīm Adham, shocking the servants into speechlessness. He calls the palace an inn, prompting the king's indignant demand for an explanation. When al-Khidr asks about previous owners of the palace, Ibrāhīm recites his lineage, but al-Khidr, unimpressed, repeats that the palace is an inn because it is simply a place where men stay briefly as they come and go out of this life.[52] In *Sir Gawain and the Green Knight,* the Green Knight's refusal to respect the court, the knights' stunned silence, and the introduction's emphasis on the quick cycles of previous reigns in British history all resemble this story, although Arthur (perhaps initially more perceptive than Ibrāhīm) identifies himself as "Þe hede of þis ostel" (253).

Geraldine Heng suggests that through romance Europeans understood the sometimes horrifying experiences of the crusades, and managed instances of their own barbarity in contrast to Islamic civility, by repressing fractures of Christian savagery into such *unheimlich* figures as giants.[53] Through a crisis of alienation, the Christian European self was represented as a monstrous giant—to the Byzantines and to the Arabs, the Latins seemed an impressive size, and moreover, the cannibalism associated with giants recalls a dearth that led to Christians eating the dead in the First Crusade. While Heng does not treat *Sir Gawain and the Green Knight,* it is no surprise that the Green Knight himself seems "Half-etayn" (140) and, like other giants of medieval romance, both strange and familiar.[54] However, the poet quickly abandons the idea that he is a giant and instead marks the signs of his civility, especially his fine clothing. The fact that the Green Knight is civilized and comes in peace means that he is not simply a figure of crusade but of social

---

[52] Farīd al-Dīn 'Attār, *The "Ilāhī-nāma" or Book of God of Farīd al-Dīn 'Attār,* trans. John Andrew Boyle (Manchester: Manchester University Press, 1976), 235–36. 'Attār also includes a brief story of Saint George (Jirjīs) and a story of al-Khidr in which the old sage Khālū confronts a young man who believes himself pure with the crushing awareness of sin; al-Khidr reproves the sage with the suggestive metaphor "do not smite him with that deadly blade" (272). 'Attār was popular in the Muslim east, and although no direct chain of transmission has been established, there has long been speculation about his influence in Middle English verse. Walter Skeat cites his work as providing an analogue of *The Pardoner's Tale,* and perhaps his best-known work, *Manteq at-Tair {The Conference of Birds}* is close to *The Parlement of Foules.* See Skeat, *The Complete Works of Geoffrey Chaucer,* 2nd ed., 7 vols. (Oxford: Clarendon Press, 1900), 3:444; and Afkham Darbandi and Dick Davis's introduction to *The Conference of Birds,* ed. and trans. Darbandi and Davis (New York: Penguin, 1984), 20–21.

[53] Heng, *Empire of Magic,* 21–35.

[54] See also Jeffrey Jerome Cohen, *Of Giants: Sex, Monsters, and the Middle Ages* (Minneapolis: University of Minnesota Press, 1999); Metlitzki, *Matter of Araby,* 192–97.

engagement with the East, just as Saint George as reflected in the Green Knight is not just a crusader but a point of contact between Muslim and Christian legends. These complex religious undertones underlie the poem's narrative arc, in which war is deflected into a game of trading. The Green Knight comes to a court that actively desires him as an outsider, as an embodiment of an "auenturus þyng, an vncouþe tale / Of sum mayn meruayle" (93–94) against which the court can define itself. The paradoxical position of an outsider with a place reserved at court leads to the uncertainty of whether the Green Knight is friend or foe, whether the contest is game or combat. The same tension is implicit in a court that on the one hand measures its wealth by eastern goods— "tars tapites" (77), Gawain's "dublet of a dere tars" (571), and his pentangle, which is a sign of Solomon (625)—but on the other hand represents in its chivalry a militant Christianity that saw crusading as the greatest calling for a knight. Arthur's urge for crusade is plain: he continues to offer battle even after the Green Knight declares that he comes in peace (275–78).

If the Green Knight's intrusion into Arthur's court and the violence of the beheading game shadow the heady fear and exhilaration of crusade, Sir Gawain's stay in Bertilak's court represents the temptations of more peaceful coexistence. This suggests that it may be worth revisiting one of the central questions raised by the poem, how best to read the relation between the two courts, Arthur's and Bertilak's. The regionality of the poem has been read through a postcolonial lens in a number of valuable recent studies analyzing Sir Gawain's travel in the west by the borders of Wales either as an exploration of colonial border hybridization or as a way of addressing the tension between regional lords and the royal court. Critics assume Hautdesert is the provincial court, arising out of the *Gawain*-poet's Cheshire milieu. Within this analytic, Hautdesert is read as a court in the borderlands, on the Welsh fringes, a satellite to the central court. In turn, Camelot as center functions as the arbiter of national or protonational values that are challenged by those of the margins. In her analysis of alliterative revivals, Christine Chism depicts the Green Knight as "provincial outsider to Arthur's court" and argues that the poem plays out a conflict "between a royal court becoming increasingly alienated from traditional seigneurial modes of chivalry and a conservative and insecure provincial gentry, whose status, livelihoods, and careers were increasingly coming to depend on careers at the royal court."[55] This sort of reading has been particularly compelling for recent work applying postcolonial theory to medieval works. Patricia Ingham's *Sovereign Fantasies* reads medieval Arthurian romances as accounts of how "medieval community is imagined not through homogeneous stories of a singular 'people,' but through narratives of sovereignty as a negotiation of differences, of ethnicity, region, language, class, and gender."[56] In her reading of *Sir Gawain and the Green Knight*, Ingham locates Bertilak's court in Wales with the Green Knight as the "exotic other" to Arthur's "centralized" Camelot, whose "opulence . . . links explicitly to the colonizing impulse of European desires."[57]

However, the insular context is not the only context. If we see the Green Knight as drawing on Saint George/al-Khidr, a number of postcolonial dynamics are altered or reversed. While England's relations with Wales were indeed colonial, colonial language simply cannot describe relations with the powerful Islamic east. Instead of the straightforward greed of future colonizers, British desire for eastern goods is the more troubled one of a culturally backward society for the products of richer and more powerful lands. In a genuinely global context, Arthur's court is not the self-evident cultural center and might in fact be inferior; hence the Green Knight's challenge becomes far more pressing. Rather than the self-satisfied gesture of colonizers, the court's adoption of the green girdle is an acknowledgment of weakness in the face of sophisticated foreign courts. Rather than a securely superior Arthur, the poem insists on the Green Knight/Bertilak's greater civility and refinement. The Green Knight's rich clothing, lovingly detailed by the poet, rivals the opulence of Arthur's court, while Bertilak's castle, although located in "countrayez straunge" (713), is as modern as any, and described as "A castel þe comlokest þat euer knyȝt aȝte" (767). Indeed, the superiority (and maturity) of the Green Knight/Bertilak allows the testing of Arthur's youthful court. The evidence of Bertilak's sophistication fits an alternative international reading where Arthur's court, ambitious but

[55] Christine Chism, *Alliterative Revivals* (Philadelphia: University of Pennsylvania Press, 2002), 66.

[56] Patricia Clare Ingham, *Sovereign Fantasies: Arthurian Romance and the Making of Britain* (Philadelphia: University of Pennsylvania Press, 2001), 9. See also Helen Young, "'Bi contray caryez this knyght': Journeys of Colonisation in *Sir Gawain and the Green Knight*," *Philament*, 2003 (http://www.arts.usyd.edu.au/publications/philament); and Rhonda Knight, "All Dressed Up with Someplace to Go: Regional Identity in *Sir Gawain and the Green Knight*," *SAC* 25 (2003): 259–84.

[57] Ingham, *Sovereign Fantasies*, 124, 127–28.

young, is considered in relation to the eastern Mediterranean with its richer, older Islamic culture.

The identification of Bertilak with Wales comes from just one stanza in Fitt II with Welsh place-names. While the geography of the journey Gawain takes may be inspired by northern marshes, the space itself is marked by foreignness more than anything else. The Welsh stanza is the middle of three stanzas describing Gawain's arduous journey. Malcolm Andrew and Ronald Waldron point out that the "beginning and the end . . . are clouded in a romantic vagueness,"[58] a vagueness that contrasts sharply with the geographical precision of the Welsh stanza. Ingham asserts that Gawain traces a "journey westward,"[59] but while Gawain does enter Wales from Logres, the later sequence of place-names indicates that Gawain is on an eastward path back out of Wales: "Alle þe iles of Anglesay on lyft half he [Gawain] haldez / And farez ouer þe fordez by þe forlondez; / Ouer at þe Holy Hede, til he hade eft bonk / In þe wyldrenesse of Wyrale" (698–701). Andrew and Waldron offer this note: "Gawain's journey takes him to Caernarvon and eastwards along the north coast of Wales. A fourteenth-century map in the Bodleian Library shows the usual route as passing through Bangor, Conway, Abergele, Rhuddlan, and Flint."[60] Wherever the Green Knight or his Chapel may be, it is not in Wales. In the next stanza, Gawain has passed beyond the named landmarks into "contrayez straunge" (713). There is no compelling reason to insist that the "contrayez straunge" are on the main island of Britain: there are evidently water-crossings, as Gawain is "fer floten fro his frendez" (714) and fights at each "warþe oþer water þer þe wyȝe passed" (715).[61] The poet seems no stranger to sea travel; in *Patience,* the speaker uses as a casual example his lord bidding him "Oþer to ryde oþer to renne to Rome" (52) and he takes for granted the unmentioned sea portion of the trip. Thus it is not necessary to restrict critical focus only to the Anglo-Welsh border, especially since

[58] Andrew and Waldron, eds. *Poems of the Pearl Manuscript,* 234 n. 698ff.

[59] Ingham, *Sovereign Fantasies,* 116.

[60] Andrew and Waldron, eds. *Poems of the Pearl Manuscript,* 234 n. 698ff. For the Gough map, they cite E. J. S. Parsons, *The Map of Great Britain Circa 1360, Known as The Gough Map: An Introduction to the Facsimile,* with "The Roads of the Gough Map" by Sir Frank Stenton (Oxford: Printed for the Bodleian Library and the Royal Geographical Society by the University Press, 1958).

[61] The *Middle English Dictionary* cites this line as an example of a more metaphorical use of the verb *fleten* (to float), as meaning "to move away from." Given the "water" and the "warþe" [shore] of the next line, the more literal meaning is to be preferred, even at the price of unsettling interpretive habit. See *MED* flēten, v.(1) 3.(a) (a).

there are reasons to read *Sir Gawain and the Green Knight* as a more cosmopolitan poem than it is usually assumed to be.

The Geographies of *Sir Gawain*'s Audiences

The argument for *Sir Gawain and the Green Knight*'s cosmopolitanism is bolstered by its geographical origins, for Cheshire men traveled widely domestically and internationally. The poem's international engagements would have resonated with upper-class English audiences, but generalizing beyond that is dangerous. Different regions and different nobles had differing relations to the larger world. The extent of the variation can be suggested by looking at three courts that have been suggested as venues for the *Gawain*-poet's activities: Richard II's, John of Gaunt's, and Sir John Stanley's.

Favoring Cheshiremen and speaking their dialect, Richard II turned in the 1390s to the Midlands and the newly created principality of Chester, making the region a cultural center (as well as a geographic center convenient to Wales and Ireland as well as England) from which to challenge London.[62] Patricia Ingham's and Christine Chism's arguments about *Sir Gawain and the Green Knight's* colonial subtext are most convincing in the context of Richard's dislocations of traditional structures of power, but Richard's recentering of England can alternatively be viewed from an international perspective. The king's court was not the magnificent center of the kingdom that it would grow to be under the Tudors, although Richard II attempted (largely successfully) to magnify the role of the king's court during his reign, with increasing formality of address, distinction of rank, and use of pageants, as part of a Europewide trend that may have started with the Islamic-Christian hybrid court of Frederick II of Sicily.[63] While royal courts may have served as regional centers, the borrowing of courtly customs back and forth shows that kings and courtiers were aware of themselves not as occupiers of the cultural center but as part of a web of royal courts competing for cultural primacy. The royal court may be seen as *primus inter pares* with strongly influential baronial courts that constituted rival cultural cen-

---

[62] John M. Bowers, *The Politics of "Pearl": Court Poetry in the Age of Richard II* (Cambridge: D. S. Brewer, 2001), 73–76; Nigel Saul, *Richard II* (New Haven: Yale University Press, 1997), 393–94; 444–45.

[63] Saul, *Richard II*, 328–47.

ters—and, as Richard moved away from London, the city itself would be another rival center.

Using provincial support, Richard fashioned an imperial monarchy, and in doing so he sought election to the Holy Roman Empire and flirted with the idea of a crusade. Michael Bennett argues: "His [Richard II's] kingship may have been peripatetic and regionally based in the 1390s, but it was universalist in ambition. Drawing inspiration from the 'matter of Britain', and from auspicious challenges and opportunities in Christendom, he was willing to be flattered into considering, if not into actively pursuing, a grand crusading vision," and furthermore, "In 1395 and 1396 the king became a focus for the ambitions and hopes of men who looked to peace and reconciliation of Christendom as a prelude to a counter-assault on the Turks and the ultimate recovery of the Holy Land."[64] Aziz Suryal Atiya has shown that crusading continued through the fourteenth century, with conflict with the Muslims exacerbated by the rise of the Ottomans; the English themselves joined forces with the French in 1396 for the key (failed) crusade of Nicopolis against the Turks.[65] Nicopolis was the culmination of a series of Europe-wide diplomatic endeavors in the later fourteenth century that had its impetus in the fall of Armenia in 1375. The last king of Armenia, Levon VI, was seeking help from England and France to mount a crusade to retake his country—the last part of the Levant to be in Christian hands—from the Muslims. As part of his efforts, he tried to broker peace between England and France, split over the papal schism. Richard II received Levon royally to his court at the end of 1385; the matter of Armenia became of some importance to the English, and allusions to Armenia were woven into the literature of the period, including Chaucer's.[66] Levon also had a strong supporter in Philippe de Mézières, adviser to Charles V and tutor to Charles VI, who started a chivalric order, the Order of the Passion, to heal the schism and to campaign for the recovery of the holy lands. Mézières had links to many European courts and his order

[64] Michael J. Bennett, "Richard II and the Wider Realm," in *Richard II: The Art of Kingship*, ed. Anthony Goodman and James Gillespie (Oxford: Clarendon Press, 1999), 204, 197.

[65] Aziz Suryal Atiya, *The Crusade in the Later Middle Ages*, 2nd ed. (New York: Kraus Reprint, 1938), 435–62; and *The Crusade of Nicopolis* (London: Methuen, 1934), 44–45.

[66] Carolyn P. Collette and Vincent J. DiMarco, "The Matter of Armenia in the Age of Chaucer," *SAC* 23 (2001): 317–58; Lee Patterson, "'The Living Witnesses of Our Redemption': Martyrdom and Imitation in Chaucer's *Prioress's Tale*," *JMEMSt* 31.3 (2001): 507–60 (540).

included Englishmen: the Despenser brothers, the earls of Huntingdon and Rutland, the dukes of York and Gloucester, John of Gaunt, and Chaucer's friend Lewis Clifford.[67] The famous Wilton Diptych, Maurice Keen argues, may be a crusading icon.[68] Richard and his court were very much aware of the Turkish threat. Richard was present at the October 1, 1397, reinterment of John Mowbray, killed by Turks outside Constantinople in 1368; sending an embassy to Constantinople in 1397, he received a letter in return from the Byzantine emperor, Manuel II, asking for help against the Turks, and though unable to comply, Richard promised troops the following year.[69] The crusading fever infected others in England as well. After relinquishing his claims to Castile, John of Gaunt became more sympathetic to peace with France and worked with Richard to effect peace in Christendom as a start toward crusading.[70]

Michael Bennett argues that Richard's "sense of providential mission was nourished by a tradition of prophecy which linked English history with its British and Arthurian past" and that his Irish expedition in 1394–95 in particular seems linked to the prophecy in Geoffrey of Monmouth's *Historia Regum Britannie* that the king who conquers Ireland will regain the Holy Land.[71] One prophetic text current in the 1390s, *The Verses of Gildas*, predicts for the king an astonishing career that culminates in a crusade against the Muslims: as Bennett describes it, "After the conquest of Ireland, the king would defeat the Scots and suppress revolt in Gascony. On his return to England, he would honour the lords who sought his grace but exile the malcontents. The king would conquer France, march through Spain and north Africa, subdue Egypt, and

---

[67] Collette and DiMarco, "Matter of Armenia," 348; see also Lynn Staley, *Languages of Power in the Age of Richard II* (University Park: Pennsylvania State University Press, 2005), 129–37. For Mézières's life and career, see Abdel Hamid Hamdy, "Philippe de Mézières and the New Order of the Passion," *Bulletin of the Faculty of Arts* (Alexandria University) 18 (1964): 45–54; A. H. Hamdy, ed., *La sustance de la chevalerie de la passion de Jhesu Crist, Bulletin of the Faculty of Arts* (Alexandria University) 18, pts. 1 and 2 (1963): 45–55, 1–104; N. Jorga, *Philippe de Mézières 1327–1405. La croisade au XIVe siècle* (Paris, 1890); G. W. Coopland, ed., *Philippe de Mézières: Le songe du vieil pelerin*, 2 vols. (Cambridge: Cambridge University Press, 1969); and Coopland, ed. and trans., *Philippe de Mézières: Letter to Richard II* (Liverpool: Liverpool University Press, 1975).

[68] M. Keen, "The Wilton Diptych: The Case for a Crusading Context," in *The Regal Image of Richard II and the Wilton Diptych*, ed. Dillian Gordon, Lisa Monnas, and Caroline Elam (London: Harvey Miller, 1997), 189–96.

[69] Michael Bennett, *Richard II and the Revolution of 1399* (Phoenix Mill: Sutton Publishing, 1999), 110, 124.

[70] Ibid., 35.

[71] Ibid., 73–74.

advance triumphantly on Babylon. After the recovery of the Holy Land, and after the pope had thrice offered to crown him, he would finally accept coronation as the emperor of the world."[72] This prophecy influenced the clerk who wrote a French letter-book in the late 1390s that included a letter dated October 13, 1395, from Richard to John of Gaunt asking about the state of Ireland. In further model letters, an exchange between John and his nephew includes news from the nephew about his father, John's brother, "who was 'in the parts of Babylon' with a very fine company. The army had torched the land around Alexandria and won a great victory in an open field near Cairo. Many Saracens had been slain, and the sultan of Babylon had been taken prisoner, 'to the great honour of our lord liege the king' and 'all the chivalry of England.'"[73]

Sir Gawain and the Green Knight subtly refers to a number of these issues. The detail of rich Armenian carpets surrounding Guinevere in the poem—"of tars tapites innoghe" (77)—is too slight to be an insistent allusion, but with the poet's playfulness it could invoke for some readers the Armenian context.[74] For those deeply concerned with Armenia and its plight at the hands of the Muslims, the poet's mention of Tars is a reminder of the desirability of eastern goods even as the challenge plot of the poem has a British king confronting a potentially Islamic rival who is ambiguously both hostile and friendly. The representation of Arthur in his youth may be a comment on Richard, who ascended the throne as a minor. If the poem is in part responding to the millenarian aspects of Richard's reign, then the entry of the Green Knight becomes a test of Richard's Roman imperial desires. By testing Arthur's desire for a challenge with a figure of Islamic provenance, the poem asks its audience to consider the worthiness of Richard's call for crusade. In comparing the strength of the Green Knight with Arthur,

[72] Bennett, "Richard II and the Wider Realm," 202; Bennett cites J. R. S. Philipps, "Edward II and the Prophets," in *England in the Fourteenth Century: Proceedings of the 1985 Harlaxton Symposium*, ed. W. M. Ormrod (Woodbridge: Boydell, 1986), 189–201 (194).

[73] British Library Harley MS 3988, fols. 39–41; cited in Bennett, "Richard II and the Wider Realm," 203. For both Gildas and the French letter-book, see also Bennett, *Richard II and the Revolution of 1399*, 73–74.

[74] Lilian Hornstein shows that "Tars" refers generally in Middle English to Tartary, from the city Tauris, which is modern Tabriz in Iran, or to Tarsus, which is in Lesser or Cilician Armenia, the part of Armenia in Christian hands until 1375. See Lilian Herlands Hornstein, "The Historical Background of *The King of Tars*," *Speculum* 15 (1941): 404–14.

and finally finding Arthur's court somewhat wanting, the poem suggests that Richard may be playing at something he does not fully comprehend. Arthur's commitment to participating in the Green Knight's challenge nearly results in the death of a knight. The subtle and witty representation of Gawain's stay at Bertilak's court—where he is both in enemy territory and yet treated as an honored guest—suggests the tension inherent in Cheshiremen's travel abroad, where they might trade with as well as fight in crusades against Muslims. The Islamic east becomes the figure both of fulfillment of ambition and threat to Richard/ Arthur. While the international aspects of the encounter between a great, young English king and an ambiguous figure tied to both the crusading Saint George and the powerful al-Khidr of Islam would have resonated with Richard's court, it would be hard to construe it as flattering. Richard II would have wanted the poem to be not about a young marginal king acknowledged by central powers but about a young king recognized as ready to become central.

The reception of the poem in Richard's court would not have been the same as in John of Gaunt's, whose court, since he was Duke of Lancaster and Knight of the Garter, was one likely venue for the *Gawain*-poet.[75] For John of Gaunt, the Green Knight would be interesting for his hybridity and ties to Spain. John's extensive ties to Iberia date from at least 1367, when he participated in an expedition in support of Pedro the Cruel. Iberia was a border zone, widely thought of as "a liminal area, the border where crusading activity took place; it was also the margin of Europe that separated Christians and Muslims."[76] Angus MacKay documents thorough cultural diffusion across the Castilian-Granadan frontier in the late Middle Ages.[77] Not only did Spain have an Islamic tradition of its own, but also it was the maritime link between England and Mediterranean markets such as Sicily, Tunis, and Alexan-

[75] Bennett, "The Historical Background," 82–83; Elizabeth Salter, "*Piers Plowman* and Alliterative Poetry," in *English and International: Studies in the Literature, Art, and Patronage of Medieval England*, ed. Derek Pearsall and Nicolette Zeeman (Cambridge: Cambridge University Press, 1988), 106–10.

[76] María Bullón-Fernández, "Not All Roads Lead to Rome: Anglo-Iberian Exchanges in the Middle Ages," in *England and Iberia in the Middle Ages, 12th–15th Century: Cultural, Literary, and Political Exchanges*, ed. María Bullón-Fernández (New York: Palgrave, 2007), 1–10 (1).

[77] Angus MacKay, "Religion, Culture, and Ideology on the Late Medieval Castilian-Granadan Frontier," in *Medieval Frontier Societies*, ed. Robert Bartlett and Angus MacKay (Oxford: Clarendon Press, 1989), 217–243.

dria.[78] Through marriage, John had a legal claim to be king of Castile, and accordingly he constructed a hybrid court. From 1371 to 1387, his court was that of a usurped king and the focus for legitimate Castilian hopes, and he made several military efforts to claim his throne.[79]

The implications of a Spanish royal court in England are too often overlooked. Forty years ago, Sydney Armitage-Smith warned that John's "strong and persistent craving for continental royalty, the keynote to his character, has been strangely neglected," and this has not changed.[80] Ignoring John's ambitions yields, in turn, the mistaken assumption that his court was unproblematically English. John married Doña Constanza, the heir of the murdered King Pedro I (lamented in Chaucer's *Monk's Tale*), and by Pedro's will her husband should have been king.[81] Pedro had a significant interest in Andalusian Moorish culture, and P. E. Russell concludes that "he probably felt closer bonds of sympathy with the Spanish Moors and Spanish Jews than with the fashionable chivalric culture of Europe north of the Pyrenees."[82] How much of his interest and knowledge of Spanish Islamic culture Pedro and his "half-oriental"[83] court passed on to his daughter and her court attendants must be a matter of speculation. Furthermore, John himself was descended from Edward I's Castilian bride Eleanor, and he seems to have associated Castile with crusading because of the *Reconquista*.[84] His struggle to claim the throne had the imprimatur of a different kind of crusade, however, since in the midst of the papal schism Castile supported Clement and John supported Urban.[85] John established a chancery to manage the affairs of the Spanish kingdom (complete with seals that showed John enthroned), and set up a mint in Gascony to make Castilian coins.[86] As John prepared to fight for his claim, Richard II began in 1386 to treat

---

[78] Olivia Remie Constable, *Trade and Traders in Muslim Spain: The Commercial Realignment of the Iberian Peninsula, 900–1500* (Cambridge: Cambridge University Press, 1994), 244.

[79] P. E. Russell, *The English Intervention in Spain and Portugal* (Oxford: Clarendon Press, 1955), 172; Anthony Goodman, *John of Gaunt: The Exercise of Princely Power in Fourteenth-Century Europe* (New York: St. Martin's Press, 1992), 49; Sidney Armitage-Smith, *John of Gaunt* (New York: Barnes & Noble, 1964), 100–102.

[80] Armitage-Smith, *John of Gaunt*, xxi.

[81] Russell, *English Intervention*, 174.

[82] Ibid., 21.

[83] Ibid., 175.

[84] Goodman, *John of Gaunt*, 136–37.

[85] Armitage-Smith, *John of Gaunt*, 304–7.

[86] Russell, *English Intervention*, 176–78; Armitage-Smith, *John of Gaunt*, 452–53.

him not as an English duke but as fellow king.[87] John and Constanza kept a number of Castilians on their household staffs; there were Castilian knights and ladies in their courts; and there were, of course, many Castilians of lower rank as well, including merchants, friars, and sailors. Even John's New Year's gifts of jewelry were in the Spanish style.[88] The effect was, as Russell notes, "to give an appropriately exotic air to the Lancastrian household . . . [and] to keep constantly in the mind of visitors . . . that they were in the vicinity of one whose greatest interests were in the Iberian Peninsula."[89] Given John's English roots, the Spanish flavor of John's court remained "foreign," as Anthony Goodman concludes, even if Constanza was sufficiently anglicized to be interested in woodwoses and to keep a Welsh jester with the possibly Arthurian name of Yevan (Yvain?).[90] Thus John's court, an obvious cultural center in England, was neither strictly English nor Spanish; it was a border where French, Spanish, English, and perhaps Welsh culture met and might have hybridized. John's court may well have provided opportunities for a poet to hear stories of al-Khidr and to perform for audiences that would recognize his appropriations of them and appreciate the tension between the familiar and the foreign. In 1388, John renounced his claim to the Castilian throne, but it was not the end of his Iberian involvements. He helped arrange for Philippa, his daughter by his first wife, Blanche, to marry Dom João of Portugal in 1387, creating yet another link by which Iberian stories could reach England: Philippa herself certainly had literary and chivalric interests.[91] In 1389, John became Duke of Aquitaine, bordering Aragon, with its own stories of al-Khidr (including a fifteenth-century Aragonese manuscript in Spanish written in Arabic characters about al-Khidr and Alexander the Great).[92]

Sir Gawain and the Green Knight would suit the image of an international Spanish court, especially the one that John created around Con-

---

[87] Goodman, *John of Gaunt*, 118, 203; Armitage-Smith, *John of Gaunt*, 302.

[88] Russell, *English Intervention*, 178–82; 179 n. 3.

[89] Ibid., 178–79.

[90] Goodman, *John of Gaunt*, 136–37, 361–62.

[91] Joyce Coleman, "Philippa of Lancaster, Queen of Portugal—and Patron of the Gower Translations?" in *England and Iberia in the Middles Ages*, ed. Bullón-Fernández, 135–65; Jennifer Goodman, *Chivalry and Exploration, 1298–1630* (Woodbridge: Boydell, 1998), 134–48.

[92] Friedländer, *Die Chadhirlegende*, 173–79. As previously mentioned, in 1393 Don John of Aragon was Richard II's rival in seeking Saint George's head.

stanza. As Pedro's court had been hybrid with substantial Moorish borrowings, Saint George/al-Khidr offered an apt figure to represent this. We do not know if John attempted to do anything with the Castilian Order of the Band, the forerunner of the Order of the Garter, but if he did the poem could be a playful anglicization of that tradition. Unlike in Richard's court, where issues of crusade and empire might shape audience response to the poem, in John's court the poem's representations of foreignness would speak to John's ambitions to rule a hybrid kingdom, Castile, that was also far from the imagined centers of the world, and that celebrated hybridity and cultural contact even while crusading.

If, however, the poem came from the context of a lesser noble's household, like Sir John Stanley's court, it would serve to underline a family claim to cosmopolitan travel—travel was necessary for a polished knight, as several chivalric handbooks made clear[93]—even if it was a court essentially English in character. From the appropriate region of the country for the poem's dialect, the Stanleys were until 1376 the hereditary master foresters for the Wirral, where Gawain wanders.[94] They owned literary manuscripts, and the Percy Manuscript, which contains the ballad *The Green Knight*, the one known work clearly derivative of *Sir Gawain and the Green Knight*, also has Stanley connections.[95] Andrew Breeze goes so far as to suggest that Sir John Stanley, rather than being simply the patron, might have been the *Gawain*-poet himself.[96] Sir John became a Knight of the Garter in 1405; Breeze suggests that the addition of the Garter motto to the manuscript reflects this development.[97] His service in Aquitaine would have brought him closer to re-

[93] Ramon Llull, *The Book of the Ordre of Chyualry*, trans. William Caxton, ed. Alfred Byles (London: Oxford University Press, for the EETS, 1926), 23; for a more qualified endorsement, see Richard Kaeuper and Elspeth Kennedy, trans. and ed., *The Book of Chivalry of Geoffroi de Charny* (Philadelphia: University of Pennsylvania Press, 1996), 90–92.

[94] For a history of the Stanleys, see W. Fergusson Irvine, "The Early Stanleys," *Transactions of the Historic Society of Lancashire and Cheshire* 105 (1954 for 1953): 45–68. For connections between Sir John Stanley and the *Gawain*-poet, see Edward Wilson, "*Sir Gawain and the Green Knight* and the Stanley Family of Stanley, Storeton, and Hooton," *RES* 30 (1979): 308–16; Ad Putter, *Introduction to the Gawain-Poet* (London and New York: Longman, 1996), 34–36; Bennett, *Community, Class, and Careerism*, esp. 215–19, 234; Gervase Mathew, *The Court of Richard II* (New York: W. W. Norton, 1968), 166.

[95] Wilson, "*Sir Gawain and the Green Knight* and the Stanley Family," 314–15.

[96] Cf. Meyer, "The Despensers and the *Gawain* Poet," 415; Bennett, *Community, Class, and Careerism*, 234.

[97] Andrew Breeze, "Sir John Stanley (c.1350–1414) and the *Gawain*-Poet," *Arthuriana* 14.1 (2004): 15–30 (17).

gions where al-Khidr stories might have been in circulation. Furthermore, in his active military career, he could have met many well-traveled men and heard their stories. For instance, in 1399 Sir John Stanley offered sureties for the release of Janico Dartasso, a Navarrese esquire who had entered Richard II's affinity and seen active service across Europe, including in the Tunisian crusade of 1390, and who had been a diplomatic messenger to Italy. Dartasso might have heard al-Khidr stories in any of these places and passed them on to his comrades.

Furthermore, a sixteenth-century biographical poem claims that Sir John sojourned in Turkey. Written by the bishop Thomas Stanley around 1562 about his family history, the poem testifies to the Stanleys' interests in and desire to be associated with the east.[98] Although it is a romanticized account with many unconfirmed details about Sir John, historian Michael Bennett is unwilling to dismiss its basic outline.[99] Among other adventures, Sir John spends six months at the Ottoman court. Not quite as considerate of his host as Sir Gawain, Sir John must leave hurriedly when the Ottoman princess warns him (with a remarkable lack of re-crimination) that she is pregnant. While details of the romance may be fabulous, Sir John could have spent time with the Ottomans. Chaucer was not being outlandishly inventive when he said that his Knight "hadde been also / Somtyme with the lord of Palatye / Agayn another hethen in Turkye" (*General Prologue*, I.64–66). Whether or not Sir John actually spent six months in the Ottoman court, the fact that the story is carefully recited in the Stanley poem testifies to the importance of the Ottoman connection in the family imagination. (A poem about a later Stanley, Sir William, also has repeated encounters with Muslims.)[100] Sir John's experience abroad educates and polishes him; the attention of the Ottoman court as witness to his worth confirms his glory. As Lavezzo argues, English marginality demands confirmation from the center.

Including the story as part of the Stanley family's self-presentation marks the importance placed on having worldly connections broad enough to extend into the Islamic sphere (though admittedly when the Stanley poem was written, Ottoman-English relations had been changed somewhat by the fall of Constantinople and the possibilities of a Protes-

---

[98] "The Stanley Poem," in James Orchard Halliwell, ed., *The Palatine Anthology: A Collection of Ancient Poems and Ballads Relating to Lancashire and Cheshire* (London: Halliwell, 1850), 211–13.

[99] Bennett, *Community, Class, and Careerism,* 215–16.

[100] "Sir W. Stanley's Garland," in Halliwell, ed., *Palatine Anthology,* 272–82.

tant-Islamic alliance against the Catholics). If Sir John was in fact the patron of the *Gawain*-poet, his court would not only have provided a milieu in which the poet could learn of al-Khidr, but it would have provided an audience sophisticated enough to appreciate Sir Gawain's delicate encounter with a foreign court teaching hard wisdom that may or may not be fully Christian. A poem like *Sir Gawain and the Green Knight* in turn lent a cosmopolitan gloss to personal and family identity.

The varied nature of these possible sites of reception of *Sir Gawain and the Green Knight* demands a shift in geographical perspective. The relationships between provinces such as Cheshire or nobles' courts and the larger world were not necessarily mediated by London and the king, and relationships to the Islamic world depended upon regional as well as national contexts. The network of relations forged by medieval trade and diplomacy were multiple and complex. Cheshire could and did have relations with the outside world independently of London, an independence reinforced when Richard II made it into a palatinate. If *Sir Gawain and the Green Knight* is to be read in terms of center and periphery, it is probably most fruitful not to consider regional courts in relation to London but to treat England itself as peripheral to the old, powerful, Mediterranean world. As Janet Abu-Lughod argues, there was a global economy with "increased economic integration and cultural efflores- cence" in the period 1250–1350 stretching from Europe to China and centered in the Middle East.[101] But while the significance of the Asian trade facilitated by the *pax Mongolica* in the late Middle Ages shaped general attitudes in England, the question of understanding how specific audiences relate to the greater world cannot be answered just by think- ing about England as an undifferentiated whole but by considering spe- cific courts and regions. In so doing, we get closer to what Ralph Hanna calls "the polyvocal and individuated voices of discrete local/regional literary cultures."[102]

The Otherness of the Green Knight

A. C. Spearing warns that "there are dangers in beginning one's study of *Sir Gawain and the Green Knight* by asking 'Who is the Green Knight?' and expecting an answer to that question will somehow 'solve'

[101] Abu-Lughod, *Before European Hegemony: The World System A.D. 1250–1350* (New York: Oxford University Press, 1991), 4.
[102] Hanna, *London Literature*, 3.

the poem."[103] Given al-Khidr's inscrutability and fame as a confounder of human reason, there is little danger that recognizing that the Green Knight embodies a representation of a figure of Saint George and al-Khidr will overly domesticate him. In taking seriously a possible Islamic derivation for the Green Knight, our reorienting of the poem yields new questions and new readings obscured by the focus on a Celtic origin for the Green Knight. Reorienting the poem makes better sense of the paradoxes of the Green Knight, his barbaric otherness *and* his civility.

Such paradoxes become particularly important in the revelations at the Green Chapel. The Green Knight forcefully uses the language of Christian penance and absolution:

> Þou art confessed so clene, beknowen of þy mysses,
> And hatz þe penaunce apert of þe poynt of myn egge,
> I halde þe polysed of þat plyȝt and pured as clene
> As þou hadez neuer forfeted syþen þou watz fyrst borne.
>
> (2391–94)

Gawain of course resists this comforting claim of absolution, insisting on his sin. Ever since J. A. Burrow raised the issue of the paired confessions before and after the nick in the neck, and the question of whether Gawain's flaws are chivalric shortcomings or Christian sins, the significance of the confession has been a matter of debate.[104] To the extent that the Green Knight is recognized as the Christian Saint George, his words are comforting, combining chivalric and Christian forgiveness, and his status as confessor is unproblematic. He teaches Gawain an important lesson about the role of sin, confession, and absolution in chivalry that can be trusted and brought back to a knightly court. But if the poem is also alluding to George's double, the Islamic part of al-Khidr's identity unsettles this. Al-Khidr can be Christianized, either by

[103] A. C. Spearing, *The Gawain-Poet: A Critical Study* (Cambridge: Cambridge University Press, 1970), 180.

[104] See Burrow, *A Reading of "Sir Gawain and the Green Knight"* (New York: Barnes & Noble, 1966), 104–10, 127–33; and W. R. J. Barron, *Trawthe and Treason: The Sin of Gawain Reconsidered* (Manchester: Manchester University Press, 1980). For contrasting views on confession and private identity, see Andrew James Johnston, "The Secret of the Sacred: Confession and the Self in *Sir Gawain and the Green Knight*," in *Performances of the Sacred in Late Medieval and Early Modern England*, ed. Susanne Rupp and Tobias Döring (Amsterdam: Rodopi, 2005), 45–63; and David Aers, *Community, Gender, and Individual Identity: English Writing, 1360–1430* (London: Routledge, 1988), 165–66, 170.

absorbing him completely into a Christian tale, as happens in the *Gesta Romanorum*, or halfway as the double of Saint George, who remains split between the religions, so the confession could still have religious worth. But the confession could also be treated as revealing moral but not strictly religious truth, just as Christian scholars used Muslim philosophy in their theology. The introduction of Aristotle's scientific works through Muslim writers—especially Averroës, who urged scholars to approach religion with the tools of logic and philosophy—had a profound effect on Christian discussion for centuries.[105] The wisdom and learning of the Islamic east (and Spain) could not, therefore, simply be rejected but had to be evaluated very carefully. The end of *Sir Gawain and the Green Knight* similarly challenges the reader, remaining troublingly between philosophy and religion.

The landscape itself witnesses this tension. Just as many chapels in the Near and Middle East were shared holy spaces, in which a single image could be interpreted in quite different ways (as in stained-glass images of Saint George/al-Khidr), the Green Chapel is more (or less) than simply Christian. The final encounter takes place by a ruined chapel, but Gawain darkly fears it is not a holy one:

> 'Now iwysse,' quoþ Wowayn, 'wysty is here;
> Þis oritore is vgly, with erbez ouergrowen.
> Wel bisemez þe wyȝe wruxled in grene
> Dele here his deuocioun on þe Deuelez wyse;
> Now I fele hit is þe Fende, in my fyue wyttez,
> Þat hatz stoken me þis steven to strye me here.
> (2189–94)

The devilish appearance of the chapel is a product of Gawain's fears, but whether he misperceives a Christian chapel because of his sin and fear, or whether he accurately perceives that the chapel is not wholly Christian, is unresolved.

This crux is foreshadowed by hints of religious tension throughout the poem. When Gawain rides to meet the Green Knight, he arms himself as a Christian champion, the pentangle proclaiming his faith in Christian resurrection as opposed to his opponent's magical or diabolical way of handling death. What he meets instead of supernatural opposi-

---

[105] Menocal, *Arabic Role*, 36–37. Menocal of course makes an argument for literary influence as well.

tion is a sophisticated and very hospitable court, in some ways greater than Arthur's. Just as Aeneas, invoked at the beginning of the poem, discovered in Dido's court the threat that love can play to nationalist and imperialist ambitions, so Bertilak's court tempts Gawain to abandon his quest. Taking his armor and replacing it with clothes of "tuly and tars" (858), they offer him dishes "sauered with spyces" (892), and he meets the lady who is "wener þen Wenore" (945). The lord presses him to stay past Christmas, and although he defers easily to Gawain's announced intention to pursue his quest, the offer to spend the time until the New Year in bed at Hautdesert leaves Gawain vulnerable. When he leaves for the Green Chapel, his guide urges him to turn away and give up the quest.

The challenge proves to have been a test of Gawain's faith in many senses—his willingness to carry out promises serious (the Green Knight's game) and trivial (Bertilak's game), but also his willingness to meet death as a Christian and his understanding of sin and forgiveness. If the poem gives the Green Knight a dual nature as Saint George and al-Khidr, it allows the poem to raise the threat of Gawain's conversion at Bertilak's attractive court and yet to deflect it into play that results only in a little nick on Gawain's neck, a nick that might, if transferred to another part of the body, suggest circumcision.[106] While the Green Knight's court is literally Christian, with its Christmas services and language of religion, coded into Gawain's adventures at the court are tropes of religious tension, similar to those in other medieval romances. In particular, the bedside conversations between Gawain and the lady recall other scenes in which conversion is figured as seduction. In *Bevis of Hampton*, the King of Armenia initially offers Bevis his lovely daughter Josian's hand in marriage if Bevis will convert, but Bevis refuses him and later refuses Josian herself.[107] It is only when Josian goes to Bevis's chamber (where he pretends to be asleep) and offers to convert herself

[106] R. A. Shoaf argues, "The *nirt* is a wound that displaces and resembles the wound of circumcision . . . and given his [the *Gawain*-poet's] audience's undoubted familiarity with the liturgical significance of New Year's Day, the *nirt* in the neck is a brilliant strategy for evoking the numerous associations of the Feast of the Circumcision." *The Poem as Green Girdle: Commercium in "Sir Gawain and the Green Knight"* (Gainesville: University Presses of Florida, 1984), 15. We would like to add that by evoking circumcision, the poem also raises the threat of Islam.

[107] *Bevis of Hampton*, lines 555–60, 1179–98, in *Four Romances of England*, ed. Ronald Herzman, Graham Drake, and Eve Salisbury (Kalamazoo: Medieval Institute Publications for TEAMS, 1999).

that Bevis agrees to the marriage. Whether her conversion is sincere or strategic is put to the test when she is wed to the Muslim King Yvor and endures years of (miraculously celibate) marriage to remain Christian.

The uncertainty in *Bevis* about who will convert whom is a recurring tension in medieval romances featuring Muslim others, where a number of romances and ballads feature Saracen women converting for love of Christian men, often prisoners.[108] Geraldine Heng rightly argues that such women are used to prove both the rightness of Christianity and the justice of Christian invasion because they answer to the desires of the inhabitants: "Part of the fantasy of empire, as colonial and conquest literature in later periods will amply teach us, is that the colonized, in the forms of their women, desire their colonizers."[109] Heng goes on to argue that as the Christians lose lands in the Levant their logic changes, creating reversed versions of the story. In the "Constance" group of stories, of which *The Man of Law's Tale* is the best known, it is a Christian woman who is desired by a Muslim prince, and her faith leads to his conversion, so it is the women who are steadfast and the men who are changeable, and Muslims who could not be conquered are seduced into Christianity.[110] If women are steadfast and men convert, then the narratives of Christian men taking Muslim wives brings the threat of Christian conversion to Islam. Sir John Mandeville, for one, claims that the Sultan of Egypt offered him great lordships and a prince's daughter if he would convert, but he refused.[111] A Stanley poem tells that when Sir William was in danger in Jerusalem, a Muslim woman offered her love in exchange for his conversion.[112] In *The King of Tars*, the question of who will convert plays out uneasily: the daughter of the King of Tars pretends to convert and lives as a Muslim until her deformed first son is born and the miracle of his transformation converts her husband to Christianity.

The three days of attempted seduction in *Sir Gawain and the Green*

[108] For analysis of these figures in romance, see Heng, *Empire of Magic*, 186–88; Siobhain Bly Calkin, *Saracens and the Making of English Identity: The Auchinleck Manuscript* (New York: Routledge, 2005), 61–95. For ballads, see Francis James Child's introductory discussion of "Young Beichan," in *The English and Scottish Popular Ballads*, 5 vols. (New York: Dover, 1965; original ed., Boston: Houghton Mifflin, 1884), 1:454–63.

[109] Heng, *Empire of Magic*, 187.

[110] Ibid., 187–99; cf. Metlitzki, *Matter of Araby*, 136–60.

[111] M. C. Seymour, ed., *The Bodley Version of Mandeville's Travels* (London: Oxford University Press for EETS, 1963), 27.

[112] "Sir W. Stanley's Garland," in Halliwell, ed., *Palatine Anthology*, 272–82. See also Child, *English and Scottish Popular Ballads*, 1:463.

Knight depict a struggle over whether Gawain will convert to this new court, whose lady is more beautiful than Guinevere (945), or whether he will win her to his side and thereby somehow escape the coming execution. Throughout, motifs from the stories of Christian knights and their captor/captive Muslim women are playfully deployed. On the first day, the lady invokes the image of a loving captor of a Christian knight when she sneaks up on him and declares, "Now ar ȝe tan astyt! Bot true vus schape, / I schal bynde yow in your bedde (1210–11). Gawain tries to invoke the convention in which loving women release their prisoners, asking her to "deprece your prysoun" (1219), but she refuses. On the second day, she reverses the scenario, teasing him with the thought that she is wholly in his power (1496), although it is clear that her profession of vulnerability is merely a stratagem. Gawain gently rejects this ploy as well, but on the third day comes the crisis. The narrator comments, "Gret perile bitwene hem stod / Nif Maré of hir knyȝt mynne" (1768–69). Mary of course was a major part of Gawain's Christian identity as represented on his shield, and the question of whether Mary will remember him suggests the question of whether he will remember her: the seductiveness of the court leading to a risk of conversion, a point driven home after the final revelations when the Green Knight offers him the chance to return not to Camelot but to Hautdesert (2467–70).

Bertilak, however, is not Islamic, and if the Green Knight is an avatar of al-Khidr, he is also Saint George. Gawain is being seduced not into apostasy but into a deeper understanding of Christian faith, one based on forgiveness of sin, not perfection, and based on humility in the face of the wider world, not naive and insular English triumphalism. However, although the confession may be a valid absolution in Christian terms, this is not sufficient to make Gawain's engagement with potentially non-Christian others vanish. Gawain's blood tie to Morgan the Goddess cannot be confessed away, and he rides back to a court with a green slash interrupting the unending knot of his pentangle. His scar and his appropriation of the green girdle, offered by the woman who tried to lead him astray, are troubling reminders of a moral complexity not acknowledged in the young and joyful court at Camelot. Gawain's return is like the crusader's return: he is changed, but it is neither recognized nor understood. Arthur and his court eagerly take up the green girdle of the Green Knight, just as the Order of the Garter took up the cross of Saint George, but whether they understand the subtle and powerful transformations of encounters with the powers beyond their borders (and the scars those encounters can leave) is not clear.

Conclusion

Like so many other speculations about the Green Knight, the argument that he is tied to al-Khidr cannot be proven, barring the miraculous discovery of both the author's identity and library. Nonetheless, there is a case to be made for a possible Islamic connection. There are not that many green, immortal figures who can appear threatening and hospitable, inscrutable initially and ultimately wise expounders of the mysteries of God. The *Gawain*-poet would probably have had opportunity and certainly have had motive to be interested in stories of al-Khidr, given the English interest in al-Khidr's avatar Saint George. Al-Khidr was one of the most important figures in Islamic mythology, and stories of him would have been ubiquitous, from Constantinople, through the Near East and North Africa, and into Spain. He had certainly passed into the Christian tradition with Latin translations of the Qu'ran, and he appears in changed form in the *Gesta Romanorum*. In addition to motive and opportunity, the poet could easily have had occasion: although the courts of the various proposed patrons would have had very different reasons to be interested in a story of an Arthurian encounter with al-Khidr, the interest in the Islamic world was certainly there. Thus, even though the link between the Green Knight and al-Khidr must remain speculative, it deserves to be part of the discussion of the poem.

The tie with al-Khidr is not simply a matter of source study, since it raises a number of interpretive questions. And it is not simply a matter of applying postcolonialism to the poem: indeed, the poem underscores how postcolonial approaches need to be adjusted to fit medieval contexts. As a recent collection of essays on the postcolonial Middle Ages, *Postcolonial Moves*, warns, "The modernity of postcolonial studies blocks certain routes to the past, and thus maintains certain nationalist and historicist exclusions."[113] In approaching medieval literature, English—even European—dominance cannot be assumed, because the global

[113] Patricia Clare Ingham and Michelle R. Warren, eds., *Postcolonial Moves: Medieval Through Modern* (New York: Palgrave Macmillan, 2003), 2.

economy is centered in the Near East, as Janet Abu-Lughod and others have argued.[114]

In these fascinating new ways of looking at the Middle Ages, we must guard against any unconscious assumption that we know what borderlands look like, and that they necessarily lie at the edges of territories with such familiar Western European centers as London or Paris. In his cogent essay on the filiative connections between postcolonialism and medieval studies, Bruce Holsinger employs this very language of borders, asking, "Can medieval symptoms of colonialism and imperialism—crusading, conversion, linguistic and cultural hybridity in the borderlands of Latin Christendom and the Mongol Empire, indigenous resistance to conquest, colonial ambivalence in the outer British Isles—be responsibly diagnosed through the lens of postcolonial theory?"[115] Holsinger's essay mounts a strong argument for an affirmative answer to the question. We concur, so long as care is taken not to import the assumptions of the modern late imperialism of the nineteenth and early twentieth centuries. For even the way Holsinger frames his question suggests that there stubbornly remains an unchallenged assumption that borderlands must lie in the hinterlands or outer reaches of Europe—despite his gesturing at the non-European empire of the Mongols—or, more tellingly, in the "*outer* British Isles" (our emphasis). Borderlands need not lie in the periphery of Christendom; Christendom itself could be the borderlands.

While the basic dichotomy between center and periphery remains important, there are no absolute centers, and so peripheries can negotiate relations with a number of different centers. Jeffrey Jerome Cohen argues, "A postcolonial Middle Ages has no frontiers, only heterogenous borderlands with multiple centers. This reconfigured geography includes Asia, Africa, and the Middle East not as secondary regions to be judged from a European standard, nor as 'sources' from which to trace influence, but as full participants in a world simultaneously larger and more fragmented—a world of intersecting, mutating, incommensurable

---

[114] For studies extending this Asian-centered system to the early modern and later periods, see Andre Gunder Frank, *ReOrient: Global Economy in the Asian Age* (Berkeley and Los Angeles: University of California Press, 1998); Kenneth Pomeranz, *The Great Divergence: China, Europe, and the Making of the Modern World Economy* (Princeton: Princeton University Press, 2000).

[115] Bruce W. Holsinger, "Medieval Studies, Postcolonial Studies, and the Genealogies of Critique," *Speculum* 77 (2002): 1195–1227 (1206).

times and places."[116] This is true not only on a continental scale, but on the scale of the kingdom as well. While London's cultural weight within England was growing and the monarchy was centralizing, London and Westminster were not the overwhelming center of England. Aristocratic courts, be they Sir John Stanley's or John of Gaunt's, had international perspectives that were not exclusively mediated by the capital and the king. These regional differences make any careful historicist work on the poem deeply dependent on speculations about the context of composition, but they drive home the theoretical point that because England's internal political structure was not that of a modern nation's, assumptions about its international and cultural relations must be altered as well.

The Green Knight captures the uncertain perspective that results. If he is at once Christian saint and Islamic friend of God, perhaps overlaid with Celtic otherworldly challenger, he can be hospitable and threatening, a teacher of what might be religious wisdom or might not. His belt can become the badge for an order of British knighthood that, save only for the scarred Gawain, has experienced only part of the adventure. For his part, Gawain wins respect for himself and for his king from a great and sophisticated lord, as is important for a knight from the edge of the world, but in doing so he is altered, tempted by the sophistication of foreign courts, confronted with religious issues, and ultimately welcomed by a court he now recognizes as understanding only partially their place in the world. *Sir Gawain and the Green Knight* offers a nuanced view of how English chivalry engages not just with a history that stretches back to Troy, but with a world centered well east of England.

---

[116] Jeffrey J. Cohen, "Introduction: Midcolonial," in *The Postcolonial Middle Ages*, ed. Cohen (New York: Palgrave Macmillan, 2001), 1–17 (7).

The Historiography of the Dragon:

Heraldic Violence in the Alliterative *Morte Arthure*

Alex Mueller

University of Massachusetts, Boston

FOR ADMIRERS OF Ernst Kantorowicz's *The King's Two Bodies*, the myth of King Arthur has an irresistible appeal.[1] Arthur's identity as *rex quondam rexque futurus* resonates with Kantorowicz's analysis of the theological character of early modern royal succession, whereby the death of a king (the body natural) is a recurrent episode in the metaphysical life of sovereignty (the body politic). Scholars have identified this juridical insistence on the sempiternity of the sovereign in late medieval incarnations of a King Arthur who never dies or dies and returns in messianic fashion.[2] Yet, as Giorgio Agamben points out, Kantorowicz fails to acknowledge the absolutist nature of sovereignty that this political theology entails. Rather than merely perpetuate the *dignitas* of the kingship, Agamben suggests that "the metaphor of the political body appears . . . as the cipher of the absolute and inhuman character

I would like to thank the readers who offered comments and suggestions for this essay in its nascent stages, especially Rebecca Krug, John Watkins, Ruth Karras, Andrew Scheil, and David Benson. An early version of this essay was presented at the annual meeting of the Medieval Academy of America, Toronto, April 2007; I am grateful for the responses from audience members and fellow presenters, particularly Michael Johnston. For their invaluable help in the late stages, I am indebted to the anonymous reviewers for *SAC*.

[1] Ernst Hartwig Kantorowicz, *The King's Two Bodies: A Study in Mediaeval Political Theology* (Princeton: Princeton University Press, 1957; repr. 1997).

[2] For a recent and full treatment, see Patricia Clare Ingham, *Sovereign Fantasies: Arthurian Romance and the Making of Britain* (Philadelphia: University of Pennsylvania Press, 2001). See also Stephen Knight, *Arthurian Literature and Society* (London: Macmillan, 1983); Martin Shichtman and James Carley, eds., *Culture and the King: The Social Implications of the Arthurian Legend* (Albany: State University of New York Press, 1994); Elizabeth T. Pochoda, *Arthurian Propaganda: Le Morte Darthur as an Historical Ideal of Life* (Chapel Hill: University of North Carolina Press, 1971).

of sovereignty."[3] In other words, the expense of the principle *le roi ne meurt jamais* is the evacuation of value from human life. By mitigating the impact of a king's death on the political body, sovereignty is simultaneously maintained and dehumanized. In this light, Arthur's legendary sempiternity is demystified as a trace of premodern statecraft.

Optimism about Arthur's return abounds in most Arthurian texts, but resistance to such political theology can be found in the early fifteenth-century alliterative *Morte Arthure*, an intimate portrayal of Arthur as a prideful sovereign. Critics have acknowledged the poem's ambivalence about war, but most have read its critiques of militaristic overreaching solely in contrast to the poem's primary sources, namely, Geoffrey of Monmouth's *Historia regum Britannie* and its vernacular translations. The influence of the Galfridian tradition upon this poem must be considered, since it is the basis for the poem's narrative content and structure, but Geoffrey's enthusiasm about the translation of empire from Troy to Rome to Britain runs counter to the *Morte*-poet's morbid dispossession of Arthur's imperial inheritance.[4]

Arthur is the natural symbol of sovereignty in the poem by virtue of his intention to reverse the track of *translatio imperii* and reclaim his Roman heritage. The origin of empire ironically becomes the coveted object of empire by Arthur, who seeks to establish an empire larger and more powerful than that of the Romans by obliterating his imperial

---

[3] Giorgio Agamben, *Homo Sacer: Sovereign Power and Bare Life,* trans. Daniel Heller-Roazen (Stanford: Stanford University Press, 1998), 91–103 (101). Cf. Kantorowicz, "Dignitas non moritur," in *The King's Two Bodies*, 383–450.

[4] What many have characterized as the poem's pacifism or ambivalence about empire-building has often been attributed to the poet's own ingenious embellishment of the Galfridian tale. As Maureen Fries has put it, the *Morte Arthure* is "indisputably Galfridian" in its direct use not only of Geoffrey's *Historia* but also of the later translations by Wace in 1155, Laȝamon at the end of the twelfth century, and Robert Manning c. 1338. See "The Poem in the Tradition of Arthurian Literature," in *The "Alliterative Morte Arthure": A Reassessment of the Poem*, ed. Karl Heinz Göller, Arthurian Studies 2 (Woodbridge: D. S. Brewer, 1981), 30–43 (34). For a concise explanation of these chronicle sources, see Mary Hamel, ed., *Morte Arthure: A Critical Edition* (New York: Garland, 1984), 34–38. See also Patricia DeMarco, "An Arthur for the Ricardian Age: Crown, Nobility, and the Alliterative *Morte Arthure*," *Speculum* 80 (2005): 464–93. In this recent article on the poem's representations of the conflict between king and noble, DeMarco rehearses the predominant scholarly perception of the relationship between the *Morte* and the Galfridian material: "The *Morte Arthure* departs from that tradition . . . both in its choice of subject matter and its method of handling the material. Amplifying what had been merely the crowning achievement of Arthur's reign in the Galfridian account, the *Morte* focuses on Britain's war against the Romans, and . . . produces a lavishly detailed portrait of military life distinguished by its extensive historical topicality and its unparalleled realism" (464).

predecessor, thereby establishing a paradoxical desire of Britain to be and not to be Rome. This attempted reclamation of an imperial origin not only inspires self-destruction but also signifies a recurrent inability to obliterate a spirit of tyranny that runs throughout the poem. The label of "tyraunt" is transferred explicitly from the Roman emperor Lucius and his legions (271, 824) to the Giant of St. Michael's Mount (842, 878, 991) and implicitly to Arthur himself.[5] Just as the Giant's tyranny "tourmentez" (842) people and causes the old widow to mourn the death of the Duchess of Brittany by "wryngande hir handez" (950), Arthur's destruction of Tuscany "turmentez þe pople" (3153) and transforms wives into widows who "wryngene theire handis" (3155). Instead of preserving the *dignitas* of the king, it is as if the greed of the tyrant never dies—when a tyrant is killed, his avaricious spirit fills a new body in the manner of the Virgilian transmigration of souls. As soon as Arthur kills the Giant of St. Michael's Mount, he becomes the Giant—as soon as he defeats the Roman emperor Lucius, he becomes a British "emperor."[6] Rather than promulgate such translations of empire, this poem denounces assertions of authority as translations of tyranny. *Translatio imperii* becomes *translatio tyrannidis*.

I want to suggest that the poem achieves this macabre message— *tyrannus non moritur*—primarily through an unstable system of chivalric machinery: the art of heraldry. Alliterative romance is replete with heraldic assertions of nobility, but the *Morte Arthure* is unique in its necrologic interpretation of such chivalric devices. Rather than simply commemorate the deeds of ancestors and confirm the noble blood of the bearers, the heraldic signs of this poem operate as visual necrologies, or lists of the dead. Just as monks would use a liturgical record of the dead in a morning office, knights ritually present the arms of the noble kins-

---

[5] All citations of the poem are from Hamel, ed., *Morte Arthure*. For different editorial readings, I refer to the following editions: Larry Benson, ed., *King Arthur's Death* (Indianapolis: Bobbs-Merrill, 1974); Valerie Krishna, ed., *The Alliterative "Morte Arthure": A Critical Edition* (New York: Burt Franklin, 1976); and Edmund Brock, ed., *Morte Arthure*, EETS o.s. 8 (London: K. Paul, Trench, Trubner & Co., 1871 (rpt. 1961, New York and London: Oxford University Press).

[6] The killings of the Giant and Lucius lead first to plunder and excessive violence and later to the "barbarization" of Arthur and his knights. After Lucius's death, Arthur's knights slaughter thousands (2274) and "tuke whate them likes" [take what they liked] (2282) from the dead bodies that are strewn across the battlefield. Then, in an act designed to shame the surviving Romans, Arthur calls forth barbers and has them shave the two senators who will accompany the coffins back to Rome, which serve as the tribute previously demanded from the Britons (2330–45).

men who died in battle. Whereas the appropriate heraldic symbol regularly secures the chivalric status of its bearer, such signs in the *Morte
Arthure* remind onlookers of the death and destruction left in their wake.
Consider the following episode after Arthur's victory at Soissons. Arthur
commands his heralds, who are normally responsible for recording the
details of battle, to act as morticians by embalming the corpses and
enclosing them in "kystys" [chests] (2302), which are decorated with
"theire baners abowne, theire bagis therevndyre" [their banners above,
their badges below] (2303).[7] In this scene, the art of heraldry becomes
the art of death, a striking equivalency that memorializes the dead as it
celebrates the living. By transforming heralds into undertakers, the
badges and banners become visual reminders of the deaths that accompany all heraldic assertions, from battle standards to coats of arms.
Rather than serve as signifiers of the stable system of knighthood and
nobility, heraldic devices in this poem emphasize the threat that martial
violence poses for the security of chivalric and sovereign identity.[8]

This heraldic signification of death renders such devices indecipherable to their witnesses—they no longer serve as reliable symbols of
noble lineage. In the description of Gawain's death, the heraldic markers
that should signal his royal blood fail: "His baners brayden down, betyn
of gowlles / His brande and his brade schelde al blody beronen" [His
banners struck down, adorned with red / His blade and his broad shield
run over completely with blood] (3945). Instead of broadcasting his
nobility, his banners and shield signify his death, with his body beaten
to the ground and his arms obscured by blood. Without his heraldic
symbols to demonstrate his gentility, Arthur consecrates Gawain's blood
himself (3991) in a desperate attempt to endow his kinsmen's blood
with what Christine Chism calls "the material transcendence of a relic."[9]
Such scenes do not suggest, as D. Vance Smith argues, that the "prox-

---

[7] I am influenced by D. Vance Smith's reading of this scene in *Arts of Possession: The
Middle English Household Imaginary* (Minneapolis: University of Minnesota Press, 2003),
198. For more on the role of heralds, see Anthony Richard Wagner, *Heralds and Heraldry
in the Middle Ages: An Inquiry into the Growth of the Armorial Function of Heralds* (Oxford:
Oxford University Press, 1939), 33ff.; Chandos Herald, *Vie du Prince Noir*, in *The Life
and Campaigns of the Black Prince*, ed. Richard Barber (Woodbridge: Boydell, 1986),
84–139.
[8] Cf. Kenneth J. Tiller, "The Rise of Sir Gareth and the Hermeneutics of Heraldry,"
Arthuriana 17.3 (2007): 74–91 (78–79); Laurie Finke and Martin Shichtman, *King
Arthur and the Myth of History* (Gainesville: University Press of Florida, 2004), 174–78.
[9] Christine Chism, *Alliterative Revivals* (Philadelphia: University of Pennsylvania
Press, 2002), 225.

imity to death" of heraldic gestures renders their signification "impossible."[10] Instead, such devices more simply signify the death that is the
necessary consequence of heraldic assertions. The profusion of Gawain's
blood, the corporeal manifestation of his nobility, obscures his martial
identity and supersedes the heraldic law that would justify his ancestry.

More than any other figure, the image of the dragon, which appears
in various forms, embodies the poem's system of heraldic signification.
It is through a reading of the dragon that the *Morte*-poet's perspective
on war has a particularly alliterative and anti-Galfridian flavor, since the
Morte-poet draws both the language used to describe the dragon and
what I call its "pedagogic" function from the late fourteenth-century
alliterative poem, *The Siege of Jerusalem*. The dragon, which is associated
with both King Arthur and the Roman Emperor Lucius, is representative of a program of slippery signification throughout the poem, which
complicates attempts to fix such signs to their referents. The result of
this programmatic slippage is a thoroughgoing critique of heraldic assertions of nobility. The *Morte*-poet attaches multiple meanings to recurring heraldic devices to attenuate martial fervor, obscure distinctions
between the conquerors and the conquered, and emphasize the collateral damage of war. The juxtaposition of signs of empire with scenes of
violence confirms the relationship between assertions of sovereignty and
the indiscriminate extermination of life.

Death Where the Dragon Is Raised

An analysis of the heraldic dragon demonstrates the way the *Morte*-
poet simultaneously draws from and unscrupulously rejects Galfridian
historiography in order to confound distinctions between the Britons
and the Romans. Like their common Trojan ancestry, the symbol of the
dragon originates in the East, but in the eyes of the Western world the
dragon became the quintessential Roman imperial standard by the end
of the second century C.E. By the fourth century, it became the chief
military ensign and was used both in battles and imperial rituals.[11] As
Mary Hamel notes, the Roman dragon symbol is "a distinct oddity" in
the *Morte Arthure* because, according to the philosophers who interpret

---

[10] Smith, *Arts of Possession*, 219.
[11] Vegetius, *Epitoma rei militaris*, ed. M. D. Reeve (Oxford: Clarendon Press, 2004),
chap. 1, sections 23, 2.7. For a full discussion of dragons and their British contexts, see
J. S. P. Tatlock, "The Dragons of Wessex and Wales," *Speculum* 8 (1933): 223–35.

Arthur's first dream in the poem, the dragon represents Arthur, not the Romans:

> The dragon þat þow dremyde of   so dredfull to schewe,
> That come dryfande ouer þe deepe   to drynchen thy pople,
> Sothely and certayne   thy seluen it es,
> That thus saillez ouer þe see   with thy sekyre knyghtez.
>
> (815–18)

[The dragon that you dreamed of so dreadful to behold, which came driving over the deep to drown your people, truly and certainly it is you, who thus sails over the sea with your trusty knights.]

This interpretation, that the dragon is Arthur, is natural since it signifies the legacy inherited from his father, Uther Pendragon, who represents the golden dragon in the Galfridian sources.[12] At this point in the poem, the *Morte*-poet clearly follows the genealogical association between the dragon and Arthur, but darkens this inheritance by claiming that Arthur will "drynchen" his people.[13] Arthur's capacity to drown his people is confirmed at the end of the poem when he orders Mordred's children to be thrown into "watyrs" (4321), which indicates that this dream is to be interpreted as a sign not only of his imperial success but also of the damage he will inflict on his kinsmen. Yet the philosophers interpret the dream as an indication that he and his knights will defeat the "tyrauntez þat tourmentez thy pople" [tyrants who torment your people] (824)—that is, the Roman Lucius and his legions—and they make no attempt to explain how or why Arthur's expedition against the Romans will lead to the destruction of his own people.[14] This is the first of many clues in the text that we should not trust this optimistic interpretation of empire-building.

[12] Chism, *Alliterative Revivals*, 209.

[13] This verb could mean "destroy," but in the context of the "deepe" and the "see," it most likely means "drown," the primary *MED* definition. The variant readings of the two extant manuscripts of *The Wars of Alexander* confirm this definition, at least for the alliterative poets. Whereas the Dublin manuscript, MS 213, olim MS.D.4.12, reads "Þe folez & þe folke þat þe flude drynched" (3072), MS Ashmole 44 reads "þe fooles & þe folke þat þe flode drouned" (3199).

[14] For a discussion of this ambiguous symbol, see John Gardner, ed., *The Alliterative Morte Arthure, The Owl and the Nightingale, and Five Other Middle English Poems* (Carbondale: Southern Illinois University Press, 1971), 254. Hamel finds it "odd that these 'sage philosophers,' subtle doctors of the seven liberal arts (808), do not explain how the Arthur-dragon is to drown his own people." See *Morte Arthure*, 285.

In the earlier description of the dream itself, which the interpreters fail to address, the dragon wields such an infectious power that "Whaym þat he towchede he was tynt for euer" [Whomever he touched was lost forever] (770). Even the symbol of the dragon itself would have inspired fear among medieval readers, since it represented evil, heresy, and even the Anti-Christ.[15] Instead of addressing these ominous overtones, however, the philosophers emphasize Arthur's destined role as glorious conqueror of Rome. Even though readers might be tempted to trust these "sage philosophers" and view Arthur's march on Rome as well intentioned and sanctioned by the *Morte*-poet, it becomes clear that the dragon also represents the collateral damage that is an unavoidable consequence of such imperial endeavors.

As the poem proceeds, the dragon is transformed from a nightmarish figure to a military standard, rendering the dragon symbol a slippery imperial signifier. Furthermore, in translating the symbol of the dragon from the dream to the battlefield, the *Morte*-poet departs from Galfridian tradition. According to Geoffrey's *Historia*, before his battle with Lucius, Arthur "also set up the golden dragon, which he had for a standard" (123).[16] Given his Pendragon legacy and the earlier dream that links Arthur specifically with the dragon, Geoffrey's association is expected, but when the dragon emblem appears for the first time in battle in the *Morte Arthure* it is unexpectedly associated with Lucius and his Roman army. The messengers from the Marshal of France announce Lucius's invasion to Arthur saying, "He drawes into douce Fraunce, as Duchemen tellez, / Dresside with his dragouns, dredfull to schewe" [He draws into sweet France, as Germans tell, dressed with his dragons, dreadful to behold] (1251–52). The dragon's status as a Roman, not an Arthurian, emblem is reaffirmed later in the poem before the battle at Sessye, when Lucius and his army "Dresses vp dredfully the dragone of golde / With egles al ouer, enamelede of sable" [Raise up dreadfully the dragon of gold with eagles on every side, adorned with sable] (2026–27). Geoffrey's account, by contrast, associates Lucius and his Romans only with a golden eagle: "In the middle he [Lucius] also ordered fixed

---

[15] Göller, "The Dream of the Dragon and the Bear," in The *"Alliterative Morte Arthure,"* 132.

[16] "Ipse quoque . . . aureum draconem infixit quem pro uexillo habebat." Neil Wright, ed., *The Historia Regum Britannie of Geoffrey of Monmouth, I: Bern, Burgerbibliothek, MS. 568* (Cambridge: D. S. Brewer, 1991). All references to Geoffrey's *Historia* are from this edition.

firmly the golden eagle, which he had brought for a standard" (125).[17] Instead of adhering to the example of his Galfridian source, Arthurian tradition, and even Edward III, who appropriated this Pendragon standard for his own marches and battles, the *Morte*-poet renders "auream aquilam" as a "dragone of golde" and "egles . . . enamelede of sable," which transfers the golden feature of the eagles to the dragon, which had earlier been associated with Arthur in his dream.[18]

This use and then later rejection of the Galfridian tradition are manifestations of the *Morte*-poet's heraldic agenda. I support the view that the *Morte*-poet departs from his Galfridian source to borrow the language of another alliterative poem, *The Siege of Jerusalem*, in order to transfer the symbol of the dragon from Arthur to Lucius. It is admittedly difficult to make arguments about "borrowings" when dealing with formulaic poetry, but the *Morte Arthure* bears more than the "superficial resemblances" to its alliterative predecessors proposed by John Finlayson.[19] Certainly, many of the verbal parallels between the poems can be attributed to a common word-hoard, but there are undeniable similarities that suggest the direct influence of alliterative poems such as *The Destruction of Troy* and *The Siege of Jerusalem* on the writing of the *Morte Arthure*.[20] To date the poem accurately to 1399–1402, Hamel has convincingly argued for a compositional sequence that begins with *The Destruction of Troy*'s reference to Geoffrey Chaucer's *Troilus and Criseyde*, and then continues through the *Siege*-poet's use of *The Destruction of Troy* and the *Morte*-poet's use of both alliterative poems.[21] Hamel shies away from making a definitive claim that the *Morte*-poet drew material di-

---

[17] "In medio etiam auream aquilam quam pro uexillo duxerat iussit firmiter poni."

[18] Ingham, *Sovereign Fantasies*, 97.

[19] John Finlayson, ed., *Morte Arthure*, York Medieval Texts (Evanston, Ill.: Northwestern University Press, 1967), 11.

[20] For a brief discussion of the nature of this "formula" problem, see Hamel, *Morte Arthure*, 46–47. The verbal parallels are so clear that George Neilson actually claims that the same poet composed these poems, in *Huchown of the Awle Ryale, the Alliterative Poet* (Glasgow: James Maclehose & Sons, 1902). J. P. Oakden argues for relationships of dependence in "The Alliterative School," in *Alliterative Poetry in Middle English* (Manchester: Manchester University Press, 1935), 85–111. In critical response to these claims, Thorlac Turville–Petre contends that "tracing verbal parallels between the alliterative poems is a profitless task" and "far from facilitating the tracing of relationships between the poems, the collocational style more often obscures the evidence and makes the process of investigation almost impossible." See *The Alliterative Revival* (Cambridge: D. S. Brewer, 1977), 5, 29.

[21] Hamel, *Morte Arthure*, 53–58.

rectly from *The Destruction of Troy*, but she reveals the numerous correspondences with *The Siege of Jerusalem*: these include the shaving of messengers, the vowing on the Vernicle, the description of Lucius's camp, the "arming of the hero," and especially the distinctive use of the dragon emblem.[22]

The dragon, therefore, plays a significant role in the dating of the *Morte Arthure*. The *terminus ad quem* for the *Morte Arthure* has been largely accepted as 1402 ever since Larry Benson dated the poem based on the poet's idiosyncratic knowledge of Italian geography and association of the dragon imagery on the Viscount of Rome's shield (2052–57) with the arms of Giangaleazzo Visconti (d. 1402), who fell into ill repute after his contribution to the defeat of crusaders at Nicopolis in 1396.[23] The hostility expressed toward the Viscount in the poem, which Benson attributes to the late fourteenth-century English enmity toward the Visconti family, combined with other historical allusions to Sir John Montague and Joan of Navarre, indicates that this poem was completed no later than 1402.[24] Given the probability that the earliest of the eight copies of *The Siege of Jerusalem* dates to the 1390s, the *Morte*-poet would have had the time necessary to consult it extensively. Ralph Hanna and David Lawton even suggest that *The Siege of Jerusalem* may predate *Troilus and Criseyde*, a scenario that would allow for nearly twenty years

[22] Ibid., 47. See also Neilson, *Huchown of the Awle Ryale*, 47–50. He uses these correspondences to identify a common author and notes that the shaving topos also appears in *Ogier le Danois* and II Samuel 10:4. See also John Finlayson, "Rhetorical 'Descriptio' of Place in the Alliterative *Morte Arthure*," *MP* 61 (1963): 1–11; Derek Brewer, "The Arming of the Warrior in European Literature and Chaucer," in *Chaucerian Problems and Perspectives*, ed. Edward Vasta and Zacharias P. Thundy (Notre Dame, Ind.: Notre Dame University Press, 1979), 221–43 (233–34). For a discussion of the Vernicle and its relationship to Roman pilgrimages, see Jonathan Sumption, *Pilgrimage: An Image of Mediaeval Religion* (Totowa, N.J.: Rowman & Littlefield, 1975), 249–50.

[23] Benson, "The Date of the Alliterative *Morte Arthure*," in *Medieval Studies in Honor of Lillian Herlands Hornstein*, ed. Jess B. Bessinger and R. R. Raymo (New York: New York University Press, 1976), 19–40 (27); George Neilson suggests that this coat of arms was a direct reference to the Visconti family and the Dukes of Milan in "The Viscount of Rome in 'Morte Arthure,'" *Athenaeum* 3916 (1902): 652–53. Hamel, *Morte Arthure*, 54.

[24] Benson suggests that the reference to "Mownttagus" (3773) as supporters of Mordred is a pointed attack on the Lollard Sir John Montague, who was lynched for his role in a conspiracy against Henry IV in 1400. See "The Date of the Alliterative *Morte Arthure*," 30–35; Hamel supports this dating by noting the unique reference to the victim of the Giant of St. Michael's Mount as the "Duchess of Brittany" (864), a title held by Joan of Navarre, who would have relinquished this title in 1403, when she became Queen of England. See Hamel, *Morte Arthure*, 54.

during which the *Morte*-poet could have drawn material from this alliterative predecessor.[25]

I want to argue that this destabilization of the dragon as a marker of martial authority is in fact a distinctly alliterative technique. The *Morte*-poet does more than simply draw on imagery from the *The Siege of Jerusalem*—he actualizes the heraldic potential of the *Siege*-dragon, a rhetorical move that complicates not simply the earlier Galfridian attribution of the dragon symbol of imperial power to Arthur, but all heraldic claims to nobility. On the textual level, the peregrination of the dragon from Britain to Rome in the *Morte Arthure* is evidence of a switch in source material, namely, from Geoffrey's *Historia* to *The Siege of Jerusalem*. This is a provocative shift since the *Siege*-dragon appears as a redoubtable sign of the Roman Empire. When Vespasian and his Roman army leave Nero in Rome to exact Christian vengeance upon Jerusalem, they "Lauȝte leue at þat lord, leften his sygne, / A grete dragoun of gold" [took leave of that lord, lifting his insignia, a great dragon of gold] (283–84). And in the later description of the symbols that are set above Vespasian's tent, the *Siege*-poet juxtaposes the eagle and dragon in a way strikingly similar to the description of Lucius's standard at the battle of Sessye in the *Morte Arthure* (2026–27): "A gay egle of gold on gilde appul, / With grete dragouns grym, alle in gold" [a gay eagle of gold on a gilded apple, with terrifying dragons, all in gold] (326–27). Given the prevalence of verbal parallels between the two alliterative poems and their equivalent use of the dragon as a symbol of empire, it is evident that the *Morte*-poet looked to his source in *The Siege of Jerusalem* for attribution of the dragon-standard to the Roman imperialists.[26] More important, such a broad connotative use of the dragon to represent its destructive capacity places an emphasis on the effect of the signifier rather than the identification of the signified. In other words, whom the dragon represents matters less than the power it wields.

This indicates that the *Morte*-poet gained more than a symbol of the Roman Empire from *The Siege of Jerusalem*—he also obtained a pedagogic perspective on visual assertions of sovereignty. The employment of such heraldic symbols as the dragon and eagle calls attention to the caution-

[25] Ralph Hanna and David Lawton, eds., *The Siege of Jerusalem*, EETS o.s. 320 (Oxford: Oxford University Press, 2003), xxxv–xxxvii. All references to the poem are from this edition.

[26] For a discussion of the literary emergence of the dragon-standard, see Hamel, *Morte Arthure*, 46–52.

ary lesson they teach their observers. To understand this sensibility of imperial signification, we should turn to other references to the golden dragon in *The Siege of Jerusalem* that demonstrate a pedagogy of terror consistent with the *Siege*-poet's unapologetic representation of martial violence. The dragon-standard does not simply represent imperial power, but actually broadcasts the destruction it will inflict from as far as four miles away. As Vespasian and his army approach the walls of Jerusalem,

> A dragoun was dressed, drawyn alofte,
> Wyde gapande of gold [þe] go[llet] to s[che]we,
> With arwes armed in þe mouþe, and also he hadde
> A fauchyn vnder his feet with foure kene bladdys. . .
>
> Þe b[es]t[e] by [his] briȝtnesse burnes myȝt knowe
> Foure myle þerfro, so þe feldes schonen.
> + On eche pomel were pyȝt penseles hyȝe
> Of selke and sendel, with seluere ybetyn.
> Hit glitered as gled-fure— ful of gold riche
> Ouer al þe cite to se— as þe sonne bemys.
>
> (393–96, 415–20)

[A dragon of gold was prepared, raised high to behold the wide gaping gullet armed with arrows in the mouth, and also he had under his feet a falchion with four keen blades . . . Men might recognize the monster by his brightness from four miles away, so much the fields shone. On each pommel were placed high pennons of silk and cendal, beaten with silver. As the sun beams, it glittered like a glowing fire full of rich gold, visible above the whole city.]

Calling attention to the gaping mouth of the dragon, the *Siege*-poet reveals knowledge of earlier models, such as that of the western Roman emperor Otho IV, who at the battle of Bouvines in 1214 displayed a cloth standard that would enlarge when the wind would blow through its wide-open jaws.[27] By constructing the standard this way, the dragon swells to a formidable size as it is carted toward the enemy during a march or siege. The detail of the description of the emblem, as well as phrases such as "burnes myȝt knowe / Foure myle þerfro" and "Ouer al

---

[27] J. Heller, ed., *Willelmi Chronica Andrensis,* in *Monumenta Germaniae Historica, Scriptores* (Hanover, 1879), 24.684 ; Tatlock, "The Dragons of Wessex and Wales," 224.

þe cite to se," indicates that this dragon is designed to be seen from afar and inspire fear in those who witness its approach. Within the context of an impending siege, the wide-open mouth signifies a subjugation of its victims, in which the restriction of the city's food supply will effect a shift of its inhabitants from eaters to the eaten—this becomes disturbingly literalized in the example of Mary and the eating of her son (1081–88). With the aid of sun-reflecting shields, the Roman army presents a dragon whose golden gaping mouth represents their greedy desire to pillage the city for its legendary riches and exterminate its inhabitants.

The implication that the raising of the dragon leads to the consumption of human flesh is supported by manuscript evidence. Recent editors Hanna and Lawton emend the line that begins with "Wyde gapande of gold" as "[þe] go[llet] to s[che]we," a reading that amplifies the description of the dragon's mouth, because they suspect that the line is a corruption of the original that followed the example of its French source in *La Vengeance de Nostre-Seigneur*.[28] However, Kölbing and Day read the b-line as "gomes to swelwe" [to swallow men], since this is how it appears in the majority of the manuscripts, which instead identifies the dragon's food of choice and method of human destruction.[29] The juxtaposition of the gold mouth with the act of swallowing is also supported thematically later in the poem, when the Jewish inhabitants of the city resort to eating their gold in order to hide it from the Roman invaders (1165–68).

Read this way, the sign of the dragon communicates more than just impending defeat—it broadcasts comprehensive corporeal annihilation. The raising of this standard is then a sign of its bearers' intent to fight to the death in the same way that Henry III used the dragon emblem in 1257 to express his imperial resolve in defeating the Welsh.[30] Vespasian's dragon then promises a similar unrelenting *exterminium* to the Jewish inhabitants of Jerusalem.

> [On] a bal of brennande gold   þe beste was [a]s[sised],
> His taille trayled þeraboute   þat tourne scholde he neuere

[28] Hanna and Lawton, *Siege of Jerusalem*, 114.

[29] See line 390 of E. Kölbing and Mabel Day's edition, *The Siege of Jerusalem* (Oxford: Oxford University Press, 1932).

[30] Hamel, ed., *Morte Arthure*, 49. Matthew Paris in his *Chronica Majora* refers to Henry III's dragon-standard as a sign "qui . . . exterminium generale Walliae minabatur" [which threatened the destruction of the Welsh people]. See Tatlock, "The Dragons of Wessex and Wales," 226; Matthew Paris, *Chronica Majora*, vol. 5, ed. Henry R. Luard, Rolls Series 57 (London: HMSO, 1880), 648.

> Whan he was lifte vpon lofte,   þer þe lord werred
> Bot ay lokande on þe londe,   till þat + lauȝte were.
> Þerby þe cite myȝt se   no s[agh]tlyng wolde rise
> Ne no trete of no trewes,   bot þe toun ȝelde.
>
> (401–6)

[The beast was placed on a sphere of burnished gold; his tail trailed around it so that he should never turn when he was lifted up high, ever looking on the land where the lord warred, until it would be taken. Thereby the city might see that no settlement would arise, neither treaty nor truce, unless the town would yield.]

Again, the emphasis on the display of the standard so that "þe cite myȝt se" indicates the pedagogic function of the sign, but here the message of the dragon is made explicit. As long as the emblem is raised, the Romans will fight to the death and not consider a truce unless the inhabitants plead for mercy and grant the city to their besiegers.[31] This kind of symbolic overkill transgresses the rules of siegecraft and emphasizes the cruelty of those who bear this imperial signifier. The *Siege*-poet's use of the dragon standard is particularly clever: by demonstrating its terrifying potential, he highlights the indiscriminate violence that is the necessary consequence of such assertions of the Roman Empire.

The association between the sign of the dragon and Roman imperial destruction is vivid in *The Siege of Jerusalem*, but in the *Morte Arthure* the relationship between the dragon and the Romans at first glance seems to be an afterthought. I want to suggest that this is not the case, however. Whereas the dragon is earlier aligned with Arthur in its battle with the bear and remains consistent in the Galfridian sources, later in the poem when Arthur meets Lucius in battle, the dragon becomes a Roman signifier. Yet in each appearance of the dragon, it retains its didactic power for its victims by highlighting the consequences of martial violence. In the dream, the *Morte*-poet embellishes his Galfridian sources to claim that the dragon will "drynchen" his own people, and when the dragon appears as a standard in battle, a succession of scenes

---

[31] As Hamel notes, such a presentation of this sign of doom "would be superfluous in the normal medieval siege, the laws of which ordinarily proclaimed no quarter to the inhabitants, 'bot þe toun ȝelde.'" See *Morte Arthure*, 49; M. H. Keen, *The Laws of War in the Late Middle Ages* (London: Routledge & Kegan Paul, 1965), 120–21.

of the bodily dismemberment of the contending warriors follows. The notion that militaristic aggression leads to an endless cycle of destruction resonates with premodern and modern theories of violence.[32] In a sermon on the feast of Saint Laurence, Saint Augustine argues that violence against wrongdoers will beget violence against the righteous.[33] Echoing this sentiment in her famous reflection, *On Violence*, Hannah Arendt remarks, "The practice of violence, like all action, changes the world, but the most probable change is to a more violent world."[34] As a symbol of destruction in both poems, the dragon signifies the reproductive and arbitrary nature of violence, thwarting readings that would valorize any particular military campaign, British or Roman.

The *Morte*-poet's dependence upon *The Siege of Jerusalem* is supported further by his use of the dragon's gaping mouth and its consumption of victims. This correspondence of the dragon signifier with violence reaches an interpretive climax in the perplexing ekphrasis of the aforementioned shield of the Viscount of Rome:

> He drisside in a derfe shelde   endenttyd with sable,
> With a dragone engowllede,   dredful to schewe,
> Deuorande a dolphin   with dolefull lates,
> In seyne that oure soueraygne   sulde be distroyede
> And all don of dawez   with dynttez of swerddez;
> For thare es noghte bot dede   thare the dragone es raissede.
>
> (2052–57)

[He dressed in a strong shield edged with sable [adorned] with a dragon with gaping jaws, dreadful to behold, devouring a dolphin with a doleful expression, as a sign that our sovereign should be destroyed and that his days should be

---

[32] For a recent discussion of violence in medieval literature, see Albrecht Classen, "Violence in the Shadows of the Court," in *Violence in Medieval Courtly Literature: A Casebook*, ed. Albrecht Classen (London and New York: Routledge, 2004), 1–36.

[33] Augustine, *Political Writings*, ed. E. M. Atkins and R. J. Dodaro (Cambridge: Cambridge University Press, 2001), 113. It is also provocative to note that *The Siege of Jerusalem* was likely composed by an Augustinian canon at Bolton Priory. See Ralph Hanna, "Contextualizing *The Siege of Jerusalem*," *YLS* 13 (1999): 109–21 (115–16); Elisa Narin van Court, "*The Siege of Jerusalem* and Recuperative Readings," in *Pulp Fictions of Medieval England: Essays in Popular Romance*, ed. Nicola McDonald (Manchester: Manchester University Press, 2004): 151–70 (164–65); "*The Siege of Jerusalem* and Augustinian Historians: Writing About Jews in Fourteenth-Century England." *ChauR* 29.3 (1995): 227–48; Chism, *Alliterative Revivals*, 156–60.

[34] Hannah Arendt, *On Violence* (New York: Harcourt Brace Jovanovich, 1970), 80.

ended by dints of swords, for there is nothing but death where the dragon is raised.]

It is important to mention here that Hamel emends Robert Thornton's scribal "engowschede" to "engowllede" (2053), which originates from the heraldic vocabulary of *engoulé de geule*, meaning "with gaping jaws."[35] While the usual pattern of alliteration in such verse, aa/ax, might seem to call Hamel's emendation of "engowschede" into question, as Hoyt Duggan notes, Robert Thornton's texts of *The Siege of Jerusalem* and *The Parlement of the Thre Ages* demonstrate that he was "an unusually careful copyist" and "content to copy irregularly alliterating lines," which suggests that he reproduced in his *Morte Arthure* an irregularity found in his exemplar.[36] Certainly his exemplar could have been corrupt, as Judith A. Jefferson and Ad Putter speculate, but Hamel's emendation is supported further by the fact that it retains the *en-* prefix that accords with the aural context of the word, which is riddled with *en-* modifiers: "enuyous" (2047), "enuerounde" (2051), "and "endenttyd" (2052).[37] The authority of Hamel's emendation of Thornton is confirmed by the fact that the image of the dragon devouring a dolphin thematically evokes *The Siege of Jerusalem*'s dragon, which is described as having a gaping mouth that consumes humans. Whereas the open mouth of the dragon

[35] See Hamel, ed., *Morte Arthure*, 49, 316. For more on *engoulé de geule,* see Gérard Brault, *Early Blazon: Heraldic Terminology in the Twelfth and Thirteenth Centuries with Special Reference to Arthurian Heraldry* (Oxford: Clarendon Press, 1972), 178–79. Benson and Krishna in their editions do not emend *engowschede*, which the *OED* defines as "stout, fleshy." The *OED* claims that *engowschede* derives from the Old French *engoussé*, but, as Hamel notes, forms of this word appear in rare instances. Frédéric Godefroy in his *Dictionnaire de l'ancienne langue française*, 10 vols. (Paris: F. Vieweg, 1880–1902), cites two occurrences of the word. For the mid-fifteenth-century instance, see "engousser"; for the next occurrence, see "engoursé" (3:176). This second instance comes from a nineteenth-century edition of fables from the Middle Ages, which defines this word as "gros, gras, bien portant." Adolf Tobler and Erhard von Lomätsch in their *Altfranzösisches Wörterbuch* (Wiesbaden: F. Steiner, 1956) contest this gloss and suggest *engonser* or *engonssier*. Since none of these glosses is relevant in describing the dragon in a heraldic manner, the *MED* suggests *encowschede*, a relative of the heraldic *couchant*, which means "lying down with head erect." But since no heraldic description includes the notions of both *vorant* and *couchant* as in "deuorande a dolphin," Hamel substitutes *engowllede* because it matches the prototype of the dragon from *Siege*, which describes it as "wyde gapande . . . gomes to swelwe" (Kölbing and Day, ed. *Siege of Jerusalem* , 390). Hamel further suggests that the "sch" may have been used because of its proximity to "schelde" in the line above and "schewe" at the end of the line.

[36] Hoyt Duggan, "Alliterative Patterning as a Basis for Emendation in Middle English Alliterative Poetry," *SAC* 8 (1986): 73–105 (76).

[37] Judith A. Jefferson and Ad Putter, "Alliterative Patterning in the *Morte Arthure*," *SP* 102 (2005): 415–33.

surely originates in a tradition of dragon-standards whose gaping jaws caught the wind and inflated their bodies, it is only in *The Siege of Jerusalem* and the *Morte Arthure* that these dragons are described as possessing the capacity to swallow their foes.

The switch from the human to dolphin victim is a curious change that reaffirms the *Morte*-poet's continual employment of subtle connotations, but this alteration also serves to critique the nature of sovereignty and obscure distinctions between the conquerors and the conquered in war. The enigmatic ekphrasis of the shield is reminiscent of Aeneas's confusion in deciphering the famous shield he receives in Virgil's *Aeneid*, an episode that has sparked considerable critical comment.[38] The *Morte*-poet provides a similarly complex ekphrasis of the imperial implications of the dragon on the Viscount's shield that incorporates both antithetical martial ethics and specific historical references. To understand the hermeneutic possibilities of this dragon symbol, we should examine the Viscount's shield within its historical context. In his attempt to date the poem, Larry Benson reveals the poet's extraordinary knowledge of Italian geography. For confirmation, he turns to the chronicle of Adam of Usk, who was intimately familiar with Italian affairs in his exile in Rome. In his chronicle, Adam describes the traditional Visconti shield as one that depicts a snake devouring a man, which suggests that the *Morte*-poet's illustration of the Viscount of Rome's shield points to the Visconti family in Italy.[39] In response to this possibility, Karl Lippe contends: "Although one can argue that 'snake' and 'dragon' are used indiscriminately, various reasons for such alterations can be suggested: either

---

[38] Interpretations of the scene divided twentieth-century critics into two camps: those who read the shield as an example of Augustan triumphalism and those of the so-called Harvard School, who identify the darker symbols that connote a more pessimistic view of Roman *imperium*. Whereas critics such as Philip Hardie read the shield as a justification and prophecy of the Roman imperial universe, the Harvard School Virgilians interpret the shield, and the epic as a whole, as representative of the costs of empire both for victor and victim. For an example of the optimistic reading of the future of the Roman Empire in the *Aeneid*, see Philip Hardie, *Virgil's Aeneid: Cosmos and Imperium* (Oxford: Clarendon Press, 1986), 336–76. For the pessimistic perspective of the Harvard School, see S. J. Harrison, "Some Views of the *Aeneid* in the Twentieth Century," in *Oxford Readings in Vergil's Aeneid*, ed. S. J. Harrison (Oxford: Oxford University Press, 1990), 1–20; Adam Parry, "The Two Voices of Virgil's *Aeneid*," *Arion* 2 (1963): 66–80; Wendell Clausen, "An Interpretation of the *Aeneid*," *Harvard Studies in Classical Philology* 68 (1964): 139–47; Michael Putnam, *The Poetry of the Aeneid* (Cambridge, Mass.: Harvard University Press, 1965).

[39] E. M. Thompson, ed., *Chronicon Adae de Usk*, 2nd ed. (London: H. Frowde, 1904), 75. See also Benson, "The Date of the Alliterative *Morte Arthure*," 27.

the author did not know the historically correct arms, he wanted to avoid an allusion which he felt was too pointed, or he wanted to ensure a particular interpretation, as is the case here. In this instance the charge functions as a symbol which means 'that our sovereign was to be destroyed.' "[40] The dolphin in particular was commonly known in the fourteenth century as a heraldic sign of the Dauphin, the one who would inherit the kingdom of France. By depicting the dolphin's death at the jaws of the dragon and interpreting this scene in the following line as a "seyne that oure soueraygne sulde be distroyede," the shield, representing the dragon as a symbol of imperial destruction and the dolphin as a symbol of the victims of empire, then serves as a warning about the consequences of such assertions of sovereignty over France.[41]

Numerous interpretive possibilities defy attempts to fix a clear referent for the dragon, and when we consider the multiple uses of the dragon as a night terror, battle standard, and shield symbol, we can conclude that maintaining continuity and clarity was not the concern of the *Morte*-poet. In fact, there are other compelling aspects of *The Siege of Jerusalem* and its historiographic perspective that would have provided more than enough reason to reject the Galfridian sources.

A literary device of *The Siege of Jerusalem* that the *Morte*-poet clearly found attractive was the didactic representation of violence through such symbols of destruction as the dragon. In *The Siege of Jerusalem*, the graphic descriptions of dismemberment, mutilation, and cannibalism

---

[40] Karl Lippe, "Armorial Bearings and Their Meaning," in *The "Alliterative Morte Arthure": A Reassessment of the Poem*, ed. Göller, 96–105 (100).

[41] Ibid., 100–101. Hamel even goes so far as to suggest that the Viscount's shield points to Edward III, who famously desired the French throne. Is this, then, the sole reason for the *Morte*-poet's decision to shift the dragon signifier from the Britons to the Romans? Hamel believes this to be the case because "there would have been no particular reason for rejecting his chronicle [i.e., Galfridian] sources in favor of *The Siege of Jerusalem*," especially while Edward III was in power, since at the battle of Crecy in 1346, he bore the dragon-standard as a symbol of English kingship for the last time before the Tudors took it up a century later (53). She further suggests that the *Morte*-poet may have felt compelled to make a late revision to his poem in 1401, when Owen Glendower, possibly motivated by the Galfridian account, appropriated the sign of the dragon for his emblem. According to this logic, the fact that a rebel to English sovereignty had adopted the dragon for his own would have compelled the *Morte*-poet to turn to his source in *The Siege of Jerusalem*, which attributed the dragon to the Romans. She concludes by claiming that this late revision "creates a certain ambiguity that further revision might have clarified." See *Morte Arthure*, 53–54. Ingham disputes Hamel's claim that the dragon-standard "fell into disuse," since there was a continuous Welsh textual tradition that supported the Galfridian account of the dragon as a symbol that "was actively used by those contesting, rather than proclaiming, Plantagenet rule." *Sovereign Fantasies*, 97–98.

obscure differences between the Jews and Romans, the besiegers and the besieged, so much so that even the bodies of the prominent Roman leaders Sir Sabyn and Vitellius end up in ditches (1202–4) and contaminated water (948) that also serve as the final resting places for their Jewish victims. The *Siege*-poet's thematic use of death as the great equalizer and graphic descriptions of the casualties of war as a means to terrify his audience affords him a corporeal space on which he can inscribe a warning about the inextricability of violence from imperialism.[42] In the same way, the *Morte*-poet complicates binary oppositions such as Britain/Rome and sovereign/subject through graphic scenes of corporeal violence and signifying play.

For example, if we return to the description of the Viscount of Rome's shield, we find an unsettling message for the one occupying the position of "sovereign." The poet glosses the heraldic symbol, asserting that the dragon eating the dolphin is a sign that "oure soueraygne" should be destroyed. The immediate context gives no clue to whom "oure" refers; as a signifier, then, it can be attached to several possibilities at once. If we read it as self-reflexive, the sovereign could refer to Lucius, but if we read it in the pedagogic manner of a battle-standard, the symbol is a warning to Arthur. And if we read on, we find a conclusion that confounds a strong interpretation either way: "For thare es noghte bot dede thare the dragone es raissede." In other words, the identification of the actual "soueraygne" is not relevant—rather it is the assertion of sovereignty that causes destruction. Since both Arthur and Lucius in different episodes throughout the poem represent the dragon, then neither can expect anything other than "death where the dragon is raised." And to complicate the matter further, the dragon immediately performs as promised by presaging the violent death of the one who had most recently raised the symbol: the Viscount of Rome. Sir Valiant fulfills his vow from the beginning of the poem by piercing the Viscount with a lance:

> Abowne þe spayre a spanne   emange þe schortte rybbys,
> That the splent and the spleen   on the spere lengez.
> The blode sprente owtte and spredde   as þe horse spryngez,
> And he sproulez full spakely,   bot spekes he no more.
>
> (2060–63)

---

[42] For a more extensive discussion of the anti-Galfridian nature of *The Siege of Jerusalem*, see Alex Mueller, "Corporal Terror: Critiques of Imperialism in *The Siege of Jerusalem*," *PQ* 84.3 (2005): 287–310.

[A span above the waist between the short ribs so that the armor plate and the spleen hung on the spear. The blood spurt out and spread as the horse springs, and he sprawls out swiftly, but he speaks no more.]

The forensic detail and description of the course of the lance through the short ribs and the spleen highlights the specifics of the Viscount's destruction, and the emphasis on the remains of the spleen lingering on the lance, the spraying blood, and convulsing body intensifies the pedagogic function of the act. On a literal level, the Welsh king Sir Valiant has avenged the wrongs of an old enemy, but the juxtaposition of the sign of the dragon and the extended account of the Viscount's death, which surpasses even that of Lucius (2252–54), reveal the all-encompassing destruction that results from such assertions of sovereignty.

And if we explore the many historical valences of the "Viscount" in the fourteenth century, we can corroborate such a focus on comprehensive and indiscriminate violence. The attribution of the "dolphin" to the "Viscount" confounds historical identifications and reaffirms the *Morte*-poet's predilection for signifying play. As noted above, the "soueraygne" as "dolphin" could refer to the future King of France, but if we examine further the significance of the textual reference to the "Viscount," this sovereign could be the actual King of France, who was the father-in-law of Giangaleazzo Visconti, Sire of Milan. A "Viscount of Rome" did not exist in the fourteenth century, but the title, which was used throughout the Holy Roman Empire, was made famous by the Visconti family, whose name originated in the office of *vice comes* of the emperor.[43] Since Giangaleazzo was also the son-in-law of the King of France, the dolphin on the Viscount's shield gestures toward Giangaleazzo's familial connections to French royalty.[44] For the *Morte*-poet, such a dual identification

[43] Benson, "The Date of the Alliterative *Morte Arthure*," 26. According to the *OED*, the first English use is by Trevisa in 1387, and the second is in *Morte* around 1400.

[44] Neilson was the first to contend that the "Viscount" in the poem actually referred to the Visconti family, which explained the change in his name from "Viscount of Rome" (326) to "Viscount of Valence" (2047). According to Neilson, Valence actually refers to Vallenza, which was under Visconti control, and therefore Giangaleazzo Visconti was both the "Viscount of Rome" because he filled the office of *vice comes* for the emperor and the "Viscount of Valence" because he was the lord of Vallenza. See "The Viscount of Rome in the 'Morte Arthure,'" 652–53. George B. Parks contests this connection because he assumes that *Morte* was composed in the 1360s, noting that it would have been too early for a reference to Vallenza because it did not come under Visconti control until 1382. He further suggests that the reference "would hardly be tactful for the poet to refer to a contemporary ruling family as miscreants and rightfully slain by one of Arthur's knights." See "King Arthur and the Roads to Rome," *JEGP* 45

of the "dolphin" is evidence of his historical awareness and insistence on the unreliability and self-destructive nature of such imperial signifiers. After all, if the Viscount of Rome refers to Giangaleazzo and the dolphin on his shield depicts his father-in-law, the macabre description of the Viscount of Rome's death fulfills what his shield predicts: "es noghte bot dede thare the dragone es raissede." The dolphin, the Viscount of Rome, Giangaleazzo, and the King of France are left dead in the dragon's wake.

Such references to historical figures are compelling, but the poem eludes any definite identifications. As the above analysis demonstrates, such arguments are ultimately circuitous and not provable, which indicates that the *Morte*-poet is not interested in condemning or praising particular sovereigns. For instance, if we follow the Visconti lead even further, we can reaffirm the *Morte*-poet's fetish for contradiction. Even though the Viscontis may have been held in high regard in the 1360s, when the English court was in the midst of marriage negotiations between their prince and a daughter of Galeazzo II, by the end of the fourteenth century, the Viscontis had fallen out of English favor. Giangaleazzo murdered his uncle Bernabó in 1385, an act that English writers, including Chaucer, emphatically condemned. The Monk of the *Canterbury Tales* records the deed this way:

> Thy brother sone, that was thy double allye,
> For he thy nevew was and sone-in-lawe,
> Withinne his prisoun made thee to dye . . .[45]

His familial treason soon became a martial treason of the kind that caused him to be seen as an Aeneas or Antenor who betrayed Troy. Froissart asserts that in 1396 Giangaleazzo played a significant role in the defeat of the Christian army at Nicopolis because he had informed his allies, the Turks, of the approach of the crusaders. Perplexed that Giangaleazzo "would seek love or alliance with a king miscreant," Frois-

---

(1946): 164–70 (165). Benson notes that if we assume an early composition of the *Morte*, the reference to the Viscount's domain of "Viterbe to Venyse" (2025) would also have been anachronistic, since it was not until 1399 that the Viscontis acquired Pisa and expanded their territory south to Viterbo. If we date the poem to 1400, however, this identification presents no problems. See "The Date of the Alliterative *Morte Arthure*," 27.

[45] *The Monk's Tale*, VII.2403–5, in Larry D. Benson, gen. ed., *The Riverside Chaucer* (Boston: Houghton Mifflin, 1987). See Benson, "The Date of the Alliterative *Morte Arthure*," 28.

sart suggests that he "held the opinion and error of his father, declaring and maintaining that they should neither worship nor believe in God."[46] His treason had heretical implications that would have incited the ire of the small number of crusaders who had survived the massacre at Nicopolis. Even though Adam of Usk held the Visconti leadership in high regard, Benson suggests that Giangaleazzo's perfidy would have been the likely inspiration for the *Morte*-poet's dismemberment of the Viscount: "Our poet, whose attitude towards Lucius's pagan allies indicates that he shared the crusading zeal that led to the disaster at Nicopolis, very likely shared Froissart's opinion of the Visconti."[47] While it is appropriate to posit the *Morte Arthure* as well as *The Siege of Jerusalem* as contributors to late fourteenth-century crusade polemic, the Viscount's violent death is too symbolically complex to characterize as a fantasized act of Christian vengeance. As Benson admits, the negative perspective of the Viscontis was far from universal and it is not evident that the *Morte*-poet made any connection between the Sire of Milan and the Visconti. To account for this ambiguity, Benson suggests that the *Morte*-poet may have been "simply confused."[48] While Benson's hypothesis is a possibility, the symbolic portability of the dragon, the evocative gloss of "oure soueraygne," and the dissonant use of violence to portray the Viscount's death combine to reveal a pattern of obscurity that denies clear distinctions between conquerors and victims and highlights the death incurred in such assertions of sovereignty. This "confusion" is then a fusing of historiographic voices that is embodied by the sign of the dragon: the dragon is both Roman and Briton, sovereign and victim, glorious and cruel.

Heraldic Historiography

The death that the dragon signifies is the theme of the *Morte*-poet's heraldic rewriting of British history. In highlighting the corporeal violence and the sacrifice of the innocent, the act of raising the dragon is a translation of tyranny. This new heraldic hermeneutic consequently

---

[46] "quéroit amour et alliance à un roi mescréant. . . . Et tint l'opinion et erreur de son père, car ils disoient et maintenoient que jà ne adoreroient ni creroient (croiroient) en Dieu qu'ils pussent." J. A. Buchon, ed., *Chroniques de Froissart*, vol. 13 (Paris, 1825), 333, 339. See also Benson, "The Date of the Alliterative *Morte Arthure*," 28.

[47] Ibid., 28–29.

[48] Ibid., 29.

evacuates the authority of coats of arms and recitations of lineage in scenes of battle. As the maculation of Gawain's arms makes clear, heraldic symbols fail to legitimize the nobility of their bearers. This interpretive obscurity defies what Smith has noted as the basic function of heraldry, which was to distinguish aristocratic households, a practice that was believed to have begun in ancient Troy. According to a household treatise in Cambridge University Library MS Dd.10.52, heraldic symbols began to flourish because "ther was so huge a multitude of people that oon might not be knowe from a nothir."[49] If knights could trace their lineage back to Troy through one of these original symbols, their noble heritage could be reasonably assured. A number of contemporary alliterative poems remind their aristocratic readers of this ancient origin, including *Sir Gawain and the Green Knight*, *Winner and Waster*, *St. Erkenwald*, and especially *The Destruction of Troy*. The *Morte Arthure* is no exception. Trojan lineage is invoked in multiple ways throughout the poem, from the heraldic assertions of Sir Priamus and Sir Clegis to the dream of the Nine Worthies and the epilogue to Arthur's death. Yet in each case, the *Morte*-poet reinterprets these heraldic devices, transforming them into signs of death and destruction rather than certificates of nobility and authority.

In order to understand this heraldic historiography, we should turn first to the dream of the Wheel of Fortune and Nine Worthies, an episode that establishes Arthur's imperial lineage. We hear the accounts not only of such doomed conquerors as Alexander and Julius Caesar but also of Hector of Troy, the glorious ancestor of Arthur.[50] Hector holds special significance because of his central role in the contemporary alliterative romance *The Destruction of Troy*, a text that emphasizes his death as much as his life.[51] It is then no surprise to readers of alliterative ro-

---

[49] I rely on Smith's reading of this household treatise, Cambridge University Library, MS Dd.10.52, fol. I, in *Arts of Possession*, 63.

[50] As Lee Patterson suggests, Fortune's wheel "expresses a historiography of recurrence," whereby Alexander's example is incessantly repeated in figures both pagan and Christian in a way that does not privilege one victim of imperial desire over another. See "The Historiography of Romance and the Alliterative *Morte Arthure*," *JMRS* 13 (1983): 1–32; reprinted as "The Romance of History and the Alliterative *Morte Arthure*," in *Negotiating the Past: The Historical Understanding of Medieval Literature* (Madison: University of Wisconsin Press, 1987), 197–230 (225).

[51] While the Galfridian treatment of Trojan historiography upholds Hector as a great king and virtuous warrior, the Hector who takes center stage in this romance is a corpse that Priam desperately attempts to keep living for Trojan eyewitnesses through a complex method of preservation that incessantly pours balm into his head (8726–32). See John Clerk of Whalley, *The Destruction of Troy: A Diplomatic and Color Facsimile Edition, Hunterian MS V.2.8 in Glasgow University Library*, ed. Hiroyuki Matsumoto (Ann

mance that Hector is one of the nine who laments his fall: "And nowe my lordchippes are loste and laide foreuer!" [And now my lordships are lost and laid low forever!] (3293). Even though this comment parallels that of the other eight conquerors, his status would have been of particular interest for an English-reading audience, which would have considered him to be a historical ancestor. In fact, his position on the wheel encourages readers to view this scene within the context of his previous appearances in the poem, in which he is invoked as a proof of nobility.

The most striking of these instances occurs during the foraging expedition, often characterized as a romance subplot, in which Gawain meets a foreign knight named Priamus.[52] A fierce battle ensues and Gawain emerges victorious, but not without suffering a grave wound. In the

---

Arbor: University of Michigan Press, 2002). Any future citations are from Matsumoto's edition. This macabre machinery ultimately fails to preserve Troy, a result that fashions Hector instead as the ultimate casualty of war and symbol of the destruction that will plague Trojan progeny. Hamel observes that Hector's self-description in the *Morte Arthure* departs from the popular tradition of viewing him as a chivalrous knight. Instead, Hector identifies himself as a courtly lover: "On ʒone see hafe I sitten als souerayne and lorde, / And ladys me louede to lappe in theyre armes" [On that seat have I sat as sovereign and lord, and ladies loved to twine me in their arms] (3291–92). The *Morte*-poet likely drew this description from a misreading of *The Destruction of Troy*'s illustration of Priam's sons, in which Hector is lauded for both his martial prowess and his popularity among "ledys": "Was neuer red in no Romance of Renke vpon erthe / So well louty with all ledys þat in his lond dwelt" [There was never read in any romance of a man upon the earth, so well loved by all the people that dwelt in his land] (3897–8). Since "ledys" is a translation of Guido delle Colonne's "regnicolis" (86) or "dwellers in his kingdom" in the *Historia destructionis Troiae*, it is probable that Clerk did not have "ladies" in mind. See Guido de Columnis, *Historia Destructionis Troiae*, ed. Nathaniel Edward Griffin (Cambridge, Mass.: Mediaeval Academy of America, 1936). The reference to "Romance" may have led the *Morte*-poet to misconstrue the context as courtly and substitute the "a" for "e" in "ledys," a common misreading of a cursive hand. Since no other illustration of Hector as a womanizer exists, this error in reading suggests that all of the formulaic parallels between the battle scenes of each poem may not solely originate in a common word hoard and may be evidence of a relationship of dependence. A separate oral tradition may have fostered the image of a licentious Hector, but given the *Morte*-poet's tendency to use multiple sources at once, particularly in this scene where he combines the trope of the Nine Worthies with the Boethian Wheel of Fortune, it is more likely that he drew from *The Destruction of Troy* extensively to illustrate the horrors of war and capitalize upon the didactic power of the image of Britain's glorious ancestor. See Hamel, ed., *Morte Arthure*, 51–52. For more on the *Morte*-poet's unique use of *Fortuna* and the Nine Worthies, see Anke Janssen, "The Dream of the Wheel of Fortune," in *The Alliterative Morte Arthure: A Reassessment of the Poem*, ed. Göller, 140–52; Finlayson, *Morte Arthure*, 13.

[52] For a full discussion of this episode, see Patterson, *Negotiating the Past*, 217–29. He suggests that the *Morte*-poet draws on two sources in this scene, the *Fuerres de Gadres* and *Fierabras*. The *Fuerres* is attached to the *Roman d'Alexandre* and can be found in E. C. Armstrong, ed., *The Medieval French Roman d'Alexandre, vol. 2: Version of Alexandre de Paris*, Elliott Monographs 37 (Princeton: Princeton University Press, 1937), 60–127.

conventional heraldic manner, the strange warrior identifies his noble lineage through his father, who, he asserts, "es of Alexandire blode, ouerlynge of kynges, / The vncle of his ayele sir Ector of Troye" [is of Alexander's blood, overlord of kings, the uncle of his heir, Sir Hector of Troy] (2603–4). This claim establishes a common bloodline between the combatants and highlights the reflexive nature of the figure of Hector and the name "Priamus"—it is only natural that his name evokes Hector's father, Priam. By expressing his lineage in such a way that a Priam is a successor of Hector rather than vice versa, the reader is invited to reverse the future-driven track of genealogy and delve into the classical past.[53] As a representative of the ancient Trojan world, Priamus's alterity remains intact, allowing him to speak a lesson that could have been expressed by none other than Hector himself:

> I was so hawtayne of herte   whills I at home lengede,
> I helde nane my hippe-heghte   vndire heuen ryche;
> Forthy was I sente hedire   with seuen score knyghttez
> To asaye of this were,   be sente of my fadire.
> And I am for cyrqwitrye   schamely supprisede,
> And be aw[n]tire of armes   owtrayede fore euere.
>
>   (2612–17)

[I was so haughty of heart while I lingered at home, I held none as tall as my hip under rich heaven; forth was I sent hither with seventy knights to experience this war, by assent of my father. And I am for pride shamefully captured, and by adventure of arms disgraced forever.]

His pride and insistence on performing chivalric deeds have led to his shame and grievous wound at the hands of an unknown knight. This speech serves as a cautionary tale about such a desire for the possession of "price cetees" (2609), "tresour," and "londes" (2610), but unfortunately, its message does not translate into Gawain's chivalric sensibility. Instead he chooses to test Priamus's nobility by calling himself a "knafe"

For *Fierabras*, see the edition by A. Kroeber and G. Servois (Paris: F. Viewig, 1860); R. H. Griffith, "Malory, *Morte Arthure*, and *Fierabras*," *Anglia* 32 (1909): 389–98; John Finlayson, "The Alliterative *Morte Arthure* and *Sir Firumbras*," *Anglia* 92 (1974): 380–86.

[53] As Patterson notes, "He is not a Saracen but a classical warrior, heir to the heroic virtues of the antique world. . . . He embodies, in short, the virtue of the non-Christian world as it is later to be manifested in the figure of the Nine Worthies." See *Negotiating the Past*, 220.

(2621) of Arthur's entourage, a statement that inspires Priamus's exclamation of disbelief:

> Giffe his knaves be syche,   his knyghttez are noble!
> There is no kynge vndire Criste   may kempe with hym on;
> He will be Alexander ayre,   that all þe erthe lowttede,
> Abillere þan euer was   sir Ector of Troye!
>
> (2632–35)

[If his knaves be such, his knights are noble! There is no king under Christ who may battle with him; he will be Alexander's heir, to whom all the world bowed, abler than ever was Sir Hector of Troy!]

Once again he invokes the figure of Hector, but this time, to establish the imperial inheritance of Arthur and assert a type of martial kinship between him and the Round Table. Priamus juxtaposes "knaves" with "knyghttez" and "kynge," positing a triangular syntactical relationship that grammatically lessens the degrees of difference between each. Since the accepted hierarchy of the Round Table and fealty between knights and lords defy such an image of equality, Priamus calls Gawain's bluff, but the trick reminds the reader of the signifying slippage that has occurred throughout the poem—Gawain maintains the oppositional identities of enemy/kinsman and knave/knight just as the dragon is both British/Roman and Arthur is both tyrant/victim.

Priamus's articulation of his heritage establishes common blood and martial intentions with Gawain, an intimacy that is paradoxically obscured and intensified by their mutual wounding. The *Morte*-poet describes Priamus's slashing of Gawain in a "dreamlike slowness" that meticulously records the damage the venomous sword inflicts on his armor (2564–73).[54] In addition to an emphasis on the violence of this act, the illustration evinces a fetish for armorial bearings and details the destruction of the shoulder piece that is decorated with his coat of arms. Priamus's sword not only damages this genealogical sign but also cuts into the vein that spurts blood that further obscures it: "his vesturis ryche / With the valyant blood was verrede all ouer" [his rich clothes were spotted all over with the valiant blood] (2572–73). This blow causes Gawain's bodily fluid to efface the symbol of his noble Trojan heritage and equalize him with his wounded foe, whose liver could be

---

[54] Chism, *Alliterative Revivals*, 220.

observed "with þe lyghte of þe sonne" [with the light of the sun] (2561) after receiving a similar slash from Gawain's sword. For both knights, their mutilated bodies now become the main concern—their armor and their lineage have failed them.[55] Their subsequent conversation, in which they discover shared kinship with Hector, leads to a revival scene, whereby Priamus assumes the role of his namesake and uses a magical fluid to resurrect their wounded bodies (2686–716). No sooner than Gawain and Priamus are revived, they are propelled into another battle in which they fight on the same side (2990, 2997). This martial violence is heightened in Arthur's assault on Metz and Como, until it reaches a climax in Tuscany, the moment when Arthur achieves the height of his tyranny. The revivals of Gawain and Priamus reinvigorate the British host, but they employ their new power to pillage towns, tear down city walls, "turmente[n] þe pople," and cause widows to wring their hands in anguish (3151–55), language that invokes the destructive power of the dragon. Such actions suggest that these Trojan signifiers beget further violence more than they establish nobility.

In fact, the recitation of lineage as a marker of virtue and prowess rings hollow in this poem from beginning to end. For instance, early in the poem, when Sir Clegis confronts the King of Syria in battle, the King refuses to engage in battle until Clegis presents his right to bear arms. Insulted, Clegis responds angrily:

> I trowe it be for cowardys   thow carpes thes wordez!
> Myn armez are of ancestrye   enueryde with lordez
> And has in banere bene borne   sen sir Brut tyme,
> At the cité of Troye,   þat tyme was ensegede,
> Ofte seen in asawtte   with certayne knyghttez,
> For þe Brute broghte vs   and all oure bolde elders
> To Bretayne þe braddere   within chippe-burdez.
>
>   (1693–99)

[I believe it is for cowardice you say these words! My arms of ancestry are acknowledged by lords and have been borne in banner since Sir Brutus's time, at the city of Troy, that time it was besieged, often seen in assault by certain

---

[55] As Chism suggests, "Interior and exterior, body and armor reverse and intermingle" (221) in the same way that Priamus and Gawain reconcile as equals after the combat.

knights, from which Brutus brought us and all our bold elders to Great Britain aboard ships.]

And despite an eloquent account of his ancestry back to Troy, the origin of such heraldry, his justification of nobility falls on deaf ears.[56] The King of Syria retorts, "saye what þe lykez" (1700) and resolves to fight Clegis's forces in mass rather than engage him in a tournament-style battle. In a historical context in which such contestations for arms—like the famous Scrope-Grosvenor trial of 1386—were commonplace, the King of Syria's response demonstrates skepticism of imperial self-fashionings and claims to Trojan origins. Troy has clearly lost the legitimizing power that provides the structure of Galfridian historiography and approves the creation of British sovereignty out of the ashes of Rome. Trojan blood is no longer an unquestionable marker of virtue—rather, it is a shameful inheritance.

From the enigmatic sign of the dragon to the assertions of Trojan heritage, the heraldic claims to nobility and sovereignty in the poem are consistently reconceived as markers of death. Even though *translatio imperii* ultimately fails and Arthur's pursuit of his Roman inheritance places him as one among many other fallen conquerors, such as Julius Caesar, the invocation of lineage retains an influential signifying power. Arthur's tyranny is enhanced through this heraldic recognition that his potential destruction of Rome becomes a metaphorical act of patricidal violence against his own bloodline. During one of the most moving moments in the poem, Arthur mourns Gawain's death as a corporeal expression of the damage inflicted by *translatio imperii*. This point is exemplified by the fact that at the same time that Arthur's knights view him as a passively weeping widow, Arthur perceives himself as complicit in the death of Gawain and his royal line. In response to their request that he cease his mourning, Arthur refuses and instead engages in a rhetorical dismemberment of his own body: " 'For blod' said the bolde kynge 'blynn sall I neuer, / Or my brayne to-briste or my breste oþer!' "

---

[56] Ibid., 208–9. Chism further suggests that "this unreliability of the signs that designate nobility infects the poem as a whole." For extended discussion of the scene's socioeconomic and chivalric implications, see Geraldine Heng, *Empire of Magic: Medieval Romance and the Politics of Cultural Fantasy* (New York: Columbia University Press, 2003), 128–46. For the scene's allusion to the Scrope-Grosvenor trial, see Keen, "Chaucer's Knight, the English Aristocracy, and the Crusade," in *English Court and Culture in the Later Middle Ages*, ed. V. J. Scattergood and J. W. Sherborne (London: Duckworth, 1983), 45–62.

['For blood,' said the bold king, 'cease shall I never, until my brain or my breast completely burst'] (3981–82). Arthur's unrestrained mourning is his only vehicle to escape the bodily fragmentation that he perceives as the consequence of his complicity in the violence that has slain his kinsman and innocent victims.[57] The bloodied sovereign's characterization of his kinsman's blood as "ryall rede" (3990) articulates a devastating consequence of his death: the end of a royal line. Arthur combines the unsettling image of his bloodied beard with an imagined dismemberment of his body to express the damage his sovereign fantasies have incurred. Through this ritual of mourning, Arthur's physical and political bodies coalesce into one indivisible entity—the destruction of one entails the destruction of the other. Such an image supports Agamben's reading of the biopolitical nature of the sovereign body. In defiance of Kantorowicz's distinction of the king's two bodies, Agamben suggests that the private and public *corpores* of the king are inseparable.[58] The sovereign body is envisioned as physically reacting to a disruption in *translatio imperii*. For Arthur, Gawain's death leaves his line to the progeny of his "other" nephew, Mordred, the "Malebranche," a genealogical consequence that exemplifies the fragmentation of Arthur's political realm.

As the end of the poem confirms, Arthur's identity as sovereign cannot be interpreted solely with a Galfridian hermeneutic. After Arthur orders the extermination of Mordred's line, Arthur's body is not translated to the Isle of Avalon—instead, he is entombed in a sepulcher be-

---

[57] Arthur further insists that "He es sakles, supprysede for syn of myn one. . . . / O rightwis riche Gode, this rewthe thow beholde, / Þis ryall rede blode ryn appon erthe! / It ware worthy to be schrede and schrynede in golde, / For it es sakles of syn, sa helpe me oure Lorde!" [He is innocent, destroyed for my own sin. . . . Oh great, righteous God, behold this grief, this royal red blood run upon the earth! It is worthy to be shrouded and enshrined in gold, for it is innocent of sin, so help me our Lord!] (3986, 3989–92). His repetition of "sakles" reiterates Gawain's innocence, while his continuing reference to "blode" calls attention to his blood-stained beard and the blood he has caused to run upon the earth through his martial endeavors. Through the physical act of smearing Gawain's blood on his face and the imagined fragmentation of his own body, Arthur again fashions Gawain and himself as victims of his own sin.

[58] Agamben, *Homo Sacer*, 184; Kantorowicz, *The King's Two Bodies*. For a Lacanian reading of this scene, see Ingham, *Sovereign Fantasies*, 95. She argues that the imagined dismemberment of the body is "aggressive disintegration" and a means of refiguring "aggressive intentions." See Jacques Lacan, *Écrits: A Selection*, trans. Alan Sheridan (New York: W. W. Norton, 1982), 4, 11. The *Morte*-poet even may have appropriated such a fusion of the state of the empire with the sovereign body from the alliterative *Siege of Jerusalem*, in which the biopolitical connection is literalized in Titus's "crippling" reaction to the news of his father Vespasian's ascendancy to the imperial throne (1027–33).

fore the eyes of grieving witnesses (4332–41). No ethereal transfer of the body politic to future generations is implied or allowed—the poem ends instead with a hollow evocation of his Trojan ancestors (4342–46):

> Thus endis Kyng Arthure,   as auctors alleges,
> That was of Ectores blude,   the kynge son of Troye,
> And of sir Pryamous the prynce,   praysede in erthe:
> Fro thethen broghte the Bretons   all his bolde eldyrs
> Into Bretayne the brode,   as þe Bruytte tellys.
>
> (4342–46)

The juxtaposition of Arthur's Trojan heritage with his burial encourages readers to view this heraldic expression of lineage more as a lamentable necrology than the establishment of a future line. A sense of wistful resignation permeates this scene since Arthur has ended his life not as a king to be praised, but as a tyrant who had become a victim of the imperial fantasy that "þe Bruytte tellys" [the *Brut* tells] (4346). As is the case with many of the signifiers throughout this poem, the reference to the "Bruytte" is not to be understood simply as Geoffrey's *Historia*. While it certainly reaffirms its Galfridian source, the tragic ending of the poem encourages readers to grapple with the many histories of Brutus and his Trojan origin that do not promise imperial glory. As I have suggested, this ambivalence can be tracked both through invocations of Trojan origins and the heraldic violence, components of the alliterative tradition that the *Morte*-poet recasts for chilling effect. As a conduit of antithetical historiographic discourses, the *Morte Arthure* demonstrates that assertions of sovereignty, while temporarily glorious, are inextricable from the violence that is inflicted upon aggressor and victim. Rather than delight in the destruction that Arthur inflicts upon his Roman imperial predecessor, the *Morte*-poet presents to his British contemporaries a stark representation of empire that cannot be reconciled with the idealizations of the Galfridian tradition.

The production of alliterative romances such as the *Morte Arthure* and *The Siege of Jerusalem* suggests a larger investment in critiques of war, heraldic assertions, and *translatio imperii* in the late fourteenth and early fifteenth centuries. Such pessimistic gestures emerge with remarkable frequency in alliterative romance during this period, distinguishing these provincial texts from historiographies that justify England's sovereignty by claiming an imperial ancestry that originates in ancient Troy and Rome. As poems that speak from the literary and topographical periphery of London's cultural center, these alliterative romances engage in careful critiques of warfare and chivalry that may have alienated their noble audiences. For instance, the writer of the *Destruction of Troy* identifies his audience as an aristocratic patron in the opening folium. He promises that in the thirty-sixth book he will provide both the "nome of the knight þat causet it to be made / & the nome of hym that translatid it out of latyn in to englysshe." The poet fulfills his promise to identify himself as the translator, albeit cryptically, as John Clerk of Whalley, through the initia of the books, which spell "M. I[O]HANNES CLERK DE WHALELE."[59] However, he leaves out the name of his knightly patron, an interesting and suggestive omission given the pessimism of the romance.[60]

The fact that neither the *Morte Arthure*, *The Siege of Jerusalem*, nor any other surviving alliterative romance, for that matter, provides the name of its author suggests that the genre itself may have been perceived on some level as hostile to aristocratic claims to sovereignty. Though these militaristic narratives are clearly written to delight their readers with chivalric accounts of Hector's martial prowess, Vespasian's siege of Jerusalem, and Arthur's Roman conquest, they belie such martial fervor with descriptions of violence and commentary on the suffering of innocent victims that are not consistent with chivalric sensibilities.

[59] While this discovery provided a name and place for the author, it did not specify which "John Clerk" wrote the poem, since John Clerk was a common name in the late fourteenth and early fifteenth century in the area of Whalley. See Turville-Petre, "The Author of *The Destruction of Troy*," *MÆ* 57 (1988): 264–69.

[60] For a discussion of the enhanced pessimism of this translation of Guido's *Historia*, see Alex Mueller, "Linking Letters: Translating Ancient History into Medieval Romance," *Literature Compass* 4.4 (June 2007): 1017–29. As a product of the Guido-tradition, *The Destruction of Troy* exhibits what James Simpson has identified as "a division of power between aristocrats and the learned, whom I shall call 'clerics'; this recognized division of power allowed clerics a permissible voice that is trenchantly opposed to aristocratic military, martial, and bureaucratic practice." See *The Oxford English Literary History, Volume 2, 1350–1547: Reform and Cultural Revolution* (Oxford: Oxford University Press, 2002), 98–99; Simpson, "The Other Book of Troy: Guido delle Colonne's *Historia destructionis Troiae* in Fourteenth- and Fifteenth-Century England," *Speculum* 73 (1998): 397–423; for the earlier twelfth-century opposition between the clergy and the military, see Ad Putter, *"Sir Gawain and the Green Knight" and French Arthurian Romance* (Oxford: Clarendon Press, 1995), 197–201.

COLLOQUIUM:
Manly-Rickert Seventy Years On

Vance Ramsey on Manly-Rickert

Henry Ansgar Kelly
UCLA

I T IS FITTING TO LEAD OFF a discussion on the editing of the *Canterbury Tales* seventy years after the Manly-Rickert edition was published in 1940 with an account of the only monograph ever published on their work, Roy Vance Ramsey's large book, *The Manly-Rickert Text of the "Canterbury Tales."*[1] Ramsey's study was sixteen or seventeen years in the making, and though he arguably knew more about their project than any other person, not much attention was paid to it when it came out, and it was never reviewed. At my suggestion, a new edition has been issued to coincide with the Manly-Rickert anniversary, in a friendlier format (specifically, with the addition of running titles).[2] Unfortunately, Ramsey himself could not participate, having passed away in 2006.

In his preface, Ramsey cites Derek Pearsall's expression of his great debt to Manly and Rickert, "whose eight-volume edition of *The Canterbury Tales* provided an indispensable foundation of the *Variorum Chaucer*, and who deserve more than the occasional carping at their inaccuracy in return for the plundering to which they have been subjected."[3] Ramsey applauds Pearsall's sentiments, and pledges himself to try to do justice to their achievements, while at the same time explaining any shortfalls

---

[1] *The Text of the "Canterbury Tales," Studied on the Basis of All Known Manuscripts*, by John M. Manly and Edith Rickert, with the aid of Mabel Dean, Helen McIntosh, and others; with a chapter on illuminations by Margaret Rickert, 8 vols. (Chicago: University of Chicago Press, 1940); Roy Vance Ramsey, *The Manly-Rickert Text of the "Canterbury Tales"* (Lewiston, N.Y.: Edwin Mellen Press, 1994).

[2] Roy Vance Ramsey, *The Manly-Rickert Text of the "Canterbury Tales,"* rev. ed., with a foreword by H. A. Kelly (Lewiston, N.Y.: Edwin Mellen Press, 2010). The text and pagination are the same as in the 1994 edition, except for correction of typographical errors.

[3] Ramsey, *The Manly-Rickert Text*, viii; Derek Pearsall, *The Nun's Priest's Tale, Variorum Chaucer*, vol. 2, part 9 (Norman: University of Oklahoma Press, 1984), xv; Ramsey misquotes Pearsall as saying "*the* indispensable foundation," but the correct citation is in his article, "Paleography and Scribes of Shared Training," *SAC* 8 (1986): 107–44 (107 n. 1).

he perceives in their work. He remains convinced that their data are absolutely necessary for truly critical editions of the *Canterbury Tales*. Of course, Ramsey weaves many of his own ideas into his book, often arguing that they are contingent upon or implied by the conclusions of Manly and Rickert. I believe these ideas deserve a response.

Chapter 1 begins with "an overview of the misunderstandings and misrepresentations of Manly-Rickert from its first appearance to the present, then surveys the far-from-satisfactory editions of the *Canterbury Tales* from 1721 to the latest ones," and Chapter 2 gives an explanatory chronology of the project.[4] In appendixes, titled collectively, "Critics of Manly-Rickert," Ramsey gives a critical review of all the previous assessments that other scholars have given to Manly-Rickert. Jill Mann has recently written that "the defects of Manly and Rickert's editorial assumptions and methods, which have been analyzed with devastating thoroughness by George Kane, deprive [their edition] of the authoritative status to which it might seem to be entitled."[5] Mann cites Ramsey's book in a note "for a defence of the Manly and Rickert edition and a moving account of the difficulties they faced,"[6] but without adverting to Ramsey's critique of Kane.[7] In fact, Ramsey says that his whole book can be seen as an implicit reply to many of Kane's criticisms.[8] He hopes he will be forgiven his occasional polemical stances, which reflect not only his devotion to Manly and Rickert's accomplishments but also his felt need to fight fire with fire.

As Ramsey explains in his preface, his study is not a simple analysis of Manly-Rickert but rather a guide to their discoveries and the uses to which they can be put. He draws not only on the edition itself but also on correspondence and other documents of the time. For instance, he cites Manly as writing in 1929 that nearly all that had been written about the production of books in the fifteenth century was wrong.[9] He describes the role of Manly and Rickert in founding the systematic dating of fifteenth-century English manuscripts by making photographic copies available for comparison, and their pioneering use of ultraviolet

[4] Ramsey, *The Manly-Rickert Text*, xi.

[5] Jill Mann, "A Note on the Text," in Geoffrey Chaucer, *The Canterbury Tales* (London: Penguin, 2005), lxi, citing George Kane, "John Matthews Manly and Edith Rickert," in Paul G. Ruggiers, ed., *Editing Chaucer: The Great Tradition* (Norman, Okla.: Pilgrim Books, 1984), 207–29.

[6] Mann, ed. *Canterbury Tales*, lxviii n. 2.

[7] Ramsey, *The Manly-Rickert Text*, 638–53.

[8] Ibid., 653, cf. 646.

[9] Ibid., 135.

light in examining manuscripts.[10] All of this is still relevant for making editorial decisions.

The main problem with their edition is one that is brought out by Manly himself, writing in the preface: "It has been more difficult than usual to bring into harmony parts of the work composed and typed at widely different periods. We hope, nevertheless, that our readers will make allowances for these restrictions and consider the difficulties under which we have worked."[11] This has not been done by most readers, and it is Ramsey's goal to help the process.

One great difficulty was that Manly and Rickert were forced to compile their edition of the text of the *Tales*, set forth in volumes 3 and 4, long before they were ready, with the idea of publishing it early to gain funding for the rest of the project. Each section of the edited text was done not by way of the best-text method but by recension and without emendation. Much of the criticism of Manly-Rickert stems from the belief that all of the discoveries of volume 2 were available when volumes 3 and 4 were compiled.[12] The result of the early fixing of the text is that the apparatus at the bottom of volumes 3 and 4 is of little use, compared to the incomparably important listing of all variants in volumes 5–8, though the textual notes are still valuable.[13] Nevertheless, Ramsey defends the text as being the best text of the *Tales* in closeness to what Chaucer wrote, apart from the fascicles of the *Variorum Chaucer*, which were edited by a method, using Hengwrt as a base, inspired by a suggestion of Manly-Rickert.[14] Needless to say, Ramsey is very critical of other editions, pointing out, for instance, that the *Riverside* third edition completely disregards Manly-Rickert and is at a fourth remove from the manuscripts.[15] He refutes the widespread idea that Robinson (hence also *Riverside*) based his edition on the Ellesmere text.[16]

Ramsey considers Manly and Rickert's most important hypothesis (he calls it a "discovery") to be their idea that Chaucer released links and tales during his lifetime, a process that Ramsey terms "Stage 1" of the

[10] Ibid., 69, 474, 71.
[11] Manly and Rickert, eds., *The Text*, 1:xiv; cited by Ramsey, *The Manly-Rickert Text*, 112.
[12] Ramsey, *The Manly-Rickert Text*, 112.
[13] Ibid., 119–20.
[14] Ibid., 94–95, 656–57.
[15] Ibid., 590, 598, cf. 43–56.
[16] Ibid., 23, 48. A recent repetition of this idea is in Simon Horobin, *The Language of the Chaucer Tradition* (Woodbridge: D. S. Brewer, 2003), 3.

dissemination of the text.[17] This early piecemeal escape of texts precludes any possibility of a single original text of the *Canterbury Tales*—a difficulty with which Manly and Rickert themselves struggled throughout their project.[18] There followed "Stage 2" (the production of whole copies from pieces by independent scribes) and "Stage 3" (the production, mainly in shops, of copies from full exemplars).

Another lesson that Manly and Rickert learned too late for their text edition was the danger of focusing on just a few variants. As the edition was being finalized in the last two years before its 1940 publication, Ramsey notes, "Manly . . . was clear about how wrong the idea about 'significant variants' was, and he had probably become clear enough about how dubiously large contamination loomed in his reading of some of the textual evidence."[19]

"Contamination" here refers to a scribe's supposed practice of inserting readings into his text from exemplars other than the main copy-text. The alternative explanation to such contamination was what Manly and Rickert called "acco," that is "accidental coincidence," or, to use Walter Greg's term, "convergent variation"—meaning the appearance of the same variants in unaffiliated manuscripts, resulting from independent copying errors. More important were unique variants, an emphasis that Ramsey has developed.

So, by the end of Chaucer's life, there had never been a single scribal version of the entire *Canterbury Tales*, but only a scribal original of each link and each tale ("leaving aside for now the further and also very difficult problem of authorial revisions of links and tales which affected even this").[20] This realization led to their new solution of early release and they had to start over in writing up their history of the text in volume 2.[21] To take an example, there are twelve lines of transmission for *The Franklin's Tale*, and we can be reasonably sure, Ramsey says, that a fair number began before 1400.[22]

[17] Ramsey, *The Manly-Rickert Text*, xi, 94.

[18] Opinion is still divided on this issue. See Daniel W. Mosser, " 'Chaucer's Scribe,' Adam, and the Hengwrt Project," *Design and Distribution of Late Medieval Manuscripts in England*, ed. Margaret Connolly and Linne R. Mooney (Woodbridge: York Medieval Press, 2008), 11–40; and Peter Robinson, "The History, Discoveries, and Aims of the *Canterbury Tales* Project," *ChauR* 38 (2003): 126–39.

[19] Ramsey, *The Manly-Rickert Text*, 84.

[20] Ibid., 160.

[21] See Manly and Rickert, eds., *The Text*, 2:36, for Manly's tentative statement, cited by Ramsey, *The Manly-Rickert Text*, 264 n. 109.

[22] Ramsey, *The Manly-Rickert Text*, 291.

Manly and Rickert came to doubt that Ellesmere and Hengwrt were written by the same scribe, in spite of their nearly identical-seeming scripts. This idea went against the consensus that developed as soon as Manly and Rickert had made photos of the two manuscripts available for comparison, a consensus still largely accepted.[23] Ramsey, building on his earlier studies,[24] takes the Manly-Rickert doubt and turns it into a strong affirmation that different scribes produced Hengwrt and Ellesmere. His 1982 article was countered by M. L. Samuels in 1983,[25] who challenged Ramsey to name a certain example of seeming identity of hands. Ramsey's response in 1986 pointed to the Glasgow manuscript of Chaucer, avowedly by Geoffrey Spirleng of Norwich and his son Thomas, in which, as Manly and Rickert say, "The two hands are so much alike that it is not always possible to distinguish them."[26] He also set forth the case for considering two further manuscripts of the *Tales,* London, BL MS Harley 7334 and Oxford, Corpus Christi College MS 198, as being by different copyists, rather than the recently celebrated Scribe D alone. In this he agrees with Manly and Rickert, who said that Harley 7334 was written in a single "excellent book hand," similar to the hand in Corpus, "but not the same."[27]

Let me repeat here Ian Doyle's warning that "there can be no absolute certainty that one scribe did not imitate another indistinguishably," which, he notes, would favor Ramsey's case.[28] One argument for non-

---

[23] Ibid., 474–75.

[24] R. Vance Ramsey, "The Hengwrt and Ellesmere Manuscripts of the *Canterbury Tales*: Different Scribes," *SB* 35 (1982): 133–54; and Ramsey, "Paleography and Scribes."

[25] M. L. Samuels, "The Scribe of the Hengwrt and Ellesmere Manuscripts of *The Canterbury Tales*," *SAC* 5 (1983): 49–65.

[26] Manly and Rickert, eds., *The Text,* 1:184; see Ramsey, "Paleography and Scribes"; see also Ramsey, *The Manly-Rickert Text,* 220–30. See, further, A. I. Doyle, "The Copyist of the Ellesmere Canterbury Tales," in *The Ellesmere Chaucer: Essays in Interpretation*, ed. Martin Stevens and Daniel Woodward (San Marino, Calif.: Huntington Library Press, 1995), 49–67, esp. 50–51.

[27] Manly and Rickert, eds., *The Text,* 1:220; see Ramsey, *The Manly-Rickert Text,* 415, 423–24. Ramsey's arguments about the two manuscripts in "Paleography and Scribes" are contested by J. J. Smith, "The Trinity Gower D-Scribe and His Work on Two Early *Canterbury Tales* Manuscripts," in *The English of Chaucer and His Contemporaries: Essays by M. L. Samuels and J. J. Smith*, ed. Smith (Aberdeen: Aberdeen University Press, 1988), 51–69. For a recent study affirming the identity of the scribe, see Jacob Thaisen, "The Trinity Gower D Scribe's Two *Canterbury Tales* Manuscripts Revisited," in Connolly and Mooney, eds., *Design and Distribution of Late Medieval Manuscripts,* 41–60.

[28] Doyle, "The Copyist of the Ellesmere," 50; 66 n. 8; see also Doyle and M. B. Parkes, "A Paleographical Introduction," in *The Canterbury Tales: A Facsimile and Transcription of the Hengwrt Manuscript, with Variants from the Ellesmere Manuscript*, ed. Paul G.

identity is different spellings, used consistently even with presumably varied exemplars, and consistently different uses of brevigraphs and accidentals.[29] Samuels holds that the Ellesmere spellings are just the same scribe adjusting to more trendy forms, but Ramsey maintains that such features would be ingrained in a scribe and not easily changed over the course of a few years, and the forms of letters especially would not be affected by different exemplars.[30]

However, Ramsey's more important criterion is the different standards of fidelity in the respective manuscripts. The richly produced Ellesmere manuscript is throughout six times "more unfaithful" to its presumed exemplars than is the plain-Jane Hengwrt. Half of the changes in Ellesmere can be ascribed to editorial attempts at improvement, but the other half to inadvertence, that is, scribal sloppiness, and failure to proofread properly.[31] To take the example of *The Nun's Priest's Tale*, the ratio of unique variants (those variants that occur in no other manuscript) between Hengwrt and Ellesmere is 13 to 1; Ellesmere con-

---

Ruggiers (Norman: University of Oklahoma Press, 1979), xix–xxxix (xxxv). Doyle notes that Ramsey did not cite this view, despite its appositeness, in either "The Hengwrt and Ellesmere Manuscripts" or "Paleography and Scribes."

[29] Consistency in the face of presumed multiple exemplars, as in the case of Hengwrt and Ellesmere, would rule out the factor of "constrained selection" of forms from an exemplar. For this concept, see Alan J. Fletcher, "The Criteria for Scribal Attribution: Dublin Trinity College, MS 244, Some Early Copies of the Works of Geoffrey Chaucer, and the Canon of Adam Pynkhurst Manuscripts," *RES* 58 (2007): 597–632, esp. 619–20, summarizing Michael Benskin and Margaret Laing, "Translations and *Mischsprachen* in Middle English Manuscripts," in *So Meny People Longages and Tonges: Philological Essays in Scots and Mediaeval English Presented to Angus McIntosh*, ed. Benskin and M. L. Samuels (Edinburgh: The Editors, 1981), 55–106.

[30] One of Ramsey's spelling examples is "else," spelled "ellis" in Hg 100 percent of the time, but "elles" in El 88.7 percent of the time ("Paleography and Scribes," 115). Statistics on "else" are given by Simon Horobin and Linne R. Mooney, "A *Piers Plowman* Manuscript by the Hengwrt/Ellesmere Scribe and Its Implications for London Standard English," *SAC* 26 (2004): 65–112, for Hg, El, and their *Piers* text, Cambridge, Trinity College MS B.15.17, which uses "ellis" 100 percent of the time, aligning it with Hg and its "less modern" spelling (89–90). However, Fletcher, "The Criteria for Scribal Attribution," who does not cite Ramsey, has similar figures for these three manuscripts (like Horobin and Mooney, he finds one instance of "elles" in Hg, where Ramsey found none), but he also finds that another earlier suggested Pinkhurst MS, a copy of Chaucer's *Boece* (Aberystwyth, National Library of Wales, MS Peniarth 393D), uses the supposedly later "elles" 100 percent of the time (625). Fletcher's figures also show that the Mercery petition of 1387/88 (London, TNA, PRO SC 8/20/997), attributed by Mooney to Pinkhurst, accords most closely with El ("ellis" once, "elles" three times).

[31] Ramsey, *The Manly-Rickert Text*, 327. For criticisms of his assumptions about variants, see Smith, "Trinity Gower," 52–53; Mosser, "Chaucer's Scribe," 12 n. 4; Takako Kato, "Corrected Mistakes in Cambridge University Library MS Gg.4.27," in Connolly and Mooney, eds., *Design and Distribution of Late Medieval Manuscripts*, 61–87.

stantly "improves" the text.[32] However, far from asserting that the El scribe was second-guessed by an editor, Ramsey believes that such changes were the work of the scribe: "Because such 'smoothing' of the meter is both very local and very regular, it seems of itself strong evidence that the editor responsible for this kind of change and for the other local kinds was the scribe himself and not some supervisor who, though Manly, Rickert, Doyle, Parkes and others believe that one 'must' have directed the work of the scribe, has left no physical trace or any other kind that I can discover and who seems to me to cry out for a trim with Occam's Razor."[33] This puts Ramsey somewhere between those who believe that El had an editor and those who, like Jill Mann, believe that it was not edited at all.[34]

Ever since paleographers were able to see Ellesmere and Hengwrt side by side, they have remarked that Ellesmere looks more old-fashioned, a judgment in which Ramsey concurs (ignoring Samuels's assertion of its trendier spellings), but other considerations have persuaded some, including Manly and Rickert themselves, that Hengwrt is earlier. This argument continued in the 1970s between M. B. Parkes and A. I. Doyle in their discussions held in connection with their "Paleographic Introduction" to the *Variorum Chaucer* facsimile and transcript of Hengwrt. Their debate and disagreement are commemorated only by "a rather vague footnote" (as Ramsey calls it),[35] but Ramsey reveals that Parkes supported an earlier date for Ellesmere because of the handwriting, whereas Doyle favored a later date because of other evidence.[36]

---

[32] Ramsey, *The Manly-Rickert Text*, 200–201.

[33] Ibid., 316–17.

[34] Jill Mann, "Chaucer's Meter and the Myth of the Ellesmere Editor of *The Canterbury Tales*," *SAC* 23 (2001): 71–107. Here she sets out "some of the evidence for scribal disturbance of meter in *both* El and Hg" (73). For a follow-up to questions she raises, see Donka Minkova and Robert Stockwell, "Emendation and the Chaucerian Metrical Template," in *Chaucer and the Challenges of Medievalism: Studies in Honor of H. A. Kelly*, ed. Minkova and Theresa Tinkle (Hamburg: Peter Lang, 2003), 129–39. Mann conjectures (78) that Manly and Rickert were insistent on seeing an editor in El because they believed Hg to be written by the same scribe and wished to privilege it over El; this would not be necessary if they came to suspect different scribes at work, as Ramsey says they did.

[35] See Doyle and Parkes, "Paleographical Introduction," xx n. 4.

[36] Ramsey, *The Manly-Rickert Text*, 475; cf. 137–39, 343. Linne R. Mooney, "Chaucer's Scribe," *Speculum* 81 (2006): 97–138, suggests that Adam Pinkhurst wrote Hg in the late 1390s or 1400 and El sometime after 1408 (115), and lists scholars who place El before 1400 (97 n. 2); they include Estelle Stubbs, *The Hengwrt Chaucer Digital Facsimile* (Scholarly Digital Editions, 2000), who dates the preparation of both Hg and El to the same time, perhaps under the supervision of Chaucer himself.

Ramsey's solution is to date Ellesmere later than Hengwrt but written by an older scribe, perhaps none other than Chaucer's own scribe Adam, whom Chaucer criticized for the mistakes he made in copying his *Troilus* and *Boece*.[37] The younger scribe who produced Hengwrt, he suggests, was a disciple of Adam's, more conscientious and careful than he.[38] He conjectures that Hengwrt was written for Chaucer's son Lewis when he was at Oxford in the mid-1390s, from individual tales and links supplied periodically by Chaucer, and that Lewis had it with him in Wales when he went there in 1403.[39]

Ramsey suggests further that another important early manuscript of the entire *Tales*, Cambridge Dd, was also written at or near Oxford, but based on slightly later texts, c. 1398–99, also supplied by Chaucer himself but given to his other son, Thomas.[40] Ramsey finds the Dd scribe second in accuracy only to Hengwrt, contrary to Manly and Rickert, who mistakenly concluded that he was careless. Ramsey attributes their mistake to their reliance on contamination as an explanation for apparent anomalies in the text of a manuscript.[41] He backs up his conclusions, here and elsewhere, by drawing on Charles Moorman's statistical study

[37] Ramsey, *The Manly-Rickert Text*, 476–77.

[38] Ibid., 471–72. Fletcher, "The Criteria for Scribal Attribution," speaks of a possible Pinkhurst school for manuscripts that manifest many of the features that have been supposed to render Pinkhurst's hand distinctive (598). The existence of such "scribal schools" in London in the period is contested by Simon Horobin, "The Criteria for Scribal Attribution: Dublin, Trinity College MS 244 Reconsidered," *RES* 60 (2009): 371–81 (380).

[39] Ramsey, *The Manly-Rickert Text*, 471, 520–21, 537–40. For an earlier speculation about a pre-1400 date for Hengwrt, see Ralph Hanna, "The Hengwrt Manuscript and the Canon of *The Canterbury Tales*," *EMS* 1 (1989): 64–84, who suggests, like Ramsey, that the manuscript was put together from exemplars received serially during Chaucer's lifetime (71–72); see also Hanna's Introduction, and Kathleen L. Scott, "An Hours and Psalter by Two Ellesmere Illuminators," both in Martin W. Stevens and Daniel Woodward, eds., *The Ellesmere Manuscript of Chaucer's Canterbury Tales: A Working Facsimile* (Woodbridge: D. S. Brewer, 1989), 1–15 (9–10); 87–119 (esp. 104–6). The Welsh connection of Hengwrt in Lewis's time is refuted by Jill Mann, note 15 in her contribution below.

[40] Ramsey, *The Manly-Rickert Text*, 404–5. See also 540, where Ramsey makes clear his supposition that Chaucer kept his originals and sent only copies. In Ramsey's hypothetical reconstruction of events, neither the copies nor the originals survived. I should note here that the attribution of the hand of Dd to Richard Wytton by Ramsey and others is countered by Orietta Da Rold, "The Significance of Scribal Corrections in Cambridge, University Library MS Dd.4.24 of Chaucer's *Canterbury Tales*," *ChauR* 41 (2007): 393–438, since it seems that the scribe was not working within a university milieu (410); and she finds it questionable that he was an amateur (411). See also Da Rold's contribution below.

[41] Ramsey, *The Manly-Rickert Text*, 379–80.

of the *Canterbury Tales* manuscripts, published in 1993 (and which, like Ramsey's own book, was never reviewed).[42]

I conclude by signaling Ramsey's statement: "I do *not* believe that study of the manuscripts and of Manly-Rickert will be enough for an editor [of the *Canterbury Tales*]. Manly and Rickert did not believe so and neither do I. Thoroughly mistaken, however, are those such as Donaldson and Kane who have triumphantly claimed that because the study of the textual evidence cannot solve all of the problems, then such a study can responsibly be renounced by an editor." He censures Donaldson in particular as an editor of the *Tales*, because, even though he started with Hengwrt as base, it was "not because of a strong belief in it (his free way of changing its readings argues otherwise) but simply because Manly-Rickert had started a controversy about it and no one had used it as base before" (606). But he neglected to take into consideration the implications of piecemeal dissemination as set forth by Manly-Rickert and the textual relations of the manuscripts, and simply "proceeded to exercise his 'learning, taste and judgment' to change the readings whenever and wherever he saw fit" (ibid.). "Contrary to the absolutists," he continues, "no intelligent person can doubt that learning, taste, and judgment must be exercised by any editor worthy of the name, *but they should be the very last resort of an editor and not the first.*"[43]

Ramsey is very clear in staking out his positions and the evidence he presents for them. Doubtless many of his positions can be opposed or modified by counterevidence, but so far this has not been done, or done adequately, and the time to do so, I say, has arrived, and the time to take Manly and Rickert's monumental work in hand again has also arrived, now using Ramsey as a guide.

---

[42] Charles Moorman, *The Statistical Determination of Affiliation in the Landmark Manuscripts of the "Canterbury Tales"* (Lewiston, N.Y.: Edwin Mellen Press, 1993).

[43] Ramsey, *The Manly-Rickert Text,* 605–7.

Manly and Rickert and the
Failure of Method

A. S. G. Edwards
De Montfort University

VANCE RAMSEY, in his extended defense of Manly and Rickert's *The Text of the Canterbury Tales*, makes the following assertion: "Contrary to the absolutists, no intelligent person can doubt that learning, taste and judgment must be exercised by any editor worthy of the name, *but they should be the very last resort of an editor and not the first*."[1] I doubt whether anyone with experience of editing Middle English texts (as Ramsey had not) would formulate the problems of editorial intervention in such a categorical way. Nor is it clear what "absolutists" (whatever the term is intended to mean) he has in mind. And if "learning, taste and judgment" are to be the "last" resort of the editor, what is to be the first?[2]

It is worth applying this last question to the editorial activities of Manly and Rickert, that is, to those portions of their work specifically concerned with presenting a text of the *Canterbury Tales*, volumes 3 and 4. These volumes have important practical implications for their larger undertaking. One might reasonably assume that the very first procedural matter that any editor would wish to establish would be the choice of the base text, which will provide the lemmata for the edition, that is, the forms against which other witnesses will be collated. Normally such a base text would also provide, in general terms, the orthographic forms for the text, what are now termed its "accidentals."

The term "accidentals" derives from the influential editorial theory

---

[1] Roy Vance Ramsey, *The Manly-Rickert Text of the Canterbury Tales* (Lampeter: Edwin Mellen Press, 1994), 606–7.
[2] Ramsey also asserts that "the manuscripts themselves constitute the court of last resort for any theories about the text" (vii). It is not clear what is left.

337

of W. W. Greg in his classic paper "The Rationale of Copy-Text."[3] Although Greg draws his examples in this essay from Renaissance texts, his formulations drew on considerable experience of Middle English works and he had also made extended study of the problems of manuscripts of the *Canterbury Tales*.[4] According to Ramsey, Greg had also been in correspondence with Manly and Rickert in the 1920s and 1930s.[5] It is clear that the experience of medieval literature helped to shape his thinking.[6] The idea of copy-text makes a clear distinction in textual authority between the accidentals (the spelling forms) of a base text and its substantive readings. Greg suggests that generally the earliest surviving witness (that closest in time to the author's original) provides authority for accidentals, while questions of substantive variation between witnesses can be assessed on a case-by-case basis using a full range of editorial resources (including doubtless "learning, taste and judgment").

Greg's formulation offers a clear and flexible statement of method: establish the choice of copy-text to provide a formal basis for a text, but emend its substantive readings on appropriate grounds. It is a statement of method that, in the case of the *Canterbury Tales*, invalidates the lengthy and fruitless debate over the textual superiority of Hengwrt or Ellesmere that Manly and Rickert conduct through assertion rather than the presentation of evidence.[7] For any edition of the work must perforce

[3] First published in *SB* 3 (1950–51): 19–36, and reprinted in slightly modified form in his *Collected Papers*, ed. J. C. Maxwell (Oxford: Clarendon Press, 1966), 374–91.

[4] See, further, A. S. G. Edwards, "W. W. Greg as Medievalist," *Textual Cultures* 4.2 (2009): 54–62.

[5] See Ramsey, *The Manly-Rickert Text*, 82.

[6] See Fredson Bowers, "Greg's 'Rationale of Copy-Text' Revisited," *SB* 31 (1978): 90–161, esp. 161.

[7] They make this claim in two key statements: "Although [Ellesmere] has long been regarded by many scholars as the single MS of most authority, its total of unique variants, many of which are demonstrable errors, is approximately twice that of [Hengwrt]. . . . And again, while it has a few lines not in any other MS, and shows some editorial changes that could have been made by Chaucer, it has many others that are questionable and some distinctly for the worst, even involving misunderstanding of the context. Since it is very clear that an intelligent person, who was certainly not Chaucer, worked over the text when [Ellesmere] was copied, the unsupported readings of this MS must be scrutinized with the greatest care." "Because of its great freedom from accidental errors and its entire freedom from editorial variants, [Hengwrt] is a MS of the highest importance." *The Text,* 1:150, 276. These claims have been effectively rebutted by George Kane, "John M. Manly and Edith Rickert," in *Editing Chaucer: The Great Tradition*, ed. Paul G. Ruggiers (Norman: University of Oklahoma Press, 1984), 207–29, 289–91; and Jill Mann, "Chaucer's Meter and the Myth of the Ellesmere Editor of *The Canterbury Tales*," *SAC* 23 (2001): 71–107.

take Ellesmere as its copy-text on wholly pragmatic grounds: it is early, dialectally consistent and, more compelling, it is the more complete of the two (Hengwrt lacks of course *The Canon's Yeoman's Tale* and much of *The Parson's Tale* and the *Retraction*), and it offers a more convincing order. Any debate about the superiority of particular readings in Hengwrt (or indeed other manuscripts) remains a matter of individual editorial judgment. Most editions now begin by identifying their "base text" or "copy-text" (the terms are often used synonymously). Such a statement might reasonably be seen as the "first resort" of any editor.

But not Manly and Rickert. Their textual methodology of course predates Greg's paper, but it has always been editorial convention to identify the text on which an edition is based. They do not. They do identify the grounds for one aspect of their textual procedure. They state: "As the basis for collation we chose Skeat's 'Student's Edition.' "[8] Although they give no more details, the edition they used is presumably W. W. Skeat's one-volume *Student's Chaucer,* an edition that takes as its texts those established in his six-volume edition of *The Works of Geoffrey Chaucer,* published in 1894.[9] But what does "the basis for collation" mean here?

Clearly it signifies something other than copy-text.[10] Skeat's edition, the "basis for collation," did have a base text, in El. But Skeat felt able to regularly disregard El's orthographic forms. He consistently changed its spellings (he had a tendency to replace El's *y* with *i*, its consonantal *u* with *v*, to remove diphthongs, and he engaged in other forms of regularization, such as replacement of thorn by *th*). In addition, he did not signal rejected readings in the conventional manner by the use of square brackets, which at least potentially poses some difficulty in collation in invariably distinguishing his emendations from the readings of his base text. And Skeat employed the Bradshaw Shift, repositioning Fragment VII (B^2) immediately after Fragment II (B^1).[11] Thus there would have

---

[8] Manly and Rickert, eds., *The Text,* 1:5.

[9] W. W. Skeat, ed., *The Student's Chaucer* (Oxford: Clarendon Press, 1895), 419–717; and *The Complete Works of Geoffrey Chaucer,* 6 vols. (Oxford: Clarendon Press, 1894). On the connection between the two, see E. P. Hammond, *Chaucer: A Bibliographical Manual* (New York: Macmillan, 1908), 147.

[10] Joseph A. Dane makes this point in his "Copy-Text and Its Variants in Some Recent Chaucer Editions," *SB* 44 (1991): 164–83, and, more extensively, in his "On the Presumed Influence of Skeat's Student's Chaucer on Manly and Rickert's *Text of the Canterbury Tales," Analytical & Enumerative Bibliography,* n.s. 7 (1993): 18–27.

[11] For general discussion of Skeat as editor, see A. S. G. Edwards, "W. W. Skeat," in *Editing Chaucer,* ed. Paul G. Ruggiers, 171–89, 280–85.

been obvious difficulties in using "the basis for collation" as the base text. But Skeat did not provide their base text.

Manly and Rickert never discuss their departures from the text of Skeat's *Student's Chaucer*. But they did not use the Bradshaw Shift. They eliminate all forms of punctuation that appear in Skeat; their text is wholly unpunctuated, a decision never explained. And quite often the orthography of their text differs from that of the *Student's Chaucer*. For example, for the first forty-eight lines, these differences in spelling occur between the two editions (Manly and Rickert's reading provides the lemma):

1. Aprill} Aprille; soote} sote
2. roote} rote
3. euery} every
5. sweete} swete
6. euery} every
8. half} halfe
9. foweles} fowles
10. nyght} night; eye} ye
12. pilgrymages} pilgrimages
13. palmeres} palmers
14. kouthe} couthe
15. euery} every
18. seeke} seke
22. deuout} devout
24. compaignye} companye
25. auenture} aventure
26. felaweship} felawshipe; pilgryms} pilgrims
31. euerichon} everichon
34. oure} our; deuyse} devyse
35. nathelees} natheles; haue} have
37. thynketh} thinketh; acordant} acordaunt
42. bigynne} biginne
45. riden} ryden; loued} loved; chiualrye} chivalrye

These readings seem typical both of Skeat's general practice and Manly and Rickert's disinclination to adhere to the orthographic forms that he imposed upon El.

If it is clear that to Manly and Rickert "basis for collation" was not the same as "base text" or "copy-text," the obvious questions arise. On what was their text based? Does this text provide the basis for their lemmata, or does Skeat? And, if the former, what difficulties, if any, might be involved in translating variants from one set of lemmata (Skeat) to another (their base text)?

To attempt to answer the first question: What is the basis of Manly and Rickert's text? None of the readings of Skeat's edition detailed above occur in El, his base text. Indeed, they seem to have no authority. In creating their own text, Manly and Rickert were clearly justified in rejecting them. And virtually all of Manly and Rickert's forms listed above occur in El. Only one of the thirty-one orthographic variants from Skeat in these lines does not appear there; in line 37, Skeat follows the Ellesmere reading "acordaunt," while Manly and Rickert read "acordant." It is not clear why they did so. Hence, in effect, the basis (the copy-text) for Manly and Rickert's text seems to have been a version of Skeat's *Student's Chaucer* that was read against El to restore most of the orthographic forms of that manuscript.

Manly and Rickert never explain why they adopted their apparent procedure to establish the accidentals of their text. The nearest they come to explaining their methodology is in the preface, when they acknowledge the work of "Miss Mabel Dean of our staff," who had studied dialect and spelling: "Miss Dean first attempted to discover whether the more carefully written MSS of the first two decades of the fifteenth century showed any regularity or approximation towards a common standard, with a view to making use of these results of the spelling of our text. She discovered that there was strong evidence of the prevalence of common habits which, if systematized, approximated very closely the spelling found in the Hengwrt and Ellesmere MSS. This was accordingly adopted as our standard."[12] As a statement of method, this leaves rather a lot to be desired. How, for example, does one "systematize" the orthography of different manuscripts? What are the distinctive characteristics of such a "standard"? Can the results be classified dialectally? Does this "systematization" have any implications for our understanding of Chaucer's metrics? None of these questions seems to be answered by Manly and Rickert. What is wholly beyond dispute is that the orthographic forms in their edition are frequently not those of Skeat's edition,

---

[12] Manly and Rickert, eds., *The Text*, 1:x.

their "basis for collation." It is unclear at what stage in their work they undertook this evidently extensive correction of Skeat's text.

The use of a text as a "basis for collation" that is then replaced by a copy-text—that printed in volumes 3 and 4 of their work—creates obvious possibilities for error in the process of the necessary consequent adjustment of the forms of the variant readings. Obviously if the lemmata are changed, then of course the forms of the variants will also change. Some readings inadvertently may get omitted in the process of adjustment. For example, it is startling to find that, early in their collation record, they omit a substantive Ellesmere variant: at line I, 92, Manly and Rickert's text reads *is*; Ellesmere reads *in*; the variant does not appear in the Corpus of Variants.[13]

Further difficulties obtain when one considers another aspect of Manly and Rickert's method, their system of collation. What are the principles upon which readings are selected for inclusion in their Corpus of Variants? They claim that this corpus "record[s] all the variants of all the MSS, with the exception of such spelling variants as are universally recognized to have no value for purposes of classification." They later claim: "We made a large collection of conflate readings and of scribal errors of all sorts and intended to include them in these volumes, but they would require many more pages and they would hardly serve their purpose unless accompanied by facsimile illustrations of the errors. We shall therefore reserve these collections for possible future publication."[14] This statement seems rather puzzling. Since scribal error provides a crucial element in establishing textual relationships, it is not clear why such readings should be suppressed.

To illustrate the problem, one can return to the opening lines of the *Canterbury Tales*. Further examination of Manly and Rickert's changes to Skeat shows that their tendency to restore El forms is not a consistent process. Thus, on folio 1r (1:1–48), a number of El's readings are either silently changed or mistranscribed. In the following list, Manly and Rickert's text (3:3–4) provides the lemma:

1. his} hise
12. Than} Thanne; pilgrymages} pilgrimage
14. kouthe} kowthe (Skeat: couthe)

[13] Ibid., 3:6; 5:8.
[14] Ibid., 1:xiii, 3:vi.

15. from] fram (Skeat: from)
17. holy] hooly (Skeat: holy)
18. that] þat[15]
19. Bifel] Bifil
37. acordant] acordaunt
40. weren] were
45. chiualrye] chiualrie (Skeat: chivalrye)
46. curteisye] curteisie (Skeat: curteisye)

Skeat records 1, 12 (both), 19, and 40 above as rejected readings, as he does a number of orthographic forms from El that Manly and Rickert retained in their text; and in 37 (as noted above), he retains an El spelling that they rejected. But it is clear that, if what happens here is typical, their text leaves quite a lot to be explained in terms of its orthographic forms. Where do these departures from El come from? And this confusion extends beyond orthography to substantive readings. For example, in line 12, they print *pilgrymages* for Skeat's *pilgrimages*. But Skeat records this as an emendation to El, which reads *pilgrymage*. The text (3:3) does not record the emendation, nor does the Corpus of Variants (5:3) note the rejected El reading.

Nor is it clear, on the basis of their statement, what principles obtain for the actual inclusion of readings. Take, for example, the very first reading in their Corpus of Variants 5:3). In compressed form, it reads:

1. Aprill] Aprilł . . . Apprilł . . . April . . . Aprił . . . Aperil . . . Apreyłł . . . Aueryłł . . . Auerełł . . . Aprile . . . Aprylle . . .

It might seem that all these are "spelling variants as have no value for purposes of classification." If so, why are they included? One notes particularly variants involving barred *l* or *ll*. What significance is perceived as attaching to them? Or again, on the same page, the following: "8. his half] h. halff." What significance attaches to such an orthographic variant? How can such trivial orthographic variants assist in "purposes of classification"? Manly and Rickert assert that "any attempt to include spelling and dialect forms would complicate the [collation] record to the point of uselessness" (2:10). How, then, is the recording of such forms as those above to be explained?

[15] Thorn seems generally to have been changed to *th* throughout the text, even though Manly and Rickert do preserve it on occasion in their variant readings.

No ready answer suggests itself to this question or to the others I have raised in this short essay. What seems clear is that if candor and method are criteria that have any place in an edition, they are not manifest in Manly and Rickert's. One could proceed with further questions. What, for instance, is the relationship between the variants they print at the foot of each page of their edition and those in their Corpus of Variants? But to attempt to answer that would be as fruitless.

If, then, Manly and Rickert's text seems open to serious methodological objections, and if, as has often been maintained, their theories about the transmission of Chaucer's text are not susceptible to confident interpretation, and if their apparent predisposition to prefer Hengwrt over Ellesmere seems misguided, is there anything that is salvageable from their work seventy years later?

One possibility that seems to have been surprisingly ignored lies in the implications of Greg's theory of copy-text. For in some ways the debate initiated by Manly and Rickert over the asserted superiority of Hengwrt has been futile. Given the incomplete and anomalous state of Hengwrt, it can scarcely serve, on simply pragmatic grounds, as the base text for any edition of the *Canterbury Tales*, however much Ellesmere's readings may require emendation. Indeed, Manly and Rickert show little understanding of the distinction between the pragmatics of copy-text—the selection of a base manuscript on criteria of early date, physical completeness, and dialectal congruence with its putative place of origin—and the potential freedom to emend the copy-text where the evidence of the variants suggests such a possibility.

Indeed, it is the general failure to consider the evidence of their Corpus of Variants that remains one of the great paradoxes of Manly and Rickert's achievement. Certainly they seem to have paid little attention to these data, and subsequent scholarship has been largely content to ignore it as well. It exists simply as a corpus of rejected readings, not as an assemblage of evidence that might be analyzed, where recension is not possible, to establish directions of error and to infer originality, in the manner employed most notably by George Kane in editing *Piers Plowman*. As I have indicated, there are problems with the Corpus of Variants. But even if its evidence may need to be rechecked before particular conclusions can be reached, it offers considerable potential for analysis in directional terms at a number of cruces.

"Learning, Taste and Judgment" in the Editorial Process:

Vance Ramsey and Manly-Rickert

Jill Mann
Girton College, Cambridge
University of Notre Dame

T HE TITLE OF ROY VANCE RAMSEY'S BOOK raises expectations that it will help to make sense of Manly and Rickert's daunting edition of the *Canterbury Tales*. To some extent, these expectations are fulfilled. Chapter 2 provides a fascinating and illuminating history of the Manly-Rickert project: much pathos is (justifiably) wrung from the account of the practical and financial difficulties under which the two scholars worked, culminating in Rickert's death a year before the publication of the edition and Manly's death a few months after it. It also helps to know that volumes 3 and 4, containing the text of the *Canterbury Tales*, were completed first, under pressure from the university administration to show some results. Ramsey summarizes the "fundamental discoveries" that Manly and Rickert made: "(1) the greater closeness of Hg to the original scribal copies of most of the links and tales than El or any other extant manuscript; (2) the fact that apart from the constant groups the manuscripts tend to shift their textual affiliations from one locus to another; and above all (3) the Stage 1 piecemeal disseminations of links and tale beginning in the midst of Chaucer's composition and revision of them and the consequent Stage 2 gathering of the links and tales to serve as exemplars for making full manuscripts of the *Canterbury Tales*."[1] In addition, Ramsey stresses the importance of the detailed descriptions of the *Canterbury Tales* manuscripts provided in volume 1, which pioneered the serious study of vernacular manuscripts.

[1] Roy Vance Ramsey, *The Manly-Rickert Text of the "Canterbury Tales"* (Lewiston, N.Y.: Edwin Mellen Press, 1994), 628–29. Further references to Ramsey's book are given parenthetically in the text.

As Ramsey's (2) suggests, the most intimidating part of the Manly-Rickert edition is the Classification of Manuscripts in volume 2, which presents a bewildering picture of shifting manuscript affiliation not only between the individual tales but also within them. The genealogical method, instead of presenting a tidy stemma that would indicate the relative authority of individual manuscripts by placing them on a line of transmission, seems instead to have produced a jostling throng in which significant relationships are hard to make out. In such circumstances, the principles on which the editors judge one reading rather than another as the more likely to be original are unclear (and the scanty nature of Manly-Rickert's textual commentary does not help). For this reason, they have in the past been accused of "counting heads" (that is, giving weight to the number of manuscripts that preserve a reading), rather than classifying manuscript relationships by means of agreement *in error*. It is here above all that the Chaucer scholar looks for aid from Ramsey's book, and to a certain extent receives it. Ramsey explains these shifts in affiliation not by contamination (*ctm*), which Manly and Rickert slowly discarded as an explanation, but as the surviving traces of the Stage 1 circulation of the tales, which resulted in strange amalgamations of material as scribes and would-be owners cobbled together tales and links (each with their own sets of scribal errors) that Chaucer was still revising. This confusion is (allegedly) the justification for Manly and Rickert's classification of manuscripts by shared readings (variants), despite the fact that many of these readings will undeniably have arisen by accident (Greg's "convergent variation," Manly-Rickert's "accidental convergence" or "*acco*"), because of the tendency for scribes to make the same kinds of error independently of one another. On pages 195–204, Ramsey takes the reader through a discussion of unique variants (those shared by no other manuscript), genetic variants (those that are transmitted by one manuscript to its descendants), and convergent variants (those that recur in different manuscripts by chance), and concludes that because of the last-named, only "the laws of probability" can reveal manuscript affiliations (though not right readings). For this reason, Ramsey has constant recourse to Charles Moorman's statistical analyses of the affiliations of *Canterbury Tales* manuscripts.[2] Using his own chart of variants in *The Nun's Priest's Tale* (199) as an example, Ramsey shows

---

[2] Charles Moorman, *The Statistical Determination of Affiliation in the Landmark Manuscripts of the Canterbury Tales* (Lewiston, N.Y.: Edwin Mellen Press, 1993).

how Manly and Rickert established the existence of "constant groups" among the manuscripts, and why they suggested four lines of transmission for this tale (203). However, apart from the (small) "constant groups," Ramsey acknowledges that his chart "makes clear that few of the manuscripts share a high enough percentage of their variants with one another to point to any very close *genetic* relationship between themselves and the others" (201; my italics), and in the case of the fourth group, which contains some very important manuscripts (Hg, El, Dd, Gg), it also makes clear "just how tenuous the relations between them are." "In such cases (and this one is fairly typical)," he goes on, "Manly and Rickert were dealing with numbers and percentages too small to allow their conclusions to be other than quite tentative, certainly too tentative to construct a stemma of four branches matching their suggested four lines of transmission" (204).

Ramsey's concern here seems to be to defend Manly and Rickert against the accusation that their laborious collations and classifications did not result in a stemma; having established its impossibility, he moves on to other topics. But it is just here that the subject becomes interesting. For it is of course the construction of a stemma that is supposed to guide an editor in identifying original readings, as opposed to scribal variants. In the absence of a stemma, how did Manly and Rickert distinguish (probable) right readings from scribal corruptions? They (and Ramsey) are silent on this, but from their Textual Notes it appears that they were often swayed by the occurrence of a reading in different lines of transmission (rather than by the number of manuscripts that contained it). So, to go back to *The Nun's Priest's Tale*, if a reading were attested in three of the four lines of transmission that they identify, they would be inclined to accept it as original.[3] But the tenuousness of the relations between the manuscripts in the fourth group, of which Ramsey is fully aware, makes this sort of procedure doubtful, to say the least. Each of the manuscripts in this group might itself represent a separate line of transmission, which would upset the calculations considerably. And if (as Manly and Rickert claimed to have "discovered," and Ramsey repeatedly emphasizes) the manuscripts reflect different stages of composition, why should not more than one variant have a claim to authenticity?[4]

---

[3] See also the account given by Ralph Hanna, *Pursuing History: Middle English Manuscripts and Their Texts* (Stanford: Stanford University Press, 1996), 137, with a useful diagram.

[4] As Ramsey acknowledges (605).

Ramsey's book contains a running attack on editors such as George Kane and Talbot Donaldson (not to mention Bentley and Housman), who think that it is possible to determine what an author wrote by the exercise of "learning, taste and judgment" (606). Of course, Ramsey acknowledges, these qualities must be deployed "by any editor worthy of the name, *but they should be the very last resort of an editor and not the first*" (606–7; Ramsey's italics). The first resort is "a full and careful study of all the available evidence—in the present case and above all, the manuscripts and Manly-Rickert" (606).[5] Early in his book, Ramsey promises to outline in Chapter 8 the procedure that anyone who wants to edit Chaucer properly should follow. When the promised outline finally arrives (601–7), it is disappointingly vague and general: first, the editor should "study the manuscripts themselves" (how, exactly?), and also "anything else which promises to be of material aid, first and foremost Manly-Rickert" (601), especially volumes 1 and 2. The next step is to compare the *Variorum Chaucer* editions of individual tales with Manly-Rickert (601), but *not* in order to follow the *Variorum* practice of sticking as closely as possible to Hg (602–3). The would-be editor will bear in

[5] This may be a good place to testify to my own careful study of Manly-Rickert by recording a substantial omission in their text of *Melibee*, which has to the best of my knowledge escaped notice for the last seventy years. See Manly-Rickert 4:180, where *Mel* 2504 is omitted (through eyeskip caused by repetition of "And after this than shal ye kepe yow" at the beginning of 2504 and 2505). Other typographical errors in the text of Manly-Rickert (confirmed as such by the appearance of the correct reading as the lemma at the appropriate point in Manly-Rickert's Corpus of Variants) are as follows (correct reading given second): *KnT* 1305 table atthamaunt > table of atthamaunt; *KnT* 3507 this > al this; *KnT* 3089 passen > to passen; *RvT* 4314 his whete > the whete; *MLT* 501 the desert > desert; *MLT* 625 as hir lyf > right as hir lyf; *MLT* 817 wo is me > so wo is me; *MLT* 1134 day to day > day to night; *WBP* 170 drynken on > drynken of; *WBP* 844 I wol bishrewe > I bishrewe; *WBT* 1002 what > what that; *WBT* 1140 mount Kaukasous > mount of Kaukasous; *SumT* 1846 My body > The body; *ClT* 675 kan worse > worse kan; *ClT* 1199 as a tigre > as is a tigre; *Sq-FranL* 692 He > And he; *PardT* 475 ynough > noght ynough; *PardT* 773 the sighte > that sighte; *PardT* 782 By > Ey; *PrT* 566/1756 the world > this world; *Mel* 1087/2277 in a desert > in desert; *Mel* 1342/2532 greet deliberacioun > greet diligence and greet deliberacioun; *CYT* 1055 to quyte yow with > to quyte with; *CYT* 1457 This > This is; *ManT* 279 o ire o recchelees > o ire recchelees; *ParsT* 255 ouer synnes > oure synnes; *ParsT* 363 sooth > dooth; *ParsT* 432 as in thynges > is in thynges; *ParsT* 781 the cure > cure; *ParsT* 861 she were > it were.

In other cases, both El and Hg have a reading that is not recorded as a variant in Manly-Rickert's Corpus of Variants, so it may reasonably be supposed that the reading in Manly-Rickert's text is an error: *GP* 355 he was > was he; *MilT* 3699 me > my; *MLP* 116 reuerence > thy reuerence; *MLT* 898 hir wyf > his wyf; *WBP* 194 wyn and ale > wyn or ale; *ShT* 173/1363 But > And; *SNT* 219 and with an angel > with an angel; *ParsT* 726 For > For certes (El only). At *KnT* 2998, "nay" is an obvious error for "nat" (the reading of both El and Hg), and at *ManT* 31 "dawsen" should be "daswen."

mind the different stages in the production of the *Canterbury Tales* and the likelihood of authorial revisions (603–5). At this point, "quality of writing" can be invoked (605), but Ramsey offers no guidance in how to recognize scribal error or to choose between different variants.

Much of Ramsey's book is devoted to detailed characterization of selected key manuscripts: El, Ha[4], Gg, Dd, Cp, La, Pw, Hg. Here, if anywhere, we might expect to find the "objective" evidence that Ramsey promises the manuscripts will provide, and that is to outweigh the "subjective" criteria of meter and poetic merit. Unfortunately, despite their frequent use of statistical charts, these sections are riddled with subjectivity. For Ramsey, the number of unique variants (readings shared with no other manuscript) in a manuscript becomes a major indicator of that manuscript's accuracy in copying its exemplar (since the exemplar's readings are likely to have left traces somewhere else in the lines of transmission). So far, so good, but Ramsey then uses the fact that El has more unique variants than Hg (though both have a strikingly low number in comparison with almost all other manuscripts)[6] to establish Hg's claim to offer the "best text" of the *Canterbury Tales*, and to support Manly and Rickert's assertion that El is an "edited" text. The "edited" nature of El is reiterated throughout the book (from page 40 on), but despite Ramsey's assertion that he has "demonstrated" it in Chapter V.B, he supplies no evidence. The nearest we get is a sample list of unique variants from *The Knight's Tale* (328), as to which Ramsey says that he will leave the reader to decide "whether or not the changes look deliberate" (327). The list (with some spelling corrections, and the El version given in full as the second of the two) is as follows:

871   And eek hir yonge suster Emelye
      And eek hir *faire* suster Emelye

876   I wolde haue toold fully the manere
      I wolde *yow* haue toold fully the manere

931   I wrecche which þat wepe and waille thus
      I wrecche which þat wepe and *crie* thus

1063   And Palamon this woful prisoner
      And *this* Palamoun this woful prisoner

---

[6] See Ramsey's chart on page 186 and his statement on page 315.

1156 What wiltow seyn thow woost nat yet now
      What wiltow seyn thow *wistest* nat yet now

1472 With Nercotikes and opye of Thebes fyn
      Of Nercotikes and Opie of Thebes fyn

1514 In to the groue ful hastily he sterte
      In to *a* groue ful hastily he sterte

1560 Thus hath youre Ire oure lynage al fordo
      Thus hath youre ire oure *kynrede* al fordo

Leaving aside entirely the question of which of these paired readings is the more likely to be original, I have to say that I cannot see *any* motive for deliberate change in any of them. The usual motive cited in the case of El is a desire to "smooth" the meter (both Ramsey and the *Variorum* editors make this claim while citing El lines that do nothing of the sort, and ignoring Hg lines that are more regular than El's). But the El variants in these lines, with the exception of 1156, do not improve the meter, and in the case of 1063 the El variant destroys it.

Ramsey never gives an account of Chaucer's meter, and the few clues he lets drop suggest that this is because his notion of it is woefully inadequate. In the first place, he often speaks of it in terms of syllables rather than stresses (e.g., page 46, where he speaks of the first line of *GP* as a nine-syllable line).[7] His few references to stress are muddled and obscure: on page 358, he speaks of the "familiar 4-beat line." On page 325, he suggests that El adds "And of" at the beginning of *CYT* 817, "Oure cementyng and fermentacioun," in order to avoid "a possible 'nine-beat line.'"[8] This shows a deplorable degree of muddle. In its non-El version, the line has neither nine beats (stresses) nor nine syllables (perhaps Ramsey did not know that "-ioun" is disyllabic?); it is a perfectly regular line of five stresses (and ten syllables) and so could not possibly call forth any metrical "smoothing" from El.

I have elsewhere presented detailed evidence to refute the notion that

---

[7] It has in fact ten syllables (counting the final -e on "soote") and is more accurately described as a "headless" line, in which the first weak stress is omitted. This is a perfectly admissible variation in Chaucer's meter; see below, note 10.

[8] The addition is more likely induced by the preceding "And of" at the beginning of line 816. I am told this has been changed in the new edition of Ramsey's book (which I have not seen) to "a possible 'four-beat line.'" The larger problem remains.

El is an "edited" text,[9] and there is no space to repeat it here. I have also given elsewhere my own account of the metrical principles governing Chaucer's verse in the *Canterbury Tales*,[10] making use both of close study of scribal practice in the manuscripts and of the computerized analyses of pronunciation/nonpronunciation of final -e by Barber and Barber,[11] as well as of other detailed analyses by Halle and Keyser, Hascall, and Kane and Cowen.[12] The point to be made here is that meter is *not*, as Ramsey seems to think, a "subjective" matter. Its rules are as "objective" and as recoverable by close study and analysis as anything else in textual studies. And they are one of the few tools that we have for discerning which of the many manuscript variants are likely to be original—if we give Chaucer his due as the consummate metrist that close study of his text (in manuscripts as well as editions) by anyone with an ear for poetry shows him to be.

Ramsey's defense of Hg goes far beyond Manly-Rickert to embrace not only Hg's text but also its jumbled tale-order,[13] which he defends

[9] "Chaucer's Meter and the Myth of the Ellesmere Editor of *The Canterbury Tales*," *SAC* 23 (2001): 71–107.

[10] See my edition of *The Canterbury Tales* (London: Penguin, 2005), lxv. The *Canterbury Tales* line is a line of five stresses, usually arranged in a weak-strong pattern. Variations in this pattern that occur with some frequency are: the inversion of weak and strong stress at the opening of a line or after the midline break; the absence of a weak stress at the opening of a line (a so-called headless line); and the absence of a weak stress between two strong stresses, especially at the midline break, where the perception of a tiny pause between the two strong stresses may be deemed to take its place. In certain circumstances (specified by Hascall in the article cited in note 12), two syllables may constitute a single metrical position.

[11] Charles Barber and Nicholas Barber, "The Versification of *The Canterbury Tales*: A Computer-Based Statistical Study," *LeedsSE*, n.s. 21 (1990): 81–103, and n.s. 22 (1991): 57–83. Despite Ramsey's heavy reliance on the computerized analyses of manuscript affiliations that Charles Moorman carried out, he does not seem to know of Barber and Barber's study.

[12] See Morris Halle and Samuel Jay Keyser, "Chaucer and the Study of Prosody," *CE* 28 (1966): 187–219; Dudley L. Hascall, "Some Contributions to the Halle-Keyser Theory of Prosody," *CE* 30 (1968): 357–65 (Hascall's modifications were accepted by Halle and Keyser, *English Stress: Its Form, Its Growth, and Its Role in Verse* [New York: Harper and Row, 1971], 172 n. 15). See also the introductory section, "The Grammar of Chaucer's Final *E* in Relation to Editorial Problems of Metre," in the Cowen and Kane edition of Chaucer's *Legend of Good Women*, 112–23. Further modifications to the Halle-Keyser theory are discussed in Gilbert Youmans, "Reconsidering Chaucer's Prosody," in *English Historical Metrics*, ed. C. B. McCully and J. J. Anderson (Cambridge: Cambridge University Press, 1996), 185–209. For a helpful survey of theories of English meter, which includes a measured assessment of the advantages and disadvantages of the Halle-Keyser theory (34–46), see Derek Attridge, *The Rhythms of English Poetry* (London: Longman, 1982), 34–46.

[13] This includes accepting that Hg's botched transformations of *Sq-FranL* to a Sq-Mer link, and of *MerE-SqH* to a Mer-Fran link, represent Chaucer's first thoughts (Ramsey,

by extending the "Marriage Group" to include *MkT*, *ManT*, and *SNT*, supposedly constituting "a more general exploration of the characters, points of view and relationships of men and women with one another in this world, finally to end with a turning away from such earthly matters to heavenly ones" (549). At this level of generality, one could justify *any* arrangement of tales (and the judgments involved, be it noted, are of a purely "subjective" nature). Ramsey does not, however, claim that Hg represents Chaucer's final intentions for the *Canterbury Tales*, but rather Manly and Rickert's "Stage 1," when Chaucer was trying out various ideas, whereas El represents, in some tales at least, a later, revised version.[14] Editorial convention would dictate a preference for an author's *last* thoughts about a text as those that should be honored in print, but this cuts no ice with Ramsey, who insists that El is a scribal compilation of tales and links, whereas Hg is (he speculates) a collection assembled from tales and links sent by Chaucer to his son Lewis in Wales (similarly, Dd represents tales sent to Thomas Chaucer in Oxford).[15] Such speculations founder on the simple fact that Ramsey's belief in Hg's Welsh provenance (520) is baseless.

Leaving such fanciful hypotheses aside, however, Manly and Rickert's notion that the chaotic state of the *Canterbury Tales* manuscripts, and the texts they contain, reflects the release of tales and links piecemeal, as Chaucer composed and revised them, is not in itself implausible, and

---

Manly-Rickert Text, 544, 558–59, 563–64, 603), with the implicit (and absurd) supposition that Chaucer later realized that "Marchant certeyn" could be neatly turned into "Frankeleyn," with concomitant improvement of the meter. Daniel Mosser's recent reconsideration of the possibility that the Hg order might represent an early stage of Chaucer's intentions acknowledges the spurious nature of these two links in their Hg versions. " 'Chaucer's Scribe,' Adam, and the Hengwrt Project," in *Design and Distribution of Late Medieval Manuscripts in England,* ed. Margaret Connolly and Linne R. Mooney (Woodbridge: York Medieval Press, 2008), 11–40 (36).

[14] See Ramsey, *The Manly-Rickert Text,* 166, 287–91, 469, 528–32. This would account for the presence in El of the lines not contained in Hg: e.g., *KnT* 2779–82; *MilT* 3155–56, 3721–22; *WBP* 575–84, 609–12, 619–26, 717–20; *FranT* 1455–56, 1493–98.

[15] See Ramsey, *The Manly-Rickert Text,* 377–80, 397–406, 519–24. Ramsey's claim (523) that Hg's "earliest feature connects it with Wales" is based on Manly-Rickert's reading of a word written by dry point on fol. 13v as 'builth,' which they identify as the name of a town in Wales. Simon Horobin has reminded me that A. I. Doyle and M. B. Parkes explained that this word should be seen the other way up, as *smug* or *snug* (*The Canterbury Tales: A Facsimile and Transcription of the Hengwrt Manuscript, with Variants from the Ellesmere Manuscript,* ed. Paul G. Ruggiers (Norman: University of Oklahoma Press, 1979), xlvii. Hg's earliest connections are with Cheshire, and its association with Wales began only in the seventeenth century, when it entered the library of Robert Vaughan of Hengwrt (ibid., xlviii).

neither is the notion that Hg is a hasty assemblage of individual tales and links from a number of different sources. But this idea is of little or no assistance to an editor in determining which readings are likely to be original. Faced with (for example) Hg's lack of the "Adam stanza" at the beginning of *MkT* (added in the margin by a later hand), an editor still has to decide (by the exercise of intelligence and knowledge of scribal habits) whether it was omitted by scribal error or whether it was added in revision.[16] Conversely, an editor must decide whether the lines that appear in Hg but not in El, or vice versa, or the links that appear in neither but are contained in other manuscripts, are the result of scribal interference or authorial changes—and if the latter, whether they are more likely to have been added or cancelled in revision.[17] Furthermore, apart from these additional lines and links, it is very hard to identify lines that show traces of authorial revision. The section "Early and Revised Versions" in volume 2 of Manly-Rickert (which Manly makes clear represents Rickert's theories rather than his own) finds significance in a series of minute alterations that are indistinguishable, to me at any rate, from ordinary scribal variants.[18] Ramsey uses a similar list of minor scribal alterations as a starting point for arguing that "indications of authorial revision" (513) can be detected in some variants that Hg and El (and other manuscripts) share in *The Friar's Tale* (Hg/El variants in square brackets).

1296 Which nedeth nat rehercen at [for] this tyme

1308 Of contractes and [and eek] of lakke of sacramentz

1322 A slyer boy was [nas] noon in Engelond

[16] Hanna, in *Pursuing History,* plausibly suggests that it was lost by eyeskip (since the next stanza also begins with "Lo") (151).

[17] For example, *GP* 252a–b appear in Hg but not in El; see note 14 above for examples of lines that appear in El but not in Hg. *The Man of Law Endlink* and *The Nun's Priest's Endlink* appear in neither Hg nor El.

[18] See, for example, the *d* variants cited on pages 496–97 (the *d* reading being the first given in each case), or Rickert's list of the trivial changes that "produced a better rhythm" at *KnT* 1749 (to wepe > for to wepe), 1765 (thogh that > althogh that), 1858 (have spoke > spak), 1861 (hath gyffen > yeueth), 2478 (Weep now > Now weep), 2527 (place > paleys), 2621 (for to reste > reste), 2627 (Whan > Whan that). It is hard to imagine Chaucer suddenly and belatedly realizing that a line would scan better if he changed "to" to "for to" or vice versa. Rather, these are typical examples of scribal variation, made by scribes with little or no metrical sense.

1331 Ne neuere shullen terme of alle [*om.*] hir lyues

1450 To wite wher men wol [wolde] yeue me any thyng[19]

1556 It is nat his entente trust [trust thow] me wel

1559 This cartere thakketh [taketh][20] his hors vpon [on] the croupe

1596 And answere there by my procuratour [procutour][21]

On the shaky basis of the suggestion that "the author himself" might have been responsible for these variants, Ramsey argues that the change from singular to plural in *FrT* 1663–64 is a product of authorial revision:

Manly-Rickert text: And prayeth that this somnour hym repente
                    Of his mysdedes er that the feend hym hente
1663 this somnour] this somnours Hg; thise Somonours El
    hym] hem Hg[1] El
1664 his] hir Hg[1] El hym] hem Hg El

Hg[1] signals corrections of the original text over erasures in Hg. These scribal corrections (which overlook an inconsistent "this" in 1663), combined with (Ramsey's blind faith in) "the excellence of the Hg text," suggest to him that Hg's exemplar here was "the original scribal copy marked up by Chaucer in such a way as to leave some doubt about whether he had finally settled on the singular or the plural in the last two lines" (516). But it could equally have been a defectively copied original, corrected by Chaucer in a similarly confusing way (although El managed to read it aright). The second thoughts would then belong to the Hg scribe, rather than to Chaucer.[22]

    The main point to be made here, however, is that Ramsey's argument

---

[19] El actually reads "wolde me yeuen" here.

[20] The variant clearly arises from the replacement of "thakketh" with an easier reading.

[21] This variant also clearly has scribal causes—to wit, the omission of an abbreviation for r + vowel.

[22] My own view would be that El's plural is original, and that the singular results from the scribes' being influenced by their knowledge of the presence of the individual pilgrim Summoner.

is highly subjective. He imagines Chaucer making a change from singular to plural because "on second thought" he found the reference to the individual pilgrim Summoner "too direct and open" to fit the pilgrim Friar (515). The invocation of manuscript authority ("the excellence of Hg" 516) does not counter this subjectivity, but is co-opted in support of it, despite the fact that in lines 1663–64 Hg's "excellence," even on Ramsey's account of the matter, consists solely in the corrections that bring its text partially into line with El. Edith Rickert had the good sense to acknowledge that her own case for revised versions would depend on "the knowledge and taste of the reader" (496), exercised in response to the evidence she put forward. Ramsey's arguments similarly from first to last call for the exercise of the "learning, taste and judgment" whose operations he wishes to defer. Unfortunately, these are just the areas in which his arguments generally prove deficient.

To conclude: the lasting value of Manly-Rickert is that (1) it demonstrates the impossibility of using recension to reconstruct the text of the *Canterbury Tales*, and (2) it provides a huge amount of raw data concerning the *Canterbury Tales* manuscripts and their readings. Anyone wanting to quarry these data for particular purposes would be well advised *not* to take Ramsey as a guide.

Opportunity's Knock and Chaucerian Textual Criticism

Tim William Machan
Marquette University

T HE 1980S WAS A HEADY DECADE for textual critics. If bad hair, John Hughes films, and MTV defined a generation, Jerome McGann and D. F. McKenzie defined an entirely new way of looking at literature, its transmission, and its authorship. Introducing concepts like the "ideology of final intentions" and the "sociology of texts," they diverted textual criticism from the study of isolated variants and texts to what might be called holistic consideration of the life of literary works. How do the processes of production and reception contribute to the definition of authors, texts, and works? they asked. And how do textual-critical decisions prefigure and transcend interpretive ones?

Textual criticism of medieval literature shared in this renaissance, with the sociological emphasis fostering an enthusiasm for the relevance of codicological work to the interpretation of medieval poetry. This approach applied the details of manuscript provenance and transmission (as well as the affiliation to readings) of, say, the *Parliament of Fowls* to suggest that the concluding roundel might well be in part a scribal attempt to tie up a Chaucerian poem of doubt and uncertainty.[1] Seeking to define the broad scribal culture in which Chaucer's works circulated, scholars even identified individual scribes and the texts they copied. In this regard, perhaps the most controversial and discussed textual-critical issue involved the composition of the *Canterbury Tales* and, more particularly, the significance of the Hengwrt and Ellesmere manuscripts. It seemed as if half the world's Chaucerians regarded the former as the most authoritative, and the other half the latter. All things seemed possible.

[1] Ralph Hanna, "Representing Chaucer as Author," in *Medieval Literature: Texts and Interpretation*, ed. Tim William Machan (Binghamton, N.Y.: MRTS, 1991), 17–40.

But when all things are possible, of course, they are not also necessarily probable. To look back at the decade of textual-critical controversy now—nearly thirty years since the publication of McGann's *A Critique of Modern Textual Criticism*—particularly from the vantage of Chaucerian studies, is to confront the fact that for all its ferment, the period promised more than it ever delivered. And it is not so much that its controversies have been resolved as that they have been allowed to fade from view.

The Hengwrt-Ellesmere issue, to which Vance Ramsey devoted significant energy, is a case in point. Manly and Rickert had presumed that large shops were responsible for the production of most of Chaucer's work and had focused their attentions on the circulation of texts and readings, not documents. In various ways, critics like C. Paul Christianson and Ralph Hanna demolished such presumptions by identifying coteries and individual professional scribes whose efforts circulated in booklets. Such critics put manuscripts back in the hands of those who produced them and made it possible to go beyond the question "What does this mean?" to "How does this mean?" What was at issue in the Hengwrt-Ellesmere dispute, then, was not merely the more authorial readings or tale order but the composition, transmission, and character of the *Canterbury Tales*. It was not about a manuscript as an abstract site of work but about manuscripts as material culture and how the texts we read, medieval or modern, above all reproduce the conditions of their existence. To what extent is Chaucer's metrical virtuosity owing to the influence of an early medieval editor, and how would such influence affect our understanding of his individual achievement? In what ways did the circulation of manuscripts among isolated scribes determine medieval readers' sense of Chaucer? If the tale orders and readings of later manuscripts could all be traced to Hengwrt, would this be the closest witness we have to a holograph for readings and tale order? Is Chaucer's poetry what we can reconstruct or what was read? What *was* Chaucer's poetry in a historical, material sense?

This textual-critical ferment yielded two editorial ideas with terrific possibilities for scholars and students alike. In an offhand way in 1985, Derek Pearsall noted that Chaucer had left the *Canterbury Tales* as "a partly assembled kit with no directions. This is how, ideally, it should be presented, partly as a bound book (with first and last fragments fixed) and partly as a set of fragments in folders, with the incomplete information as to their nature and placement fully displayed."[2] Pearsall's point, of course, is that while the first fragment obviously begins the collection and the tenth just as obviously concludes it, what happens between these bookends is much less clear. Indeed, the manuscripts' varying contents, readings, tale orders, and spurious links manifest a work that was fundamentally open and malleable in the Middle Ages.

Over the years, Pearsall's metaphor and proposed edition have resonated favorably with many Chaucerians who otherwise share little common critical ground.[3] It would seem that conceptually an unfinished edition has much to recommend it. Practically, things have been otherwise, for such an edition has never been produced. Indeed, the standard edition today for teaching as well as scholarly purposes is the resolutely bound *Riverside*, which may have appeared in 1987 but which, as a revision of F. N. Robinson's 1957 and 1933 editions, in many ways rested on textual-critical decisions made long before arguments about the sociology of the text. While the sequential numbering of *Canterbury Tales* fragments may acknowledge the poem's incompleteness, in every other way the layout of the book overrides the very uncertainty that Pearsall foregrounds. Following the example of Robinson 1 and 2, for instance, *Riverside* prints only one of what it acknowledges to be two versions of the Prologue to *The Nun's Priest's Tale*, thereby eliding signs of the poem's partially assembled status. By adjoining an epilogue to the tale, the *Riverside* likewise fosters the notion that Fragment VII is complete— even though the notes acknowledge that the epilogue was probably cancelled. In the spirit of the decade, Pearsall proposed an edition that reflects the identity of the *Canterbury Tales*, but the *Riverside Chaucer* in effect merely nods to this identity, which it then reshapes into a polished product. The edition gets the kit both ways—unfinished and finished.[4]

---

[2] *The Canterbury Tales* (London: Allen and Unwin, 1985), 23.

[3] For example, Philippa Hardman, review of *The Canterbury Tales, RES* 38 (1987): 542–43 (542); Phyllis Portnoy, "The Best-Text/Best-Book of Canterbury: The Dialogic of the Fragments," *Florilegium* 13 (1994): 161–72 (166); Ralph Hanna, *Pursuing History: Middle English Manuscripts and Their Texts* (Stanford: Stanford University Press, 1996), 180; Ann W. Astell, *Chaucer and the Universe of Learning* (Ithaca: Cornell University Press, 1999), 227; David C. Greetham, *Theories of the Text* (Oxford: Oxford University Press, 1999), 242; Míceál F. Vaughan, "Chaucer's *Canterbury Tales* and the Auchinleck MS: Analogous Collections?" *Archiv* 242 (2005): 259–74 (265); and Marijane Osborn, *Time and the Astrolabe in the Canterbury Tales* (Norman: University of Oklahoma Press, 2002), 97.

[4] This same kind of double consciousness underwrites interpretive treatments that accept the poem as unfinished and then proceed as if this condition has little or no impact on interpretation. For example, Stephanie Trigg, *Congenial Souls: Reading Chaucer from Modern to Postmodern* (Minneapolis: University of Minnesota Press, 2001), 83; Os-

Editorial opportunity knocked again in Michael Murphy's presentation of the *Canterbury Tales*.[5] Published in 1991 (so that we might attribute it to the long 1980s), Murphy's edition arose from very specific circumstances—the fact that he taught at Brooklyn College, which has a significant population of immigrants and first-generation college students. It is a population of students, in other words, who are not necessarily born to the manner of academic training and traditions, reading verse aloud, or translating archaic English. In response, Murphy crafted not a translation, as he was careful to note, but simply a modern-spelling text with marginal glosses for words that either had changed meaning since the fourteenth century or had fallen out of use. In theory, then, he tried to make Chaucer's poetry accessible to students, while in practice doing what has been done to accidentals for years for Shakespeare's works as well as those of more recent writers. In Murphy's edition, the opening of the *Canterbury Tales* thus reads:

> When that April with his showers soote
> The drought of March hath pierced to the root
> And bathéd every vein in such liquor
> Of which virtue engendered is the flower.

Marginal glosses explain the archaic *soote* and medieval senses of *vein* and *liquor*, while a footnote translates line 4.

Murphy's "reader-friendly" edition eventually expanded to include the *General Prologue* and sixteen tales, and he has also modernized both *Troilus and Criseyde* and Henryson's *Testament of Cresseid*. The *Canterbury Tales* volume remains in print, in both its original form and in two selections, and all the modernizations are available online, linked to major research pages like the Chaucer Meta-Page.[6] Yet they cannot be said to have made much of an impact on the teaching and reading of Chaucer's poetry. According to WorldCat, the *Canterbury Tales* edition resides in just 173 libraries worldwide. By contrast, *The Riverside Chaucer*, which

---

born, *Time and the Astrolabe,* 270; Seth Lerer, "The Canterbury Tales," in *The Yale Companion to Chaucer* (New Haven: Yale University Press, 2006), 243–94 (244–45); Lee Patterson, ed., *Geoffrey Chaucer's "The Canterbury Tales": A Casebook* (New York: Oxford University Press, 2007), 8–9.

[5] Michael Murphy, *The General Prologue and Twelve Major Tales in Modern Spelling* (New York: University Press of America, 1991).

[6] See his *Canterbury Quintet: The General Prologue and Four Tales: A Reader-Friendly Edition* (New York: Conal and Gavin, 2000), and *Canterbury Marriage Tales: The Wife of Bath, The Clerk, The Merchant, The Franklin* (New York: Conal and Gavin, 2000).

has been issued in multiple formats, seems to be present in about 1,200 libraries, with the paperback *Canterbury Tales* selection in 100 more. And these numbers of course do not include what must be thousands upon thousands of copies (new and used) circulating among students and faculty.

My point is not simply to plug Murphy's edition. It is to suggest that the 1980s issue that motivated him—the accessibility of a medieval poet to contemporary students—is one that motivates everyone who teaches Chaucer's works and that even if we reject Murphy's solution, the difficulties he identified remain. While I am sure there are some undergraduates who can pick up the *Riverside* and read Chaucer without difficulty, I suspect there are many more, including some coming from accomplished high schools and attending selective universities, who find even the sterilized texts of the *Norton Anthology*, the Penguin editions, or the Broadview edition off-putting, if not incomprehensible. Indeed, the notion that students today are somehow better equipped to read Chaucer in the original is belied by the fact that the number of glosses in the eighth edition of the *Norton* has increased from that in the first, whether the word in question is an archaic one like *forsoothe* or an obscurely spelled one like *shirreve*. As the rate of glossing to poetry in all modern editions threatens to overwhelm the texts, it affirms the texts' inscrutability to modern readers. Teachers often say—I have often said—that Chaucer's English is worth the little effort that it takes to learn, but I wonder what a systematic survey of students' views on this issue would reveal, particularly of students in lower-division survey courses. And I worry that as a rationale this argument is reminiscent of the arguments that made generations of earlier students study Latin, only to result in Latin losing its centrality to the curriculum. Reading the *Canterbury Tales* in the original language may be much easier than reading the *Aeneid*, but when the argument for doing so is that endurance will lead to delayed gratification, Middle English becomes as dead as Latin.

A consistent response to Murphy's work has been that he does not provide what faculty desire: the possibility of teaching Chaucer in the original Middle English. Fair enough. But the various modern editions that ordinarily appear in classrooms do not themselves offer an authentic, unadulterated Middle English experience. By its nature, editing is a transformation, an unpacking, something that renders an original in an ersatz version accessible to those (in this case) without access to original manuscripts and without the ability to read them anyway.[7] Editing provides a stand-in that may be good, bad, or indifferent but that is never the same as an author's holograph or early printed copies. And this is as true of the *Riverside* and the *Norton* as it is of Murphy's edition: all offer their own interpretations prior to that of any reader or teacher. The *Norton* readily acknowledges that its texts are regularized and modernized,[8] while the *Riverside*, like many scholarly editions of medieval works, supplies punctuation and capitalization, silently expands abbreviations, regularizes stanzaic and paragraph structure, substitutes *th* for *þ* and *gh* for *ʒ*, and distributes *i/j* and *u/v* according to modern conventions. However comforting it may be to imagine that the *Norton* text or even the *Riverside* is authentically Chaucerian in ways that Murphy's is not, the fault line between ersatz editions that we consider Chaucerian and those we do not lies somewhere else.

Certainly, I do not mean to imply that textual criticism has been completely sedentary these three decades. The *Canterbury Tales* Project is a novel idea with much potential, and there have likewise been valuable studies of individual medieval manuscripts.[9] But despite the dynamic opportunities of the 1980s, textual criticism by nature is a conservative process. Since its first edition in 1962, for example, the *Norton* has lost several Chaucerian pieces and added only the Man of Law's epilogue and Troilus's "Song"; the texts it does include, as well as many of their glosses, remain largely the same. During this same period, we have developed all manner of new critical approaches that have themselves served as opportunities to compete for students in an academic market increasingly focused on student recruitment and retention. Indeed, Chaucer's concerns with gender or class speak directly to students' own concerns and render him competitive with more recent

---

[7] Even those who can read medieval manuscripts do so as creatures of the twenty-first century, not the fifteenth, when (the textual criticism of the 1980s showed) the *Canterbury Tales* dynamically interacted with historical conceptions of authors, works, and texts.

[8] Stephen Greenblatt, ed., *The Norton Anthology of English Literature*, 8th ed., vol. A (New York: W. W. Norton, 2006), xxii. Cf. Barry Windeatt, ed., *Troilus and Criseyde* (London: Penguin, 2005), lxiii; Jill Mann, ed., *The Canterbury Tales* (London: Penguin, 2005), lxvi; and Robert Boenig and Andrew Taylor, eds., *The Canterbury Tales* (Ontario: Broadview, 2008), 37.

[9] See, for example, Peter Robinson, "The History, Discoveries, and Aims of the Canterbury Tales Project," *ChauR* 38 (2003): 126–39; Andrew Taylor, *Textual Situations: Three Medieval Manuscripts and Their Readers* (Philadelphia: University of Pennsylvania Press, 2002); and see, further, Daniel Wakelin in this colloquium.

writers. Yet we can also undermine this competitiveness when we insist on teaching from the same kinds of editions. It is worth recalling that the modern Chaucer edition and course are not set in stone but are just over a century old. As the controversies of thirty years ago showed, textual criticism, despite its conservative nature, offers its own novel opportunities for students as well as scholars.

"Maked na moore":
Editing and Narrative

Daniel Wakelin
Christ's College, Cambridge

S EVENTY YEARS ON, the edition of the *Canterbury Tales* created by John M. Manly, Edith Rickert, and their collaborators stands as an impressive historical monument. It is historic in the sense of important—a historic occasion in Chaucerian scholarship. But it is also historic in the sense of being no longer current, for its text seems seldom to be cited (although its manuscript descriptions remain of great value for codicologists and palaeographers today studying manuscripts of the *Tales*); and it has become historic in the sense of being an object for historical study and storytelling, part of Chaucerian reception history, like Thynne's edition, or of the history of scholarship, like the *Oxford English Dictionary*. Earlier responses were, rightly, engaged, from the posthumous prize to Manly, through the expositions and corrections by Dempster and Rydland, to the muted dismissals of later editors.[1] Passions often ran high—most notably the passionate blame and praise of Kane and Ramsey. But after seventy years, might passions now be spent?[2] We would no longer scarify or defend the editorial practice of the Rolls Series, say; to do so would suggest a strange lack of perspective. Recent scholarship has found a new perspective from which to dis-

[1] Respectively, C. H. Beeson, George La Piana, and J. S. P. Tatlock, "Report of the Committee on Award of the Haskins Medal," *Speculum* 17 (1942), 453–54; various articles by Germaine Dempster, such as "Manly's Conception of the Early History of the Canterbury Tales," *PMLA* 61 (1946): 379–415; Kurt Rydland, "The Meaning of 'Variant Reading' in the Manly-Rickert *Canterbury Tales*: A Note on the Limitations of the Corpus of Variants," *NM* 73 (1972): 805–814; Larry D. Benson, gen. ed., *The Riverside Chaucer* (Boston: Houghton Mifflin, 1987), 1120; Geoffrey Chaucer, *The Canterbury Tales*, ed. Jill Mann (London: Penguin, 2005), lxi.

[2] George Kane, "John M. Manly (1865–1940) and Edith Rickert (1871–1938)," in *Editing Chaucer: The Great Tradition*, ed. Paul G. Ruggiers (Norman, Okla.: Pilgrim Books, 1984) 207–229; Roy Vance Ramsey, *The Manly-Rickert Text of the "Canterbury Tales"* (Lewiston, N.Y.: Edwin Mellen Press, 1994).

cuss Manly and Rickert's work: the historian's mode, the recovery and interpretation of Manly and Rickert's work within the wider histories of university professionalization, evolutionary theory, gender in the academy, and so on.[3] From the perspective of 2010, it seems time to treat this edition of 1940 as an object of historical curiosity and narrative.

After all, one of the most striking features of Manly and Rickert's edition is the way in which it reports its own history from the outset, turning itself into an object of historical inquiry. The editors tell the story of their work in detail in several places in volumes 1 and 2. They describe searching for exemplars, making photostats, filling in cards, even taking two weeks' vacation or enjoying the respites of transatlantic travel (1:vii–xvii, 1:1–9, 2:1–10).[4] The technology of photostats, ocean liners, and notices in *Country Life* and the cast of Misses and Sirs and earls off in colonial Kenya all mark this edition, seventy years on, as a quaint relic of "history," of a world we have lost.[5] Much of this effect is an accident of hindsight and belatedness. But not all: Manly and Rickert chose to tell us more about their work than other editors of the time— who tellingly often used "I" only when they were uncertain, and wrote only terse prefaces of thanks for photostatting.[6] And by narrating the process of editing so fully, Manly and Rickert make it look contingent, bound by circumstances, even subjective. Moreover, they make it sound—wittingly or not—like the travails of the manuscript transmission they narrate. Their search for exemplars oddly echoes the efforts of the scribes who "picked up" tales here and there (quoted below), their rue for sloppy collations by students (1:3), and their dream of photographic reproduction to avoid typesetting errors (1:xiv) recall Chaucer's worries for miswriting. In fact, the weird self-reflexiveness of the edition

---

[3] See the overview by Elizabeth Scala, "John Matthews Manly (1865–1940), Edith Rickert (1871–1938)," in *Medieval Scholarship: Biographical Studies on the Formation of a Discipline*, ed. Helen Damico, 3 vols. (New York: Garland, 1995–2000), 2:297–311.

[4] All references in parentheses come from John M. Manly, Edith Rickert and others, ed., *The Text of the "Canterbury Tales," Studied on the Basis of All Known Manuscripts*, 8 vols. (Chicago: University of Chicago Press, 1940).

[5] Ramsey, *The Manly-Rickert Text*, 57–81, 89–92, fills in this fascinating history.

[6] Contrast, for example, the taciturn personal details in Woodburn O. Ross, ed., *Middle English Sermons Edited from British Museum MS. Royal 18.B.xxiii*, EETS o.s. 209 (London: Oxford University Press, 1940), vii (8 lines of personal thanks), xvii–xviii, xxxviii–xxxix ("I" around tentative hypotheses); or similarly Henry Watson, trans., *Valentine and Orson*, ed. Arthur Dickson, EETS o.s. 204 (London: Oxford University Press, 1937), vii (brief thanks), xi, xvi, xvii, lxiii ("I" for speculating or conceding ignorance). Comment on the process of editing—whether personal or merely factual, about conventions and so on—seems rare in EETS editions of the late 1930s and early 1940s.

goes even further than that, for in recounting the making of a text the edition does something like that famous text about texts, the *Canterbury Tales* itself.[7]

The oddest likeness between Chaucer's labor and his editors' comes in the death of one editor, Rickert, before the edition was complete, just as Chaucer died with the poem still undone. Manly reports that on May 30, 1938, Rickert "handed me a paper setting forth the views she had long held on the preservation of some traits of Chaucer's early drafts," and she was "full of confident hope that she would live to see the whole work completed," but "alas!"—a moment of pathos striking in an editorial paratext—within two days she died (1:viii). The edition has been described therefore as "a memorial for Edith Rickert."[8] It is interesting that the manuscript which Manly and Rickert so influentially saw as crucial, the Hengwrt manuscript, looked to them as though it recorded Chaucer interrupted by illness or something else "insurmountable"— such as death?—in the midst of *The Cook's Tale* (3:446): "Of this Cokes tale maked Chaucer na moore."[9] We must not romanticize Hengwrt as being written exactly while Chaucer lay dying, in an apoplexy about *swyving* for a living, with Pinkhurst waiting in titillation for the next lines.[10] Yet there is a curious analogy between the death of the author and the death of the editor—and Manly too died just after publication. These deaths seem to seal off the edition, like the poem, as past, as history, to be maked no more.

Moreover, it is curious that what Rickert left unfinished was her work

[7] Derek Pearsall, "Authorial Revision in Some Late-Medieval English Texts," in *Crux and Controversy in Middle English Textual Criticism*, ed. A. J. Minnis and Charlotte Brewer (Cambridge: Brewer, 1992), 39–48, notes also that the chaotic structure of the edition gives the reader "the sense, as in the *Canterbury Tales*, that almost anything could happen" (40).

[8] Sylvia Tomasch, "Editing as Palinode: *The Invention of Love* and *The Text of the Canterbury Tales*," *Exemplaria* 16 (2004): 457–76 (469). Though Tomasch muses on editing as mourning not primarily for people but for "the loss of the text (often compounded as the loss of the author)" (459).

[9] Aberystwyth, National Library of Wales, MS Peniarth 392, fol. 57v. A similar note appears in London, British Library, MS Harley 7333, fol. 60r ("¶ Off þis tale / chauncier made namore"), and in a different position in Princeton, University Library, MS 100, fol. 60v: "Squyers tale for Chawser made no more".

[10] Simon Horobin, "Adam Pinkhurst, Geoffrey Chaucer, and the Hengwrt Manuscript of the *Canterbury Tales*," *ChauR* 44 (2010): 351–67, questions the notion that Chaucer died during the copying of Hengwrt (357–59). For a contrasting view, see Daniel W. Mosser, "'Chaucer's Scribe,' Adam, and the Hengwrt Project," in *Design and Distribution of Late Medieval Manuscripts in England*, ed. Margaret Connolly and Linne R. Mooney (Woodbridge: York Medieval Press, 2008), 11–40 (36–38).

on Chaucer's rewriting, which was—if not in the small matters she proposes, then in larger matters—also unfinished. And just as his unfinished revision prompted posthumous scribal editing, so Rickert's own unfinished analyses are edited after her death by Manly.[11] At the end of volume 2, Manly turns to the arguments for even "more extensive revision on the part of Chaucer," but he removes the arguments from the anonymity of collaboration to record that they "originated entirely with Professor Rickert" and are "Miss Rickert's own words" (2:501, 2:511). Indeed Manly distances himself from these arguments by noting that he "was never convinced of the truth" of them and argued with her about them (2:501, 2:511–12).[12] Thus he frames her story of revision within a conversation, just as the pilgrims' stories are framed by their conversations and by Chaucer's editorial disclaimers. He also sets apart Rickert's work as the tales are set apart in manuscripts, with its own underlined title at the top of a new page, like a rubric (2:502), and a line left blank at its end (2:511). And as scribes altered Chaucer's work, Manly alters Rickert's, reproducing it only "in large part" and not whole (2:501), for it was "better not to print the part of Miss Rickert's paper" that was less persuasive (2:514).[13] This moment typifies the way that *The Text of the Canterbury Tales* undoes its own arguments about textual history by noting its own textual history of doubt and contingency.

The moment also typifies one of the most useful things that *The Text of the Canterbury Tales* highlights: the possibility that, just as the 1940 edition itself unfolded over time and is susceptible to narrative description, so too might the *Canterbury Tales* be described emerging over time, in the hands of the poet, and then of the scribes. Manly and Rickert begin with the commonsensical hypothesis that poems develop over time in stages, increments, and improvements—as works by Petrarch, Boccaccio, Rolle, and Gower are recorded as doing (2:30–36). So, some of Rickert's seventeen suggestions about revision after publication (2:505–8) are quite plausible as suggestions about Chaucer's honing of

---

[11] And see also Martin M. Crow and Clair C. Olson, eds., *Chaucer Life-Records* (Oxford: Oxford University Press, 1966), v–vii, on editing other literary remains from this project. Ramsey, *The Manly-Rickert Text*, for example, 174–75, suggests that some other parts of *The Text of the Canterbury Tales* were also more Rickert's work than Manly's.

[12] Although an earlier part of the same volume has already stated that these arguments have "strong reasons" in their support (2:115, 2:135).

[13] Although he helpfully prints the textual variants on which it was based, allowing readers to analyze her arguments independently (2:514–18).

his style in stages before publication.[14] This is not to endorse—or not fully—Manly and Rickert's claim that Chaucer issued individual tales during revision. As later studies have shown, there is little firm evidence of preissued drafts in the manuscripts.[15] Manly and Rickert's description of this early circulation is a bit fanciful: the death of Chaucer's wife in 1387 deprived him of company at home, beyond little Lewis, so that he felt compelled to share his work in progress with friends (2:36–38). (This may be another curious echo of the death of Rickert and the isolation of revising work without a beloved female companion.)[16] But they also describe the allusions or textual alternatives that reveal that some elements of the poem were known to readers in Chaucer's own lifetime or were altered by him—scars of time so deep that even *The Riverside Chaucer* does not conceal them: for example, weaving earlier stories such as that of Palamon and Arcite into the *Tales*; switching the tales of the Wife of Bath, Shipman, and others; expanding or shortening the account of the Nun's Priest in the frame-narrative (2:115, 2:133–35, 2:189–90, 2:350, 2:410–13).[17] Many of the stories Manly and Rickert tell are problematic in their particular details and deductions. One might note inconsistencies: for instance, the couplet "And yaf a certeyn ferme for the graunt / Noon of his bretheren cam ther in his haunt" (3:12, A.252^{b-c}, noted after A.252) is once guessed to have been added "perhaps in the margin" (2:95–96), but later is described as "perhaps" being "rejected" by Chaucer or being "cancelled" (2:423, 3:424,

---

[14] If unprovable from the manuscript evidence. For a useful distinction between revision of previously published work and work that betrays the processes of revision prior to full publication, see Geoffrey Chaucer, *Troilus and Criseyde: A New Edition of "The Book of Troilus,"* ed. B. A. Windeatt (Harlow: Longman, 1984), 38–40.

[15] For example, N. F. Blake, *The Textual Tradition of the Canterbury Tales* (London: Edward Arnold, 1985), 36–37, citing Germaine Dempster, "On the Significance of Hengwrt's Change of Ink in the Merchant's Tale," *MLN* 63 (1948): 325–30 (329), suggests that when the manuscripts betray disruption in the exemplar for *The Merchant's Tale,* this disruption reveals that scribes were copying not a prepublished earlier draft but Chaucer's own last holograph. (But the disorderly state of the holograph suggests if not Chaucer's revision of work already issued, then stages in the making of his work—say, a pause as he reaches the line "Lat vs namoore wordes her of make" and devises the slightly forced dénouement of the tale.) As it happens, Manly and Rickert in the relevant places (2:282–83, 3:375, 3:413, 6:491) do not explain this disruption at their fragment E, lines 2318–19 (Benson, gen. ed., *The Riverside Chaucer,* IV.2318–19). Horobin, "Adam Pinkhurst, Geoffrey Chaucer," 360, explains it well.

[16] I am not alleging that Manly and Rickert were lovers—although Elizabeth Scala, "Scandalous Assumptions: Edith Rickert and the Chicago Chaucer Project," *Medieval Feminist Forum* 30 (2000): 27–37, offers judicious speculation about their relationship.

[17] See also Benson, gen. ed., *The Riverside Chaucer,* 826, 862, 910–11, 1126, 1132, 1133.

5:21).[18] Or one might question the speculation that the lines "Another NONNE with hire hadde she / That was hir chapeleyne and preestes thre" (A.163–64, on 3:9) were left incomplete, for no variants are recorded in the apparatus to support such a conjecture (cf. 2:95; 3:422–23, 5:13). Yet the inconsistencies continue the honest uncertainty of the histories being deduced, and even the unprovable conjecture about the Nun's Priest raises a thought-provoking question: Why did Chaucer not describe him in the *General Prologue*? And overall *in principle,* there is real intellectual merit in thinking about Chaucer at work on the poem in a biographical narrative, even with the uncertainty necessary in all biography.[19] Though Manly and Rickert undertook to make an edition of the *Canterbury Tales*, a stripping away of the detritus of passing time from the text, in fact they revealed the poem as something formed over time.[20] This is no surprise, for in all the interruptions and changes of plan among the pilgrims, Chaucer dramatizes the process of a literary work emerging over time. Understanding this is one of the main intellectual challenges set by both *The Text of the Canterbury Tales* and the *Canterbury Tales* itself—a challenge that still feels difficult.

Moreover, Manly and Rickert not only tell stories about Chaucer's work, but they also tell stories about the work of the scribes who preserved it. As they seek to apply their genealogical method to the relationship of the manuscripts in volume 2, the genealogy unravels. Genealogy, as usually practiced, weaves multiple narratives into one whole. But Manly and Rickert's accounts of manuscript relations in volume 2 unspool these threads quite dramatically (as they note: 2:39–41). This unspooling is what makes their edition dizzyingly unreadable, even though it in fact takes that most readable form, narrative—or indeed a collection of narratives, again like the *Canterbury Tales*.

They begin the story of scribal transmission with an account of the "constant groups," which have had some influence in textual studies of

[18] Benson, gen. ed., *The Riverside Chaucer*, 1122, places it in square brackets and cites Manly and Rickert cutting it "on the assumption that Chaucer dropped the couplet in revision."

[19] On such endeavors, see, recently, Daniel Birkholz, "Biography After Historicism: The Harley Lyrics, the Hereford Map, and the Life of Roger de Breynton," in *The Post-Historical Middle Ages*, ed. Elizabeth Scala and Sylvia Federico (New York: Palgrave Macmillan, 2009), 161–189 (174), in general; and Derek Pearsall, *The Life of Geoffrey Chaucer: A Critical Biography* (Oxford: Blackwell, 1992), 226, in particular.

[20] And in some relation to (changing) authorial intention, as Pearsall, "Authorial Revisions," 47–48 adds, in an argument that this one parallels.

the *Tales*;[21] but the constancy is modified within just a few sentences as tending to hold "through a long stretch" (2:49). A long stretch, however, is not the whole stretch and therefore is not constant; and immediately other problems with these groups are conceded (2:49–51), especially the *d* group (2:63–70) and some ungrouped manuscripts (2:70–77).[22] But most problematically, having established these groups, Manly and Rickert then proceed to survey the poem tale by tale, link by link, not as an overview but following the sequence of the tales themselves (or one possible sequence), and for several sections the textual relations are reanalyzed and retold as little stories. Genealogy proves insufficient to illustrate how individual manuscripts, and even individual parts of the text, seem to have more than one ancestor; so Manly and Rickert end up instead focusing on the activities of scribes rather than on reconstructing the text. So, for example, the transmission of the Franklin's tale is a particularly complex story, as they note (2:300), and dissolves into several little stories, of people who "used the same exemplar" and "continued to follow this exemplar probably to 1050" (2:302); the ancestor of one tradition "edited considerably," introducing various "changes," while other manuscripts "made their own" (2:302). These little stories are hard to read: they feel like the mythical novel written in algebra, for the sentences mix subjects that are mere sigla with verbs that express real human action and agency; and the verbs are not always in the past tense customary of narrative. But when we read that, for example, "Ln edits much independently" and "Ha² . . . corrects by Mg" (2:303), there are human narratives implied: the stories of one scribe who edited his manuscript with a great deal of independence, or another who corrected his manuscript by checking a second. And there are people implied in those sigla: for example, Hg and Cx are not abstractions but are the scribe of the manuscript known as Hg, whom we now call Adam Pinkhurst, and the printer of Cx, William Caxton. Manly and Rickert offer a remarkable resource for such stories about these people.

Even when they reach the most vexing editorial conundrum, "The Order of Tales" (2:475–94), a section that would seem to require some lofty overview, the perspective is again not that of a map but of an

---

[21] Blake, *The Textual Tradition*, 37. Their groups influence even studies that branch out as individually as Charles A. Owen Jr., *The Manuscripts of "The Canterbury Tales,"* Chaucer Studies, vol. 17 (Cambridge: Brewer, 1991).

[22] Pearsall, "Authorial Revisions," 39.

itinerary. They narrate how the various scribes ordered the poem. Yet once more a clear genealogy for the text unravels, and we are left tracing single threads in its transmission, which do not necessarily knit up. Twice they narrate the confusion and haphazard problem-solving of the scribe of Hg (1:266–68, 1:271–74).[23] Then the tales as ordered in other manuscripts were "picked up from different sources" or a "selection picked up at random" (2:487). And so to understand these shifts in the order of tales, it is vital to trace narrative threads. For example, *Gamelyn* should not appear in manuscript Ch, as that is "entirely anomalous and contrary to its affiliations," but it can be understood by tracing how *Gamelyn* was here "a late insertion, in different ink and on a special quire" (2:488; cf. 1:86, 1:89). Similarly, the order of tales in manuscript Gl would be "Very puzzling" were there not an evident shift in exemplar from one "point," when two tales were "overlooked" until they were later "added" (2:486–87). Although passive verbs, these verbs tell an unfolding story of points in time and different actions by Geoffrey Spirleng and his son, the scribe of this copy whose story is narrated fully elsewhere (1:184–86).[24] From all this, Manly and Rickert conclude—rather extremely—that Chaucer had no "general plan" for the order of tales, almost in rebellion against the bureaucratic order of his day job (2:490): but, as others have noted, the real rebellion seems to be that of Manly and Rickert, whose orderly bureaucratic oversight of the entire textual tradition uncovers only disorder,[25] and individual histories.

For establishing the text by genealogy, or for boiling down the historical detritus to distill the authorial text, these histories are distracting; indeed, Manly and Rickert call the details tedious (2:489) and in *The Riverside Chaucer* Manly and Rickert are said to be "reduced to offering a narrative account."[26] But that conversion of editing into storytelling is not a reduction but a vital precedent for Middle English palaeography

---

[23] Their story of his uncertainty and "quandary" in making Hg (2:477–78) is still reiterated in the most recent codicological research: see, for example, Mosser, " 'Chaucer's Scribe,' Adam, and the Hengwrt Project," 16–18, with references to other studies.

[24] See also Richard Beadle, "Geoffrey Spirleng (*c*.1426–*c*.1494): A Scribe of the *Canterbury Tales* in His Time," in *Of the Making of Books: Essays Presented to M. B. Parkes*, ed. P. R. Robinson and Rivkah Zim (Aldershot: Scolar Press, 1997), 116–46.

[25] Sealy Gilles and Sylvia Tomasch, "Professionalizing Chaucer: John Matthews Manly, Edith Rickert, and the *Canterbury Tales* as Cultural Capital," in *Reading Medieval Culture: Essays in Honour of Robert W. Hanning*, ed. Robert M. Stein and Sandra Pierson Prior (Notre Dame, Ind.: University of Notre Dame Press, 2005), 364–83 (372–75).

[26] Benson, gen. ed., *The Riverside Chaucer*, 1120.

of the last seventy years, which has tended to be formed as a tale collection of case studies and microhistories. Opening the manuscripts of the *Canterbury Tales,* what are most striking are these narratives unfolding over time. Of course, for reasons that other people have long pointed out, the text itself in Manly and Rickert's edition is flawed and obsolete—consigned to history, no longer worth arguing about. But the other volumes of *The Text of the Canterbury Tales* remain intellectually provocative for reminding us that Chaucer's composition and the scribes' copying might be susceptible to narrative presentation, and for reminding us, too, that editions are subjects for stories, subject to history, in a similar way. Manly and Rickert retraced what Chaucer traced—that we might tell stories about storytellers.

Should We Reedit the *Canterbury Tales*?

Orietta Da Rold
University of Leicester

E IGHT VOLUMES, clad in pale blue cloth with gilded frame and letters on the spine, constitute a bibliographical point of reference for textual scholars who have worked on the *Canterbury Tales*. The importance of *The Text of the Canterbury Tales: Studied on the Basis of All Known Manuscripts* lies precisely in the task the title describes. Manly and Rickert aimed to prepare a new edition with a text: "based throughout upon the evidence afforded by all the extant MSS and such early editions as represented MSS no longer in existence."[1]

Manly and Rickert's decision to work from the textual evidence of all the known surviving manuscripts was revolutionary, because no other earlier editorial projects of the *Canterbury Tales* had fully undertaken such an impressive survey of the surviving witnesses.[2] By dedicating two volumes to the description of the manuscripts and incunabula (vol. 1) and detailed analysis of the textual affiliation of the witnesses with special attention to the relationship between manuscripts (vol. 2), they gave these matters more attention than had ever been given. Their edition of the poem appears in volumes 3 and 4, which also contain a brief *apparatus criticus* and notes. The remaining four volumes give the textual vari-

---

[1] John Manly and Edith Rickert, eds., *The Text of the Canterbury Tales: Studied on the Basis of All Known Manuscripts*, 8 vols. (Chicago: University of Chicago Press, 1940), 1:1.

[2] In the editorial history of the *Canterbury Tales*, from the medieval to the Victorian periods, editors always looked for and collated known available manuscripts that would contribute to, and above all justify, the production of a new edition of the poem, but few were able to provide such breadth and depth of information on the manuscripts and their textual affiliation. For an overview of early editorial practices, see the essays in Paul G. Ruggiers, ed., *Editing Chaucer: The Great Tradition* (Norman, Okla.: Pilgrim Books, 1984). Skeat, of course, was pioneering in his interest in the manuscript textual evidence, but he did not achieve the comprehensiveness of Manly-Rickert. See W. W. Skeat, ed., *The Complete Works of Geoffrey Chaucer*, 6 vols. (Oxford: Clarendon Press, 1894), 4:viii–xx.

ants, grouped according to tales and links; this too was novel, and is a practice seldom adopted even by recent editors.[3] The edition was then a major contribution to the textual criticism of the *Canterbury Tales*, even though it did not have an immediate impact on the scholarly community.[4] In particular, the difficulty of interpreting the data and sifting through the complex *apparatus criticus* and variants have not given editors, scholars, and students easy access to the critical mass of information that Manly and Rickert collected.[5]

Manly and Rickert attempted a new approach to the editing of Chaucer's work, and if the text they established did not find favor among editors, nevertheless their work on the affiliation of the manuscripts,[6]

[3] See, for instance, the decision by the editors of *Canterbury Tales* in *The Riverside Chaucer* to offer only selected variants in their "Textual Notes": Larry D. Benson, gen. ed., *The Riverside Chaucer* (Oxford: Oxford University Press, 1988), 1117–38.

[4] For a recent acute view of the editors' textual practices, see Edwards in this colloquium. For other appraisals of the edition see C. Brown, "Review of Manly and Rickert 1940," *MLN* 55 (1940): 606–21; Joseph A. Dane, "The Presumed Influence of Skeat's Student's Chaucer on Manly and Rickert's Text of the *Canterbury Tales*," *Analytical & Enumerative Bibliography* 7 (1993): 18–27; G. Kane, "John Manly (1865–1940) and Edith Rickert (1871–1939)," in *Editing Chaucer*, ed. Paul G. Ruggiers, 207–29; Charlotte C. Morse, "What the Clerk's Tale Suggests About Manly and Rickert's Edition— and the *Canterbury Tales* Project," in *Middle English Poetry: Texts and Traditions: Essays in Honour of Derek Pearsall*, ed. A. J. Minnis (Woodbridge: York Medieval Press, 2001), 41–56.

[5] The challenge of working with Manly and Rickert's volumes 5–8 was recently taken up in Jill Mann, ed., *The Canterbury Tales* (London: Penguin, 2005), lxiii. For a discussion on the incomplete state of the variants in these volumes, see K. Rydland, "The Meaning of Variant Reading in the Manly and Rickert Canterbury Tales: A Note on the Limitation of the Corpus of Variants," *NM* 73 (1972): 805–14; see also Mann and Edwards in this colloquium.

[6] According to Manly and Rickert, the manuscripts can be textually grouped in four categories: *a, b, c,* and *d,* with some exceptions, such as: California, San Marino, Huntington Library MS El. 26 C 9 (Ellesmere), Cambridge, University Library MS Gg.4.27, Aberystwyth, National Library of Wales MS Peniarth 392 D (Hengwrt), which relates to London, British Library MS Harley 7334 and London, British Library MS Additional 35286. These groups were determined on the basis of persistent and consistent variation across certain manuscripts: for instance, in the *a* group, Manly and Rickert included Austin, University of Texas, Humanities Research Centre MS 143 (Cardigan), University of Manchester, John Rylands Library MS English 113, Tokyo, Takamiya MS 24 (Devonshire), London, British Library MS Egerton 2726 and Cambridge, University Library MS Dd.4.24. These manuscripts share an affiliation based on similar textual variation in errors. Manly and Rickert's groups are not related chronologically with one another; the manuscripts in the *a* group are not older than the ones in the *d* group, but it is implied that the textual quality of the manuscripts in these groups is variable. Their textual quality is measured against how authoritative the text in each group is. Thus *quality* is Manly and Rickert's criterion for understanding the closeness of a given manuscript to Chaucer's intention: a good text is close to the original and a bad text is a copy corrupted by scribal errors. For instance, the *c* and *d* groups contain a text "inferior" to that of the *a* group. This grouping is also associated with the order of the tales, which

their argument for the textual importance of Aberystwyth, National Library of Wales MS Peniarth 392 D (Hengwrt),[7] and their research on the manuscripts of the *Canterbury Tales* have influenced textual and literary scholars, palaeographers, and book historians.[8] Manly and Rickert's contribution to the textual criticism as well as our understanding of the material production of the manuscripts of the *Canterbury Tales* is worth considering in more detail. But even more challenging would be to consider afresh *new* editorial projects in which the textual and material dimension of the *Canterbury Tales* do not sit in separate volumes, but work together to ask new and ambitious research questions of the poem. This interaction can only be achieved in an electronic environment, which allows the integration of text and manuscripts in imaginative ways. The reconciliation of these two aspects is pivotal in exploring further issues of authorship and canonicity in the *Canterbury Tales* and Chaucer's other works alike.

Existing electronic projects, such as the Canterbury Tales Project, have aimed to refine Manly and Rickert's understanding of how the texts of the surviving manuscripts relate to one another.[9] The *General Prologue*, the Wife of Bath's *Prologue*, *The Miller's Tale,* and *The Nun's Priest's Tale* have been transcribed in order to provide an electronic collation of multiple textual variants to complement Manly and Rickert's manual collation.[10] These electronic editions are certainly valuable, and

---

Manly and Rickert considered derived from scribal engagement with the fragmented and unorganized texts left by Chaucer. See Manly and Rickert, eds., *Text of the Canterbury Tales,* 2:40–44, 49–77 and 474–94.

[7] See, for example, Donald C. Baker, "The Relationship of the Hengwrt Manuscript to the Variorum Chaucer Text," in *The "Canterbury Tales": A Facsimile and Transcription of the Hengwrt Manuscript with Variants from the Ellesmere Manuscript,* ed. Paul G. Ruggiers (Norman: University of Oklahoma Press, 1979), xvii–xviii.

[8] See, for instance, G. S. Ivy's discussion of the manuscripts of the *Canterbury Tales* in "The Bibliography of the Manuscript Book," in *The English Library Before 1700: Studies in Its History,* ed. Francis Wormald and C. E. Wright (London: Athlone Press, 1958), 32–65; see also A. I. Doyle, "English Books In and Out of Court from Edward III to Henry VII," in *English Court Culture in the Later Middle Ages,* ed. V. J. Scattergood and J. W. Sherborne (London: Duckworth, 1983), 163–82; Charles A. Owen Jr., *The Manuscripts of the Canterbury Tales* (Cambridge: D. S. Brewer, 1991); and Roy Vance Ramsey, *The Manly-Rickert Text of the "Canterbury Tales"* (Lampeter: Edwin Mellen Press, 1994).

[9] See, for example, Peter Robinson, "Stemmatic Analysis of the Wife of Bath's Prologue," in *The Canterbury Tales Project Occasional Papers,* ed. N. F. Blake and P. Robinson (London: Office for Humanities Communication, 1997), 69–132.

[10] Peter Robinson, ed., *The Wife of Bath's Prologue on CD-ROM* (Cambridge: Cambridge University Press, 1996); Elizabeth Solopova, ed., *The General Prologue on CD-ROM* (Cambridge: Cambridge University Press, 2000); P. Robinson, ed., *The Miller's*

one of the most important achievements is to provide complete textual evidence of the transcribed tales to aid future editors.[11] As Manly and Rickert's classification was essential to explain the eclectic editorial approach they had chosen, it would seem that a refinement of their textual affiliation would offer new evidence to establish a new text, provided that all the tales and links are transcribed and available to scholars. However, can we go beyond this text-based approach? Can we start again with fresh questions: Do we need a new edition of Chaucer's *Canterbury Tales*, especially after the excellent and affordable edition by Jill Mann?[12] Do we need a new Complete Works? If so, what would constitute the text we are editing? And how would we go about editing it, and for whom?

Manly and Rickert's consideration of the affiliation of the manuscripts and the organization of the tales is a major departure from earlier assessments,[13] and it leads to some important suggestions about authorial intention and the state of the text and the canon. Manly and Rickert argued that none of the surviving manuscripts could be dated earlier than Chaucer's death, but they also note that some of the tales could have circulated at the end of the fourteenth century and that Chaucer may have revised them.[14] This assessment opened up an interesting debate among scholars who believed that Chaucer "published" his work during his lifetime and those who opposed this argument, believing instead that the single pile of paper left by Chaucer was edited and published by his literary executors.[15]

Tale on CD-ROM (Leicester: Scholarly Digital Editions, 2004); and Paul Thomas, ed., *The Nun's Priest's Tale* (Birmingham, UK: Scholarly Digital Editions, 2006).

[11] For an appraisal of the project's editorial assumptions, see Joseph A. Dane, *The Myth of Print Culture* (Toronto: University of Toronto Press, 2003), 124–42.

[12] Mann, ed., *The Canterbury Tales*.

[13] For example, Skeat's A, B, C, D groups, see Skeat, ed., *Complete Works of Chaucer*, 4:viii, and Brusendorff's explanation of the "Oxford," "All England," "Cambridge," and "London" groups. Aage Brusendorff, *The Chaucer Tradition* (New York: Oxford University Press, 1925), 63–108.

[14] Manly and Rickert, eds., *Text of the Canterbury Tales*, 2:30.

[15] Most notably, Ralph Hanna, "The Hengwrt Manuscript and the Canon of The *Canterbury Tales*," *EMS* 1 (1989): 64–84, argues for "some public circulation during Chaucer's lifetime" (72). For the opposite view, see N. F. Blake, *The Textual Tradition of the "Canterbury Tales"* (London: Edward Arnold, 1985). The suggestion that Chaucer may have supervised some early manuscripts was, however, later reconsidered by Blake; see N. F. Blake, "Geoffrey Chaucer and the Manuscripts of the *Canterbury Tales*," *JEBS* 1 (1997): 95–122; see also, more recently, Stubbs, "'Here's One I Prepared Earlier': The Work of Scribe D on Oxford, Corpus Christi College, MS 198," *RES* 58 (2007): 133–53, and Mosser, "'Chaucer's Scribe,' Adam, and the Hengwrt Project," in *Design*

The question of prior circulation and authorial revision is important in developing an editorial rationale, because the answers to these questions will influence the choice of how to edit the text. If Chaucer did not publish any texts during his lifetime, an editor could consider the establishment of the final version intended by the author. However, if Chaucer issued multiple copies of his text and then altered them, how could an editor justify one single authorial text? Then a case might be made for more than one edition, representing different stages of publication. The *Canterbury Tales* has generally been understood and edited as one text with one order and one authorial textual tradition, and mostly has been edited eclectically to recover authorial intention.[16] This has occurred despite the variation in textual content and in the order of the tales across the surviving manuscripts, and it differs from the editorial approaches taken to other major Middle English texts. The editors of Langland's *Piers Plowman,* for example, have acknowledged that the poem is to be edited according to different versions, reflecting authorial revisions and augmentations.[17] What is at stake here is whether or not Chaucer contributed to the production of any manuscripts and whether he revised his text after publication. Germaine Dempster refined Manly and Rickert's suggestions on precirculation of the tales and observed that Chaucer circulated and revised his text before his death.[18] Her argument did not fare well with textual scholars and editors. However, Blake has also suggested that we may be reconsidering the way we edit Chaucer, by editing different versions of the text, relating to different stages of textual composition. This method would be particularly interesting if it were true that Chaucer supervised the production of some of the manuscripts of the *Canterbury Tales.*[19] Can an editor take this consider-

---

and Distribution of Late Medieval Manuscripts in England, ed. Margaret Connolly and Linne R. Mooney, 11–40.

[16] Compare, for instance, the eclectic method in Benson, gen. ed., *The Riverside Chaucer,* with the best-text method in N. F. Blake, ed., *The Canterbury Tales* (London: Edward Arnold, 1980).

[17] For an overview, see Ralph Hanna, *William Langland,* Authors of the Middle Ages, vol. 3 (Aldershot: Variorum, 1993).

[18] Germaine Dempster, "Manly's Conception of the Early History of the *Canterbury Tales,*" *PMLA* 61 (1946): 379–415; "A Chapter of the Manuscript History of the *Canterbury Tales*: The Ancestor of Group D; the Origin of Its Texts, Tale-Order, and Spurious Links," *PMLA* 63 (1948): 456–84; and "A Period in the Development of the *Canterbury Tales* Marriage Group and of Blocks B2 and C," *PMLA* 68 (1953): 1142–59. On this, see also C. Brown, "Three Notes on the Text of the *Canterbury Tales,*" *MLN* 56 (1941): 163–75, and "Author's Revision in the *Canterbury Tales,*" *PMLA* 57 (1942): 29–50.

[19] Blake, "Geoffrey Chaucer and the Manuscripts of the *Canterbury Tales.*"

ation further and imagine the reader's experience when confronted with multiple versions of texts incorporating codicological and palaeographical details? Would readers be confused? Or would their experiences be augmented by the challenge of the idea that what they read in *The Riverside Chaucer* is not all that Chaucer intended? Can an editor open the door onto the rich material textuality that the production of medieval manuscripts offers? I think at this stage in the scholarly debate on the *Canterbury Tales*, it is possible to ask these questions, and it is precisely the significance of this material aspect of the textual transmission that I would like to consider in my concluding remarks.

Manly and Rickert's approach to the text has provided much information on the manuscripts themselves. The value and importance of their descriptions of the manuscripts of the *Canterbury Tales* are undeniable; textual scholars are still indebted to their detailed descriptions of such features as watermarks, collation, date, writing, ink, supervision and correction, illumination, binding, present condition, order of the tales, affiliations and textual character, dialect and spelling, special features, and provenance.[20] Although it is also true that seventy years after the first publication of these descriptions, manuscript studies have advanced considerably and more research has become available on individual scribes and on medieval book culture in general,[21] the fact remains that when scholars look at a manuscript of this Chaucerian poem, Manly and Rickert's work is the initial point of departure and it is yet to be superseded.[22] Their descriptions are at times frustrating; because of their wide influence, their assessments are often simply accepted rather than appraised.[23] For instance, their opinions on nomenclatures and considerations of scribal production are quite obscure. A case in point is the

[20] It is worth reading the overall discussion and rationale behind the selection of these features, which very much interrelate with the textual significance of each individual manuscript. Manly and Rickert, eds., *The Text of the Canterbury Tales*, 1:9–28.

[21] The literature is vast, but see A. I. Doyle and M. B. Parkes, "The Production of Copies of the *Canterbury Tales* and the *Confessio Amantis* in the Early Fifteenth Century," in *Medieval Scribes, Manuscripts, and Libraries: Essays Presented to N. R. Ker*, ed. M. B. Parkes and Andrew G. Watson (London: Scolar Press, 1978), 163–210. For an overview, see also Ralph Hanna, *London Literature, 1300–1380* (Cambridge: Cambridge University Press, 2005), 1–43 in particular, and of course Linne R. Mooney, "Chaucer's Scribe," *Speculum* 81 (2006): 96–138.

[22] Seymour's catalogue, although valuable, does not contain the wealth of information that Manly and Rickert provide. See M. C. Seymour, *A Catalogue of Chaucer Manuscripts: The Canterbury Tales*, vol. 2 (Aldershot: Scolar Press, 1997).

[23] See, for instance, Ramsey's arguments about the scribe who copied Cambridge University Library MS Dd.4.24, in *The Manly-Rickert Text*, 377–406.

scribe of Cambridge University Library MS Dd.4.24, who Manly and Rickert regarded as an amateur. I have argued elsewhere that Manly and Rickert are incorrect, and that the scribe was probably working in the London-Westminster area as a professional in some form of administrative capacity.[24] Scribes have been arbitrarily labeled "amateur" or "professional," precluding any sophistication in better describing and understanding their role in the book production and circulation of exemplars during the fifteenth century with reference to the *Canterbury Tales*. Nevertheless, it is this specific area of research relating to the history of the manuscript production that is currently yielding the most exciting new work on the text of the *Canterbury Tales* on two counts. First, studies of the manuscripts have revealed that textual collation may not be sufficient to appreciate how a text is transmitted. Close codicological examinations have brought to light a complex material matrix that ought to be considered if a new edition of the poem is to be undertaken. For example, the rearrangement of folios in paper quires in Cambridge University Library Dd.4.24 and the alternation of thick and fine parchment in Oxford, Corpus Christi College MS 198 may pose questions about the kind of exemplars available, the order of the text, and the agency behind the changes themselves.[25]

Second, a new edition should reconsider the issue of circulation of exemplars from the perspective of the history of the book, which studies the text as belonging to a written culture, in which the act of collecting exemplars, copying texts, and making books influences the consumption of literature and the transmission of the text, and is worthy of investigation and editorial consideration. Thus the manuscript transmission of the *Canterbury Tales* would not be explained only in terms of stemmata and textual relationships, but as a cultural complicated web of human relationship in which scribes, patrons, readers, and perhaps the author himself are involved in the circulation of the text.[26]

[24] Orietta Da Rold, "The Quiring System in Cambridge University Library Ms Dd.4.24 of Chaucer's *Canterbury Tales*," *The Library*, 7th ser. 4.2 (2003): 107–28; "The Significance of Scribal Corrections in Cambridge University Library, Ms Dd.4.24," *ChauR* 41 (2007): 393–436.

[25] Da Rold, "The Quiring System"; Stubbs, "'Here's One I Prepared Earlier'"; and Orietta Da Rold, "Materials," in *The Production of Books in England, 1350–1530*, ed. Alexandra Gillespie and Daniel Wakelin (Cambridge: Cambridge University Press, forthcoming).

[26] The AHRC-funded project, "The Identification of the Scribes Responsible for Copying Major Works of Middle English Literature," will provide a new set of evidence for further consideration of the close relationship between scribes and exemplars in Lon-

This evidence will bring new challenges to the work of an editor of Chaucer's text. Editors will have to think about additional important questions: How would these new data influence our understanding of a text? How can our editorial method and rationale take these issues into consideration? Is it possible to include the material text in our editorial practices? If so, how would this be done? Could this lead to a new edition of Chaucer's text? Or perhaps to many editions, which can show different levels of authorial engagement with the text? What about an edition of the *a, b, c,* and *d* groups? How might that be carried out? Technology seems to have advanced different ways of making new interesting texts available, but can it stretch as far as accomplishing challenging integrations that perhaps have not yet been fully imagined? Manly and Rickert's edition went a long way in the study of the textual tradition of the *Canterbury Tales.* It is now our turn to take this further by questioning the tradition of authorial variation and intention from a material perspective, reconsidering the complex web of agencies that lay behind the production of these manuscripts, and to reopen the debate on these questions. We should ask ourselves whether we want all these agencies to influence a new edition of Chaucer's texts and, if so, whether the Web is the place to publish such a complex undertaking. I believe that this is a debate worth having regardless of or in spite of the final answer.

---

don at the end of the fourteenth and beginning of the fifteenth centuries. I would like to thank Estelle Stubbs for very interesting conversations on this subject.

REVIEWS

Suzanne Conklin Akbari. *Idols in the East: European Representations of Islam and the Orient, 1100–1450.* Ithaca: Cornell University Press, 2009. Pp. xii, 323. $49.95.

Suzanne Akbari's study of Western views of Islam throughout the European Middle Ages is synoptic in the best sense, working comfortably with texts in Latin, Old French, Italian, German, and Middle English, and exhibiting an equally capacious grasp on secondary scholarship in an equal variety of languages. It usefully extends and carefully intervenes in the areas of scholarship laid out by the generalist studies of Richard Southern and John Tolan. Akbari examines religious polarization and geographic diversity, which combine and recombine throughout the medieval period to inform concepts of the Saracen in romance, historical, scientific, and geographical writings, and in so doing constructs an archaeology of knowledge for later incarnations of orientalism.

Akbari innovatively foregrounds her study with the spatial and cognitive geographical schema of the encyclopedists, extending them to literary texts. This spatial emphasis throughout comprises the book's most original contribution, and Akbari uses spatiality and orientation in a variety of fluid and figurative ways in the course of her study, both incorporating it into her methodology and organizational schema for the order of chapters and exploring the use of spatial metaphors and thinking within the texts she studies. The chapters trace a journey between earth (in the first chapter) and paradise (in the last chapter), taking in the complex reorganizations of space exerted by actual bodies—of Jews, of Muslims, of relics—deployed as identitarian boundary markers by Christian writers from the High to the late Middle Ages. The introduction situates the study's overall scholarly intervention into the dominant discourses of Saidian Orientalism and Foucauldian imaginative geography and the archaeology of knowledge, differentiating from later orientalisms a medieval "orientalism" that combines polarizing religious discourses with spectrum-organized geographical ones. In other words, Akbari argues that more modern East/West versions of orientalism do not fit the state of affairs in the Middle Ages where discourses of alterity were also informed by conceptualizations of geographic locations, regions, and climatological zones. These conceptualizations stress contiguity within a terrestrial continuum and productively complicate the more familiar orientalist religious agonisms. Akbari plays these competing impulses of religious polarization and geographical conceptualization against each other as she examines the idea of medieval knowledge production about the Saracen/East as a process, continually in flux, continually reorganizing itself in particular textual nodes—literary, religious, encyclopedic, and cartographic. The aim of this book therefore is the description of the parameters within which this knowledge production occurs and the tracing of dominant currents within it.

Chapter 1, "The Shape of the World," examines the different encyclopedists—including Isidore of Seville, Bartholomaeus Anglicus, and Pierre D'Ailly—whose models of the world took in tripartite, quadripartite, regional, and zonal images, and informed such later writers as Gower and Mandeville. The reading of *Mandeville's Travels* as a series of dispersive centers is particularly useful and catches at the heart of that narrative's productive inconsistency and expansiveness. Chapter 2, "From Jerusalem to India," moves to the Alexander romance, exploring the *Liber Floridus*, *The Roman de toute chevalerie,* and *Kyng Alisaunder*, to describe a later medieval transition from a Jerusalem-centered world to one drawn rather toward India and the exotic reaches of the East, both of which serve as objects of cultural desire, fantasy, and fear. Chapter 3 uses climate theory to overview the diasporic Jewish body: at once culturally central and dispersed, nowhere and ubiquitous, and thus illuminates the popularity of texts describing the destruction of Jerusalem as the defining narrative for Christian views of Judaism.

Chapter 4, "The Saracen Body," launches the central argument of the book as it centers on literary images of the Saracen body in the crusade romance of *Fierabras* and the *King of Tars*. Once again, Akbari uses climate theory to outline the nature and composition of the Saracen as a figure of bellicose energy and fury. As she compares one version to another, she describes a counterplay between the expected religious polarizations (Christian vs. Muslim) and, surprisingly, more nuanced regional discourses in representations of Saracens. Akbari distinguishes Saracens by gender and focuses on the productive and dangerous corporealities they come to represent as she explores the Male Saracen and Fierabras and the Female Saracen and Floripas. Particularly fascinating is her discussion of the long liminal space in which Floripas's conversion occurs and the differences between the various versions with their traceable, historically different concerns. Akbari's reading of the *King of Tars* deploys ideas of hybridity and metamorphic conversion to explore the utility of the idea of the Saracen to the problematics of Christian identity, boundary-making, and self-transformation.

Chapter 5, "Empty Idols and a False Prophet," comes to grips with two interwoven ideas of Islam's idolatry, learned and popular, fanciful and realistic, differentiated in previous scholarship but here persuasively shown to be working in tandem. Akbari compares popular romance (*The Sowdone of Babylone*), chanson de geste (*The Chanson de Roland*), and drama (the *Jeu de saint Nicholas* and the Digby *Mary Magdalene*) to show how oppositions between Christian spirit and Muslim letter/idol are established and policed. The chapter ends with a fascinating reading of the ambiguous "space of the Prophet" Muhammad, a place of cognitive and physical suspense that allows Christian writers such as Dante to invert Muslim narratives of the mi'raj (heavenly ascent) and resituate Islam in the agonizing suspensions of the inferno, where Islam can function as a false copy of Christian truth. Chapter 6, "The Form of Heaven," centering on images of Paradise and the Muslim afterlife, is an energetic, original synthesis of unfamiliar materials and one of the most illuminating readings of Dante I have yet come across. It stages a series of actual transactions and appropriations between Muslim religious, philosophical, and cultural texts, including the *Kitab al-mi'raj* and its Italian and French translations, *The Book of the Ladder*—and Christian ones, such as Dante's *Paradiso*. It is one of the only places in the book where Muslim writing is identified as actually having had an impact on Christian self-articulation. Akbari juxtaposes Averroës, Saladin, Dante, and Bacon to describe cultural transmissions sparking not only anxiety but also desire, appropriation, and productive differentiation. The conclusion helpfully regathers the strands to describe the transition from medieval forms of orientalism to the very different renderings of the effeminate Turk and the Moor that obsess the early modern period.

Akbari's study is often original, admirably researched, synthetic and synoptic and moves forward very substantially studies in this important area. The comparable studies by Southern, Tolan, Metlitzki, and Menocal have different emphases and do not engage in the same kind of conceptual historicism about developing ideas of geography, space, and cultural difference. *Idols in the East* will be noticed and used by medievalists and will be useful to generalists and nonmedievalists. It is a substantial accomplishment and a valuable contribution to its field.

CHRISTINE CHISM
UCLA

VALERIE ALLEN. *On Farting: Language and Laughter in the Middle Ages.* New York: Palgrave Macmillan, 2007. Pp. xiii, 239. $69.95.

SUSAN SIGNE MORRISON. *Excrement in the Late Middle Ages: Sacred Filth and Chaucer's Fecopoetics.* New York: Palgrave Macmillan, 2008. Pp. xiii, 271. $89.95.

"I know you like to think your shit don't stink, but lean a little bit closer and your roses really smell of pooh-pooh," sings Hayseed Dixie, amplifying what cultural thinkers have been saying for decades: that we like to locate our identity in the rose garden of culture or consciousness, as far away as possible from the waste we produce. In psychoanalytic thought, Freud had uncovered not only sexual but also anal repression, and Kristeva has described the abjection of waste; anthropological work has drawn out the links between dirt and the sacred; feminists have analyzed the association between women and bodies, and men and mind; and posthuman theory has criticized the scientific conception of humans as reducible to pure information in virtual reality. The treatment of bodily emissions—of "what I permanently thrust aside in order to live," in Kristeva's words—has been shown to reveal what a culture does not want to be, and by inversion its innermost values. But academics have been slow to explore this promising approach and actually research the excrement, farts, blood, sweat, and tears that make up the underside of a life. That this is beginning to change in studies of medieval English literature must have something to do with Chaucer, who, unlike the canonical medieval authors in other languages, so relished descriptions of the nether regions of bodily functions. Medievalists are also already well used to being seen as playing in the mud, working on an allegedly smelly and unhygienic period, and so might have a higher tolerance for filthy research topics.

In the past few years, there have been numerous articles and essays on bodily waste in medieval Britain, but Valerie Allen and Susan Signe Morrison have published the first monographs on farting and excrement, respectively. They both argue for a revaluation of that which we would rather not talk about, as a way of getting a different perspective on history. And like true pioneers, they are both swept away by the wealth of material from different cultures and literatures that they uncover. In this new area of academic gold-digging, there are plenty of nuggets and not just shiny flashes in the pan.

Excrement and gold share a common logic anyway, these books argue. Modern capitalists like to confine them both to the private sphere, rather than freely distributing them or dreaming of turning shit into money, like medieval alchemists and waste collectors. That excrement and farts contributed to establishing the distinction between public and private is a major point made in both books. Allen and Morrison show that defecation was consigned to the private sphere and shielded from public view. For each individual, the regulation of her emissions also worked to separate her proper body from external matter. The wish to stay away from others' excretions or even farts (in a prebacterial culture that believed disease could be spread via smell) helped to create notions of privacy. Both Allen and Morrison also observe a close relationship between vocal and anal emissions of the body, between language and farts, linguistic taboos and obscene vocabulary. Excretion is even surprisingly often compared to pilgrimage in medieval writing, for its transformative and purging role.

Allen makes these and other stimulating attempts to understand medieval views of bodily wind in the first half of *On Farting*, an entertaining yomp through literary occurrences of the fart in the context of music, smell, health, hell, and money. Unlike excrement, she points out, farts are not so much a material substance as a performance. Chaucer—especially in *The Miller's Tale*, where Nicholas farts in Absolon's face, and in *The Summoner's Tale,* with its logical conundrum of how to divide a fart between twelve friars—makes repeated appearances, in the company of Dante and a rich seam of scatological jokes, but also of Aristotle and Plato, and nineteenth-century court records and freak shows. The second half features a long chapter on etymology, veering far off farting into a woolly defense of folk etymology over academic etymology, ostensibly to show that there may be a link between "farthing" and "farting." To demonstrate that there was a *perceived* connection between those words would have been more effective than trying to unhinge modern histori-

cal linguistics. And finally, there is an extended case study of the historical evidence for the thirteenth-century Suffolk liegeman Roland the Farter, who earned his name by paying his fees with "a jump, a whistle and
a fart" before the king once a year—presumably as entertainment.
Much like playing the harp or juggling, farting was a valued skill for
court performers.

Morrison, writing just after Allen's pioneering work, is much more
ambitious in her claims. Drawing heavily on a range of critical literature
throughout, she argues for filth as a whole new area of literary and
cultural studies, even including a manifesto for waste studies or "fecopoetics." More pedestrian than Allen's glorious prose, this volume laud-
ably aims to construct a more traditional argument. The first section
sets out three ways of considering waste, invoking in passing theorists
like Bataille, Freud, Deleuze and Guattari, Kristeva and Mary Douglas:
as a part of a rhizomatic body in a network of significations spreading
in all directions (again compared to pilgrimage); as a material manifestation of sin; and as gendered. A second section loosely revolves around
the role of excrement in Chaucer, but it places much more emphasis on
comparative material from mystical and medical writing, material history and manuscript illustrations (which, sadly, are not reproduced).
Here there is some discussion of *The Prioress's Tale* with its dead boy in
the Jewish privy, the Host's association of the Pardoner's relics with
excrement, and the ecologically sound cohabitation of human and animals in all their materiality in *The Nun's Priest's Tale*. The book is completed by three more general chapters on the possibilities of waste
studies, which hint at their great potential without going into much
detail.

So what do we learn about medieval toilet habits? Morrison includes
more material history on the nitty-gritty of defecation. People did their
business in outhouses or privies, using straw, leaves, or washable rags
for cleaning their bottoms. In cities, castles, and convents, their drop-
pings would either be flushed out into nearby waters or emptied by
highly-paid professionals who would then sell the dung to farmers. In
the country, the circuit from bottom to field was presumably shorter.
Farting in company had as much fun and embarrassing potential as
today. Roland the Farter and his colleagues were a kind of human
whoopee cushion.

And can we learn anything about medieval culture more generally
from these studies? While both books are adamant that we can, they

fail to make a clear argument for this, as opposed to simply stating it. In the view of this anally retentive viewer, they lack a firm editing hand that would rein in the anecdotes and draw out a wider perspective. There is plenty of potential for generalization, as the sketches of waste and money, waste and privacy, waste and self, and the many allusions to contemporary theoretical issues indicate. Unfortunately, however, the "New Middle Ages" series has become notorious for offering little copy-editing or proofreading, and has failed these two authors completely. Morrison has even been allowed to get away with howlers like "a more bothermore adversary" (44), "Carolyn Walker Bynum" (71 and passim), and, my Freudian favorite, Thorhall in a quotation from *Njal's Saga* walking not out of a room, but "out of the book without a limp" (49). But more important is the failure to edit the copious ideas into coherent arguments. If being human is about negotiating production and retention, as these books are so keen to assert, then they err on the side of production. Perhaps unsurprisingly, resistance to the "proper" topics of historical inquiry often goes hand in hand with resistance to the strictures of academic style. But if it is hard enough for a book on farts to be taken seriously, challenges to the conventions of Anglophone scholarly publishing make it all the harder.

And that books on farts and excrement are taken seriously is important. Both *On Farting* and *Excrement in the Middle Ages* show what material there is to uncover at the rear end of history, and neither provides a definitive analysis. Aside from stringent argumentation, there is much more basic work to be done on different medical, religious, courtly, literary, legal, political, and cultural conceptions of the body and its waste throughout medieval Europe, on the material culture of bodily emission from spittoons to handkerchiefs, on the relationship between texts and the matter they are written on, on hygiene and statecraft, tears of devotion, menstruation and birth, bad skin and bad breath, communal bathing and bloodletting. The body has been shown to have been of crucial concern to medieval people, and studying it will yield as many important insights into their beliefs and lives as studying their battles and bibles has done. Indeed, bodies will turn out to have been *part* of their battles and bibles. Bottoms deserve their turn in the spotlight.

BETTINA BILDHAUER
University of St Andrews

ROBERT W. BARRETT JR. *Against All England: Regional Identity and Cheshire Writing, 1195–1656*. Notre Dame: University of Notre Dame Press, 2009. Pp. xvii, 306. $35.00 paper.

Robert Barrett's monograph opens a new debate over Cheshire's regional identity in the Middle Ages, seen in opposition to London as England's political and cultural center. His approach is topographical and historicist, making use of the *longue durée* (1195–1656), set apart from previous center-based diachronic studies of what critics often see as "national discourse." Barrett attends to "the intranational tensions between Cheshire and the larger English community" (15) and focuses on "dialogic" Cestrian identity (17). The study is divided into two parts, with three chapters on Chester and two on Cheshire.

"Chester the City" includes an overview of Chester's identity in monastic writing and two types of civic performance at the beginning and end of the chosen period. In *De laude Cestrie* (c. 1195), the Benedictine monk of Saint Werburgh, Lucian, constructs an "allegorical topography" of the "cloistered city." Lucian's achievement is to celebrate "urban renewal," "shifting portions of the city's topography around in an attempt to consolidate the abbey's influence" (32). Literary devices such as the rhetorical triads ("groups of threes designed to convey the image of triple identities subsumed within a greater unity") are, according to Barrett, less likely to be influenced by Welsh tradition than an attempt to reflect the Holy Trinity. The number three also justifies Lucian's etymology for Chester's Latin name, the tri-syllabic word *Cestria* (derived from the phrase *Dei castra*, "camp of God"). Chester becomes the center of the world, a new Jerusalem imagined as a cross (if imperfect, as Bridge Street and Northgate do not form a continuous line), made up of two lines signifying the Old and New Testaments through the churches that mark them: the Old Testament line is marked by Eastgate (Saint John's church) and Watergate (Saint Peter's), as a reflection of the passage between the "precursor of the Lord and his gatekeeper," while the New Testament is marked by Northgate (Saint Werburgh's) and Bridge Street (Saint Michael's), as a link to the Virgin Mary and the Archangel (41). Henry Bradshaw's *Life of St. Werburge* (c. 1506–13) reflects this local monk's attempt to present Chester as "a site of organic and spiritual unity" (44). Bradshaw's text intervenes in the "long-running struggle between the mayor and the abbot for control of Chester" as his focus is on the "conflicting jurisdictions of Chester's local courts"

(47). The initial victory went to the mayor, and the monastery's secular influence ceased with the Dissolution in 1539–40. Bradshaw's text was revived for the national scene through its publication in 1521 by Richard Pynson, the King's Printer, possibly due to its perceived utility for the "nationally coordinated anti-Lutheran" movement (53). Barrett considers that the *Life* was "primed for such appropriations" from the beginning, and its use was both local and national (58). While Lucian's and Bradshaw's texts are perfect markers of the beginning and end of Barrett's chosen period, it remains difficult to ascertain, at least for the nonspecialist reader, how dissimilar their texts were from monastic productions in other regions.

The following two chapters focus on the civic performances of the Whitsun plays and *Chester's Triumph in Honor of Her Prince* in 1610, which marked the first Chester horse races. In Play 5 of the Whitsun cycle (the Cappers' *Moses and the law; Balaam and Balaack*), the phrase "cittye, castle, and ryvere" (5.274) indicates the adaptation of the original story to local topographical details observed by actors standing on the performing wagon in Chester. Play 1, the Tanners' *Fall of Lucifer*, is used as a case study for Lucifer's rebellion, which "engages with local anxieties about political ambition" (81–82), while Lucifer risks "disenfranchisement" much as Chester's citizens did in the sixteenth century due to a multiplicity of jurisdictional boundaries. Play 13, *The Blind Chelidonian: The Raising of Lazarus,* shows evidence that the character of Caecus (the blind beggar in John 9:1–38) responds to and opposes the Tudor poor laws passed by Henry VIII in 1531 and Chester's Mayor Gee's 1539 Assembly order concerning the poor. These readings are provocative and engaging, modifying previous assumptions about this cycle of civic drama. Barrett links characters from the Whitsun plays and those in *Chester's Triumph*, in particular Saint George. *Chester's Triumph* displays the self-aggrandizing possibilities offered to citizens such as Robert Amery who were involved in its production. It was of course unfortunate that Prince Henry did not attend this event, since the production was designed to celebrate his elevation to the titles of Prince of Wales and Earl of Chester. However, the audience's attention was directed away from Prince Henry's absence, to think instead of Chester's secular authorities, and their efforts to assert the region's participation on the national political scene.

"Heraldic Devices / Chivalric Divisions" contains Barrett's review of *Sir Gawain and the Green Knight* from the perspective of the Scrope-

Grosvenor trial of 1385–91, in particular the "multiple regional communities" represented in this debate and their relation to local topography (149). The trial consisted in assessing the rights of Sir Robert Grosvenor of Hulme, Cheshire, and Sir Richard Scrope of Bolton, Yorkshire, to the heraldic arms *Azure, a bend Or*. Following the trial, Grosvenor's local regional affinities lost out to Scrope's display of national support. Barrett uses this context as a background to his regional analysis of the poem. He concludes that "heraldic vulnerability precedes that of the body" (153) when Gawain is disarmed at Bertilak's castle. The removal of Gawain's arms signifies his loss of identity through the removal of his heraldic insignia and leads Barrett to state that "the pentangle fails to signify across regional boundaries" (159). While the analyses of the passages describing the Green Knight's and Gawain's armor as signifiers of identity are persuasive, the idea that armor-less and device-less Gawain is unrecognizable to his hosts is debatable. The poem seems more concerned with the enactment of complex chivalric, courtly, and pious virtues symbolized by the pentangle than with the actual presence of Gawain's armor or heraldic device in his daily encounter with Bertilak and his lady. Frustratingly, a number of other interesting points related to regional differences are raised in this chapter, some sadly relegated to endnotes (see notes 21, 60, 68). Similarly, the relevance of studying the poem in its literary context is rather dismissed as a marginal point (see note 67).

In Chapter 5, "Celebrating Regional Affinities in the Stanley Family Romances," Barrett looks at how the Stanley poems "serve as records of individual negotiations between overlapping spatial identities (Cestrian, Lancastrian, northern, western, English, Scottish, etc.)" (174). The Bosworth Field poems (*Bosworth Field, Lady Bessy,* and *The Rose of England*) are considered alongside the Flodden Field poems (*Flodden Field* and *Scottish Field*), and the history of the family entitled *The Stanley Poem.* The discussion starts with Thomas Lord Stanley's celebration as Henry VII's supporter at Bosworth in *The Rose of England* poem, as the text is said ultimately to "subordinate local celebration to national ends" (177). In *Flodden Field,* Barrett sees the loss of the Stanley estates in Cheshire and Lancashire as a topographical representation of the poem's focus away from international conflict and return to "intranational strife" (193). Barrett supports the idea that chivalric romance "plays a part in Civil War politics," whether in a consolatory fashion or to offer "scripts for action," as was the case with the "romance" accounts of Charlotte

Stanley's defense of Lathom House against the Parliamentarians in 1644 (196–97).

Overall, this is a provocative and engaging study, which challenges previously held critical views of Cheshire and its literature. While some readers may object to the limited scope of each chapter, it is clear that Barrett's monograph is pathbreaking and proposes fertile avenues for further research.

RALUCA L. RADULESCU
Bangor University

CANDACE BARRINGTON. *American Chaucers*. New York: Palgrave Macmillan, 2007. Pp. xv, 224. $74.95.

Candace Barrington's stated purpose in *American Chaucers* is to examine "the intersections between the 'father of English letters' and American popular culture" (1). She casts her net wide, dealing with such disparate genres as grand opera, memoir, college pageant, spiritualist performance, and contemporary film. Her goal is to demonstrate "how Chaucer's difficult alterity and canonical cachet combine to create a chameleon text suitable for adaptation to various American concerns and values" (1). This goal may seem a bit vague, but it is actually an extension of the title of the book—an acknowledgment that when talking about Chaucer and American popular culture one must always keep in mind the plurality of the father of English letters.

Barrington begins her work on "American Chaucers" with a useful treatment of how the poet was anthologized in the United States. In this chapter, she differentiates the British from the American anthology by noting that where the British anthology emphasized an Arnoldian aesthetic and developed a "historical continuum culminating in contemporary poets," American anthologies "tended to arrange the poems thematically . . . decontextualiz[ing] the medieval setting" (21). British editors focused on how poetry could "promote higher virtues," while American editors promoted the extent to which the anthology was a marker of "good breeding" (35). British poems thus become cultural capital available to be mined "and cashed in for social and economic improvement" (35).

Chapter 2, comprising almost a third of the book, deals with Percy MacKaye and his work *The Canterbury Pilgrims*. Narrating the fascinating story of how MacKaye's dramatic piece moved from play to pageant to comic opera between 1902 and 1917, Barrington demonstrates his desire to embody in Chaucer a "serious vernacular poet urgently needed to unify the increasingly diverse American culture" (92). Chaucer's "ideal" relationship to his audience provides a model for MacKaye's desideratum, an American "civic theater." His failure to realize his dream is the result of bad luck, the increasingly commercial drive of theater (with which MacKaye was complicit) and the emergence of a counter-tradition in the person of Eugene O'Neill.

In chapter 3, Barrington treats *Flying with Chaucer*, a fifty-six-page memoir written by James Hall some eleven years after World War I. In it Hall narrates how he found a volume of the *Canterbury Tales* while interred in a makeshift detention facility in Landshut, Germany. The volume, pocketed as he escapes from the prison, is in Barrington's words, "not only a reliquary for preserving . . . aristocratic sensibility, but also becomes a talisman for transporting Hall to the past and for transmitting that otherwise lost sensibility to the future" (114). Indeed, Hall claims that he wrote the start of *Flying with Chaucer* in the blank back pages of the book he was carrying. His ambition was to pass the book (and thus his words) on to his children. Barrington writes feelingly of how Hall's ambivalence about war and his sense of loss are communicated through half a dozen Chaucerian passages in his memoir. But the larger implications of Hall's work remain elusive as Barrington at once claims that his work is a *"vox clamantis in deserto"* and an expression of the larger cultural forces of the interwar period.

Barrington's focus seems to narrow even more as she turns to the issue of gender and twentieth-century American attitudes toward Chaucer. In a chapter entitled "Geoffrey and the American Flapper," Barrington expresses her desire to discover "women's role in disseminating Chaucer" (118). Her exemplary moments are the production of a Chaucerian pageant at a women's liberal arts college in Massachusetts and the spiritualist Chaucerian performances of Katherine Gordon Sanger Brinley, "a writer of little note who took her ability to recite Chaucer on the road" (126). The stories of the pageant and Brinley are fascinating, but they tend to overwhelm any sustained analysis about why they are important. The result is that statements such as "The exchange of Chaucer from woman to woman . . . occurred outside institutionalized venues, an indication of women's marginalization in mainstream academia until the second half of the twentieth century" remain merely evocative and promising when they could give rise to deeply useful cultural insights (123).

Barrington's final intervention, a treatment of Brian Helgeland's *A Knight's Tale*, is the shortest (ten pages) and weakest chapter of the work. One would certainly understand, given the title of her book, why she should wish to categorize the film as quintessentially American. But even a cursory look at the film's production notes demonstrates its global nature. The company that produced it, Columbia, is American, but is owned by a Japanese corporation, Sony. Paul Bettany, who plays Chaucer, is English. The so-called American soundtrack is actually performed by British and Irish groups, and the movie was shot in the Czech Republic. Hence her argument that the movie "speaks to and valorizes [an] American culture of risk-taking" seems less than persuasive (especially as she notes that "risk-taking . . . was not the exclusive provenance of the United States"). In fact, the film seems to point to the extent to which early twenty-first-century film is ultimately a global enterprise even if the message of the movie is one with which Americans would have been sympathetic.

Barrington's book is ultimately quite useful insofar as it provides a point of departure for the study of the reception of Chaucer in the United States from the early nineteenth century into late modernity. As suggested above, a bit more cultural work would have gone a long way toward teasing out the meanings of these American Chaucers. And the distinction between "Academic" and popular Chaucer that initially enables Barrington's argument is put under more and more pressure as the work progresses (particularly in Chapter 4). But Barrington has written an engaging, provocative, and mostly convincing account of how the father of English literature was adapted to the needs of a country that could at once claim him as its own and consider him a foreigner.

THOMAS PRENDERGAST
College of Wooster

ANKE BERNAU and BETTINA BILDHAUER, eds. *Medieval Film*. Manchester: Manchester University Press, 2009. Pp. 241. £55.00; $84.95.

This collection of essays contributes to the study of medievalisms by focusing on medieval film, a paradoxical genre the editors define in three

ways: films set in the Middle Ages; films with medieval themes, characters, or allusions; and (most elusively) films that "resist adhering to
chronological history" (3). By working with this expanded notion of
medieval film, these essays demonstrate why it is no longer necessary to
limit our judgment of cinematic depictions of the medieval past to how
well they achieve historical accuracy. Not only do film narratives set in
the Middle Ages help us to see how difficult it is to create a history
not influenced by contemporary conventions and concerns, but medieval
film's pretense of transporting the audience to an authentic past (that is
in truth unavailable) reveals "the narrative and cinematic manipulations
underlying all historical films" (4). As these various essays explore, these
manipulations bring together the moment of history being depicted, the
moment of the historical moment's being filmed, the moment of its
screening, and the moment of its reinterpretation, causing each moment
to shape the other moments and confounding any ability to create a
historically accurate moment. The essays take three approaches: understanding the ways in which medieval film defamiliarizes standard film
conventions; understanding how medieval films can convey contemporary political concerns; and understanding how medievalism shaped film
history and film theory.

Four essays explore the significant ways that films set in the medieval
period manipulate such standard conventions as setting, music, and language. The artificiality of these cinematic conventions can be invisible
when films are set in more historically accessible periods. Medieval film,
however, foregrounds the partial availability of historical authenticity.
Because films set in the Middle Ages portray events, places, and characters that must be re-created, these films manage to reveal the inevitable
intervention implicit in any filmic depiction of the past. Sarah Salih
demonstrates the particular trouble attempts at authenticity pose for
films set in the Middle Ages. Because medieval artifacts and other visual
representations survive into the film era as broken, dirty, colorless ruins,
filmmakers are faced with a dilemma: either portray the premodern
world from a contemporary perspective by providing audiences with the
dark and grim setting that accords with these remains, or present
medieval artifacts as new and freshly painted, as they would have been
seen by medieval men and women, but then fail to meet audience expectations. Thus, the films that are most medieval in spirit may feel the
least visually authentic. For example, *Camelot* (1967), an apparently in-
authentic version of the Middle Ages, successfully captures medieval

attitudes toward the past when it reuses and juxtaposes texts and materials looted from the past. Andrew Higson's essay continues Salih's trajectory by arguing that associations of the Gothic with the Middle Ages frequently influence the sort of audience to which medieval films appeal. Because audiences have come to define the Middle Ages as "dangerous and dirty," the small subset of British heritage films set in the Middle Ages tend to earn "a more populist and masculine appeal" than similar films set in Victorian or Edwardian England, which tend to be depicted as clean and prim (203).

The two further essays in this line of inquiry examine the ways in which medieval films defamiliarize our assumptions about what audiences hear when they see a film set in the Middle Ages. Alison Tara Wilson examines the apparent dissonance between a film's medieval setting and its nonmedieval, contemporary music. As she demonstrates, such music can provide commentary affirming or challenging the film's medieval ethos. Carol O'Sullivan examines how films set in the Middle Ages deal with the problem of presenting different languages to a modern, frequently monolingual, audience. Whether filmmakers resolve the challenge by using only the language of the target audience, by inserting stray medieval morphemes (such as the *ye*, *thee*, and *-eth* associated with Middle English), or by using subtitles for multilingual exchange, the intervention foregrounds language difference. In both cases, the essays remind us that aural components do not necessarily enhance a film's historical authenticity; nor should the failure to achieve historical authenticity be a black mark against the film.

Two essays in *Medieval Film* examine the use of medieval narratives to consider contemporary political concerns. Marcia Landy looks at the ways in which four Italian films—two dating from the Fascist era and the other two from the 1960s—reimagine the Middle Ages to draw out their own particular political and cultural interests. Richard Burt takes a narrower approach with a detailed examination of para-mimetic elements in two films that appropriate the Bayeux Tapestry. In doing so, he argues that while *Robin Hood: Prince of Thieves* (1991) undermines its purported third-world multiculturalism by replicating the values of United States imperialism, *El Cid* (1961), an ostensibly more tradition-bound film, breaks with the logic of cultural dominance.

Finally, by exploring the ways in which medievalism shaped twentieth- and twenty-first-century cinema and film theory, three essays reflect the recent move in medieval studies to demonstrate the early influence of medievalism and medieval studies on contemporary critical theory. Thus Bettina Bildhauer demonstrates that much film theory relies on medievalism because early film theorists seized on clichés about the medieval past in order to present the Middle Ages' pre-print culture sometimes as an analogous state to which film aspired, sometimes as a foil to the "liberated movement of the camera" (53). Similarly, John Ganim provides a wide-ranging overview of the unsettling ways in which medievalism and film noir shaped each other. Most notably, he demonstrates how film noir's "medieval undercurrent" allows this modern film genre to question cinematic and ethical assumptions. And Anke Bernau explores how a film such as D. W. Griffith's *Birth of a Nation*, which ostensibly has nothing to do with the Middle Ages, can be shown to have derived many of its premises and aesthetic issues from medievalism. By building its nationalist discourse on dichotomies that set the medieval into opposition with the modern, the film's multiple medievalisms ultimately "unravel the oppositions and unmake the categories on which the rhetoric of nationhood is founded" (105).

Throughout, these essays provide provocative reminders that medieval film, like all pastness, forever recedes into inaccessibility and, like all cinema, cannot erase the marks of its anachronistic intervention. By providing a multiplicity of approaches and daring readings, this collection extends and sharpens the critical analysis of both medieval films and medievalism.

CANDACE BARRINGTON
Central Connecticut State University

ROSALIND BROWN-GRANT. *French Romance of the Later Middle Ages: Gender, Morality, and Desire.* Oxford: Oxford University Press, 2008. Pp. xi, 254. £55.00; $110.00.

In this welcome study, Rosalind Brown-Grant scrutinizes fifteen prose romances written after 1390, many of them commissioned by the court of Burgundy, all of them initially produced for aristocratic audiences. She excludes Arthurian romances, *Perceforest*, *Mélusine*, and *Jehan de Saintré,* among other works, limiting herself to what she calls "historico-realist romances" that were produced in the "moralizing" climate of late medieval Burgundy. Brown-Grant's thoughtful analyses offer a real service for scholars seeking greater familiarity with these important but rather neglected works. I count myself among those who cannot claim to have read all the romances analyzed here, some of which have only recently been published in modern editions or are difficult to access.

In Chapter 1, "'Recit d'armes et/ou d'amour': Love, Prowess, and Chivalric Masculinity," Brown-Grant examines seven tales of *innamoramento,* in which a young knight proves his valor before a high-born woman: *Ponthus et Sidoine, Cleriadus et Meliadice, Rambaux de Frise, Blancandin, Jehan d'Avennes, Gilles de Chin,* and *Olivier de Castille.* These romances, she argues, focus less on heterosexual love than did their literary predecessors, instead highlighting friendships with other knights, politically expedient marriages, and military prowess channeled for the common good, *"la chose publique."* Brown-Grant locates similar values in contemporary manuals of chivalry and chivalric biographies, such as Ramon Llull's *Livre de l'ordre de chevalerie,* Geoffroi de Charny's *Livre de chevalerie,* Jean de Bueil's *Le Jouvencel,* the biographies of Boucicaut and Lalaing, and Ghillebert de Lannoy's *Instruction d'un jeune prince* and *Enseignement paternels.* Although the manuals of chivalry express a variety of attitudes toward love, ranging from the "positively laudatory" in de Charny to the "downright hostile" in de Lannoy (29), Brown-Grant notes that they share common views on the importance of knighthood as a cornerstone of the social good and that these ideals are echoed in their romance counterparts.

In Chapter 2, "Youthful Folly in Boys and Girls: Idyllic Romance and the Perils of Adolescence in *Pierre de Provence* and *Paris et Vienne,*" Brown-Grant compares the representation of adolescence in these later medieval romances with its treatment in earlier "idyllic romances" such as *Floire et Blanchefleur* and *Galeran de Bretagne.* Whereas the earlier romances idealize youthful passion, the later romances stress the dangers that young people's headstrong emotions and strong physical urges can have on their families' well-laid plans for marriage and social ascension. As in Chapter 1, Brown-Grant sets these late medieval texts in the context of contemporary didactic writings, in this case treatises such as Aldobrandino of Siena's *Régime du corps,* Henri de Gauchi's French translation of Giles of Rome's *De Regimine principum,* Philippe de Novare's *Des quatre tens de d'aage d'ome,* and the writings of Christine de Pizan—works that underscore the disruptive nature of youthful passions and the importance of parental authority.

Chapter 3, "Husbands and Wives in Marital Romance: The Trials of Male Adultery, Bigamy, and Repudiation," demonstrates the influence of late medieval clerical writings about marriage on selected romances. Following Duby, Brown-Grant describes the contrast between an "aristocratic" model viewing marriage principally as a means of consolidating territory and power among noble families and an ecclesiastical or "clerical" model stressing the indissolubility of bonds, the consent of both partners, and the mutual obligations of respect and solace between husband and wife. In keeping with her insistence on the influence of late medieval didactic tracts, Brown-Grant maintains that certain late medieval romances reflect clerical rather than aristocratic ideals as they examine male behavior in marriage.

One might argue that earlier medieval romances also frequently reflect clerical values and scrutinize conjugal relationships. For example, Tristan's *Thomas* presents a rather "clerkly" critique of passionate love, and the later volumes of the *Lancelot-Grail* go even further in condemning adultery. The husband's behavior could be considered problematic, in different ways, in *Erec et Enide, Yvain, Eliduc,* and the *Roman de Jehan et de la Belle Flore* (a source for the *Roman du Comte d'Artois),* to name a few examples. The late medieval romances that Brown-Grant studies may constitute an evolution rather than a departure from earlier models. Nonetheless, her analysis of particular texts is compelling, as she demonstrates how the *Roman du Comte d'Artois* and *Gillion de Trazegnies* pay particular attention to the "correction" of unworthy behavior by husbands toward wives and how each of three manuscript versions of the *Seigneurs de Gavre* portrays the exemplary marriage and governance of a son who offers a powerful corrective lesson to the impetuous, harsh behavior of the father. Brown-Grant's remarks about the clerkly model of marriage are informed by recent scholarship on the legend of Saint Joseph, whose portrait as compassionate, understanding husband becomes prominent during this period.

The final chapter, "Incestuous Desire versus Marital Love: Rewriting the Tale of the 'maiden without hands,'" examines the most negative representation of passion in three versions of the *Manekine*: Philippe de Rémi's thirteenth-century verse romance, *La Manekine* (c. 1240); Jehan Maillart's *Roman du Comte d'Anjou* (1316), a verse recasting of Philippe; and, finally, Jehan Wauquelin's prose *Manekine* (mid-fifteenth century). As in the previous chapters, Brown-Grant contrasts an earlier, more "courtly" romance, in which love is presented either as a malevolent force or an ennobling passion, with later, moralizing tales that incorporate either elements of hagiography, as does the *Roman du Comte d'Anjou*, or didactic precepts from the "mirror of princes" tradition, as does Wauquelin's romance. Her demonstration of Wauquelin's borrowings from Giles of Rome's *De Regimine principum* is particularly persuasive, since, as she points out, Wauquelin himself retranslated Henri de Gauchi's French translation of Giles for Philippe le Bon in 1450; it remains unedited in a luxurious illuminated manuscript. Setting Giles's remarks about the negative effects of endogamous marriage and the positive virtues of royal marriage for the realm against the narrator's commentary in Wauquelin's romance, Brown-Grant presents perhaps her most convincing case about the influence of moralizing, didactic literature on late medieval fiction.

The greatest strengths of Brown-Grant's book are her stimulating comparative analyses of little-studied romances in the light of particular contemporary didactic treatises. Reading a romance such as *Ponthus et Sidoine*, with its embedded "mirror of princes," against Geoffroi de Charny; comparing the *Seigneurs de Gavre* to Jean Gerson's treatise on marriage and to his laudatory description of Saint Joseph; or viewing Wauquelin's portrait of marriage through the lens of Giles: through such critical juxtapositions, Brown-Grant helps to flesh out the cultural context of late medieval French romance. Brown-Grant's arguments are less compelling when she attempts to make overly broad generalizations about gender relations in either earlier or later romances. As she demonstrates, the later texts are characterized by a remarkably diverse range of representations; this is no less true for the portrayal of male and female roles in dozens of earlier verse romances and in the vast thirteenth-century prose cycles. The important romances excluded from her study (among them *Mélusine* and *Saintré,* both remarkable for their generic hybridity and problematization of traditional gender roles) would doubtless complicate Brown-Grant's sometimes overly schematic analyses. Finally, Brown-Grant seems at times too eager to reduce the arguments of earlier critics into pat formulas, overlooking the nuances of their critical analyses. A spate of stimulating studies by scholars such as Sylvia Huot, Sylvie Lefèvre, Danielle Régnier-Bohler, Michèle Szkilnik, and Jane Taylor about these and other works has raised the level of critical discourse about late medieval narrative, whose representation of the ethical issues surrounding gender, clerical discourse notwithstanding, may prove to be as complex as that of earlier romances. Brown-

Grant makes an important contribution to this ongoing project by contextualizing late medieval Burgundian romances under the sign of vernacular didactic literature, thus inviting further critical reflection about the social and moral functions of narrative and about the *mise en roman* of ethics and gender.

ROBERTA KRUEGER
Hamilton College

MARGARET CONNOLLY and LINNE R. MOONEY, eds. *Design and Distribution of Late Medieval Manuscripts in England*. York: York Medieval Press, 2008. Pp. xiii, 336. £60.00; $115.00.

Editors of themed essay collections must routinely have difficulty devising appropriate collective titles as volumes on the same theme multiply. *Design and Distribution of Late Medieval Manuscripts in England* will do well enough for this one, partly because the quality of the contributions is mostly very high: it would be unreasonable to complain seriously. But a reviewer has the responsibility of making clear the actual content of a collection. In the present case, the bias is predominantly Middle English and textual, most of the essays deriving from the 2005 York Manuscripts Conference. Only two of the thirteen are centrally concerned with the physical design of manuscripts in the sense of layout, decoration, and illustration. Design is elsewhere interpreted as relating to the choices a scribe makes when deciding how to transmit text in writing. As for distribution, the introduction asserts that late medieval producers of manuscript books were as concerned with marketing, audiences, intended use, and the like as those involved, shortly afterward, with the printed book trade. This claim is not really substantiated by the essays here, and a better word than "distribution" might have been "circulation," or simply "copying."

The book is usefully organized into three sections, by subtheme. We start with "Designing the *Canterbury Tales*: Chaucer's Early Copyists": three fairly heavyweight essays for those who wish to keep up with the latest thinking on the early textual transmission of the *Tales*, especially following the identification of the Hengwrt/Ellesmere scribe as Adam Pinkhurst, who must be Chaucer's own scribe Adam. Dan Mosser,

"'Chaucer's Scribe': Adam and the Hengwrt Project," examines physical and textual evidence in the Hengwrt manuscript to see what we can deduce about authorial presence or absence in its direction. His tentative conclusion is that Chaucer is quite likely to have been involved at some stage of Hengwrt's production—perhaps at a distance—"but certainly not to the extent of 'finishing' it" (38). Jacob Thaisen writes about "The Trinity Gower D Scribe's Two *Canterbury Tales* Manuscripts Revisited." This is a close examination of the orthography (and, in support, codicology) of these manuscripts (Oxford, Corpus Christi College, MS 198, and London, British Library, MS Harley 7334) in relation to the nature of the exemplars the scribe employed. Thaisen presents evidence for, among other things, the very early integration of the noncanonical *Tale of Gamelyn* into the *Canterbury Tales* tradition—perhaps even before Chaucer's death—and stresses generally that "other manuscripts than Pinkhurst's contain authoritative material unrecorded in his" (60). Takako Kato's "Corrected Mistakes in Cambridge University Library MS Gg.4.27" is rather different in being wholly textual. Its concentration on types of scribal error occurring as part of the copying process (which she categorizes in detail) is scholarship of a kind practiced before manuscript studies came into vogue. MS Gg.4.27 is a textually important Chaucer manuscript, and so Kato's conclusions about the scribe's performance—that the majority of his errors are the result of carelessness rather than insufficient understanding of his exemplar—are valuable for understanding its place in the textual tradition.

In the second grouping, "Designing Devotion: Individual and Institutional," no more than one of the four essays has to do with Middle English. This is Alexandra Barratt's "Singing from the Same Hymn-Sheet: Two Bridgettine Manuscripts," which expertly characterizes the physically contrasting London, Lambeth Palace Library MS 3600, and BL, MS Harley 494 (which belonged to Anne Bulkeley), and analyses their complicated textual overlap, testifying to common source materials. The former was undoubtedly made at Syon Abbey, and Barratt, who traces the court and abbey connections of Anne Bulkeley's family, shows that the latter manuscript was very likely compiled there also, in the 1530s. The other three essays in this section are Sherry L. Reames, "Late Medieval Efforts at Standardization and Reform in the Sarum Lessons for Saints' Days"; Amelia Grounds, "Evolution of a Manuscript: The Pavement Hours"; and Julian Luxford, "'Secundum originale examinatum': The Refashioning of a Benedictine Historical Manuscript."

Reames, in a groundbreaking piece of research, bases her convincing conclusions on a survey of a large number of Sarum breviaries and lectionaries; Luxford skillfully compares the "Founders' Book" of Tewkesbury Abbey (c. 1510) with a manuscript reproduction made almost a century later, which accurately reproduces the textual and pictorial content of the original while endeavoring to make it resemble a (decidedly nonmedieval) printed book. Grounds's essay is unfortunately less well judged in that she writes somewhat repetitively for a less specialist audience, and frustratingly does not provide a complete list of the devotional images later inserted into the Pavement Hours, although this is the very interesting phenomenon she is discussing. The editors must take some of the blame for this.

"Development and Distribution: Mapping Manuscripts and Texts" returns us firmly to Middle English. Linne R. Mooney, "Locating Scribal Activity in Late Medieval London," expertly investigates the different types of writer engaged in copying vernacular texts in the capital, bringing out the amount of work likely to have been undertaken by freelance or foreign scribes, or government officials working out of hours. Especially interesting is her account of the different geographical areas in question, including the numerous liberties located within the City walls. Michael G. Sargent's "What Do the Numbers Mean? Observations on Some Patterns of Middle English Manuscript Transmission" is another authoritative survey, densely footnoted, drawing on earlier scholarship to demonstrate, with bar charts, the rising then falling rate of manuscript production of the most copied works of Middle English literature, from the dates of their composition on into the early sixteenth century. His results confirm the importance of early Lancastrian London in terms of both level of book production and canon formation. Sargent does not, however, provide charts for the Wycliffite Bible or the prose *Brut*, and relevant data for the latter are not included in John J. Thompson's "The Middle English Prose *Brut* and the Possibilities of Cultural Mapping." Thompson is mainly concerned to establish the cultural centrality of the *Brut* in the fifteenth and sixteenth centuries in the face of its later dismissal by "serious" historians, and restricts his specific remarks to small groups of linked *Brut* manuscripts—most interestingly a group apparently produced along the Welsh/English border—as examples of what could be done on a larger scale.

Mapping is also the theme of two of the final three essays, but the evidence adduced by Margaret Connolly and Ralph Hanna is very different. In "Mapping Manuscripts and Readers of *Contemplations of the Dread and Love of God*," Connolly undertakes a detailed exploration of the readership of this much-copied devotional text on the basis of ownership inscriptions. She shows, valuably, that the *Contemplations* was almost certainly not only compiled within a scholarly environment, probably Carthusian, but professionally copied and circulated also. The inscriptions suggest a predominantly religious readership in the fifteenth century giving way to lay ownership in the sixteenth. In contrast, Hanna's "Yorkshire Manuscripts of the *Speculum Vitae*" uses the dialect-mapping methodology of the *Linguistic Atlas of Later Mediaeval English* to demonstrate that the most textually accurate copies of this long didactic verse treatise are also those that are closest linguistically to the author's likely area of origin in the northern half of the West Riding of Yorkshire or the southern part of the North Riding. "This disposition of the copies, almost too neat to be true, most likely reflects some variety of institutionally controlled transmission" (291). The collection concludes with George R. Keiser, "Vernacular Herbals: A Growth Industry in Late Medieval England." In a clear and useful introduction to a difficult field (and using a mixture of codicological, textual, and ownership evidence), Keiser covers both the development and circulation of standard texts and the phenomenon of "designer herbals," where compilers select from or conflate existing texts to meet their particular requirements.

Design and Distribution contains many valuable essays and will be much referred to. It has its share of misprints, but is otherwise a handsome weighty volume exemplifying the best standards of modern book production. There are two detailed high-quality indexes, one of manuscripts, the other general.

OLIVER PICKERING
Leeds, UK

JOSEPH A. DANE. *Abstractions of Evidence in the Study of Manuscripts and Early Printed Books*. Aldershot: Ashgate, 2009. Pp. viii, 184. £55.00; $99.95.

Joseph Dane's investigation of evidence in medieval manuscripts and early printed books from a bibliographical and theoretical perspective is very much a sequel to his *The Myth of Print Culture* (2003) and a contribution to recent discussions in bibliography and history of the book. The book is structured in two parts: "Inference and Evidence in Medieval Books" and "What Is a book?" Both are prefaced by an introduction on the difficulties of using electronic resources and catalogues to identify books as well as researching specific bibliographical evidence regarding these books. "What is that thing before us? How does it relate to what we think and speak about? How does one appeal to it? or address it?" (20), Dane asks, and how can a researcher defeat the standardization of books, which is imposed by catalogues and databases? Dane argues that such tools do not regard the book as a unique entity but rather a book as many others. These are important questions that shift from the location and identification of the object into a larger theoretical framework on materiality and textuality, thus leading Dane to explore the "abstractions" of evidence. The term, by the author's own admission, is "deliberately equivocal" and relates to evidence "removed or taken away" (9) from the materiality of the book and from, so it seems, its context.

In the following chapters, Dane presents self-contained case studies that introduce readers to a wide range of texts and issues. Chapter 1 reconsiders Littlewood and Greg's formula in calculating print runs of sixteenth-century copies of *Everyman*, arguing that the calculus was very much influenced by assumptions that ultimately cannot be proved. Chapter 2 is a cogent and lucid appraisal of Kane's editorial approach to the "Prologue" of Chaucer's *Legend of Good Women* with specific reference to the treatment of the text in Cambridge, University Library, MS Gg 4.27. Chapters 3 and 4 conclude the first section of the book by focusing on medieval vernacular drama, reconsidering its editorial history in constructing textual and authorial identity. In Chapter 4, for instance, Dane reviews the creation of the abstract notion of the "Wakefield Master" in an interesting excursus through the critical editions of the Towneley plays and related scholarly publications from the nineteenth century to the present day.

The second part of the monograph starts with a discussion of the production of erroneous facsimiles of printed books and examines the lasting impact of such errors in the critical and scholarly use of the text reproduced. Dane here reconsiders the dangerous authority that a facsimile can exert. He fears that facsimiles are becoming "the primary substitute for the literary 'thing itself'" (93), especially given the wide use of Early English Books Online. The succeeding chapters focus on detective work and detailed bibliographical examination of books with mistaken identity. Dane chases two misbound title pages of Thynne's 1542 edition of Chaucer's *Works* and reattributes them to the correct book. He reconsiders De Ricci's bibliographical note on the 1476 edition of Boccaccio's *De Casibus virorum illustrium* by Colard Mansion. In Chapter 8, he evaluates the duality of the use of Caxton in scholarly discourse, on the one hand as a synonym for the printed book itself and on the other biographically, as an individual. He concludes that our understanding and rating of the man and the object can at times be diametrically opposed, with the object being more highly regarded than the man. The final two chapters reconsider how books are subject to manipulation to "conform to abstract and evolving notions of what they should or ought to be" (139): a bibliographical case in point is the Huntington Library's 1484 printed edition of Bonaventura's *Opuscula*. This is a book that is difficult to describe because the print-run of this edition had a table of contents that varied in its content, making it difficult to indicate in the catalogue precisely what the book contains. Therefore the book is catalogued, Dane would argue, according to "idealised" parameters, which may not accurately describe the actual contents of the Huntington copy. The conclusion is a defense of the unique nature of each book as a material object, because a book, known via a catalogue, is rarely, or almost never, what a scholar is expecting to see. Catalogues cannot substitute for the unique impression that the handling of the physical book unveils.

There is much of interest to Chaucerians in this new book by Dane. The discussion of Kane's methodology and the tale of mistaken identity in Thynne's editions are methodologically inspiring. Readers working on the Huntington collections will also find compelling bibliographical evidence and observations in many of the essays. Some will already be familiar with essays and chapters that have appeared before, but the material included here allows for an overall assessment of the importance of bibliographical and textual matters, and nine of the chapters are previously unpublished.

While the theoretical discussion of idealized texts and their relationship to real objects and books is stimulating, the book reads more as a collection of essays than a structured argument. It may be unfair to note this when in the introduction the author includes an apologia and explains: "These chapters are not organized to produce a scholarly narrative, seamless or otherwise, nor to construct a step-by-step argument"

(10). In fact, an argument runs throughout the book, but it could have been more forcefully advanced by offering the contexts for the textual evidence presented; instead, context is explicitly removed from the discussion. A more integrated discussion, with evidence placed in context, would have allowed some reconciliation of the insurmountable divide between bibliography and literary criticism (86). Materiality and abstraction are interesting concepts and ought to be integrated and contextualized in a wider literary and historical background to allow scholars to understand fully why this evidence matters in our cultural, literary, and historical understanding of the past.

ORIETTA DA ROLD
University of Leicester

ANDREW GALLOWAY and R. F. YEAGER, eds. *Through a Classical Eye: Transcultural and Transhistorical Visions in Medieval English, Italian, and Latin Literature in Honour of Winthrop Wetherbee.* Toronto: University of Toronto Press, 2009. Pp. viii, 436. $80.00.

The editors of *Through a Classical Eye* point out in their introduction Winthrop Wetherbee's significance as a latter-day successor to the "giants of early twentieth-century medieval (and other) 'philology' and literary study, especially Erich Auerbach, Ernst Robert Curtius, C. S. Lewis and Leo Spitzer" (4). And certainly this festschrift will remind everyone of Wetherbee's decisive contributions to the study of the twelfth-century Latin classics and "the adapters and creative mis-readers of the classical Latin tradition, Jean de Meun, Dante, Chaucer and Gower" (5). A bibliography of Wetherbee's publications (19–24), a concluding essay (415–18) by a close friend, Robert Morgan, and a list of prestigious contributors complete the presentation of Wetherbee's character and achievements. Needless to say, the contributors usually document their debt to Wetherbee and note where their contribution fits into the pattern of his own interests.

The essays assembled fall into three groups: *"auctores"* (four essays), "Italy and the world" (six essays) and "England and Beyond" (nine essays). In *"auctores,"* Joseph Pucci gives us a taste of his forthcoming book, *Augustine's Ancient Affections,* in arguing that Catullus's mesmerizing use of words sat deeper in the souls of late antique writers than we have hitherto believed. I find the uses of Catullus by Fortunatus writing to Agnes, Abbess of the Convent of the Holy Cross, slightly more compelling than those signalized in Augustine's *Confessions* 1.5.5, but this is still a striking article. Danuta Shanzer contributes a learned set of glosses on problematic points in the notorious "Irish" text of the seventh century, the *Hisperica Famina*. Jeremy Tambling unites Bernard Silvester, Augustine, Derrida, and Dante in quest of creation, matter, good, evil, and the allegory of *selva oscura*, the heartland of much of Wetherbee's work. R. F. Yeager concludes this portion of the volume with a probing of the unusually frequent metaphor of shipwreck in Alan of Lille's *De planctu naturae*, showing how the term "contributes to Alain's poetic endeavor to create 'a mode of allegory both cosmological and sacramental'" (101).

In "Italy and the World," the key part of the feast is the first essay, in which Rita Copeland provides an arresting comment on the way impersonal didactic "technai" in the Middle Ages replaced the personal charisma of teachers. She achieves great effect by way of a study of the unique link between "technai" and charisma in Guido Faba's *Rota Nova*. This is an essay everyone should read and it displays excellently the author's ability to think quite outside the normal routines of study and to illuminate all our detailed work. In the first of two essays dealing with Dante, Giuseppe Mazzotta provides a wide-ranging set of ideas on "the incommensurability between divine wisdom and human knowledge" (136), justice, and "geometry and its relations to art, ethics, history and geography" (141) in connection with *Paradiso* VIII–XX. He concludes that "the *Divine Comedy* [is] a text radically unlike the epic poems of Homer and Virgil," as Dante "brings thought to its outermost boundaries and asks of us that we edge to the limits of ourselves [herein producing] a poetic text wherein borders are not construed as barriers" (142). Warren Ginsberg follows this up with a complex set of links in Dante between geography, rhetoric, and dialectic (talking of *Inferno* XVI) and between Dante, Boccaccio, and Chaucer. Teresa A. Kennedy then "seeks to explore the contradictions in Boccaccio's understanding of Greek classicism as a humanist philological project on the one hand, and its genealogical and rhetorical relationship to vernacular themes and motifs including Byzantium and the Islamic world on the other" (165). She concludes that "Boccaccio's Greek philology, the echoes of Troy and Thebes, of Griselda and Criseida, all destabilize the categories of knowledge that Petrarch's Latin philology seeks to establish" (182). Jim Rhodes next situates two stories from Boccaccio's *Decameron* (I.3 and X.9) in the double-sided development of Western views of Islam: hostility and polemic on one side, praise of the virtuous Islamic hero (Saladin) on the other. David Wallace concludes this part of the volume by considering the story of Griselde in light of the relationship between Petrarch and Boccaccio, and the "imaginative kinship" Chaucer found with these writers.

Nine essays conclude the academic portion of the volume, offering pointed insights into territory that Wetherbee discussed in his *Chaucer and the Poets* (1984) and elsewhere, as the contributors note. Thomas C. Stillinger seeks "to situate Chaucer on the threshold between the Middle Ages and the Renaissance" (224). Christina Von Nolcken proposes to "think about [Chaucer's] Miller in conjunction with the Wycliffite Bible translation itself," rather than simply in the context of "a Wycliffite Biblicism" (239). Frederick Ahl "examines selected aspects of Chaucer's wordplay from [the] perspective [of an] assess[ment of] what happens to his poetry when we remove the wordplay, as some translators have done, and then [by] show[ing] some ways in which Chaucer's poetry follows the practices of classical Roman writers" (267). Alastair Minnis deals with "the most robust put-down in the entire *Canterbury Tales*," suffered by the Pardoner (287), exploring "the cultural sources and significance" of the humor that Chaucer brings into play. An understanding of "the powers some 'real' relics and healing shrines were believed to possess," Minnis argues, may help to "understand the manner in which the Host fictionalizes his opponent's testicles as the prize exhibit in his collection" (288). I like Minnis's conclusion (306): "Top-down research, based on high-culture texts, will not get us very far into the breech. Rather we need to exploit the resources of popular religion and folklore, to work from the bottom up"! Disa Gambera then examines the wounds a woman who is gazed at inflicts upon the gazer in regard to Fragment I of the *Canterbury Tales* (but her analysis touches many other parts of the *Tales*). Yoshiko Kobayashi contextualizes John Gower's contrasting of "the present state of misery with a former happiness" in Book I of his *Vox Clamantis* with Ovid's elegiac lament in his *Tristia* about the passing of *his* former happiness when writing his famous amatory elegies. María Bullón-Fernández follows this up with a wide-ranging examination of two "versions of Pygmalion": Ovid's *Metamorphoses* 10.238–97 and John Gower's *Confessio Amantis* 4.371–450. Thomas D.

Hill then examines a phrase in the Middle English poem *Cleanness*, and James Simpson concludes the collection with an investigation of *involucrum* and *otium* in "a little-known but interesting early fifteenth-century work, *Reason and Sensuality*, which is itself apparently insouciant about its *oisiveté*" (391).

All in all, this is a difficult collection and one that seldom approaches the broad sweep and easy relevance that Wetherbee launched in his magisterial *Platonism and Poetry in the Twelfth Century: The Literary Influence of the School of Chartres*, now thirty-eight years old. It is not a volume to be picked up by the ordinary interested reader. Nevertheless, all the essays do mine veins within the ore zones that Wetherbee touched upon, and to those familiar with the detail and background of each presentation there will be much that is cogent and of value to ruminate over. It seems to the present reviewer, however, a far cry from the enthusiasm of his first meeting with Wetherbee, in the reviewer's room, around 2 A.M. at a Kalamazoo conference shortly after the publication of *Platonism and Poetry*. What took place then was an animated conversation about big matters that seemed so important and profound. What we have here is mostly small matters, close and complex and detailed. However, there are two sides to scholarship, and Wetherbee easily encompasses both. For those who do not know his work, the present volume is certainly one to place on the shelf, next to *Platonism and Poetry in the Twelfth Century* itself.

JOHN O. WARD
University of Sydney

GEOFFREY W. GUST. *Constructing Chaucer: Author and Autofiction in the Critical Tradition*. New York: Palgrave Macmillan, 2009. Pp. xiv, 286. $95.00.

This book urges that the persona be reenshrined in Chaucer studies: "Let us undertake to rescue Chaucer's persona from the ghetto, returning it to the center of critical discussion—where it belongs" (196). By "Chaucer's persona," Geoffrey Gust has in mind the persona presented in the *Thopas-Melibee* link, the subject of his final chapter, entitled "Claiming the 'Popet.'" It is argued that a sophisticated awareness of the usage of personae was current in the Middle Ages, but then was lost to view as later periods became obsessed with reading Chaucer's work and the "popet" as straight autobiography. The rediscovery of persona awareness permits a critical restoration, and the persona is for Gust a far more justifiable trope than the postmodern concern with "subject" or "voice," partly because it is authentically medieval, and because it means the same thing anyway only under a "variant terminology" (38). Unfortunately, this simple blurring of categories is characteristic of a study that, while frequently sophisticated in its mode of expression, betrays some conceptual naïveté.

It is never really made clear why the persona is such a vital entity, beyond the generalizing insistence that, if we take the "Chaucer" who appears in his works at face value, we will not be attuned to the complexity and "productive indeterminacy" of the Chaucer text (75). It would be difficult for any modern student of Chaucer to dissent from this, and indeed much of this book is a reception history of the unenlightened search for "Chaucer the Man" that characterized criticism from the sixteenth to the mid-nineteenth centuries (with the honorable exception of Dryden). But Gust's desire to forge new directions in Chaucer criticism sits unconvincingly alongside the exposé of this tradition, which is hardly blocking the way any longer: the claim that "it is still broadly true that . . . some Chaucerians see in the narrator a kind of direct relationship with Chaucer the Man himself" (44) is not only vague but for support tellingly resorts via an endnote to an article published in 1974. Gust has in effect imperfectly welded two projects, one on the Chaucer tradition, and the other entering the field of contemporary critical debate; while the first is performed competently, the second suffers in the process.

This is partly because, the final chapter aside, Gust never develops his own persona-based readings. Time and again we are told of "possibilities" that deserve "more support and exploration, and might inspire much future research" (119), or of "issues that deserve further discussion [which] I have only been able to explore . . . in a limited fashion in this chapter" (135). Such issues include a nonautobiographical reading of "Lenvoy to Scogan" and the possibility of a "tongue-in-cheek quality" to Chaucer's Retraction (117). One might retort that one reason for these limitations is the amount of space the book dedicates to reception matters, to the exclusion of the detailed treatment that would justify a range of interpretations hardly begun. The curious tone of exhortation

412

throughout—"critics would do well to explore further the fact that . . ." (106)—makes one ask why Gust has not done the exploring himself. Again, Chapter 1 indicates the Ph.D. origin of the whole in its dutiful survey of writing relating to the persona from classical times to Salman Rushdie, space that could have been used more productively in the passage from thesis into book. And in spite of the claim to consider both persona-history and persona-theory, the emphasis on the former is to the detriment of a theoretical underpinning that would bolster the contemporary critical intervention.

Where Gust does get down to some detailed critical work is in his final chapter. After sprinkling the term "queer" and passing references to queer theory around in earlier chapters as cognates for "productive indeterminacy"—"I would call [Sir Nicholas Harris] Nicolas's life-writing usefully 'queer' in its function" (of "undercut[ting] unequivocal, positivistic readings of complex texts and records") (75)—the author here attempts to substantiate the earlier claim that "persona-theory and queer-theory overlap in significant ways" (123). The result is an attentive reading of the "Prologue" to *Sir Thopas* and of gender questions prompted by Chaucer's use of terms like "elvyssh" and "popet," though the fact that this "autofiction" is mediated through the Host's obsessive concern with proper masculinity is not sufficiently considered. But it is the wider intervention that Gust attempts to make with this reading that sums up some of the problems with the book. "The time has come to end the silence" (194), we are told, and to expose "the failure, or outright refusal of critics to take up the gauntlet and fully address the implications of the persona-construct" (196). "Chaucer's Challenge," hitherto shamefully avoided by the profession at large and proclaimed in the book's extraordinary peroration, lies in the fact that "he dares us to address the full implications of his narrative I-persona" (194). These "implications" are not only that the Chaucer-persona is queer—and even Glenn Burger is accused of evasion in ducking the challenge here—but that in presenting such a persona Chaucer is forcing critics to examine their own constructed personae (or "scholarly personalities") and the (ideological) interests they serve. But the reference to ideology is, as previously (81, 108), superficial ("I, too, bring my own ideologies to my research"), something the author possesses rather than is possessed by, and merely equated with the ambition "to try and push the bounds of Chaucerian interpretation to new limits" (196). The desire may be sincere, but one could have done without the final pages, declaiming in conspiracy-theory mode against the unspecified but presumably numerous Chaucerians still engaged in cover-up, latter-day Speghts and Lelands fearful for the good name of the Father of English Poetry and needing a stiff dose of Roland Barthes. "In simple terms, *the persona is not the poet*" Gust tells us in his own italics early in the book (44), and rhetoric rather than analysis too often takes over in trying to get us much further.

STEVE ELLIS
University of Birmingham

CAROL FALVO HEFFERNAN. *Comedy in Chaucer and Boccaccio*. Cambridge: D. S. Brewer, 2009. Pp. xi, 151. £45.00; $90.00.

The title of Carol Falvo Heffernan's addition to Brewer's Chaucer Studies series is admirably straightforward. Yet, as Heffernan shows, the nature of comedy in Chaucer and Boccaccio is not so straightforward, but spans a multiplicity of subgenres. This multiplicity reinforces the complexity of late medieval comedy, which incorporates both the exalted cosmological vision of Dante's *Commedia* and the low plotting of the French fabliaux. Both Chaucer and Boccaccio immerse themselves in this variety, and Heffernan reminds us of their shared comic inheritance and the various parallels between the two authors' works.

An unavoidable question, which this study attempts to answer, concerns Chaucer's knowledge of the *Decameron*. The answer to this question has changed in recent decades, shifting from J. E. Severs's resounding "no," through Donald McGrady's "perhaps," to Heffernan's "very likely." Indeed, Heffernan builds upon recent commentary in this area by N. S. Thompson, John Finlayson, Helen Cooper, Leonard Michael Koff and Brenda Deen Schildgen, among others, all of whom in some form or another have recommended that we reconsider the long-established view that Chaucer did not know Boccaccio's mercantile epic directly. Heffernan states that in an earlier study she "also was burdened by caution" (67), but apparently is so no longer. While Heffernan is right to argue that "the accumulation of so many parallel details cannot be explained away as the result of coincidence" (67), in order to state definitively that Chaucer knew the *Decameron* firsthand some new concrete evidence is needed. This is not forthcoming, yet one would be unwise to disregard Heffernan's accumulation of intertextual parallels. Consequently, Heffernan, like many others who have addressed this question, is forced to adopt a subjunctive tone; the caveat "might have" or variants thereupon necessarily recur often. We need not be "burdened by caution," although this is not to say that we should ignore caution either—Heffernan manages to maintain a careful balance in this respect.

The opening chapter lays the historical groundwork for those that follow. It revisits the possibility that "Chaucer could have met Petrarch at Padua or nearby Arqua and Boccaccio at Florence or Certaldo" (10) during his first recorded ambassadorial visit to the peninsula in 1372–73. However, neither Petrarch nor Boccaccio mentions a meeting with a young English poet in their correspondence of this period, which leads one toward the view that such a meeting did not take place. Nevertheless, these possibilities remain tantalizing, as Heffernan notes: "One would like to think there was a meeting between Chaucer and Petrarch at which Chaucer received the Latin version of the *Clerk's Tale*, Petrarch's translation of the last tale of the *Decameron*" (10). Heffernan also examines the critical reception of Chaucer's works in Italy in the late medieval and early modern periods, as a counterpoint to the customary accounts of the presence of Italian texts in England. This is very interesting, especially the discussion of Gerolamo Ghilini's seventeenth-century essay on Chaucer and Stefano Surigone's fifteenth-century eulogy. Heffernan suggests moreover that there "is reason to think Chaucer's writing might have been known to Italians even earlier" (7) due to wider Anglo-Italian cultural and mercantile connections, and argues that the "absence of manuscripts and early printed texts of Chaucer from Italian libraries is not necessarily evidence that he was not known in Italy" (9). It is not entirely clear, however, how the discussion of Italian knowledge of Chaucer reinforces the overall argument for Chaucer's reading of Boccaccio and their mutual comic inheritance. The chapter concludes with a discussion of the links and distinctions between Chaucer's London, and Boccaccio's Florence and Naples (13–19), providing interesting and necessary accounts of each city's culture(s) and how these cultures inform the biographies of the two authors.

Chapter 2 details Chaucer and Boccaccio's shared comic inheritance, which stretched from antiquity to the late medieval fabliaux. This continuum begins with Aristotle's theory of comedy as detailed in the *Poetics*, a work that—while it was not directly available to Chaucer and Boccaccio—influenced certain Latin comedies, which were available, at least in reworked forms, to authors of the later Middle Ages. Further-more, as Heffernan points out, the "grammarians of the late classical period (i.e. Diomedes, Evanthius, Donatus) were important transmitters of ancient thinking about drama . . . to the Middle Ages" (28). Both Boccaccio and Chaucer were familiar with late medieval *artes rhetoricae*, while Dante's concept of comedy was known to Boccaccio, if not to Chaucer (if indeed the *Epistle to Can Grande*, in which the definition appears, was written by Dante). The chapter concludes with a discussion of the development of the novella and its possible influence upon Chau-cer's English fabliaux.

Chapter 3 follows on from its predecessor by considering the parallel comic tales of the *Decameron* and the *Canterbury Tales*, comparing *The Miller's Tale* and *The Reeve's Tale* with Boccaccian analogues (*Decameron* III.4 and X.6, respectively). The chapter then compares *The Shipman's Tale* and *The Merchant's Tale* to their supposed French sources. The source of the former is allegedly a no-longer-extant French fabliau, while that of the latter is Matthew of Vendôme's *Comedia Lidie*. Heffernan argues that *Decameron* VIII.1 is a more probable source than a poten-tially nonexistent fabliau, while *Decameron* VII.9—itself a reworking of the *Lidie*—is as likely a source as Matthew's original. The number of detailed comparisons in this chapter do incline one toward Heffernan's view that "for his comic tales in verse, Chaucer borrowed as much from Italian prose novellas as he did from French fabliaux" (71).

Chapter 4 discusses antifraternal satire, focusing on Chaucer's Par-doner and Boccaccio's Fra Cipolla (VI.10). The chapter is set against the "burst of antifraternal writing in all the European vernacular literatures" (73) following papal recognition of the mendicant orders in the thir-teenth century. Heffernan compares the recurrence of antifraternalism in the *Canterbury Tales* and the *Decameron* to Dante's attacks in the *Para-diso*, and perhaps most influentially, Jean de Meun's figure of Faus Sem-blant. However, Heffernan makes an important distinction between Chaucer's and Boccaccio's portrayals of the friars: "Boccaccio's tales are not particularly concerned with the spiritual consequences of corrupt friars" (87), which is partly due to Boccaccio being "more comfortable than is Chaucer with the implicit parallel between the verbal artistry of his corrupt preacher and his own" (89). It is perhaps no coincidence that Fra Cipolla dupes the citizens of Certaldo, the alleged birthplace of Boccaccio.

The final chapter readdresses C. S. Lewis's question of what Chaucer really did to Boccaccio's *Filostrato*. According to Heffernan, this "consists primarily in [Chaucer's] introduction of comedy into the Italian's romance of unhappy love" (101). The main catalyst for this comedy is Pandarus. By making Boccaccio's Troiolo and Criseida less forthcoming, Chaucer necessitates the transformation of Pandaro into a more experienced, crafty figure, which in turn necessitates his devising the kinds of plots found in fabliaux and Latin comedy such as the twelfth-century *Pamphilus*. However, this is not the only form of comedy in *Troilus and Criseyde*; it also "includes the divine comedy of the hero's translation to the celestial eighth sphere" (101). Chaucer, nevertheless, calls his poem a *tragedye*, but one that becomes "richer and more complex by adding comedy" (127).

Heffernan's study concludes by noting how Chaucer's addition of comedy to the *Troilus* points toward the fabliaux of the *Canterbury Tales*, and acknowledges that Chaucer's comedy "is not so much derivative of Boccaccio's as part of a common European comic tradition that both poets inherited" (129). The study closes by comparing how each poet, in his own way, turned away from comedy, Chaucer in the *Retraction*, and Boccaccio by shifting his attention to Latin humanism.

Despite the difficulty of providing fresh evidence, and the concomitant, necessary dependence upon informed conjecture, Heffernan's study manages to draw together the various parallels, inheritances, and analogues between Chaucer's and Boccaccio's comic tales, and in doing so provides readers with the opportunity to make a decision based upon a convincing accumulation of links that surely goes beyond mere coincidence.

WILLIAM T. ROSSITER
Liverpool Hope University

GREGORY HEYWORTH. *Desiring Bodies: Ovidian Romance and the Cult of Form*. Notre Dame: University of Notre Dame Press, 2009. Pp. 376. $38.00 paper.

Gregory Heyworth crafts a powerful monograph about Ovid's influence on major authors from the Middle Ages and Renaissance (Marie de France to Milton, with 1170 to 1670 as the proposed range). Among the pleasures and benefits of this book are the historical range and the sequence of ("romance") texts it addresses, spanning different European cultural and political moments. The involvement of intellectual history and philosophy (Aristotle, Augustine, Wyclif and many others) make the book a bit highfalutin for undergraduates (even the personal acknowledgments use words like "ontogeny"), and so the book is geared to advanced graduate students and scholars. Yet all the arguments are direct and tangible and always textually based, so with some guidance the individual essays can be assigned to seniors and M.A. students working on particular texts, such as *Romeo and Juliet* or Petrarch's *Rime*, or *The Knight's Tale*. Heyworth sometimes writes as if he were Ernst Curtius, and this depth and range of allusion across European and classical literature is exciting and, most important, "profitable" (to put it in terms relevant to Heyworth's own study of culture and value) because Heyworth re-creates for us the "intellectual history and social and generic forms" (ix) that directly informed the poets he studies. He explains their inheritances and cultural imperatives—how they struggle with art/genre and confront ideas of honor, virtue, governance, and social and personal order. This kind of work must be distinguished from a criticism that *imposes* a favored theory or ideology through an indignant interrogation (and predictable indictment) of the past. That is not at all what this very good book does.

Heyworth masters the turn of phrase that drives home the argument at critical times: "Culture is a history of pretense," "an account not of how things were but of how people desired them to be" (xi). Oscar Wilde pleasingly figures here, as Heyworth traces how Ovid's exploration of "forms changed into new bodies" (adjusting a common understanding of the complex syntax of *Metamorphoses* 1.1) informs the history of culture in relation to literary and social forms of civilization, against which personal desire and individual identity often clash. My paraphrase does no justice to Heyworth's bold ambition. He puts it better: "Every generation breaks the icons of the last, then worships the shards. But by worshiping the Ovidian *cultus*, later poets ended up deconstructing the cultural values whose continuity many thought they were preserving" (xiii). We thus learn about the historical situations of texts and poets such as Marie de France, whose elusive biography and deceptively simple narratives are very hard to contextualize politically and historically. Focusing on hunting, wounding, desire, and violence, Heyworth studies "Bisclavret," "Guigemar," and "Eliduc," lais that dramatize the disruption of the pretences of civilization and the "body politic" (30). "The habitus [a term Heyworth uses to mean the social form of the body] that Marie investigates is that of the political outcast, the individual whose wounded, transformed body contributes its form to the social values of autarky and non-conformity that, while alien to epic, become central to romance" (28). Heyworth reads Marie not only through Ovid but Aristotle, Icelandic saga, John of Garland, the *Ancrene Riwle,* and a host of other texts. Culture, form, and body are woven lyrically through the book, variously manifested and defined; the *Metamorphoses* (viewed productively in relation to Augustan moral law and absolute polity) is a work of "culture as resistance to the tendentiousness of form" (xvii) and "form is the shape of the body translated onto an object of human desire" (9). The fluidity of these terms accords well with Ovidian flux itself and with the conflicts of art and body that animate all the works under study.

In "Economies of Romance," Heyworth explores the works of Chrétien de Troyes, discerning the relationships between culture, creativity, leisure, work, patronage, charity, romance, and profit, all issues rooted in Paul, Aristotle, and Augustine. Heyworth traces the opposition of *los* ("honor through action") to *repos* (63) and shows how the genre of romance itself, as conceived and discussed by Chrétien in his important prologues, emerges from real material events in twelfth-century history, which take their part in the poet's struggle to resolve the conflicts of love and honor. This is no "Marxist reading," where that would mean a facile application of class resentment by a naïf or a true believer. Rather, Heyworth examines the actual language of the texts—generously quoted, translated (he often revises the popular published translations he provides), and explicated in philological detail—and allows the poetry itself to tell its story. Heyworth uses Marx as he uses Cicero or Aristotle, as an intellect that studied men, work, and thought. He thus writes free from the droning social justice politics that drive so much medieval criticism that subordinates and perverts literature.

In "States of Union," Heyworth turns to Chaucer's *Knight's Tale* and *Franklin's Tale*, exploring the reverberations of Ovid's doctrine that "coercive power and love do not go well together," Chaucerian "maistrie," and the tensions between the "fustian amenities of imperial greatness and the workaday bullydom of domestic 'mastery'" (106). Horace, Cicero, Gower, and Wyclif are summoned, as well as Aristotle, to contextualize deeply the themes of governance and control that inform the political and domestic spheres; Heyworth also associates Richard II to Augustus, thus keeping relevant and present the cultures and polities that the poets worked in and reacted to. A stunning reference to the obscure Elias of Triplow on God, authority, and community (141–42), plus telling reference to the "late-Soviet crisis of unity" (175), bespeaks Heyworth's tireless range.

The next three chapters take on no less a pantheon than Petrarch, Shakespeare, and Milton, as Part II confronts other genres that nonetheless contain "strong romance elements," reflecting a "hybridization of literary forms" best understood "in terms of bodily metamorphosis" (179). Petrarch, like Ovid, pieces together "fragments of various genres" into "a more or less coherent mosaic." Involved here is the history of the physical composition of the *Rime* "written, rewritten, and reordered obsessively over a period of thirty years" (183) and, of course, the body of Laura and the quest for an Ovidian *carmen perpetuum.* Troping on related issues of genre and time, Heyworth reads *Romeo and Juliet* as a play that "succeeds as a romance because it confirms the besetting, archetypal anxiety of all lovers" that "they will not be able to transform the accident of a single meeting into the necessity of a life together" (230). Phaëton and Narcissus and Echo figure prominently here, and Heyworth earns his wry conclusion about the play's *chronotope*: "who could bear a middle aged Romeo and Juliet" (259). Milton boldly challenges decorum in involving Ovidian love in his epic, as Heyworth explores Milton's relations to science and astronomy and reveals the poet's struggle with knowledge and poetic ambition.

The three centerpieces of Hayworth's accomplishment, which itself defies the paraphrasing rhetoric of the book-review genre—are the intellectual contextualizations of the works he studies, the dramatic and detailed engagement with Ovidian love, bodies, forms, polity, and "culture," and the old-school, detailed close reading of the poets' words and stories. These chapters endlessly provoke study of some of the major works of literature in the medieval and Renaissance canon. It is thus a scholar's book but also a teacher's book. I believe readers, like this reviewer, will look forward to ongoing engagement with its dramatic arguments and to assigning its chapters to students, for whom they will model excellence in scholarship.

MICHAEL CALABRESE
California State University, Los Angeles

ORDELLE G. HILL. *Looking Westward: Poetry, Landscape, and Politics in "Sir Gawain and the Green Knight."* Newark: University of Delaware Press, 2009. Pp. 203. $51.50.

In this richly textured, stimulating but rather exasperating book, Ordelle Hill claims that scholarship on *Sir Gawain and the Green Knight* has looked in the wrong direction. In his view, "it is the west that has given the poet a cultural tradition, a journey, people and places, and a beheading game" and "the failure of critics to look westward is the very problem the *Gawain*-poet is addressing, a cultural bias that no good can come from the west" (22). This is unfair and tendentious. It is a point of rare scholarly consensus that the *Gawain*-poet hailed from the North West Midlands. Furthermore, there is little in *SGGK*, or in this book, to support the claim that the poet was concerned to address such a cultural bias.

Hill's real point is that critics have not looked far *enough* westward, and failed to acknowledge the relevance of Wales and the Welsh Marches. His concept of the "west," however, tends to elide the cultural distance between the West Midlands, the frontier marcher lordships, and Wales. The West Midlands were wholly English in culture and looked eastward. The orientation of the region gave its inhabitants, not least the alliterative poets, their self-consciousness as "westerners." Yet Hill tends to present the *Gawain*-poet as somehow Anglo-Welsh. He similarly identifies Henry of Grosmont, duke of Lancaster, the other protagonist in his study, as a borderer. Though born near Abergavenny, Grosmont spent almost all his life in England and on the Continent and can scarcely be regarded as a "neighbor" of the *Gawain*-poet.

In Chapter 1, Hill offers a Welsh perspective on *SGGK*, beginning by reminding his readers that "the Arthurian legend developed in Wales." More interesting is his claim that Welsh influence can be found in the alliterative verse of the west midlands, most notably in the *Gawain*-poet's "bob and wheel." In the second section, Hill offers a generally rewarding discussion of similarities in "themes and images" between *SGGK* and the poetry of Iolo Goch and Dafydd ap Gwilym. Still, it is a little perverse for him to present a clear difference—the Welsh poets' direct references to people and events of the time—as demonstrating a "political awareness present also in the *Gawain*-poet" (40). The focus of the final section of a chapter on Welsh poetry is Grosmont's *Le Livre des Seyntz Medicines*. In another circular argument, Hill rehearses the intriguing correspondences between *Le Livre* and *SGGK* as if they support the idea that the texts are related products of a distinctive and hybrid borderland culture. A more natural conclusion is that the two writers drew on cultural resources, chivalric and Christian, which transcended locality.

In Chapter 2, Hill explores Gawain's journey to the Green Chapel. Though the poet presents him traveling through "Logres," that is, England, and doubtless imagined an English Camelot, Hill focuses on possible routes from Caerleon in South Wales and claims that the poem's audience "would have recognized the 'gate' [Gawain] traveled." Yet the only textual clue is Gawain's sudden appearance in North Wales and his riding eastward along the coast to the Wirral. Hill reads too much into this brief episode, with North Wales allegedly prompting reflection on the English conquest of Wales, appropriation of Welsh cultural heritage and the iron ring of Edward I's castles, the brief notice of Anglesey reviving memories of conflict and "historical reconciliations" (65), and the allusion to "wyldrenesse of Wyrale," calling to mind more prosaic issues of maladministration. The *Gawain*-poet certainly presents his hero's journey as a test of his physical and spiritual strength. Still, there is no textual evidence to support the view that his sojourn in Wales was especially educational or that he began to acquire there "a sensitivity to other cultures and people" (75).

In *SGGK*, according to Hill, "People and places begin to emerge from the mist of Arthurian myth as part of the vital and historical landscape of the fourteenth century" (78). The first part of the third chapter provides a useful review of the personalities and politics of fourteenth-century England and of the correspondences between historical figures and events and the characters and plot of the poem. It was a world in which life imitated art: Edward III identified with Arthur; round tables and knightly orders were formed; nobles variously challenged and championed the king; and traitors were beheaded and memorialized. The Mortimers, with their Welsh bloodline, loom large. The colorful lives of the Bohuns, Fitzalans, Montagues, and Despensers, who also held marcher lordships, might have been brought into this frame. Naturally enough, Hill focuses on the house of Lancaster, especially Thomas of Lancaster, the cousin and antagonist of Edward II, and Henry of Grosmont, stalwart of Edward III, paragon of chivalry, and possibly a "model both for the young Gawain and the older Bertilak" (91). The second part of the chapter, on the sites of the poem, is more a travelogue. Hill is perhaps right that, though seemingly "pared out of papure purely," Hautdesert was a "real" castle. He claims that all the architectural details can be found "in one or several" of Grosmont's castles in the Welsh Marches and the Midlands. The site of the Green Chapel is likewise felt to be "real." Hill usefully describes a number of possible sites, including the favorites, Ludchurch and Wetton Mill, on the Cheshire and Staffordshire border. He proposes a new possible site, Deepdale Cave, near Buxton.

In the fourth and final chapter, Hill draws threads together. After exploring the significance of beheading in Celtic tradition, he suggests a direct Welsh source for the beheading game in *SGGK*. He also seeks to associate the development of the English practice of beheading traitors, beginning with Simon de Montfort in 1265 and Llywelyn ap Gruffudd in 1282, with Wales and the Welsh Marches. The execution of Roger Mortimer, earl of March, in 1330 is significant, he gamely notes, "not because it involved beheading, but because it did not" (129). The beheading that cast the longest shadow, and the most pertinent to Hill's study, is that of Thomas of Lancaster in Yorkshire in 1322. Still, Hill is sure that "the west is the key to understanding the significant beheadings of the thirteenth and fourteenth centuries," adding that, with characteristic circularity of argument, "it is no coincidence that the *Gawain*-poet makes Wales and the west the setting for his beheading game" (131–32).

Hill began his project seeking links between the *Gawain*-poet and Henry of Grosmont. Though he soon came to realize that there was "no direct evidence, external or internal" (13) of a connection, he clearly remained drawn to the notion that the *Gawain*-poet wrote with Grosmont in mind, perhaps under his patronage or after his death. This is not implausible. Still, "looking westward," in the sense of looking to the Welsh Marches and Wales, does not help the case. The worlds of the *Gawain*-poet and Grosmont doubtless intersected, but in Midlands, military, and courtly contexts. In addition, Hill's focus on Wales has encouraged some odd readings of the poem. While he raises interesting questions, especially as to how the kings and magnates of the fourteenth century dealt with the bloody consequences of recent internecine strife, he pushes too hard to find somewhat anachronistic political meanings. This is unfortunate because Hill is an enthusiastic guide to *SGGK* and, beneath it all, a sensitive reader.

MICHAEL BENNETT
University of Tasmania

T. E. HILL. *"She, This in Blak": Vision, Truth, and Will in Geoffrey Chaucer's "Troilus and Criseyde."* London and New York: Routledge, 2006. Pp. ix, 147. £65.00; $115.00 cloth. £20.00; $35.95 paper.

As T. E. Hill's title notes, Criseyde wears black, and of course, it is indeed significant that she wears black: she is a widow, wearing her mourning weeds, and the blackness of her dress, within Chaucer's protean characterizations, develops key aspects of her character—her inscrutability, her confusion, and, yes, perhaps her cruelty. Hill considers Criseyde, as well as Troilus and Pandarus, from a philosophical perspective, and his text bears with it traces of philosophical prolixity, such as in his thesis: "In *Troilus and Criseyde,* Chaucer addresses difficulties concerning representation and will inherent in the perspectivist model of perception and cognition by couching the activities of *scientia* within a wider framework of covenantal causality as it is expressed in the theological doctrine of the dialectic of divine power that differentiates between God's absolute omnipotence and his self-delimiting ordained power, or his 'capacity and volition' " (3). By reading *Troilus and Criseyde* in concert with the insights of philosophers both classical (Aristotle, Augustine, and Boethius) and medieval (Holcot, Strode, the Mertonians, Bradwardine, and Wyclif), Hill illuminates the text's participation in scholastic and theological debates on perception and thus enlightens readers' understanding of the very mixed motives of its three primary characters.

The structure of *"She, This in Blak"* is simple and effective: following Chapter 1, "Introduction and Background," Hill devotes a chapter each to Troilus, Pandarus, and Criseyde, and then concludes with a brief analysis of *Troilus and Criseyde*'s Epilogue. Hill's readings of the characters are mostly persuasive, if not revolutionary. He sees Troilus as "represent-[ing] the traditional perspectivist attitude toward perception and cognition, one in which the proper connection between *res* and *verbum* is assumed to be substantial, certain, and causally determined" (3), whereas Pandarus "is portrayed as the practitioner of a more 'modern' calculatory approach to truth, where the relationship between object and concept is only knowable within an estimated latitude" (3). For Hill, Criseyde is a "voluntarist *viator* who accepts the darkness in which the universe of the knowable is bound, and who is able to act in a context of uncertainty by trusting to the intuited intentionality of her will when the resources of reason have been exhausted" (4). The readings of the characters in their respective chapters expand these initial observations fruitfully, paying close attention to the ways in which perceptions influence their understanding of the cosmos and of their place in it, as well as the manner in which love challenges their ability to perceive. These readings of the characters do not diverge from many such interpretations of Troilus as passively sincere, Pandarus as amorously manipulative, and Criseyde as "slydinge of corage" (5.825), but they succeed in providing another context for understanding the characters' shifting motivations.

Sound in its conception and execution, the argument of *"She, This in Blak"* nonetheless extends in some clunky ways, especially when Hill's analysis becomes virtually an allegorical framework for reading the characters as representatives of varying philosophical perspectives. Consequently, textual moments are occasionally overinterpreted or ignored when they do not fit neatly into his schema. When Troilus uses an economic metaphor to describe the vagaries of love—"Youre hire is quyt ageyn, ye, God woot how!" (1.334)—Hill sees extraordinary philosophical depth:

That Troilus mixes economic imagery here with that of sacramental theology is notable in view of William Courtenay's observation that scholastic objections to the notion of the ascribed value of the sacraments may have been influenced by traditional Church teaching on the just price of goods and services, which was based on the concept of inherent value (*bonitas intrinseca*). Surely Troilus's jibe would have had a special resonance in Chaucer's time: a period when rapid monetization combined with devaluating currencies, fluctuating market prices, and widespread counterfeiting destabilized values for goods, land and labor and caused deep anxieties across the European social fabric. (27)

It is certainly within the realm of reasonable interpretations that this idiom might take on a "special resonance" in fourteenth-century England, but the ubiquity of the idiom, in its typical deployment as a linguistic shorthand, argues against its addressing variable cultural conditions.

Another such example occurs when Pandarus tells Troilus, "for the am I bicomen . . . swich a meene / As maken wommen unto men to comen; / Al sey I nought, thow wost wel what I meene" (3.253–56). Hill affirms multidisciplinary import in "meene": "The play on the word 'meene,' which indicates in its first use both a means and an intermediary, and in its second the act of signifying, has various resonances—logical, mathematical, economic, and scientific—that identify Pandarus as the instrument of a perceptual and epistemological relativism of late fourteenth-century natural philosophy" (44). These readings exemplify Hill's tendency to overdetermine the philosophical register of even the text's clichéd expressions and to find evidence for his argument where it might not appear.

For such a dense argument, Hill's monograph is remarkably short, coming in at exactly 100 pages of text (with another 47 of notes, bibliography, and index). It would benefit greatly from extending its discussion of *Troilus and Criseyde* with contemporary gender criticism, since the ways in which perception is linked to gender passes largely unnoticed within these pages. Sadly, the notes and bibliography are blighted by numerous errors. The documentation style of the notes can most forgivingly be described as eclectic. In the bibliography, errors on page 131, chosen randomly after I noticed many problems, include those of alphabetical order (Harwood should follow Hanning, not precede it) and a reluctance to indicate that *Troilus and Criseyde* is used as a title.

"She, This in Blak" succeeds in its goal of opening *Troilus and Criseyde* to insights from scholasticism, philosophy, and perspective studies, and the nuanced readings of Troilus, Pandarus, and Criseyde ameliorate most of my concerns about the exaggerated nature of occasional interpretations. Chaucer's masterpiece continues to challenge readers due to his obfuscation of his characters' motivations, and Hill outlines key vantage points through which to understand the inscrutable.

Tison Pugh
University of Central Florida

Daniel Hobbins. *Authorship and Publicity Before Print: Jean Gerson and the Transformation of Late Medieval Learning*. Philadelphia: University of Pennsylvania Press, 2009. Pp. xii, 335. $49.95.

Daniel Hobbins wants us to consider what it meant to write and publish in a manuscript culture, specifically in the late medieval period and solely through the writings of the theologian and chancellor of the University of Paris, Jean Gerson (1363–1429). The author's thesis is that by viewing Gerson above all as a writer, we gain access not only to Gerson's historical significance but also to that of his era, which Hobbins argues was neither an age of declining scholasticism nor of nascent humanism, but participated in both. This is an interesting and original approach—a contribution to the relatively young fields of authorship studies, the history of reading and writing, and studies of medieval manuscript production, as well as to Gerson studies in general. For those who, until now, have turned to Gerson only for his theology, this book has an oddly secular tone. But Hobbins would be the first to acknowledge that the changing trends he identifies in late medieval writing and authorship, as exemplified by Gerson's theories and practices of writing, evolved to fulfill theological responsibilities and pastoral requirements.

Given the constraints Hobbins faces—the loss of early copies of Gerson's works and the disappearance of his personal library (a lone copy of the works of John Cassian survives)—Hobbins's pursuit of late medieval writing culture via the chancellor's writings, which he labels "an act of recovery," is well served by his broad knowledge of the Gersonian corpus. One derives added benefit from Hobbins's book by keeping constantly in mind that the trends he describes were taking place a mere handful of decades before the dawn of printing.

Hobbins examines the emergence of the university master from his natural habitat, the university, to fill a broader role in society. Whereas Aquinas, according to Hobbins, was barely read beyond the walls of the university or monastery, Gerson was acutely aware of a new nonacademic public, able to read and eager for his opinions on issues of moral theology. Initially, Gerson was not easily moved to compose original works. His brother Jean the Celestine once wrote that Gerson found the holy doctors of the past to be "proven" and thus sufficient for the "complete perfection of life." In fact, Gerson often needed to be "pestered" to write, and in some circumstances seemed to care so little about what he wrote that he did not even bother to keep personal copies. After long consideration, Gerson began writing "for the cause of faith" (1).

Gerson largely abandoned the old scholastic genres and decried the scholastic practice of overreliance on written tradition. "Tell us not what others have written, but what you yourself say or believe," he warned fellow clerics, who were in the habit of heaping citation upon citation (63). To express his own opinion on the moral issues of the day, Gerson favored the tract (*tractatus*)—whose impact is traced in Chapter 5—for its brevity, portability, and ease of distribution. Gerson, perhaps to the detriment of his permanent written legacy, had a "voracious appetite" for examining the leading questions of his day as matters for practical theology. A noteworthy chart in *Authorship and Publicity Before Print,* which plots the frequency with which late medieval authors treated contemporary controversies in tract format, shows Gerson the obvious frontrunner in his use of this popular genre. Hobbins makes a strong case, especially for the final ten years of Gerson's life, that the chancellor was "long on creativity but short on execution" and that he missed his chance to write "something truly timeless." Ironically, as Hobbins observes, just such a lasting work was attributed to Gerson in the *Imitation of Christ,* now restored to Thomas à Kempis. But how much the pursuit of reputation, fame, and literary ambitions (all phrases Hobbins used) might actually have characterized Gerson remains to be seen. According to Jacob Wimpheling (1450–1528), whom Hobbins sees as turning Gerson "from man into marble" by idealizing him, Gerson busied himself with what was "useful and necessary to praising God, to strengthening the faith . . . to building morals, and to saving souls" (70).

The last two chapters of this book specifically address publishing before print, in particular the influence of the councils of Constance and Basel on manuscript distribution, and the triumphs, as well as the hazards, of publishing in a pre-print culture. Gerson's written legacy was indubitably strengthened by the popularity of his works within a network of Celestine and Carthusian monasteries in France and the Empire. To an important degree, survival of a text depended on whether anyone wanted to make copies (whereas a book automatically exists in as many copies as its print run). Furthermore, once a manuscript left the author's desk, it moved quickly out of his control. Faulty copies were hard to contain and scribes might modify the text they copied, whether willfully or inadvertently. One can experience just how independent any given work might be of its author through an intriguing example that Hobbins relates from the Council of Constance, where a scribe finished a copy of Gerson's *On Mystical Theology* on July 30, 1415, without Gerson necessarily having brought the work there himself or even known of its presence, much less examined it for accuracy. Precisely because of the uncertainties and accidental circumstances pervading late medieval book culture, I take exception to Hobbins's relatively heavy reliance on the Joan of Arc tract *Super facto puellae* (more commonly known as *De mirabili victoria*) as evidence of Gersonian writing culture. A favorable opinion of the Maid by France's greatest contemporary theologian might have satisfied the needs of propaganda, but with no autograph manuscript and no solid manuscript history until several years after the events had passed, a greater measure of caution is needed before attributing this work to Gerson.

For ease of use, I would have preferred footnotes referring to Gerson's works to include a short title of the work cited rather than the ubiquitous *OC* for *Oeuvres complètes*, especially where eleven substantial volumes are involved. Back matter includes a list of Gerson manuscripts in Carthusian and Celestine monasteries.

This is a well-executed and innovative study that introduces Jean Gerson to scholars of late medieval book culture, and medieval book culture (including Gerson's pivotal role) to scholars of Gerson. In focusing on Gerson as a writer, Hobbins has found an unexpectedly rich thread to fuse a previously compartmentalized Gerson into a single figure. But I can imagine that if Hobbins pursues his subject further he will indeed uncover "new" Gersons, equally worth the read.

DEBORAH FRAIOLI
Simmons College

LAURA L. HOWES, ed. *Place, Space, and Landscape in Medieval Narrative.* Knoxville: University of Tennessee Press, 2007. Pp. xxix, 208. $43.00.

Described by editor Laura Howes as part of "an ongoing investigation of place and spatial relationships in medieval culture" (viii), *Place, Space, and Landscape in Medieval Narrative* offers its readers twelve essays on the spatial practices of medieval texts from the English, French, Italian, Latin, and Spanish literary traditions. What unites the collection is a sense of space as "defined by movement and by human experience" (viii), a viewpoint indebted to thinkers like de Certeau, Foucault, and Lefebvre. Howes's brief introduction is largely devoted to a summary of the volume's contents; for a fully developed statement of purpose, the reader must turn to John Ganim's "Landscape and Late Medieval Literature: A Critical Geography." Building on Foucault's sense that space should be understood as "dialectical, dynamic, and creative" (xv),

Ganim offers up a survey of twentieth-century approaches to spatial questions, one in which medievalists rub shoulders with theorists of space. His review of spatial thinkers is welcome, but more significant is his observation that "domestic" space in the texts of the Western Middle Ages undergoes "a certain orientalization" (xxi). The biblical cycles are "a test case" for this observation, re-creating through performance "a memory of the originary geography of the Holy Land itself" (xxi). Ganim thus resituates these heavily localized celebrations in a newly global context: "England mounts performances in which the spaces of the city become as if the places of the Holy Land at a time when the possibility of pilgrimage and reconquest grows increasingly unlikely" (xxiv). The as-yet-undeveloped postcolonial reading of medieval English drama will clearly begin here.

After Ganim's essay, *Place, Space, and Landscape* splits into three sections, the first of which concerns itself with readings of historical locales. Lisa Cooper takes on twelfth-century Bruges in "Making Space for History: Galbert of Bruges and the Murder of Charles the Good," identifying in Galbert's chronicle accounts of the count's murder a "careful attention to physical space of all kinds" (5). Particularly noteworthy is Cooper's conclusion that Galbert saw "the mind as but one more space that could be laid open by the historiographer's piercing and omniscient eye" (16), an "imaginative penetration of space" that involves the "stretching of historical 'fact' beyond the limits of 'objective' reality" (21). In "A Camp Wedding: The Cultural Context of Chaucer's *Brooch of Thebes*," William Askins is ostensibly writing about fourteenth-century Plymouth, location of the 1386 wedding of John Holland and Elizabeth Lancaster. But he devotes relatively little space to Plymouth *as* space, preferring instead to situate Chaucer's "Complaint of Mars" and "Complaint of Venus" in time, reading the wedding as the occasion for the two poems. As a result, his essay seems out of place in the overall scheme of the anthology. Lawrence Warner's "Adventurous Custance: St. Thomas of Acre and Chaucer's *Man of Law's Tale*" concentrates on a single building, London's Church of St. Thomas of Acre. As a structure "in which the mercantile and the military are inextricably fused" (45), St. Thomas of Acre represents in situ the romance and bourgeois dynamics driving Chaucer's version of the Custance story. Although Warner is ultimately unable to establish a direct connection between poet and church, his essay nonetheless offers a convincing portrayal of a deeper cultural context for the *Tales*.

The second section of the book moves from historical to fictional spaces. In Thomas Heffernan's "'The sun shall be turned to darkness and the moon to blood': How Sin and Redemption Affect Heavenly Space in an Old English Transfiguration Homily," an anonymous sermon "illustrates the complex understanding that English monastics of the late tenth century had of the relationship of sin to the natural world" (75). Heffernan's piece is a solid source study, but it resembles Askins's essay in having only a tenuous connection to the models of spatial practice outlined in the introductions of Howes and Ganim. Michael Calabrese returns to form with "Controlling Space and Secrets in the *Lais* of Marie de France," a comparison of Marie's investment in the creation of a literary "safe space" (81) with her characters' literal "search for a secret, private space where, if only fleetingly, love and honor can be free" (81–82). One of the strongest pieces in the anthology, Calabrese's essay explores the "acts of concealing and revealing, of entering and exiting, and of opening and closing" that "animate" the *Lais* (83). His excellent close readings here will no doubt quickly find their way into the classroom. Kenneth Bleeth's "Chaucerian Gardens and the Spirit of Play" is likewise noteworthy for its immediate pedagogical utility. Surveying the gardens in *Troilus* and the *Tales*, Bleeth argues for a Chaucer "decidedly less sanguine" than his predecessors "about the possibility of creating self-sufficient realms of play within the greater world" (109). His interpretations of Criseyde's and Emily's gardens as utterly contingent enclosures merit special commendation for their attention to questions of sex and gender.

The rationale for the last section of *Place, Space, and Landscape* is ambiguous: these five essays are grouped under the rubric "Landscape, Power, Identity"—but those issues are also present in many of the earlier essays in the volume. Without a clear justification, this section of the anthology feels weaker than the first two: for example, Gregory B. Kaplan's "Landscapes of Discrimination in *Converso* Literature" and Catherine Cox's "Eastward of the Garden: The Biblical Landscape of *Sir Gawain and the Green Knight*" both treat the spaces of their texts as mere signs pointing to greater truths. Landscapes are glossed over in these essays as the critics move quickly to nonspatial concerns. Sylvia Federico is more focused on space in her "Place of Chivalry in the New Trojan Court: Gawain, Troilus, and Richard II," identifying the romance bedroom as a sign of "Trojan deviance" (171) and Ricardian failure. But her contribution originates in a 1999 conference paper and thus reads as overly familiar; in a sense, Federico has scooped herself with her 2003 *New Troy: Fantasies of Empire in the Late Middle Ages*. Robert Hanning's "Before Chaucer's *Shipman's Tale*: The Language of Place, the Place of Language in *Decameron* 8.1 and 8.2" ends the anthology on a strong note by juxtaposing the "contrasting spatial frames"—urban and rural—of his chosen Boccaccian *novelle* (182). His reading of Ambrugia's bedroom in 8.1 stands out here for its careful coordination of class and sex/gender analysis. However, the essay that remains truest to the goals of the collection is Kari Kalve's " 'Truth is therinne': The Spaces of Truth and Community in *Piers Plowman* B." Kalve's careful parsing of Langland's landscapes demonstrates how "inside spaces . . . are almost entirely harmful, closing people off from community and from spiritual interaction . . . The work of the social and spiritual institutions . . . must be done openly, even though such openness inevitably leads to difficulties" (141). The Tower of Truth is the poem's only wholly positive interior space, and—in a typical Langlandian move—it remains utterly inaccessible in this life.

As is the case with most scholarly anthologies, the utility of *Place, Space, and Landscape* will vary according to its readers' particular interests. However, I can say that each piece in the volume has its merits. My highest recommendation is reserved for the essays of Cooper, Warner, Calabrese, Bleeth, Kalve, and Hanning: by choosing to engage fully with the dynamic spirit of Ganim's introduction, the work of these six scholars points the way for future analyses of space in medieval literature.

Robert W. Barrett Jr.
University of Illinois at Urbana

Andrew James Johnston. *Performing the Middle Ages from "Beowulf" to "Othello."* Turnhout: Brepols, 2008. Pp. viii, 344. 70.00; $95.00.

Performing the Middle Ages from "Beowulf" to "Othello" is a courteous and well-written book, though not exactly a book about performance. Rather, the book seems to be about male aristocratic or chivalric subjectivity. Although Johnston has a few paragraphs about a performative theory of subjectivity in the introduction, the fact that he does not return to this concept in several chapters of the book makes the use of the term "performance" in his title rather gratuitous. It may also, lamentably, throw scholars interested in his subject matter off the trail. The term "performance" may serve as something of a catch-all (as I discuss below), since, indeed, the unifying subject matter can be difficult to discern, given, as the author is, to interesting but rather lengthy digressions. Hence, perhaps, the book may be best looked at as four or five significant chapters on some of the key texts of our discipline grouped together within a vibrant purple cover.

Each chapter is lengthy, digressive, generally rewarding, and offers as much perspective on the critical reception of the texts as on the texts themselves. This is why I call it a courteous book, because Andrew James Johnston has read his comrades carefully and thoroughly, displaying a scholarly generosity in doing so. Rarely does one find this type of close reading of critical material any more, since single-sentence generalizations have become almost normalized. Johnston follows the argument of even the most thorny and unwieldy secondary scholarship closely, and, with adeptness, locates the lacunae to allow him to situate his own critical intervention. In this way, he pays great respect to the discipline, ensuring that he is not repeating former arguments but in fact is building upon them. And since he is working with some of the most canonical texts of the discipline, his task in sorting through the critical tradition is huge and his achievement in doing so impressive. Any critic cited in this text might consider herself or himself fortunate to have such an interlocutor as Johnston.

However, there are also some drawbacks to such tenacious commitment to the literary discipline. When Johnston does engage with extra-literary issues that have an impact upon a literary event—for instance, the issue of confession in *Sir Gawain and the Green Knight*—he tends to cite other literary critics for material on confessional practices rather than consult Duns Scotus or Wyclif himself. At one point, Johnston criticizes Michel Foucault for his transhistorical and abstracted theory of confession, remonstrating that "he does not deign to wallow in the mire of medieval theology, penitential literature, or historical sources" (142). Such a statement might aptly be applied to Johnston himself. There is a surprising paucity of citations to primary texts outside the literary ones that constitute the material of his chapters. In his chapter on *Othello*, in one of his characteristic digressions, Johnston spends some twenty pages examining the myth of Cortés's apotheosis as a deity by the sixteenth-century Aztecs (this is by way of contesting Stephen Greenblatt's one-sided application of "improvision" to the European conquistadors and arguing that one might as well locate the theme of "colonial" apotheosis in a medieval romance, Chrétien de Troyes's *Perceval*). Astonishingly, although he cites several historians' interpretation of Cortés's letters, he seems never to have consulted the letters himself, as he fails to refer to them, nor are they listed in his bibliography. Since the letters appear important enough to Johnston to merit such space in making his point, they surely merit their own scrutiny. While Johnston is intent upon examining the "binary" logic that divides the Middle Ages from modernity, he seems relatively content to maintain the rather flimsy distinction between the literary and historical disciplines as they have been traditionally constructed.

The achievement of this book is not in bringing new sources to bear upon well-known texts but in offering new insights into some of the major critical conundra of major texts. Hence, this book will matter a great deal to people who have staked out a position on debates such as Wealhtheow's reference to Hrothulf and the Danish succession in *Beowulf*, the seemingly obtuse narrator of Chaucer's *Knight's Tale*, the validity of Gawain's confession in *Sir Gawain and the Green Knight*, the ostensible "orality" of *Le Morte Darthur*, and Othello's self-fashioning and "Moorish" identity. These are of course some of the, if not *the*, major debates in all five of these works, so Johnston has not shied away from plunging himself headfirst into controversial waters. His examination of these debates does, eventually, lead to his main argument: that these texts all exhibit a self-knowledge about the "loss" of a culture of a univocal heroic identity even as they seem to represent heroic knightly figures. Rather than locate such self-consciousness in modernity, Johnston demonstrates how this nostalgia underwrites all of these canonical texts and therefore contests the construction of an unreflective, unknowing Middle Ages. Johnston also explains his use of the term "performance" here: he argues that the "Middle Ages" is always already constituted as a lost object that these texts draw upon in their narrative strategies. Hence, the pastness of medieval chivalric identity is acknowledged and reified by the texts themselves. Even Othello is "a highly self-conscious master of chivalric narrative" (298). I do not think many will quarrel with this thesis today as the self-consciousness of medieval texts has long been on the table and we are now nearly two decades past once-seminal articles such as Lee Patterson's "On the Margin: Postmodernism, Ironic History, and Medieval Studies" (1990) and David Aers's "A Whisper in the Ear of Early Modernists" (1992), both of which Johnston cites. Thus the conclusion of the book may be less important than its performance: its responsible dissections of the critical tradition, its massive bibliography of secondary sources, its precise and nuanced readings of extremely slippery passages in major texts, its long and learned digressions into tangential issues. An astute editor might have pruned away the excess to bring the argument into focus, but in this case the branches may captivate and sustain our attention more than the tree.

MARGARET PAPPANO
Queen's University

SARAH A. KELEN. *Langland's Early Modern Identities*. New York: Palgrave Macmillan, 2007. Pp. xiii, 225. $79.95.

When Palgrave publishes a book with a title such as *Langland's Early Modern Identities*, one expects another theoretical dismantling of the author function or a foray into identity studies. However welcome such studies would be, though, they would falter in the absence of any comprehensive study of the reception history of *Piers Plowman*. Notwithstanding its Palgravesque title, or that publisher's lack of much interest in producing books with a reasonable price; decent font, margin, or page size; and running heads indicating what chapter or page numbers the endnotes refer to, Sarah Kelen's book fills this gap. *Langland's Early Modern Identities* skillfully weaves the major strands in the reception of the poem from the sixteenth century's sustained interest in its author's identity, through Florence Converse's 1903 juvenile novel *Long Will*. The result is a careful, solid, and engaging work of scholarship that all Langland scholars, not to mention anyone interested in reception history, Chaucer, sixteenth-century religious controversies, editorial history, and Augustan antiquarianism, ought to read. At a mere 150 pages of main text, this is a more slender volume than one might have wished, but *Langland's Early Modern Identities* does not miss a note of the tune it plays. The surprises here are to be found in the contexts that Kelen establishes as the most productive for analysis of the material. Students of the poem's history might have known about Elizabeth Cooper's extracts in her *Muses Library* of 1737, for instance, but how many have known how fully situated Cooper's project was in contemporary scientific rhetoric, especially concerning geological datings of the earth (83–85)?

Langland's Early Modern Identities proceeds in roughly chronological order, but the primary structure is thematic. Kelen lays the groundwork by citing evidence for *Piers Plowman*'s continued popularity in the sixteenth and seventeenth centuries, when, she says, seven extant manuscripts containing the poem in part or full, and annotations of a handful of medieval manuscripts, appeared. True enough, and widely rehearsed; but what of Cambridge, Gonville and Caius MS 201/107, a complete manuscript, apparently copied from Rogers's 1561 edition; or two manuscripts, Trinity College, Cambridge R.3.14 and London, British Library, Additional 34779, in which Tudor-era readers added missing lines; or the scores of annotations of surviving Crowley and Rogers editions (cf. 34)? Obviously these supplements to Kelen's evidence only bolster the argument that *Piers Plowman* was vital in this era, but they point to unexplored worlds particularly worthy of attention given their absence from the conversation to date.

Chapter 1 surveys the beginnings of "the idea of Langland as the author (and authorizer) of the poem" in the Tudor linking of the poet with Wyclif (41), an idea Kelen connects with the presentation of Langland as a prophet of the Reformation. While obviously this, long the default approach to the topic, works well in general terms, only a single figure, John Bale, fits it without qualification. Robert Crowley in fact said that Langland was *not* a prophet; his denials are "not entirely convincing" to Kelen (34). Most of the other materials that do take *Piers Plowman* to be prophetic evince no interest in its author's identity. Then we turn to a few Catholic readers, who can figure only as exceptions to the dominant trend. This is the one chapter in which I feel Kelen's overarching claim—that this era's dominant mode was to identify Langland as prophet—is not borne out by her careful individual analyses.

Chapter 2, which concerns the ways in which the figure Piers the Plowman, rather than *Piers Plowman* or its author, "provided an authorizing model for the literature of complaint" (45), will be the starting point for all future scholarship on these many "plowman texts": *The Plowman's Tale, I Playne Piers*, and the rest. The phenomenon is major, is almost exhaustively treated here (George Gascoigne's 1576 *The Steele Glas* is the only obvious omission I noted), and, alas, becomes boring in its predictability. Eventually Kelen finds little else to do with it other than repeat the point that "in all of the sixteenth-century Plowman texts, the Plowman speaks as an outsider" (68), "Piers . . . has similar roles in all of these appearances" (69), and so on a few more times through page 74.

The fascinating Chapter 3 turns to the eighteenth century and "Langland Anthologized," a phenomenon that "worked to move Langland more squarely into the narrative of English letters" in which literary origins were found in the medieval rather than classical era (82). Foundational here is Cooper's *Muses Library*, which "presents *Piers Plowman* favorably as a point of literary origin, but unfavorably as a product of an age less refined than Cooper's own" (85). Kelen argues that Cooper, as well as Thomas Warton and his nemesis, Joseph Ritson, anthologized the confession episode of B.5 because it was the "most 'Chaucerian'" (94) in its satire of contemporary morals. I would have welcomed treatment of Gerald Langbaine's late-1640s manuscript anthology (Oxford, Bodleian Library, MS Wood donat. 7), or of Pope's scheme for an English literary tradition that included the "School of Provence," comprising Chaucer's visions, the *Roman de la Rose*, *Piers Plowman*, and tales from Boccaccio (cf. 81), but this is still one of the freshest accounts of *Piers Plowman*'s reception available.

The following two chapters continue that high standard. "Langland Recontextualized," after breezing through some eighteenth-century accounts of Langland's language by figures such as George Hickes and Thomas Percy, focuses on Thomas Whitaker's 1813 edition of the C-text. On the one hand, Whitaker archaized the text by using black letter, adopting odd spellings, and printing what he took to be the poet's first version; on the other, he presented Langland as "a social commentator still relevant to the nineteenth century" (114), casting the poet in his own image as a country vicar. In Kelen's reading, Whitaker's poor editorial performance is mitigated by his recognition that *Piers Plowman* was not just a series of "visions," but made up a coherent whole. Kelen, like her object of study, is groundbreaking in this sensitive interpretation, which is salutary in its refusal to follow the usual approach of judging editors' achievements according to twentieth-century ideas about language alone.

In Chapter 5, Chaucer returns to prominence as Langland's alter ego. Kelen offers a lively account of the story that Chaucer assaulted a friar (who in one version had written a satiric "mummery" about him as a response to *The Plowman's Tale*), followed by in-depth treatments of William Godwin's and Florence Converse's takes on the two poets, both fictional even though Godwin saw himself as writing biography. Langland's relationship to Chaucer figures more or less prominently throughout the eras discussed in this book. Kelen's implicit point, I suspect, is that all accounts of these poets rely upon decisions—about chronological or artistic priority, about religious affiliations, about literary value—that are at their core rooted in circular beliefs about biography, which is to say, in fictions. All scholars of Middle English should acquaint themselves with the historical formations of those fictions, a task for which they now have an invaluable guide in Sarah Kelen's *Langland's Early Modern Identities*.

LAWRENCE WARNER
University of Sydney

PEGGY KNAPP. *Chaucerian Aesthetics*. New York: Palgrave Macmillan, 2008. Pp. x, 242. $79.95.

In recent years, there has emerged a growing interest among literary scholars in returning to the questions of aesthetics and form that historicism, in its various guises, seemed to neglect or willfully exclude. This return usually has been accomplished in one of two ways: either the critic begins with theories of the aesthetic and proceeds to the literary text, or the critic engages in some kind of close scrutiny of the text and its engagement with (or construction of) aesthetic and formal categories like "beauty" or "genre" or "character" or "style." Peggy Knapp takes the first route, opening her *Chaucerian Aesthetics* with two wide-ranging considerations of aesthetic theory, both medieval and post-Enlightenment, including thinkers like Augustine, Thomas Aquinas, and Bonaventure, Kant, Wittgenstein, Gadamer, and Scarry, as well as cognitive theorists like Antonio Damasio and Daniel Dennett. These opening accounts guide the more thematic readings of Chaucer's poetry that follow in five wide-ranging chapters. The theoretical approach has many advantages, not the least of which is its capacity to articulate Chaucerian practice—the various ways in which Chaucer deploys aesthetic devices and forms. This approach can also make connections among the aesthetic values of the distant past, the recent past, and the present day, creating connective tissue that firmly links Augustine and Aquinas to Kant, Wittgenstein, and others. Knapp foregrounds this potential of aesthetic theory by frequently performing a kind of *translatio* on the aesthetic values she derives from medieval thinkers—as she does, for instance, with the term *claritas*, which she links to Elaine Scarry's notion of "greeting," the welcome that beauty extends to the viewer. Knapp's goal seems to be to create a network of interwoven aesthetic features, held together across time by this *translatio*, within which she can situate Chaucer's poetry in order to establish the fundamentally transhistorical nature of its generosity and openness—its capacity to speak to readers in the past and in the present. Along the way, she prosecutes various literary critical arguments, addressing both local questions of interpretation and larger disputes about the nature of the literary text itself.

It would be impossible in a short review to survey adequately the formidable array of aesthetic categories and concepts that Knapp deploys in her interpretations of Chaucer's poetry. She begins with medieval categories like verisimilitude, *integritas* (formal coherence), proportionality, *claritas* (luminosity), and usefulness (for moral reasoning), and joins them to notions like "epistemic hunger" (from Dennett), "aspect formation" and the "language game" (from Wittgenstein), "capacious regard" and "greeting" (from Scarry), the "luminous detail" (from Pound), and "free delight" (from Kant). The sheer volume of ideas at work here is at once impressive and destabilizing. It is always a severe challenge to distill the philosophical thought of many centuries into a short space, and Knapp is to be congratulated for her remarkable account of aesthetics from the Middle Ages to the present. As an introduction to a book titled *Chaucerian Aesthetics*, however, this pastiche of ideas comes dangerously close to muddying the waters, threatening to overwhelm what should be at the core of the book: Chaucer's *own* notion of the aesthetic as it is expressed in his vocabulary, use of aesthetic devices, and references to aesthetic concepts like the imagination or, most famously, "sentence and solaas." Because each of the thinkers referenced emerges from a slightly different philosophical tradition, with different vocabularies and definitions, different trajectories and goals, the result of Knapp's extensive citation can be confusion. The substitution of modern terms for medieval categories seems in this light to neglect the contexts in which the vocabulary on both sides of the divide was forged, contexts that reveal much about how aesthetics was understood at different moments in history. Given the rich and nuanced language for describing the imagination in the Middle Ages—so elegantly articulated by Knapp—one wonders why it is necessary to seek terms from different historical moments in order to explain how Chaucer viewed his own relationship to the sensible. Understanding how he negotiated this "language of the sensible" in relationship to his own artistic practice is crucial to understanding the development of vernacular literary notions of aesthetics. That said, I do not mean to imply that it is always inappropriate to link Chaucer's poetic practice to modern aesthetic thinking; certainly, recent thinkers open up new ways of looking at Chaucer that would have been unimaginable for Augustine or Aquinas. Chaucer was an innovator, after all. My criticism is largely about the *extent* of Knapp's project of *translatio*, the multiplicity of her categories, and the degree to which that multiplicity verges on obscuring rather than illuminating Chaucer's vision of the aesthetic.

Knapp's chapters on Chaucer are organized around categories familiar to readers of historicist Chaucerian criticism: genre, persons, women, laughter, and community. Chapter 3 is titled "Playing with Language Games" and focuses on genre in the *Canterbury Tales*, particularly in relation to literary realism; here Knapp is especially interested in the ways in which art offers both imaginative freedom and bounded forms. In Chapter 4, Knapp engages the significant question of Chaucer's relationship to persons, arguing that he uses "luminous details" to imagine for his characters "rich inner lives." This psychological realism uses beauty to forge connections between persons, not only readers and characters, but also readers and individuals whom they encounter in the real world. In Chapter 5, beautiful persons give way to beautiful women, and to the problem of female beauty for medieval thinkers. Knapp focuses on Criseyde above all, though she does discuss the Miller's Alisoun, Virginia, Custance, Griselda, May, Dorigen, Canacee, Cecilia, and Prudence. Crucially, she demonstrates how Criseyde's beauty creates a tension between the sensible and the intelligible, between its visceral appeal and its symbolic character, pointing out that in some ways, "the sensible image may be responded to as beautiful only until it becomes intelligible" (118)—a striking insight that encourages a rethinking of medieval understandings of the beautiful, the sensuous, and the reasonable. The next chapter, "The Aesthetics of Laughter," turns to the genres of fabliau and parody. Knapp elucidates six notions about humor with which she discusses Chaucer's comedy, including the idea that laughter involves both the sensible and the intelligible, the notion that comedy produces imaginative freedom, the fact that jokes produce surprises and suspense, the relation of proportionality to comedy, the idea that jokes can be laughed at in a disinterested way, and the topicality of humor. Finally, the last chapter deals with notions of community, and the way in which Chaucer's "generous inclusiveness" works to create an imaginary community held together by aesthetic force. It is in this community that Knapp finally locates beauty, as a category linking the sensible and the intelligible, the aesthetic and the social, in a distinctly Chaucerian way.

Although I have criticized *Chaucerian Aesthetics*, my criticisms arise from its admirable ambition. Knapp set out not only to think through Chaucer's poetry in relation to the aesthetic but also to rewrite the history of literary aesthetics from the Middle Ages to the present and to propose an aestheticism—a critical mode of thought—for medievalists. Each of these projects could have been a book in itself, and it is a testimony to Knapp's intelligence and experience that she manages to keep all of these balls in the air at once. This volume is written by someone with deep reservoirs of knowledge to draw upon, knowledge of the Middle Ages, of Chaucer, of literary criticism, and of philosophical aesthetics. Chaucer scholars will want to read it carefully, both for what they can learn on its pages and for the kind of inspiration the book provides. Knapp argues that Chaucer uses the aesthetic to teach his audience new ways to feel pleasure and to conceive of their social worlds; in much the same way, her book shows its audience new and unexpected ways to look at familiar texts. Her Chaucer is generous, inclusive, optimistic, and filled with *caritas* for his community—and that is precisely how her book presents itself to its audience, as a record of thinking generously designed to share a new vision of a familiar poet.

MAURA NOLAN
University of California, Berkeley

V. A. KOLVE. *Telling Images: Chaucer and the Imagery of Narrative*. Stanford: Stanford University Press, 2009. Pp. xvii, 368. $65.00.

Telling Images, the long-awaited sequel to *Chaucer and the Imagery of Narrative: The First Five Canterbury Tales* (Stanford, 1984), confirms V. A.

Kolve's status as one of his generation's preeminent scholar-critics of Middle English literature. Although six of its eight chapters have been previously published, having them packaged so conveniently and beautifully with their 157 illustrations and 112 pages of supporting notes and index makes the wait worthwhile.

Unlike the first installment, which focused on the opening two fragments of the *Canterbury Tales*, *Telling Images* includes chapters not only on other Chaucerian works (Chapter 1, "Looking at the Sun in Chaucer's *Troilus and Criseyde*"; and Chapter 2, "From Cleopatra to Alceste: An Iconographic Study of *The Legend of Good Women*"), but also on the God-denying fool ubiquitous in medieval psalters and on the so-called medieval religion of love (Chapter 8). In lieu of a formal conclusion, which could have provided greater coherence to what Kolve acknowledges to be a collection of "occasional pieces" (xvi), this chapter serves as the author's "Retraction," discussing "my personal situation for the first time, confessing to a dilemma I have never wholly resolved: how to teach and write 'from within' Christian systems of thought without appearing to acquiesce in beliefs I do not share" (xvii). The struggle with this dilemma clearly informs the volume's nuanced humanism, which characterizes Kolve's scholarship since its auspicious beginning with *The Play Called Corpus Christi* (Stanford University Press, 1966).

Methodologically, *Telling Images* does not break new ground as did the 1984 volume, which included opening chapters detailing Kolve's hypotheses regarding the audience of medieval imagery and a theory of narrative images. In our review (*SAC* 7 [1985]: 212–18), Ronald B. Herzman and I praised the book's comprehensive readings but questioned some of its assumptions and worried about its juxtaposition of literary and visual images wrenched from their historical, geographic, social, and functional contexts. Nevertheless, the chapters were important meditations on the thorny issues that arise when scholars seek to negotiate the complex relationships between medieval artistic and literary cultures and to calculate the extent to which visual and verbal images did not just reflect but fully informed an assumed late medieval aesthetic. Kolve's notion of a narrative image is an important and useful hermeneutic tool. Unfortunately, the present volume does not forward the methodology delineated twenty-five years earlier, despite significant advancements by both literary (e.g., Mary Carruthers) and art (e.g., Jeffrey Hamburger) historians studying how images functioned in particular contexts for specific patrons and communities of viewers and readers.

The older methodology tends to deploy visual analogues primarily to illustrate literary readings and not as works worthy of meticulous scrutiny in their own right. Picking and choosing from an impressive repertoire of images, Kolve highlights the crucial detail that supports his reading, while ignoring other, sometimes more visually prominent forms. Such use of visual evidence will disappoint but not surprise art historians, who are accustomed to literary critics privileging word over image.

As a work of literary criticism, *Telling Images* should be judged by its success in advancing our understanding of Chaucer, particularly in its two new chapters on *The Merchant's Tale* (both titled "Of Calendars and Cuckoldry"). The first (Chapter 4, subtitled "January and May in *The Merchant's Tale*") begins by assuming that the pear tree incident is "the tale's 'governing image'—the first image likely to come to mind as readers or listeners think back on what they remember of the tale" (93). For me, the tale's most memorable image is not this scene but the revealing and typically understated Chaucerian moment when May tears Damian's love letter "And in the pryvee softely it caste" (IV.1954); for purposes of this review, however, I will become the reader Kolve imagines. He immediately draws our attention to a woodcut depicting two lovers in the foliage of a tree above a blind old man embracing its trunk. Interestingly, although printed by Caxton, the image illustrates not his edition of the *Canterbury Tales* but his *Fables of Esope* (1484). Kolve here misses the opportunity to address a crucial question concerning Chaucer and medieval visual culture: Why were the *narratives* of the *Canterbury Tales* not illustrated in the fifteenth century (as were the poems of Gower and Lydgate)? No other illustrations of his "governing image" are reproduced, furthermore; instead, the chapter focuses on representations of the months of January and May in the calendars of books of hours and psalters. An extensive overview of the iconography of January, for example, discusses the two- or three-headed January as a gatekeeper holding a key and January as a wealthy man feasting. Not all the illustrations support the analysis, but Kolve does cite an image in a book of hours (Bourges, c. 1500?) that "offers a more perfect fit" (113). Seeking an image to "fit," however, demonstrates how the literary interpretation precedes and shapes the visual evidence, much of which does not contribute substantially to comprehending January as *character* beyond what the literary analogues and poetic text manifest. That the tale is "underwritten by calendar images for January" (114) is surely an over-statement.

The second of the new chapters (Chapter 5, subtitled "The Sun in Gemini and *The Merchant's Tale*") is more successful in visualizing fresh perspectives on Chaucer's tale. The wide-ranging survey of calendar images is fascinating, leading Kolve to note that "Castor and Pollux, pictured *as the Gemini,* constitute an overlooked vein of homoerotic imagery in medieval art" (132). Thirteen pages into the chapter's argument, however, he anticipates an impatient reader by asking: "All very interesting, no doubt. But what . . . has any of this to do with *The Merchant's Tale?*" (132). The answer is discovered in yet another iconographic tradition that represents the Gemini twins as male and female, who "shed their clothes too, and as the centuries go by, enter more deeply into the surrounding woods" (142). The trajectory of the argument is now clear, and after discussing another twelve images, Kolve arrives at the tale's youthful lovers: "May's desire for Damian proves as compulsive, urgent, and without moral scruple as his desire for her. . . . For Chaucer, as for many a manuscript painter from the thirteenth century on, the sun in Gemini enabled certain kinds of events. It was thought of as a sexually empowering, procreative sign" (150). The chapter continues with further explications of the garden scene's tree imagery, including manuscript representations of the Jesse Tree, before concluding that *The Merchant's Tale* "imagines the coupling in a tree in terms of what I shall call 'calendar realism': an event in harmony with a larger natural order, restoring the balance in something gone wrong" (169). This is an important critical insight, a reading that helps situate the tale in a seasonal, naturalistic context, balancing—without replacing—readings that associate January's "fresshe gardyn" with Eden and the Fall.

Some readers may lack the patience to work through the chapters, closely examine their illustrations, and attend to their digressions, but this would be unfortunate, because there is a great deal to be learned from them. Moreover, for those who share Kolve's affection for the abundant, diverse, and productive visual culture of the later Middle Ages, as I do, a fresh look at the previously published chapters will also reward. For example, Chapter 7, *"The Second Nun's Tale* and the Iconography of St. Cecilia"—published almost thirty years ago—remains one of the best studies of this understudied tale. Rereading it in *Telling Images* underscores the comprehensive knowledge of medieval iconography and keen critical insights that Kolve continues to share with his readers through his engaging and elegant prose.

RICHARD K. EMMERSON
Manhattan College

JILL MANN. *From Aesop to Reynard: Beast Literature in Medieval Britain.* Oxford: Oxford University Press, 2009. Pp. xii, 380. £60; $110.

From Aesop to Reynard traces a temporal and textual set of relations among several genres of beast literature, focusing most often on beast epics and fables. Organized roughly chronologically, the book moves across more than a millennium from the emergence of Aesopic tales in classical Latin traditions through the emergence of beast epic in the eleventh century and onward to Henryson's "epicized fables" in the fifteenth century. The study's argument does not fall victim to chronology by structuring its vast materials simply to trace sources, influences, and the development of forms. Instead, Mann's chronology is the starting point for discovering quirky particularities, interventions from further genres, complex cross-currents, disappearances, and rediscoveries. *From Aesop to Reynard* is importantly introductory in its broad coverage and accessible arrangement of information about hundreds of works whose interrelations truly deserve the trendy term "rhizomous." At the same time, in its extended analyses of its most central texts, this book contributes substantially to scholarship on the stakes of beast literature: how we might understand its invocations of animals, what its social uses were, and how it could be bent to particular occasions and agendas.

Although *From Aesop to Reynard* is far more than a genre study, one of Mann's productive approaches to beast literature is through genre considerations. Aiming to trace "not *what* animals mean, but *how* animals mean" (1), she begins by drawing some basic distinctions between beast fable and beast epic. The fable strives for insight into the ways of the world, into how things happen, not insight into how conditions might change or how characters develop. "The fable renounces novelty; new narratives lead to old conclusions, revealing themselves as variations on the ancient themes" (43). Serving this purpose, the use of animal protagonists conveys inevitability: whatever language the animals may deploy to defend or gloss their actions, these actions prove to be governed by animal natures such as the predator's violence and the prey's meekness. Two aspects of fable particularly resonate with aspects of beast epic: for both genres, language is untrustworthy, masking motives and misrepresenting situations to the advantage of speakers; and both genres endorse "the power of nature—the inescapable basis of both human and animal existence, which sets unbreachable bounds to ambition and pretentiousness" (306). These consonances help explain how the two genres can so fully cross-pollinate despite other traits that are distinctive to beast epic, such as its astonishing verbosity, its vaunted amorality, and its satirical take on behavior.

Each chapter discusses interconnections among a few forms and genres: Chapter 4 sets *The Owl and the Nightingale* in the context of bestiaries, animal debates, and fables; Chapter 6 argues that Chaucer's *Nun's Priest's Tale* owes less to beast fable than to beast epic as exemplified in *The Vox and the Wolf* and the *Roman de Renart*. Peripherally related materials from sermons, proverbs, lays, and romances are worked into these discussions with a fine sense of timing and proportion. For example, when the Owl retells the lay of *Laüstic* in *The Owl and the Nightingale*, the lay's nightingale is treated not as an innocent victim of human passions but instead as the guilty instigator of illicit human love, rightly killed for her fault. Mann argues that here, as with the Owl's and the Nightingale's invocations of familiar fables, the birds' twisted perspective emphasizes their physical existence as birds: they "treat beast literature as if it was simply a mine of information about each other's disgraceful past" (177). The effect is partly comic: the birds misread their subordination to allegoresis in fable, and they act absurdly insofar as they act like humans. Yet the effect is also to set against their allegoresis another way of taking their representation: they refer to themselves as natural creatures with habits that derive from their differing species. Their natures provide an incompatible crosscurrent to the anthropomorphizing aspects of their presentation.

This example of Mann's persistent attentiveness to the category of nature marks an advance over much of the scholarship on beast literature, which too often has little to say about animals except that they are merely figures for human concerns. Figurative tropes assign meaning to both of their elements (nightingale and poet, for example); the best of tropes spark oscillations and exchanges between their poles of meaning. Mann's analysis is attentive to these oscillations where animals are concerned, although the category of "nature" itself calls for further examination. Publications in environmental studies, for example, Kate Soper's *What Is Nature?* and the collection *Engaging with Nature* edited by Barbara Hanawalt and Lisa Kiser, have shown that invocations of nature tend to be richly hypothetical and figurative. In Mann's analysis of beast literature, nature lies beyond the reach of debate: this literature invokes "the determining power of nature," "the neutral realities of natural history," and "true physical reality" (129, 172, 306). Instead of a vital point of analysis, nature can seem in these passages an uncontested category free from cultural construction.

Beast epic's mobilization (or demobilization) of ethical argument offers another field of investigation that Mann handles gracefully but with a certain dismissiveness. Introducing beast epic as essentially a comic form, Mann attributes its verbosity to its characters' deployment of rhetoric as a weapon: "Linguistic dominance, it appears, both ensures physical dominance and sets the seal on it. . . . In this resolutely amoral world, there is little point in analysing the animals' behaviour in moral terms" (45, 50). Instead, episodes are structured by "the inexorable operation of the law of comic reversal" (51); therefore they appropriately conclude with witticisms rather than with morals. Particularly in working out the relation of beast epic to beast fable, this explanation helpfully confronts the beast epics' conjunction of extraordinary verbosity and extreme violence. At the same time, the epic's relation to morality in fable and the very verbosity of beast epic would make deeper sense if the beast epics were not entirely closed to moral significance. How might Mann take on board or refute James Simpson's argument that beast epic is not simply amoral? For Simpson ("Consuming Ethics: Caxton's *History of Reynard the Fox*," in *Studies in Late Medieval and Early Renaissance Texts in Honour of John Scattergood* [2005]), the Reynard episodes may be investigating how moral principles come under threat: "We can only take the ethical seriously by setting it within a complex psychological and discursive field. We can only take it seriously, that is, by seeing it as threatened" (335). The genius of Reynard, in Simpson's view, is that he puts tremendous pressure on ethics by appealing to moral principles such as pity for others and then deploying those principles to justify his amoral and pitiless self-interest.

From Aesop to Reynard will be a lasting landmark for scholars of beast literature. Mann's masterly presentation of medieval texts, editing, and critical work will make this book an indispensable resource and point of reference. Complementing its immense field of reference, *From Aesop to Reynard* concentrates on a small set of representative works in order to foreground some of the most important questions for ongoing critical work on beast literature.

SUSAN CRANE
Columbia University

JOANNA MARTIN. *Kingship and Love in Scottish Poetry, 1424–1540*. Aldershot: Ashgate, 2008. Pp. x, 200. £50; $99.95.

In her impeccably researched book, Joanna Martin makes an important contribution to our understanding of both canonical and less frequently read Scottish texts of the fifteenth and early sixteenth centuries by concentrating on the relation between the themes of royal governance and love. The preface describes her approach as "historicist and cultural," explaining that "the amatory content of each work is related to the intellectual and political context . . . or to the interpretive context(s) provided by the manuscripts or prints in which it survives." Among the most valuable aspects of her study, in fact, are the detailed analyses of codicological matters that shed light on the production and early reception of each work. The most important political context that she identifies is the uninterrupted succession of royal minorities from James I through James VI. Given this troubled history, it is significant that the texts she studies witness "a recurrent concern . . . with the youth and consequent vulnerability" of the king "to personal misgovernance." The "advice to princes" genre is so central to the literary culture of medieval and early modern Scotland, and sexuality such a perennially worrisome issue, that Martin's sharp focus on the love-life of young kings—both fictional and real—lends coherence to her study.

This brief review can only touch on the main outlines and conclusions of the book. The introduction convincingly argues that "love is fundamental to the advisory and ethical" (1) concerns of many works from late medieval Scotland. Although some of the poetic texts she studies were composed with royal readers in mind, the surviving manuscripts and early prints were often produced or circulated outside the court, in households that were politically active. Thus Chapter 1 treats *The Kingis*

Quair and *The Quare of Jelusy* from Oxford, Bodleian Library, MS Arch. Selden B.24. The former text turns out to be the most "optimistic" work Martin studies, presenting the young king's "reasoned love as efficacious in an unstable world" (28). The *Quare*, however, is more disturbing in its "suggestion that there can be no effective resistance against tyranny" (36), though it remains hopeful about the possibility of the reader's self-reformation. Chapter 2 examines *Lancelot of the Laik* (c. 1460–79), an incomplete work surviving in a single manuscript. Based on the noncyclic French *Lancelot*, the Scots adaptation is more concerned than the original with the relation between sexual desire and governance. Martin remains alert to subtle changes of emphasis in the Scottish text, which "make the conventional collocation of love and chivalry into a way of exploring the ethical order of the self" (60). Chapter 3 focuses on another little-read work, *The Buik of King Alexander the Conquerour*, an incomplete survival that nonetheless reaches nearly twenty thousand words. Its epilogue seems to suggest that the surviving text is a revised version dated 1499 of an earlier translation by Gilbert Hay from perhaps around 1460. Compared to its French source, the Scottish work gives greater emphasis to Alexander as a youthful king, "a powerful reminder of the work's genesis in fifteenth-century Scotland" (61). Especially striking is the Scottish poet's increased attention to "royal amorousness" (67). Although the young Alexander is presented as a *puer senex*, he is a more ambiguous figure later in the poem, which "resists clear alignment with either the wholly positive or negative aspects of the Alexander tradition" (78).

Chapter 4, one of the most interesting, turns to Henryson's *Orpheus and Eurydice*, emphasizing that Orpheus is presented as a "young and passionate monarch" (79) in a way that emphasizes the political significance of the legend. The fable offers a "pessimistic end" (102) when the lover-king succumbs to temptation; the *moralitas* at least offers the hope that the reader can successfully use reason to rule over desire. Chapter 5 discusses *The Thre Prestis of Peblis*, a text whose immediate historical context is unclear, owing to its late survival in the Asloan MS (c. 1515–30). Yet its "political and amatory themes" have "ideological consonance" with the other later fifteenth-century texts that Martin studies (103). The work is a framed series of tales told by three priests who draw on material from estates satire, using both comic and serious modes of exemplification to discuss "social problems, just kingship, and personal morality" (129). Chapter 6 examines *King Hart* (c. 1500), a text attributed to Gavin Douglas in the late sixteenth-century Maitland Folio MS, though not by the scribe who copied the poem. (Modern scholars generally follow Priscilla Bawcutt, who in a 1959 article argued decisively against attributing the poem to Douglas; it should be noted that in note 7 on page 132 Martin misidentifies the author of this article.) Although the poem is a personification allegory, Martin convincingly argues that if we take seriously the literal sense of the narrative about a wayward king, its treatment "of the problems of minority rule," including "court factionalism and the education of the prince," are "more historically and culturally engaged than has previously been recognized" (131). The poem's dark comedy seems pessimistic about the possibility of "royal and personal reformation." Because it was not a product of the royal court, however, the poem need not have succumbed to "the pressure of having to confidently predict the emergence of good kingship" (152), as Martin observes. The epilogue, after a brief consideration of the advisory poetry of William Dunbar (the truncated discussion of the famous poem celebrating the marriage of James IV and Margaret Tudor in 1503, it must be said, is disappointing), goes on to examine relevant early sixteenth-century work by Sir David Lyndsay and two much lesser known poets, John Bellenden and William Stewart. Again, given her topic, it is disappointing that Martin does not devote more space to *Ane Satyre of the Thrie Estaitis*, though her discussion of Lyndsay's early poetry draws welcome attention to some fascinating works that most readers of this journal would find congenial.

This book is more likely to appeal to specialists than to a wider audience because of the sharply focused nature of Martin's topic and also because her approach declines to draw on recent theoretical approaches to gender and sexuality. Some readers may find that the effort to determine the extent to which each work is either "optimistic" or "pessimistic" is unnecessarily constraining. If the works examined in the epilogue seem especially pessimistic and "express a profound lack of confidence in this advisory and poetic project" (177), a different kind of historicist approach might insist that these writers participate in a larger crisis of authority in fifteenth- and early sixteenth-century Scotland, one in which *all* the traditional institutions of power were coming apart at the seams much as they were elsewhere, and thus the pattern of royal minorities was as much an effect as a cause. Yet the book is convincing within the limited parameters it sets for itself, and students of older

Scots literature must remain in Martin's debt for her painstaking attention to some relatively unexplored material.

R. JAMES GOLDSTEIN
Auburn University

ALASTAIR MINNIS. *Translations of Authority in Medieval English Literature:*
Valuing the Vernacular. Cambridge: Cambridge University Press,
2009. Pp. xv, 272. £50.00; $90.00.

R. N. Swanson's liberating evocation of a medieval church that, for all
its canons and councils, remained minimalist in its definitions of faith,
may be imagined as the setting for Alastair Minnis's latest book, which
takes as one of its points of departure the fact that, for various reasons,
medieval intellectual life as pursued in the courts and schools left so
much incomplete. Judicious silence, anxious irresolution, pragmatic inconsistency—all staple elements of theological discourse in its professional modes—created a fertile ground in which vernacular writing
could discover and ply its distinctive creativity. "Thinking in poetry," to
borrow J. A. Burrow's phrase, thrived in the late medieval period because, where theology in particular was concerned, the topics that exercised the thinkers, and that concern Minnis in this study, left so much
work for the poets and other extramural writers to do. The role of good
works in ensuring salvation, the remit of indulgences, the exegesis of
scriptural passages, or the affective charge of religious relics—all challenged authors to bring arguments to conclusions unforeseen by university disputants, or to no conclusions at all, or to expose the provisionality
or the reductiveness of such argument (hence Chaucer's burlesquing of
the Strode/Wyclif debate on predestination in Troilus's agonized, but
detrimentally unprofessional, philosophizing). The fact that even a dead
vernacular poet might be well ahead of a living, professional theologian
is soberly brought home to the reader of Thomas Gascoigne, who, in
the course of a discussion of chastity, solemnly rehearses arguments the
speciousness of which had been exposed decades earlier by the Wife of
Bath.

That particular example of the way in which an argument could re-
sound so differently in Latin and English does not feature in the present

451

study, but this book is concerned with a rich variety of similar engagements. Over the course of the discussion, Minnis investigates many possibilities for reciprocity and mirroring between Latin and vernacular, treating both not merely as spoken and written languages, but also as textual, cultural, and institutional practices; and he imagines these discursive worlds as intimately involved, rather than being opposed to one another. Thus he is concerned not only with the ways in which "Middle English carried on the business of Latin intellectual culture" (x), but also with the extent to which "medieval Latin [might] be deemed a vernacular or a group of vernaculars" (xi); and in this context it is salutary to remember how long Latin remained an occupational dialect among schoolmen, and thus how much thinking (and surely even dreaming) must have been macaronic during this period and long afterward.

The first chapter, "Absent Glosses," provides a speculative overview of the unsystematic way in which fragments of intellectual culture trickled into English during the late fourteenth century. Using the efflorescence of contemporary French vernacular translation as one of his points of reference, Minnis concludes that England did not witness such *grands projets* because "the *translatio studii* ideal was tainted by the Lollards" (37). The very coherence of that conclusion may mean that it finds resistance even as it enables much further, fruitful discussion. But Minnis does some characteristically energizing intellectual history throughout the rest of the book, providing what amounts to an extensive commentary on selected passages, or showing how particular vernacular texts grow out of, and bear the weight of, contested traditions of thought. Chaucer and, to a greater extent, Langland focus the next two chapters in which Minnis revisits and historicizes uncertainties surrounding the salvation of righteous heathens and the authority of pardons. Chapters on Walter Brut and Margery Kempe follow, knitted together by their subjects' differing expressions of nonprofessional authority. In the final chapter, Minnis further models the enterprise of "valuing the vernacular" by extending the term's frame of reference to include "popular cultural beliefs and practices," and pursuing their interactions with practices sanctioned by the Church. Using religious relics as his testing ground, he mounts a rich discussion that extends from Chaucer to More and that ends with an exhortation to his readers to investigate "between the lines of the élite documents" so as to "access the rich mother lodes of vernacular religion" (162).

Together with the many incidental pleasures afforded by a book that

452

is redolent throughout of its author's long familiarity with the creativity of scholastic thought, Minnis's greatest achievement here is to make this revisiting of textual cruces look easy: it is liberating, for example, for those who have lived long with *Piers Plowman* to follow him safely through the dark wood of critical explication surrounding the tearing of the pardon in B.VII. His reading of this passage is paradigmatic of the critical demystification that he conducts throughout the book, robustly calling into question as it does the notion that Langland was necessarily embroiled in the particular theological debates that some modern critics would like to foist on him. Although the solution that Minnis proposes—that the words of the pardon from Treuthe should be "read and glossed with reference to the Atonement" (87)—emerges rather abruptly from the dense and compelling argument that precedes it, it is valuable to have further evidence of Langland as a "radical conservative" whose thinking was readily accommodated by the established latitudes of theological discussion. The consequences of such engagements for writing itself, and poetry in particular, are not Minnis's chief concern, although there is a tantalizing glimpse of what such consequences might be in his salutary reminder that "the idea of the pardon mutates along with the idea of the plowman . . . during this Passus it seems to have changed in size and content" (81). Such a discussion refreshes our understanding of how the most radical achievement of Langland's poetry was not the particular conclusions that might be teased out of it, but the way in which it enabled thought itself to assume postures unimagined in other discourses. Langland was free not merely to flout the rules governing coherence in other genres of discourse—such as the conduct of a university *disputatio*, or the setting out of a literary *quaestio*—but also to invent his own, and to leave them undisclosed, with no traces in contemporary literary theory. As Minnis acknowledges in the following chapter on Brut, the language question by itself may be a red herring here. A more pertinent explanation must lie with what he briefly but significantly considers toward the end of this chapter, namely, the institutional contexts in which such thinking and writing were taking place. In the course of this discussion, he expends a good deal of energy in trying to rechristen the kind of theology that Brut produced. Having appraised "vernacular theology" elsewhere in the discussion, he experiments here with "non-institutional theology," "anti-institutional theology," and "unofficial theology." I would suggest that the term "extramural" still has a good deal of purchase in this context.

Minnis describes this book as a "compilation" (xi), and it could be argued that the chapters, each of which has been imagined as "an essay in the politics of *translatio auctoritatis*" (1), are centripetally rather than sequentially related. But this, one might equally retort, is faithful to the nature of the phenomenon under investigation, namely, the loosely related episodes and contexts in which Latin and vernacular cultures circled one another in late medieval England. And that phenomenon in turn is but one early instantiation of the way in which so much in English intellectual life has flourished while remaining stubbornly unauthorized.

MISHTOONI BOSE
Christ Church, Oxford

ESTHER CASIER QUINN. *Geoffrey Chaucer and the Poetics of Disguise.* Lanham, Md.: University Press of America, 2008. Pp. xii, 251. $42.00.

This book is the result of an evidently long and deep engagement with the poetry of Geoffrey Chaucer. Its central thesis is that Chaucer deployed a poetics of disguise in order to criticize those in power around him, with a particular focus on the abuses of Richard II. This poetics, it is argued, comprises an amalgam of techniques, from the creation of composite figures, to the very subtle and playful use of "auctoritees," to the use of seeming praise. These all enable Chaucer to criticize without risking disfavor. One of the main methodologies that Quinn uses to tie together all of these aspects is to trace the recurrence of what she sees as key words. Thus Chaucer's work is always read as referring to one historical event or another, and his characters are often contemporary figures in disguise. If the result is at times intriguing, it is ultimately not convincing and indeed often infuriates with its speculative connections and allusions.

Chapter 1 is a synthetic presentation of the politically and socially turbulent decades of Chaucer's most productive literary period, from the 1370s onward. It suggests that the use of terms such as "traitour," "pardoun," "lawe," "treasoun," and "oath" are productively read against the backdrop of such political turmoil. Four words are afforded particular attention in the following chapters: "love," "deth," "synne," and "trouthe."

Chapter 2, "Dream Worlds," is an analysis of three of Chaucer's dream-vision poems. Each is given an extended descriptive exposition. The *Book of the Duchess*, which is seen as an occasional poem on the death of Blanche of Lancaster, is described as a "deeply felt, subtly nuanced work of art, a treasure in itself and the beginning of what was to become a vast, varied, intricate, and wide-ranging body of poetry extending far beyond the courtly world" (28). The *House of Fame* further explores the dynamics of the dream vision and shows a Chaucer who has a clearer sense of his own individuality, as a person and a poet. For Quinn, a line like *HF* 1878, "I wot myself best how y stonde," provides a key to the *House of Fame* and Chaucer's "poetics of disguise." Love is the central theme in the *Parliament of Fowls,* and through the debate of the birds Chaucer explores the theme of choice. Here Quinn rightly highlights the fact that the formel eagle is not indecisive but rather delays her decision for another year. The *Parliament* explores, in her historical reading, a number of related issues, such as the meaning and kinds of love, the responsibilities of kingship, class, and gender differences, and the importance of choice.

In Chapter 3, "Pagan Worlds," Quinn looks at the *Troilus, The Legend of Good Women*, and briefly at *Anelida and Arcite*. The *Troilus* has Chaucer explore more fully "the interrelatedness of love, war, and politics" (55), especially through the freedom offered by his disguised *auctor*, Lollius. One aspect of the poem on which Quinn concentrates is the astrological content; given that astrology was popular at the court of Richard II, this is read as a veiled criticism of such practices: "Chaucer conveys his criticism of the English aristocracy's interest in astrology and veils his own negative views, not only by representing the two most devious Trojans as astrologers but by introducing astrological allusions at crucial points in the narrative. Moreover, by alternately referring to pagan deities and planetary bodies, thus calling to mind the misbehavior of the gods and the blameless movements of the stars, he was able to be critical without seeming to be" (65). *The Legend of Good Women* is read with the Prologue and individual Legends together, the former being the key to understanding the latter. The Prologue, with its tyrannical Cupid and pacifying Alceste, and the Legends, with their false and treacherous men, lend themselves to being read as having a "resemblance to contemporary situations" (85).

Chapter 4, "Moving Toward Canterbury," is the longest in the book, and reads the *Canterbury Tales* as the most developed and ingenious phase of Chaucer's poetics of disguise. The tales are treated in groups, divided between those set in a pagan past, fabliaux, rhyme royal tales, tales without women, Chaucer's own tales, unfinished tales, tales of pilgrims who lack portraits, the penultimate tale, and tales that are variants of these. As such, Quinn aims to cover almost all of the *Tales* and she certainly succeeds in providing a broad reading of the whole work. Each tale is given a fairly brief but concentrated close reading, tying together many different thematic and narrative strands.

The final chapter looks at the short poems and these too, though proving somewhat more difficult to fit into a set of historical circumstances, are read as examples of disguised treatments of Chaucer's contemporaries. So, the *Complaint unto Pity* expresses Chaucer's anxieties as he contemplated the troubled reign of Richard II, and the structuring of the poem provides a key to its meaning. The idealized lady and idealized king merge and "Pite" is transformed from a quality one hopes to find in a lady to one that a subject hopes to find in a ruler.

The connections made in this book between specific passages and historical events will fail to convince many, and more severe reviewers would (and will) spend more time on them. What is peculiar about this book is the way that Quinn pursues such politically inflected readings almost wholly in the absence of any (at least declared) ideological concerns. While such an approach is refreshing, and its pleasure *is* peculiar, it threatens to destabilize the reading at many points. For example, while there is some attention to Chaucer's sources, they are usually rather hastily treated in order to get to a general point, as on page 34, where the figure of Ganymede in *The House of Fame* "calls to mind passages in the *Aeneid*, *Metamorphoses*, and the *Purgatorio*, [but] differs markedly from all of them and suggests the poet's own service to the king." There are too many steps taken at once here, too much elided in poetic and political terms to render the observation fully meaningful. The concept of "disguise" is never adequately defined and its use becomes at various points a matter of convenience rather than necessity. The bibliography, too, is in need of some updating: Bryan and Dempster's *Sources and Analogues* could now be supplemented with or replaced by Correale and Hamel's two-volume anthology. However, even if the stated aims of the book fail to convince, one is never in any doubt that the object of discussion is firmly and fiercely the poetry itself. Quinn opens by citing the magnificent lines of Wallace Stevens, in "Notes Toward a Supreme Fiction," and it is as good a place as any to end:

> From this the poem springs: that we live in a place
> That is not our own.

K. P. CLARKE
Pembroke College, Cambridge

RALUCA L. RADULESCU and CORY JAMES RUSHTON, eds. *A Companion to Medieval Popular Romance*. Cambridge: D. S. Brewer, 2009. Pp. xiv, 209. £50.00; $95.00.

Cory Rushton closes this interesting volume by observing that "the journey of the popular romance has been from the center to the margins and then back again" (179). In so doing he exemplifies much of what is striking about the book; above all, its literary-historiographical self-consciousness. In recent decades, the study of medieval "popular" romance has expanded apace: as Rosalind Field notes in the opening to her chapter, more than twenty years ago Derek Brewer was moved to comment on the dramatic "explosion of interest" in the anonymous romance (9). This volume thus makes appropriately frequent reference to the collections of Ad Putter and Jane Gilbert (*The Spirit of Medieval Popular Romance*, 2000) and Nicola McDonald (*Pulp Fictions of Medieval England*, 2004), and to the numerous books (published in the same series as the present volume) that have come from the biennial "Medieval Romance" conference, now in its twelfth iteration. This conference itself has done a great deal to expand the field, with an explicit focus on insular, non-Arthurian romance, in both English and the French of England. That being so, it is fascinating to note the degree to which the subject still carries the burden of prior scholarly dismissal; almost all contributors to this volume spend at least a few hundred words clearing the ground for their arguments, and Derek Pearsall is more than once made to pay the price for expressing earlier prevailing views in the most memorable and distinctive manner. What makes this such a meaty problem is the relative lack of disagreement between the two scholarly positions adumbrated: when Radulescu and Rushton state in their introduction that "our effort to redeem medieval popular romance forms an integral part of the modern project of recuperating 'medieval popular culture'" (3), they make no controversial claims for the literary or aesthetic merit of the texts under consideration; instead, as others have done, they shift the grounds of interpretation to the historicist and theoretical fields. This is effectively a volume about medieval popular romance and the twenty-first-century academy's approaches to it; with that in mind, some readers will be more troubled than others by the implications of the observation that "scholars of medieval popular romance continue to unearth attitudes and behaviours that are not always completely articulated in these texts and indeed not always acknowledged even as a possibility" (4).

Definition of the texts (and characteristics) that constitute the genre is another area of self-consciousness, though there is little dispute about the nature of our shared uncertainties in clarifying both "romance" and "popular" (not to mention "medieval"). The editors offer a usefully brief summation, that "in this Companion we define 'popular romance' as those texts in Middle English, sometimes with origins in Anglo-Norman versions, which show a predominant concern with narrative at the expense of symbolic meaning" (7). One suspects (sympathetically) that this formulation may have been redrafted more than once; other contributors in turn define their field in different ways, although the overall effect is complementary and reinforcing rather than conflicting. The near-absence of insular French texts is, however, something of a shame, and perhaps chiefly an inheritance from that earlier scholarship the volume is so keen to overturn, which regarded literature in English as necessarily for an unsophisticated audience, inherently "popular" in contrast with the "courtliness" of French. Rosalind Field, who has of course done so much to create and advance the study of insular French romance, is given the opportunity to demonstrate (in typically impressive and convincing fashion) that Anglo-Norman romance can be "popular" too, deploying the narratives of Boeve/Bevis and Gui/Guy to illustrate "the translation of popular romance from one vernacular into popular romance in another" (15). However, this insight is rather lost to view in the remainder of the volume, or reduced to a token gesture toward "their Old French predecessors" (97), and in turn it illuminates the inherent difficulty of defining the genre's boundaries. The threatened executions of Lunet in *Ywain and Gawain* and of Guinevere in the stanzaic *Morte Arthur*, and the false charges in *Bevis* and *King Horn*, all of which are cited as "failures in the chivalric code" (108) characteristic of the genre, are of course all present in their sources (and two of those sources, the Vulgate prose *La Mort le roi Artu* and Chrétien de Troyes's *Yvain*, are unanimously classed as "courtly" by critics).

Where this volume is unambiguously successful, however (and it is never less than interesting), is in its unusually concrete focus on the manuscript and later print contexts of the romances, and on technical questions, in the shape of Ad Putter's rather brilliant chapter on prosody and Karl Reichl's judicious and clarifying argument in "Orality and Performance." These chapters exemplify the overriding virtue of the whole volume, which is that in contrast with most "companions" to a field, it is packed with information and with complex (and compressed) argument, to a degree that will make it a useful quick reference tool for scholars of all levels, rather than a textbook aimed at the beginning undergraduate. In this context, the survey style of some of the chapters becomes a positive boon, and speaks explicitly to the volume's hope of encouraging future work. This is a book that continually invites one to follow up its thumbnail descriptions, rapid arguments, and thematic threads; the frequent sense of being at the current forefront of scholarship in the field is not, I think, illusory. Some of these chapters will perhaps date more readily than others, through no fault of the authors' own: Thomas Crofts and Robert Rouse do rather an impressive job of demonstrating the difficulties (and even inappropriateness) of applying theories of nationalism to the popular romance, with the result that even this (partisan) reviewer begins to wonder whether that particular obsession has had its day. Meanwhile, Phillipa Hardman's fascinating chapter on the possibilities opened up by considering popular romance as children's literature (and children's literature as worthy of examination) is an important contribution that promises to develop our understanding of the genre.

This is a valuable volume, and one that amply proves the case that it addresses a "perceived gap" (2), even in what is now rapidly becoming a crowded field. The uncertainties and multiplicity of perspectives with which it leaves the reader are entirely fruitful; one of the warmer effects of that literary-historiographical self-consciousness is that the reader too is encouraged to feel part of a community of scholars, engaged on a shared project.

LAURA ASHE
Worcester College, Oxford

SAMANTHA J. RAYNER. *Images of Kingship in Chaucer and His Ricardian Contemporaries*. Cambridge: D. S. Brewer, 2008. Pp. x, 178. £45.00; $90.00.

Interest in the relationship between Richard II's court and some of the richest poetry of his time seems inexhaustible. King Richard himself showed much more evident interest in other art forms, and the poetry of Chaucer, Gower, Langland, and, it seems, the *Gawain*-poet was produced not in, but on the edges, of his court. However, the relationship between court and poetry is no less intriguing for that. In *Images of Kingship in Chaucer and His Ricardian Contemporaries*, Samantha J. Rayner notes both the absence of a royal poetry of Ricardian kingship and the heterogeneity of her various poets' standpoints in relation to the royal court, but she sees kingship as a shared concern across their poetry. More suggestively, Rayner adopts a broad and decentered perspective on her theme to find common ground in her poets, reflecting that they "unite . . . in their focus on the individual subject's place in a kingdom beset with corrupt practices and unstable leadership" (160). Reading this study, I was usually more interested in the variety of individual subject positions projected by the poetry than in this unifying thesis, and Rayner's readings do bring out some of that diversity.

Rayner divides her book up simply, allocating one chapter each to Gower, Langland, the *Gawain*-poet, and Chaucer, and framing these with a very brief introduction and conclusion. The Gower chapter discusses only Book 7 of *Confessio Amantis* and the Chaucer chapter—much less predictable and more ambitious in its selections—accounts for fully half of the book. The first chapter finds Gower dealing very directly with kingship. Rayner concentrates on the five virtues of "policy" and the exempla that illustrate them in *Confessio*, Book 7. Around this discussion, she considers the context of the book within the confessional frame narrative of Amans and Genius, and aligns herself with the most illuminating critical accounts of the complex relationship between royal government and individual ethics in Gower's poem. Rayner concludes that "Gower's achievement in the *Confessio* is to make the issue of kingship relevant to every estate" (34) by way of an extremely broad concept of governance encompassing royal power and individual will.

The discussion of *Piers Plowman* dwells on the vision of the "feeld ful of folk," the parliament of rats and mice, and Lady Mede (36–49). The plowing of the quarter acre and Truth's pardon are then talked through with regard to good subjecthood, a complement to good kingship (49–52). The rest of the chapter deals briefly with the remainder of the poem under this remit, Rayner remarking at the end that "Langland is not concerned especially with the role of the king" but above all with "the responsibility of each individual to reform" (60). Given the theme of her study, I wondered whether Rayner might have done more to show *how* Langland positions state politics in a merely supporting role. She mentions Christ's apocalyptic kingship, for instance, and might have engaged with work such as Kathryn Kerby-Fulton's *Reformist Apocalypticism and Piers Plowman* further to consider how, and how far, Langland takes politics away from temporal kingship.

The next chapter touches on all four works of the *Pearl* manuscript, but kingship is off the radar for some time while Rayner concentrates on less specific topics, such as "a sense [in *Pearl*] of a persona searching for order in a world that is bound by mysteries" (68). Coming to her main theme, Rayner concludes uncontroversially that *Pearl* and *Cleanness* relate earthly courts to the heavenly one. Her reading of *Sir Gawain and the Green Knight* is more contentious, in the first place because she presents it as more obvious than many would allow. She finds the "innate stability and moral healthiness" (80) of Arthur's court to be as good as self-evident, and she takes insufficient account of readings attuned to the social flaws in the poem. Instead, she rebuffs a caricature of such readings in which Gawain's quest ends in "disaster" that exposes "the latent corruption of Camelot" according to the critic's "determined effort to see defeat . . . at every point of the story" (80). Rayner's course takes her into some challenging interpretations of her own, as when Arthur's "yonge blod and his brayn wylde" "fits with an impression of a court that is stable and secure in its fashioning" (77). Nevertheless, this section in the book is one that conveys most strongly a sense of Rayner's own critical voice driving a single argument.

Rayner's long chapter on Chaucer is broken into three fairly discrete sections, covering, respectively, the dream visions, *Troilus and Criseyde*, and the *Canterbury Tales*. Rayner finds *The Book of the Duchess* to be a decorous and sensitive work for a royal prince. She passes over *The House of Fame* as a poem mainly about writing, dismissing Fame's political authority (elsewhere much discussed) as something set "outside of a recognisable reality" (98). *The Parliament of Fowls* is read as playfully topical, and she applies the same approach with more industry to the Prologue of *The Legend of Good Women*. Rayner's *Troilus* is a sophisticated

461

poem for a sophisticated audience, an audience that prefers to take its politics obliquely. Several of the *Canterbury Tales* are then taken in turn, and Rayner's outlook here is as upbeat as in her discussion of *Sir Gawain*. Theseus is wise and well meaning, Genghis Khan's reign in *The Squire's Tale* is "unblemished" (127), and *The Franklin's Tale* offers an egalitarian endorsement of nobility of character. Having said this, Rayner is fully alert to the darkness of *The Manciple's Tale*.

Rayner makes a praiseworthy bid to bring together works by four major poets of the late fourteenth century, but her study declares its own limits in that "it will concentrate only on what can be found about kingship in the works themselves, without comparison to . . . other contemporary texts" (4). Rayner is interested in topical hypotheses about occasions for composition, but she eschews historicism more broadly conceived and approves Edward I. Condren's verdict that Chaucer's "poetry usually frees itself of the fourteenth century and requires for its appreciation only a deep knowledge of human nature" (85). This approach, and a corresponding lack of attention to how political discourses work, creates an unresolved tension in a study aiming to deal with a topic as complicated and historically contingent as kingship.

Elliot Kendall
University of Exeter

Nicole R. Rice. *Lay Piety and Religious Discipline in Middle English Literature.* Cambridge: Cambridge University Press, 2008. Pp. xvii, 247. £50.00; $90.00.

Everyone would agree that the passage of monastic spirituality into lay possession is one of the great narratives of the later Middle Ages. In 1989, Vincent Gillespie observed: "The fifteenth century witnessed an extensive and consistent process of assimilation by the laity of techniques and materials of spiritual advancement which had historically been the preserve of the clerical and monastic orders." In the essay that followed, he provided a groundbreaking codicological analysis, showing how techniques of ordering and organizing the page facilitated access to these clerical texts by a wider readership ("Vernacular Books of Religion," in *Book Production and Publishing in Britain, 1375–1475*, ed. J.

Griffiths and D. Pearsall, 1989), 317–44 [317]). Since then, research on book ownership and provenance has used predominantly physical evidence to illustrate how widely texts originally monastic in direction were owned by lay people.

Now this cultural shift from monastic to lay has been newly explored from a textual point of view. Nicole Rice's book describes fully and analyzes thoughtfully the gradual shift in spiritual reading, and indeed in the provision of spiritual guidance, from professed religious to laymen or women. She provides a succession of often surprising close readings, readings that juxtapose devotional texts and literary ones, since, as she says, Chaucer and Langland "often ask the very questions that didactic authors seek to answer" (xii).

In this analysis, Rice brings to light what must always have been implicit in this or any account of cultural change: opposition and resistance. Her work makes one wonder why such resistance has not been more widely acknowledged. Of course there must often have been reluctance toward what amounted to transfer of spiritual authority from clerical to lay hands. And of course works of spiritual guidance would have demonstrated different positions with regard to the degree of spiritual authority assigned to lay people.

To illustrate these resistances, Rice examines two different kinds of spiritual works, the first structured around "the requirements of orthodoxy," the second impelled by "the impulses of reform." *Abbey of the Holy Ghost* and *Fervor Amoris* fall into the first category (both 1375 to 1400–25). Rice's readings aim to show the essential conservatism of these texts. Particularly striking is her accompanying analysis of Chaucer's *The Shipman's Tale*, included in order to demonstrate one of her central themes, the closeness of lay and religious estates. She compares the merchant and the monk, alike in their "shared hybridity," their "partial transformation" of their respective ways of life (45), and their "skeptical perspective on the possibility of converting material to spiritual capital" (41). Read in this light as a series of mishaps resulting from lay identification with an imperfect religious figure, the tale makes painfully clear the mixture of contemporary attitudes toward religious life: admiration, emulation, criticism, all simmering together to produce what Rice calls a "fraught period" for the categories of lay and clerical.

The second group of religious texts, those that provide new forms of lay religious authority, Rice labels "dialogic." This category includes *Life of Soul* (a dialogue proper), *Book to a Mother* (not a dialogue, but a text that establishes "an intimate rhetorical relationship" between the author and his mother-addressee, which is then extended to a wider lay audience), and Walter Hilton's *Epistle on the Mixed Life* (displaying an advisory relation between author and addressee). All these works can be described as conversations in which "mutual affection fosters the growth of clerical understanding." All three precede Arundel's constitutions of 1407–9 and hence they illustrate the complexity of the debate on scriptural access and offer relatively open positions on this matter. Importantly, all three are conceived "to reshape traditional relations between learners and teachers" (80).

Working independently, both Rice and Jessica Brantley have identified the dialogue as what seems the central formal mode employed in the late medieval cultural shift from religious to lay reading. Brantley's book *Reading in the Wilderness: Private Devotion and Public Performance in Late Medieval England* (Chicago, 2007) examined London, British Library MS Additional 37049, a Carthusian manuscript that, like Rice's texts, illustrates the passage of monastic reading into lay possession. The scribe of the manuscript several times converted his texts into dialogues between two persons and illustrated them marginally with two speaking figures. One might see registered here both verbally and visually the participation by laity in monastic religious culture—a participation not entirely unproblematic, since the dialogues contain questions and challenges.

Throughout her book, Rice is concerned to make visible not only how reading was shared, but how authority was. In one of the book's most striking sections, she juxtaposes two female participants in the preaching tradition: the Wife of Bath, who is called "self-interested," and the addressee of *Book to a Mother*, whose chaste widowhood, in cooperation with the parish priest (her son, the author, is presumed to be a member of the regular clergy), can constitute an exemplary state for all. Thus in Rice's terms, the "preaching widow" opposes the "clerical widow." The *Book* daringly adopts the Wycliffite position, advising that with good living all men and women can preach, but the author defuses it by adding "for oure Ladi was þe beste prechour þat euer was, saue Crist, and ȝut sche spak but fewe wordis. Þus modur, preache þou, desiringe alle men to do þus" (125)—that is, first do, then preach. Rice claims that *Book to a Mother* shows the possibility of an embodied lay authority alongside the official clerical one, but we might wonder if what is being offered women is so very different from Thomas Aquinas's strictures, cited by

Rice, which allowed women to teach but only privately. As *Book to a Mother* puts it, "tellinge hem þat liueþ wiþ þe, wiþ goode desires of þin herte or wiþ goode wordis or wiþ goode werkis" (123).

Rice concludes her book by examining *in toto* the contents of four manuscripts that contain the individual works she has discussed earlier. Here she succeeds in showing how various were the pre-1400 positions on these central topics: enclosure as a spiritual practice, lay pastoral care, and—most important—preaching and teaching. Oxford, Bodleian Library MS Laud 210, for instance, includes not only *Life of Soul* and *Book to a Mother,* works Rice has classed as reformist, but (added later) the conservative *Abbey of the Holy Ghost,* plus a series of catechetical guides and a Wycliffite tract. Does the manuscript embody a position? Only, perhaps, what Vincent Gillespie has suggested: that all its elements might be called "forms of living."

In her examination of these forms of living, these spiritual and literary texts, Rice is able to make her readers see freshly both the texts themselves and the cultural situation that produced them, marked by the absolute primacy it accorded the ideal of religious life. Yet these writings also show the beginnings of attempts to shift that ideal somewhat, though "without undermining priestly intellectual, pastoral, and penitential power" (x). Rice's subtle and imaginative construction of this historic moment has produced a deeply interesting view of its struggles and accommodations over the possession of spiritual authority.

MARY C. ERLER
Fordham University

LARRY SCANLON, ed. *The Cambridge Companion to Medieval English Literature, 1100–1500.* Cambridge: Cambridge University Press, 2009. Pp. xix, 294. £45; $80 cloth, £17.99; $29.99 paper.

In many ways, the field of medieval English literary studies was redefined in 1999 by *The Cambridge History of Medieval English Literature,* edited by David Wallace. Iconoclastic in its toppling of the evolutionary model of literary history, in which a very few authors' stars shone in the medieval darkness, the *History* also erected a multicultural, polyglot, formally diverse Middle English as a field of weight in its own right, an argument underscored by the monumentality of the book itself, with nearly eleven hundred pages and weighing in at over 3.5 pounds. Since that volume's appearance a decade ago, we have seen at least nine other histories and companions to Middle English literature, not to mention the many casebooks and guides devoted to single authors or particular genres (I know of eight published on Chaucer alone, and there may well be more). This is an abundance of riches, and the growth of such guides seems to attest to a flourishing field. More cynically, this number might suggest that publishers are more interested in channeling their resources into the lucrative market of guides for entry-level readers and undergraduate libraries than into furthering more specialized scholarship. But this proliferation does prompt the question: Do we really need another such resource book like *The Cambridge Companion to Medieval English Literature* at this moment?

The answer rests with what we want in a companion (an answer, alas, that can be as contradictory in reference materials as it is in life). Are we students, or perhaps beginning college teachers, needing to hoover up in a hurry the basic outlines of a period, a genre, or an author's canon—looking, in short, for a Virgil to offer us instruction and then to lead us out of the dark wood so that we can share what we have seen with others? Do we want a companion to make a journey with us as our friend and confidant, a trusty Achates who helps to do the dirty work—reminds us when exactly Chaucer visited Italy or how the C-text diverges from the B-text—but never sets himself up as a rival to the main action? Or are we specialized readers ourselves, seeking a companion to challenge us with further novel speculation and elaboration, knowing that the risk of such a guide is that its pedantry may resemble the long-winded eagle of *The House of Fame?*

Certainly the compactness of *The Cambridge Companion to Middle English Literature* works against any flights of the eagle. And while pretending to understated conservatism—"err[ing] on the side of what seemed conventional wisdom" (6)—this *Companion* is too lively to be considered simply a second-in-command. Instead, it is a true guide, efficiently orienting advanced undergraduates/graduates/new instructors in the terrain of current literary study of Middle English. The *Companion* is divided into two sections. "Part I: Contexts, Genres, and Traditions" begins by providing two different ways to locate late medieval literature, linguistically in the status of Middle English as a vernacular (Wendy Scase) and socially in the milieu of patrons and readers of Middle English texts (Richard Firth Green). Cogent introductions to genres follow, including religious writing (Richard Newhauser); romance (Christine Chism); dialogue, debate, and dream literature (Steven Kruger); drama (Sarah Beckwith); lyric (Ardis Butterfield); and Lollard writings (Rita Copeland). "Part II: Authors" then introduces readers to William Langland (Ralph Hanna), the *Gawain*-poet (Sarah Stanbury), John Gower (Diane Watt), Geoffrey Chaucer (Larry Scanlon), Julian of Norwich (Lynn Staley), Thomas Hoccleve (Ethan Knapp), John Lydgate (James Simpson), Margery Kempe (Rebecca Krugg), Sir Thomas Malory (David Wallace), and Robert Henryson (Sally Mapstone).

The expectation is that these essays should provide a double focus, a summary of major issues as well as a gesturing to critical cruces left unresolved. On the whole, the contributors deliver this. Kruger gives an excellent overview of sources and critical approaches to the dream vision; Chism creates order upon the unwieldy, errant body of romances through different taxonomies based on style, sources, and audience; Newhauser valiantly offers coherence to what the editor admits is a "catch-all" chapter, ranging from hagiography and devotional works to confessional manuals and other *pastoralia*. But the risk in the chapters of Part 1 is that we are given a hurried list of texts, some flitting past as title alone.

Understandably, the narrower compass set by the chapters devoted to single authors allows for more depth. Simpson deftly itemizes the standard criticisms in Lydgate's reception as well as the features that ought to make the poet a promising subject for future study, and then gives two fresh close readings that point outward to larger themes. Wallace cleverly navigates the entire *Morte Darthur* while also giving tastes of individual incidents by focusing on "the contradictions and specious wordplay that uphold [Malory's] Arthurian society" (238). And somehow Scanlon is able to bring something fresh to an introduction on Chaucer, wisely using the weight of Chaucer's authority to spark a discussion of his career and influence.

It is also refreshing to encounter not just wisdom but joy. Stanbury evokes well the sense of wonder the *Gawain*-poet exudes in his beautifully intricate narratives. Beckwith's unadulterated enthusiasm for the Towneley cycle or *Mankind* does in miniature what the best companions should do: it encourages the reader to return to the original with fresh energy. The editor should be commended for assembling a dream team in his contributors, for it is lovely to get a pithy statement on Langland from Hanna or Lollards from Copeland, without it feeling like a retread of past work.

As a collection, this volume seems a bit of a departure from the typical *Cambridge Companion* formats. Usually those books are either devoted to particular authors or specific genres. "Medieval English Literature" is neither; in fact, each of those individual words of the title generates its own set of critical challenges. What period of "medieval" are we discussing? The title page states 1100–1500, but, on closer inspection, the time-spread is even narrower, 1350–1500. Granted, 1066 does make a linguistic break as well as a political one, but we do then consign to the shadows the very rich—one might say, relative to what was happening literarily on the Continent, significantly richer—period of Old English. Similarly, what exactly is "English" literature? Several authors—Scase, Chism, and Butterfield, as well as the editor in his Introduction— recognize the trilingual nature of England in this period, but even with that acknowledgment this volume is about literature written in Middle English, not simply written within England, or by English people. (That said, a special chapter for Middle Scots poet Robert Henryson, and not, by extension, Middle Scots poets King James I, William Dunbar, or Gavin Douglas, seems rather odd.) And finally, what, precisely, are we calling "literature"? Pastoral and Lollard writings have fruitfully been the subjects of scholarly vigor in the last thirty years, but *The Layfolks' Catechism* and *Jacob's Well* are not literature. Similarly, Julian of Norwich and Margery Kempe quite justifiably receive their own chapters, but neither would have considered her text as being literary in the way that Chaucer, Gower, or the *Gawain*-poet (much less most modern readers) would have. If we are going to throw open the door to mystical theologians as literature, then why not provide a chapter for the *Cloud*-author, Walter Hilton, or Richard Rolle? Why not give hagiographers John Capgrave or Osbern Bokenham a chapter of their own?

But these are minor quibbles. A simple title change to "Middle English" would obviate most of them. These questions speak not so much to these editorial decisions as to the practicalities of teaching medieval literature today. Julian and Margery, for instance, along with their many merits as writers and thinkers, are also very likely to appear on syllabi due to the growth of interest in women writers. Similarly, the inclusion of Henryson alone among the Middle Scots authors must rest in part with the likelihood of *The Testament of Cresseid* being taught alongside Chaucer's *Troilus*.

Moreover, the editor is correct that "it is hard to deny, as brute philological fact, the profusion of writing in English after 1300 and the marked increase after 1350. From a more literary standpoint, it is equally hard to deny that the period before 1350 offers little of the array of major individual authors which we can find in the period afterward" (3). But it is also a brute fact that *Sir Orfeo*, much less *The Wanderer*, is much harder for students (and instructors not trained as medievalists) to read in the original.

This observation about "major individual authors" points to another welcome feature of the *Companion*: its unapologetic celebration of the author, which challenges the picture of the field painted by the *Cambridge History* ten years ago. We are once again reminded that Middle English does have its great authors, several of them in fact, although the *Cambridge Companion* balances this with other critical approaches, particularly in Butterfield's elegant discussion of lyric.

Perhaps the only disappointment of the *Companion*, then, is that, as when Virgil abruptly departs at the summiting of Mount Purgatory, we are left wanting more: more space in the roundup chapters to allow for close reading; more chapters, so that other authors or anonymous masterpieces might find a place somewhere in the volume; more pages for discussing the contexts of Middle English literature, so that the role of patronage and the state of literacy might more fully be addressed.

KAREN GROSS
Lewis & Clark College

WINTHROP WETHERBEE. *The Ancient Flame: Dante and the Poets*. Notre Dame: University of Notre Dame Press, 2008. Pp. xii, 304. $35.00 paper.

In *The Ancient Flame: Dante and the Poets,* Winthrop Wetherbee argues that Dante's *Commedia* reflects direct, unmediated reading of the Latin *Poeti*—Virgil, Lucan, Ovid, and Statius—and that Dante's poetic power derives in great part from his imaginatively participating in their tragic understanding of the human world as conditioned by inescapable destiny and loss. Such an experience is a necessary precondition to assimilating and finally emulating their poetry, but as recorded in the poem,

Dante's encounter with these poets is fraught with spiritual and poetic dangers: the bleak moral vision formulated by them has the potential to engulf Dante and prevent his development of an authentic voice. Nevertheless, the tension between Dante's sense of absolute difference from his models and his dependence on them as poetic masters is crucial to his artistic development, and Dante's engagement with them "defines a process of self-discovery that is in effect an existential counterpart to the spiritual journey which is his primary theme" (4). In the *Inferno*, where ancient poetry most resists his appropriation, Dante's poetry registers the degree to which he at times succumbs to the power of Virgil and, more ominously, Lucan. *Purgatorio* and *Paradiso* show Dante's increasing ability to construct a poetry that is faithful both to the best aspirations of his models and his own vocation as a Christian, vernacular poet.

Chapter 1 opens these matters by comparing the description of Camille's tomb in the Old French *Eneas* with Dante's episode of Paolo and Francesca (*Inferno* V). Both resonate with dense echoes of Virgil's *Aeneid*, especially the death of Dido, and both balance epic against romance. But *Inferno* V, which demonstrates the limits of romance in light of Dido, is only an initial stage in Dante's complex encounter with Virgil and his Roman successors, who offer Dante distinctive yet linked perspectives: Virgil, whose *Aeneid* Dante experiences as a "compelling and authoritative" narrative of sacred history (16); Lucan, whose bitterness about Roman destiny in the *Pharsalia* underpins Dante's own questioning of Virgilian authority; Ovid, whose approach to metamorphosis may have instructed Dante's own more probing explorations; Statius, whose epic admits but fails to integrate the private and spiritual within his pagan context. In contrast to typological critics or those who read classical echoes in Dante's works by means of medieval grammarians or mythographers, Wetherbee aims to show how Dante experienced and mastered an authorizing tradition that was nevertheless historically alienated from his own.

The remaining chapters of the book examine in more detail the stages by which Dante comes to terms with these models, "the depth to which his allusions plumb the archive of poetic knowledge embodied in their texts" (23), with different *Poeti* represented at successive moments of Dante's journey. Virgil and Lucan dominate *Inferno*. So Chapter 2 demonstrates the "power of the remembered *Aeneid* to shape Dante's experience" (37) in the early cantos of *Inferno*. In Canto III, for instance, when he appropriates Virgil's comparison of damned souls to autumn leaves, Dante incorporates himself into the image as the bough that "sees all its spoils upon the ground" (III.113–14). Dante's Virgilian language shows him imaginatively experiencing damnation, to the point that he risks losing his sense of "the sustaining love of God" (37), represented by Beatrice, and subjects himself to the intense psychological confusion dramatized by his loss of consciousness. Virgil, then, is not simply an agent sent by Beatrice to help in Dante's salvation, or a voice of Roman triumphal destiny, but a source of Dante's participation in the limits of paganism and alienation. Virgil's authority is itself limited, yet challenging Virgil may draw Dante into the excesses modeled by the poetry of another epic writer, Lucan. Chapter 3 examines the relation between Virgil and Lucan, a connection exemplified in Dante's fable of Virgil's summoning by Lucan's Erichtho. In Lucan's *Pharsalia,* the witch provides a way for Lucan to express his religious skepticism, his despair at the end of republican Rome, and his repudiation of Virgil's vision of Roman history. Dante's version of Erichtho introduces Lucan's radical pessimism and his artistic energy to the *Inferno,* where he "sanctions an indulgence of anger and an emphasis on horror and the grotesque for which Vergil offers no precedent" (63). Erichtho enters the scene at Inferno IX, though Dante's succumbing to a Lucanian mode is most visible in the cruel metamorphoses of *Inferno* XXIV and XXV, while his progress as an artist and pilgrim, his transformation of his models, is measured by Dante's handling of Ulysses and Ugolino. Chapter 4 presents *Purgatorio*'s opening canto as a final salute to Lucan; thus Dante's Cato is as rigid and egocentric as Lucan's, but through this figure Dante finally attributes to Lucan a spiritual capacity denied fulfillment by his historical setting.

If Cato is a figure in stasis, and his canto a "coda" to *Inferno,* the remaining cantos of the *Purgatorio* are devoted to transformation. The poets treated here are Virgil and two *Poeti* only touched on in *Inferno,* Ovid and Statius. Chapter 5 begins with Ovid, whose approach to metamorphoses underpins Dante's. In *Purgatorio,* Ovidian narratives are rewritten and resolved in spiritual terms: so the narrative of Jacopo del Cassero's flight leads him to a moment of recognition and repentance evoking Ovid's episode of Narcissus, but without its despairing outcome. Moreover, from Ovid, Dante learns to trust his imaginative faculty, even as he moves beyond Virgil, who increasingly represents a static poetic tradition. Chapter 6 examines the figure of Statius, whose

Thebaid presents a conflict-ridden world governed by malign powers. His "history" struggles, nevertheless, to articulate spiritual values new to epic tradition. Hypsipyle, in particular, represents the "divided vision of human life" in the poem (186), a woman of great humanity who nevertheless is subject to a violent historical narrative that leaves her desiring only death. In this she represents her creator, and, Wetherbee argues, just as Statius delivers her providentially from slavery, so Dante delivers his own character, Statius, and endows him with a narrative that justifies his epic in a spiritual sense. Chapter 7 ends *Purgatorio* by examining, in the Terrace of Lust and the Earthly Paradise, the refinement of desire in the exercise of poetry, a process beginning with the lustful, continuing with Matelda, and concluded only after Beatrice plays Iarbas to Dante's Dido. In the final chapter, on *Paradiso*, Wetherbee finds allusions to all the *Poeti*, most importantly Virgil, though Ovid, too, is clearly important for Dante's mature poetic vision. In this final stage of the journey, "imaginative desire is transformed into spiritual aspiration" (239), while human poetry attains its limit—a point made even as Dante invokes Boethius and Horace, and revises his own Virgilian epic simile of *Inferno* III, now comparing the separation of leaves from bough to the transitory nature of human language.

This is a richly suggestive and generous book with much to say about Latin epic tradition, about recent classical scholarship, about Dante and his readers. Its sweeping argument is anchored by evocative readings of individual passages, each leading to new and fruitful ways of considering both the *Commedia* and the poems informing it. Although Wetherbee does not organize his chapters around them, his references to female characters emblematic of their authors' artistic and ethical concerns are especially thought-provoking—Dido, for Virgil (but also, tantalizingly, Amata); Erichtho for Lucan; Philomela (among others) for Ovid; Hypsipyle for Statius. Further, the book demonstrates how a modern reader may value the classical tradition while rejecting the violent heroic values that it has been thought to advocate. The book makes a fine addition to Notre Dame's William and Katherine Devers Series in Dante Studies and its helpfulness to readers of Dante is enhanced by extensive footnotes, an index, and lists of passages cited from the *Poeti* and the *Commedia*.

REBECCA S. BEAL
The University of Scranton

Books Received

Aers, David. *Salvation and Sin: Augustine, Langland, and the Fourteenth Century*. Notre Dame: University of Notre Dame Press, 2009. Pp. 304. $38.00 paper.

Archibald, Elizabeth, and Ad Putter, eds. *The Cambridge Companion to the Arthurian Legend*. Cambridge: Cambridge University Press, 2009. Pp. xx, 261. $90.00; $28.99 paper.

Barański, Zygmunt G., and Theodore J. Cachey Jr., eds. *Petrarch and Dante: Anti-Dantism, Metaphysics, Tradition*. Notre Dame: University of Notre Dame Press, 2009. Pp. xii, 414. $42.50 paper.

Boenig, Robert, and Andrew Taylor, eds. *The Canterbury Tales: A Selection*. Peterborough, Ontario: Broadview Press, 2009. Pp. lviii, 400. $19.95 paper.

Borroff, Marie, and Laura L. Howes, eds., Marie Borroff, trans. *Sir Gawain and the Green Knight*. New York: W. W. Norton, 2010. Pp. xxix, 237. $22.00.

Butterfield, Ardis. *The Familiar Enemy: Chaucer, Language, and Nation in the Hundred Years War*. Oxford: Oxford University Press, 2009. Pp. xxx, 444. £60.00; $99.00.

Copeland, Rita, and Ineke Sluiter, eds. *Medieval Grammar and Rhetoric: Language Arts and Literary Theory, AD 300–1475*. Oxford: Oxford University Press, 2009. Pp. xii, 972. £95.00; $175.00.

Correale, Robert M., and Mary Hamel, eds. *Sources and Analogues of the Canterbury Tales II*. Cambridge: D. S. Brewer, 2009. Pp. xvi, 824 paper. £30.00; $60.00.

Davis, Kathleen, and Nadia Altschul, eds. *Medievalisms in the Postcolonial World: The Idea of "the Middle Ages" Outside Europe*. Baltimore: Johns Hopkins University Press, 2009. Pp. 456. $70.00.

Fellows, Jennifer, and Ivana Djordjević, eds. *Sir Bevis of Hampton in Literary Tradition*. Woodbridge: Boydell and Brewer, 2008. Pp. xii, 207. £50.00; $95.00

Finke, Laurie A., and Martin B. Shichtman, eds. *Cinematic Illuminations: The Middle Ages on Film*. Baltimore: Johns Hopkins University Press, 2009. Pp. 464. $60.00 cloth; $30.00 paper.

Goodall, Peter. *Chaucer's Monk's Tale and Nun's Priest's Tale: An Annotated Bibliography, 1900–2000*. The Chaucer Bibliographies. Toronto: University of Toronto Press, 2009. Pp. xlviii, 338. $110.00.

Hanna, Ralph, ed. *Speculum Vitae: A Reading Edition*. 2 vols. EETS o.s. 331. Oxford: Oxford University Press, 2008. Pp. xcvi, 674. £70.00; $150.00.

Hazell, Dinah. *Poverty in Late Middle English Literature: The* Meene *and the* Riche. Dublin: Four Courts Press, 2009. Pp. 233. €49.50; $70.00.

Jefferson, Judith, and Ad Putter, eds. *Approaches to the Metres of Alliterative Verse*. Leeds: Leeds Texts and Monographs n.s. 17, 2009. Pp. 311. £40.00.

Kaeuper, Richard W. *Holy Warriors: The Religious Ideology of Chivalry*. Philadelphia: University of Pennsylvania Press, 2009. Pp. xi, 331. $59.95.

Kaufman, Alexander L. *The Historical Literature of the Jack Cade Rebellion*. Farnham: Ashgate, 2009. Pp. ix, 231. £55.00; $99.95.

Kerby-Fulton, Kathryn, ed. *Women and the Divine in Literature Before 1700: Essays in Memory of Margot Louis*. Victoria: ELS Editions, 2009. Pp. xi, 279. $30.00 paper.

Murphy, Michael, and James Clawson. *Companion to Medieval English Literature: Some Themes, Motifs, and Conventions*. New York: Conal and Gavin, 2009. Pp. 240. $14.95 paper.

Patterson, Lee. *Acts of Recognition: Essays on Medieval Culture*. Notre Dame: University of Notre Dame Press, 2009. Pp. xii, 356. $38.00 paper.

Rigby, S. H. *Wisdom and Chivalry: Chaucer's "Knight's Tale" and Medieval Political Theory*. Leiden: Brill, 2009. Pp. xvi, 329. €114.00; $169.00.

Somerset, Fiona, ed. *Four Wycliffite Dialogues*. EETS o.s. 333. Oxford: Oxford University Press, 2009. Pp. lxxi, 151. £110.00; $60.00.

Travis, Peter W. *Disseminal Chaucer: Rereading "The Nun's Priest's Tale."* Notre Dame: University of Notre Dame Press, 2010. Pp. xi, 443. $40.00.

Urban, Malte, ed. *John Gower: Manuscripts, Readers, Contexts*. Turnhout: Brepols, 2009. Pp. xii, 242. €60.00; $87.00.

Vázquez, Nila, ed. and trans. *The "Tale of Gamelyn" of the "Canterbury Tales": An Annotated Edition*. Lewiston, N.Y.: Edwin Mellen Press, 2009. Pp. vi, 466. $129.95.

An Annotated Chaucer Bibliography, 2008

Compiled and edited by Mark Allen and Bege K. Bowers

Regular contributors:

Anne Thornton, *Abbot Public Library* (Marblehead, Massachusetts)
Michelle Allen and Stephen Jones, *Ball State University* (Indiana)
George Nicholas, *Benedictine College* (Kansas)
Debra Best, *California State University at Dominguez Hills*
Gregory M. Sadlek, *Cleveland State University* (Ohio)
David Sprunger, *Concordia College* (Minnesota)
Winthrop Wetherbee, *Cornell University* (New York)
Elaine Whitaker, *Georgia College & State University*
Elizabeth Dobbs, *Grinnell College* (Iowa)
Andrew James Johnston, *Humboldt-Universität zu Berlin*
Teresa P. Reed, *Jacksonville State University* (Alabama)
William Snell, *Keio University* (Japan)
Denise Stodola, *Kettering University* (Michigan)
Brian A. Shaw, *London, Ontario*
William Schipper, *Memorial University* (Newfoundland, Canada)
Martha Rust, *New York University*
Warren S. Moore III, *Newberry College* (South Carolina)
Cindy L. Vitto, *Rowan College of New Jersey*
Brother Anthony (Sonjae An), *Sogang University* (South Korea)
Ana Saez Hidalgo, *Universidad de Valladolid* (Spain)
Stefania D'Agata D'Ottavi, *Università per Stranieri di Siena* (Italy)
Martine Yvernault, *Université de Limoges*
R. D. Eaton, *Universiteit van Amsterdam* (The Netherlands)
Cynthia Ho, *University of North Carolina, Asheville*
Margaret Connolly, *University of St. Andrews* (Scotland)
Rebecca Beal, *University of Scranton* (Pennsylvania)
Mark Allen and R. L. Smith, *University of Texas at San Antonio*

John M. Crafton, *West Georgia College*
Bege K. Bowers, *Youngstown State University* (Ohio)

Ad hoc contributions were made by several contributors at the Freie Universität Berlin: Sven Duncan Durie, Philipp Hinz, Elisabeth Kempf, and Mareen Liske; and by Nathan Philip Hauser of Georgia College & State University. The bibliographers acknowledge with gratitude the MLA typesimulation provided by the Center for Bibliographical Services of the Modern Language Association; postage from the University of Texas at San Antonio Department of English; and assistance from the library staff, especially Susan McCray, at the University of Texas at San Antonio.

This bibliography continues the bibliographies published since 1975 in previous volumes of *Studies in the Age of Chaucer*. Bibliographic information up to 1975 can be found in Eleanor P. Hammond, *Chaucer: A Bibliographic Manual* (1908; reprint, New York: Peter Smith, 1933); D. D. Griffith, *Bibliography of Chaucer, 1908–1953* (Seattle: University of Washington Press, 1955); William R. Crawford, *Bibliography of Chaucer, 1954–1963* (Seattle: University of Washington Press, 1967); and Lorrayne Y. Baird, *Bibliography of Chaucer, 1964–1973* (Boston: G. K. Hall, 1977). See also Lorrayne Y. Baird-Lange and Hildegard Schnuttgen, *Bibliography of Chaucer, 1974–1985* (Hamden, Conn.: Shoe String Press, 1988); and Bege K. Bowers and Mark Allen, eds., *Annotated Chaucer Bibliography, 1986–1996* (Notre Dame, Ind.: University of Notre Dame Press, 2002).

Additions and corrections to this bibliography should be sent to Mark Allen, Bibliographic Division, The New Chaucer Society, Department of English, University of Texas at San Antonio 78249-0643 (Fax: 210-458-5366; e-mail: mark.allen@utsa.edu). An electronic version of this bibliography (1975–2007) is available via The New Chaucer Society Web page at http://artsci.wustl.edu/~chaucer/ or directly at http://uchaucer.utsa.edu. Authors are urged to send annotations for articles, reviews, and books that have been or might be overlooked.

Classifications

Abbreviations of Chaucer's Works

ABC	*An ABC*
Adam	*Adam Scriveyn*
Anel	*Anelida and Arcite*
Astr	*A Treatise on the Astrolabe*
Bal Compl	*A Balade of Complaint*
BD	*The Book of the Duchess*
Bo	*Boece*
Buk	*The Envoy to Bukton*
CkT, CkP, Rv–CkL	*The Cook's Tale, The Cook's Prologue, Reeve–Cook Link*
ClT, ClP, Cl–MerL	*The Clerk's Tale, The Clerk's Prologue, Clerk–Merchant Link*
Compl d'Am	*Complaynt d'Amours*
CT	*The Canterbury Tales*
CYT, CYP	*The Canon's Yeoman's Tale, The Canon's Yeoman's Prologue*
Equat	*The Equatorie of the Planetis*
For	*Fortune*
Form Age	*The Former Age*
FranT, FranP	*The Franklin's Tale, The Franklin's Prologue*
FrT, FrP, Fr–SumL	*The Friar's Tale, The Friar's Prologue, Friar–Summoner Link*
Gent	*Gentilesse*
GP	*The General Prologue*
HF	*The House of Fame*
KnT, Kn–MilL	*The Knight's Tale, Knight–Miller Link*
Lady	*A Complaint to His Lady*
LGW, LGWP	*The Legend of Good Women, The Legend of Good Women Prologue*
ManT, ManP	*The Manciple's Tale, The Manciple's Prologue*
Mars	*The Complaint of Mars*
Mel, Mel–MkL	*The Tale of Melibee, Melibee–Monk Link*
MercB	*Merciles Beaute*
MerT, MerE–SqH	*The Merchant's Tale, Merchant Endlink–Squire Headlink*

MilT, MilP, Mil–RvL	The Miller's Tale, The Miller's Prologue, Miller–Reeve Link
MkT, MkP, Mk–NPL	The Monk's Tale, The Monk's Prologue, Monk–Nun's Priest Link
MLT, MLH, MLP, MLE	The Man of Law's Tale, Man of Law Headlink, The Man of Law's Prologue, Man of Law Endlink
NPT, NPP, NPE	The Nun's Priest's Tale, The Nun's Priest's Prologue, Nun's Priest's Endlink
PardT, PardP	The Pardoner's Tale, The Pardoner's Prologue
ParsT, ParsP	The Parson's Tale, The Parson's Prologue
PF	The Parliament of Fowls
PhyT, Phy–PardL	The Physician's Tale, Physician–Pardoner Link
Pity	The Complaint unto Pity
Prov	Proverbs
PrT, PrP, Pr–ThL	The Prioress's Tale, The Prioress's Prologue, Prioress–Thopas Link
Purse	The Complaint of Chaucer to His Purse
Ret	Chaucer's Retraction {Retractation}
Rom	The Romaunt of the Rose
Ros	To Rosemounde
RvT, RvP	The Reeve's Tale, The Reeve's Prologue
Scog	The Envoy to Scogan
ShT, Sh–PrL	The Shipman's Tale, Shipman–Prioress Link
SNT, SNP, SN–CYL	The Second Nun's Tale, The Second Nun's Prologue, Second Nun–Canon's Yeoman Link
SqT, SqH, Sq–FranL	The Squire's Tale, Squire Headlink, Squire–Franklin Link
Sted	Lak of Stedfastnesse
SumT, SumP	The Summoner's Tale, The Summoner's Prologue
TC	Troilus and Criseyde
Th, Th–MelL	The Tale of Sir Thopas, Sir Thopas–Melibee Link
Truth	Truth
Ven	The Complaint of Venus

WBT, WBP, WB–FrL	*The Wife of Bath's Tale, The Wife of Bath's Prologue, Wife of Bath–Friar Link*
Wom Nob	*Womanly Noblesse*
Wom Unc	*Against Women Unconstant*

Periodical Abbreviations

AdI	*Annali d'Italianistica*
Anglia	*Anglia: Zeitschrift für Englische Philologie*
Anglistik	*Anglistik: Mitteilungen des Verbandes deutscher Anglisten*
AnLM	*Anuario de Letras Modernas*
ANQ	*ANQ: A Quarterly Journal of Short Articles, Notes, and Reviews*
Archiv	*Archiv für das Studium der Neueren Sprachen und Literaturen*
Arthuriana	*Arthuriana*
Atlantis	*Atlantis: Revista de la Asociacion Española de Estudios Anglo-Norteamericanos*
AUMLA	*AUMLA: Journal of the Australasian Universities Language and Literature Association*
BAM	*Bulletin des Anglicistes Médiévistes*
BJRL	*Bulletin of the John Rylands University Library of Manchester*
C&L	*Christianity and Literature*
CarmP	*Carmina Philosophiae: Journal of the International Boethius Society*
CE	*College English*
ChauR	*Chaucer Review*
CL	*Comparative Literature* (Eugene, Ore.)
Clio	*CLIO: A Journal of Literature, History, and the Philosophy of History*
CLS	*Comparative Literature Studies*
CML	*Classical and Modern Literature: A Quarterly* (Columbia, Mo.)
CollL	*College Literature*
Comitatus	*Comitatus: A Journal of Medieval and Renaissance Studies*
CRCL	*Canadian Review of Comparative Literature/Revue Canadienne de Littérature Comparée*

DAI	*Dissertation Abstracts International*
DR	*Dalhousie Review*
ÉA	*Études Anglaises: Grand-Bretagne, États-Unis*
EHR	*English Historical Review*
EiC	*Essays in Criticism: A Quarterly Journal of Literary Criticism*
EJ	*English Journal*
ELH	*ELH: English Literary History*
ELN	*English Language Notes*
ELR	*English Literary Renaissance*
EMS	*English Manuscript Studies, 1100–1700*
EMSt	*Essays in Medieval Studies*
Encomia	*Encomia: Bibliographical Bulletin of the International Courtly Literature Society*
English	*English: The Journal of the English Association*
Envoi	*Envoi: A Review Journal of Medieval Literature*
ES	*English Studies*
ESC	*English Studies in Canada*
Exemplaria	*Exemplaria: A Journal of Theory in Medieval and Renaissance Studies*
Expl	*Explicator*
FCS	*Fifteenth-Century Studies*
Florilegium	*Florilegium: Carleton University Papers on Late Antiquity and the Middle Ages*
FMLS	*Forum for Modern Language Studies*
Genre	*Genre: Forms of Discourse and Culture*
H-Albion	*H-Albion: The H-Net Discussion Network for British and Irish History, H-Net Reviews in the Humanities and Social Sciences* http://www.h-net.org/reviews/home.php
HLQ	*Huntington Library Quarterly: Studies in English and American History and Literature* (San Marino, Calif.)
Hortulus	*Hortulus: The Online Graduate Journal of Medieval Studies* http://www.hortulus.net/
IJES	*International Journal of English Studies*
JAIS	*Journal of Anglo-Italian Studies*
JEBS	*Journal of the Early Book Society*
JEGP	*Journal of English and Germanic Philology*

JELL	*Journal of English Language and Literature* (Korea)
JEngL	*Journal of English Linguistics*
JGN	*John Gower Newsletter*
JHiP	*Journal of Historical Pragmatics*
JMEMSt	*Journal of Medieval and Early Modern Studies*
JML	*Journal of Modern Literature*
JNT	*Journal of Narrative Theory*
JRMMRA	*Quidditas: Journal of the Rocky Mountain Medieval and Renaissance Association*
L&LC	*Literary and Linguistic Computing: Journal of the Association for Literary and Linguistic Computing*
L&P	*Literature and Psychology*
L&T	*Literature and Theology: An International Journal of Religion, Theory, and Culture*
Lang&Lit	*Language and Literature: Journal of the Poetics and Linguistics Association*
Lang&S	*Language and Style: An International Journal*
LeedsSE	*Leeds Studies in English*
Library	*The Library: The Transactions of the Bibliographical Society*
LitComp	*Literature Compass* http://www.literaturecompass .com/
MA	*Le Moyen Age: Revue d'Histoire et de Philologie* (Brussels, Belgium)
MÆ	*Medium Ævum*
M&H	*Medievalia et Humanistica: Studies in Medieval and Renaissance Culture*
Manuscripta	*Manuscripta* (St. Louis, Mo.)
Marginalia	*Marginalia: The Journal of the Medieval Reading Group at the University of Cambridge* http:// www.marginalia.co.uk/journal/
Mediaevalia	*Mediaevalia: An Interdisciplinary Journal of Medieval Studies Worldwide*
MedievalF	*Medieval Forum* http://www.sfsu.edu/~medieval/ index.html
MedPers	*Medieval Perspectives*
MES	*Medieval and Early Modern English Studies*
MFF	*Medieval Feminist Forum*
MichA	*Michigan Academician* (Ann Arbor, Mich.)

MLN	Modern Language Notes
MLQ	Modern Language Quarterly: A Journal of Literary History
MLR	The Modern Language Review
MP	Modern Philology: A Journal Devoted to Research in Medieval and Modern Literature
N&Q	Notes and Queries
Neophil	Neophilologus (Dordrecht, Netherlands)
NLH	New Literary History: A Journal of Theory and Interpretation
NM	Neuphilologische Mitteilungen: Bulletin of the Modern Language Society
NML	New Medieval Literatures
NMS	Nottingham Medieval Studies
NOWELE	NOWELE: North-Western European Language Evolution
Parergon	Parergon: Bulletin of the Australian and New Zealand Association for Medieval and Early Modern Studies
PBA	Proceedings of the British Academy
PBSA	Papers of the Bibliographical Society of America
PLL	Papers on Language and Literature: A Journal for Scholars and Critics of Language and Literature
PMAM	Publications of the Medieval Association of the Midwest
PMLA	Publications of the Modern Language Association of America
PoeticaT	Poetica: An International Journal of Linguistic Literary Studies
PQ	Philological Quarterly
RCEI	Revista Canaria de Estudios Ingleses
RenD	Renaissance Drama
RenQ	Renaissance Quarterly
RES	Review of English Studies
RMRev	Reading Medieval Reviews http://www.rdg.ac.uk/ AcaDepts/ln/Medieval/rmr.htm
SAC	Studies in the Age of Chaucer
SAP	Studia Anglica Posnaniensia: An International Review of English
SAQ	South Atlantic Quarterly
SB	Studies in Bibliography: Papers of the Bibliographical Society of the University of Virginia

SCJ	*The Sixteenth-Century Journal: Journal of Early Modern Studies* (Kirksville, Mo.)
SEL	*SEL: Studies in English Literature, 1500–1900*
SELIM	*SELIM: Journal of the Spanish Society for Medieval English Language and Literature*
ShakS	*Shakespeare Studies*
SIcon	*Studies in Iconography*
SiM	*Studies in Medievalism*
SIMELL	*Studies in Medieval English Language and Literature*
SMART	*Studies in Medieval and Renaissance Teaching*
SN	*Studia Neophilologica: A Journal of Germanic and Romance Languages and Literatures*
SoAR	*South Atlantic Review*
SP	*Studies in Philology*
Speculum	*Speculum: A Journal of Medieval Studies*
SSF	*Studies in Short Fiction*
SSt	*Spenser Studies: A Renaissance Poetry Annual*
TCBS	*Transactions of the Cambridge Bibliographical Society*
Text	*Text: Transactions of the Society for Textual Scholarship*
TLS	*Times Literary Supplement* (London, England)
TMR	*The Medieval Review* http://www.hti.umich.edu/t/tmr/
Tr&Lit	*Translation and Literature*
TSLL	*Texas Studies in Literature and Language*
UTQ	*University of Toronto Quarterly: A Canadian Journal of the Humanities* (Toronto, Canada)
Viator	*Viator: Medieval and Renaissance Studies*
WS	*Women's Studies: An Interdisciplinary Journal*
YES	*Yearbook of English Studies*
YWES	*Year's Work in English Studies*
YLS	*The Yearbook of Langland Studies*

Bibliographical Citations and Annotations

Bibliographies, Reports, and Reference

1. Allen, Mark, and Bege K. Bowers. "An Annotated Chaucer Bibliography, 2006." *SAC* 30 (2008): 425–516. Continuation of *SAC* annual annotated bibliography (since 1975); based on contributions from an international bibliographic team, independent research, and *MLA Bibliography* listings. 302 items, plus listing of reviews for 90 books. Includes an author index.

2. Allen, Valerie, and Margaret Connolly. "Later Medieval: Chaucer." *YWES* 87 (2008): 278–313. A discursive bibliography of Chaucer studies for 2006, divided into four subcategories: general, *CT*, *TC*, and other works.

See also nos. 93, 109, 288.

Recordings and Films

3. Bowers, John M. *The Western Literary Canon in Context, Parts I–III.* The Great Courses, no. 2120. Chantilly, Va.: The Teaching Company, 2008. 6 CD-ROMs; 1 booklet; iv, 209 pp. Audiovisual recording of thirty-six lectures by Bowers (on topics ranging from the Bible to Tolkien and postcolonialism), illustrated with occasional still pictures and linguistic examples. One thirty-minute lecture (Lecture 17, "Chaucer— The Father of English Literature") pertains to Chaucer's place in literary tradition, particularly his relationships with medieval Continental literature and his establishment and reception as "father" of English literature. The booklet (pp. 76–80) includes an outline of the lecture, with brief summary and study questions.

4. D'Arcens, Louise. "Deconstruction and the Medieval Indefinite Article: The Undecidable Medievalism of Brian Helgeland's *A Knight's Tale.*" *Parergon* 25.2 (2008): 80–98. D'Arcens addresses Helgeland's film as an entry point for deconstructing medievalist studies. Such studies, she suggests, reflect a latent Platonism that regards the Middle Ages as a stable standard against which to measure texts and contemporary textual adaptations.

5. Dell, Helen. "Past, Present, Future Perfect: Paradigms of History in Medievalism Studies." *Parergon* 25.2 (2008): 58–79. Dell contends that Brian Helgeland's film *A Knight's Tale* offers an alternative to capitalistic perpetual accomplishment, the model of desire that critics associate with the film. This alternative is courtly love, a paradigm drawn from the *Lancelot* of Chrétien de Troyes.

6. Forni, Kathleen. "Popular Chaucer: The BBC's *Canterbury Tales*." *Parergon* 25.1 (2008): 171–89. Forni lauds the BBC's modernized television adaptation of *CT* (2003) for its appeal to a wide audience while retaining fidelity to the original texts; for its intertextuality; and for its highlighting of aspects of Chaucer that appeal to contemporary audiences.

7. Lerer, Seth. "Chaucer's English." *The History of the English Language*. 3 parts. The Great Courses, no. 800. Chantilly, Va.: The Teaching Company, 1998. 6 DVDs or 18 audio CDs. Part 1. Lecture 10. Approx. 17 min. Lerer's lecture on the opening eighteen lines of *GP*, commenting on diction and etymology, verse form, and linguistic conditions at the time. The Teaching Company released a second, revised edition with the same title in 2008 (The Great Courses, no. 2250).

8. ———. "Dialect Jokes and Literary Representation in Middle English." *The History of the English Language*. 3 parts. The Great Courses, no. 800. Chantilly, Va.: The Teaching Company, 1998. 6 DVDs or 18 audio CDs. Part 1. Lecture 11. Approx. 29 min. Seth Lerer's lecture on dialect diversity in Middle English, identifying distinguishing features and examining *RvT* and the *Second Shepherd's Play* for their representations of dialect. The Teaching Company released a second, revised edition with the title "Dialect Representations in Middle English" in 2008 (The Great Courses, no. 2250).

9. Matthews, David. "What the Trumpet Solo Tells Us: A Response." *Parergon* 25.2 (2008): 119–27. Matthews responds to articles about Brian Helgeland's film *A Knight's Tale*, suggesting that medieval studies should be open to medievalism studies, rather than placing the fields in opposition.

10. Nicolson, J. U., trans. *The Canterbury Tales*. Classic Literature. [Ashland, Ore.]: Blackstone Audio, 2008. 17 CD-ROMs. Approx. 21 hrs. Also released by [Solon, Ohio]: Playaway Digital Audio, 2008, on a preloaded digital audio player. "Unabridged" audio recording of Nicolson's 1934 modern English translation of *CT*, narrated by Martin Jarvis and others.

11. Raffel, Burton, trans. *The Canterbury Tales: A New Unabridged Translation*. North Kingston, R.I.: BBC Audiobooks, 2008. Sound Library. 18 CD-ROMs. 22 hrs., 23 min. An audio reading of Raffel's 2008 translation of the complete *CT* (*SAC* 32 [2010], no. 36); disc 1 includes the general introduction by John Miles Foley and Raffel's translator introduction. Six readers narrate the tales: Bill Wallis, Ric Jerrom, Mark Meadows, Cameron Stewart, Maggie Ollerenshaw, and Kim Hicks.

12. Sutherland, John. *Classics of British Literature, Part 1*. The Great Courses, no. 2400. Chantilly, Va.: The Teaching Company, 2008. 2 CD-ROMs. Audiovisual recording of twelve lectures by Sutherland (from Anglo-Saxon roots to *Paradise Lost*), illustrated with occasional still pictures and linguistic examples. Two thirty-minute lectures pertain to Chaucer: Lecture 2, "Chaucer—Social Diversity," concerning *GP* and the linguistic, prosodic, and socioeconomic conditions of Chaucer's time; and Lecture 3, "Chaucer—A Man of Unusual Cultivation," concerning Chaucer's life and career, with commentary on *CT*, especially *KnT*, *MilT*, and *WBPT*.

13. Trigg, Stephanie. "Medievalism and Convergence Culture: Researching the Middle Ages for Fiction and Film." *Parergon* 25.2 (2008): 99–118.Trigg identifies two conflicting motivations for the making of Brian Helgeland's film *A Knight's Tale*: the desire for academic research to provide legitimacy and the desire to create a new fictional narrative to engage a contemporary audience. This and similar popular narratives contribute to the current popular distribution of medieval knowledge, an area of focus for medievalism studies.

See also nos. 15, 216, 336.

Chaucer's Life

14. Bestul, Thomas H. "Did Chaucer Live at 177 Upper Thames Street? The Chaucer Life-Records and the Site of Chaucer's London Home." *ChauR* 43 (2008): 1–15. Bestul reexamines the relevant evidence and shows that Chaucer lived at 179 Upper Thames Street rather than at 177. The study illuminates the history of scholarly politics and of conflicting "historical paradigms" behind the 1966 *Chaucer Life-Records*, pointing to the inevitability of error in such a monumental project.

15. Grahame, Lucia, and Bob Taylor. "Geoffrey Chaucer." *Poets*. Famous People, Incredible Lives. Wheeling, Ill.: Film Ideas, 2008. 1

DVD. Includes biographies of Homer, John Milton, Omar Khayyám, and Chaucer. The latter (approximately seven minutes) comments on Chaucer's life and works, accompanied by visual materials.

See also nos. 12, 170, 299, 317.

Facsimiles, Editions, and Translations

16. Boenig, Robert, and Andrew Taylor, eds. *The Canterbury Tales*, by Geoffrey Chaucer. Broadview Editions. Buffalo, N.Y.: Broadview Press, 2008. 502 pp. 11 b&w illus. Complete text of *CT* newly edited from the Ellesmere manuscript, with an introduction (pp. 9–38), brief bibliography, and eleven "background documents" that include selections from sources and historical records. Glosses to the Middle English are included in the margins to the text, with brief notes at the bottom of the page.

17. Cannon, Christopher. "Foreword to the 2008 Edition." In Larry D. Benson, gen. ed. *The Riverside Chaucer*. Oxford: Oxford University Press, 2008, pp. iva–ivh. Foreword to the reissue of the paperback version of *The Riverside Chaucer*, assessing the legacy of the *Riverside* text in light of editorial theory and modern computers.

18. Courtauld, Sarah, Abigail Wheatley, and Susanna Davidson. *"The Canterbury Tales": From the Story by Geoffrey Chaucer*. Illus. Ian McNee. Usborne Classics Retold. London: Usborne, 2008. 158 pp. Retellings (in prose, unless otherwise noted) of *GP, KnT, MilT, RvT, MLT, WBT, FrT, MerT, SqT, FranT, PardT, Th* (in verse), *NPT, CYT, ManT*, and *Ret*. The book shortens and bowdlerizes the works for an adolescent audience and "tidies up some of the loose ends that Chaucer left hanging" (p. 8). It reorders the sequence of descriptions in *GP*, alters the the narrator and Host, and rewrites the links between tales. Illustrations include black-and-white silhouettes of the pilgrims and characters.

19. Cuddington, Richard, trans. *Chaucer's "Canterbury Tales": In Bite-Size Verse*. Brighton: Book Guild, 2008. x, 500 pp. b&w illus. Verse retelling of selections from *CT* (all but *Mel, SNPT, CYPT, ManPT*, and *ParsPT*) with reduced plots, simplified rhetoric, and modernized English in ballad stanzas. Cuddington adapts the links to unify the selections, which are arranged in the following order: *CT* Parts 1, 2, 7, 6, 3, 4, and 5.

20. Echard, Siân. *Printing the Middle Ages*. Material Texts. Philadelphia: University of Pennsylvania Press, 2008. xvi, 314 pp. Echard studies the "postmedieval life of medieval texts" as they are embodied in material form, exploring strategies for representing the authenticity of the texts and for reimagining them for new audiences. The book includes chapters on design features in editions of *Piers Plowman* and *Pierce the Plowman's Crede*, typographical representations of Old English, illustrations in *Bevis of Hampton* and *Sir Guy of Warwick*, the Trentham manuscript of Gower's works, juvenile adaptations of Chaucer's *CT*, the domesticating of Froissart's *Chroniques* into English, and a coda on "digital avatars of medieval manuscripts" (with comments on the *Canterbury Tales Project*). The chapter on Chaucer explores the role of sentiment in children's versions of *CT*, from Mary Eliza Haweis's *Chaucer for Children* (1877) to the "decline of interest" in such versions in the 1930s.

21. Galbraith, Steven K. "'English' Black-letter Type and Spenser's *Shepheardes Calender*." *SSt* 23 (2008): 13–40. Printing in black-letter type rather than italic was a form of nationalism.

22. Harbus, Antonina. "A Renaissance Reader's English Annotations to Thynne's 1532 Edition of Chaucer's *Works*." *RES* 59 (2008): 342–56. The heavily annotated copy of Thynne held by the Beinecke Rare Book and Manuscript Library at Yale University shows what a sixteenth-century reader found of interest in Chaucer's storytelling, language, and moral vision.

23. Kuskin, William. "'The loadstarre of the English language': Spenser's *Shepheardes Calender* and the Construction of Modernity." *Textual Cultures: Texts, Contexts, Interpretation* 2.2 (2007): 9–33. The prefaces to Spenser's *Shepheardes Calendar* (1579) and to Thomas Speght's *Workes of Chaucer* (1598) share similarities with Lydgate's *Fall of Princes* and thus belie the claims made for a break in continuity with the past in sixteenth-century England, indicating instead a seamless "textual culture" across the period between the Middle Ages and Renaissance.

24. ———. *Symbolic Caxton: Literary Culture and Print Capitalism*. Notre Dame, Ind.: University of Notre Dame Press, 2008. xxvi, 390 pp. Kuskin presents a manifesto on history-of-the-book studies as well as on the need to rethink Chaucerian reception. The volume is divided into three sections: "Capital and Literary Form," "Authorship and the Chaucerian Inheritance," and "Print and Social Organization." The second section includes two chapters: "Chaucerian Inheritances: The Transformation of Lancastrian Literary Culture into the English Canon,"

a succinct history of Caxton's two editions of Chaucer; and "Uninhabitable Chaucer: Patronage and the Commerce in the Self," an argument that Chaucer's canonical status in the fifteenth century made it difficult for new writers to claim Chaucer's legacy.

25. Maciulewicz, Joanna. "Translations and Imitations of Medieval Texts in Neoclassicism: Chaucer as a 'Rough Diamond' That 'Must First Be Polished ere He Shines.'" In Liliana Sikorska, ed., with the assistance of Joanna Maciulewicz. *Medievalisms: The Poetics of Literary Re-Reading*. Studies in English Medieval Language and Literature, no. 21. Frankfurt am Main: Peter Lang, 2008, pp. 113–31. Maciulewicz examines neoclassical rewritings of medieval texts, focusing on Dryden's and Pope's reworking of Chaucer (*CT* and *HF*). Close readings show that eighteenth-century revisions seek to elevate Chaucer to promote national literature and, simultaneously, to polish and/or modernize Chaucer's language for contemporary readers. These rewritings of Chaucer "reveal as much about the time in which they were created as about Chaucer's own period."

26. Núñez Méndez, Eva, ed. *A Spanish Version of Chaucer's "Troilus and Criseyde"/Versión española del "Troili y Criseida" de Chaucer*. Lewiston, N.Y.: Edwin Mellen Press, 2008. iv, 649 pp. Translation of *TC* into modern Spanish, with facing-page copy-text reprint of Barry Windeatt's text of Corpus Christi College, Cambridge University, MS 61. The translation is arranged in stanzas, but without rhyme or regular meter. The introduction (pp. 1–5) comments on *TC* as a translation of Boccaccio's *Filostrato*. The apparatus includes a list of manuscripts, a bibliography (pp. 581–95), and a glossary of Middle English words with brief definitions in modern English and Spanish (pp. 599–649).

27. Stinson, Timothy. "The Rise of English Printing and Decline of Alliterative Verse." *YLS* 22 (2008): 165–97. Pynson's 1492 edition of *CT* illustrates the editor's role in decline of verse forms.

28. Summit, Jennifer. *Memory's Library: Medieval Books in Early Modern England*. Chicago: University of Chicago Press, 2008. x, 343 pp. Investigating the period between 1431 and 1631, Summit argues that libraries—particularly the Parker, the Cotton, and the Bodleian— enabled early modern projects of historical and cultural redefinition concurrent with Reformation ideology and encouraged perceptions of the alterity of the Middle Ages. Methods of acquisition, cataloguing, and textual scholarship directly supported this self-fashioning. Manuscript-based texts such as Thomas Speght's edition of Chaucer's *Works* suggest

the simultaneous inclusion and defamiliarization of the past embedded in the libraries' reinvention of communal memory.

29. Wiggins, Alison. "What Did Renaissance Readers Write in Their Printed Copies of Chaucer?" *Library*, 7th ser., 9 (2008): 3–36. Annotations by sixteenth- and seventeenth-century readers show an ongoing interest in Chaucer as a source of *sententiae* and a focus of antiquarian interest; they also shed light on the role of women readers and on the household as a reading center. Their net effect is to confirm and refine our sense of Chaucer's authority.

30. Wilcockson, Colin, ed. and trans. *"The Canterbury Tales": A Selection*. London: Penguin, 2008. li, 585 pp. Prose translations of *GP*, *KnT*, *MilPT*, *RvPT*, *WBPT*, *ClPT*, *MerPT* (and epilogue), *FranPT*, *PardPT*, and *NPPT*, with Middle English texts from *The Riverside Chaucer* on facing pages. Includes bottom-of-page explanatory notes, a chronology, and an introduction (pp. ix–li), with commentary on the selections and on the translation, along with suggestions for further reading. The Caxton woodcuts accompany the selections.

See also nos. 34, 47, 164, 191, 192, 204, 227, 237, 242, 278, 287.

Manuscripts and Textual Studies

31. Clermont-Ferrand, Meredith, ed. *Jean d'Angoulême's Copy of "The Canterbury Tales": An Annotated Edition of Bibliothèque Nationale's Fonds Anglais 39 (Paris)*. Lewiston, N.Y.: Edwin Mellen Press, 2008. xxxv, 473 pp. Clermont-Ferrand edits d'Angoulême's copy of *CT*, providing continuous lineation (15,080 lines), sidebar glossing, and bottom-of-page explanatory notes. The introduction (pp. vii–xxxv) comments on editing a "bad" copy of *CT*, various exemplars of the fifteenth-century manuscript known as Paris *fonds anglais* 39, its additions and deletions, John Duxworth as scribe, and d'Angoulême as patron, explaining the importance of the manuscript to the "variorum" tradition of editing *CT*.

32. Connolly, Margaret, and Linne R. Mooney, eds. *Design and Distribution of Late Medieval Manuscripts in England*. Manuscript Culture in the British Isles. York: York Medieval Press, 2008. xiii, 336 pp. Thirteen essays by various authors, with a brief introduction by the editors. The collection treats English scribes, manuscripts, and the production and circulation of texts from 1350 to 1600. Addressing design and *CT*, the

first section contains three essays that focus on early copyists of the poem; see nos. 33, 35, and 40.

33. Kato, Takako. "Corrected Mistakes in Cambridge University Library MS Gg.4.27." In Margaret Connolly and Linne R. Mooney, eds. *Design and Distribution of Late Medieval Manuscripts in England* (*SAC* 32 [2010], no. 32), pp. 61–87. Kato assesses accuracy of the text of *CT* that appears in Cambridge University Library MS Gg.4.27. Quantifies and categorizes the scribe's errors, paying particular attention to the mistakes that the scribe himself corrected.

34. Meyer-Lee, Robert J. "Manuscript Studies, Literary Value, and the Object of Chaucer Studies." *SAC* 30 (2008): 1–37. Interrogates the "ghost of judgment" that haunts the study of Chaucerian manuscripts as well as formalist analysis of Chaucer's works, commenting on implications for editing and teaching.

35. Mosser, Daniel W. " 'Chaucer's Scribe,' Adam, and the Hengwrt Project." In Margaret Connolly and Linne R. Mooney, eds. *Design and Distribution of Late Medieval Manuscripts in England* (*SAC* 32 [2010], no. 32), pp. 11–40. Considers whether the Hengwrt manuscript (Aberystwyth, National Library of Wales, MS Peniarth 392D) of *CT* was produced during Chaucer's lifetime. Mosser finds conflicting evidence of authorial involvement among corrections to the text, particularly in regard to ordering of the tales.

36. Raffel, Burton, trans. *The Canterbury Tales*. New York: Modern Library, 2008. xxxvii, 626 pp. Modern English translation of *CT* (based on Robinson's second edition), following Chaucer's prose and pentameter and modernizing his syntax. Raffel relies on off-rhymes, slant-rhymes, and blank verse to approximate Chaucer's couplets and other verse forms and uses occasional accent marks to encourage rhythm. Some names of the pilgrims are modernized (the Franklin is the "Landowner," the Manciple is the "Provisioner," etc.). Brief informational notes appear at the back of the book (pp. 599–626); an introduction by John Miles Foley (pp. xv–xxvii) emphasizes Chaucer's innovation and diversity. See also nos. 11 and 410.

37. Reis, Huriye. "*The Canterbury Tales* in Turkish: A Cultural Translation." *Çeviribilim ve Uygulamaları Dergisi* (Journal of Translation Studies, Hacettepe University) 11 (2001): 47–58 (in English, with English and Turkish abstracts). Two translations of Chaucerian works into Turkish—*GP* (1993), by Barçin Erol, and *CT* (1994), by Nazim Ağil— illustrate the "cultural approximation necessitated by the act of

translation." Reis assesses specific passages from these translations, focusing on matters such as diction, proverbial expressions, and cultural expectations.

38. Tavormina, M. Teresa, ed. *Sex, Aging, and Death in a Medieval Medical Compendium: Trinity College Cambridge MS R.14.52, Its Text, Language, and Scribe*. Medieval and Renaissance Texts and Studies, no. 292. Tempe: ACMRS (Arizona Center for Medieval and Renaissance Studies), 2006. 2 vols. xxvi, 930 pp. Edition and comprehensive study of Trinity College, Cambridge, MS R.14.52, which was produced by the Hammond scribe. Includes five essays by various authors on physical features of the manuscript, an edition in ten sections by various editors, topical discussion of each section, a glossary of medical terminology, and an index to the discussions. Recurrent references to Chaucer, especially his medical and scientific knowledge. See no. 283.

39. Thaisen, Jacob. "The Merchant, the Squire, and Gamelyn in the Christ Church Chaucer Manuscript." *N&Q* 253 (2008): 265–69. Oxford, Christ Church College, MS 152 encloses *Gamelyn* in an inserted quire and supplies the long ending of *MerT* and Link 17 on substitute bifolia. Considered in relation to corresponding "fault lines" in Hengwrt and Ellesmere, this evidence suggests that these texts were present at the beginning of the manuscript tradition of *CT*.

40. ———. "The Trinity Gower D Scribe's Two *Canterbury Tales* Manuscripts Revisited." In Margaret Connolly and Linne R. Mooney, eds. *Design and Distribution of Late Medieval Manuscripts in England* (*SAC* 32 [2010], no. 32), pp. 41–60. Linguistic analysis of the two copies of *CT* made by the copyist known as "Scribe D" (Oxford, Corpus Christi College, MS 198, and British Library MS Harley 7334). Thaisen focuses on orthography, especially the distribution of common lemmata, and comments on codicological aspects, including the placing of *SqT*.

See also nos. 20, 289, 328, 329.

Sources, Analogues, and Literary Relations

41. Azinfar, Fatemeh Chehregosha. "Usurping the Voice of Authority: Chaucer's Reply to Dante." In *Atheism in the Medieval Islamic and European World: The Influence of Persian and Arabic Ideas of Doubt and Skepticism on Medieval European Literary Thought*. Bethesda, Md.: Ibex Publishers, 2008, pp. 233–65. Azinfar reads the comic treatment of Dante

in *HF* as a skeptical rejection of religious authority and discusses depictions of theological contradiction in *Mars*, *Venus*, and *WBP*. Chaucer's rationalism aligns him with other skeptics and atheists, medieval and modern.

42. Boitani, Piero. *Letteratura europea e medioevo volgare*. Bologna: Il Mulino, 2007. 537 pp. Medieval vernacular literature, which inherits and deeply reelaborates themes and modes of Latin culture, is at the origin of "European" literary production. Italy followed soon after France in establishing a vernacular literary tradition, anchored by the great personalities and the artistic achievements of Dante, Petrarch, and Boccaccio. The new vernacular works adapt *topoi*, characters, and genres of classical tradition, modifying some fundamental images and concepts such as the cavern, the temple, the labyrinth, and, especially important, fame. The vitality and impact of Italian medieval culture are evident in that culture's ongoing influence, from Chaucer to twentieth-century poets (Pound and Eliot) and beyond.

43. Justman, Stewart. "The Secularism of Fiction: A Medieval Source." *Literary Imagination* 10 (2008): 127–41. Justman considers the transmission of Eastern narratives (especially Petrus Alphonsi's *Disciplina Clerica*, but also *Thousand and One Nights* narratives) to Western Europe—particularly to Boccaccio and Chaucer—exploring how the "category of fiction" took shape and separated from religious propaganda. The Crusades established the cultural contact, but "good stories," untrammeled by claims of historical or moral authenticity, "showed the impossibility of reducing others to fixed types."

44. Spencer, Alice. *Dialogues of Love and Government: A Study of the Erotic Dialogue Form in Some Texts from the Courtly Love Tradition*. Newcastle: Cambridge Scholars, 2007. x, 234 pp. 3 b&w illus. Studies the "Boethian dialogue model in literature concerned with courtly love," treating the literature as examples of dialogue rather than dream vision and examining the relationship between the hierarchical, upward-leading erotics of this literature and its worldly, political implications and applications. Considers the Platonic, Augustinian roots of form and theme in Boethius's *Consolation of Philosophy* and the pervasive influence of the treatise on Dante and on French and English writers—Machaut, Froissart, Usk, Gower, the *Pearl*-poet, and more. Discusses narcissism and the dream of Morpheus in *BD* and assesses autocratic power and the *marguerite* tradition in *LGWP*. Chaucer's poems explore ironies.

45. Williams, Deanne. "Boethius Goes to Court: The *Consolatio* as

Advice to Princes from Chaucer to Elizabeth I." In Catherine E. Léglu and Stephen J. Milner, eds. *The Erotics of Consolation: Desire and Distance in the Late Middle Ages* (*SAC* 32 [2010], no. 124), pp. 205–26. Williams considers adaptation of the *Consolatio* for courtly audiences in a number of works, including *HF*, *WBT*, and the "oft overlooked Boethian poems" *Form Age, For, Truth, Sted,* and *Gent.* These overlooked poems were particularly popular in fifteenth- and sixteenth-century anthologies and with courtly readers.

See also nos. 3, 68, 172, 199, 206, 208, 209, 213, 223, 228, 233, 241, 253, 270, 272, 275, 276, 292, 294–96, 298, 302, 304, 309, 310, 313–15, 320, 327.

Chaucer's Influence and Later Allusion

46. Anderson, Judith H. *Reading the Allegorical Intertext: Chaucer, Spenser, Shakespeare, Milton.* New York: Fordham University Press, 2008. x, 436 pp. Anderson considers intertextuality to be both a result of authorial intent and an inevitability of language, assessing various kinds of influence, imitation, allusion, and citation. Allegory is a "process of thinking," a kind of metaphor that is "continued" or "moving" through plot. Allegory informs the intertextual relationships among the four "landmark" authors discussed in seventeen revised or reprinted essays and two new essays (both on Milton). Chapter 7 "substantially revises" a 1971 essay on *NPT* and Spenser's *Muiopotmos,* and six other essays, originally published between 1982 and 2006 and here lightly revised, pertain to Chaucer's impact on Spenser.

47. Blandeau, Agnès. *"The Canterbury Tales* et *The Clerkenwell Tales:* De la poésie à la prose de Peter Ackroyd, une expérimentation de la forme." *BAM* 74 (2008): 71–90 (in French). Comparing Chaucer's and Ackroyd's styles, Blandeau shows Ackroyd's indebtedness to Chaucer's use of images and sense of detail.

48. Chance, Jane. "Subversive Fantasist: Tolkien on Class Difference." In Wayne G. Hammond and Christina Scull, eds. *The Lord of the Rings, 1954–2004: Scholarship in Honor of Richard E. Blackwelder.* Milwaukee, Wis.: Marquette University Press, 2006, pp. 153–68. In his fiction, Chance contends, Tolkien subverts traditional class distinctions, and his studies of Chaucer reflect a similar sensibility.

49. Collette, Carolyn P. "'Faire Emelye': Medievalism and the Moral

Courage of Emily Wilding Davison." *ChauR* 42 (2008): 223–43. 3 b&w illus. Considered in the light of key themes of Victorian medieval-ism and of her own early identification with Chaucer's Emily, Davison's actions—especially those leading to her untimely death—stand as ex-pressions of her ethical commitment, rather than as deeds of the "wild enthusiast" for which historians have frequently taken her.

50. Corrie, Marilyn. "Fortune and the Sinner: Chaucer, Gower, Lyd-gate, and Malory's *Morte Darthur*." *LitComp* 5.2 (2008): 207–19. Depic-tions of Fortune and Fortune's effects in Malory's *Morte Darthur* have much in common with depictions in works by his English predecessors. Corrie comments on Chaucer's *Bo*, *TC*, *KnT*, and *MkT*.

51. Cullen, Dolores L. *Ensnared by His Words: My Chaucer Obsession*. McKinleyville, Calif.: Fithian, 2008. 155 pp. b&w illus. Narrative auto-biography of the author's fascination with Chaucer, recounting the writ-ing and publishing of three books on allegory in *CT*. Includes Cullen's thoughts about the reception of Chaucer among academic and popular audiences.

52. Fresco, Karen. "The Place of Christine de Pizan's *Enseignemens moraulx* in Paris BnF fr. 1551." In Juliette Dor and Marie-Élisabeth Henneau, eds. *Christine de Pizan: Une femme de science, une femme de lettres*. Études christiniennes, no. 10. Paris: Champion, 2008, pp. 289–300. Fresco draws attention to the imitation of Chaucer's *enchâssement* (encase-ment, enshirement) in Christine's *Enseignemens moraulx* BnF fr. 1551.

53. Gray, Douglas. *Later Medieval English Literature*. Oxford and New York: Oxford University Press, 2008. xiii, 712 pp. Gray surveys "literature written in English from the death of Chaucer to the earlier sixteenth century," with numerous references to Chaucer's legacy and influence during the period. Introductory chapters on intellectual and cultural history are followed by sections on prose, poetry, Scottish writ-ing, and drama, with a subsection dedicated to "Chaucerian" poems—i.e., "poems of the Chaucerian apocrypha." See also no. 369.

54. Grund, Peter. "*Sidrak and Bokkus*: An Early Modern Reader Re-sponse." *Anglia* 125 (2007): 217–38. Describes the unique copy of por-tions of *Sidrak and Bokkus* found in Bibliotheca Philosophica Hermetica, Amsterdam, MS M199, an early modern alchemical miscellany. Accom-panying the selections, manuscript annotations refer to a wide variety of texts, indicating early modern reading habits. The notes include two quotations from the third printing of Thynne's edition of Chaucer (c.

1550), two from *MkT* (on Lucifer and Cresus), and one from *CYT* (a reference to an "erthen pot").

55. Guy-Bray, Stephen. *Loving in Verse: Poetic Influence as Erotic.* Toronto: University of Toronto Press, 2006. xviii, 132 pp. Argues that poetic influence can be regarded as an erotic or romantic relationship between male couples, focusing on literature of Dante, Spenser, and Hart Crane and questioning notions of literary influence promulgated by T. S. Eliot and Harold Bloom. Chapter 2, "Chaucer and Spenser and Other Male Couples" (pp. 28–60), considers how Book 4 of Spenser's *Faerie Queene* dramatizes "the process by which heteroeroticism drives out homoeroticism." Spenser changes his sources—Chaucer's *SqT* and *Amys and Amylion*—to present a narrative in which "attachments between men are ultimately superseded by marital and familial attachments . . . just as Spenser uses the *Knight's Tale* to recast the *Squire's Tale.*" See also no. 370.

56. Hutchins, Christine E. "Chaucer and the Problem of 'Recreative' Poetry in Renaissance England." *Ben Jonson Journal* 15 (2008): 248–70. Late sixteenth-century Elizabethan reception of Chaucer focused as much on his "recreational" talents as a vernacular poet and stylist as on his doctrinal or philosophical themes. Constructed as a "prodigal" poet as well as a laureate, Chaucer was at the center of a Renaissance debate concerning the validity of pleasure versus instruction in vernacular literature.

57. McInnis, David. "Repetition and Revision in Shakespeare's Tragic Love Plays." *Parergon* 25.2 (2008): 33–56. Suggests that Chaucer's *TC* influenced Shakespeare's *Romeo and Juliet* before serving as the source of the playwright's *Troilus and Cressida.* Shakespeare explores ways to respond to source material in the two works. His *Troilus,* in particular, is an experimental work.

58. Norris, Ralph. *Malory's Library: The Sources of the "Morte Darthur."* Arthurian Studies, no. 71. Cambridge: D. S. Brewer, 2008. [viii], 187 pp. Norris tallies and assesses the major and minor sources of Malory's *Morte Darthur,* suggesting that Malory was more widely read than is usually assumed. Chaucer's influence (especially *WBT, FranT,* and *KnT*) is neither close nor sustained in plot, but echoes of language and various sequences of ideas indicate that Malory had read works by Chaucer (along with Lydgate's *Pageant of Knowledge* and various Middle English romances) in addition to the major French romances. See also no. 403.

59. Osborough, W. N. *Literature, Judges, and the Law.* Dublin: Four

Courts Press, 2008. viii, 171 pp. Explores literary allusions used in the courts of law in Britain and Ireland, revealing how literature conceptually informs practical life. Osborough briefly mentions Chaucer when discussing etymology in a nineteenth-century case involving compensating a hotel employee upon termination. The court concluded that the hotel employee would not be considered a "menial" laborer, since in *ShT* only ordinary servants are labeled as *meynee*.

60. Perkins, Nicholas. "Haunted Hoccleve? *The Regiment of Princes*, the Troilean Intertext, and Conversations with the Dead." *ChauR* 43 (2008): 103–39. Hoccleve's authorial identity develops through "borrowings and echoes" derived from *TC*: "Boethian dialogue; diseased language; and gendered subjects." These allusions work as conjurings—understood as both invocation and exorcism—of the "spectral Chaucerian corpus."

61. Ruppert, Timothy. "'Is not the past all shadow?': History and Vision in Byron, the Shelleys, and Keats." *DAI* A69.02 (2008): n.p. Places Chaucer in a tradition of English visionary literature that culminates in the second generation of Romantic poets.

62. Sidhu, Nicole Nolan. "Henpecked Husbands, Unruly Wives, and Royal Authority in Lydgate's *Mumming at Hertford*." *ChauR* 42 (2008): 431–60. Building on medieval "gender comedies," including Chaucer's (especially *WBP* and the fabliaux), Lydgate anticipates the family-state analogy that pervades early modern political theory. By giving the complaints of abused husbands a court hearing, the *Mumming* establishes wifely shrewishness as a public "problem" even as it figures the passive henpecked husband as the "ideal subject" of royal authority.

See also nos. 3, 24, 29, 45, 70, 178, 231, 289, 321.

Style and Versification

63. Burrow, J. A. *The Poetry of Praise*. Cambridge Studies in Medieval Literature, no. 69. Cambridge and New York: Cambridge University Press, 2008. vii, 196 pp. Burrow explores the functions and rhetoric of praise in classical, medieval, and Renaissance poetry, with commentary on its relative paucity in modern tradition. Focuses on medieval English panegyric verse, love poetry, and devotional poetry, with particular attention to *Beowulf* and Chaucer's works, though ranging widely in Old and Middle English poetry and assessing Spenser's *Faerie Queene* and

Tennyson's *Idylls of the King*. The discussion of Chaucer (pp. 101–49) concentrates on the poet's rhetorical uses of intensifiers and other forms of "epideictic magnification" (both serious and satirical), examining *GP*, *HF*, praise of women and leaders, and descriptions of individuals, particularly Troilus and Criseyde.

64. Cole, Kristin Lynn. "Rum, Ram, Ruf, and Rym: Middle English Alliterative Meters." *DAI* A68.12 (2008): n.p. Cole contends that metrical groupings of works from the "Alliterative Revival" are faulty and that these groupings reflect inappropriate application of phonology common in the "poetic dialects" of Chaucer and Gower.

65. Duffell, Martin J. "Some Observations of English Binary Metres." *Lang&Lit* 17 (2008): 5–20. Provides statistical analysis of 300-line samples from the verse of eight poets who wrote in English (Chaucer, Shakespeare, Milton, Pope, Wordsworth, Tennyson, Longfellow, and Browning), comparing percentages of inversion and "erosion" among iambic pentameter, iambic tetrameter, and trochaic tetrameter. Applies principles derived from Russian metrical analysis and from parametric theory. The Chaucerian sample is the opening of *GP*.

66. Fujiki, Takayoshi. "Chaucer's Proverbs and His Comic Art in Some Fabliaux." *Sapientia* 39 (2005): 59–72 (in Japanese, with English abstract). Fujiki considers comic "misapplication of proverbs" in *TC* (Pandarus), *MilT* (John), *MerT* (January), and *SumT* (the friar), suggesting that Chaucer capitalized on his audience's expectation of proverbs to characterize some users as foolish.

67. Hirabayashi, Mikio. "On the Rhetorical Expressions of G. Chaucer: European Poems and Aesthetics." *Daito Bunka Daigaku Kiyo, Jinbun Kagaku (Bulletin of Daito Bunka University: The Humanities)* 45 (2007): 157–73. Lists examples from Chaucer's works of rhetorical devices recommended by Aristotle and/or used by Ovid, demonstrating Chaucer's place in the rhetorical tradition of Western European literature.

68. Holton, Amanda. *The Sources of Chaucer's Poetics*. Aldershot, Hampshire; and Burlington, Vt.: Ashgate, 2008. x, 168 pp. Studies Chaucer's stylistic techniques, comparing several texts (*KnT, MLT, PhyT, MkT, ManT*, and *LGW*) with sources to show that Chaucer employed a style that was remarkably consistent across genres, rather than appropriating the styles of source texts. Chaucer's narrative elements are tightly controlled and chronological, although commentary and complaint sometimes modify the impression of control. Rhetorical figures articulating aspects of narration abound, with similes outnumbering

metaphors (which are usually conventional). This consistency (with the notabable exception of *MkT*) qualifies the traditional belief that Chaucer adapted his techniques to reflect differences among *CT* narrators. Echoes of the styles of sources remain, however, particularly when the source is Ovid.

See also nos. 27, 47, 163.

Language and Word Studies

69. Benson, C. David. "Teaching Chaucer in Middle English." In Stephen J. Harris and Bryon L. Grigsby, eds. *Misconceptions About the Middle Ages*. Routledge Studies in Medieval Religion and Culture, no. 7. New York: Routledge, 2008, pp. 240–53. Benson advocates teaching Chaucer in Middle English because the liveliness and vitality of Chaucer's language are lost in translation.

70. Considine, John. *Dictionaries in Early Modern Europe: Lexicography and the Making of Heritage*. Cambridge and New York: Cambridge University Press, 2008. xiv, 393 pp. Surveys the making of English, German, Latin, and Greek dictionaries from 1500 to 1650, including the contributions of Franciscus Junius (among others). Discusses the unpublished manuscript of Junius's glossary to Chaucer and the place of Chaucer's lexicon in Junius's *Etymologicum anglicanum*.

71. Crespo-García, Begoña. "Specific and Non-Specific Nouns in Late Middle English: When Robert Grows from Man to Herb." *ES* 89 (2009): 587–606. Crespo-García gauges the "scientific register" of *Astr* and *Equat* in contrast with medical handbooks, examining etymology and specificity in the common nouns and nominalized forms in these works. The astrological treatises reflect a specialized audience.

72. Gillmeister, Heiner. "The Origin of Imperative Constructions and Chaucer's Nonce-words *viritoot*, *virytrate*, and *phislyas*." *PoeticaT* 4 (1975): 24–49. Gillmeister derives *viritoot* (*MilT* 1.3770) and *virytrate* (*FrT* 3.1582) from hypothetical French words **viretost* (early-riser) and *viretart* (slug-a-bed), respectively, and derives *phislyas* (*MLE* 2.1189) from unattested ME **fille-li-as* (loaded dice), suggesting that *CkT* was once intended to follow *MLT*. He argues that these words developed from imperative constructions under specific sociolinguistic conditions.

73. Hirabayashi, Mikio. "The Influence of French and Other Languages on Chaucer's English." *Daito Bunka Daigaku Kiyo, Jinbun Kagaku*

(Bulletin of Daito Bunka University: The Humanities) 42 (2004): 221–58 (in Japanese, with English abstract). Argues that, despite the influence of French on the idioms, spelling, and pronunciation of Chaucer's English, the "basic structure of English as a Germanic language . . . remained intact."

74. Hsy, Jonathan Horng. "Polyglot Poetics: Merchants and Literary Production in London, 1300–1500." *DAI* A68.07 (2008): n.p. Hsy explores the use of English, French, and Latin by writers such as Chaucer, Gower, and Margery Kempe in conjunction with the polyglot mercantile culture of London. Argues that these writers "hybridize" multilingual traditions to form "hybrid personas."

75. Iyeiri, Yoko. "Unsupported Negative *Ne* in Later Middle English." *N&Q* 253 (2008): 21–23. Analysis of *Bo, Mel,* and *ParsT* reveals that preverbal *ne* unsupported by a postverbal *not* appears most often with "forms of *be, will,* and *witen*"; moreover, this construction is more likely to appear in subordinate clauses than in main clauses.

76. Jucker, Andreas H. "Politeness in the History of English." In Richard Dury et al., eds. *English Historical Linguistics 2006: Selected Papers from the Fourteenth International Conference on English Historical Linguistics (ICEHL 14), Bergamo, 21–25 August 2006. Volume II: Lexical and Semantic Change.* Amsterdam: John Benjamins, 2008, pp. 3–29. Arguing that contemporary "negative" politeness may function in public only, Jucker surveys historical functions of politeness in English. Analyzes Chaucer's use of *thou* and *you* in *ClT* as "retractable," i.e., variable by situation, rapidly shifting, and dependent on levels of "politeness and respect" as well as on "affection and intimacy."

77. Miura, Ayumi. "The Impersonal Verb *Listen* in Chaucer's Works: Implications of Its Textual Distribution." *Lexicon* (Tokyo) 36 (2006): 24–40. Studies the distribution of Chaucer's impersonal verb *listen* (to be pleasing), focusing on disparities between distributions in prose and verse, usage in formulaic expressions, and transition from impersonal to personal usage.

78. ———. "New Impersonal Verbs in Some Late Fourteenth-Century English Texts." In Masachiyo Amano, Michiko Ogura, and Masayuki Ohkado, eds. *Historical Englishes in Varieties of Texts and Contexts: The Global COE Programme, International Conference 2007* (*SAC* 32 [2010], no. 94), pp. 187–200. Identifies and tabulates "new" impersonal verbs used by Chaucer, Gower, Langland, and the *Gawain*-poet, describing factors that affected their usage, especially imitation of Old French forms.

79. Molencki, Rafał. "The Rise of *Because* in Middle English." In Masachiyo Amano, Michiko Ogura, and Masayuki Ohkado, eds. *Historical Englishes in Varieties of Texts and Contexts: The Global COE Programme, International Conference 2007* (*SAC* 32 [2010], no. 94), pp. 201–15. Discusses the "sudden emergence" of and rapid growth in the use of the "adverbial subordinator" *because* in Middle English writing, including the works of Chaucer.

80. Momma, Haruko, and Michael Matto, eds. *A Companion to the History of the English Language.* Blackwell Companions to Literature and Culture, no. 54. Malden, Mass.; and Oxford: Wiley-Blackwell, 2008. xxxiii, 690 pp. Fifty-nine essays by various authors on topics ranging from the Indo-European roots of English to linguistic theory of the twenty-first century, from "the history of the history of English" to various geographical Englishes, and from English lexicography to sociolinguistics. Recurrent references to Chaucer, with one section focusing on his use of language: John F. Plummer's "'In swich englissh as he kan': Chaucer's Literary Language" (pp. 445–54) addresses Chaucer's dialect and flexible uses of various registers. The volume includes a timeline, a glossary of linguistic terms, and an index.

81. Nohara, Yasuhiro. "Explaining the Disappearance of Extinct Words Associated with the Concept 'Dream.'" *English Review* (Momoyama Gakuin University) 8 (1993): 71–87 (in Japanese, with English abstract). Argues that function shifts and the development of impersonal constructions reduced the nouns and verbs associated with dreaming in the development of English. Nohara focuses on the loss of forms of *sweven* and *meten* from Middle English, drawing examples primarily from Chaucer.

82. ———. "The Numerals in Chaucer." *English Review* (Momoyama Gakuin University) 10 (1995): 41–65 (in Japanese, with English abstract). Surveys the verbal representation of numerals in Chaucer and elsewhere in Middle English and comments on the Germanic basis of composite representations (e.g., "four and twenty") and the development of French-influenced forms (e.g., "twenty-four"). Chaucer relies heavily on composite representations.

83. ———. "On Correlative Comparison Construction in *The Canterbury Tales.*" *Journal of Human Sciences* (Momoyama Gakuin University) 24.1 (1988): 35–67 (in Japanese). Tallies and assesses Chaucer's uses of comparative constructions using *as* in *CT* (e.g., "as . . . as," "as . . . as is a . . ."), including their functions as set phrases.

84. ———. "On 'Strengthening of Negations' [in *The Canterbury Tales*]." *Journal of Human Sciences* (Momoyama Gakuin University) 23.2 (1988): 47–68 (in Japanese). Tallies and assesses Chaucer's uses of multiple negation in *CT*.

85. ———. "Plural Forms Viewed from the Chaucerian Age." *English Review* (Momoyama Gakuin University) 16 (2001): 143–66 (in Japanese, with English abstract). Explores the development and uses of plural nouns from Old to Modern English. Modern English plural usage was already established for the most part in Chaucer's Middle English.

86. ———. "Pronouns of the Second Person in Chaucer." *English Review* (Momoyama Gakuin University) 13 (1998): 35–49 (in Japanese, with English abstract). Surveys Chaucer's uses of *ye* and *thou* forms in *CT*, discussing plurality, formality, and other usage.

87. ———. "A Transition of 'Independent Adverbs' from Present-Day English, Through Shakespeare's, Spenser's, and Chaucer's English, to Old English." *English Review* (Momoyama Gakuin University) 17 (2002): 49–76 (in Japanese, with English abstract). Diachronic exploration of the morphology and function of English "independent" (as opposed to interrogative and conjunctive) adverbs, with examples from Old English, Chaucer, Spenser, Shakespeare, and Sidney Sheldon. Nohara focuses on uses of *-ly* and *-lich* suffixes.

88. Pakkala-Weckström, Mari. "'No botmeles bihestes': Various Ways of Making Binding Promises in Middle English." In Andreas H. Jucker and Irma Taavitsainen, eds. *Speech Acts in the History of English*. Amsterdam: John Benjamins, 2008, pp. 133–62. Pakkala-Weckström examines the speech act of promising and the special conditions needed to constitute a binding promise in Middle English, drawing examples from several of Chaucer's works: *FranT*, *ClT*, *WBT*, *TC*, *FrT*, and *ShT*. Certain formulaic words and expressions constitute a binding promise, and the "intentions of the promiser are of secondary importance" (158). The words considered include *sweren*, *trouthe*, *biheste*, *plighten*, and *trouthe*.

89. Rozenski, Steven, Jr. "'Your ensaumple and your mirour': Hoccleve's Amplification of the Imagery and Intimacy of Henry Suso's *Ars moriendi*." *Parergon* 25.2 (2008): 1–16. Addresses word choice in Thomas Hoccleve's English translation of Henry Suso's *Ars moriendi*, a Latin text. Chaucer's use of the word *similitude* shows that it had entered the English language; however, Hoccleve translates both *imago* and *similitudo* as "image."

90. Sauer, Hans. "Interjection, Emotion, Grammar, and Literature."

In Masachiyo Amano, Michiko Ogura, and Masayuki Ohkado, eds. *Historical Englishes in Varieties of Texts and Contexts: The Global COE Programme, International Conference 2007* (*SAC* 32 [2010], no. 94), pp. 387–403. Surveys the structure, frequency, and functions of interjections in the English language, tracing discussion of this word class in linguistic commentary and in *Beowulf*, *MilT*, and modern comic books.

91. Sweeney, Mickey. "Generating Enthusiasm: Performing Chaucer in the Small Liberal Arts College Classroom." *SMART* 15.1 (2008): 47–54. Presents performance strategies for improving linguistic knowledge among undergraduate Chaucer students.

92. Walling, Amanda. "Vicious Praise: Flattery in Late Medieval English Politics and Poetry." *DAI* A68.09 (2008): n.p. Looks at flattery "as a practice" (for communicating with superiors) and "as a discourse" (the conventional railings against the practice) in a variety of Middle English texts. Chapter 3 examines *Mel*, *MerT*, and *NPT* as "conjunctions of flattery and antifeminism."

See also nos. 7, 8, 40, 59, 64, 72, 144, 153, 168, 191, 195, 198, 200–202, 273, 280, 281, 302, 303, 320.

Background and General Criticism

93. Allen, Valerie. *The Age of Chaucer*. Cambridge Contexts in Literature. Cambridge: Cambridge University Press, 2004. 128 pp. Introduction and study guide to Chaucer and his works (especially *CT*), with emphasis on connections with contemporaneous history and literature. Includes advice on how to approach medieval texts; extracts from the literature with discussion; a description of critical approaches; suggestions for writing assignments; bibliography; and additional resources.

94. Amano, Masachiyo, Michiko Ogura, and Masayuki Ohkado, eds. *Historical Englishes in Varieties of Texts and Contexts: The Global COE Programme, International Conference 2007*. Studies in English Medieval Language and Literature, no. 22. New York and Frankfurt am Main: Peter Lang, 2008. xi, 403 pp. Twenty-eight essays by various authors on linguistic aspects of Old and Middle English, including three that pertain to Chaucer; see nos. 78, 79, and 90.

95. Anderson, Miranda. "Chaucer and the Subject of the Mirror." In Miranda Anderson, ed. *The Book of the Mirror: An Interdisciplinary Collection Exploring the Cultural History of the Mirror*. Newcastle: Cambridge

Scholars, 2007, pp. 70–79. Anderson illustrates the use of mirror metaphors, common in medieval literature and theology alike, in Chaucer's texts (e.g., *SqT*, *KnT*, *Rom*, *For*, and *Wom Unc*). Humanity's internal mirror should reflect the image of God, but human reason can be impeded by erroneous and feminized traits (imagination, vanity). Only the active will can prevent such erroneous reflections of spiritual reality.

96. Bale, Anthony. "From Translator to Laureate: Imagining the Medieval Author." *LitComp* 5.5 (2008): 918–34. Surveys medieval notions of authorship from the twelfth century to the late fifteenth century, commenting on topics such as anonymity, laureateship, Mandeville's *Travels*, *The Cloud of Unknowing*, *The Book of Margery Kempe*, and the development of a modern idea of authorship in early print culture. Recurrent and sustained attention to Chaucer's works and to reception of them.

97. Bate, Jonathan, and Susan Brock. "The CAPITAL Centre: Teaching Shakespeare (and More) Through a Collaboration Between a University and an Arts Organization." *Pedagogy: Critical Approaches to Teaching Literature, Language, Composition, and Culture* 7 (2007): 341–58. Overview of workshops conducted under the auspices of CAPITAL (Creativity and Performance in Teaching and Learning), a combined effort of the University of Warwick and the Royal Shakespeare Company. The authors also comment on a "study day" dedicated to *CT* involving academics, actors, and students.

98. Battles, Dominique, and Paul Battles. "Building a Better Introduction to a Medieval English Literature Course." *SMART* 15.1 (2008): 39–46. Advice to instructors teaching undergraduate-level introductions to medieval English, including strategies for avoiding "Chaucer fatigue."

99. Bliss, Jane. *Naming and Namelessness in Medieval Romance*. Studies in Medieval Romance. Rochester, N.Y.; and Cambridge: D. S. Brewer, 2008. xi, 253 pp. Bliss surveys the variety of ways that names, naming, and namelessness in romance "contribute to our understanding" of the genre, focusing on Middle English narratives but also discussing French and Anglo-Norman analogues. She identifies a number of "naming patterns and tendencies," uses them to define or clarify generic features of romance, and explores onomastic themes. References to Chaucer's works recur throughout, with brief sustained commentary on *MLT* (pp. 150–54).

100. Bloom, Harold, ed. [Cornelius, Michael G., vol. ed.] *Geoffrey*

Chaucer. Bloom's Classic Critical Views. New York: Infobase, 2008. xiii, 416 pp. An anthology of eighty-three responses to Chaucer and his works excerpted from commentaries written from the fourteenth through the twentieth centuries: fourteenth (2), fifteenth (9), sixteenth (20), seventeenth (4), eighteenth (10), nineteenth (35), and twentieth (3). Includes a brief introduction by Bloom (xi–xiii), a biography and chronology of Chaucer, and an index to the volume.

101. Bovaird-Abbo, Kristin Lee. "Chaucer's Arthuriana." *DAI* A69.06 (2008): n.p. Considers Chaucer's use of Arthurian legend, from his use in *TC* of the traditional French conception of Lancelot for Troilus to his examination of the subtext the legend provides for the fabric of fourteenth-century English society. In particular, the author looks at the use of a Gawain figure in *Th* and *WBT*.

102. Bryant, Brantley L. "Common Profit: Economic Morality in English Public Political Discourse, c. 1340–1406." *DAI* A68.09 (2008): n.p. Chaucer and other writers of the "middle strata" of English society (Gower and Langland) "imagine economic activity" in ways that are much like the views recorded in documentary writing. Such writings by societal, administrative, and governmental authors were a site of resistance to "royal demands for acquiescence."

103. Burrow, J. A. *Medieval Writers and Their Work: Middle English Literature, 1100–1500.* 2nd ed. Oxford and New York: Oxford University Press, 2008. 156 pp. Revised version of the 1982 original, with new material and updating of notes and bibliography.

104. Buschinger, Danielle, and Arlette Sancery, eds. *Mélanges de langue, littérature et civilisation offerts à André Crépin à l'occasion de son quatre-vingtième anniversaire.* Médiévales, no. 44. Amiens: Presses du Centre d'Études Médiévales, Université de Picardie-Jules Verne, 2008. Includes eight essays that pertain to Chaucer; see nos. 149, 161, 203, 254, 257, 273, 302, and 323.

105. Cannon, Christopher. *Middle English Literature: A Cultural History.* Cultural History of Literature. Malden, Mass.: Polity, 2008. xi, 256 pp. Surveys the forms, topics, and contexts of Middle English writing, clarifying its construction from various literary traditions set against a number of social, economic, and political conditions. The discussion is divided into five broad categories (Technology, Insurgency, Statecraft, Place, and Jurisdiction). The appendices include suggestions for further reading, a chronology, notes and bibliography, and an index. Cannon

refers to Chaucer and his works frequently, emphasizing Chaucer's self-fashioning and how it was viewed by subsequent writers.

106. Clifton, Nicole. "Teaching & Learning Guide for: [*sic*] Teaching and Studying the Middle English Romance: New Directions, Affiliations, and Pleasures of the Text." *LitComp* 5.1 (2008): 158–64. Pedagogical portfolio (containing material such as bibliography, sample syllabi, and discussion questions) for the study of Middle English romances, including several works by Chaucer.

107. Cole, Andrew. *Literature and Heresy in the Age of Chaucer*. Cambridge Studies in Medieval Literature, no. 71. Cambridge and New York: Cambridge University Press, 2008. xx, 297 pp. Post-Wycliffite writing has a different character from that which preceded it. Writers of the late fourteenth and early fifteenth centuries, including Chaucer, produced works with this novel character, often defined as heretical. Cole connects Chaucer's use of the vernacular and his interest in translation to Wycliffism. The prologue to *Astr* is the primary focus, with some attention to *MLE*. See also no. 352.

108. Cooper, Lisa H., and Andrea Denny-Brown, eds. *Lydgate Matters: Poetry and Material Culture in the Fifteenth Century*. The New Middle Ages. New York: Palgrave Macmillan, 2008. 223 pp. Eight essays by various authors, an introduction by the editors, an afterword by D. Vance Smith, and an index. The essays consider Lydgate's poetry in relation to "the role of material goods and the material world in the formation of late-medieval identity." References to Chaucer appear throughout. Two essays include sustained attention to his works: see nos. 170 and 221. See also no. 353.

109. Corrie, Marilyn, ed. *A Concise Companion to Middle English Literature*. Blackwell Concise Companions to Literature and Culture. Oxford: Blackwell: 2007. Reissued as a print-on-demand volume, Malden, Mass.: Wiley-Blackwell, 2009. xii, 268 pp. 3 b&w illus. Eleven essays on topics concerning late medieval English literature and its contexts: Signs and Symbols (Barry Windeatt), Religious Belief (Marilyn Corrie), Women and Literature (Catherine Sanok), The Past (Andrew Galloway), Production and Dissemination (Alexandra Gillespie), The Author (Jane Griffiths), Language (Jeremy J. Smith), Translation and Adaptation (Helen Cooper), Contemporary Events (Helen Barr), Manuscripts and Modern Editions (Daniel Wakelin), and The Afterlife of Middle English Literature (David Matthews). The index lists numerous references to Chaucer.

110. Denny-Brown, Andrea. "Fashioning Change: Wearing Fortune's Garments in Medieval England." *PQ* 87 (2008): 9–32. Denny-
Brown analyzes sartorial changes accompanying the figure of Fortune
from the twelfth century through the late medieval period, considering
(along with works by other authors) Chaucer's *For*, *Bo*, *Form Age*, *Wom
Unc*, *BD*, and *MerT*. Chaucer's uses of Fortune direct attention to goods
in the feudal system, assess wonder elicited by Fortune's goods, and
associate late medieval female "consumer behavior" with Fortune's ste-
reotypical characteristics.

111. Dinshaw, Carolyn. "The Heterosexual Subject of Chaucerian
Narrative." *Medieval Feminist Newsletter* 13 (Spring 1992): 8–10. Reports on how notions of heterosexual normativity can be used in classroom discussions of *BD*, *TC*, and *CT*.

112. Dor, Juliette, and Marie-Élisabeth Henneau, eds. *Femmes et pèler-
inages/Women and Pilgrimages*. The Way to Santiago, no. 2. [Santiago de
Compostela]: Compostela Group of Universities, 2007. 235 pp. Collection of essays in French and English that examine factual and fictive
female pilgrims, focusing on their representation in spiritual and courtly
literature. Two essays pertain to Chaucer; see nos. 153 and 155.

113. Foster, Michael. *Chaucer's Narrators and the Rhetoric of Self-Repre-
sentation*. New York and Frankfurt am Main: Peter Lang, 2008. 196 pp.
Foster revisits the question of Chaucer's narrator as a fictional construct,
gauging responses that the verisimilitude of Chaucer's narrative might
have invited in a contemporary audience. In *WBP*, Jankyn's actions as
a reader comment on Chaucer's narrator and his literary and scholarly
competence. In the dream visions, the narrators' attitudes toward reading create a Chaucer-like persona who relies on authority rather than
experience (*HF*), who is emotionally limited (*PF*), and who has a textual
relationship with Love (*LGWP*). *TC* contrasts the communal experience
of an aural audience with the experience of a silent, solitary reader.

114. Galler, Matthias. *"O Death, thou comest when I had thee least in
mind!": Der Umgang mit dem Tod in der mittelenglischen Literatur*. Texte
und Untersuchungen zur Englischen Philologie, no. 34. Frankfurt am
Main: Peter Lang, 2007 (in German). 419 pp. Galler studies the theme
of death in Middle English literature and argues against the "pessimistic" dictum that the people and works of the late Middle Ages were
primarily concerned with the transience of life, the dominant approach
on this subject since Johan Huizinga's *The Waning of the Middle Ages*.
Instead, Galler traces a distinctly "optimistic" perception of death

founded on Christian salvation history, considering texts such as *BD*, *KnT*, *TC*, *PardT*, *LGW*, and several Middle English romances. He also discusses "questions of life and death beyond Christian tenets" (p. 399), examining Celtic narrative traditions and texts from classical philosophy and mythology.

115. Gibson, Angela L. "Fictions of Abduction in the Auchinleck Manuscript, the 'Pearl' Poet, Chaucer, and Malory." *DAI* A68.08 (2008): n.p. Considers *TC*, *MLT*, and *LGW* in the larger context of the idea of *raptus* and its implications for national and other borders and for female status.

116. Gillespie, Vincent. "Afterword: On Allegory, Allegoresis, and the Erotics of Reading." In Mary Carr, K. P. Clarke, and Marco Nievergelt, eds. *On Allegory: Some Medieval Aspects and Approaches*. Newcastle: Cambridge Scholars, 2008, pp. 231–56. Surveys distinctions between the restrictive "allegory of theologians" and the expansive "allegory of the poets," arguing that Chaucer's poetry is a radical form of the latter. Chaucer's works decenter the author and thereby pose "new kinds of imaginative syllogism" that prompt readers to various "wrong" readings and evoke parallels between political and readerly rebelliousness. Gillespie comments on *HF*, *Mel*, and the Host's response to *ClT*.

117. Harriss, Gerald. *Shaping the Nation: England, 1360–1461*. New Oxford History of England. Oxford: Clarendon Press; New York: Oxford University Press, 2005. xxi, 705 pp. b&w illus. Harriss studies English social and political history from the Hundred Years' War to the Wars of the Roses as a period of cultural transformation that established the "shape of English society and government" that "it was to retain until the Civil War." Recurrent attention to Chaucer's life and works as well as to those of other authors of the period, including discussion of court patronage, the rise of vernacular literature, literature among the "gentry," and literary impact on political models. Includes a chronology, a bibliography, and an index. See also no. 373.

118. Hernández Pérez, Mª Beatriz. "Geoffrey Chaucer y el mecenazgo femenino en la corte inglesa bajomedieval." *Liminar: Estudios sociales y humanísticos* 6.2 (2008): 15–30 (in Spanish). Examines Chaucer's works, particularly *BD* and *LGW*, in connection to female patronage networks in the late fourteenth century in England, France, and the Iberian Peninsula. Argues that the new cultural and political role of many aristocratic women had an impact on Chaucer's depiction of female characters and amorous subjects.

119. Iamartino, Giovanni, Maria Luisa Maggioni, and Roberta Fac-chinetti, eds. *Thou sittest at another boke . . . : English Studies in Honour of Domenico Pezzini*. Milan: Polimetrica, 2008. 488 pp. This festschrift includes twenty-five essays, four of which pertain to Chaucer. See nos. 199, 244, 301, and 335.

120. Kaylor, Noel Harold, Jr., and Richard Scott Nokes, eds. *Global Perspectives on Medieval English Literature, Language, and Culture*. Kalamazoo, Mich.: Medieval Institute, 2007. xv, 310 pp. A festschrift for Paul Szarmach, celebrating the internationalization of medieval studies. Twelve essays by various authors, on topics ranging from Old and Middle English language and literature to the Narnia Chronicles of C. S. Lewis and the Mayan epic *Popol Vuh*. For two essays that pertain to Chaucer, see nos. 296 and 309.

121. Knapp, Peggy A. *Chaucerian Aesthetics*. The New Middle Ages. New York: Palgrave Macmillan, 2008. x, 242 pp. Applies Kantian aesthetic principles to "display the interanimation of sensible detail with intelligible order" in *TC* and *CT* and considers the two poems in light of Hans-Georg Gadamer (on art of the past), Ludwig Wittgenstein (intellectual play), and Antonio Damasio and Daniel Dennett (cognitive theory). "Why Aesthetics?" is the topic of the initial chapter, and the second chapter explores Augustinian roots of Chaucer's ideas of beauty in verisimilitude, coherence, proportionality, clarity, and usefulness, along with distrust of imagination. Five subsequent chapters apply these concerns to *TC* and *CT*, focused on topics of play and genre, "individual personhood" and typicality, the lures and joys of female beauty, humor and disinterestedness, and community and nuances of social good.

122. Labbie, Erin Felicia. *Lacan's Medievalism*. Minneapolis: University of Minnesota Press, 2006. xiii, 264 pp. Jacques Lacan's "methodologies follow those established by the medieval scholastic scholars who sought to determine the potential for the human subject to know and represent real universal categories"; and his seminars engage medieval discourses on universals, realism, and nominalism. Labbie assesses Boethius, troubadour verse, Marie de France's *Bisclavret*, Jean d'Arras's *Melusine*, *Sir Gawain and the Green Knight*, and Chaucer's *ClT* and *Astr*. Reads Griselda as "singular, sovereign and universal," while Walter is a "dependent, dialogically engaged, figure"—two aspects of desire. *Astr* (along with Chaucer's many scientific allusions) presents a "complex struggle with the potential for science to solve or create human prob-

lems"; the focus is on the incompleteness of the treatise and on its stated goal: "to slay envy." See also no. 381.

123. Lacey, Robert. "Geoffrey Chaucer and the Mother Tongue, 1387." In Robert Lacey. *Great Tales from English History: Chaucer to the Glorious Revolution, 1387–1688.* London: Little, Brown, 2004, pp. 1–5. Appreciative commentary on *CT*. Chaucer's "cheery and companionable writing" in the vernacular "sets out the ideas" for the rest of Lacey's volume of anecdotal history.

124. Léglu, Catherine E., and Stephen J. Milner, eds. *The Erotics of Consolation: Desire and Distance in the Late Middle Ages.* The New Middle Ages. New York: Palgrave Macmillan, 2008. viii, 241 pp. Ten essays by various authors explore topics related to the *Consolatio* of Boethius and its impact within vernacular traditions. The essays are divided equally under two headings: "Consolation and Desire" and "Consolation and Loss." For two essays that pertain to Chaucer, see nos. 45 and 320.

125. Lundeen, Stephanie Thompson. "Medieval English Poetry and Performance." *DAI* A69.05 (2008): n.p. Considers Chaucer's works in the context of medieval poetry, approached here as "instantiations of performance," i.e., understood as interplay among author, performer, audience, and the material form of the texts.

126. Manion, Lee Basil. "'In another kynde': Modes of Recognition in Late Medieval English Literature." *DAI* A68.12 (2008): n.p. Uses *KnT* and *TC* (among other works) as case texts for a study of recognition within various forms of medieval romance. In particular, Manion argues that these Chaucerian texts use recognition as a means of speculating on the limits of interpersonal knowledge.

127. Martin, Molly Anne. "Isn't the Gaze Male? Gender and the Visual Experience in the Romances of Chaucer and Malory." *DAI* A68.08 (2008): n.p. Using the medieval concepts of "intromissive optics" and the passive viewer, Martin suggests that Chaucer in *TC*, *KnT*, and *MerT* employs conventions from outside the romance genre at the moment of sight. She contrasts this technique with that of Malory, who works within and "validates" the romance genre.

128. Mehl, Dieter. "Old Age in Middle English Literature: Chaucer, Gower, Langland, and the *Gawain*-Poet." In Christa Jansohn, ed. *Old Age and Ageing in British and American Culture and Literature.* Studien zur englischen Literatur, no. 16. Münster: LIT Verlag, 2004, pp. 29–38. Explores the representation of old age in *WBPT*, *MerT*, *PardT*, *Piers Plowman*, *Sir Gawain and the Green Knight*, *Confessio Amantis*, and the

Book of Margery Kempe, arguing that the motif of old age falls into three distinct categories: "the comical figure of the impotent lover, the ugly witch[,] or the disturbing reminder of death" (p. 37). Instances of "the realities of ageing" are rare, but traces of this experience can be found in Chaucer and Langland and particularly in the *Book of Margery Kempe*.

129. Neal, Derek G. *The Masculine Self in Late Medieval England.* Chicago: University of Chicago Press, 2008. xiii, 303 pp. Examines frames of cultural reference (legal, domestic, physical, and literary—especially romance), arguing that "two versions of masculinity defined the socially performed lives of men in late medieval England." The first version was normative and stabilizing, based on trust and honesty among males. The other—more "rebellious, aggressive, sensual"—coexisted with the first, creating tension between exterior social performance and internal desire. Neal discusses several Middle English romances and refers at times to Chaucer's *RvT*, Pardoner, and Parson.

130. Niebrzydowski, Sue. *Bonoure and Buxum: A Study of Wives in Late Medieval English Literature.* New York: Peter Lang, 2006. 239 pp. Niebrzydowski documents "significant attention," positive and negative, paid to wives and wifehood in the literature and architecture of fourteenth- and fifteenth-century England. The volume is structured to "follow the life cycle of a wife," from the canon law of eligibility to topics such as marital contracts, sex education, childbirth and motherhood, and depictions of life with a husband—drawing on art, literature, and history for examples of the freedoms and constraints of female marital life. The wide variety of texts (conduct literature, homilies, historical records, cycle plays, the *Book of Margery Kempe*, and more) indicates how wifehood was "constructed by patriarchal textual discourses." Includes sustained discussions of *ClT*, *MerT*, *MLT*, and especially *WBPT*. See also no. 402.

131. Owen, Corey Alec. "The Passions of Sir Gawain: Patience and the Idiom of Medieval Romance in England." *DAI* A68.10 (2008): n.p. Uses Chaucer (selections from *CT*) and Langland to contextualize "patient heroism" in medieval romances, especially *Sir Gawain and the Green Knight*.

132. Pugh, Tison. *Sexuality and Its Queer Discontents in Middle English Literature.* The New Middle Ages. New York: Palgrave Macmillan, 2008. xii, 220 pp. Pugh theorizes "the compulsory nature of queerness in creating heterosexuals," exploring how a number of masculine characters in Middle English literature are "rendered queerly normative due

to external forces that reimagine their masculinity as little more than a phantastically inadequate performance." Individual chapters discuss the Dreamer in *Pearl*, the Host in *CT*, Walter and the audience in *ClT*, the protagonist of *Amis and Amiloun*, and that of *Eger and Grime*. The discussion of the Host was previously published in 2006 (see *SAC* 30 [2008], no. 167); for Walter, see no. 224. See also no. 408.

133. Quinn, Esther Casier. *Geoffrey Chaucer and the Poetics of Disguise*. Lanham, Md.: University Press of America, 2008. xii, 251 pp. Identifies how and where Chaucer's poetry engages contemporary society and politics, as well as how it adjusts to changes in these arenas. As a court poet, Chaucer was knowledgeable about worldly affairs but unwilling to comment or criticize openly. Close reading of *BD*, *HF*, and *PF* shows how Chaucer used the dream-vision form to speak out "without seeming to." In *TC*, *LGW*, and *Anel*, he used "the distant past as a cover for his reflections on his own time." Developing "new forms of disguises" in *CT*, he strove to avoid censure while commenting on courtly imbroglios and general ethical concerns. Quinn discusses several of Chaucer's short poems (especially *Pity*, *Mars*, *Purse*, and the Boethian poems) and comments on the chronological development of Chaucer's "poetics of disguise."

134. Raskolnikov, Masha. "Confessional Literature, Vernacular Psychology, and the History of the Self in Middle English." *LitComp* 2 (2005): 1–20. Surveys recent discussions of the role of confession in constructing a vernacular sense of self in late medieval English writing, with recurrent references to Chaucer's works.

135. Rayner, Samantha. *Images of Kingship in Chaucer and His Ricardian Contemporaries*. Chaucer Studies, no. 39. Cambridge: D. S. Brewer, 2008. 177 pp. Examines depictions of kingship among the Ricardian poets—Gower, Langland, the *Gawain*-poet, and Chaucer—as reflections of common concerns in a time of turbulence, considering royalty in several of Chaucer's works. In *BD*, the royal birds are refracted versions of royalty, but still quite human in their common experiences. *TC* reveals much about poetic representation by what it does not say, while direct counsel opposes royal tyranny in *LGW*. In *CT*, Chaucer reacts to worldly turbulence by turning from support of the monarchy and asserting the importance of the individual as an English citizen and a subject of sovereign God. Comments on *KnT* and *NPT* in particular.

136. ———. "'Perced to the Roote': Challenges in Teaching Chaucer at UK Universities." *LitComp* 5.2 (2008): 195–206. Surveys peda-

gogical tools for teaching Chaucer to secondary and undergraduate students, maintaining that "the future looks promising for medieval studies." Includes a summary of studies that address the topic and contrasts practice in the United Kingdom and the United States.

137. Robertson, Elizabeth Ann. "Practicing Women: The Matter of Women in Medieval English Literature." *LitComp* 5.3 (2008): 505–28. Summarizes Aristotelian affiliations of women with matter (rather than form) and, following Bourdieu, explores how this affiliation and its "practices" are enacted in Middle English literature. Chaucer engages "contemporary historical practices about the law, marriage, and contemporary debates about preaching women" in *WBT*, *MerT*, and *SNT*.

138. Salas Chacón, Alvaro. "Art, Politics, or Religion? (Allusions to the Virgin Mary in *The Canterbury Tales*)." *Káñina* (Costa Rica) 17.2 (1993): 105–9. Surveys Chaucer's Marian allusions and critical commentary on them. Suggests that Chaucer wrote his Marian poetry (*ABC*, *PrT*, *SNT*, and allusions elsewhere) for political and aesthetic reasons, not out of religious devotion.

139. Sebastian, John T. "Chaucer and the Theory Wars: Attack of the Historicists? The Psychologists Strike Back? Or a New Hope?" *LitComp* 3.4 (2006): 767–77. Surveys recent historicist and psychoanalytic approaches to Chaucer's writing, positing an impending turn toward "an emerging norm of multi- and post-theoretical criticism."

140. Sisk, Jennifer Lynn. "Forms of Speculation: Religious Genres and Religious Inquiry in Late Medieval England." *DAI* A69.05 (2008): n.p. Sisk contends that a number of late medieval works, including Fragment 8 of *CT*, "obliquely" address contemporary religious issues. These works mark a departure from more traditional (and clearly didactic) religious treatises and may even suggest that these texts merit further consideration as witnesses to intellectual history.

141. Stanbury, Sarah. *The Visual Object of Desire in Late Medieval England*. The Middle Ages. Philadelphia: University of Pennsylvania Press, 2008. 290 pp. Stanbury describes late medieval English attitudes toward images, icons, and devotion, exploring how the tensions among these attitudes are represented in art and literature. Reformist distrust of images coexisted with newly intensified devotional practice to produce awareness and anxiety about the "premodern fetishes" of devotional art. Against this backdrop, Stanbury assesses John Capgrave's *Katherine*, Walter Hilton's "Merk Ymage," Nicholas Love's *Mirror of the Life of Christ*, the *Book of Margery Kempe*, and several aspects of Chaucer's "sacra-

mental poetic": his ekphrastic descriptions, the Pardoner's relics, daisy worship in *LGWP*, the "translation" of Griselda in *ClT*, and the tension between private devotion and public spectacle in *PrT*. See also no. 420.

142. Sylvester, Louise M. *Medieval Romance and the Construction of Heterosexuality*. The New Middle Ages. New York: Palgrave Macmillan, 2008. 202 pp. Investigates how medieval romances have shaped heterosexual gender roles, studying the role of language in constructing sexuality. In close readings of *TC*, *MilT*, and *MerT*, Sylvester analyzes "transitivity" and maps dialogue between male and female characters, particularly in scenes in which characters meet and in which intercourse is initially offered. Forceful heterosexual masculinity is required for heterosexual intercourse to occur in fabliau and romance. Includes discussion of rape in medieval romance. See also no. 422.

143. Taylor, Andrew. *"The Canterbury Tales*, 1380s–90s: Geoffrey Chaucer." In *Books That Changed the World: The 50 Most Influential Books in Human History*. London: Quercus, 2008, pp. 46–49. Summarizes Chaucer's life and works, particularly *CT*, and praises Chaucer's characterizations, use of vernacular English, and depiction of a wide social range and register.

144. Williams, Tara. "Fragments and Foundations: Medieval Texts and the Future of Feminism." *LitComp* 4.4 (2007): 1003–16. Argues that a "turn to the Middle Ages" can reinvigorate feminist criticism, encouraging exploration of the "origins of gendered language," e.g., *womanhood*, *femininity*, and *wifehood*. Williams surveys the tradition of feminist approaches to medieval literature, particularly studies of Chaucer and female writers.

The Canterbury Tales—General

145. Bishop, Kathleen A., ed. *"The Canterbury Tales" Revisited—21st Century Interpretations*. Newcastle: Cambridge Scholars, 2008. xvi, 337 pp. Eighteen essays by various authors, with a foreword by David Matthews (pp. x–xiv) and a preface by the editor (pp. xv–xvi). See nos. 150, 169, 171, 185, 186, 195, 196, 211, 217, 225, 249, 256, 259, 262, 272, 274, 307, and 330.

146. Bloom, Harold, ed. *Geoffrey Chaucer's "The Canterbury Tales."* *New Edition*. Bloom's Modern Critical Interpretations. New York: Infobase, 2008. vii, 286 pp. Eleven essays previously published between 1999 and 2004. Includes essays by Fiona Somerset on *SumT* and on

clerical hypocrisy, Colin Wilcockson on *GP*, Katherine Little on *ParsT*, Lee Patterson on *PrT*, Elizabeth Robertson on *MLT*, Louise M. Bishop on *MilT*, Richard Firth Green on "changing Chaucer," Lianna Farber on *PhyT*, Peter W. Travis on *SumT*, and William F. Woods on *RvT*. The volume includes a Chaucer chronology, a bibliography, and an index.

147. Boyd, David Lorenzo. "Chaucer, Geoffrey (134?–1400)." In Claude J. Summers, ed. *The Gay and Lesbian Literary Heritage: A Reader's Companion to the Writers and Their Works, from Antiquity to the Present*. Rev. ed. New York: Routledge, 2002, pp. 147–48. Boyd summarizes the tension in medieval tradition between the promotion of homosocial bonding and the proscription of sodomy. He characterizes Chaucer's treatment of male homosexuality in *CT* as typically homophobic.

148. Bugbee, John Stephen. "God's Patients: Suffering and the Divine in *The Canterbury Tales*." *DAI* A68.12 (2008): n.p. Applies the thought of Bernard of Clairvaux to issues of human action and subjection to God and law, as seen in *ClT*, *MLT*, *KnT*, *FrT*, and *PhyT*. Argues that a fuller understanding of Chaucer's "religious background" is essential to interpretation of his work.

149. Cigman, Gloria. "Rich Man, Poor Man: Polarities of Privilege." In Danielle Buschinger and Arlette Sancery, eds. *Mélanges de langue, littérature et civilisation offerts à André Crépin à l'occasion de son quatre-vingtième anniversaire* (*SAC* 32 [2010], no. 104), pp. 111–17. Explores ambiguities of wealth and poverty in *CT* in light of contemporaneous reality.

150. Kia-Choong, Kevin Teo. "Noise, *Terminus*, and *Circuitus*: Performing Voices in Chaucer's *Canterbury Tales*." In Kathleen A. Bishop, ed. *"The Canterbury Tales" Revisited—21st Century Interpretations* (*SAC* 32 [2010], no. 145), pp. 314–33. The "polyphonic assemblage of voices" in *CT* "displaces the teleological-topographical narrative" of movement toward the heavenly city of God. The Wife of Bath, the Pardoner, and the Miller, in particular, embody noise and represent the *vox populi* that resists official culture.

151. Malo, Roberta. "Saints' Relics in Medieval English Literature." *DAI* A68.07 (2008): n.p. Discussing the use of relics as a site of "institutional control," Malo argues that in works such as *CT*, writers "use relics as tools" for affirmation or critique of the Church's position as dispenser of grace and healing.

152. Morrison, Susan Signe. *Excrement in the Late Middle Ages: Sacred Filth and Chaucer's Fecopoetics*. The New Middle Ages. New York: Palgrave Macmillan, 2008. xiii, 271 pp. Morrison constructs a cultural po-

etics of excrement to suggest that Chaucer's treatment of fecal matter, in both its literal and figurative senses, illustrates the ways that the Middle Ages viewed excrement. This cultural poetics enables the modern critic to better understand the Middle Ages, as well as the legacy that medieval attitudes toward fecal matter have left to modern culture. Morrison addresses much of *CT* (*PrT*, *NPT*, and *PardT* most extensively), focusing on fecal matter in an attempt to "correct the potential decorporealization of the medieval body."

153. ———. "Pilgrimage, Gender, and Theory: Where Are the Women Pilgrimage Poets of the Fourteenth Century?" In Juliette Dor and Marie-Élisabeth Henneau, eds. *Femmes et pèlerinages/Women and Pilgrimages* (*SAC* 32 [2010], no. 112), pp. 141–52. A number of the most famous fourteenth-century poets used pilgrimage as a genre to promote the use of vernacular language. Morrison's essay considers pilgrimage, gender, and use of the vernacular, raising questions about intertextual anxiety and the identities of pilgrim poets, including Chaucer.

154. Normandin, Shawn D. "The Opacity of Renunciation in Chaucer's *Canterbury Tales.*" *DAI* A68.08 (2008): n.p. Examines the motif of renunciation in *CT*, ranging from renunciation of poetry (*MkT*, *ParsT*, and *Ret*) to renunciation of music and high-flown rhetoric (*ManT*), renunciation of curiosity (*MilT*, *CYT*), and praiseworthy acts of renunciation (*ClT*, *FranT*). These renunciations have a variety of effects, both literary and philosophical.

155. Pericard-Mea, Denise. "Women and Pilgrimage." In Juliette Dor and Marie-Élisabeth Henneau, eds. *Femmes et pèlerinages/Women and Pilgrimages* (*SAC* 32 [2010], no. 112), pp. 25–46. Discusses female presence and company on pilgrimage routes, examining women's destinations and motivations compared to those of men.

156. Stockton, William. "Sex, Sense, and Nonsense: The Anal Erotics of Early Modern Comedy." *DAI* A68.07 (2008): n.p. Stockton discusses the "critique of cynical reason" in *CT* as part of a larger psychoanalytical discussion of the role of comedy in the formation of the foundations of civilizations.

157. Tormey, Warren. "Mining, Metalworking, and the Epic Underworld: The Corruption of Epic Heroism and the Emergence of Commercial Ethos as Represented in the Epic Line from Homer to Milton." *DAI* A69.04 (2008): n.p. Tormey examines metal and metalworking as symbols of economic forces shaping the development of epic form and

subject matter. Discusses *CT* and Dante's *Inferno* as "proto-commercial travel narratives."

158. White, Michael P. "Vegetable Love." *DAI* A68.07 (2008): n.p. Employs the metaphor of the vegetable to examine a variety of poetic works, emphasizing "metamorphic natural processes, and thus the dissolution of boundaries between states of being." Considers *CT* as an example, focusing on complicated, entertwined relationships among the pilgrims.

159. Williams, Tara. "The Host, His Wife, and Their Communities in the *Canterbury Tales*." *ChauR* 42 (2008): 383–408. Harry Bailly's remarks about his wife Goodelief constitute a community among the husbands along for the pilgrimage; they also call attention to various affiliations of wives in *CT*, e.g., the Clerk's "archewyves." As outlets for complaints about spouses, these communities based on "marital identity" have the salutary effects of revealing and addressing deficiencies of marriage.

160. Woods, William F. *Chaucerian Spaces: Spatial Poetics in Chaucer's Opening Tales*. SUNY Series in Medieval Studies. Albany: State University of New York Press, 2008. xi, 203 pp. Woods discusses the effect and significance of space and place in seven tales of *CT*, exploring place as an index of character and space as a site of characteristic potential. In *KnT*, Theseus and the narrator consider chivalry analogous to nature; in *MilT*, Alysoun's household is a world for men. Symkyn's house in *RvT* is a place of advancement, in contrast to the countryside; in *CkT*, London is part of the interior world of the characters. Custance's return to Rome in *MLT* coincides with a collapse of narrative space. The Wife of Bath projects her desires onto the landscape, but she also internalizes the world to accommodate her needs. In *ShT*, the wife makes her bedroom her own mercantile space, a parallel to the merchant's counting room.

See also nos. 6, 10–12, 16, 18–20, 25, 27, 30–33, 35–37, 39, 83, 84, 86, 93, 111, 121, 131–33, 135, 309.

CT—The General Prologue

161. Brewer, Derek. "Proximity, Prestige, and Paradox." In Danielle Buschinger and Arlette Sancery, eds. *Mélanges de langue, littérature et civilisation offerts à André Crépin à l'occasion de son quatre-vingtième anniversaire*

(*SAC* 32 [2010], no. 104), pp. 59–62. Considers friendly and hostile relationships, commenting on *GP* and *TC*.

162. Carlin, Martha. "'What say you to a piece of beef and mustard?' The Evolution of Public Dining in Medieval and Tudor London." *HLQ* 71 (2008): 199–217. Carlin documents the development of public dining in London and Westminster, drawing evidence from, among other sources, *GP*, *Piers Plowman*, and the prologue to Lydgate's *The Siege of Thebes*.

163. Farrell, Thomas J. "Hybrid Discourse in the *General Prologue* Portraits." *SAC* 30 (2008): 39–93. Analyzes the "range of discourses" in several *GP* descriptions, particularly those of the Monk, Friar, Parson, Clerk, Sergeant at Law, and Prioress. In various ways, Chaucer combines estates satire, free indirect discourse, the opinions of the narrator, and voice and "character zone" as theorized by Bakhtin to produce clear satire, approbation, and unresolved ambiguity in individual descriptions. Chaucer anticipates narrative techniques of the novel.

164. Mack, Peter, and Chris Walton, eds. *General Prologue to the Canterbury Tales*, by Geoffrey Chaucer. Oxford Student Texts. Oxford: Oxford University Press, 2008. vi, 185 pp. Textbook edition of *GP*. Includes glosses and discursive notes (at the back of the book) and discussion of approaches to the text: sources and analogues, characterization, assessment of theme and topic, and analysis of poetic technique. Also includes basic contextual materials (black-and-white illustrations of pilgrims, excerpted analogues, etc.), a chronology and discussion of language, and suggestions for classroom activities and discussion. Revised version of 1994 publication.

165. Moberly, Brent Addison. "'Wayke Been the Oxen': Plowing, Presumption, and the Third-Estate Ideal in Late Medieval England." *DAI* 69.02 (2008): n.p. Uses Chaucer (*MilT* and the absent Plowman), Hoccleve, Lydgate, and Bishop Reginald Pecock to investigate changing ideas regarding "post-plague labor practice" and the traditional concept of the plowman.

166. Nohara, Yasuhiro. "Chaucer's Play on Numbers." *Intercultural Studies* (Momoyama Gakuin University) 37 (2007): 113–39 (in Japanese, with English abstract). Cast as a dialogue between Chaucer and Nohara, the article reconsiders the discrepancy between "nyne and twenty" (*GP* 24) and the number of pilgrims in *CT*.

167. ———. "The Meaning of the Pilgrims in *The Canterbury Tales*." *Momoyama Gakuin Daigaku Kirisutokyo Ronshu* (St. Andrew's University

Journal of Christian Studies) 40 (2004): 61–108 (in Japanese, with English abstract). Considers the impulses to go on pilgrimage in late medieval England and assesses the *GP* descriptions of the pilgrims in light of contemporary motivations for pilgrimage.

168. ———. "Numerals and Intensive Adverbs in Chaucer." *English Review* (Momoyama Gakuin University) 11 (1996): 27–47 (in Japanese, with English abstract). Argues that the intensive use of "wel" in "wel nyne and twenty" (*GP* 24) helps account for the apparent discrepancy between the phrase and the number of pilgrims in *CT*.

169. Reale, Nancy M. "Companies, Mysteries, and Foreign Exchange: Chaucer's Currency for the Modern Reader." In Kathleen A. Bishop, ed. *"The Canterbury Tales" Revisited—21st Century Interpretations* (*SAC* 32 [2010], no. 145), pp. 256–80. Chaucer's *CT*, particularly *GP*, offers "as its 'utilitarian' value or 'worth' exemplary lessons on constructing social identity in the context of an emergent market system." This "bold step paved the way for modern ways of understanding the self," sensitizing readers to the importance of "language and appearance" in constructions of self.

170. Strohm, Paul. "Sovereignty and Sewage." In Lisa H. Cooper and Andrea Denny-Brown, eds. *Lydgate Matters: Poetry and Material Culture in the Fifteenth Century* (*SAC* 32 [2010], no. 108), pp. 57–70. Strohm assesses historical implications of the concern with civic and personal cleansing in Lydgate's *Troy Book* and comments on Chaucer's imagery of cleansing in *GP*, his concern with civic orderliness in *KnT*, and his personal experiences with sovereignty and civic planning as Clerk of Works.

See also nos. 7, 12, 63, 65, 180, 227, 229, 241, 242, 278.

CT—The Knight and His Tale

171. Casey, Jim. "'Love should end with hope': Courting and Competition in *The Knight's Tale*." In Kathleen A. Bishop, ed. *"The Canterbury Tales" Revisited—21st Century Interpretations* (*SAC* 32 [2010], no. 145), pp. 209–27. The price of love for Palamon and Arcite in *KnT* is violence and death, a feature of the "gender/violence/courtship paradigm" of medieval courtly literature that continues into the present, as evident in Brian Helgeland's *A Knight's Tale*.

172. Curtis, Carl C. III. "Biblical Analogy and Secondary Allegory in

Chaucer's *The Knight's Tale*." *C&L* 57 (2008): 207–22. Biblical analogies embedded in *KnT* constitute an implied critique of the pre-Christian setting: Palamon and Arcite's first sight of Emelye accords with David's first sight of Bathsheba (2 Samuel 11:2); loving Emelye reorganizes Arcite's psyche and morals as love of Christ revolutionized Paul's (Philippians 3:3–9); the representation of "womman travaillynge" in Diana's temple recalls Revelation 12:1–2 and—as a sacramental image that both heathens and Christians would recognize—Romans 1:20. Familiar to the audience although not to the characters, these analogies point to broader moral allegory.

173. ———. *Chaucer's "The Knight's Tale" and the Limits of Human Order in the Pagan World*. Lewiston, N.Y.: Edwin Mellen Press, 2008. x, 262 pp. The first two chapters of this book look at the Knight and *KnT* in the context of the "heroic life." The Allegory of Rule and the Allegory of Love offer ways to understand Palamon and Arcites's fight in the wood. The second two chapters examine the importance of Athens—its constitution, failure, and refounding—as location of the pagan world.

174. Dor, Juliette. "Quelle victoire pour Thésée sur les Amazones dans le *Conte du Chevalier* de Chaucer?" In Guyonne Leduc, ed. *Réalité et représentations des Amazones*. Paris: L'Harmattan, 2008, pp. 257–72 (in French). Feminist and postcolonial reconsideration of the figure of Emily that focuses on the Knight's adjustment of traditional material; Emily has not submitted to patriarchal values, despite the Knight's modifications.

175. Edwards, Elizabeth B. "Chaucer's *Knight's Tale* and the Work of Mourning." *Exemplaria* 20 (2008): 361–84. Edwards discusses the rites and purposes of mourning in *KnT* in relation to the psychological theories of Freud and Derrida. Contrasts the Freudian account with medieval practices of theology and Purgatory; the pagan setting is necessary to complete the "work of mourning," impossible in a fourteenth-century Christian society.

176. Ganim, John M. "Chaucer and the War of the Maidens." In Jeffrey Jerome Cohen, ed. *Cultural Diversity in the British Middle Ages: Archipelago, Island, England*. The New Middle Ages. New York: Palgrave Macmillan, 2008, pp. 191–208. The War of the Maidens, a founding myth of Czech history, may have come to England via Anne of Bohemia and may be part of the "political unconscious" of several of Chaucer's works, particularly his depiction of the Amazons in *KnT*.

177. Guidry, Marc S. "The Parliaments of Gods and Men in the

Knight's Tale." ChauR 43 (2008): 140–70. Chaucer's uses of parliamentary terminology throughout *KnT*, but especially in Saturn's counsel to Venus and in Theseus's "First Mover" speech, establish a parallel between divine and human realms, revealing "the abuse of power and authority" in both and effecting a critical assessment, in turn, of the Ricardian court and of the "norms of English political discourse."

178. Hammond, Paul. "The Interplay of Past and Present in Dryden's 'Palamon and Arcite.'" *Seventeenth Century* 23 (2008): 142–59. Hammond compares and contrasts Dryden's "Palamon and Arcite" from *Fables Ancient and Modern* with its source, Chaucer's *KnT*, finding that Dryden reworked religious and political concerns to create a "macaronic fabric" that combines classical, medieval, and Restoration motifs in an idealized whole.

179. Johnston, Andrew James. "Voyeurism and Narratorial Power: The Cultural Politics of the 'Knight's Tale.'" In Andrew James Johnston. *Performing the Middle Ages from "Beowulf" to "Othello."* Late Medieval and Early Modern Studies, no. 15. Turnhout: Brepols, 2008, pp. 94–123. Revises the author's earlier study "The Keyhole Politics of Chaucerian Theatricality: Voyeurism in the *Knight's Tale*" (*SAC* 27 [2005], no. 183), placing it in the context of a parallel discussion of *Sir Gawain and the Green Knight*.

180. Kim, Hyonjin. "Chaucer's 'Wayke Ox': Rereading *The Knight's Tale.*" *MES* 16 (2008): 77–111 (in Korean, with English abstract). Surveys critical approaches to *KnT*, particularly New Critical, Feminist, and New Historical, focusing on discussions of order and disorder in the *Tale*. *KnT* functions as a "second prologue" to *CT* and, with *GP*, asserts and affirms the diversity of human affairs.

181. Lee, Dongchoon. "*The Knight's Tale*: Forms, Incongruities, and Chaucer's Intention." *MES* 16 (2008): 43–76 (in Korean, with English abstract). Through various devices of style and narrative technique, Chaucer undermines the Knight's (and Theseus's) efforts to find or impose order on human and cosmic disruption and violence.

182. Lewis, Celia M. "History, Mission, and Crusade in the *Canterbury Tales.*" *ChauR* 42 (2008): 353–82. Together, Chaucer's two references to the Alexandrian crusade in *CT*, along with his portrait of the Knight and depictions of Custance and the Sultaness in *MLT*, expose similarities between missionary work and crusading. The Knight's participation in a pilgrimage thus endorses "personal spiritual renewal" as a greater good than seeking the religious conversion of others.

183. Wadiak, Walter Philip. "Romancing Capital: The Gift in Middle English Literature." *DAI* A69.01 (2008): n.p. Wadiak considers how Middle English romances focus on "giving and spending" as a questioning of the emergent capitalistic system, examining romances from *King Horn* through *KnT* and arguing that these works simultaneously shape and reflect the move from feudalism to capitalism.

184. White, R. S. *Pacifism and English Literature: Minstrels of Peace.* New York: Palgrave Macmillan, 2007. vii, 299 pp. White explores the role of literature in "peace studies," traces pacifist theory through the ages, and surveys pacifism in English literature from the Middle Ages to modern prose, poetry, and film. The chapter on the Middle Ages comments on Old English tradition, Anglo-Norman tradition, and works by Gower, Lydgate, Hoccleve, and Chaucer (especially *Mel* and *KnT*).

185. Zilleruelo, Art. "Chaucer's Knight as Revisionist Historian: Anachronism in *The Knight's Tale*." In Kathleen A. Bishop, ed. *"The Canterbury Tales" Revisited—21st Century Interpretations* (*SAC* 32 [2010], no. 145), pp. 194–208. Reads *KnT* as "historical narrative constructed upon a foundation of misleading anachronism . . . to lend strength to the potentially objectionable sociopolitical agenda of its narrator."

See also nos. 12, 49, 50, 58, 68, 95, 126, 127, 135, 141, 148, 160, 170, 188, 267, 268.

CT—The Miller and His Tale

186. Bishop, Kathleen A. "Queer Punishments: Tragic and Comic Sodomy in the Death of Edward II and in Chaucer's *Miller's Tale*." In Kathleen A. Bishop, ed. *"The Canterbury Tales" Revisited—21st Century Interpretations* (*SAC* 32 [2010], no. 145), pp. 16–26. Asserts several parallels between the window scene in *MilT* and reports of the sodomitical execution of Edward II.

187. Braswell, Mary Flowers. " 'A Completely Funny Story': Mary Eliza Haweis and the *Miller's Tale*." *ChauR* 42 (2008): 244–68. A series of essays and translations written between 1877 and 1886, Mary Eliza Haweis's work on *MilT* constitutes a large and uniquely positive chapter in the reception of *MilT* in Victorian England.

188. Eyler, Joshua R., and John P. Sexton. "The *Miller's Tale*, 3466–3499: Narrative Inconsistency and the First Fragment of *The Canterbury*

Tales." ANQ 21.3 (2008): 2–6. Nicholas's door in *MilT* (knocked off its hinges in one moment and then closed on its hinges a few minutes later) is a semiotic hinge in the play between public and private space, echoing Theseus's attempts to control space in *KnT*.

189. Forbes, Shannon. "'To Alisoun now wol I tellen al my love-longing': Chaucer's Treatment of the Courtly Love Discourse in *The Miller's Tale." WS* 36.1 (2007): 1–14. In *MilT*, Alison resists Absolon's efforts to compel her to perform courtly behavior and chooses her "own predicates" of behavior, thus establishing her identity and coercing Absolon to abandon his failed courtly role.

190. Kelly, Henry Ansgar. "Canon Law and Chaucer on Licit and Illicit Magic." In Ruth Mazo Karras, Joel Kaye, and E. Ann Matter, eds. *Law and the Illicit in Medieval Europe*. The Middle Ages. Philadelphia: University of Pennsylvania Press, 2008, pp. 211–24. John's incantations to protect Nicholas in *MilT* would have been considered licit uses of medicinal magic according to strictures of John Peakham, the Archdeacon of Canterbury. Kelly also comments on *FranT*, *SqT*, and *ParsT*.

191. Misaki, Noguchi. "Translating of the Polysemous Words in the Modernizations of 'The Miller's Tale' in Geoffrey Chaucer's *The Canterbury Tales." Kaetsu University Research Review* 50.2 (2007): 89–111 (in Japanese). Explores the semantic range of *hende* and of *sely* in *MilT* and examines efforts to translate the words in various modernizations, particularly those of the eighteenth century.

192. Richmond, E. B., trans. *The Miller's Tale*, by Geoffrey Chaucer. London: Hesperus, 2008. xv, 58 pp. Facing-page version of *MilPT* and the *GP* description of the Miller, with modernization in iambic pentameter facing the Middle English text from the *Riverside* edition. Contains a descriptive introduction, brief notes (pp. 53–55), and a biographical note.

193. Smith, Charles R. "Jealousy: Chaucer's Miller and the Tradition." *ChauR* 43 (2008): 16–47. Chaucer's audience would have considered the Miller's apparent lack of jealousy toward his wife in the context of a long-standing teaching that jealousy has a salutary side. According to that view, "Whoever is not jealous does not love."

194. Tolmie, Sarah. "Langland, Wittgenstein, and the Language Game." *YLS* 22 (2008): 103–29. Tolmie notes "an anti-Augustinian semiotic moment" (111) in *MilT*.

195. Zilleruelo, Erica L. "The Churlish Nature of Chaucer's *Miller's Tale*: How Language Can Define Genre." In Kathleen A. Bishop, ed.

"The Canterbury Tales" Revisited—21st Century Interpretations (*SAC* 32 [2010], no. 145), pp. 27–43. Considers several features of *MilT*, including diction, arguing that *MilT* is a "Chaucerian fabliau."

See also nos. 12, 66, 90, 142, 150, 154, 160, 165, 286, 297.

CT—The Reeve and His Tale

196. Breuer, Heidi. "Being Intolerant: Rape Is Not Seduction (in 'The Reeve's Tale' or Anywhere Else)." In Kathleen A. Bishop, ed. *"The Canterbury Tales" Revisited—21st Century Interpretations* (*SAC* 32 [2010], no. 145), pp. 1–15. Identifies several aspects of medieval legal discourse concerning rape and explores how they "inform the representation of rape" in *RvT*. Also assesses implications of modern resistance to recognizing the two rapes in *RvT*, viewing that resistance as evidence of "rape culture."

197. Campbell, Bruce M. S. *Field Systems and Farming Systems in Late Medieval England.* Variorum Collected Studies. Burlington, Vt.: Ashgate, 2008. Reprints thirteen essays by Campbell, including his "The Livestock of Chaucer's Reeve: Fact or Fiction" (*SAC* 19 [1997], no. 181), first published in 1995.

198. Epstein, Robert. " 'Fer in the north; I kan nat telle where': Dialect, Regionalism, and Philologism." *SAC* 30 (2008): 95–124. Analogous to orientalism, the "philologism" of *RvT* is rooted in "North-South binaries" that partake of and help to constitute southern condescension to northerners in England, even before the rise of a Standard Written Dialect. Informed by the theory of Pierre Bourdieu, the essay compares and contrasts the "regionalist generalizations" in *RvT*, *The Second Shepherd's Play*, and elsewhere in Middle English.

199. Petrina, Alessandra. "Seeing, Believing, and Groping in the Dark: A Reading of the *Reeve's Tale.*" In Giovanni Iamartino, Maria Luisa Maggioni, and Roberta Facchinetti, eds. *Thou sittest at another boke . . . : English Studies in Honour of Domenico Pezzini* (*SAC* 32 [2010], no. 119), pp. 223–35. *RvT* differs from its sources and analogues by developing the relationship between sight, desire, and reason, ultimately questioning the function of vision, the most important of the senses.

200. Tolkien, J. R. R. "Chaucer as a Philologist: *The Reeve's Tale.*" *Tolkien Studies* 5 (2008): 109–71. Reprints Tolkien's assessment of the dialect features of *RvT*, originally presented to the Philological Society

in Oxford (May 1931) and published in the Society's *Transactions* in 1934. This version is reprinted with attention to Tolkien's marginal comments and corrections to a copy of the original printed version.

201. ———. "*The Reeve's Tale*: Version Prepared for Recitation at the 'Summer Diversions.' Oxford: 1939." *Tolkien Studies* 5 (2008): 173–83. Reprints the "rare pamphlet version" of Tolkien's lightly abbreviated performance version of *RvT*, adapted from Skeat's edition with diacritical marks to aid pronunciation and several adjustments to emphasize dialect features of the *Tale*. In his preparatory remarks, Tolkien comments that Chaucer presents an "*East-Anglian* reeve, who is amusing *southern*, largely London, folk with imitations of *northern* speech brought southward by the attraction of the *universities*."

See also nos. 8, 129, 160.

CT—The Cook and His Tale

202. Nohara, Yasuhiro. "The Grammar of *The Cook's Tale* in *The Canterbury Tales*." *Journal of Human Sciences* (Momoyama Gakuin University) 17.3 (1981): 33–69 (in Japanese). Line-by-line, phrase-by-phrase commentary on the grammar and lexicon of *CkPT*, presented as a series of notes to a reprinting of the text from F. N. Robinson's 1957 edition.

See also no. 160.

CT—The Man of Law and His Tale

203. Aloni, Gila. "M(ons)ters In-Law: Maternal Models in *The Man of Law's Tale*." In Danielle Buschinger and Arlette Sancery, eds. *Mélanges de langue, littérature et civilisation offerts à André Crépin à l'occasion de son quatre-vingtième anniversaire* (*SAC* 32 [2010], no. 104), pp. 1–10. Explores how Chaucer's reflections on maternity expose a relationship between Christianity and other religions in *MLT*.

See also nos. 68, 99, 107, 115, 130, 148, 163, 330.

CT—The Wife of Bath and Her Tale

204. Allen, Valerie, and David Kirkham, eds. *The Wife of Bath's Prologue and Tale*, by Geoffrey Chaucer. Cambridge School Chaucer. Cam-

bridge: Cambridge University Press, 1998. 112 pp. Middle English text of *WBPT* and the *GP* description of the Wife of Bath, with notes, glossary, and discussion questions on facing pages. Includes commentary on Chaucer's life, contemporary social issues (including pilgrimage), and the rest of *CT*. Illustrations include photographs and line drawings.

205. Brandolino, Gina. "Voice Lessons: Violence, Voice, and Interiority in Middle English Religious Narratives, 1300–1500." *DAI* A68.10 (2008): n.p. Brandolino examines reciprocity between faith and interiority in a number of late medieval English vernacular texts, including *WBPT* and *SNT*. After 1215, when Pope Innocent III "issued a decree requiring all Christians . . . to make an annual private confession," works such as saints' lives, "contemplative and meditative texts," and lyrics demonstrated an irreconcilable gap between "institutional faith and interiority."

206. Cannon, Christopher. "Langland's *Ars Grammatica.*" *YLS* 22 (2008): 1–25. The Wife of Bath and Langland draw on similar "schoolroom texts" such as Matthew of Vendôme's "Tobias."

207. Cole, Meghan R. "'Wynne . . . for al is for to selle': Sexual Economics and Female Authority in Chaucer's *Wife of Bath's Prologue.*" *Sigma Tau Delta Review* 5 (2008): 17–25. Cole examines the "intricate relationship between sex, money, and power" in *WBP*, particularly as reflected in the sequence in which the Wife recalls her husbands.

208. Gaffney, Paul Douglas. "Taking Stock of Middle English Popular Romance." *DAI* A69.04 (2008): n.p. Contrasts *WBT* to popular romance narratives of the period, arguing that notions of *sentence*—i.e., of "meaning that is inscribed into a narrative by its author"—force high cultural glossing onto popular texts that may not be best suited to such glosses.

209. Green, Richard Firth. "'Allas, Allas! That evere love was synne!': John Bromyard v. Alice of Bath." *ChauR* 42 (2008): 298–311. Bromyard's denunciation of "popular views on sex" in the *Luxuria* section of his *Summa Predicantium* resonates verbally and structurally with *WBP*, suggesting that the Wife's performance functions in part as a counterattack to such sermonizing by Bromyard and others.

210. Jacobs, Kathryn. "Unlikely Sympathies: The Rapist of the Wife's Tale." *Mediaevalia* 29.2 (2008): 1–13. In the fourteenth century, rape was perceived as "natural," a relatively minor social infraction. In *WBT*, the ladies of the court do not dispute the verdict assigned the rapist-knight; they dispute only the penalty. The knight is socially reha-

bilitated, not morally reformed. The humor of his discomfiture allows for his restoration to the primarily male community of the court, a community he has embarrassed by creating a social problem and by asserting a sexual advantage over his fellow knights.

211. Martin, Jennifer L. "The *Crossing* of the Wife of Bath." In Kathleen A. Bishop, ed. *"The Canterbury Tales" Revisited—21st Century Interpretations* (*SAC* 32 [2010], no. 145), pp. 60–74. Cites instances in which the Wife of Bath crosses over between binary sets (male/female, sex/gender, authority/experience), and suggests that she cannot be seen simply as a feminist. Nor is she simply a victim.

212. Newman, Claire. "Reading or Listening to Alison? Chaucer's *Wife of Bath's Prologue.*" *English Review* (Deddington, Oxfordshire) 13.1 (2003): 2–5. Summarizes performance features of *WBP* (echoes of preaching, animal imagery, range of emotion, entertainment value) appropriate to fourteenth-century encounters with the text as an aural experience.

213. Normandin, Shawn. "The Wife of Bath's Urinary Imagination." *Exemplaria* 20 (2008): 244–63. Normandin argues that a "surplus of urine in the absence of fecal matter affects the tone" of *WBP*. Chaucer "associates the Wife of Bath with urine because antifeminist traditions often represented females as liquid, dripping creatures and because urine functioned as a deceptive medical signifier"; however, "fecal matter is better suited to aggressive satire" than is urine. Also surveys scatology in Jerome's *Adversus Jovinianum*, Chrétien de Troyes's *Cligès*, and *The Towneley Plays*.

214. Risden, E. L. "Lost in the Not-So-Fun House: Subversive Threads in the Medieval Narrative Labyrinth." The Plenary Address, 22nd Annual Meeting of the Medieval Association of the Midwest, January 2007, University of Puerto Rico at Mayaguez. *Enarratio* 13 (2006): 1–24. Risden explores how several medieval narratives "subvert" readers' expectations and "hint at the loneliness of the moral act." Includes comments on *WBP*, as well as on *Beowulf*, *Sir Gawain and the Green Knight*, *Piers Plowman*, and other works.

215. Rosenfeld, Nancy. "Who Peyntede the Leon? The Olde Wyf Confronts the Wife of Bath and Criseyde." *Atenea* (Puerto Rico) 23.1 (2003): 69–83. Parallels between Criseyde and the women of *WBPT* "interrogate the following issues: equality between the sexes, possessions (ownership), possession (jealousy), and appearance." Rosenfeld reads the loathly lady as a "synthesis" of the Wife of Bath and Criseyde and as an

expression of the ideal that the separation between appearance and reality can be transcended.

216. Steiner, Wendy. "Steppin' Out: On Making an Animated Opera Called *The Loathly Lady*." In Rosemary Feal, ed. *Profession 2008*. New York: Modern Language Association, 2008, pp. 24–32. Personal narrative about Steiner's composition of an opera inspired by *WBT*, intended for production as a full-length animated film. Includes sketches and storyboards by John Kindness.

217. Walzem, Al. "Peynted by the Lion: The Wife of Bath as Feminist Pedagogue." In Kathleen A. Bishop, ed. *"The Canterbury Tales" Revisited—21st Century Interpretations* (*SAC* 32 [2010], no. 145), pp. 44–59. Reads the Wife of Bath as ur-feminist and traces parallels between *WBP* and *WBT*. These parallels indicate the Wife's efforts to teach feminist principles.

See also nos. 12, 41, 45, 58, 62, 88, 101, 113, 128, 130, 137, 150, 160, 247, 268, 307.

CT—The Friar and His Tale

218. Culver, Jennifer. "Charity Refused and Curses Uttered in Chaucer's *Friar's Tale*." *Hortulus* 4 (2008): n.p. Argues that Chaucer's representation of the widow in *FrT* anticipates the "cursing hag" of early modern tradition, especially in responding to the summoner's refusal of her request for charity. The curse and the summoner's refusal to repent help to convey the *Tale*'s themes of intention, agency, and the power of language.

219. Griffith, John Lance. "The *Friar's Tale* and Divine Justice: The Reality and the Fiction of Righteous Anger." *NTU {National Taiwan University} Studies in Language and Literature* 18 (2007): 37–59. The exemplary value of *FrT* is rendered complex by its setting within the Canterbury fiction and by the angered antagonism between Friar and Summoner. Chaucer places the story "in a human situation . . . to engage our understanding of the way in which the sin of anger, the response to that sin, and the claim for just anger operate in the everyday world." Misused "narratives of divine anger" lead to "hell."

See also nos. 88, 148, 163.

CT—The Summoner and His Tale

See nos. 66, 147.

CT—The Clerk and His Tale

220. Carlson, Cindy. "Chaucer's Grisilde, Her Smock, and the Fashioning of a Character." In Cynthia Kuhn and Cindy Carlson, eds. *Styling Texts: Dress and Fashion in Literature*. Youngstown, N.Y.: Cambria Press, 2007, pp. 33–48. Carlson examines motifs of shame and covering in the two disrobing scenes in *ClT*, arguing that Griselda's request for a smock to cover herself before she leaves Walter indicates that she has "shown a self that cannot be shamed by Walter, by poverty, by her father."

221. Denny-Brown, Andrea. "Lydgate's Golden Cows: Appetite and Avarice in *Bycorne and Chychevache*." In Lisa H. Cooper and Andrea Denny-Brown, eds. *Lydgate Matters: Poetry and Material Culture in the Fifteenth Century* (*SAC* 32 [2010], no. 108), pp. 35–56. Denny-Brown explores roots of the medieval legends of Bicorn and Chichevache, examining how Chaucer develops the "themes of beastly appetites" in *ClT* and how Lydgate expands the theme of appetite in his *Bycorne and Chychevache*.

222. Ding, Jian-Ning. "Virtue or Strategy: Three 'Restraints' in *The Clerk's Tale*." *Foreign Literature Studies* [*WenGuo Xue Yan Jiu*] 29 (2007): 111–17 (in Chinese). Argues that Griselda's "restraint" is a subversive strategy and explores the implications of this subversion for understanding the Clerk as narrator and Chaucer as poet.

223. Harkins, Jessica Lara Lawrence. "Translations of Griselda." *DAI* A69.05 (2008): n.p. Looks at *ClT* and Boccaccio's *Decameron* 10.10, along with works of Saint Jerome, Apuleius, and Petrarch, to examine assumptions about Griselda and versions of her tale, arguing that Chaucer was aware of the Boccaccio text.

224. Pugh, Tison. "'He nedes moot unto the pley assente': Queer Fidelities and Contractual Hermaphroditism in Chaucer's *Clerk's Tale*." In *Sexuality and Its Queer Discontents in Middle English Literature* (*SAC* 32 [2010], no. 132), pp. 75–99. The Clerk's submission to the Host's tale-telling game parallels Griselda's submission to Walter: the two are queerly faithful in ways that bring into focus their "contractual hermaphroditism" and deconstruct traditional gender categories. Griselda's

fidelity reconstructs Walter's masculinity; the Clerk compels from his audience a "dissolution of gender" for the remainder of *CT*. Readers find queer pleasure despite the cruelty of the *Tale*.

225. Rossiter, William. "'To Grisilde again wol I me dresse': Readdressing *The Clerk's Tale*." In Kathleen A. Bishop, ed. *"The Canterbury Tales" Revisited—21st Century Interpretations* (*SAC* 32 [2010], no. 145), pp. 166–93. Complex intertextual relationships among *ClT* and its multiple sources, as well as the complex political implications of *ClT*, reinforce the *Tale*'s "habit of returning its readers to the multiplicity of interpretation."

226. Yoon, Minwoo. "Griselda's Body and Labor in Chaucer's Tale." *MES* 16 (2008): 113–41 (in Korean, with English abstract). Although Griselda is "translated" in three different ways in *ClT* (language, place, and social class), her labor is constant throughout. Her labors (domestic, wifely, and public) define her essential selfhood and grant her a kind of power that Walter fails to achieve.

See also nos. 76, 88, 116, 122, 130, 132, 141, 148, 154, 247, 284, 330, 337.

CT—The Merchant and His Tale

227. Innes, Sheila, ed. *The Merchant's Prologue and Tale*, by Geoffrey Chaucer. Cambridge School Chaucer. Cambridge: Cambridge University Press, 2001. 112 pp. Middle English text of *MerPT* and the *GP* description of the Merchant, with notes, glossary, and discussion questions on facing pages. Includes contextual information concerning Chaucer's life, courtly love, and the rest of *CT*, particularly the "Marriage Debate."

228. Jones, Mike Rodman. "January's Genesis: Biblical Exegesis and Chaucer's *Merchant's Tale*." *LeedsSE* 39 (2008): 53–87. *MerT*, particularly its marriage encomium, was influenced by exegetical treatments of Eve as "helper," drawn from the Augustinian tradition and from Albertanus of Brescia. Chaucer rewrites these two divergent strands, reverses their interpretations of male and female bodies, and uses their commentaries on Eve, female rationality, and feminine advice to posit a political meaning.

229. Robertson, Kellie. "Medieval Things: Materiality, Historicism, and the Premodern Object." *LitComp* 5.6 (2008): 1060–80. Surveys

materialist "thing theory" as background on how objectivities and subjectivities interacted in medieval and early modern cultures. Summarizes work to date on the topic and considers how the accoutrements of the Merchant (especially his hat) in *GP* point to "things as events whose signified is their own interiority"—not simply indications of human subjects, but subjects in their own right.

See also nos. 39, 66, 92, 110, 127, 128, 130, 137, 142, 230.

CT—The Squire and His Tale

230. Bovaird-Abbo, Kristin. "Lancelot Reborn: The Squire's Warning in *The Canterbury Tales*." *Enarratio* 13 (2006): 104–32. Intertextual relationships among *MerT*, *SqT*, and *FranT* indicate differing attitudes toward perception, loyalty, and treason, particularly focused in the depictions of squires. Chaucer's Squire condescends to the lower classes and their ignorance of romance and Arthurian tradition, whereas the Franklin cautions his young social superior to seek a more chivalric outlook.

231. Fumo, Jamie C. "John Metham's 'Straunge Style': *Amoryus and Cleopes* as Chaucerian Fragment." *ChauR* 43 (2008): 215–37. Heretofore noted for its allusions to *TC*, the romance *Amoryus and Cleopes* also develops many of the themes, motifs, and stylistic traits of Fragment 5 of *CT* (*SqT* and *FranT*), in particular "its portrayal of pagan religion, its treatment of mechanical marvels and magical illusions, its frequently awkward narrative voice, and certain of its techniques of characterization."

See also nos. 39, 40, 55, 95, 190.

CT—The Franklin and His Tale

232. Dor, Juliette. "*Le Conte du Franklin*: Chaucer décline la plainte au masculin et au féminin." In Florence Alazard, ed. *La plainte au Moyen-Âge*. Paris: Champion, 2008, pp. 181–93 (in French). Comments on Chaucer's ventriloquist complaints (in *LGW* and *TC*) and examines the length, structure, position, tone, and function of the genre in *FranT*. While they were initially types, major characters gain dimension. Dorigen's second soliloquy reflects the struggle of a female who attempts to solve the tragedy in which she is entangled.

233. Finlayson, John. "Invention and Disjunction: Chaucer's Rewriting of Boccaccio in the *Franklin's Tale*." *ES* 89 (2008): 385–402. In *FranT*, Chaucer reshapes the source material found in Boccaccio's *Filocolo* and *Decameron*, adding the "pre-story" of a courtly love marriage, increasing the pathos of Dorigen, undercutting Arveragus's "self-serving" views of honor and truth, and leaving the final question unanswered. Chaucer amplifies and humanizes the "story of the Rash Promise" and "casts into question the 'unreal' literary world of the *demande d'amour*."

234. Ganze, Alison. "'My trouthe for to holde—allas, allas!': Dorigen and Honor in the *Franklin's Tale*." *ChauR* 42 (2008): 312–29. Beyond her concern to remain bodily faithful to her husband, Dorigen also exhibits a commitment to keep faith with her word. But the *Tale*'s denouement suggests that Dorigen's ultimate interest lies less with honoring her promises than with having a reputation as someone who honors promises.

235. Hume, Cathy. "'The name of soveraynetee': The Private and Public Faces of Marriage in *The Franklin's Tale*." *SP* 105 (2008): 284–303. Chaucer, having established an egalitarian marriage ideal at the beginning of *FranT*, explores how such an ideal would be tested by real-world circumstances.

236. Noji, Kaoru. "A Reading of Chaucer's *Franklin's Tale*: The Different Understanding of 'Trouthe' in Ideal Marriage." *Bulletin of Yamamura Women's Junior College* 3 (1991): 245–62. Explicates *FranT*, focusing on the characterization of Dorigen and how it reveals the "social compromises which women are conditioned to make." The "cracks in mutual understanding" between Dorigen and Arveragus also reveal how the values of women and men differ.

See also nos. 58, 88, 154, 190, 230, 231.

CT—The Physician and His Tale

237. Aitken, Robert, ed. "Literary Trials: *The Canterbury Tales*." *Litigation* 34.2 (2008): 72–73. Brief description of *PhyT*, accompanied by a Middle English version of lines 6.105–276, without notes or glosses.

238. Kline, Daniel T. "Jephthah's Daughter and Chaucer's Virginia: The Critique of Sacrifice in *The Physician's Tale*." *JEGP* 107 (2008): 77–103. Virginius's fatal encounter with his daughter Virginia in *PhyT* can

be seen as an instance of "torture," as Elaine Scarry defines it, the "most extreme" of political situations. In Scarry's terms and from Virginius's perspective, Virginia's existence lacks legitimacy.

239. Smith, Kirk L. "False Care and the Canterbury Cure: Chaucer Treats the New Galen." *Literature and Medicine* 27 (2008): 61–81. *PhyT* expresses its narrator's concern with "fiduciary" ethics and asserts the principle that "responsible professionals abjure exploitation." Such concerns are part of the late medieval professionalization of medical practice, so the *Tale* is appropriate to its teller.

See also nos. 68, 148.

CT—The Pardoner and His Tale

240. Chaganti, Seeta. *The Medieval Poetics of the Reliquary: Enshrinement, Inscription, Performance*. The New Middle Ages. New York: Palgrave Macmillan, 2008. xvi, 245 pp. 26 b&w illus. Chaganti explores the "dialectical interaction between inscription and performance" that underlines the "poetics of enshrinement" in medieval visual art, literature, and discourse on representation. Individual chapters address *Saint Erkenwald*, the N-Town *Assumption*, *Pearl*, *PardT*, and the brief lyric "In 8 is alle my love." Chapter 5, "Reliquaries of the Mind: Figuration, Enshrinement, and Performance in the *Pardoner's Tale*" (pp. 131–53), presents *PardT* as a "self-enshrining performance," structured in a way that occludes differences between utterance and description of utterance. Chaganti also comments on the lyric "I" in *BD* and on the enshrining imagination in *BD* and *HF*.

241. Cocco, Gabriele. "'I Trowe He Were a Gelding or a Mare': A Veiled Description of a Bent Pardoner." *Neophil* 92 (2008): 359–66. Chaucer may have tapped into traditional knowledge of the Northern god Loki in creating the description of the Pardoner in *GP*. Links with Loki, who transformed himself into a mare in the Old Norse *Gylfaginning*, encourage us to view the Pardoner as homosexual and a warped trickster.

242. Croft, Steven, ed. *The Pardoner's Tale*, by Geoffrey Chaucer. Oxford Student Texts. Oxford and New York: Oxford University Press, 2006. viii, 135 pp. Textbook edition of *PardPT* and the *GP* description of the Pardoner. Includes glosses and discursive notes (at the back of the book) and discussion of approaches to the text: sources and analogues,

characterization, assessment of theme and topic, and analysis of poetic technique. Also includes a chronology and discussion of language, plus suggestions for classroom activities and discussion.

243. Egan, Rory B. "Bulles, Coillons, and Relics in *The Pardoner's Tale.*" *ANQ* 21.2 (2008): 7–11. The Host's retort to the Pardoner at the close of *PardT* reinforces a connection between the terms and concepts of testicles (false or otherwise) and relics (false or otherwise). A trilingual collection (French, Latin, and English) of terms along with allusions to the *Roman de la Rose* reinforce Chaucer's critique of the Pardoner and his enterprise.

244. Lonati, Elisabetta. "'Allas, the shorte throte, the tendre mouth': The Sins of the Mouth in *The Canterbury Tales.*" In Giovanni Iamartino, Maria Luisa Maggioni, and Roberta Facchinetti, eds. *Thou sittest at another boke . . . : English Studies in Honour of Domenico Pezzini* (*SAC* 32 [2010], no. 119), pp. 237–62. *PardT* shows the polysemous aspects of gluttony as a sin, suggesting that gluttons are similar to heretics, who use the mouth to deny sacred truths. In contrast to the Parson, the Pardoner embodies the idea that *peccata oris* are not confined to over-indulgence in food and drink but extend to other vices related to the mouth, such as swearing and perjury.

245. Malo, Robyn. "The Pardoner's Relics (and Why They Matter the Most)." *ChauR* 43 (2008): 82–102. A recognition of the Pardoner as a "parodic relic custodian" calls for a fresh look at his sexuality—relic custodians were to be celibate—and casts into relief the tension in *CT* between restrictive ecclesiastical power and "lay desire" for access to the sacred, to relics in particular.

246. McCarthy, Shaun. *The Pardoner's Tale.* York Notes Advanced. London: Pearson, 2008. 143 pp. Pedagogical commentary on *PardPT*, based on A. C. Spearing's 1965 edition (text not included). McCarthy emphasizes the "gothic" elements of *PardPT* and summarizes the poem in sections, offering section-by-section commentary, along with sidebar glosses, notes, and suggestions for further readings and films. Includes additional commentary on characterization, theme, narrative technique, language and style, and critical perspectives.

247. Minnis, Alastair. *Fallible Authors: Chaucer's Pardoner and Wife of Bath.* The Middle Ages. Philadelphia: University of Pennsylvania Press, 2008. xvi, 510 pp. Studies the Pardoner's and Wife of Bath's "deviancy" in light of late medieval theological and academic discourses, particularly the commentaries and summas of the scholastics, Lollard treatises,

and reactions to Lollard writings and trials. Neither character embodies Lollardy or Wycliffite heterodoxy, but each is radically unorthodox. The authority of the Pardoner is "fallible" because of his shocking abuses of sacerdotal privileges; the Wife's failings are linked to her usurpation of the rhetoric of clerical authority. Topics include qualifications for preaching; administration and validity of the sacraments of baptism, penance, the Eucharist, ordination, and marriage; indulgences; the role of intention; female clergy; the Pardoner's sexuality; the Wife's obscenity; and the loathly lady's discussion of gentility in relation to dominion. Though heterodox, the characters tell moral tales. Also comments on *SNT*, *ClT*, and *Mel*. See also no. 398.

248. Stockton, Will. "Cynicism and the Anal Erotics of Chaucer's Pardoner." *Exemplaria* 20 (2008): 143–64. Stockton reads the Pardoner as a "cynic" in a Marxist context: one who "submit[s] fully to an ideological structure despite knowing better." Contrasts the Pardoner's queerness with his cynicism, asking, "How queer can the Pardoner be when he guards an ideological system he does not believe in?" Psychoanalytically diagnoses the Pardoner as an anal erotic.

See also nos. 114, 128, 129, 141, 147, 150–52, 259.

CT—The Shipman and His Tale

249. Brown, Elaine. "An Exploration of the Public and Private in Chaucer's *Shipman's Tale*." In Kathleen A. Bishop, ed. *"The Canterbury Tales" Revisited—21st Century Interpretations* (*SAC* 32 [2010], no. 145), pp. 75–87. *ShT* reflects Chaucer's belief that "the dominance of a husband over his wife is too strict" in traditional marriages. Private games threaten to open out into public scandal.

250. Connors, Michael. *Chaucer's Shipman of Dartmouth. John Hawley: Merchant, Mayor, and Privateer*. Dartmouth: Richard Webb, 2008. 168 pp. 5 maps; 50 b&w and color illus. A biography of John Hawley that concludes by arguing (pp. 147–55) that Hawley was at the center of a number of satirical allusions in Chaucer's *GP* description of the Shipman. Chaucer depicts a professional mariner, which Hawley was not, but the "social commentary" of the description capitalizes on late fourteenth-century London's familiarity with Hawley.

251. Freeman, Ray. *Dartmouth and Its Neighbours*. Chichester, Sussex: Phillimore, 1990. xi, 212 pp. 120 b&w illus. A social history of Dart-

mouth and the lower Dart river valley; includes the suggestion that William Smale was the model for Chaucer's *GP* description of the Shipman.

252. Rice, Nicole R. *Lay Piety and Religious Discipline in Middle English Literature*. Cambridge Studies in Medieval Literature, no. 73. Cambridge: Cambridge University Press, 2008. xviii, 247 pp. Rice studies late fourteenth-century vernacular prose devotional guides, with attention to their relationship with works by Chaucer and Langland. Wycliffite writings and changes in religious discipline affected notions of how to live the "best life," reflected in new guides and translations. In light of these works, Chaucer's *ShT* is a "knowing response to intersections of lay spiritual desire and monastic discipline" that focuses on "confusions of material and spiritual capital." The merchant's desire for brotherhood and his closing himself in his counting room enact a longing for a monastic ideal that Daun John fails to live.

See also nos. 59, 88, 160, 286.

CT—The Prioress and Her Tale

253. Alonso García, Manuel José. "Comparación del texto de la *Cantiga número 6* de Alfonso X el Sabio, y el texto del *Cuento de la Priora*, de Chaucer, respecto a los *Milagros de Nuestra Señora*." In Armando López Castro and María Luzdivina Cuesta Torre, eds. *Actas del XI congreso internacional de la Asociación Hispánica de Literatura Medieval: Universidad de León, 20 al 24 de septiembre de 2005*. 2 vols. León: Secretariado de Publicaciones de la Universidad de Léon, 2007: vol. 1, pp. 163–82 (in Spanish). Compares Chaucer's *PrT* with Alfonso X's *Cantigas de Santa Maria* (no. 6), analyzing them in detail (from plot to prosody), and providing parallel editions of the two texts.

254. Bourgne, Florence. "La lettre du texte." In Danielle Buschinger and Arlette Sancery, eds. *Mélanges de langue, littérature et civilisation offerts à André Crépin à l'occasion de son quatre-vingtième anniversaire* (*SAC* 32 [2010], no. 104), pp. 53–58. Studies the function of medieval inscribed or letter-shaped jewels and similar objects, referring to Chaucer's Prioress and to *TC*.

255. Czarnowus, Anna. "Chaucer's Clergeon, or Towards Holiness in *The Prioress's Tale*." *SAP* 43 (2007): 251–64. In *PrT*, uncanniness and the eventual wounding of the clergeon are necessary to render the cler-

geon holy and Christlike. His experience is close to that represented in miracle plays exploring the Slaughter of the Innocents.

256. Elliott, Winter S. "Eglentyne's Mary/Widow: Reconsidering the Anti-Semitism of *The Prioress's Tale.*" In Kathleen A. Bishop, ed. *"The Canterbury Tales" Revisited—21st Century Interpretations* (*SAC* 32 [2010], no. 145), pp. 110–26. The Prioress aligns herself with the widow in her *Tale* and with the Virgin Mary. Although the clergeon is like Christ in his challenge to Jewish tradition, *PrT* is concerned with female power as well as with cultural prejudice.

257. Kendrick, Laura. "Verbal and Visual Contexts for Understanding the Prioress's Smile in the *General Prologue* to *The Canterbury Tales.*" In Danielle Buschinger and Arlette Sancery, eds. *Mélanges de langue, littérature et civilisation offerts à André Crépin à l'occasion de son quatre-vingtième anniversaire* (*SAC* 32 [2010], no. 104), pp. 197–203. Kendrick considers secular and religious contexts in which the smile of the Prioress may be understood.

258. Krummel, Miriamne Ara. "Globalizing Jewish Communities: Mapping a Jewish Geography in Fragment VII of the *Canterbury Tales.*" *Texas Studies in Literature and Language* 50 (2008): 121–42. A significant Jewish presence echoes in the wide-ranging geographies of *PrT* (Asia), *Th* (fairyland), and the Monk's stories of Peter of Spain and Antiochus (Judea). Chaucer evokes a sophisticated awareness of Jewishness that mitigates the Prioress's anti-Judaic paranoia.

259. ———. "The Pardoner, the Prioress, Sir Thopas, and the Monk: Semitic Discourse and the Jew(s)." In Kathleen A. Bishop, ed. *"The Canterbury Tales" Revisited—21st Century Interpretations* (*SAC* 32 [2010], no. 145), pp. 88–109. The violent anti-Semitism of *PrT* attracts critical attention, but a variety of brief, positive depictions of Jews occurs elsewhere in *CT*, reflecting the dynamic nature of medieval attitudes.

260. ———. "The Semitisms of Middle English Literature." *Lit-Comp* 1 (2003–04): 1–14. Surveys critical commentary on the absence and presence of Jews in late medieval English society and literature, gauging the state of discussions of works such as *PrT*, the Croxton *Play of the Sacrament*, and others.

261. Price, Merrall Llewelyn. "Sadism and Sentimentality: Absorbing Antisemitism in Chaucer's Prioress." *ChauR* 43 (2008): 197–214. Read as symptoms of a "childlike" individual "dealing with a number of psychosexual developmental issues," the Prioress's personal habits and

narrative performance register anxiety not only about boundaries of the individual human body but also about "the dangerous porosity of religious, social, and community identity that it represents."

262. Welch, Bronwen. "'Glydeth my song': Penetration and Possession in Chaucer's *Prioress's Tale*." In Kathleen A. Bishop, ed. *"The Canterbury Tales" Revisited—21st Century Interpretations* (*SAC* 32 [2010], no. 145), pp. 127–50. Explores anti-Semitism and the modern response to *PrT* in light of recurring concern with humans (the Prioress, Mary, the clergeon, and the Jews) possessed or penetrated by superior beings. Readers are overwhelmed by the desire for "piercing sweetness," even though the anti-Semitism and patriarchalism of *PrT* render this desire troublesome.

263. Zieman, Katherine. *Singing the New Song: Literacy and Liturgy in Late Medieval England*. The Middle Ages. Philadelphia: University of Pennsylvania Press, 2008. xvii, 294 pp. 6 b&w illus. Explores how liturgical training and practice, particularly the interrelated devotional activities of singing and reading, affected literacy in late medieval England. Lay devotional ritual became separated from clerical practice, and definitions of "literate" shifted from "repertory based knowledge" to development of skills—both changes resulting in an increase in "extragrammatical" liturgical activity and new uses for liturgical texts. Zieman considers the impact of such practices on the *apologia* of *Piers Plowman* C.5 and on Chaucer's *PrT* and *SNT*, examining how the poets represent contemporary anxiety about public verbal production and performance of spoken and written rituals. The pairing of *PrT* and *SNT* is paralleled by *Th* and *Mel*. See also no. 429.

See also nos. 138, 141, 152, 163.

CT—The Tale of Sir Thopas

264. Jager, Katharine Woodason. "The Practice of Makynge: Masculine Poetic Identity in Late Medieval English Poetry." *DAI* A68.11 (2008): n.p. Jager contends that medieval English poetry occupied a "hybrid" oral/written cultural space and that the poems "posit an artisanal, poetic masculinity." She uses *Th*, along with *Piers Plowman*, *Sir Gawain and the Green Knight*, and other works, to explore the status of the works and their authors.

265. Purdie, Rhiannon. *Anglicising Romance: Tail-Rhyme and Genre in*

Medieval English Literature. Studies in Medieval Romance. Cambridge: D. S. Brewer, 2008. xi, 272 pp. 9 b&w illus. Purdie explores "how and why" tail-rhyme romance developed in Middle English and defines the "temporal and geographical limits" of the subgenre. The book includes a version of Purdie's "The Implications of Manuscript Layout in Chaucer's *Tale of Sir Thopas*" (2005; *SAC* 29 [2007], no. 244).

266. Warkentin, Elyssa. "The Poet Disarming Himself: Chaucer's 'Tale of Sir Thopas' and the Death of the Author." *EAPSU Online: A Journal of Critical and Creative Work* 1 (2004): 139–56. Chaucer uses *Th* to "debunk his own textual authority" and subvert patriarchal power, enacting the "death of the author" that is completed in *Ret*.

267. Whetter, K. S. *Understanding Genre and Medieval Romance*. Burlington, Vt.: Ashgate, 2008. xi, 205 pp. 12 b&w illus. Defines medieval romance as a narrative (usually poetic) that follows a hero's encounters with "love, ladies, and adventures, culminating in a happy ending." Whetter explores these features in Middle English romances, particularly Malory's *Morte Darthur*, which combines features of romance and tragedy. Chaucer's *Th* parodies these features (except the happy ending, since *Th* is incomplete). *KnT* combines the features with philosophy; *TC*, with tragedy.

See also nos. 101, 258, 259, 263, 271, 272.

CT—The Tale of Melibee

268. DeMarco, Patricia. "Violence, Law, and Ciceronian Ethics in Chaucer's *Tale of Melibee*." *SAC* 30 (2008): 125–69. DeMarco clarifies the classical and medieval distinctions between "public" and "private" violence and explores efforts to justify each type of violence, showing that Prudence's advice to Melibee is "secular," "pragmatic," and ultimately Ciceronian. Relationships between *Mel* and its sources show that (like *WBT*, *KnT*, and Gower's *Confessio Amantis*) *Mel* offers ethical advice attuned to late fourteenth-century concerns with honor, profit, social stability, and legal tradition.

269. Foster, Michael. "Echoes of Communal Response in the *Tale of Melibee*." *ChauR* 42 (2008): 409–30. Through extensive use of "multiple dialogue introducers," Chaucer creates a "mimetic representation of speech" in *Mel* and thus invites a listening audience to be part of the

fictional conversation and, beyond that, to emulate it by taking time to "pause, consider, and discuss before acting."

270. Hull Taylor, Candace. "'A prudent feruentnesse or a feruent prudence': Reading Prudence in Classical, Patristic, and Medieval Texts." *DAI* A68.09 (2008): n.p. Examines the cardinal virtues, especially prudence, from the Socratic philosophers to the late Middle Ages. Considers *Mel* in an epilogue.

271. Mehtonen, Päivi. *Obscure Language, Unclear Literature: Theory and Practice from Quintilian to the Enlightenment*. Trans. Robert MacGilleon. Helsinki: Finnish Academy of Science and Letters, 2003. 228 pp. A "premodern conceptual history" of obscurity in literature, with emphasis on rhetorical traditions, philosophy, and exegesis. Includes comments on *Mel* and *Th* as literary examples of the "vices of narration" described in rhetorical handbooks. See also no. 394.

272. Spencer, Alice. "Dialogue, Dialogics, and Love: Problems of Chaucer's Poetics in the *Melibee*." In Kathleen A. Bishop, ed. *"The Canterbury Tales" Revisited—21st Century Interpretations* (*SAC* 32 [2010], no. 145), pp. 228–55. Explores tensions among the Boethian, Platonic form of *Mel* as a didactic dialogue, the *Tale*'s practical Aristotelian subject matter, and its status as a compilation of composite proverbs. Reflecting a literate author, *Mel* modifies its sources and opposes the orality of *Th*. Such tensions problematize the monologic underpinnings of the didactic debate genre.

See also nos. 92, 116, 184, 247, 263.

CT—The Monk and His Tale

273. Dor, Juliette. "Zénobie: Péché d'orgueil et port de la vitremyte." In Danielle Buschinger and Arlette Sancery, eds. *Mélanges de langue, littérature et civilisation offerts à André Crépin à l'occasion de son quatre-vingtième anniversaire* (*SAC* 32 [2010], no. 104), pp. 151–55. In *MkT*, Zenobia is punished for transgressing her gender; and symbols of her former power (including the *vitremyte*, here newly interpreted) become burlesque attributes.

274. Fisher, Leona. "*No man ne truste upon hire favour longe*: Fortune and the Monk's Other Women." In Kathleen A. Bishop, ed. *"The Canterbury Tales" Revisited—21st Century Interpretations* (*SAC* 32 [2010], no. 145), pp. 151–65. Affiliations between women and Fortune recur

throughout *MkT*, a facile parallel rendered ridiculous by Chaucer's depiction of the Monk and the Monk's tale-telling style.

275. Holton, Amanda. "Which Bible Did Chaucer Use? The Biblical Tragedies in the *Monk's Tale*." *N&Q* 55 (2008): 13–17. The Vulgate's sheer availability offers compelling evidence that Chaucer used the Vulgate Bible, while faint lexical echoes of the *Bible historiale* suggest ancillary use of the *historiale*. The Wycliffite Bible's candidacy may be ruled out on a number of grounds, most persuasively its late date.

276. Lindeboom, B. W. "Chaucer's Monk Illuminated: Zenobia as Role Model." *Neophil* 92 (2008): 339–50. Chaucer may have intended to end *MkT* with the account of Zenobia—extracting it from *LGW*—and thereby to offer her narrative as a remedy for the Monk's "spiritual condition," which develops over the course of *CT*. Lindeboom compares Chaucer's version of Zenobia to that in Boccaccio's *De Claris Mulieribus*.

See also nos. 50, 68, 154, 163, 258, 259.

CT—The Nun's Priest and His Tale

277. González Miranda, Emilio. "El sueño del gallo Chantecler en tres versiones de la literatura medieval europa." In Armando López Castro and María Luzdivina Cuesta Torre, eds. *Actas del XI congreso internacional de la Asociación Hispánica de Literatura Medieval: Universidad de León, 20 al 24 de septiembre de 2005*. 2 vols. León: Secretariado de Publicaciones de la Universidad de León, 2007: vol. 2, pp. 641–49 (in Spanish). Compares the dream of Chauntecleer in *NPT* with the dreams of the roosters in *Roman de Renart* and *Reinart Fuchs*.

278. Mack, Peter, and Andy Hawkins, eds. *The Nun's Priest's Tale*, by Geoffrey Chaucer. Oxford Student Texts. Oxford: Oxford University Press, 2006. ix, 165 pp. Textbook edition of *NPPT*. Includes glosses and discursive notes (at the back of the book) and discussion of approaches to the text: sources and analogues, characterization, assessment of theme and topic, and analysis of poetic technique. Also includes basic contextual materials (*GP* description of Prioress, black-and-white illustrations, excerpted analogues, etc.), a chronology and discussion of language, and suggestions for classroom activities and discussion. First published in 1996.

See also nos. 46, 92, 135, 152, 284.

CT—The Second Nun and Her Tale

See nos. 137, 138, 140, 205, 247, 263, 297.

CT—The Canon's Yeoman and His Tale

See nos. 140, 154.

CT—The Manciple and His Tale

279. Breeze, Andrew. "Chaucer and Harbledown, Kent." *LeedsSE* 39 (2008): 89–93. Despite recurrent uncertainty, the location of "Bobbe-up-and-doun" mentioned in *ManP* is surely the same place as Harble-down.

280. Coley, David Kennedy. "The Wheel of Language: Representing Speech in Middle English Narrative, 1377–1422." *DAI* A69.05 (2008): n.p. While considering how speech in narrative poetry may represent "a distinct category within linguistic discourse," Coley reads *ManT* as a Chaucerian interaction with William of Ockham's rejection of long-standing Augustinian "hierarchies."

See also nos. 68, 154.

CT—The Parson and His Tale

See nos. 129, 147, 154, 163, 190, 244.

CT—*Chaucer's Retraction*

See nos. 154, 307.

Anelida and Arcite

See no. 133.

A Treatise on the Astrolabe

281. Bello-Piñón, Nuria, and Dolores Elvira Méndez-Souto. "Complex Predicates in Early Scientific Writing." In Isabel Moskowich-Spie-

gel and Begoña Crespo-García, eds. *Bells Chiming from the Past: Cultural and Linguistic Studies on Early English*. Costerus New Series, no. 174. Amsterdam and New York: Rodopi, 2007, pp. 169–78. The authors present statistical summaries of complex predicates in *Astr* and *Equat* and hypothesize about why such scientific texts contain a relatively low percentage of these predicates.

282. Kennedy, Victor. "Astronomical References in Chaucer: What Can Modern Students Learn from Studying Ancient Texts?" *ELOPE: English Language Overseas Perspectives and Enquiries* 2.1–2 (2005): 139–54. Draws examples and discussion from *Astr* to argue that modern teachers of literature should "look to history, cross boundaries between academic fields, and use practical, as well as theoretical, teaching methods" (quotation from abstract at http://www.sdas.edus.si/Elope/abstracts2.pdf).

283. Laird, Edgar S. "Texts Concerning Scientific Instruments." In M. Teresa Tavormina, ed. *Sex, Aging, and Death in a Medieval Medical Compendium: Trinity College Cambridge MS R.14.52, Its Text, Language, and Scribe* (*SAC* 32 [2010], no. 38), vol. 2, pp. 607–80. Laird edits and describes portions of Trinity College Cambridge MS R.14.52 that pertain to scientific instruments, including several sections from Chaucer's *Astr* (conclusions 2.37, 40, 39, and 38).

284. Lerer, Seth. *Children's Literature: A Reader's History, from Aesop to Harry Potter*. Chicago: University of Chicago Press, 2008. ix, 385 pp. 23 b&w illus. Studies the currents and crosscurrents of pedagogy, moral didacticism, and entertainment in children's literature, exploring how trends in reading and interpretation recur as the subject matter of the stories and help to define their historical legacy. Focuses on literature written in English but explores international influences and premodern legacies in the classics, medieval traditions, travelogues, religious writing, fairy stories, illustration and printing history, literary prizes, canon formation, style, and more. Comments on *Astr*, *NPT*, and *ClT*.

285. Mead, Jenna. "Geoffrey Chaucer's *Treatise on the Astrolabe*." *Lit-Comp* 3.5 (2006): 973–91. Surveys critical responses to *Astr*, highlighting recent discussions that emphasize patterns of readership, pedagogical strategies, and the status of science in late fourteenth-century England.

286. Walts, Dawn Simmons. "Time's Reckoning: Time, Value, and the Mercantile Class in Late Medieval English Literature." *DAI* A68.07 (2008): n.p. Employs Jacques Le Goff's ideas of "Church time" and

"merchant's time" to consider reckoning of time and social rank in the York cycle, *Pearl*, and works of Chaucer. In particular, *Astr* suggests knowledge of time, while *MilT* and *ShT* demonstrate that an ability to understand time affords some individuals an advantage over those who lack the ability.

See also nos. 71, 107, 122.

Boece

287. Machan, Tim William, ed. *Chaucer's "Boece": A Critical Edition Based on Cambridge University Library, MS Ii.3.21, ff. 9^r–180^v.* Middle English Texts, no. 38. Heidelberg: Winter, 2008. xli, 193 pp. A critical text of *Bo*, collated "with all medieval and late-medieval authorities and also with the modern critical editorial tradition." Includes a list of glosses and an extensive introduction, with a survey of interpretive responses to *Bo*.

288. Oizumi, Akio. *A Lexicon of the "Boece." A Complete Concordance to the Works of Geoffrey Chaucer*, vols. 14.1 and 14.2. Supplement Series, nos. 4.1–2. Hildesheim, Zürich, New York: Olms-Weidmann, 2008. xvi, 803 pp. A two-volume lemmatized concordance to *Bo*, arranged alphabetically, based on *The Riverside Chaucer*. Each entry includes a headword, part of speech, references to standard dictionaries (*MED*, *OED*, and others), definitions, frequency of occurrence, a list of attested spellings (with frequencies specified), occasional cross-references, information about collocations and uses in phrases (where appropriate), and a list of occurrences, with the headwords quoted in the context of the lines in which they appear. Vol. 1: A–L; vol. 2: M–Z.

289. Wakelin, Daniel. *Humanism, Reading, and English Literature, 1430–1530.* Oxford: Oxford University Press, 2007. xi, 254 pp. Explores "reading habits" in fifteenth-century England and the extent to which they are part of the humanist movement, examining how manuscript glossing, responses, and other forms of commentary reflect philological, stylistic, and political attitudes that characterize humanism. Assesses reactions to Chaucer's *Bo* in manuscripts and Caxton's edition and comments on the awareness of Chaucer's classicizing interests among fifteenth-century writers. See also no. 426.

See also nos. 50, 110, 303.

The Book of the Duchess

290. Farber, Annika. "Usurping 'Chaucers dreame': *Book of the Duchess* and the Apocryphal *Isle of Ladies*." *SP* 105 (2008): 207–25. Reexamines the anonymous and neglected Chaucerian *Isle of Ladies*, accepted as a work by Chaucer from the time of Speght's 1598 edition of the works of Chaucer until its rejection by Skeat in his edition. Uses *Isle of Ladies* to reread Chaucer's *BD* and finds that its relationship with *BD* parallels Chaucer's own rereading and retelling of earlier works.

291. Foster, Michael. "On Dating the Duchess: The Personal and Social Context of *Book of the Duchess*." *RES* 59 (2008): 185–96. Reconsiders the traditional dating of *BD* in light of the evolving relationship between Chaucer and John of Gaunt, as affected by Katherine Swynford. The date influences our reading of the poem.

See also nos. 44, 110, 111, 114, 118, 133, 135, 240, 299.

The Equatorie of the Planetis

See nos. 71, 281.

The House of Fame

292. Green, Richard Firth. "Did Chaucer Know the Ballad of *Glen Kindy*?" *Neophil* 92 (2008): 351–58. Chaucer's allusion to the legendary Welsh bard Glascurion in *HF* (line 1209) is paralleled by details that survive in the traditional ballad *Glasgerion*, or *Glen Kindy*. Echoes of the ballad tradition are also found in Gavin Douglas's *The Palice of Honour*.

293. Quinn, William A. "Chaucer's Recital Presence in the *House of Fame* and the Embodiment of Authority." *ChauR* 43 (2008): 171–96. Chaucer's interest throughout *HF* in the nature of phantoms—from dreams to spirits of the dead—ultimately reflects a single "immediate concern: the survival of his rehearsal of the dream in script, that is, the translation of his voice into our text."

294. Sullivan, Anne Victoria. "Writing the Rites of the Goddess Fame: The Divinely Comical Conversion of Geoffrey Chaucer." *DAI* A68.10 (2008): n.p. Employing the Lacanian theory of Slavoj Žižek, Sullivan examines the relationship of *HF* to Augustine's *Confessions*, Virgil's *Aeneid*, Boethius's *Consolation of Philosophy*, and Dante's *Divine Com-*

edy, arguing that Chaucer and Dante rewrite "the pagan classical cosmos" through "incarnational astronomical poetics."

295. Whitehead, Christiania. *Castles of the Mind: A Study of Medieval Architectural Allegory.* Religion and Culture in the Middle Ages. Cardiff: University of Wales Press, 2003. xi, 324 pp. Whitehead describes the complex significations of architectural structures in medieval thought and memory, examining Christian and classical roots of such thinking. Discusses classical, scriptural, and exegetical commentaries on concrete figures (e.g., temple, ark, cloister, castle, household) and explores commonplace rhetorical uses of architecture to represent abstractions such as fortune, fame, honor, knowledge, sex, and courtly love. Focuses on examples from vernacular literary representations (especially Middle English), including sustained discussion of Chaucer's *HF* as a skeptical response to Dante's castle of honor (*Inferno* 4) and its humanist legacy.

See also nos. 25, 41, 45, 63, 113, 116, 133, 240, 299.

The Legend of Good Women

See nos. 44, 68, 113–15, 118, 133, 135, 141, 232, 297.

The Parliament of Fowls

See nos. 113, 133, 299.

The Romaunt of the Rose

See no. 95.

Troilus and Criseyde

296. An, Sonjae (Brother Anthony). "No Greater Pain: The Ironies of Bliss in Chaucer's *Troilus and Criseyde.*" In Noel Harold Kaylor Jr. and Richard Scott Nokes, eds. *Global Perspectives on Medieval English Literature, Language, and Culture* (*SAC* 32 [2010], no. 120), pp. 117–32. Allusions to and echoes of Boethius and Dante reinforce Chaucer's concern with the inevitability of sorrow and its relationship to joy in *TC*. The structure of the poem collaborates with these devices to convey the transitory nature of worldly joy that culminates in Troilus's "Particular

Judgment"—his rise to the sphere of Saturn, and Mercury's taking of him.

297. Bowers, John M. " 'Beautiful as Troilus': Richard II, Chaucer's Troilus, and Figures of (Un)Masculinity." In Tison Pugh and Marcia Smith Marzec, eds. *Men and Masculinities in Chaucer's "Troilus and Criseyde"* (*SAC* 32 [2010], no. 319), pp. 9–27. Chaucer's "portrayal of Troilus as a soliloquizing, swooning lover . . . reads like a fulsome *apologia*" for Richard II. *TC* reflects Richard's relationship with Robert De Vere and reveals his "sexless marriage" with Anne. *SNT* and *LGW* defend sexless marriage, whereas Absolon of *MilT* is Chaucer's exposé of "the comic pretenses of failed masculinity."

298. Calabrese, Michael. "Being a Man in *Piers Plowman* and *Troilus and Criseyde*." In Tison Pugh and Marcia Smith Marzec, eds. *Men and Masculinities in Chaucer's "Troilus and Criseyde"* (*SAC* 32 [2010], no. 319), pp. 161–82. Focusing on failures of the male body depicted in the consummation scene of *TC* and in the autobiographical episode of the C-text, Calabrese compares Troilus of *TC* and Will of *Piers Plowman* as masculine questors in search of truth. Pandarus "roughly corresponds" to Recklessness and Criseyde to Lady Meed.

299. Condren, Edward L. *Chaucer from Prentice to Poet: The Metaphor of Love in Dream Visions and "Troilus and Criseyde."* Gainesville: University Press of Florida, 2008. xiv, 239 pp. Condren explores similarities of theme and technique in *BD*, *PF*, *HF*, and *TC*, focusing on numerical composition and Chaucer's "self-dialogue" on poetry and love. Biographical reading of *BD* reveals that the man in black is not Gaunt but the dreamer's own mourning self; the poem was originally written to commemorate Queen Philippa and adjusted later to Blanche. The "hidden code" of *PF* affirms the theme of harmony as a form of Neoplatonic love. *HF* is a contemplation of what constitutes "poetic truth" and was written as a "formal prologue" to *TC*, the man of "auctorite" being Chaucer himself. *TC* is a "metaliterary construct" in which the characters serve as aspects of the composition process. Pandarus speaks Troilus's thoughts, and close reading discloses sexual innuendoes in speeches of the two lovers.

300. Crocker, Holly A., and Tison Pugh. "Masochism, Masculinity, and the Pleasures of Troilus." In Tison Pugh and Marcia Smith Marzec, eds. *Men and Masculinities in Chaucer's "Troilus and Criseyde"* (*SAC* 32 [2010], no. 319), pp. 82–96. Troilus's suffering in *TC* is informed by a "Christian economy" of pain that valorizes a new kind of manhood,

one that activates others through its passivity and converts weakness to strength "through a managed display." Troilus's identity "emerges from inaction," and his "masculinity is produced as masochistic to secure its privileged position." His exaltation at the end of the poem confirms the audience's enjoyment of his suffering.

301. D'Agata D'Ottavi, Stefania. "Melancholy and Dreams in Chaucer's *Troilus and Criseyde*." In Giovanni Iamartino, Maria Luisa Maggioni, and Roberta Facchinetti, eds. *Thou sittest at another boke . . . : English Studies in Honour of Domenico Pezzini* (*SAC* 32 [2010], no. 119), pp. 209–21. In *TC*, Troilus's melancholy character and his intense intellectual activity—a topos reminiscent of the first of Pseudo-Aristotle's thirty "problemata" in *Problemata Physica*, according to which all men of genius are melancholy—are especially evident in the hero's dreams. The dreams present themselves vividly to the melancholy sleeper's mind, and his interpretation of them is more problematic and subtle than that of Pandarus.

302. Dauby, Hélène. "Termes d'adresse dans *Troilus and Criseyde*." In Danielle Buschinger and Arlette Sancery, eds. *Mélanges de langue, littérature et civilisation offerts à André Crépin à l'occasion de son quatre-vingtième anniversaire* (*SAC* 32 [2010], no. 104), pp. 142–44. Assesses invocations and formulas used to address divinities, characters, and sources in *TC*.

303. Everhart, Deborah. "Chaucer's Providentialism and the Meanings of 'Hap' in *Boece* and *Troilus and Criseyde*." *CarmP* 1 (1992): 35–52. Everhart considers Chaucer's translation strategies in *Bo* and identifies his unusual one-to-one substitution of *hap* for Latin *casus* in that work. Multiple connotations of *hap* in *TC* imply a different, playful rhetoric of translation that in turn reflects the limits of language and human perception.

304. Fewer, Colin. "The Second Nature: *Habitus* as Ideology in the *Ars Amatoria* and *Troilus and Criseyde*." *Exemplaria* 20 (2008): 314–39. In *Ars Amatoria* and *Remedia Amoris*, Ovid provides "habits of thought" that give medieval thinkers a vocabulary to describe "the operations of what we would today call ideology," or the conforming of the self to conceive social institutions as realities. Pandarus in *TC* makes this Ovidian ideological operation especially clear.

305. Haruta, Setsuko. "Uncle Pandarus vs. Aunt Criseyde." *PoeticaT* 69 (2008): 27–40. Discusses the role of Criseyde as a niece and an aunt and how Chaucer depicts her mature persona.

306. Helmbold, Anita. "Chaucer Appropriated: The *Troilus* Frontis-

piece as Lancastrian Propaganda." *SAC* 30 (2008): 205–34. Surveys commentary on the frontispiece to *TC* in Corpus Christi College, Cambridge University, MS 61, and argues that it was commissioned by Henry V as part of his program to promote Lancastrian legitimacy and English vernacular writing.

307. Jensen, Charity. "Spaces of Authority: *Troilus and Criseyde* and *The Canterbury Tales*." In Kathleen A. Bishop, ed. *"The Canterbury Tales" Revisited—21st Century Interpretations* (*SAC* 32 [2010], no. 145), pp. 281–99. Although hedged in by bookish tradition, Chaucer "continually stretches the boundaries as he sets himself up as a legitimate *auctor*." Jensen assesses several of Chaucer's "self-authorising" interventions in the proems of *TC*, in *WBP*, and in *Ret*, exploring how Chaucer's submissions to traditional authority function as assertions of his own authority.

308. Jirsa, Curtis Roberts-Holt. *"Piers Plowman* and the Invention of the Lyric in the Middle Ages." *DAI* A69.02 (2008): n.p. Focuses on *Piers Plowman* (and considers *TC*), using "modern lyric criticism" as an approach to medieval narratives.

309. Kaylor, Noel Harold, Jr. "Re-examining Geoffrey Chaucer's Work in an Age of Globalization: *Troilus and Criseyde* and Chaucer's Global Perspective." In Noel Harold Kaylor Jr. and Richard Scott Nokes, eds. *Global Perspectives on Medieval English Literature, Language, and Culture* (*SAC* 32 [2010], no. 120), pp. 133–53. Kaylor contrasts themes and techniques of Dante's *Commedia* and Chaucer's *TC* (and *CT*), suggesting that a shift in "frame-of-reference" occurred between the times of the two poets. Dante is concerned with universal, absolute, and transcendent phenomena; Chaucer, with particular, relative, and temporal ones. Perhaps because of fourteenth-century calamities, the latter poet is more Einsteinian and global.

310. Keller, Wolfram R. *Selves and Nations: The Troy Story from Sicily to England in the Middle Ages*. Britannica et Americana, 3rd ser., no 25. Heidelberg: Winter, 2008. xiv, 644 pp. Keller traces the medieval tradition of Troy narratives from Benoît de Saint-Maure and Guido delle Colonne through various Middle English adaptations, including *TC*. Focuses on the literary interplay of imperial ambition—with its tendency to produce *static* notions of individual selfhood and forms of group identities—and a more flexible, vernacular sense of nationhood that provides a site for more complex explorations of individuality. The latter model originates in Benoît's Ovidian interpretation of the Troy story, whereas

the former is encapsulated in Guido's Latin attempt to contain the destabilizing effects of Benoît's account.

311. Koppelman, Kate. " 'The Dreams in Which I'm Dying': Sublimation and Unstable Masculinities in *Troilus and Criseyde*." In Tison Pugh and Marcia Smith Marzec, eds. *Men and Masculinities in Chaucer's "Troilus and Criseyde"* (*SAC* 32 [2010], no. 319), pp. 97–114. Criseyde is the "fullest subjectivity" in *TC*. Her resistance to Troilus's fantasy demonstrates the "constructed nature of masculinity" as shifting and dependent posturing. Koppelman explores Criseyde's confrontations with the "opaque network" of systems of signification that her role as courtly lady entails.

312. Martin, Molly A. "Troilus's Gaze and the Collapse of Masculinity in Romance." In Tison Pugh and Marcia Smith Marzec, eds. *Men and Masculinities in Chaucer's "Troilus and Criseyde"* (*SAC* 32 [2010], no. 319), pp. 132–47. In medieval optical theory of intromission and in medieval romances, gazed-upon objects are understood to be more active than they are in modern theorizing of scopophilia. Tracing interdependencies of the romance genre and the masculine gaze in *TC*, Martin argues that romance vision in Chaucer's poem strains the genre and challenges gender distinctions.

313. Marzec, Marcia Smith. "What Makes a Man? Troilus, Hector, and the Masculinities of Courtly Love." In Tison Pugh and Marcia Smith Marzec, eds. *Men and Masculinities in Chaucer's "Troilus and Criseyde"* (*SAC* 32 [2010], no. 319), pp. 58–72. Marzec surveys portrayals of Hector as a knightly paragon of prowess and virtue in sources and analogues of *TC*, arguing that Chaucer's Troilus is a distinctly "courtly" figure in contrast to his brother. The contrast critiques courtly love.

314. Mieszkowski, Gretchen. "Revisiting Troilus's Faint." In Tison Pugh and Marcia Smith Marzec, eds. *Men and Masculinities in Chaucer's "Troilus and Criseyde"* (*SAC* 32 [2010], no. 319), pp. 43–57. Mieszkowski surveys masculine lovers in medieval romance, showing that fainting and passive love "acquired feminine gender" only after the fourteenth century. Modern discussions of *TC* that treat Troilus as "feminized" both mistake his role as an idealized lover (not a "result driven" one such as Diomedes) and overlook medieval nuances in the consummation scene.

315. Milowicki, Edward, and Rawdon Wilson. "Ovid's Shadow: Character and Characterization in Early Modern Literature." *Neohelicon* 22 (1995): 9–47. Ovid's *Metamorphoses* is crucial to the development of

characterization in Western European literature. Ovid complicates the conventional "divided consciousness" of earlier characterizations through relativism, rationalization, rhetoric, reduction, and legalism. Andreas Capellanus, Chrétien de Troyes, and Chaucer (examples drawn from *TC*) carry these techniques into the Renaissance and anticipate the development of the novel.

316. Modarelli, Michael. "Pandarus's 'Grete Emprise': Narration and Subjectivity in Chaucer's *Troilus and Criseyde*." *ES* 89 (2008): 403–14. Modarelli examines the characterization of Pandarus in *TC*, particularly the way he acts "with the agency of an author"—one in a "trinity" of authors that includes the narrator and the poet. Using Tzvetan Todorov's formulation of "constructive reading," Modarelli argues that the character of Pandarus "has no psychological determinism" and thus is open to multiple readings, depending on the "socio-cultural attitudes and beliefs of various readers."

317. Paxson, James J. "Masculinity and Its Hydraulic Semiotics in *Troilus and Criseyde*." In Tison Pugh and Marcia Smith Marzec, eds. *Men and Masculinities in Chaucer's "Troilus and Criseyde"* (*SAC* 32 [2010], no. 319), pp. 73–81. Troilus's secret entry into Criseyde's bedroom in Pandarus's house alludes to King David's surprise of the Jebusites when conquering their city (2 Samuel 5); it attests to Troilus's masculine heroism and derives in part from Chaucer's experiences in draining marshes when he was Clerk of Works.

318. Pugh, Tison. "Vectoring Genre and Character: A Pedagogical Model for Chaucer's *Troilus and Criseyde* and Other Multigeneric Texts." *Pedagogy* 8 (2008): 348–61. Pugh discusses the value of "vectored" writing assignments for undergraduate analyses of "multigeneric" texts, focusing on *TC*. "Vectored analysis"—defined here as the "examination of a text from at least two converging yet separate perspectives"—encourages students to engage in "vibrant exploration of textual interplay." The article describes the use of genre/character graphs for discussion of *TC*.

319. ———, and Marcia Smith Marzec, eds. *Men and Masculinities in Chaucer's "Troilus and Criseyde."* Chaucer Studies, no. 38. Cambridge: D. S. Brewer, 2008. ix, 200 pp. Twelve essays by various authors on gender construction in *TC*, with an introduction (pp. 1–8). See nos. 297, 298, 300, 311–14, 317, 321, 322, 324, and 325. See also no. 409.

320. Rosenfeld, Jessica. "The Doubled Joys of *Troilus and Criseyde*." In Catherine E. Léglu and Stephen J. Milner, eds. *The Erotics of Consola-*

tion: Desire and Distance in the Late Middle Ages (*SAC* 32 [2010], no. 124), pp. 39–59. Rosenfeld concentrates on language of lovers and language of clerks ("erotic and intellectual discourses"), arguing that *TC* affirms the value of earthly happiness during life, as well as the inevitable instability of earthly matters.

321. Shoaf, R. Allen. " 'The Monstruosity in Love': Sexual Division in Chaucer and Shakespeare." In Tison Pugh and Marcia Smith Marzec, eds. *Men and Masculinities in Chaucer's "Troilus and Criseyde"* (*SAC* 32 [2010], no. 319), pp. 183–94. Shoaf comments on male separation anxiety in *TC* and Shakespeare's *Troilus and Cressida*, suggesting that the profundity of the poets' realizations underlies their aesthetic power.

322. Sturges, Robert S. "The State of Exception and Sovereign Masculinity in *Troilus and Criseyde*." In Tison Pugh and Marcia Smith Marzec, eds. *Men and Masculinities in Chaucer's "Troilus and Criseyde"* (*SAC* 32 [2010], no. 319), pp. 28–42. Sturges applies Giorgio Agamben's theory of sovereignty to *TC*, exploring shifting figures of sovereignty in the poem (the people, parliament, Hector) and measuring the extent to which Troilus and Criseyde live in a "state of exception" (an Agambenian political concept), subject to gendered versions of sovereignty.

323. Vial, Claire. " 'Quick-eyed love, observing'—Le rire de Troilus, entre mépris du monde et amour des hommes." In Danielle Buschinger and Arlette Sancery, eds. *Mélanges de langue, littérature et civilisation offerts à André Crépin à l'occasion de son quatre-vingtième anniversaire* (*SAC* 32 [2010], no. 104), pp. 312–16 (in French). Examines the laughter of Troilus in light of the tradition of *contemptus mundi* and stresses links between *TC* and pilgrimage literature.

324. Weisl, Angela Jane. " 'A Mannes Game': Criseyde's Masculinity in *Troilus and Criseyde*." In Tison Pugh and Marcia Smith Marzec, eds. *Men and Masculinities in Chaucer's "Troilus and Criseyde"* (*SAC* 32 [2010], no. 319), pp. 115–31. Criseyde shows more of a "mannes herte" than does Troilus in the consummation scene of *TC*. Throughout the poem, she chooses masculine, active self-interest rather than feminine, passive submission. In characterizing Criseyde, *TC* explores and exploits several oppositions—dishonor/death, masculine/feminine, epic/romance, Greece/Troy, war/love—thereby destabilizing gender.

325. Yvernault, Martine. " ' . . . *hold of thi matere/The forme alwey, and do that it be like* . . .' (II, 1039–40): L'entrée en matière dans le *Troilus*

and Criseyde de Chaucer." *BAM* 74 (2008): 29–55 (in French). Considers the nature, function, and value of the incipits and proems in *TC*.

326. Zeikowitz, Richard E. "Sutured Looks and Homoeroticism: Reading Troilus and Pandarus Cinematically." In Tison Pugh and Marcia Smith Marzec, eds. *Men and Masculinities in Chaucer's "Troilus and Criseyde"* (*SAC* 32 [2010], no. 319), pp. 148–60. Zeikowitz articulates the "largely unnarrated 'ocular logic' of the exchanges between Troilus and Pandarus" in Book 1 of *TC* and "teases out the subtle homoeroticism underlying their interaction." The essay focuses on the cinematic technique of "suturing," whereby the audience is drawn into a character's perspective without initially being aware of the point of view.

See also nos. 26, 50, 57, 60, 63, 66, 88, 101, 111, 113–15, 121, 126, 127, 133, 135, 142, 161, 215, 231, 232, 254, 267.

Lyrics and Short Poems

See no. 133.

An ABC

327. Dor, Juliette. "L'*ABC* de Chaucer: Traduction et transformation." In Frédéric Duval and Fabienne Pomel, eds. *Guillaume de Digulleville: Les pèlerinages allégoriques*. Rennes: Presses Universitaires de Rennes, 2008, pp. 401–23 (in French). Dor compares *ABC* with its source, revealing that Chaucer's translation is a rewriting that achieves intense dramatic power. Transformations of the figure of Mary, some shifts in the poem's tone, and ironical remarks invite us to reconsider the poem's significance and to revise some definitions in the *Middle English Dictionary*. Includes a French translation of *ABC*.

See also no. 138.

Adam Scriveyn

328. Gillespie, Alexandra. "Reading Chaucer's Words to Adam." *ChauR* 42 (2008): 269–83. Despite their empirical basis, the conclusions Linne R. Mooney draws regarding Adam Pinkhurst's relationship to Chaucer ultimately depend on literary evidence, which should remind

scholars that while particular communities of readers make a work "particularly meaningful," poetic language enables a variety of readings, in the light of which any particular meaning may become "unstuck," if not "undone."

329. Olson, Glending. "Author, Scribe, and Curse: The Genre of *Adam Scriveyn*." *ChauR* 42 (2008): 284–97. Reading *Adam* as a specimen of the genre of book curses reveals a tension in *Adam* between the incipient humanist idea of the author, "whose inventions transcend their scribal incarnations," and the reality in late medieval London of authors' dependence on an increasingly professionalized and hence powerful cadre of scribes.

Against Women Unconstant

330. Veck, Sonya. "Chaucerian Counterpoise in *The Canterbury Tales*: Implications of Newfangleness and Suffisaunce for the 21st Century Reader." In Kathleen A. Bishop, ed. *"The Canterbury Tales" Revisited— 21st Century Interpretations* (*SAC* 32 [2010], no. 145), pp. 300–313. Veck comments on recurrent thematic opposition between newfangleness and sufficiency or steadfastness in *wom Unc, Truth*, and *CT*. She suggests that Chaucer complicates the opposition with examples in which "a dash of inconstancy or newfangleness would work well" (e.g., *MLT* and *ClT*).

See also nos. 95, 110.

The Complaint of Chaucer to His Purse

331. Lindeboom, B. W. "Chaucer's *Complaint to His Purse*: Sounding a Subversive Note?" *Neophil* 92 (2008): 745–51. Comments on discussions of Chaucer's *Purse* that relate the poem to Lancastrian politics, offering further corroboration that *Purse* is subversive.

The Complaint of Mars

332. Brantley, Jessica. "Venus and Christ in Chaucer's *Complaint of Mars*: The Fairfax 16 Frontispiece." *SAC* 30 (2008): 171–204. 13 b&w illus. The artist of the Fairfax frontispiece manipulates similarities between traditional depictions of Venus "rising from the sea" (*anadyomene*) and Christ in baptism. The visual echoes express a form of "Christian

skepticism" that parallels questions about free will and determinism evident in Chaucer's *Mars*. The illustration and the poem capitalize in similar ways on the rich ambivalences of mythographic traditions.

See also no. 41.

The Complaint of Venus

See no. 41.

The Former Age

See nos. 45, 110.

Fortune

See nos. 45, 95, 110.

Gentilesse

See no. 45.

Lak of Stedfastnesse

See no. 45.

Truth

See nos. 45, 330.

Chaucerian Apocrypha

333. Ames, Alexander Vaughan. "Transcending Chaucer: Authority and Apocryphal *Canterbury Tales*." *DAI* A68.08 (2008): n.p. Applies notions of links between tale and teller to apocryphal tales, an approach suggested by the medieval notion of *auctoritee*. Concludes that post-medieval editions of *CT* do not "accurately" reflect the medieval understanding of the work as "a contextually contingent conversation."

334. Bolens, Guillemette. "Narrative Use and the Practice of Fiction

in *The Book of Sindibad* and *The Tale of Beryn.*" *Poetics Today* 29 (2008): 309–51. Bolens explores David Rudrum's notion of "narrative use" (fiction as a speech act that is used for a purpose) and applies it to *The Book of Sindibad, The Seven Sages of Rome*, and especially *The Tale of Beryn*. Narrative use is an overt concern throughout *Beryn*, which, through its frame, encourages law students to become expert in the use of fiction.

335. Conti Camaiora, Luisa. "*The Floure and the Leafe*: A Source of Keatsian Inspiration." In Giovanni Iamartino, Maria Luisa Maggioni, and Roberta Facchinetti, eds. *Thou sittest at another boke . . . : English Studies in Honour of Domenico Pezzini* (*SAC* 32 [2010], no. 119), pp. 305–18. The theme of doubleness in *The Floure and the Leafe* appears to have been especially attractive for Keats, whose attention was always drawn to the relationship between life and art. He found in the medieval poem an interesting "authority" that allowed him to transform an ancient poem, written in the form of a debate, into a modern lyrical composition.

336. Gayk, Shannon. "Teaching Chaucer's Legacy." *SMART* 15.1 (2008): 91–104. Pedagogical strategies for exploring how Chaucer's early reception and apocrypha can be used to "engage students in some of the larger issues of literary history and canon formation," with comments on how to use twentieth- and twenty-first-century media adaptations of *CT*.

337. Parsons, Ben. " 'For my synne and for my yong delite': Chaucer, the *Tale of Beryn*, and the Problem of *Adolescentia*." *MLR* 103 (2008): 940–51. Not just a continuation of *CT*, the *Tale of Beryn* engages Chaucer's work critically. Assigned, in the anonymous Interlude, to the Merchant on the return journey, *Beryn* challenges the Clerk's notion of male adolescence as a stage of pre-identity that will lead to maturity. The sense of adolescence as a force to be controlled in *Beryn* may connect with efforts to stem Lollardy by focusing on the young and their education.

See also nos. 53, 290.

Book Reviews

338. Adams, Jenny. *Power Play: The Literature and Politics of Chess in the Late Middle Ages* (*SAC* 30 [2008], no. 100). Rev. Laura Kendrick,

SAC 30 (2008): 335–37; Daniel E. O'Sullivan, *Encomia* 29–30 (2007–8): 9–10; Mark N. Taylor, *Review of Politics* 70 (2008): 120–23.

339. Akbari, Suzanne Conklin. *Seeing Through the Veil: Optical Theory and Medieval Allegory* (*SAC* 28 [2006], no. 59). Rev. Max Staples, *Parergon* 25.1 (2008): 191–93.

340. Alexander, Michael. *Medievalism: The Middle Ages in Modern England* (*SAC* 31 [2009], no. 48). Rev. Eric Daffron, *SCJ* 29 (2008): 932–33; Marysa Demoor, *TMR* 08.09.16, n.p.

341. Allen, Elizabeth. *False Fables and Exemplary Truth in Later Middle English Literature* (*SAC* 29 [2007], no. 86). Rev. Elizabeth Scala, *MFF* 44.2 (2008): 152–55.

342. Ashton, Gail. *Chaucer's "The Canterbury Tales"* (*SAC* 31 [2009], no. 147). Rev. Conrad van Dijk, *H-Albion* (May 2008), n.p.

343. ———, and Louise Sylvester, eds. *Teaching Chaucer* (*SAC* 31 [2009], no. 82). Rev. Louise D'Arcens, *SAC* 30 (2008): 337–40; Malcolm Hebron, *The Use of English* 59 (2008): 261–65; Tison Pugh, *TMR* 08.02.21, n.p.

344. Bale, Anthony. *The Jew in the Medieval Book: English Antisemitisms, 1350–1500* (*SAC* 30 [2008], no. 230). Rev. Bryan Cheyette, *TLS*, March 31, 2008, p. 24; Jeffrey J. Cohen, *SAC* 30 (2008): 340–43; Lisa Lampert-Weissig, *Speculum* 83 (2008): 659–60.

345. Bardsley, Sandy. *Venomous Tongues: Speech and Gender in Late Medieval England* (*SAC* 30 [2008], no. 196). Rev. Raquel Gutiérrez Estupiñán, *SCJ* 29 (2008): 304–5.

346. Blamires, Alcuin. *Chaucer, Ethics, and Gender* (*SAC* 30 [2008], no. 105). Rev. David Matthews, *MP* 106 (2008): 117–27.

347. Bowers, John M. *Chaucer and Langland: The Antagonistic Tradition* (*SAC* 31 [2009], no. 37). Rev. Christopher Cannon, *RES* 59 (2008): 139–40; Emily Runde, *Comitatus* 39 (2008): 233–34; James Simpson, *SAC* 30 (2008): 343–46; Pamela Luff Troyer, *Rocky Mountain Review* 62.2 (2008): 96–98; Lawrence Warner, *TMR* 08.05.20, n.p.

348. Bullón-Fernández, María, ed. *England and Iberia in the Middle Ages, 12th–15th Century: Cultural, Literary, and Political Exchanges* (*SAC* 31 [2009], no. 15). Rev. James D'Emilio, *TMR* 08.01.06, n.p.; Jordi Sánchez-Martí, *SAC* 30 (2008): 350–53.

349. Burger, Glenn. *Chaucer's Queer Nation* (*SAC* 27 [2005], no. 143). Rev. David Matthews, *MP* 106 (2008): 117–27.

350. Butterfield, Ardis, ed. *Chaucer and the City* (*SAC* 30 [2008], no. 108). Rev. Jay Ruud, *SMART* 15.2 (2008): 147–51.

351. Carlson, David R. *Chaucer's Jobs* (*SAC* 28 [2006], no. 8). Rev. William Askins, *Speculum* 83 (2008): 182–84.

352. Cole, Andrew. *Literature and Heresy in the Age of Chaucer* (*SAC* 32 [2010], no. 107). Rev. Linda R. Bates, *Marginalia* 8 (2007–8): n.p.

353. Cooper, Lisa H., and Andrea Denny-Brown, eds. *Lydgate Matters: Poetry and Material Culture in the Fifteenth Century* (*SAC* 32 [2010], no. 108). Rev. Robert J. Meyer-Lee, *TMR* 08.09.23, n.p.

354. Correale, Robert M., and Mary Hamel, eds. *Sources and Analogues of the "Canterbury Tales."* Vol. 2 (*SAC* 29 [2007], no. 46). Rev. K. P. Clarke, *N&Q* 55 (2008): 523–24.

355. Cox, Catherine S. *The Judaic Other in Dante, the "Gawain" Poet, and Chaucer* (*SAC* 29 [2007], no. 231). Rev. Heather Richardson Hayton, *CLS* 45 (2008): 247–52.

356. Craun, Edwin D., ed. *The Hands of the Tongue: Essays on Deviant Speech* (*SAC* 31 [2009], no. 204). Rev. Virginia Langum, *Marginalia* 8 (2007–8): n.p.

357. Davis, Isabel. *Writing Masculinity in the Later Middle Ages* (*SAC* 31 [2009], no. 271). Rev. Anne Laskaya, *TMR* 08.05.02, n.p.; Robert J. Meyer-Lee, *Speculum* 83 (2008): 975–77; Cory James Rushton, *MÆ* 77 (2008): 331–32; Ulrike Wiethaus, *JBSt* 47 (2008): 912–14.

358. Desmond, Marilynn. *Ovid's Art and the Wife of Bath: The Ethics of Erotic Violence* (*SAC* 30 [2008], no. 199). Rev. Heather Richardson Hayton, *CLS* 45 (2008): 247–52; Duncan Kennedy, *MLR* 103 (2008): 160–61; Marylène Possamaï-Perez, *MA* 114 (2008): 730–31; Catherine Sanok, *Speculum* 83 (2008): 188–89.

359. Duncan, Thomas G., ed. *A Companion to the Middle English Lyric* (*SAC* 29 [2007], no. 105). Rev. Klaus Bitterling, *ES* 89 (2008): 615–19.

360. Edwards, Robert R. *The Flight from Desire: Augustine and Ovid to Chaucer* (*SAC* 30 [2008], no. 278). Rev. Heather Richardson Hayton, *CLS* 45 (2008): 247–52.

361. Ellis, Steve, ed. *Chaucer: An Oxford Guide* (*SAC* 29 [2007], no. 108). Rev. Julia Boffey, *YES* 38 (2008): 262–63.

362. Evans, Ruth, Helen Fulton, and David Matthews, eds. *Medieval Cultural Studies: Essays in Honour of Stephen Knight* (*SAC* 30 [2008], no. 115). Rev. Pamela O'Neill, *Parergon* 25.1 (2008): 208–10.

363. Farber, Lianna. *An Anatomy of Trade in Medieval Writing: Value, Consent, and Community* (*SAC* 30 [2008], no. 117). Rev. Martine Yvernault, *MA* 114 (2008): 136–37.

364. Fradenburg, L. O. Aranye. *Sacrifice Your Love: Psychoanalysis,*

Historicism, Chaucer (*SAC* 26 [2004], no. 133). Rev. David Matthews, *MP* 106 (2008): 117–27.

365. Fyler, John M. *Language and the Declining World in Chaucer, Dante, and Jean de Meun* (*SAC* 31 [2009], no. 101). Rev. Robert Boenig, *M&H* 34 (2008): 171–73; K. P. Clarke, *RES* 59 (2008): 456–57; Robert R. Edwards, *SAC* 30 (2008): 358–61; Norm Klassen, *MÆ* 77 (2008): 342–44; Tim William Machan, *Speculum* 83 (2008): 984–85.

366. Galloway, Andrew. *Medieval Literature and Culture* (*SAC* 31 [2009], no. 102). Rev. Rachel E. Frier, *MFF* 44.2 (2008): 171–74; Matthew Giancarlo, *TMR* 08.03.12, n.p.; Norbert A. Wethington, *Enarratio* 13 (2006): 133–35.

367. Gillespie, Alexandra. *Print Culture and the Medieval Author: Chaucer, Lydgate, and Their Books, 1473–1557* (*SAC* 30 [2008], no. 23). Rev. A. E. B. Coldiron, *Speculum* 83 (2008): 438–40; Siân Echard, *SMART* 15.2 (2008): 153–56; Kathryn Kerby-Fulton, *SAC* 30 (2008): 361–64; Linne R. Mooney, *JEBS* 11 (2008): 29–41; Nigel Mortimer, *MÆ* 77 (2008): 131–33; Stephen R. Reimer, *Textual Cultures* 2.2 (2007): 136–39.

368. Grady, Frank. *Representing Righteous Heathens in Late Medieval England* (*SAC* 30 [2008], no. 280). Rev. Suzanne Conklin Akbari, *SAC* 30 (2008): 364–68.

369. Gray, Douglas. *Later Medieval English Literature* (*SAC* 32 [2010], no. 53). Rev. Ruth Ahnert, *Marginalia* 8 (2007–8): n.p.

370. Guy-Bray, Stephen. *Loving in Verse: Poetic Influence as Erotic* (*SAC* 32 [2010], no. 55). Rev. Natalie Katerina Prestwich, *UTQ* 77 (2008): 177–78.

371. Hamaguchi, Keiko. *Non-European Women in Chaucer: A Postcolonial Study* (*SAC* 30 [2008], no. 120). Rev. Kathryn L. Lynch, *Speculum* 83 (2008): 706–8.

372. Hanna, Ralph. *London Literature, 1300–1380* (*SAC* 29 [2007], no. 116). Rev. Jordi Sánchez-Martí, *Atlantis* 29 (2007): 167–72.

373. Harriss, Gerald. *Shaping the Nation: England, 1360–1461* (*SAC* 32 [2010], no. 117). Rev. Douglas Biggs, *Speculum* 83 (2008): 1004–5.

374. Hodges, Laura. *Chaucer and Clothing: Clerical and Academic Costume in the General Prologue to "The Canterbury Tales"* (*SAC* 29 [2007], no. 170). Rev. Susan Carroll-Clark, *Medieval Clothing and Textiles* 2 (2006): 176.

375. Hopkins, Amanda, and Cory James Rushton, eds. *The Erotic in the Literature of Medieval Britain* (*SAC* 31 [2009], no. 110). Rev. Kath-

leen Coyne Kelly, *SAC* 30 (2008): 372–75; Yvette Kisor, *TMR* 08.05.01, n.p.

376. Horobin, Simon. *Chaucer's Language* (*SAC* 31 [2009], no. 69). Rev. Richard Dance, *SAC* 30 (2008): 375–78.

377. Howes, Laura L., ed. *Place, Space, and Landscape in Medieval Narrative* (*SAC* 31 [2009], no. 112). Rev. Sara V. Torres, *Comitatus* 39 (2008): 308–10.

378. Kabir, Ananya Jahanara, and Deanne Williams, eds. *Postcolonial Approaches to the European Middle Ages: Translating Cultures* (*SAC* 29 [2007], no. 52). Rev. Christine Chism, *UTQ* 77 (2008): 223–25.

379. Kaylor, Noel Harold, Jr., and Philip Edward Phillips, eds. *New Directions in Boethian Studies* (*SAC* 31 [2009], no. 215). Rev. Winthrop Wetherbee, *TMR* 08.03.07, n.p.

380. Kerby-Fulton, Kathryn. *Books Under Suspicion: Censorship and Tolerance of Revelatory Writing in Late Medieval England* (*SAC* 30 [2008], no. 125). Rev. Cindy Carlson, *Rocky Mountain Review* 62.2 (2008): 98–100; Andrew Cole, *SAC* 30 (2008): 378–84; Alexandra Gillespie, *EHR* 123 (2008): 715–17; Ryan Perry, *CollL* 35.4 (2008): 222–24; Steven Rozenski Jr., *Comitatus* 39 (2008): 293–95; Rosalynn Voaden, *Speculum* 83 (2008): 447–49.

381. Labbie, Erin Felicia. *Lacan's Medievalism* (*SAC* 32 [2010], no. 122). Rev. Emma Campbell, *TMR* 08.12.05, n.p.

382. Lavezzo, Kathy. *Angels on the Edge of the World: Geography, Literature, and English Community, 1000–1534* (*SAC* 30 [2008], no. 192). Rev. Jane Beal, *SCJ* 29 (2008): 1159–61; Hugh Magennis, *CollL* 35.3 (2005): 180–90.

383. Lerer, Seth. *Inventing English: A Portable History of the Language* (*SAC* 31 [2009], no. 73). Rev. Anne Curzan, *Michigan Quarterly Review* 47 (2008): 133–40; Peggy A. Knapp, *Speculum* 83.3 (2008): 725–26.

384. ———, ed. *The Yale Companion to Chaucer* (*SAC* 30 [2008], no. 131). Rev. Robert R. Edwards, *JEGP* 107 (2008): 416.

385. Lightsey, Scott. *Manmade Marvels in Medieval Culture and Literature* (*SAC* 31 [2009], no. 118). Rev. A. G. Pluskowski, *TMR* 08.05.16, n.p.

386. Lindeboom, B. W. *Venus' Owne Clerk: Chaucer's Debt to the "Confessio Amantis"* (*SAC* 31 [2009], no. 158). Rev. Alcuin Blamires, *MLR* 103 (2008): 506–7; Conrad van Dijk, *MÆ* 77 (2008): 129–30; Russell Peck, *Speculum* 83 (2008): 726–28.

387. Lipton, Emma. *Affections of the Mind: The Politics of Sacramental*

Marriage in Late Medieval English Literature (*SAC* 31 [2009], no. 240). Rev. Suzanne M. Edwards, *MFF* 44.2 (2008): 144–46; Bernard O'Donoghue, *SAC* 30 (2008): 384–87; Tara Williams, *TMR* 08.11.12, n.p.

388. Machan, Tim William, ed., with the assistance of A. J. Minnis. *Sources of the Boece* (*SAC* 29 [2007], no. 271). Rev. Gregory Heyworth, *Textual Cultures* 1.2 (2006): 170–71.

389. McCormack, Frances. *Chaucer and the Culture of Dissent: The Lollard Context and Subtext of the Parson's Tale* (*SAC* 31 [2009], no. 274). Rev. Julia Boffey, *TLS*, June 6, 2008, p. 22; Anne Hudson, *MÆ* 77 (2008): 373–74; Katherine Little, *TMR* 08.04.28, n.p.; Karen Winstead, *RES* 59 (2008): 607–8.

390. McMullan, Gordon, and David Matthews, eds. *Reading the Medieval in Early Modern England* (*SAC* 31 [2009], no. 56). Rev. Ruth Ahnert, *Marginalia* 7 (2008): n.p.; Malcolm Hebron, *The Use of English* 59 (2008): 261–65; Maura Nolan, *TMR* 08.10.15, n.p.

391. McSheffrey, Shannon. *Marriage, Sex, and Civic Culture in Late Medieval London* (*SAC* 30 [2008], no. 133). Rev. Ian Forrest, *EHR* 123 (2008): 714–15; R. N. Swanson, *SCJ* 29 (2008): 305–7.

392. McTurk, Rory. *Chaucer and the Norse and Celtic Worlds* (*SAC* 29 [2007], no. 48). Rev. Andrew Breeze, *LeedSE* 39 (2008): 135–37; Craig R. Davis, *JEGP* 107 (2008): 130.

393. Mann, Jill, and Maura Nolan, eds. *The Text in the Community: Essays on Medieval Works, Manuscripts, Authors, and Readers* (*SAC* 30 [2008], no. 49). Rev. Philip F. O'Mara, *SCJ* 29 (2008): 297–99.

394. Mehtonen, Päivi. *Obscure Language, Unclear Literature: Theory and Practice from Quintilian to the Enlightenment* (*SAC* 32 [2010], no. 271). Rev. James J. Paxson, *Speculum* 83 (2008): 732–33.

395. Meyer-Lee, Robert J. *Poets and Power from Chaucer to Wyatt* (*SAC* 31 [2009], no. 57). Rev. Anthony Bale, *MP* 105 (2008): 698–704; Richard Firth Green, *SAC* 30 (2008): 387–89; Ad Putter, *TLS*, July 4, 2008, p. 9; Randy P. Schiff, *JBSt* 47 (2008): 160–62; Lynn Staley, *Speculum* 83 (2008): 470–71; Daniel Wakelin, *MÆ* 77 (2008): 133–34.

396. Mieszkowski, Gretchen. *Medieval Go-Betweens and Chaucer's Pandarus* (*SAC* 30 [2008], no. 285). Rev. Sealy Gilles, *Speculum* 83 (2008): 218–19.

397. Miller, Mark. *Philosophical Chaucer: Love, Sex, and Agency in the "Canterbury Tales"* (*SAC* 29 [2007], no. 164). Rev. R. James Goldstein, *Southern Humanities Review* 42.1 (2008): 83–88; David Matthews, *MP* 106 (2008): 117–27.

398. Minnis, Alastair. *Fallible Authors: Chaucer's Pardoner and Wife of Bath* (*SAC* 32 [2010], no. 247). Rev. Seth Lerer, *TLS*, July 4, 2008, p. 10.

399. Mitchell, J. Allan. *Ethics and Exemplary Narrative in Chaucer and Gower* (*SAC* 28 [2006], no. 101). Rev. Jacob Thaisen, *ES* 89 (2008): 364–65.

400. Morgan, Gerald. *The Tragic Argument of "Troilus and Criseyde"* (*SAC* 30 [2008], no. 286). Rev. Nigel Mortimer, *YES* 38 (2008): 264–65.

401. Newhauser, Richard, ed. *The Seven Deadly Sins: From Communities to Individuals* (*SAC* 31 [2009], no. 229). Rev. Jessica Rosenfeld, *TMR* 08.06.12, n.p.

402. Niebrzydowski, Sue. *Bonoure and Buxum: A Study of Wives in Late Medieval English Literature* (*SAC* 32 [2010], no. 130). Rev. Marie-Françoise Alamichel, *MA* 114 (2008): 435–36; Helen Phillips, *MÆ* 77 (2008): 330–31.

403. Norris, Ralph. *Malory's Library: The Sources of the "Morte Darthur"* (*SAC* 32 [2010], no. 58). Rev. Carolyne Larrington, *TLS*, July 11, 2008, p. 31.

404. Passmore, S. Elizabeth, and Susan Carter, eds. *The English "Loathly Lady" Tales: Boundaries, Traditions, Motifs* (*SAC* 31 [2009], no. 219). Rev. Misty Schieberle, *TMR* 08.11.13, n.p.

405. Patterson, Lee, ed. *Geoffrey Chaucer's "The Canterbury Tales": A Casebook* (*SAC* 31 [2009], no. 164). Rev. C. David Benson, *SMART* 15.2 (2008): 157–59.

406. Phillips, Susan E. *Transforming Talk: The Problem with Gossip in Late Medieval England* (*SAC* 31 [2009], no. 123). Rev. Brian Murdoch, *L&T* 22 (2008): 122–24; Nicole Nolan Sidhu, *SAC* 30 (2008): 390–93; Janet Hadley Williams, *Parergon* 25.1 (2008): 244–45.

407. Prendergast, Thomas A. *Chaucer's Dead Body: From Corpse to Corpus* (*SAC* 28 [2006], no. 46). Rev. Alexandra Gillespie, *N&Q* 55 (2008): 524–25.

408. Pugh, Tison. *Sexuality and Its Queer Discontents in Middle English Literature* (*SAC* 32 [2010], no. 132). Rev. Carl Phelpstead, *TMR* 08.09.19.

409. ———, and Marcia Smith Marzec, eds. *Men and Masculinities in Chaucer's "Troilus and Criseyde"* (*SAC* 32 [2010], no. 319). Rev. Daniel Wakelin, *MÆ* 77 (2008): 133–34.

410. Raffel, Burton, trans. *The Canterbury Tales* (*SAC* 32 [2010], no.

36). Rev. Tom Shippey, *Wall Street Journal*, November 21, 2008, n.p.; Alexander Theroux, *Los Angeles Times*, November 26, 2008, p. F8.

411. Rudd, Gillian. *The Complete Critical Guide to Chaucer* (*SAC* 25 [2003], no. 133). Rev. Linda R. Bates, *Marginalia* 6 (2006–7): n.p.

412. Rust, Martha Dana. *Imaginary Worlds in Medieval Books: Exploring the Manuscript Matrix* (*SAC* 31 [2009], no. 34). Rev. Jessica Brantley, *SAC* 30 (2008): 393–96.

413. Salih, Sarah, ed. *A Companion to Middle English Hagiography* (*SAC* 30 [2008], no. 140). Rev. Virginia Blanton, *Speculum* 83 (2008): 742–44.

414. Sanok, Catherine. *Her Life Historical: Exemplarity and Female Saints' Lives in Late Medieval England* (*SAC* 31 [2009], no. 298). Rev. J. Patrick Hornbeck II, *JBSt* 47 (2008): 651–52; Larry Scanlon, *SAC* 30 (2008): 396–99.

415. Scanlon, Larry, and James Simpson, eds. *John Lydgate: Poetry, Culture, and Lancastrian England* (*SAC* 30 [2008], no. 71). Rev. Mary-Rose McLaren, *Parergon* 25.1 (2008): 248–50.

416. Scase, Wendy. *Literature and Complaint in England: 1272–1553* (*SAC* 31 [2009], no. 127). Rev. Ad Putter, *TLS*, July 4, 2008, p. 9.

417. Schibanoff, Susan. *Chaucer's Queer Poetics: Rereading the Dream Trio* (*SAC* 30 [2008], no. 145). Rev. Kathryn L. Lynch, *SAC* 30 (2008): 399–402; David Matthews, *MP* 106 (2008): 117–27.

418. Schoff, Rebecca L. *Reformations: Three Medieval Authors in Manuscript and Movable Type* (*SAC* 31 [2009], no. 128). Rev. Elizabeth Evershed, *MÆ* 77 (2008): 349–50.

419. Spearing, A. C. *Textual Subjectivity: The Encoding of Subjectivity in Medieval Narratives and Lyrics* (*SAC* 29 [2007], no. 143). Rev. Elizabeth Scala, *TMR* 08.04.07, n.p.

420. Stanbury, Sarah. *The Visual Object of Desire in Late Medieval England* (*SAC* 32 [2010], no. 141). Rev. Dallas D. Denery II, *H-Albion* (December 2008), n.p.

421. Strohm, Paul. *Politique: Languages of Statecraft Between Chaucer and Shakespeare* (*SAC* 29 [2007], no. 257). Rev. R. A. Griffiths, *EHR* 123 (2008): 1530–31; Frank A. Napolitano, *SCJ* 29 (2008): 295–96.

422. Sylvester, Louise M. *Medieval Romance and the Construction of Heterosexuality* (*SAC* 32 [2010], no. 142). Rev. Lisa Perfetti, *MFF* 44.2 (2008): 174–77.

423. Thomas, Alfred. *A Blessed Shore: England and Bohemia from Chaucer to Shakespeare* (*SAC* 31 [2009], no. 137). Rev. Michael Kuczynski,

TMR 08.10.12, n.p.; David Mengel, *SAC* 30 (2008): 405–8; Andrew Taylor, *Speculum* 83 (2008): 1038–39.

424. Turner, Marion. *Chaucerian Conflict: Languages of Antagonism in Late Fourteenth-Century London* (*SAC* 31 [2009], no. 138). Rev. Julia Boffey, *TLS*, June 6, 2008, p. 22; John M. Bowers, *SAC* 30 (2008): 408–11; David Matthews, *MP* 106 (2008): 117–27; Maura Nolan, *Speculum* 83 (2008): 769–70.

425. Van Dyke, Carolynn. *Chaucer's Agents: Cause and Representation in Chaucerian Narrative* (*SAC* 29 [2007], no. 151). Rev. David Matthews, *MP* 106 (2008): 117–27; Diane Watt, *MÆ* 77 (2008): 130–31.

426. Wakelin, Daniel. *Humanism, Reading, and English Literature, 1430–1530* (*SAC* 32 [2010], no. 289). Rev. Mishtooni Bose, *MÆ* 77 (2008): 347–49; Simon Horobin, *JEBS* 11 (2008): 275–77.

427. Williams, Deanne. *The French Fetish from Chaucer to Shakespeare* (*SAC* 28 [2006], no. 94). Rev. Theresa Coletti, *Speculum* 83 (2008): 1058–59.

428. Yeager, R. F., ed. *On John Gower: Essays at the Millennium* (*SAC* 31 [2009], no. 291). Rev. Conrad van Dyk, *TMR* 8.10.17, n.p.; Tamara Stasik, *Encomia* 29–30 (2007–8): 55–57.

429. Zieman, Katherine. *Singing the New Song: Literacy and Liturgy in Late Medieval England* (*SAC* 32 [2010], no. 263). Rev. Elisabeth Dutton, *TLS*, July 31, 2009, p. 27; Andrew Galloway, *H-Albion* (October 2008), n.p.

Author Index—Bibliography

INDEX